HIGH
&
LOW

HIGH & LOW

MODERN ART · POPULAR CULTURE

KIRK VARNEDOE · ADAM GOPNIK

THE MUSEUM OF MODERN ART, NEW YORK

A NOTE ON THE TEXT: THE STRUCTURE OF THIS BOOK AND THE IDEAS IN IT WERE CONCEIVED COLLABORATIVELY. KIRK VARNEDOE WAS THE PRINCIPAL AUTHOR OF "WORDS," "GRAFFITI," AND "ADVERTISING," AND ADAM GOPNIK THE PRINCIPAL AUTHOR OF "CARICATURE," "COMICS," AND "CONTEMPORARY REFLECTIONS." "INTRODUCTION" AND "CODA" WERE CO-AUTHORED.

PUBLISHED IN CONJUNCTION WITH AN EXHIBITION OF THE SAME TITLE DIRECTED BY KIRK VARNEDOE AND ADAM GOPNIK

THE MUSEUM OF MODERN ART, NEW YORK
OCTOBER 7, 1990–JANUARY 15, 1991

THE ART INSTITUTE OF CHICAGO
FEBRUARY 20–MAY 12, 1991

MUSEUM OF CONTEMPORARY ART, LOS ANGELES
JUNE 21–SEPTEMBER 15, 1991

THE EXHIBITION IS SPONSORED BY AT&T.

AN INDEMNITY FOR THE EXHIBITION HAS BEEN RECEIVED FROM THE FEDERAL COUNCIL ON THE ARTS AND THE HUMANITIES.

EDITED BY JAMES LEGGIO
DESIGNED BY STEVEN SCHOENFELDER
PRODUCTION BY TIM MCDONOUGH
SET IN TYPE BY TGA COMMUNICATIONS, NEW YORK
COLOR SEPARATIONS BY REPROCOLOR LLOVET, BARCELONA
PRINTED AND BOUND BY CAYFOSA, BARCELONA

PUBLISHED BY THE MUSEUM OF MODERN ART
11 WEST 53 STREET, NEW YORK, NEW YORK 10019

DISTRIBUTED IN THE UNITED STATES AND
CANADA BY HARRY N. ABRAMS, INC., NEW YORK
A TIMES MIRROR COMPANY

DISTRIBUTED OUTSIDE THE UNITED STATES AND
CANADA BY THAMES AND HUDSON LTD., LONDON

PRINTED IN SPAIN

FRONTISPIECE:
O'GALOP. *LE COUP DE LA SEMELLE BIBENDUM.* 1910–11 (FROM A DESIGN OF 1905); RECONSTRUCTED 1987. STAINED GLASS, 9'8⅛" × 7'11½" (295 × 242 CM). THE CONRAN SHOP, LONDON; FORMERLY THE MICHELIN BUILDING

COVER BY STEVEN SCHOENFELDER, AFTER A DESIGN BY ALEKSANDR RODCHENKO OF 1923 (REPRODUCED P. 58)

BACK COVER, FROM TOP:
JEAN DUBUFFET. *DHOTEL SHADED WITH APRICOT.* 1947 (P. 147)
CY TWOMBLY. *LEDA AND THE SWAN.* 1961 (P. 96)
FERNAND LÉGER. *THE SYPHON.* 1924 (P. 288)
ROY LICHTENSTEIN. *OKAY, HOT-SHOT.* 1963 (P. 207)

CONTENTS

116457

With this catalogue and the exhibition it represents, AT&T celebrates 50 years of formal association with the arts.

That association is founded on our belief that communication is the beginning of understanding. That refers, of course, to the technology that lets information loose on the world. But it also refers to the arts, which color that world from a uniquely human perspective.

It is that gift of expression and its promise of understanding that prods our support. It is the illumination of our own ignorance that fuels the search.

The arts, after all, exist not to explain, but to question. To unearth not the answers, but the possibilities. To remind us not of what we are, but what we can be.

R. E. Allen
*Chairman of the Board
and Chief Executive Officer
AT&T*

"High and Low: Modern Art and Popular Culture" continues a tradition that has been important to The Museum of Modern Art throughout its history: thematic exhibitions that examine the fundamental premises of modern art, and link the innovations of its pioneers to the explorations of younger, contemporary artists. This kind of exhibition is particularly demanding, and the present project, so ambitious and heterogeneous in its scope, was only made possible by the dedication of an extraordinary number of individuals and institutions, to whom I express very warm thanks.

The exhibition was conceived by Kirk Varnedoe, Director of the Department of Painting and Sculpture, and by Adam Gopnik, staff writer and art critic for *The New Yorker*. Kirk Varnedoe assumed the directorship of Painting and Sculpture in August of 1988. He had already proposed this exhibition as a project to be accomplished at a later date, after he had settled into his new responsibilities. For compelling reasons, however, the exhibition's schedule was substantially advanced. Mr. Varnedoe accepted this change with admirable grace, even though he knew the intense pressures it would entail. We were very fortunate that his collaborator, Mr. Gopnik, who had helped to develop the initial plan for the exhibition and was exploring some of the issues it would pose, was also prepared to accelerate his work to meet these difficult deadlines. The commitment of time and thought Mr. Gopnik made to realizing this project is as impressive as the critical judgment, intelligence, and insight he brought to it.

FOREWORD

It is an enormous tribute to Mr. Varnedoe's professional discipline, energy, and organizational skill that he could balance so effectively his heavy new duties as Director of Painting and Sculpture and the more than full-time task of preparing an unusually large and complex exhibition and catalogue. He managed to do so without any compromise of the high standards of performance, of intellectual rigor and aesthetic sensibility which we have come to expect from him. Despite far too many extra hours of work in late evenings, early mornings, and on weekends, he also maintained his customary humor, composure, and civility.

It was clear from the outset that if this complex and challenging conception was to be realized in the proper fashion, the Museum would require as its partner in the enterprise a corporate sponsor with both courage and vision. Very substantial resources had to be committed to a project that promised to be demanding and somewhat unorthodox, and which involved taking risks. Happily, AT&T responded to this prospect in the best spirit imaginable.

The year of the exhibition's opening, 1990, marks the fiftieth anniversary of AT&T's patronage of the arts, which began with sponsorship of The Telephone Hour on radio in 1940. In the history of its involvement with the arts, AT&T has evidenced a particular concern to promote and foster communication, in the deepest sense of that word. Its present leaders recognized in "High and Low" an effort to chart some of the most important linkages between seemingly disparate sections of modern society, and between the flights of the modern individual imagination and a broader sphere, encompassing both day-to-day life and technological progress in our era. They accorded us exceptionally generous funding for the exhibition's many expenses, and furthermore undertook to sponsor the series of events by performance artists that accompanies the show. In addition, AT&T provided Kirk Varnedoe and his staff with a computer network to facilitate management of the wide array of research data and documentation the show required.

For this invaluable spirit of support and of partnership, we extend our warmest thanks to Robert E. Allen, Chairman and Chief Executive Officer; Marilyn Laurie, Senior Vice President, Public Relations; and R. Z. Manna, Corporate Advertising and Event Marketing Director. Zack Manna, with whom we have had the pleasure of working on other projects as well, has been an essential liaison between our institution and AT&T. We owe him an immense debt of gratitude for the enthusiasm he showed from our first discussions about this exhibition, and for his active cooperation at every stage of its preparation.

The responsiveness of lenders is the most crucial element in an exhibition like this one. We were able to avail ourselves of their generosity to borrow so many major works because of an insurance indemnity provided by the Federal Council on the Arts and the Humanities. As so often in the past, we deeply appreciate the advice and assistance of its Indemnity Administrator, Alice M. Whelihan.

It is our hope that the exhibition, and this publication, will throw new light on a central concern of modern artists of yesterday and today, and in so doing will fully reward the faith in this project of all who have lent their support and encouragement.

Richard E. Oldenburg
Director, The Museum of Modern Art

This exhibition project has called upon, and has received in extraordinary measure, the goodwill, cooperation, and assistance of artists, museum professionals, archivists, collectors, and dealers around the world, as well as colleagues in every part of the staff of The Museum of Modern Art. In most of the remarks that follow, I will be speaking not only for myself but also for Adam Gopnik, the co-author of this book, and the co-director of the exhibition "High and Low: Modern Art and Popular Culture," in acknowledging these diverse contributions.

In the initial stages of the endeavour, my colleagues took a leap of faith, in agreeing to commit both floors of the Museum's special-exhibition space, as well as many of the institution's resources, to the idea of a thematic exhibition dealing with the interchanges between modern art and popular culture. They also showed great forbearance in licensing us to define this idea (which has broad ramifications in all phases of modern creativity, including architecture, film, and photography) in the narrower terms that concerned painting and sculpture — a narrowing that we hoped would serve to focus on the issues at hand in the sharpest and most telling fashion. The first person to thank in this regard is Richard E. Oldenburg, Director of The Museum of Modern Art. He has been fully supportive, from the moment of the exhibition's proposal through every phase of the development of the show and

ACKNOWLEDGMENTS

its publications. He was also subjected to many pressures that were properly my own burden. He shielded me from them, and has been a constant source of sympathetic encouragement. For their crucial concurrence in the beginning premises of the project, I also wish to thank Riva Castleman, Deputy Director for Curatorial Affairs, as well as the Directors of the other curatorial departments—John Elderfield, John Szarkowski, Stuart Wrede, and Mary Lea Bandy—and the members of their departments who comprise the committee on exhibitions.

At the risk of repeating Richard Oldenburg's Foreword, I wish to thank AT&T for an act of faith as well. I am particularly grateful to Zack Manna, Corporate Advertising and Event Marketing Director, for his enthusiastic openness to the concept of this show, and for his help in obtaining the funding necessary to realize it in the best fashion; I appreciate as well the positive reception and helpful comments offered by Marilyn Laurie, Senior Vice President, Public Relations. It has been a pleasure to work with them, and that experience has been made all the more easy and productive because

of the work of the Museum's Deputy Director for Development and Public Affairs, Sue Dorn, and of John Wielk, Manager of Exhibition and Project Funding. I also appreciate the careful attention given to the contractual aspect of this relationship by our General Counsel, Beverly Wolff. And in this, as in many other matters related to this exhibition, a great debt of thanks is owed to James Snyder, Deputy Director for Planning and Program Support, who has been constantly attentive to every aspect of the project.

A crucial part of the support from AT&T was the sophisticated AT&T computer system provided, early on, to the staff working on the exhibition. This StarLAN system was enormously valuable in expediting all our work, and among the many individuals at AT&T that worked hard to get our network up and running—as well as to help train our staff in its use—we particularly thank Stratos Colman, Sloan Weitzel, Arthur Salvadore, and Genevieve Dudley for their assistance.

Also near the beginning of the exhibition's preparation, we were pleased to have the commitments of both The Art Institute of Chicago and the Museum of Contemporary Art, Los Angeles, as the venues for the show's tour. James Wood, Director of The Art Institute of Chicago, and Richard Koshalek, Director of the Museum of Contemporary Art, have been strongly supportive, and have proved valuable partners in this enterprise. We are grateful, too, for the help given us by their curators, Charles Stuckey in Chicago, and Paul Schimmel in Los Angeles.

Though the subject of the exhibition appeared broad and general, its successful elucidation depended on obtaining the loan of a very specific list of masterworks. Yet given the conditions of recent years—escalating art prices, and steadily more frenetic activity on the international exhibition circuit—such loans have become increasingly difficult to obtain. This is especially true for a thematic exhibition which requires the kind of irreplaceable works many museums would normally consent to lend only to a monographic show dedicated to the artist in question. I am therefore particularly grateful to the museums and collectors who responded positively to our entreaties for loans, even when the granting of such requests required that exceptions be made to long-standing restrictions. The Trustees of the Tate Gallery, London, and that institution's Director, Nicholas Serota, kindly made such an exception, as did Suzanne Pagé, Director, Musée d'Art Moderne de la Ville de Paris; Prof. Dr. Werner Schmalenbach, Director, Kunstsammlung Nordrhein-Westfalen, Düsseldorf; and Evan Turner, Director, The

Cleveland Museum of Art. In each case, the extra measure of generosity has permitted a special masterpiece to enhance the quality of the exhibition, and we are most grateful.

This debt is redoubled in the case of those who made multiple loans to bolster different parts of the exhibition. Among these latter I should cite particularly the Philadelphia Museum of Art and offer special gratitude to Anne d'Harnoncourt, Director, as well as to Ann Temkin, Curator of Twentieth-Century Art, for their patience with my many requests, and for allowing rarely lent works of the highest quality to be a part of this exhibition. Gérard Regnier, Director of the Musée Picasso, Paris, and Paule Mazouet, Curator, generously consented to send several key works by Picasso. Christian Geelhaar, Director of the Kunstmuseum Basel, and Dieter Koepplin, Director of its Kupferstichkabinett, also showed great kindness in allowing us to borrow a number of key Cubist works. Requests for such works, many of which had only the year before appeared in William Rubin's landmark exhibition "Picasso and Braque: Pioneering Cubism," were especially difficult to honor; we are also grateful to Jean-Hubert Martin, Director of the Musée National d'Art Moderne at the Centre Georges Pompidou, and Isabelle Monod-Fontaine, Curator, for agreeing to lend us once again major works by Picasso and Braque, as well as a significant list of other rarely lent paintings and sculptures by modern masters. I would also like to thank Jean-Hubert Martin for the spirit of collegial cooperation in which he worked with me to consider how best to resolve possible conflicts between "High and Low" and his own, partially parallel project for an exhibition on modern art and advertising.

Thanks are also owed to Wim Beeren, Director, Stedelijk Museum, Amsterdam; Rosa Maria Malet, Director, and Teresa Montaner of the photograph department, Fundació Joan Miró, Barcelona; Katharina Schmidt, Director, Städtisches Kunstmuseum, Bonn; Douglas G. Schultz, Director, Albright-Knox Art Gallery, Buffalo; Siegfried Gohr, Director, and Evelyn Weiss, Chief Curator, Museum Ludwig, Cologne; Richard Brettell, Director, Dallas Museum of Art; Julia Brown Turrell, Director, Des Moines Art Center; James Cuno, Director, Hood Museum of Art, Dartmouth College, Hanover, New Hampshire; Norbert Nobis, Deputy Director, and Dietmar Elger, Curator, Sprengel Museum, Hannover; Dominique de Menil and Walter Hopps of The Menil Collection, Houston; Earl A. Powell III, Director, Maurice Tuchman, Curator, and Judi Freeman, Associate Curator of Twentieth-Century Art, at the Los Angeles County Museum of Art; Masaharu Ono, Curator, The National Museum of Art, Osaka; Philippe de Montebello, Director, and William Lieberman, Chairman of Twentieth-Century Art, The Metropolitan Museum of Art, New York; J. Carter Brown, Director, and Jack Cowart, Curator, National Gallery of Art, Washington, D.C.; Duncan Robinson, Director, Yale Center for British Art; and Mary Gardner Neill, Director, and Sasha Newman, Associate Curator

of European and Contemporary Art, Yale University Art Gallery. I am especially grateful to Ms. Neill and Ms. Newman, not only for their help with works from their collection, but also for their assistance with requests from the Yale Center for British Art, and for their cooperation in our request to borrow the Claes Oldenburg sculpture *Lipstick*. Professor Donald Quinlan, Master of Morse College, Yale University, and the students of Morse College, are also to be thanked for allowing *Lipstick* to leave its normal emplacement for several months.

While our relationship with institutions such as these may permit us to reciprocate their generosity in the future, we have made perhaps even more difficult demands on the many private collectors who have lent to the exhibition, and we owe them our most profound gratitude. Among them we would especially thank S. I. Newhouse, Jr., for the several loans to which he agreed, and for his support of the show in general. I also wish to express particular thanks to those lenders who made the extraordinary gesture of sending us once again Cubist works that had previously appeared in "Picasso and Braque," or paintings by Andy Warhol that had been included in the Museum's recent retrospective of the artist: Peter Ludwig, Irving Blum, Robert and Meryl Meltzer, The Estate of Andy Warhol, and an anonymous collector. For their help in working with other private lenders, thanks are also due David McKee, James Corcoran, and Paula Cooper, as well as Werner Spies, who was particularly supportive in his cooperation with our effort to obtain Max Ernst collages. To all the lenders, including those not named specifically here, goes our warmest gratitude, for making the exhibition possible. (A list of the lenders appears on page 453.)

Both in regard to loan requests and in seeking information about the availability of works, we depended on the kindness of a great many people. The personnel of the auction houses Sotheby's and Christie's were particularly cooperative, and we are grateful to Christopher Burge and Michael Findlay of Christie's, as well as to David Nash, John Tancock, Anthony Grant, and Marjorie Nathanson of Sotheby's. Heiner Bastian also provided help that was greatly appreciated, as did Angela Westwater and Gian Enzo Sperone. Special thanks is owed Jeffrey Deitch, both for his liaison work with private lenders and for his generous help with matters of valuation. In this latter regard, we once again called as well on the help of Ernst Beyeler, and appreciated his prompt attention to our queries. Alexandr Lavrentiev, Joe Walker, Chris Ursitti, and Paul McGinnis also assisted in a very valuable way with matters central to our representation of the Russian avant-garde.

One of the great pleasures of the preparation of the show involved dealing with a number of the artists whose works were central to its theme. Richard Hamilton was a generous host at his home outside London, and Elizabeth Murray graciously helped with our selection of works and with research. We also appreciate the aid of Saul Steinberg, and of Alexander Liberman. Cy Twombly was a valuable friend of the project, and enriched it by key loans. Jasper Johns and Robert Rauschenberg were similarly responsive to our requests for works from their collections. In two cases, we were fortunate to have access to the studios and files of artists in New York, and this was of immeasurable help. The cooperation of Roy Lichtenstein, both by lending and by assisting our research into his sources in comic-book illustration, was unstinting and greatly appreciated. Claes Oldenburg and Coosje van Bruggen were wonderfully patient with many demands for access to notebooks and collections of ephemera, and offered information and criticism that helped shape our understanding of the work. Sarah Taggert, Jasper Johns's assistant, Patricia Koch, Roy Lichtenstein's assistant, and David Platzker, assistant to Claes Oldenburg and Coosje van Bruggen, helped us a great deal in all these matters, and we thank them, as well as David White, curator for Robert Rauschenberg, for the aid they provided.

The research underlying this exhibition has led, not only to artist's files and to expected sources in museums and libraries, but also into areas less familiar to most art historians, in the worlds of advertising, graffiti, and comics especially. In these territories, chasing down references, photographs, and documents, we have depended on the guidance of many friends, old and new. In our work on the Michelin company and its avatar Bibendum, we were initially aided by Sir Terence Conran, whose firm now owns the former Michelin headquarters in London. Through the cooperation of Sir Terence, we were put in touch with the stained-glass firm of Goddard & Gibbs, who crafted, on commission from Michelin especially for the exhibition, a replica of an original 1910–11 Bibendum window (see the frontispiece, p. 2). Jean-Pierre Vuillerme, of Michelin, S.A., was the key person who supported the firm's cooperation with our project, and we are deeply appreciative of the help he gave, as well as of the archival assistance offered by Albert D'Arpiany in Clermont-Ferrand, and of the help provided by Michel Bonny of the Michelin office in London.

In the research on early twentieth-century journalism and photographic ephemera, we very much appreciate the assistance of Maurice Guibert, of L'Ivre d'Antin in Paris, and of Andreas Brown, of the Gotham Book Mart in New York. Michel Melot of the Bibliothèque Nationale, and Marie de Thézy and Christina Huvé of the Bibliothèque Historique de la Ville de Paris, were also very helpful, as were: Wendy Schadwell of the New-York Historical Society; Bonnie Yochelson and Terry Ariano of the Museum of the City of New York; Margaret Luchars of the Cooper-Hewitt Museum; Richard Hill of the New York Public Library; Leslie Furth, Associate Curator for Research at The Phillips Collection, Washington, D.C.; and the staffs of the Print Division of the New York Public Library, Butler Library and Avery Library at Columbia University, and St. Mark's Library at the General Theological Seminary.

Outside of these institutions, a great many individuals also helped guide research, and direct us to sought-after materials. Among these, we offer our gratitude to Jeffrey Weiss, Gertje Utley, Michelle Facos, Marie-Aline Prat, Arline Meyer, Susan Cooke, Mitchell Merling, and Bruce Altschuler, as well as to Elizabeth Childs of the State University of New York at Purchase, James L. Coen of Columbia University Business School, and Miyeko Murase of Columbia University. Aimée Brown Price of the City University of New York, Benjamin H. D. Buchloh of the Massachusetts Institute of Technology, William Camfield of Rice University, and Leo Steinberg of the University of Pennsylvania all generously shared with us information pertaining to their special scholarly knowledge. An extra note of thanks is also due Emily Braun, for alerting me to, and helping me resolve, a problem in her field of expertise.

In the area of comics and cartoon illustration, we were blessed with the cooperation of those in the creative, as well as the production and collecting, domains of the business. Both Garry Trudeau and Robert Crumb were generous with their time and knowledge, and several of the draftsmen associated with D.C. Comics in the early 1960s—John Romita, Joe Kubert, Irv Novick, Bernard Sachs, and Russ Heath—provided us with invaluable insights into that world. Historians of comics, including Maurice Horn, Joyce Brabner (herself a comics artist), Catherine Yronwode, and Richard Marschall, editor of Nemo, all lent their support. In the pursuit of original editions of the appropriate comics, we had help from Arnie Koch of Golden Age Express, and the collectors Mark Hanerfeld and Mike Tiefenbacher. Research into the archives of D.C. Comics was greatly assisted by Joe Orlando and Angelina Genduso; we also thank Michael Wolff and Tony Silver for their cooperation with this special part of the exhibition project.

Similarly, our work with the subject of graffiti was helped by the photographer Henry Chalfant, and by the interviews we were able to have with the former subway graffiti writers who work under the professional names A-One, Lee, Crash, and Daze.

In addition to Mr. Chalfant's documentary images of graffiti, we also depended on the work of several other photographers. Bryan Burkey, Jim Strong, Rick Dingus, and Ken Kirkwood all produced photos that contributed to the catalogue, and François Sautour of the photo agency Roger-Viollet in Paris provided additional help. At the Museum, we put heavy demands for photography on our own Department of Rights and Reproductions, and owe great thanks to Richard Tooke, Mikki Carpenter, Kate Keller, and Mali Olatunji for responding to these demands in exemplary fashion.

There is virtually no part of the Museum which did not feel, at one time or another, the pressures of this exhibition; and the realization of both the show and its catalogue would not have been thinkable without the smooth, committed cooperation of a great many people in all corners of the institution. Closest to home, the demands of research, documentation, and organization put a heavy strain on those who work most closely with me, and on others in the Department of Painting and Sculpture. Lisa Nadel, Executive Secretary, took charge of the vast amounts of typing and filing necessary to keep loan correspondence functioning properly, and handled foreign phone calls with special diplomacy; after her departure, Helen Selsdon assumed these duties in exemplary fashion, and Joanna Watsky also assisted in this crucial area. Cora Rosevear, Associate Curator, and Judith Cousins, Research Curator, lent special help with works from the Museum's collection, and Lynn Zelevansky, Curatorial Assistant, was of invaluable aid in matters that overlapped with her work on the "Picasso and Braque" exhibition. Carolyn Lanchner also provided valuable assistance in dealing with several sensitive loans, and with questions relating to her expertise in the work of Miró. I owe a particular debt to Anne Umland, Assistant to the Director, who not only did a thousand things to keep the exhibition project on track, and bore the brunt of our entry into the computer age, but who organized the business of my office in such a fashion as to allow me to keep focused on the show, and at the same time to maintain the day-to-day management of the Department. Her can-do attitude and impeccable efficiency helped preserve sanity even in the most stressful moments, and I am deeply appreciative.

The myriad responsibilities that attended the collecting, crating, shipping, and receiving of the works to be included in the exhibition came to rest on the desk of Carrie DeCato, the Registrar of the show. We were lucky indeed to have her experienced, professional hand at the tiller. Her careful, admirably thorough control of all these tasks was aided by Eloise Ricciardelli, and by Aileen Chuk, Ramona Bannayan, and Mary Klindt. The insurance arrangements surrounding transportation, and countless other matters related to the proper functioning of the exhibition, fell to Richard Palmer, Coordinator of Exhibitions. Working with Eleni Cocordas, Associate Coordinator of Exhibitions, and with his assistant Rosette Bakish, Dick fulfilled his job, as he has so often, in the heat of countless upsets and menacing deadlines, with the most unflappable professional calm and astuteness.

Drawing on the resources of the Museum's own collection, both for loans and for documentation, we have been admirably propelled along in our work by the support of colleagues in the Library, including the Director, Clive Phillpot, Janis Ekdahl, Hikmet Dogu, Eumie Imm, and Terry R. Myers; in the Department of Photography, Peter Galassi, Susan Kismaric, and Lisa Kurzner; in the Department of Prints and Illustrated Books, Wendy Weitman; in the Department of Architecture and Design, Robert Coates; and in the Department of Drawings, Beatrice Kernan. Special thanks are owed to Magdalena Dabrowski of the Department of Drawings, not only for help with material in her charge, but also for her aid with loans from Russia.

In all questions pertaining to the conservation of works in the exhibition, we have benefited from the keen eyes, sound advice, and skill of those in our Department of Conservation. Antoinette King, Director of the department, has been of great help, and we also extend particular thanks to Conservators James Coddington, Carol Stringari, and Karl Buchberg, and Associate Conservators Anny Aviram, Pat Houlihan, and Lynda Zycherman.

If the handling of objects is the most tangible and immediately physical part of the work of an exhibition, perhaps the least tangible—yet crucially important—aspect of such a project is the dispersal of information about it. Without the proper organization of press information and photographs, an enormous part of the exhibition's intended impact would be lost. For getting out the word, and for their careful attention to the best presentation of the show on all fronts, great thanks are owed to Jeanne Collins, Director of Public Information, and to Jessica Schwartz, Associate Director, as well as to the other members of that department, including Jennifer Carlson, Edna Goldstaub, Christopher Lyons, Hilarie Sheets, Julie Zander, and Victoria Garvin.

Shaping the impact of the exhibition on the visiting public is also, in areas of critical importance, the responsibility of the Department of Education. It has been a pleasure to work with Philip Yenawine, Director of Education, and with Emily Kies-Folpe, Museum Educator, Special Programs, in the preparation of the wall texts, exhibition brochure, and surrounding educational programs that do so much to help guide the Museum's visitors to the best appreciation and understanding of the ideas and artworks the exhibition presents.

The presentation of the exhibition itself has been in the talented hands of Jerry Neuner, Production Manager. Jerry's consummate professionalism, his keen grasp of the requirements of different objects and ideas, and his relentless resistance to any form of despair or panic, combine with his considerable creative talents to make of him an ideal collaborator in exhibition design. This exhibition has presented especially challenging situations with regard to diverse materials and the need for subtle juxtapositions, and I am deeply grateful for his help in clarifying its presentation. Thanks, too, to his assistants, Karen Meyerhoff and Douglas Fieck, for all that they contributed.

Turning from the show itself to the publications surrounding it, I convey my gratitude to Ellen Harris, Deputy Director for Finance and Auxiliary Activities, for her patience in the face of the extreme delays that attended the writing of the catalogue texts, and for her constant readjustments in the face of mounting pressures. I have appreciated her efforts to rationalize the publishing process, and to arrive at a book that would serve the show, and the Museum, in the best fashion. The editing of the texts has been the work of James Leggio, and I am grateful to him for a close and helpful reading as well as for his characteristically scrupulous attention to matters of quality. The complexities of dual authorship and the large scope of the manuscript placed extreme demands on all involved, and he has borne the brunt of those demands. In the face of these exceptional pressures, he nonetheless dedicated himself to an unimpeachably thorough command of every phase of the editing process, and did a remarkable and much appreciated job of saving the book from countless errors that continually threatened its fabric. On the side of illustrations, quality control has been the task of Tim McDonough, and he has conquered this task with quiet, flawless aplomb. His calm hand in the project, and my knowledge of the high standards he always upholds, have been the source of great reassurance in hours of darkness during the long months it took to produce the book. Steve Schoenfelder designed the book, and I cannot say enough regarding my admiration for his ability, and regarding the joy of working with him. Laboring under unusual constraints, Steve has consistently solved every problem and responded to every challenge. He has been open to all suggestions, but finally firm in his own vision as well, and the results have been made to look, by one of his patented miracles, as if these words and pictures somehow fell together naturally. Steve's work has been overseen and assisted by Michael Hentges, Director of Graphics, in the best spirit. Michael and Gregory Gillbergh have also taken charge of the graphics for the exhibition's installation, and of coordinating all printed matter pertaining to it. They have done an excellent job, and it has been a pleasure to work with them.

In addition to the catalogue at hand, other publications will also accompany the exhibition. Most notably, a volume titled *Modern Art and Popular Culture: Readings in High and Low*, with contributions by nine authors, will be co-published by The Museum of Modern Art and Harry N. Abrams, Inc. I am grateful for the work done on that volume by Harriet Bee of the Museum's Department of Publications, and I am especially in the debt of Joan Pachner for the intense burst of work she contributed, on short notice, to rescue the volume from dire last-minute problems. The book could never have been brought to completion without her saving intervention at a crucial point. Further information about the contributions of the nine authors, and of the work of those responsible for producing that companion publication, may be found in its own Acknowledgments.

A brochure guide to the exhibition will also be published, in the form of a newspaper. This guide, as well as the exhibition display's reproductions of the pages that Cubist artists saw, and used in their works, around 1912–14, were made possible through the generosity of *The Star-Ledger* of Newark, New Jersey. We are deeply grateful to Mark W. Newhouse, Vice President, for the time and resources he has committed to both of these projects, and for the excellent work done by his technicians.

In addition to the guide to the exhibition, a separate brochure will also appear, to introduce the series of performances arranged to accompany the exhibition

and organized by RoseLee Goldberg. I am grateful to RoseLee for accepting my invitation to prepare this series and its brochure, and for the extensive work she has done to coordinate an exceptionally talented group of artists as participants. Her special expertise in this area has added another dimension to the concept of the exhibition, and I have enjoyed having her as a collaborator in this area. The many people on the Museum staff who helped with the performance series are acknowledged in its brochure, and I add my appreciation for their cooperation.

I reserve my final expressions of gratitude for those with whom I have worked most directly, for the past two and a half years, in producing "High and Low." If, familiarly, "every picture tells a story," then certainly every object in this exhibition, and every illustration in its catalogue, has at least one, if not many, tales to tell—of mountainous paperwork, countless phone calls and letters, intricate arrangements, constant cross-checking, innumerable lists, and hours of labor beyond counting. The people best equipped to tell those tales, and least likely to forget them, are the two talented, indefatigable Curatorial Assistants who did the nuts-and-bolts organizational work, and more, in this project. Jennifer Wells took charge of all matters pertaining to loans. Despite conflicting demands from other exhibitions also in her care, and with professional sang-froid in the face of numerous crises, she did an impeccable job of keeping track of every aspect of the exhibition. Her sharp eye, and relentless research efforts, also made signal contributions to the curatorial shaping of the exhibition in many areas. Mary Beth Smalley oversaw the preparation of the material for this publication, and thus assumed the burden of initially setting in order our ever-changing demands for illustrations, and of following through down to the last details of altered footnotes and figure references. Both Jennifer and Mary Beth have been besieged with tasks, and called upon for exertions that stretched well beyond normal hours, in order to wrestle into order a vast amount of material. Each has done superb work, and has well earned the professional admiration, and warm thanks, of all who were involved in the exhibition.

The partners Adam Gopnik and I have had in our research have been Matthew Armstrong, doctoral candidate at the Institute of Fine Arts of New York University, and Fereshteh Daftari (Ph.D., Columbia University). We had vast ground to cover, and little time to cover it. These two researchers threw themselves at the task, scouring libraries here and abroad, pursuing leads like detectives, locating acres of obscure literature, reading and summarizing hundreds and hundreds of articles. The annotated bibliography in this book gives some indication of the scope of their work, but cannot fully convey all that we owe to them. Their creative initiatives, and willingness to go the extra mile, along with their never-say-die commitment to thoroughness and accuracy, have been the indispensable resources behind the texts of this book. Many of the most telling discoveries owe to their work, from Matt's pursuit of Lichtenstein's sources and Duchamp's elusive urinal to Feri's in-depth recovery of the literature on graffiti; and much more of their work had to be left behind in the final cuts. To them, all homage and appreciation.

A special acknowledgment is due Lily Auchincloss, whose generous participation made a tremendous difference in helping us bring the work on this publication to a successful conclusion. I extend my warmest personal appreciation to her for this suppport.

I thank my wife, Elyn Zimmerman, for bearing with me through the considerable sacrifices that were made to move this project toward completion and for the help she gave me in focusing my ideas in the manuscript of this book. And my concluding note of thanks is succinct, in recognition of a debt that is dauntingly extensive, to my collaborator and co-author, Adam Gopnik. We shared ideas and initiatives in the conception and throughout all the aspects of preparing this exhibition. He made it happen, and he made it fun.

Kirk Varnedoe
Director, Department of Painting and Sculpture
The Museum of Modern Art

Bob Gottlieb, the editor of *The New Yorker,* showed, throughout the frantic year that it took to produce this book, extraordinary patience with what must have seemed to him at times to be an incomprehensibly preoccupied "Talk" reporter; I thank him for his generosity, for his clarity, and for his friendship. Charles McGrath—deflator of the fake crescendo, defender of the extended metaphor—who has for several years drawn the extremely short straw of editing my own contributions to the magazine, also agreed to run his peerless pencil through my contributions to these pages. Whatever felicities of style appear are, as always, mostly his; whatever infelicities remain, mostly mine. At *The New Yorker*, where several passages in this book originally appeared, all in very different form, I would also like to thank Roger Angell, Eleanor Gould, Mark Singer, and, especially, Alec Wilkinson, for everything that they have tried to teach me about style; and Martin Baron and his fact-checkers, for everything that they tried to teach me about truth. Other passages in this book also first appeared in different form at different places: at *Art Journal*, I thank Judith Wechsler and Rose Weill for their editorial intelligence; at *The New York Review of Books*, I thank Barbara Epstein for her wit and for her reach.

In addition to seconding all of Kirk Varnedoe's thanks to the staff of The Museum of Modern Art, and particularly to all the people on the fifth and sixth floors who shared the pressures and deadlines of this book and show, I would like to add my own special, intense, and heartfelt thanks to Matthew Armstrong and Fereshteh Daftari.

My father and mother, Irwin and Myrna Gopnik, taught me long ago to think about style change as a form of social passage. I thank them for that and for all else besides. I would also like to thank Richard Avedon, whose wisdom, counsel, and uncompromising standards are a constant source of strength, and of hope; and Mary Shanahan, who can look at anything and gently make sense of it all.

From the moment that he first asked me to share this journey with him, Kirk Varnedoe has been, as ever, an inspiring teacher, and an incomparable learner. His contagious appetite for ideas and images and experience makes him as ideal a companion as he is a collaborator; my thanks to him go deeper, and extend further, than I can ever say. Martha Parker, despite being engaged on a professional journey of her own at least as demanding as this one, still managed, somehow, to read every page, calm every fear, correct every excess, and grace every moment.

Adam Gopnik

Many of the works reproduced in this book are not included in the exhibition of the same title. A checklist of that exhibition is available from The Museum of Modern Art.

In the captions, the dimensions of works of art are given first in inches and then in centimeters; height precedes width, which is followed in the case of sculpture by depth. Dimensions for works on paper indicate sheet size, unless otherwise noted.

1. Morris column, place Denfert-Rochereau, Paris, c. 1910

Go back to Paris around the turn of the century, and follow an artist as he returns from the Louvre to his studio at the end of the day. Exiting the galleries onto the quai, still charged by the grandeur of the Panathenaic frieze, the dynamism of the Victory of Samothrace, or the masterly countenances in Rembrandt, he dreams of an art that will revive their ideals and rival their grasp of human experience. Yet, crossing the boulevards and public parks, he recognizes that the experience with which he must contend will not be theirs, but his. He wants to be of his time, and find languages of form appropriate to the world of machines, science, and social revolution that is emerging all around him.

We know where such musings will lead. We know that the modern world then forming has since yielded a mass society more complex than anyone could foresee. But we also know that one of the most distinctive forces within that society has been a tradition of art that allowed the individual imagination unparalleled freedom, and yielded difficult, exasperating, and even hermetically resistant objects of invention—from austere abstractions to wildly distorted human faces, fur-lined teacups, paintings of soup cans, and rooms full of glowing bands of moving words.

Above all, we know that crucial ciphers in the combination that would unlock this artist's dilemma, and help bring forth that new force of invention, were to be found neither in the monuments he left at the museum nor in the privacy of the atelier to which he returned. Beside, beneath, and behind him in that stroll, in the apparently trivial and marginal things taken for granted along his path—in the cheap reproductions he brushed past on his way out of the museum, in the brightly colored commercial posters along the boulevard and in the shop windows of the department stores, in the newspapers and cartoon journals of the morning, stacked up in kiosks along the quai, and even in the mean scrawlings on the walls of the darkened side streets—was an alphabet for art's new language. There, in germ, lay another telling power of the coming age—modern urban culture, a phenomenon as vulgar and polyglot in its energies as the modern artist seemed cloistered and exclusive in his meditations.

But if the artist in question happened to be Georges Seurat, and he cast an interested glance toward the rashes of posters then coming to cover city walls, a key contact between these apparently opposite domains would have been made. Or if he were Giacomo Balla,

INTRODUCTION

and looked down to study the scribbles that marred a door along the way, another channel would have been opened. And above all, if our artist were Pablo Picasso or Georges Braque, and stopped to consider the look of poster columns, billboards, and newspapers in the years just before World War I, then the moment that would usher those pieces of the urban stroller's world into the mainstream of the modern imagination would have been at hand—and shortly a spark would arc over to create a permanent circuit between high art and the low culture of the modern city.

This book traces the story of that circuit: the evolving relationship, from then till now, between modern art and popular culture. It is a book about people and objects, not terms and categories. But since virtually every word in its title—"modern" or "art" or "culture" or "popular," not to mention the labels "high" and "low" themselves—is subject to debate and diverse interpretations, we should start by saying how we intend to use these terms, in order to make clear what we will and will not be after.

Start with the primary term: by "modern art" we mean that tradition of expanded freedom for the individual imagination which began in the era of our artist's Parisian walk, and which includes Seurat, Balla, Picasso, and Braque, as well as Léger, Duchamp, Miró, Ernst, Magritte, Rodchenko, Johns, and the other painters and sculptors we discuss. We call their work "high" art, not to glamorize it or quarantine it (nor to deny that there are notable differences of purpose and of quality within that roster), but because these artists and their work are the primary material with which any history of art in this century must contend. Achievements in this lineage have always involved, in one way or another, a consciousness of the traditional "high" ceremonial and religious art enshrined in places like the Louvre, and entailed some sense of obligation—even if that obligation was expressed through emphatic rejection and the urge to start afresh—to the grand manner of art.

"Low" is more problematic. There have been many different forms of representation that were unconcerned with the grand Western traditions, and considered inferior by accepted standards of art, but which modern artists have revalued and drawn upon for inspiration. This book will not attempt to deal with all or even most of these—not the carvings of tribal cultures, for example, nor the playroom drawings of children, nor the imagery created by the insane, nor the bridges and grain silos of industrial engineers, nor the art of rural folk limners or visionary amateurs. All these are

2. George Herriman. Panels from *The Family Upstairs*, November 22, 1910

topics for another day. Our interest is in forms and styles associated with the rise of urban culture in industrialized nations that involve self-conscious, streetwise, or commercial—as opposed to ostensibly "naïve"—creation. Guided by what we see as principal interests of modern artists, we will look at four varieties of this kind of popular culture: graffiti, caricature, comics, and the broad domain of advertising, including newspaper ads, billboards, catalogues, and sales displays with their transformations of everyday objects.

Some of these forms of representation are often included in the umbrella term "mass culture," and by adopting instead the word "popular" as a label of convenience we do not mean to imply that there is something spontaneously generated or democratically appealing about all of this material. Advertising and comics, for example—both clearly commercial enterprises, making images for sale or to promote selling—are aspects of what we might call an "overlord" culture, directed by a few people toward a broad audience. Caricature and graffiti, by contrast, seem to belong to what we might call "underbelly" culture, a tradition of social criticism or raw, outlaw drawing. And while advertising and comics flowered in the modern era, through the technologies of mass reproduction, caricature and graffiti are much older forms of expression, made individually if often anonymously. But just because of these differences, a consideration that groups the four areas together can allow us to see two distinct yet parallel aspects of modern art: the way it responded to unfamiliar, developing aspects of the modern world, like billboards; and also the way it devised new forms to address that world, from sources that were familiar but ignored or long belittled, like graffiti.

We call all these areas of representation "low," not to denigrate them out of hand (on the contrary, we hope to show that within their realm artists can be found who made work of originality and intensity) but to recognize that they have traditionally been considered irrelevant to, or outside, any consideration of achievement in the fine arts of our time—and in fact

have commonly been accepted as opposite to the "high" arts in their intentions, audiences, and nature of endeavor. Throughout the chapters ahead, "low," like "high," should be understood as a working, shorthand convention rather than as a definition of a fixed class of things. Yet we recognize that the imperative need to have reliable, solid distinctions between high and low—whether as a challenge for future achievement or as a lost ideal—haunts the theoretical literature concerned with the different levels of culture in modern society.

In 1910 the cartoonist George Herriman created a comic strip, *The Family Upstairs* (fig. 2), that ran for two years on a single premise. In this strip, a family named the Dingbats, who live in an apartment in an unnamed city, are obsessed with curiosity about the goings-on of their upstairs neighbor. The Dingbats are convinced that some mad, enormous world of dangerous licentiousness and wonderful possibility exists right there above their heads. The attempt to get one small, fleeting look at The Family Upstairs becomes the Dingbat family grail, involving in the quest policemen, private detectives, Rube Goldberg–type contraptions, and endless strategizing. The Dingbats will do anything to find out—anything, that is, except simply go upstairs and knock on the door.

Much writing on the subject of modern art and popular culture has tended to have somewhat the same persistent but static plot—only here the mystery has always resided *down*stairs, below the floorboards of those who write books and undertake social theorizing about the literature, imagery, and amusements of the "common people" of mass society. And while the Dingbats' obsession lasted only two years, the debate over popular culture—about where it comes from, what it means, and what effects it may have both on its participants and on those who try to resist it—has been going on at least since the Romantic era, when modern democracy and modern industry together began to change life in the Western nations. Ever since it was first drawn on the map of modernity, around the middle of the last century, the frontier dividing high from low culture has been an indispensable topic for pundits, both as a major fault line of anxiety and as a meeting point for otherwise opposite ideologies; its imminent disappearance has been lamented as often as its entrenched existence has been loathed. This split has been damned by elitists who have felt that the only true culture is by definition high, and limited to the enlightened few, as well as by apostles of uplift who have felt that a good society requires a unified culture, in which all participate. But the line of distinction has nonetheless been a constant cause for alert concern, for fear that its location might become more ambiguous, or its separations less certain.

Countless events have transformed the terms of this controversy. In the mid-nineteenth century, with the spread of literacy, the popular press and dime novels posed a whole new challenge to literature, while lithography, and then photography and photomechanical reproduction, broadened the public for images. Since 1900, radio, or film, or talking films, or television, have each been greeted in their turn as agents of revolution in modern society's apprehension of the arts, while political developments, such as the ascendancies of fascism, communism, or monopoly capitalism, have provided pressing reasons to reconsider culture's fate within mass society. After each of these changes, thinkers of diverse stripe have considered the matter anew, and by now the literature they have produced has taken on a life of its own; thick volumes, and full scholarly careers, may be devoted simply to surveying and analyzing aspects of this body of thought. (The annotated bibliography included here can provide an initial guide through those thickets.) But this book was conceived in part from a frustration with the sense of stalemate that pervades this literature. For all the sweeping ideas, subtle nuances of analysis, and arresting personalities involved in theorizing about high and low culture in modern society, it seems that a few stereotyped responses are repeated over and over again, with a dismayingly permanent narrowness.

A large part of this tradition of writing rests on the idea that low, popular culture in modern society constitutes a separate, definable body of phenomena, with its own essential nature (however bastardized or inauthentic); and on the belief that this nature is not just irredeemably inferior to the spirit of high culture, but intrinsically noxious. The world of cheap pleasures is a bad thing, we are told, because it supplants something precious we once had, or at least puts it in imminent danger of extinction. In this view, popular culture is essentially parasitic in nature and inevitably trivializes the true culture it draws upon. And that skepticism is shared by two very different political persuasions. One, a conservative outlook, originates in nineteenth-century criticisms of the leveling effects of democracy, and typically sees the expansion of classes who satisfy themselves with "shallow" amusements as a threat to the independent-minded individualism associated with great traditions of the past. This view links high artistic achievement with the kind of focused patronage to be

found in markedly stratified societies, and typically involves a nostalgia for a past of ostensibly enlightened support from the castle and the court.

Others with more egalitarian convictions, though, welcome the demise of the castle and the court, and regret instead the passing of the cottage and the village: what they see imperiled by modernity is the possibility of any genuinely popular folkways or common culture of customs, generated by the people themselves or answering to their real needs. This view blames the failings of the extant, ersatz pop culture not (as the conservatives do) on the crass natures of its consumers, but on the manipulations of powerful minorities who control the production and dissemination of tabloid newspapers, popular music, television serials, and so on. One of the most influential of these

3. Newsstand, Paris, 1924

lines of criticism insists, for example, that the term "culture industry," as opposed to simply mass or popular culture, more properly identifies the manufactured evil at hand.[1]

Modern popular culture is scorned, then, both because it menaces true high art and because it overwhelms true low customs. It is feared for its addiction to novelty, which seems bound to chase out tradition and overthrow established values; and at the same time (and often by the same critics) damned for its profoundly conservative tendency to swamp or co-opt any genuine alternatives, and to maintain the interests of its makers against any possibility of meaningful change.

Those who reject modern popular culture for these

4. **Berenice Abbott.** *Hardware Store, 316–318 Bowery, Manhattan.* **1938. Gelatin-silver print, 7⅝ × 9½″ (19.4 × 24.1 cm). The Museum of Modern Art, New York. Photography Study Collection**

different reasons also tend to agree that modern art must define itself in strictest opposition to this force—in order, some say, to achieve an ideal and lofty expression, untainted by the common, the tawdry, or the facile; or else to maintain, as others would wish, a permanent role of inassimilable dissent against society's dominant powers.

A wholly opposite attitude, however, can also be found in the writing on popular culture. Extolling democracy itself as a primary value, supporters of this alternative viewpoint look with suspicion on any attempt to define degrees of intrinsic quality distinguishing high from low culture. They see such efforts as the work of a self-proclaimed elite out to impose false hierarchies where no authentic ones exist. And in their insistence on the falsity of ranking one social group's forms of diversion as more worthy than another's, such enthusiastic populists are often joined by those with a more clinical, anthropological approach, who support a catholic, inclusive notion of culture and consider virtually all manifestations of a society equally deserving of attention and study. Here an uninflected leveling impulse, or a doggedly perverse will to stand conventional hierarchies on their head, takes the place of any attempt to make discriminations about enduring value and importance among the creations of low culture, or to follow the intricate, peculiar history of their engagement with high art. The real differences in ambitions and procedures at the two levels of creation,

hypertrophied in the first views we mentioned, are ignored or denied in these.

The theoretical literature on the division between high and low in modern life could appear to leave room for countless hybrid permutations among a set of terms such as elitist, populist, nostalgist, conservative, radical, optimist, and skeptic. Yet the basic positions we have just sketched persist with monotonous regularity, and the schematic nature of their typologies makes this literature a poor guide to the subject matter we are about to explore. In general, such theoretical writing about modern popular culture has shown a sublime lack of curiosity about the particulars of its subject. Bland assertions about the "corrupting" or "hegemonic" social role of jazz, or the movies, or comics, abound, unaccompanied by any sense of the variety within these categories, or investigation of the diverse individuals and histories that have shaped them. (If we only take, for example, a characteristically confident condemnation of kitsch that derides "movies, tap-dancing, slick commercial fiction, comics, [and] popular songs,"[2] and replace its categories with real people—such as Charles Chaplin and Pier Paolo Pasolini, or Fred Astaire, or Paul Bowles and P. G. Wodehouse, or George Herriman, or Duke Ellington, and so on—we see how complexly riven may be the ground on which such theories claim to stand.) And specifically, this body of writing has paid very little attention to modern visual art. Instead, it tends to extrapolate les-

5. Times Square, New York, 1938

sons from meditations on the state of the novel, or drama, or music, and then to apply these, in procrustean fashion, to painting, sculpture, and architecture.[3] This book sets out with an opposite set of premises: in it the visual arts are primary, and the particulars of their history are the central focus.

For such a vast subject, we will adopt a purposely delimited approach. The story of the interplay between modern art and popular culture is one of the most important aspects of the history of art in our epoch. It was central to what made modern art modern at the start of this century, and it has continued to be crucial to the work of many younger artists in the last decade. Yet just because the subject can be so unwieldy and seemingly all-pervasive, we must accept at the outset a principle of draconian selectivity and sacrifice if we hope to give a coherent account within the compass of this one book. High modern painting and sculpture constitute our primary topic. The book will give as much sense as possible of the corresponding particularities of relevant "low" worlds around modern art, but will not aspire to offer a full chronicle of such things as comics or advertising over the past hundred years, much less essay any broad sociological history of popular culture. We feel that the way to open new avenues into this field of study is to ask focused questions about a limited number of key instances, and let the lessons learned there reverberate elsewhere—

rather than to attempt to make global statements, or simply to enumerate every known aspect of the subject at hand. We focus, therefore, on only a few places, principally Paris and New York, with occasional excursions in the directions of London, Berlin, Moscow, or Los Angeles. This is not meant to imply that art from these centers constitutes either the whole or the essence of modern art. On the contrary, since we insist that each case must be considered in its separate details, we cede that terrain to others, to carry on this kind of investigation in the art of those other places— and in other domains such as architecture, photography, or performance art.

Our goal is to examine the transformations through which modern painters and sculptors have made new poetic languages by reimagining the possibilities in forms of popular culture; and, as a corollary, to acknowledge the way those adaptations in modern art have often found their way back into the common currency of public visual prose. To demonstrate that process, we will focus on aspects of style, including small items like sans-serif typefaces or Benday dots, and broader strategies such as gigantism or the mind-arresting transformation of objects. This means that we will not be dealing principally with art that happens to be made from "low" materials such as scrap metal, old cars, or postcards, or with art that simply depicts popular-culture motifs, such as movie marquees, diners, or rock stars. Nor is our story about the influence

6. **Bryan Burkey.** *Times Square, New York.* 1990. Dye-transfer print, 16 × 20″ (40.6 × 50.8 cm). Collection the artist

7. **Bryan Burkey.** *Times Square, New York.* 1990. Dye-transfer print, 16 × 20″ (40.6 × 50.8 cm). Collection the artist

on modern art of things as ubiquitous and multifaceted as "photographic imagery," or "cinema," or "jazz." In order to express a feeling for such new things, whether it was the syncopation of boogie-woogie or the abstruse conundrums of altered ideas of space and time, modern artists had first to search the resources available in existing, developed languages of form, to find appropriate pictorial or plastic devices—they had, in other words, to make up a style. And their stylistic inventions often propelled the movements of specific manners and strategies from low to high and back again: billboards affect avant-garde painters whose work later affects billboard designers, for example; or techniques of sales display get picked up in structures of art that in turn change the look of commerce.

Obviously, these internal histories of exchanged forms take place within, and are affected by, external contingencies of uses and conflicts and politics; and a large part of our work involves recounting those outside circumstances. We hope to take objects that have too often been isolated as "timeless" or "transcendent" and resituate them within the changing, dynamic contradictions of real life. What we will not do, though, is take things that are by nature historical in the deepest sense—individual choices, whims of taste, and the unpredictable fates of objects bought and sold in the marketplace—and make them prisoner to static categories or comfortably untestable abstractions. Wherever possible, we want to deal with all our themes, regardless of their scope and ramifications, as they manifest themselves in individuals and in visible properties of particular things; this is a book, as we said, about people and objects.

Our chronicle begins with the first moment of direct incorporation of material from modern popular culture into the fabric of modern art, in the Cubists' inclusions of newspaper snippets and typography from commercial labels. After tracing the consequences of their work with the ephemera of printed words—as a compressed demonstration of some basic patterns of interchange between high art and the new commercial givens of the city—we take up other artists' engagement with the older, preexisting forms of graffiti and caricature; then we return to specifically modern phenomena by considering caricature's twentieth-century stepchild, the comics. The broadest, most inclusive history, that of the complex exchanges between modern art and the various practices of advertising—print ads, displays, catalogues, packaging, and so on—is the last of these separate but related stories that follow modern art history up to about 1970.

A chapter is set aside, at the end, to deal with developments in recent art, from 1970 to 1990. This is not to suggest some fateful rupture in history; on the contrary, one purpose of the other, preceding chapters will be to help make better sense of what is taking place now. We recognize, though, that we cannot have anything like the same perspective on last month's or last year's exhibitions that we can have on works of early modern art, or of the immediate postwar era. Inevitably, writing on such contemporary work involves more recounting of lived experience, and less analysis of established achievements. We also want to avoid a false sense of continuity. The art of the last ten or twenty years seems different in part because artists have insisted that it is. A great many contemporary artists who have made a point of addressing their work to the nature of popular culture have willfully set themselves apart from their predecessors, asserting that their own time is shaped by different social forces, and that their art acts to criticize, not simply extend, modernism's earlier attitudes toward phenomena such as advertising. Their critique of what early modern art achieved, and that art's implicit critique of them, merit separate consideration.

At each step of our journey, we are going to try to forestall the construction of any grand theoretical frameworks, and indulge instead our curiosity about particulars. We want to go back and extend, in a way, that turn-of-the-century artist's journey through the world of modern urban culture—to learn more about the histories of those mundane things that lay on the fringes of his visual consciousness and have since, in part because of modern art, become so central to our vision of the world we live in. When Picasso and Braque started clipping Parisian newspapers, was there anything special about those papers, and if so why? What did graffiti look like then? When did people start paying attention to it, and who first thought it might be like art? Is caricature just a part of graffiti, and an immemorial bit of human malevolence, or does it have some history we can chart that would help us understand some of the strange faces and bizarre bodies in modern art? We know some of these things in general: we know that Roy Lichtenstein borrowed images from comic books, for example, and that Marcel Duchamp and Francis Picabia presented mundane functional objects as sculptures and portraits. But what kind of comics were chosen, who drew them, and what other comic styles were available then? And what did people outside the art world, like merchants with shop windows or sales catalogues, think about the display and personalization of objects like toilets and automobile accessories? It's fairly common knowledge, too, that Fernand Léger, Stuart Davis, Richard Hamilton, and James Rosenquist all responded to advertising; but was advertising at all the same thing in these separate cases? And if not, what made the differences? Individually, some of these inquiries may seem a little blunt, even simple-minded; but collectively, they and others like them may save us from the stalemates of empty theorization, and from the self-imposed plight of the Dingbats. The best big answers often arise from the smallest and most obvious first questions; starting with the turn of this page, we propose to go downstairs and knock.

1. Pablo Picasso. *Table with Bottle, Wineglass, and Newspaper*. 1912. Pasted paper, charcoal, and gouache on paper, 24⅜ × 18⅞" (62 × 48 cm).
Musée National d'Art Moderne, Centre Georges Pompidou, Paris. Gift of Henri Laugier

n the beginning was the word, and the word was BAL. Or perhaps it was BACH. At some point in the early autumn of 1911, Georges Braque picked up a common stencil and used it to paint onto a Cubist picture either the three letters, B, A, and L, that indicated a popular-dancing ball, or the four, B, A, C, and H, that named the eighteenth-century composer. Braque was winding up a vacation when he tried this little experiment, and by the time he returned to Paris he had with him two completed pictures that bore these words respectively (figs. 2, 3). We will never be certain which came first, the reference to the provincial fête or the homage to the master of the fugue;[1] and the ambivalence is entirely appropriate. When Braque lifted that stencil off the canvas, he had set into a painting where all else was high cerebration and subtly refined ambiguity a word of immediate, unmistakable legibility, rendered in a style of typography usually seen on packing crates and crude commercial signage. From that moment onward, the line that divided the high tradition of art from the world of posters and cheap entertainment— that held BACH apart from BAL—would be transgressed and redrawn with sharply increasing frequency. Braque's lettering, undertaken in an already charged climate of interchange between himself and Picasso, initiated a sequence of events that was decisive for the whole future process of modern art's engagement with the materials of popular culture.

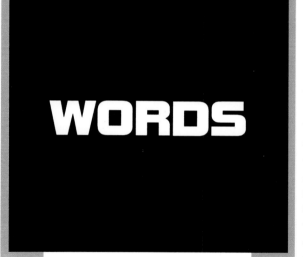

By the end of 1911, Braque and Picasso had been involved for almost three years in a constant round of mutual studio visits, shoptalk, and shared secrets that had produced a radical new painting style, Analytic Cubism, which at moments seemed headed toward pure abstraction. The collaboration had been so complete that outsiders could barely tell some of their works apart; for a time, the two even signed canvases only on the back, to preserve the sense of a shared, objective research project. But during those years, each had served the other not just as partner and prime audience, but also as chief competitor; and in late 1911, their fraternal rivalry was about to enter a phase of serve-and-volley exchanges that would change the way their game was structured.

During that summer, they had both been painting still lifes and figure pictures that used newspapers and books as accessories, and which therefore included typographical elements from journal mastheads. But Braque broke the parity of their shared style with his stencil, when he set down its impersonal and semi-mechanical letters so squarely and flatly across the surface of his canvases, independent of any apparent reference to a depicted piece of printed matter. Picasso at first "replied" by similarly adding words or phrases to his paintings (fig. 4); but then he upped the innovative ante in a different way, in the spring of 1912, by gluing into a still life a piece of oilcloth with a photomechanically printed chair-caning pattern (fig. 5). For months Braque made no similar change in his methods. Then in the following September, when the two were vacationing together near Avignon, Braque purposefully waited until Picasso had left town before trying out a further wrinkle, gluing a piece of imitation wood-grain decorator's paper into a drawing. And after he saw that initiative, Picasso in turn added still another twist, by creating more eclectic compositions from printed wallpapers, colored paper, and especially pieces clipped from newspapers (fig. 9).

Meanwhile, the painter Juan Gris had formulated his own responses to Picasso's *Still Life with Chair Caning,* in a painting with glued-on pieces of mirror, and in another that included a snippet of printed text, both of which he exhibited in October 1912.[2] By the turn of the year, Braque, Picasso, and Gris were all working intensively with the idea of gluing found paper elements into their works; and from then until Braque departed for his wartime military service in 1914, all three of these artists churned out a large body of paintings and pasted-paper images (the French term is *papiers collés*) that seemingly rerouted the printed ephemera of the café table and the city streets into the studio and onto the easel—incorporating, among other things, news headlines, movie bills, cigarette wrappers, package labels, and ads for razors, furs, lingerie, lamps, and liqueurs (figs. 1, 6, 16–19, 36, 41, 47–54). Braque's few, austerely stenciled letters had opened the way for a gaudy, loquacious array of found ephemera; and from this yearlong round of one-upsmanship had emerged a fundamentally revised notion of what the activity of making art was, and what art might be about.

The new cut-paper assemblages and paintings with letters were centrally concerned with the words of the modern world. The primary sources from which they drew their phrases, letters, and fragmentary syllables were the daily newspapers. Mastheads, headlines, advertisements, and illustrations appear throughout this phase of Cubism (see figs. 1, 6, 8, 9, 16, 23, 31, 32, 35, 36, 47, 48, 49). And beyond just providing raw

2. **Georges Braque.** *Le Portugais (The Emigrant).* 1911. Oil on canvas, 46 × 32″ (117 × 81 cm). Kunstmuseum Basel. Gift of Raoul La Roche, 1952

3. **Georges Braque.** *Homage to J. S. Bach.* 1911. Oil on canvas, 21¼ × 28¾″ (54 × 73 cm). Collection Carroll Janis and Conrad Janis, New York

are the newspapers.''[3] Apollinaire in fact singled out the newspapers, in 1918, as representative metaphors of the new art's spirit of wide-ranging, unprejudiced exploration of life—an ''encyclopedic liberty . . . not less than that of a daily newspaper which on a single sheet treats the most diverse matters and ranges over the most distant countries.''[4]

The particular newspapers in question, the Parisian journals of the era of World War I, were a distinctive novelty of the age. What Apollinaire and his painter friends found when they unfolded the press each morning were the results of a period of prodigious ex-

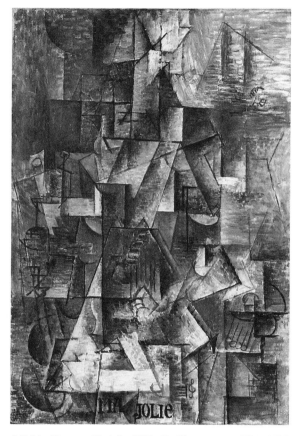

4. **Pablo Picasso.** *Ma Jolie.* 1911–12. Oil on canvas, 39⅜ × 25¾″ (100 × 65.4 cm). The Museum of Modern Art, New York. Acquired through the Lillie P. Bliss Bequest

material for the *papiers collés*, the newspaper is a dominant, constant motif in these works, a central element in their conjuring of the experience of city life. In incorporating this material and imagery, the Cubists were using a new kind of artistic process as a way to embrace a specifically modern phenomenon. Their associate, the poet Guillaume Apollinaire, had the same aim in mind in 1913, when he evoked the city in terms of ''prospectuses, catalogues and posters which shout aloud / Here is poetry this morning and for prose there

5. **Pablo Picasso.** *Still Life with Chair Caning.* 1912. Collage of oil, oilcloth, and pasted paper on canvas (oval), surrounded by rope, 10⅝ × 13¾″ (27 × 35 cm). Musée Picasso, Paris

pansion and transformation in journalism—the first modern "media explosion," based on a mix of news, features, and commerce, which had its origins in the mid-nineteenth century. In 1836 Émile de Girardin had altered the face of news publishing in Paris by halving the price of his *La Presse*, with the aim of supporting the paper primarily through the sale of space for advertising.[5] This modern approach restructured the trade: henceforth selling the readers to the advertisers would be as important as selling the paper to the readers. Dependence on more ad pages went hand in hand with a need for increased circulation figures and brought changes in both the look and the content of the press. Girardin also pioneered, for example, the inclusion of serial suspense novels in the daily papers, as an audience-building device. (These *romans feuilletons*

were cliff-hanging narratives, not unlike television serials, and were similarly lamented as mind-rotting trivialities.)[6] Soon the advertising sections of the papers swelled, and changed in appearance: in the 1850s and 1860s French papers broke the rigid column-width requirements that still shaped their American counterparts and "opened their pages to large display ads with more imaginative use of novel type faces."[7] The look of the front, editorial sections remained more sedate and homogeneous into the early Third Republic (fig. 10), but after that they were enhanced by new *fin-de-siècle* technologies such as photomechanical illustration (figs. 7, 12). At the same time, the tone and content of the news changed, as wire-service connections relayed hot information from the distant flashpoints of a world that was becoming steadily more

6. **Juan Gris.** *Le Journal.* 1914. Oil, pasted paper, and pencil on canvas, 21⅝ × 18⅛" (55 × 46 cm). Judith Rothschild Collection

7. *Le Journal,* **November 18, 1912, p. 1**

unstable and bellicose in the years before 1914. The front page thus became more complexly fragmented, and the back pages more crowded with attention-getting type and illustrations.

Along with developments in commerce and technology, the other crucial factor in the advent of the new Parisian press was the law passed by France's Third Republic on July 29, 1881. This legislation eliminated government censorship and thereby affirmed a general right to publish, which had not existed either under the Second Empire or under the early years of the Republic in the 1870s.[8] Coming at a time when

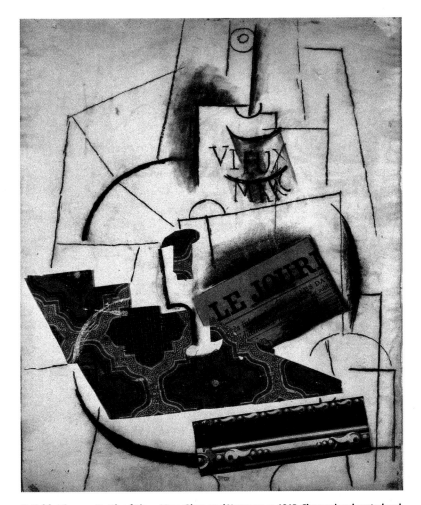

8. **Pablo Picasso.** *Bottle of Vieux Marc, Glass, and Newspaper.* 1913. Charcoal and pasted and pinned paper on paper, 24¾ × 19¼″ (63 × 49 cm). Musée National d'Art Moderne, Centre Georges Pompidou, Paris. Gift of Henri Laugier

9. Pablo Picasso. *Guitar, Sheet Music, and Glass.* **1912. Pasted paper, gouache, and charcoal on paper, 18⅞ × 14¾″ (47.9 × 36.5 cm). Marion Koogler McNay Art Museum, San Antonio**

those condemned to exile for the insurrection of the Commune in 1871 were being allowed to return to France, and when political debate was reheating after a long period of repression and quiescence, the law of 1881 opened the way for a proliferation of newspapers of all political stripes, and for sharp competition in an expanded field.

The drive to sell papers in this climate encouraged sensationalist writing, and led to an expansive new form of mass journalism, reaching out from Paris by rail to a far-flung audience. "By the 1890s," Daniel Pope recounts, "the French penny press had outstripped in circulation all other newspapers in the world. In the early years of the new century, the four major Paris dailies extended their circulation range throughout the nation. By 1914, they published a total of about four-and-a-half million copies daily, some forty percent of the total circulation of France's newspapers."[9]

The boom in newspapers served new styles of politics, concerned to excite and direct mass opinion.

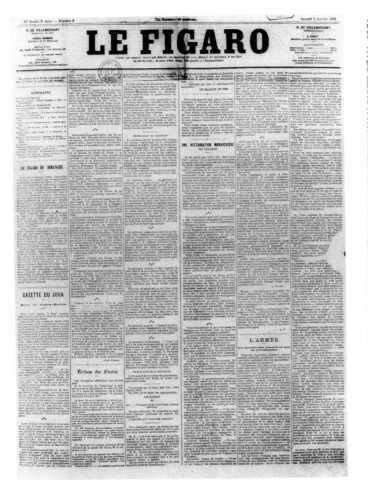

10. *Le Figaro,* January 2, 1875, p. 1

11. *Le Figaro,* January 2, 1875, p. 5

One need only think of the public polemics of the Dreyfus affair, at the turn of the century (epitomized by the memorable front-page headline of Émile Zola's *J'accuse*), to measure how crucial a factor in social contention the newspapers of Paris had become.[10] They spread out for their readers a parallel, processed version of contemporary reality, more sensational, urgent, and temporally compressed than an individual's experience could ever be. And as diverse interests sought to exploit the power of the press to manipulate opinion, the credibility of the Parisian journals was frequently undermined, by scandals which revealed frequent distortions of facts and widespread corruption by secret subsidies.[11]

This newly heterogeneous, opinionated, and competitive press was also closely linked to, and dependent upon, the rise of modern advertising; and in the early years of the twentieth century the newspapers began to grow in size in order to accommodate more ads. The standard four-page format was first expanded to six by *Le Figaro* in 1895, with two others following suit in 1901. ("The sixth page of a paper is a wall" was a maxim of the admen who "posted" their notices there, and who complained of the helter-skelter disorder in these ad groupings.)[12] The paper the Cubists clipped and represented most frequently, *Le Journal*, was the most expansive of these new exemplars of commercial-

12. *Le Journal,* December 1, 1912, p. 1

13. Newsstand, Paris, before 1914

14. *Le Journal,* December 2, 1912, p. 9

15. *Le Journal,* December 3, 1912, p. 10

16. **Georges Braque.** *Glass and Bottle.* 1913–14. Charcoal and pasted paper on paper, 18⅞ × 24⅜" (48 × 62 cm). Private collection, Switzerland

ized journalism; it was the only one regularly to print more than eight pages.[13] Then, in the years just before the war, the overlap and interpenetration of sales and news, implicit in the newspapers since Girardin, became their visible form: ads appeared on the same pages with bulletins and features, and the

17. **Georges Braque.** *Glass and Packet of Tobacco: Bock.* 1912–13. Charcoal and pasted paper on paper, 12¼ × 9½" (31 × 24 cm). Kunstmuseum Basel, Kupferstichkabinett. Gift of Raoul La Roche, 1963

dailies began to be more flashily composed with multiple typefaces. Newspapers advertised themselves assiduously (many of the mastheads the Cubists included were ubiquitous features of the cityscape, on kiosk signs, posters, and painted walls); and the line between reporting and promotion became less easy to draw.[14]

Such corrupted mixtures of sensationalism, commerce, and entertainment were doubtless what the German historian Oswald Spengler had in mind when he looked on the rise of the Parisian genre of modern newspaper as one of the most telling signs of the decadence and impending downfall of Western civilization.[15] For a young foreigner like Picasso, though, this extraordinary, particularly Parisian phenomenon may have exercised a different fascination: the local newsstand was a fountainhead of urban modernity, the focal point of a new kind of massive daily disgorgement of information and persuasion run together, in fast-changing styles of type, layout, and political and commercial appeal (fig. 13). The displays of these kiosks had in fact become so crowded and opulent by 1911 that they were considered to be contributing to the downfall of bookstores, and the Prefect of the Seine was considering a law to suppress the foldout "wings" on which these arrays were set forth.[16] In tearing scraps from newspaper pages around 1912–14, Picasso and the other practitioners of *papier collé* were dipping their cups directly into the commercially stimulated flow of sensation, of simultaneity and fast-paced change,

18. **Juan Gris.** *The Bottle of Banyul.* 1914. Pasted paper, oil, and pencil on board, 15 × 11¼″ (38 × 28.5 cm). Collection Mr. and Mrs. James W. Alsdorf, Chicago

19. **Pablo Picasso.** *Pipe, Glass, and Bottle of Rum.* 1914. Pasted paper, pencil, and gouache on cardboard, 15¾ × 20¾″ (40 × 52.7 cm). The Museum of Modern Art, New York. Gift of Mr. and Mrs. Daniel Saidenberg

20. *Le Journal,* December 3, 1912, p. 7

with all the threats of political unrest and the seductions of consumer allurements that made up contemporary urban consciousness.

When the Cubists looked into the daily papers, though, they did not single out the most modern aspects. These journals were in fact uneasy conglomerates, where the urgently current jostled the quaintly outmoded; and the artists responded to them as

such. The Cubists clipped both bold headlines about war and banal come-ons for cheap liqueurs, often from the same edition. They generally avoided, however, the "modernized" elements of illustration (figs. 14, 15) and virtually never extracted any of the pervasive photographic imagery (fig. 12). In picking advertising copy from the back sections, they consistently passed over the impressive large spreads that were then beginning to appear as banners for big-

21. *Le Journal,* December 7, 1912, p. 10

22. *Le Journal,* December 3, 1912, p. 9

23. **Pablo Picasso.** *Bottle and Glass.* 1912. Pasted paper, charcoal, and pencil on paper, 23⅝ × 18⅛″ (60 × 46 cm). The Menil Collection, Houston

name brands (fig. 21), to land on cruder, unfashionable squibs for less prestigious items and enterprises (figs. 22, 23). Looking over an issue of *Le Journal* for December 9, 1912, Picasso even steered past a fountain-pen ad that had already allied itself to Cubism as the style of the moment (fig. 24), to take a thoroughly bland column of type from the same page. In this and other ways, these artists encapsu-

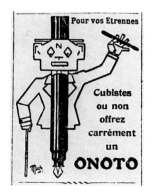

24. Advertisement from *Le Journal,* December 9, 1912, p. 7

lated a particular sense of their moment, and of the feel of modern times in general: a sense of contradictory variety, in which the day-to-day emergence of the future, in the news, took place amid the trickling residue of styles passing out of mode.

In some important respects, the Cubists seem to have made choices that were willfully regressive, or at least against the grain of what many thought was "progressive" in art. Certainly neither the idea of putting words into pictures nor the notion of artists' interest in public printed matter were in themselves exceptional in Paris at the time. A *fin-de-siècle* vogue for flattened design, partly abetted by *japoniste* influences, had led artists such as Toulouse-Lautrec and Pierre Bonnard to experiment with poster layouts that unified type and image (figs. 25, 26). In fact, French advertising prided itself precisely on such meldings of progressive aesthetics and commerce. The walls the Cubists walked by would have been blanketed with "modern" combinations of stylistic simplification and innovative typefaces (fig. 27), and Picasso himself had been adept at just this sort of modish text-and-image design as a beginner in Barcelona (fig. 28). But he and Braque and Gris said goodbye to all that. Ignoring or avoiding the considerable part of their urban environment where "good taste" and commercial utility were held to coexist compatibly or to merge, their collages and *papiers collés* set up instead miniature worlds in which the two domains of art and industry held their separate characters, and abutted each other without cushion. The most studiously recondite little structure of lines representing a bottle, for example,

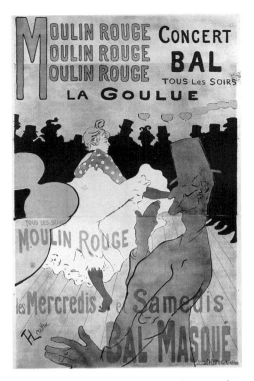

25. **Henri de Toulouse-Lautrec.** *Moulin Rouge (La Goulue).* 1891. Lithographic poster, 6'3³⁄₁₆" × 46¹⁄₁₆" (191 × 117 cm). The Art Institute of Chicago. The Mr. and Mrs. Carter H. Harrison Collection

26. **Pierre Bonnard.** *L'Estampe et l'affiche.* 1897. Lithograph, 32⁵⁄₈ × 24¹⁄₄" (82.8 × 61.2 cm). The Museum of Modern Art, New York. Purchase Fund

27. Posted wall, Dijon, 1901

28. **Pablo Picasso.** *Menu of Els Quatre Gats.* 1899. Printed, 8⅝ × 6½″ (22 × 16.5 cm). Museo Picasso, Barcelona

could be overlaid with the most baldly direct label, or ad, or headline (figs. 29, 33).

The parts of the printed environment to which these artists were drawn were "anonymous" productions, like beer and bouillon labels, with no self-conscious claims to artistry; and the typefaces they typically favored—thick, sans-serif heavyweights—were the fusty blunderbusses in the modernizing commercial armory. Picasso and Braque, and Gris following their lead, seem to have had a reprobate affection, even a certain nostalgia, for these banal elements of mass-produced design; the world of typography and advertisements they sought out had in general a vulgar, unpretentious energy.

The way the material was employed, however, was unmistakably radical, even if against the "progressive" grain: the products of modern society were there to change art, instead of vice versa. It is often remarked (without enough regard for the particular dexterities asked, and pleasures accorded, by a new form of "drawing" with scissors and a newly spontaneous manner of working with instantly re-arrangeable elements) that the cut-and-paste methods of *papier collé* bypassed the skills of the artist's hand. But it needs reemphasizing just how drastically, and pointedly, the Cubists rejected the particular veneration of individualized handcraft, and the accompanying notions of the reforming artist, which many had thought were key to progress in modern art.

The renewal of the decorative arts, in the face of the threat of industrialization, had been a prime preoccupation of tradesmen and governments alike in the later nineteenth century. And in the Arts and Crafts movement, or related guild-like enterprises

29. **Georges Braque.** *Bottle of Marc.* 1912. Charcoal and conté crayon on paper, 19 × 12¼″ (48 × 31 cm). Kunstmuseum Basel, Kupferstichkabinett. Gift of Raoul La Roche, 1963

that coincided with modernist circles from Vienna to Helsinki at the start of this century, art conceived and wrought by the dedicated individual was seen as a saving holdout against the debasements of mechanical production. Hope for an integrated, organic

30. Page of typography by **Kolomon Moser** from *Beispiele Künstlerischer Schrift Herausgegeben von Rudolf v. Larisch* (Vienna: Anton Schroll & Co. Verlag, 1900), pl. 22. The Museum of Modern Art, New York. Architecture and Design Study Collection

society was vested in programs that called for artists to beautify all aspects of life, including furniture, décor, and typography (fig. 30)—often in the manner of a unifying, harmonious style such as the organic curves of art nouveau.[17] No more direct slap in the face of such ideals can be imagined than Picasso and Braque's motley selections of fake chair caning, imitation wood grain, cheap machine-made wallpaper, and simple, blunt commercial typefaces. Using stencils, and adopting common tricks of the commercial decorator's trade (such as the combing of paint to produce the effect of wood grain), Picasso and Braque—who were seen at times even to dress alike in workers' overalls—cast their artistic lot with the workaday commingling of the artisanal and the mechanical, against the pretensions of those who held lofty ideals for the decorative arts, or who made a cult of refined handwork. They built oblique conundrums from labor-saving shortcuts, and made a thinker's art from workers' artifices. And when they reintroduced color into their paintings after a long period of near-monochrome images, they experimented with the use of a commercial paint, Ripolin enamel (as for example in figs. 45 and 52)—in part to obtain a vivid chromatics that stepped outside the high-art tradition, but also, it seems, because this paint dried with a smooth, uniform impersonality of surface that denied any sense of painterly finesse.[18] The world of commercial design, like the newspaper, contained a broad variety of possibilities, and from both they chose the materials and styles that seemed least tinged with the pretensions of art, and least self-consciously "modern."

Along with the preference for a specific range of type styles came the isolation of a particular kind of poetics. The Cubists were drawn to the compact punch of words that worked for a living, modern ideographs that carried their meaning along in their very form: logos, labels, and mastheads, where typographic styles had been made to evoke a "brand" identity. These artists obviously favored the special slang of headlines and subheads, where pithy "teasers" harangued like sideshow barkers (LA BATAILLE S'EST ENGAGÉE ["The Battle Is On"], figs. 7, 9). At the same time, though, they did not simply acquiesce to the economies of commercial language. As Robert Rosenblum first pointed out in detail, Picasso, Braque, and Gris worked to subvert this rough-and-ready efficiency of communication, by breaking up, cropping, and rearranging the found words into fragments and combinations that, through puns and in-jokes, released multiple private meanings lurking within the exhortations of public words.[19]

Up through the 1950s, when historians and critics of Cubism discussed such lettering, they talked primarily about its general function of reintroducing "reality," or its formal role of affirming the flatness of the picture plane. Rosenblum, however, saw more clearly than his predecessors that these are, almost literally, speaking images. Put simply, these words ask to be read: Picasso, Braque, and Gris took a vocabulary from the news and business of the day, and used it to add linguistic, conceptual, and even political dimensions to their works. And to say what these works mean, we are in part obliged to puzzle out the literal sense and local associations that at-

31. Pablo Picasso. *Student with a Newspaper.* 1913–14. Oil and sand on canvas, 28¾ × 23½" (73 × 59.5 cm). Private collection, Switzerland

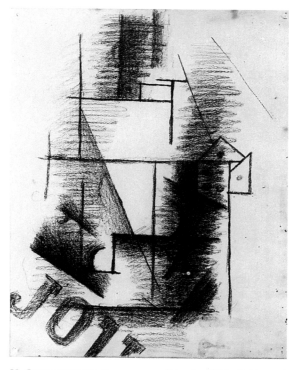

32. Georges Braque. *Newspaper and Dice: Jou.* 1912–13. Charcoal on paper, 12¼ × 9½" (31 × 24 cm). Kunstmuseum Basel, Kupferstichkabinett. Gift of Raoul La Roche, 1963

tached to the words they selected.

Rosenblum pointed out, for example, how these Cubists played with the simple word JOURNAL (figs. 6–9)—which denoted specifically the daily *Le Journal,* from whose masthead the type style was taken, and which also served as the generic French term for newspaper—by splitting it into words for day (JOUR), for urinal (*urinal* in French as in English, here contracted to URNAL [fig. 31]), and for play (the French *jeu* and *jouer* transposed into JOU [fig. 32]; a further

permutation would yield *jouir*, the verb for enjoying ecstatic pleasure, or, specifically, orgasm). And he went on to point out other covert messages in the headlines and advertisements these artists selected. The headline UN COUP DE THÉÂTRE, for instance (fig. 34), could be clipped to form UN COUP DE THÉ (fig. 33), thus changing "a dramatic turn of events" (referring to an episode in the Balkan Wars) into a line evoking the phrase *un coup de dés* ("a toss of the dice"), which in turn resonates with the title of Stéphane Mallarmé's Symbolist masterwork, the poem *Un coup de dés jamais n'abolira le hasard* ("A toss of the dice will never abolish chance"). Or (since Picasso's French at the time was laughable, and the chances that he had read this poem, as opposed simply to

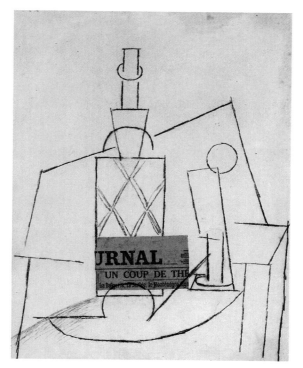

33. Pablo Picasso. *Table with Bottle, Wineglass, and Newspaper.* 1912. Pasted paper, charcoal, and gouache on paper, 24⅜ × 18⅞" (62 × 48 cm). Musée National d'Art Moderne, Centre Georges Pompidou, Paris. Gift of Henri Laugier

34. *Le Journal,* December 4, 1912, p. 1

35. **Georges Braque.** *Woman with a Guitar.* **1913. Oil and charcoal on canvas, 51¼ × 28¾"
(130 × 73 cm). Musée National d'Art Moderne, Centre Georges Pompidou, Paris. Gift of Raoul
La Roche**

knowing its title, are slim) the strategically omitted
letters may have conjured something more prosaic,
associated with café consumption: a cup (*coup[e]*),
or in slang a "hit" or "dose" (*coup*), of tea; or even,
by aural connection, the salad of raw vegetables ordered as *un crudité*. Braque could also change the
wake-up call in the masthead RÉVEIL (the source of
the bugler's "reveille" in English) into the evocation
of a dream, RÊVE, while retaining a word, ORGAN[E],
from the subheading, for sexually suggestive placement in his figure of a woman (fig. 35)—making this
elusive lady with a guitar either the organ of a dream
(with a pun on the musical instrument), or the bearer
of a dream organ.

For this way of editing and recombining the world
of print, there were sources of inspiration ready to
hand, if one only had the inclination to take them

seriously. Over-posted walls offered a daily display of
inadvertent reeditings and juxtapositions (fig. 27),
even if these urban "eyesores" had become less
widespread than they had been in the previous century. (The two front-page photographs in Gris's
Glasses, Teacup, Bottle, and Pipe on a Table [fig. 36]
show the before-and-after effects of clean-up laws
that controlled or forbad posting on most public
monuments and walls.)[20] On the poster columns of
the boulevards (fig. 37), or even in the kiosks themselves, where layers of overlapping, folded journals
were held up in racks (fig. 38), the abutting of different scales and typefaces, and untoward cropping or
surprise juxtaposition of words and word fragments,
were commonplace. Picasso's clipping from a front
page, for example, could follow almost directly the
lines along which the paper was apparently folded

36. **Juan Gris.** *Glasses, Teacup, Bottle, and Pipe on a Table.* 1914. Oil, pasted paper, and charcoal on canvas, 25⅝ × 36¼″ (65 × 92 cm). Kunstsammlung Nordrhein-Westfalen, Düsseldorf

vertically (fig. 7). His fragment may have been pre-selected in this case, and similar serendipities doubtless cropped up on every newsstand and café table.

The punning usage of the words and word fragments in the Cubist *papiers collés* was likewise unremarkable in itself; it found its parallels in an unexceptional branch of French schoolboy wit. Yet in the Cubist context these smirking little puns and double-entendres are set within a fabric of formal play with ambiguity and multiplied meaning that allows us to reckon them, like the similarly street-common wordplay of James Joyce, as central elements in the innovative force of the art. The jokes with words, and the paper scraps themselves, are both taken from the realm of the everyday, and both are important not *despite* their commonplace nature, but *because* of it. That workaday banality is a

central part of what made them attractive to the artists, both in themselves and as powerful antidotes to overrefined artistic conventions.

The remarkable thing was not just to have seen that occlusions and overlays of printed matter could contain such puns, but to have decided as well that this seemingly random profusion, and the strain of often sophomoric or smutty wordplay it could yield, could have any traffic with the world inside a Cubist image—a world that by 1911 had reached a point of austere cerebral refinement that seemed forbiddingly remote from the boulevard. But having perfected an exquisite, chamber-music harmony, Picasso and Braque seem to have decided that the perfect next step was to add a kazoo counterpoint.

In formal terms, the high Analytic Cubism of 1910–11 was approaching the kind of serene bal-

37. Morris column, place Denfert-Rochereau, Paris, c. 1910

ance that could have become formulaic; the introduction first of trompe-l'oeil and caricatural elements, then of lettering, disrupted that balance and the solemn, near-monochromatic atmospheric unity. In the *papiers collés* and collages of late 1912 and after, no traditional notion of binding atmosphere or consistent brushstroke was allowed to remain operative among the elements of a work. What could constitute pictorial unity, or balance, was precisely what was most radically reconceived here, in ways that determined not only their formal modernism, but also the modern, distinctively urban feel of the works.

The difference is, at one level, architectural. The work of 1911 conjures the interplay of a system of similar structural elements, and has evoked comparisons with scaffoldings or fire-escape structures; it has its affinities with (and likely drew upon) distant visions of irregularly accreted buildings, both in chunky vernacular masonry from provincial towns like Céret and Horta de Ebro, and in rooftop vistas of Paris. But the world of the *papiers collés* is more aggressively about the big city's word-covered planes—poster hoardings, café windows, painted walls of buildings, the pages of the newspapers themselves—as the sites not of interlocked structural logics and conundrums, but of floating surface collisions and layerings of styles.

There is a new kind of unity of contrasts in the content as well. One of Picasso's first reaches into typography, in the *Ma Jolie* (fig. 4) of 1912, announces the spirit involved: it is one in which the coexistence of sharply different levels of legibility, and the juxtaposition of the invented and the found, is as welcome as the overlap between an intimate personal relationship (Picasso's new love, Eva Gouel)

39. Picture postcard of Le Havre, 1912

and the refrain of a current popular song (the words *ma jolie* ["my pretty"], Picasso's sobriquet for Eva, came from a tune called "Dernière Chanson").[21] The "label" of *Ma Jolie* seems, of course, incongruous. Yet it is a sign of neither absurdity nor irony, but of affection, and it is used as such again and again by

38. Newspaper display, Paris, before 1914

40. Pablo Picasso. *Souvenir du Havre.* 1912. Oil and enamel on canvas (oval), 36¼ × 25⅝" (92 × 65 cm). Private collection

the artist. The trite term of endearment seems to have taken on a new shine from the here-today, gone-tomorrow song; and it seems to have been borrowed as the special token of a private crush precisely because of its public, ephemeral nature, in the way teenagers still adopt a Top Ten tune as "their" song. Something so freshly minted and innocent of any role in established culture has a particular availability for appropriation; and a specially piquant kind of pleasure derives from finding a secret hidden in something everyone knows, but which (like the edited headlines) no one else understands in the terms

41. Pablo Picasso. *Bouillon Kub.* **1912. Oil on panel, 10⅝ × 8¼″ (27 × 21 cm). Private collection, Switzerland**

42. (Above) Paris, c. 1912

43. (Right) Illustration from J.-B. Fonteix and Alexandre Guérin, *La Publicité moderne* **(Paris, 1922), p. 124**

shared by the initiates. The platitude that was shopworn but now a novelty, and generic but now specific, could be at once public and covertly intimate. And that shared private delight must have been redoubled when this song snippet was imported as an identifying tag line into an art whose visual language seemed dauntingly obscure to all but a few. Picasso was almost certainly amused by this, just as he was doubtless pleased to spoof his own enterprise by labeling a nearly indecipherable Cubist image based

44. Pablo Picasso. *Landscape with Posters.* **1912. Oil and enamel on canvas, 18⅛ × 24″ (46 × 61 cm). The National Museum of Art, Osaka**

45. **Pablo Picasso.** *The Scallop Shell: Notre Avenir est dans l'air.* 1912. Oil and enamel on canvas (oval), 15 × 21¾" (38 × 55.5 cm). Private collection

on elements from a Normandy journey with the banner SOUVENIR DU HAVRE (fig. 40)—adopting a line anyone would recognize from kitsch postcards (fig. 39) to identify a subject only he and Braque would understand.

Similarly, the small circle of the Cubists and their friends delighted in finding "their" mark emblazoned on vast walls and displayed in every café, in their adopted club logo, the ad for Kub brand bouillon cubes (figs. 41, 44). A derogatory term (Cubism) given to their art by its enemies, allied to a brand name with wholly other origins, became a private joke of elective affinity that let them see the city fabric as peppered with advertisements for themselves, and perhaps to imagine their actually rather small-time art "business" as a full-fledged part of the urban commercial landscape (fig. 42).[22]

In three paintings of spring 1912 Picasso also incorporated fragments of the title of a brand-new, tricolor brochure exhorting France to improve its military aviation: *Notre Avenir est dans l'air* (figs. 45, 46). The slogan "Our Future Is in the Air" fused two meanings which Picasso almost certainly saw as applying to his and Braque's endeavor: the events of tomorrow were "in the air," or "in the wind" all around; and also, destiny led upward, along the path of the pioneer aviators, toward the conquest of the skies. Picasso could adopt even this last message as a private motto; for regardless of his attitude toward this militarist pamphlet[23] (which he may well never have read beyond the cover), he and Braque were both caught up in the general public infatuation with aviation, and specifically taken with the

Wright brothers as model inventor-adventurers; Picasso even addressed Braque affectionately as "Wilbourg" (for "Wilbur").[24] Just at the time Picasso painted the still lifes that include the cover of *Notre Avenir est dans l'air*, he made his first experiment in

46. Cover of *Notre Avenir est dans l'air* (Clermont-Ferrand, 1912)

collage, the *Still Life with Chair Caning*; and thus may have felt a special affinity with the way the collaborating Wrights had made a decisive leap of invention with extremely simple means, rethinking basic principles and using parts available to anyone. Here, as with *Ma Jolie*, the impulse to "subvert"

47. **Juan Gris.** *Breakfast.* **1914. Pasted paper, crayon, and oil over canvas, 31⅞ × 23½″ (80.9 × 59.7 cm). The Museum of Modern Art, New York. Acquired through the Lillie P. Bliss Bequest**

wordplay and then simply rerouted to private purpose. This seemingly most cloistered art of formal experiment was happy to articulate its identity, in quite literal ways, through the tag lines, slogans, and logos of the profane world of publicity. Gris, for example, even imagined his own name set in headline type, as a kind of alternative signature (fig. 47).

The anonymity of such found signatures, adopted signs, and assumed identities was, like the smooth surface of the Ripolin enamel, apparently a desirable relief from the Romantic notion of artistic subjectivity and its accompanying cult of the personal style. Instead, with borrowed words and labels, the artist could blend in with his urban environment, turning up in disguises, expressing his wit, his tastes, and his ideas through appropriated vehicles. This affection for a different style of individuality—covert, playful, and urbane—may have been what drew Gris and others to the popular mystery stories that featured the enigmatic Fantômas, a character omnipresent but never seen. Gris's inclusion of a cover from one of the Fantômas books in a café still life (fig. 48), and the mysterious figure hidden behind the paper in *The Man at the Café* (fig. 49), may be homages not simply to the pleasure taken in this notably unprestigious form of literature, but to the specific model of the elusive subversive who melds into the flux of cosmopolitan life.[25]

public language may have been puckish, but lacked malevolent irony: the pithy, mind-catching slogan could be embraced in all its upbeat, intentional

48. **Juan Gris.** *Fantômas (Pipe and Newspaper).* **1915. Oil on canvas, 23½ × 28⅞″ (59.8 × 73.3 cm). National Gallery of Art, Washington, D.C. Chester Dale Fund**

49. Juan Gris. *The Man at the Café.* 1914. Oil and pasted paper on canvas, 39 × 28⅜″ (99 × 72 cm). Collection Mrs. William R. Acquavella

The *papiers collés* used public material in the construction of private languages. They also assimilated without apparent prejudice signs for several different kinds of information and pleasure in urban life. Regardless of taste, few today would flinch at the notion that Cubist art by Picasso, Braque, and Gris has a level of complexity, of pleasurable depth and difficulty, that makes its cultural achievement worthy of consideration beside that of Bach's richly contrapuntal music. What still may be difficult to take in about these works, however, and what seems potentially richest as a model for modern creativity, is their catholic inclusiveness—the way they encompass BACH and BAL and BASS with such equanimity. In assemblages where the most recondite and the most obvious signs can collaborate, each on their own terms, so too a performance of classical music (announced by a poster where the name of the violinist Jan Kubelík added another Kub pun; fig. 50), a popular fête (BAL), and a foreign beer (BASS, the English ale; fig. 51) can each be attended to without any spurious leveling unity—and equally without a censoring compartmentalization of the diversity of a modern metropolitan life.[26] Ironically, in light of the émigré Picasso's crucial role, these admixtures (in part a reflection of the two artists' different temperaments and tastes) show an updated version of the kind of assured sampling of experience that outsiders often chafe at as maddeningly blasé French dandyism. The modernism they propose preaches no exclusive ideals of purity, nor does it traffic in abso-

lutes; it gladly accommodates the vulgar and novel yet apparently demands no blanket hostility to traditional culture, seemingly unperturbed by any sense of incompatibility between brandy and beer.

Replacing the more traditional subjects that had dominated Cubism in 1909–10—women with musical instruments, studio still lifes—these new assemblages of paper and paint dramatically increased the presence of an iconography of cosmopolitan sociability, or more precisely, of individual experiences associated with public places: dice and cards, daily newspapers and little avant-garde magazines, classical concerts and movie handbills, alcohol and tobacco. As many have remarked, a dominant motif in this phase of Cubism, explicit or implied, was that of the café table. It served in the way the renter's paradise of suburban gardens and Sunday sailboats served as Monet's and Renoir's motif of choice in the heyday of Impressionism: in both cases, aggressively disruptive artistic innovation concerned itself with a world of seemingly unproblematic urban recreation—and thereby appeared to associate artistic freedom with that modern kind of individuality defined by leisure-time choices.[27]

The reference to the café world in the Cubists' pasted-paper works also seems a modern continuation of the attention paid by Degas, Manet, and Seurat to the commercial amusements of the city—the world of drinking, shopping, and killing time. These artists of early French modernism had focused on the common, often tawdry, businesses of Parisian

50. **Georges Braque.** *Violin: Mozart/Kubelick.* **1912. Oil on canvas, 18 × 24″ (46 × 61 cm). Private collection, Switzerland**

51. Pablo Picasso. *Bottle of Bass, Wineglass, Packet of Tobacco, and Calling Card.* 1914. Pasted paper and pencil on paper, 9½ × 12" (24 × 30.5 cm). Musée National d'Art Moderne, Centre Georges Pompidou, Paris. Gift of Louise and Michel Leiris, the donors retaining a life interest

52. Pablo Picasso. *Violin, Wineglasses, Pipe, and Anchor.* 1912. Oil and enamel on canvas, 31⅞ × 21¼" (81 × 54 cm). National Gallery, Prague

diversion, sometimes with a positive appetite, sometimes with a more jaundiced and critical eye. And this continued conjunction of avant-garde art and cheap consumer culture, of the difficult and the easy, is potentially one of the most politically provocative aspects of the Cubist collages and *papiers collés*. But there are clearly limits to what we can "read" from the scraps of Paris these artists left us. In important ways, the vision of urban life in these collages is remarkably broad and varied; any given arrangement of news clippings and found paper can contain the range of categories of experience advertised on the movie bills Braque appropriated (figs. 53, 54): COMÉDIE, DRAME, GRAND DRAME, SENSATION, DOCUMENTAIRE. Yet for all their heterogeneous inclusiveness, these works, like Renoir's and Monet's canvases of the 1870s, take a very oblique and partial slice from a complex moment in French life. In the clipped materials, rumblings of the war to come abut the wrappers of cigarettes smoked and the whimsies of white-sale ads;[28] while adjacent notices for things we now think of as quintessential signs of the time—Mistinguett at the Folies-Bergère and the like—were left on the cutting-room floor.[29] An attempt to decrypt from these works specific messages about the epoch would seem simplistic, in a context where elusive complexity is the defining order; and it

53. **Georges Braque.** *Guitar and Program: Statue d'épouvante.* 1913. Charcoal, gouache, and pasted paper on paper, 28¾ × 39⅜″ (73 × 100 cm). Musée Picasso, Paris

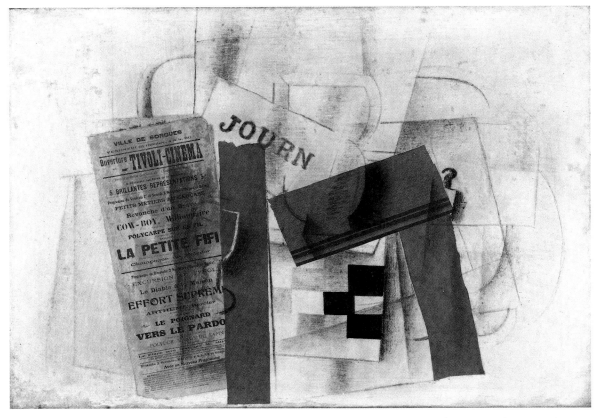

54. **Georges Braque.** *Checkerboard: Tivoli-Cinéma.* 1913. Gesso, pasted paper, charcoal, and oil on canvas, 25¾ × 36¼″ (65.5 × 92 cm). Collection Rosengart, Lucerne

would go against the grain of the way the words, and the structure of the works as a whole, consistently work to subvert single-minded clarity. The world of words the Cubists made in these *papiers collés* is not merely an edited shorthand for the one that surrounded them. It creates a shadow, or parallel, order in which fragments of an initial functional clarity are reshuffled into expanded, unexpected meanings. This was an antireductive art, and reductive explanations betray it.

Braque, Picasso, and Gris brought together familiar scraps and unfamiliar forms in order to give shape to a particular sense of urban life on the eve of World War I that was alternately ruminative and slapstick, and mingled alarms and amusements; but obviously their work has proved to offer more than simply an account of that time and place. Over the years, it has become more meaningful for us, constantly challenging and still pertinent to our experience, not simply because of its formal complexity, but because it embodies a uniquely rich engagement with modern society, dense with sociological implications and moral weight that impose themselves on us, even while they elude any pat definition. When we ask the larger questions of what such works mean, we are really probing beyond the particular message of a given clipping or label, and beyond the immediate sphere of reference of Paris in 1912–14, toward lessons that might be drawn regarding modern art's larger relationship to the social (and particularly commercial) forces that generate newspapers, billboards, advertisements, and so on. This inquiry is one that also involves, centrally, the consequences of the Cubists' innovations for subsequent artists. And later art profited importantly, not from seeing precisely what the Cubists were about, but from creatively misinterpreting their "message" in a fruitful, often contradictory variety of ways.

In their immediate impact, certainly, Cubist collages and *papiers collés* proved to be less valuable for any reflection they offered of the Cubists' particular experiences than for the new model they provided others—to engage with different areas of the language of publicity and commerce and construct sharply distinct versions of what modernity was. Since there were no accompanying manifestoes, or even interviews or statements, to clarify the purposes of the inner circle of initiators, Cubist works with words, like Cubism in general, appeared to many contemporaries to provide a language without an ideology, in a time when there were numerous ideologies in search of a language. If the inner circle who made this language never said what it meant, others nonetheless quickly saw what they could do with it.

The Futurists, for example, had made the whole issue of artistic engagement with the forces of modern life the indispensable plank in their aesthetic platform. Indeed, their call for painters and sculptors to address the look of modern cities had begun as early as the publication of their founding manifesto (in a Parisian newspaper, appropriately) in 1909; and their influence, spreading through such poets as Apollinaire and such painters as Robert Delaunay and Fernand Léger, may have been a goad to the Cubists in their opening-up to the evidences of modern life. But if the Futurists provided Picasso and Braque with needling ideas, it was certainly Picasso and Braque who generated the forms the Futurists adapted to give shape to their own visions. Futurist painters such as Umberto Boccioni eagerly transposed the quiescent architecture of Analytic Cubism's facets into imagery of violent fracturing. And when the Futurists saw the delphic syllables of the *papiers collés*—JOU, NAL, BAL—they transposed them into comic-style transliterations of noises—ZUM, ZANG, RRRRRRRRR (fig. 55).

Reducing words to noises was no idle amusement for them, but an earnest act consistent with their urge to get down to the basics of communication. Also, from their earlier devotion to Symbolist poetry, they saw in the possibility of free-floating word fragments an opportunity to manifest what they held to be deeper analogies: the running together of words associated with disparate things, animate and inanimate, would serve to capture the dawning modern sense of the simultaneity of diverse experiences— the fusion of objects, people, machines, noises, light, smells, and so on. In 1914, the Futurist painter Giacomo Balla specifically combined his fascination for noises and machines with a Cubist-inspired attention to typography, in a stage performance called *Macchina tipografica* ("Printing Press") wherein each of twelve performers acted out the role of a part of the machine, moving in rhythm and repeating a characteristic sound.[30] The curtain for this performance (fig. 56) is one of the most vivid indications of the Futurists' penchant for seizing on what had been a series of little quips in Cubism and making them into something programmatic and larger than life. Through the optic of the Futurist imagination, the running together of unrelated words and materials in collage seemed an appropriately telegraphic form for the speeded-up thinking of modern man. In Cubism, words and word fragments had generally denoted concrete objects—liqueur bottles, newspapers—but now they came to stand in for ideas and summarize unseen entities. At the same time, the syntax of their assemblage revealed the interplay of contending energies, becoming the vehicle of a forceful overlapping and compression that conveyed the impact of modern dynamism.[31]

Linking motorcars and Mallarmé in this fashion, Futurist poetics, like that of Apollinaire from within the Cubist circle, favored synthetic word-pictures. F. T. Marinetti's *Words in Freedom (Chaudronneries)* (fig. 57), for example, marshaled captured type fragments into the extended screams and chopped-off metallic complaints of unmuffled machines, while

55. Filippo Tommaso Marinetti. *Vive la France*. 1914. Ink, crayon, and pasted paper on paper, 12⅛ × 12¾″ (30.9 × 32.6 cm). The Museum of Modern Art, New York. Gift of the Benjamin and Frances Benenson Foundation

56. Giacomo Balla. Sketch for stage, *Printing Press*. 1914. Ink and pencil on paper, 8⅝ × 12¾″ (22 × 32.5 cm). Museo Teatrale alla Scala, Milan

57. Filippo Tommaso Marinetti. *Words in Freedom (Chaudronneries).* c. 1912. Ink on paper, 12 × 8¼″ (31 × 21 cm). Private collection

skewing them into tilts and collisions. Similarly, Carlo Carrà assembled from printed ephemera not the placid gaze from a café table, but an aerial view of a riotous assembly, clamoring for war (fig. 58). He also adapted Cubism's disjunctive combinations of schematic form and stenciled letters as a formula for evoking military clashes, in abstract yet didactically literal terms (fig. 59). In this way, JOU yielded to juggernaut, and BAL became *battaglia*. A new liberty with letters allowed the Italians to express their yearning for a modernity not of sociable urban pleasures, but of blood-boiling cataclysm, alive with the roar of crowds and the mingled chatter of valve tappets and machine guns.

Where the Futurists saw the elements of a new language of belligerent purposefulness, though, others who looked at Cubist works with words saw them as the perfect point of departure for an art of deadpan irony and subversive absurdity. The difference between the literal and excited noise-words of the Italians and the nonsensical, infantile word fragment that these other, French and German artists adopted as their group name—Dada—encapsulates the opposed viewpoints. German Dada artists such as Hannah Höch and Raoul Hausmann, embittered by

58. Carlo Carrà. *Interventionist Demonstration.* 1914. Collage on pasteboard, 15¼ × 11¾″ (38.5 × 30 cm). Mattioli Collection, Milan

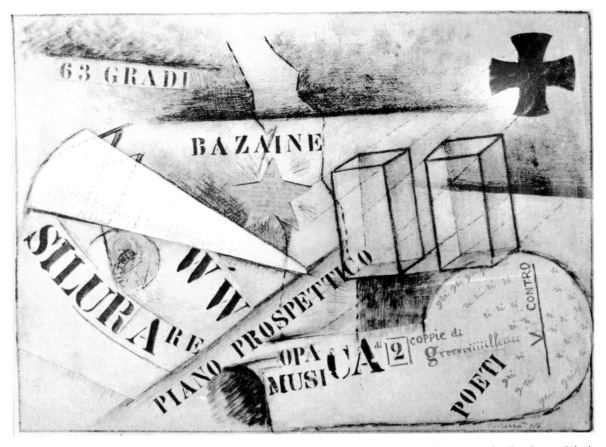

59. **Carlo Carrà.** *The Night of January 20, 1915, I Dreamed this Picture (Joffre's Angle of Penetration on the Marne against Two German Cubes).*
1915. Collage of newsprint, paper painted with white gouache, postage stamp, with pencil, charcoal, and ink, 10 × 13½″ (25.4 × 34.3 cm).
Winston-Malbin Collection

World War I and the failed revolution in Germany that followed on it, adopted the model of cut-paper assemblages as a way to turn the imagery and language of the dominant, commercially minded society against itself. Here the sense of hands-off anonymity that the Cubists had established in their use of found materials, commercial paints, and decorator's tricks, became a programmatic substitution of the mechanical for the human, as a willful denial of bourgeois ideals of subjectivity (figs. 60, 61). The Dada artists' counterlogical tableaux, whose incongruities and dislocations were intended to provoke awareness of the chaotic irrationality of contemporary life, are better taken up in a later discussion of the use of commercial imagery, in the chapter "Advertising." But their work with words and word fragments belongs here, as an alternative to the racing letters of Marinetti and the others, to show how the new adoption of public words could move toward a trenchant critique of modern life as well as a blustering affirmation. Instead of massing printed characters into exulting, rowdy crowds, the Dadaists pushed the fragmentations and ellipses of Cubist work into new, sharper alienations: isolated letters and phrases, attached to nothing, and a willfully confounding babble of messages within a tilting jumble of different scales and weights of type.

The Dada artists saw the modern language of commerce as a target for subversion, but many of them were certainly not above attention-getting

"promotional" events of their own. And in their heyday before the war, the Futurists bathed in the headlines, comfortably moving along with the most raucous energies of modern advertising. Slogans, manifestoes, and noisy demonstrations were central to their aesthetic program; in fact, they typically

60. **Raoul Hausmann.** *Dada Siegt.* **1920. Watercolor and collage on paper, mounted on board, 23⅝ × 17¾″ (60 × 45 cm). Private collection**

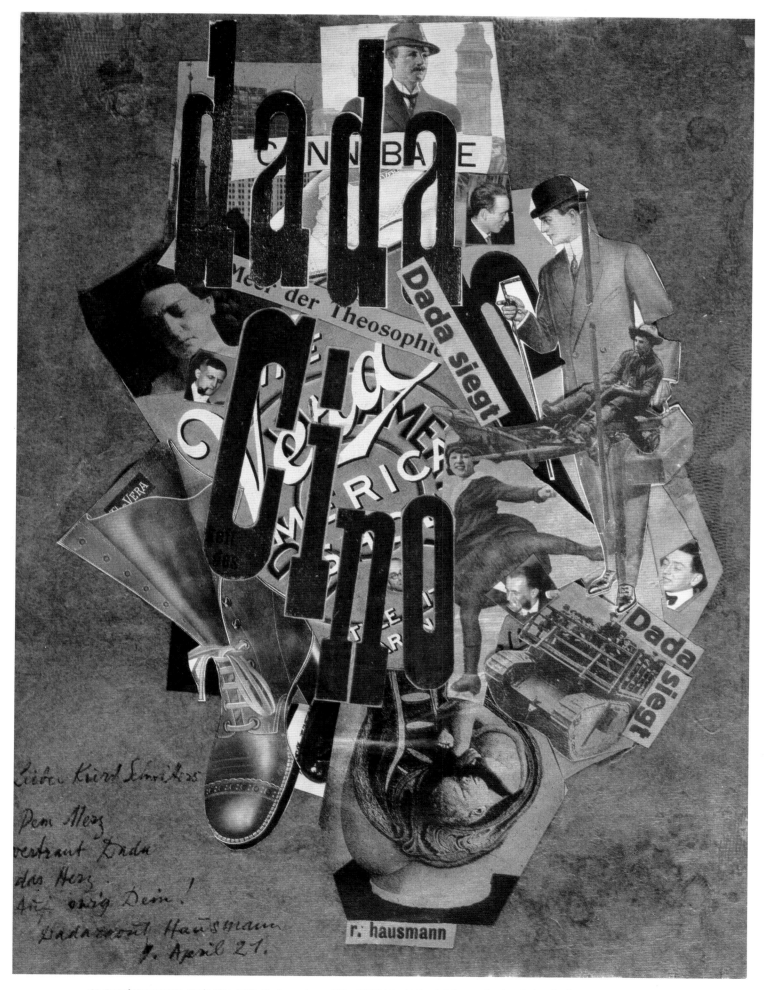

61. Raoul Hausmann. *Dada-Cino.* 1920. Photomontage, 12½ × 8⅞″ (31.7 × 22.5 cm). Private collection, Switzerland

launched a rousing "hype" before they had worked out an art to match it. For them, the new commercial and journalistic ways of motivating interest and desire seemed a signal part of modernization, and were not without implications for an artistic program dedicated to fanning the constant lust for the new. Their self-promotion carried this message across the continent; and in any event, they were hardly alone in this attitude. At a moment when avant-garde minorities all over Europe were struggling for an audience, the dominance of new modes of public persuasion provided if not a cause for celebration, at least a model of effective communication, to be turned if possible to the artists' own goals.

The language and look of publicity became a specially apt model when avant-garde art moved to step in from its fringe position and enter public life along a broad front, in Russia in the 1920s. Russian artists of the teens had shown an immediate response to Cubist adoptions of urban signage and newspaper typography. Shifting their attention from the rude signboards of small merchants to the typographic overlays of news kiosks and poster columns, Russian painters such as Kasimir Malevich made a decisive break with their earlier, primitivizing tendencies, and abandoned their affection for rustic simplicity in favor of an internationally oriented, cosmopolitan im-

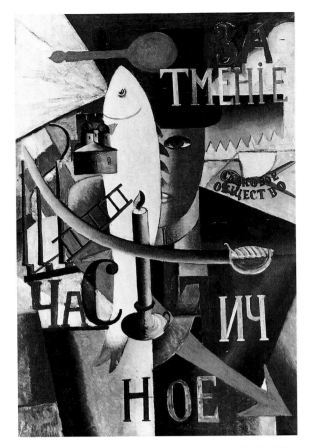

62. **Kasimir Malevich.** *An Englishman in Moscow*. 1913–14. Oil on canvas, 34⅝ × 22½" (88 × 57 cm). Stedelijk Museum, Amsterdam

63. **Kasimir Malevich.** *Woman at Poster Column*. 1914. Oil on canvas with collage, 26⅞ × 25¼" (71 × 64 cm). Stedelijk Museum, Amsterdam

agery of layered and dynamic city life (figs. 62–64). These echoes of Parisian inclusiveness were soon lost, however, in the more exclusive, focused pursuit of new extremes of abstraction. When the public word reentered Russian artistic thinking in the 1920s, it was in an altogether different context, as a consciously manipulated device of combined propaganda and commerce.

Russia of the early 1920s had its own form of *perestroika*, the New Economic Plan, which set state enterprises in competition with private, profit-hungry entrepreneurs. Civic-minded artists were called on to beat these capitalists at their own game, by the catchy design of wrappers, boxes, posters, and painted walls that would woo buyers for state products. The revolution had given them experience with improvising splices between avant-garde art and mass political indoctrination, in forms such as the agitprop trains, painted in a Cubo-Futurist manner, that were sent out into the provinces to act as mobile podiums for instructing the peasants in the principles of the new order. And when the state commercial assignments of the 1920s called for a similar combination of radical form and broad public address, that conjunction seemed not just practicable but wholly natural, even imperative, for a truly progressive art.

Modern advertising appeared to many Soviets of the 1920s, artists and poets among them, not as simply a capitalist evil, but as an objective technique that (like the Ford assembly-line methods) could be adapted to the higher purposes of Soviet society. The private artistic imagination seemed obliged to learn from such techniques in order to participate in the transformation of the culture.[32] The young Aleksandr Rodchenko, for example, was a quintessential man of the age, a painter of cosmic abstractions, then a maker of hanging sculptures that ignored gravity, and then a photographer in search of unexpected angles of vision that would change people's ideas about the order of the world. Methodical in his will to demolish all the enslaving traditions of the past, he wanted art to be a full partner in the creation of a liberated human consciousness and a more rational society. With his students in one of the art "laboratories" established by the revolution, he had undertaken a back-to-basics examination of the materials and shapes that could serve as foundations for a new art, and in the 1920s he determined to turn this analysis toward the reform of such practical things as chairs and clothing. In this context, abstract painting's former ambitions for direct access to the viewer's consciousness seemed to him readily adaptable to the task of propagating messages of reform to the broadest public. Basic geometry and boldly clarified color could be yoked with eye-catching typographic elements, and a headline-and-telegram-

64. Kasimir Malevich. *Private of the First Division.* **1914. Oil on canvas with collage, 21⅛ × 17⅝″ (53.7 × 44.8 cm). The Museum of Modern Art, New York**

65. **Aleksandr Rodchenko.** Packaging for Zebra biscuits. 1924. Printed, 14¼ × 5¹¹⁄₁₆" (36 × 14.5 cm). Private collection

66. **Headquarters of the Mosselprom firm, Moscow, 1924, with advertisements designed by Aleksandr Rodchenko, texts by Vladimir Mayakovsky**

style diction, to disrupt the numbing routines of tradition, and to open convergent routes toward the irresistible communication of the government's credo. It was only a small step more to direct that feeling toward the good of the state in concrete terms, such as the purchase of a certain kind of cigarette or light bulb (figs. 65–70).[33]

Rodchenko's frequent collaborator, as composer of the advertising copy, was the poet Vladimir Mayakovsky, who was intent on a similar reform of the word itself. Mayakovksy, who had contributed to highly simplified propaganda notices displayed in otherwise empty store windows during the war and the revolution, developed a keen appreciation for

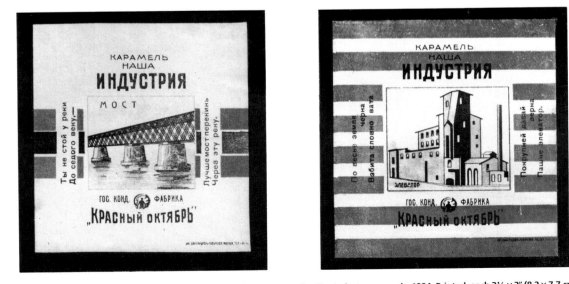

67. **Aleksandr Rodchenko,** text by **Vladimir Mayakovsky.** Wrappers for Our Industry caramels. 1924. Printed, each 3¼ × 3" (8.2 × 7.7 cm). Private collection

68. Aleksandr Rodchenko, text by **Vladimir Mayakovsky.** Advertisement for Chervonet cigarettes. 1923 (reconstructed by Vavara Stepanova, 1930). Gouache and photopaper, 4¼ × 10⅞″ (10.8 × 27.6 cm). Private collection

the "poetry" of modern advertising. He found, as did Marinetti, that the urgent condensation of slogans and headlines was a key expression of the spirit of the age; given the opportunity to promote the state's products, he determined to work directly in this new syntax, and improve upon it on its own terms. Hence he counted his formulation of the catchy tag line for Mosselprom, the state purveyor of agricultural products, *Nigde krome kak v Mosselprome* ("Nowhere Else But in Mosselprom"), as a favorite poetic achievement.[34]

69. Kiosk, Moscow, 1926, with a Mosselprom advertisement designed by **Aleksandr Rodchenko,** text by **Vladimir Mayakovsky**

For creators with these purposes in view, the startled meetings Picasso and Braque had first arranged between garrulous publicity and the hermetic avant-garde seemed to have initiated a romance of destiny. Its progeny were now to leave the café and reconquer the street—modern art, Soviet avant-garde artists believed, was born to communicate, to persuade, to change minds. Thus they determined to make a new wholeness from the Cubist and Dada incongruities, and to turn the idiom of modernism's clubhouse jokes into rhetoric that would move the masses. Painters turned graphic designers, like Rodchenko and El Lissitzky, demonstrated that the quirky incongruities of Cubist and Dada collages and *papiers collés*—the ad hoc combinations of disparate type sizes, the overlays, occlusions, and tilting planes, and the abutting of the literal and the abstract—could be understood as the first stammerings of a coherent new public language, more arresting and efficient than any before it. In their work, these devices were combined (as John Bowlt has shown) with lessons learned from indigenous Russian advertisements of the years before World War I, which had also employed bold typographic layouts and slanted lines of print.[35] The end result was a new style of graphic/linguistic expression, rigorously machine-tempered and objective, that sent the word back onto walls, boxes, and book pages, clothed in modern dress (figs. 71–73).

This in itself would be a remarkable story of reform, in which the private innovations of Braque and Picasso's little conversation in 1912 became, by a few intermediary steps and within a decade, a signal part of the official public language of a nation; and in which parts from the capitalist economic machine were cannibalized, through avant-garde art, to build its greatest rival. But the fuller story is still more complex, as the line of influence turns into the trajectory of a boomerang. The Russians' modern fusions of words and design did not simply stay at home as pro-

70. **Aleksandr Rodchenko,** text by **Vladimir Mayakovsky.** Advertisement for light bulbs at Gum, the State Department Store, Moscow. 1923 (reconstructed by Vavara Stepanova, 1930). Gouache and photopaper, 4⁷⁄₁₆ × 11³⁄₁₆″ (11.3 × 28.5 cm). Private collection

paganda; they were transmitted back to the West through magazines, books, and posters. (A Rodchenko study for the cover of one of these books, B. Arvatov's *On Mayakovsky* [fig. 71], provided the inspiration for the cover of the present volume.) Émigrés, such as El Lissitzky himself, also carried the innovations abroad. In Germany especially, Lissitzky's books and the influence of the Bauhaus spread the new look through the avant-garde, and then into broader commercial usage in advertising and packaging.

After the 1925 Universal Exposition of Decorative

71. **Aleksandr Rodchenko.** Cover design for *On Mayakovsky,* by B. Arvatov. 1923. Gouache and ink on paper, 9⅛ × 6⅛″ (23.2 × 15.5 cm). Private collection

Arts in Paris, where the Russian pavilion made a lasting impression on young European designers, the modernizing trend—by now translated into a notably looser set of lessons about asymmetry, "functionally" clean typefaces, and widened contrasts in font scales and weights—caught on in mainstream advertising and publishing, and began to affect posters, billboards, magazine covers, matchbooks, and product packaging across the continent in the late twenties and thirties. The self-styled progressive French publicists, who had generally ignored the avant-garde developments in the visual arts occurring under their noses in the teens and twenties, now found themselves taken by a flanking attack, in which the forces set loose by those same Parisian innovations—by Cubist collages and *papiers collés* most notably—came sweeping in from Russia and Germany to overrun the fort.[36] When Picasso or Braque walked down the boulevards and past the kiosks of Paris in the thirties, each passed through a public world of words that had come to echo in loud if garbled fashion, and often with a Russian or German inflection, their private dialect of 1912.[37]

The process by which all these changes took place is one that seems to involve some of the largest, most potent forces of our age: the rise of mass journalism, the advance of modern advertising, and the relation of European capitalism and American sales techniques to Soviet communism. But the more closely we look at the process, the more it appears to have been driven by the work of a few people who formed small cliques, which in turn controlled little magazines, which in turn helped constitute larger communities of taste, and so on. We can see that typography got into modern art to begin with through a private round of one-upping competition among two or three artists; and that the idea spread and transformed itself as it provided a tool for other purposes in other corners of the avant-garde, by a chain of identifiable individuals like Marinetti and

72. Aleksandr Rodchenko. Cover design for the prospectus of the first issue of *Lef*. 1923. Printed, 8⅞ × 5⅝″ (22.5 × 14.3 cm). Private collection

73. El Lissitzky. "The Sun," from *Dyla Golosa* ("For the Voice"), by Vladimir Mayakovsky (Berlin: RSFSR State Publishing House, 1923)

small groups like the Berlin Dada artists. Through transmitting agents like Lissitzky, this also seems to be the way the new typographic styles began to rebound back into broad usage in commerce. The less charted parts of the tale, though, are the later ones, where the reprise of modernized graphics by magazines and packaging designers tends to remain in the realm of collective anonymity—the magazine "business" or the advertising "industry"—because far less about the individuals and factions within those corporate entities has been published, or even acknowledged.

Luckily, though, one of the key agents in this later part of the story identified himself through his writings, and reflected on the larger history as well. Mehemed Fehmy Agha, who formed his tastes in Germany in the 1920s and thus had direct experience of the work of pioneering modern graphic designers such as Lissitzky, was called to America by the publisher Condé Nast in 1929. "Dr." Agha, as he was known, subsequently redesigned American *Vogue* and other publications in a way that helped bring the United States into the wave of modernization of type styles and layout sweeping Europe.[38] And in 1931, Agha wrote a brief but acute article

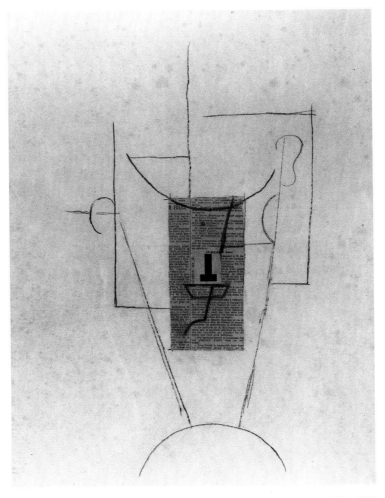

74. **Pablo Picasso.** *Head of a Man.* 1912. Ink and pasted paper on paper, 24¾ × 18½″ (63 × 47 cm). Musée d'Art Moderne, Villeneuve-d'Ascq. Gift of Geneviève and Jean Masurel

that gave an overview of one particular element in the changes he had lived through and affected: the emergence of sans serif as the official family of type-faces constituting the modern style.[39]

Picasso, Braque, and Gris, as we noted earlier, recurrently plucked out of newspapers and ads examples from a certain class of typefaces: chunky, utilitarian, and bearing either blocky serifs or none at all (figs. 16, 74). When they did that, around 1912–15, these forms were hangovers of the crude poster typefaces of the previous century (fig. 75). The first sans-serif faces, after 1800, may have owed something to the emulation of archaic stone inscriptions from antiquity, as a part of neoclassicism; but a great many of the most prominent ones had been devised out of the necessity, in the huge wooden pieces of type used for posters, to eliminate serifs that would have been especially vulnerable to the physical pressures of printing. The Cubists' selection of these workaday characters from the printer's bin, dated and utterly lacking in anything one could call style, represented what Agha called ''a light Gallic joke,'' that then was taken up in earnest by outsiders in Germany and Russia. (The Futurists, too, adopted rudely bold poster type for the masthead of their journal *Lacerba*; and Picasso responded positively by including that masthead in one of his works [fig.

76].) In the context of the broad and fast-spreading influence of Cubist and Dada innovations in collage and *papier collé*, outsiders saw the direct simplicity

75. Plate from Deberny & Peignot, *Spécimen résumé* (Paris, 1894)

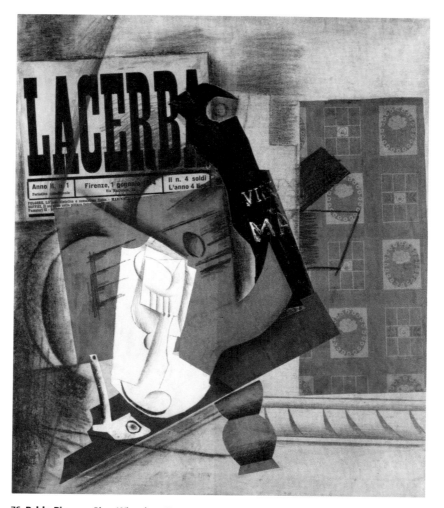

76. **Pablo Picasso.** *Pipe, Wineglass, Newspaper, Guitar, and Bottle of Vieux Marc: Lacerba.* **1914. Pasted paper, oil, and chalk on canvas, 28¾ × 23⅜″ (73.2 × 59.4 cm). Peggy Guggenheim Collection, Venice; The Solomon R. Guggenheim Foundation**

of these letters, isolated or in word fragments, as an essential element in the new look of modernity. And these eager innovators then formulated procedures that would capture that look—by imposing programmatically tilted type lines and sudden scale shifts, and also by devising new, no-nonsense, "functional" sans-serif type fonts. The vogue for the new typefaces, seemingly so attuned to the machine age in their stripped-down bareness, then spread through magazines to expositions and eventually back out into the broadest currents of public print in the 1930s.[40] Nor does the story stop there; the page you are now reading is set in a sans-serif type that was designed in 1976 and could be counted among the distant consequences of the changes we have been charting.

Agha saw that the history of sans-serif type was a wheel: starting from the lowest, least prestigious strata of public currency, moving up by artists' selection into rarefied levels of avant-garde experiment, and from there revolving back around to reenter, and transform, the widest currency of public language. His typographical mini-history involved only matters of the form and style of the modern world of words, rather than more telling issues of its content; but it points out some basic facts of twentieth-century history that are useful to recognize. Above

all, it suggests that the world of modern public language and that of avant-garde innovation are not irrevocably separate domains, but parallel historical developments, which have recurrently engaged in exchanges, in both directions. The story is one in which modern art was neither simply an enemy of modern commercial culture nor just an occasional poacher on its territory, but a partner in a complex *pas de deux* of give-and-take: the one drew from the other, and then vice versa. Agha's wheel is a pattern of linkages and transformations that moves things from one category to another, from one use to another, and from one level of consideration to another. Rather than trying to define isolating barriers and divisions, it sketches a case for the interdependence, within modern art, between playful aesthetic innovation and powerful social activism, and between things that seem merely utilitarian, even shopworn, and things that, in the hands of an artist, can become potent, meaningful, and complex. In this sense, the little tale about type may also be a typical tale—and its wheel-like motion worth remembering in the larger cycle of modern art's interchanges with popular culture. Those who prefer their categories static—with low, utilitarian graphics remaining comfortably distinct from the language of high art, or avant-garde innovations remaining

77. **Kurt Schwitters.** *The Kots Picture.* 1920. Collage, 10⅝ × 7⅝″ (27 × 19.5 cm). Sprengel Museum, Hannover

fiercely inassimilable to mundane commercial purposes—are in for frustration and disappointment in this turning world.

Agha saw the cycle of give-and-take between modern art and the world of commerce and journalism as a revolving comedy of manners. Others might view that wheel as the one on which modern art is broken, by the inexorable descent of vanguard ideals into trivial currency.[41] But any vision that would require true art to be imperviously resistant to the common life of the public market, or that would require us to separate the vanguard from the vulgar without allowance for fruitful crossover, is a vision ill suited to contend with modern history in its larger workings, and inadequate to embrace the lived experiences of modern artists.

Locally, Cubist collages and *papiers collés* show that the most hermetic formal speculations may be perfectly commensurate with cheap humor and mundane popular diversions. And even more pointedly, these little assemblages insist that an openness to unconsidered possibilities within seemingly trivial things that everyone shares may be a privileged route to the most remarkable cultural changes. The consequences of Cubism show, too, that an artist can generate from the public world of words the basis for several things at once. From it may come authentic new work of great difficulty and contrariness, or powerful new styles of mass persuasion, or disorienting languages of critique and protest, or trivial manners of decoration. And all of these may coexist without contradiction, within the same ep-

och, the same city, or even the same life, in the compass of a day or an hour. Consider in this regard a final example that belies the application of neatly separated categories: the case of the German Dada artist Kurt Schwitters, for whom Picasso's and Braque's way of assembling printed ephemera was the key to developing a personal manner of living within, but against the grain of, the provincial burgher society of Hannover.

The name for Schwitters's art, Merz, was originally just a clipping from KOMMERZ ("commerce") in one collage of the late teens. But then he decided, in a self-conscious marketing strategy, to adopt this word fragment systematically as a brand name for his work, his attitude, and himself: by the late 1920s he could say, "Now I call myself Merz."[42] Nor was this label arbitrary. In the printed world where the Cubists had found games and dreams, Schwitters found crap: Merz, though meaningless in itself, is close to the French slang, *merde*, for excrement. That combination of blank unfamiliarity and covert scatology satisfied his paradoxical aesthetic, in which zeal for pure, new, abstract languages cohabited with a hoarding instinct for society's detritus. If JOU was a serendipitous logo for the Cubists' playful subversion of public language, the Merz trademark served as an apt emblem of Schwitters's ambivalent involvement in, and contempt for, a world built on business.

Schwitters set out to make "new art forms from the remains of a former culture."[43] His mature assemblages are compiled wholly from detritus; and the signs of usage and decomposition—cuts, tears,

78. Kurt Schwitters. *The Saddler Portfolio.* **1922. Collage, 15⅛ × 22" (38.4 × 55.8 cm). Collection E. W. Kornfeld, Berlin**

79. Kurt Schwitters. *Figurine.* 1921. Collage, 6¾ × 3⅝″ (17.3 × 9.2 cm). Private collection

partiality itself—play an evident, expressive role. He often dwelt on a world gone by, fashioning mock-sentimental tributes to imagined ladies by clipping clothing ads in which the ornate typefaces and blandly idealized wood-engravings epitomized complacent materialism (figs. 77–79). A cigarette pack, with its evocations of faraway places, could be the material for a romantic dialogue with a woman's name (fig. 80). This vein of evident nostalgia, like his hoarder's sense of *horror vacui* (fig. 81), sets the work well away from the more confident, spacious

Cubist works that preceded it.

Schwitters's frugal, twine-saver's art trafficked not in words for cognacs, cafés, and concerts, but in tiny tram tickets, wrappers from much-loved chocolates, and labels from small, torn packages. It had less to do with sociability than with solitary wanderings, real and imagined, and diaristic fantasies; instead of savoring hot headlines and crude humor, it aimed to wrest more uncertain meanings from thoroughly perfunctory public notices (DOGS MUST BE KEPT ON LEASH), the most weary clichés, and snippets of re-

80. **Kurt Schwitters.** *Miss Blanche.* 1923. Collage, 6¼ × 5″ (15.9 × 12.7 cm). Collection Dr. Werner Schmalenbach, Düsseldorf

81. **Kurt Schwitters.** Untitled (Kwatta). 1928. Collage, 6¾ × 4¾″ (17 × 12.5 cm). Present whereabouts unknown

82. Kurt Schwitters. *Eva Stee.* 1937–38. Collage, 9¾ × 7½″ (24.8 × 19.4 cm). Courtesy Marlborough Fine Art, London

fuse, by displacing them from their original contexts into new, illogical relationships. His intimately scaled collages, like his poetry, cherished the genteel disorientation of these used, wholly banal things, or words, or phrases. The tender form of art that results is at once sentimental and ironic, tidy and trashy, commonplace and intensely personal.

If this is remote from Parisian sociability, it seems further still from Futurist clamor, and Russian propaganda. Schwitters's art tears, fold by fold and scrap by scrap, the words of a private, intimate dialogue from the mundane registers of the public word. Yet, surprisingly, he also had a "second identity," which belongs firmly within the story of modernization and reform encountered in Soviet propaganda and advertising. One of Schwitters's close associates and occasional collaborators was El Lissitzky; and Schwitters's writings on typography show he understood Lissitzky's lessons well: simple, clear typefaces, composed in a way that suggested machine-like impersonality, with nothing ornamental, and detached letters used as independent, abstract symbols. With

these precepts in mind, Schwitters opened his own graphic-design business in Hannover in 1924 (fig. 83). He enjoyed notable success in devising sleekly modern ads and packaging for the manufacturer of Pelikan inks (fig. 84), and eventually won—in a poignant irony that put the ragman in charge of the cloth mill—the contract for production of the city of Hannover's official printed matter.

This odd, Penelope-like double existence—making the public's print by day, and tearing it up by night—makes Schwitters a special figure in the story of art's early encounter with the public world of words. His working on two fronts embodies the bifurcated evolution of the Cubists' innovations with found language and letters. On the one hand, the "liberation" of words, which snatched them from their public contexts and scattered their fragments within a composition of abstracted form, gave new options to those modernizers who sought an insistently unsubjective and impersonal art, bent variously on declamation, criticism, and persuasion. On the other, the model of an art built on private jokes and

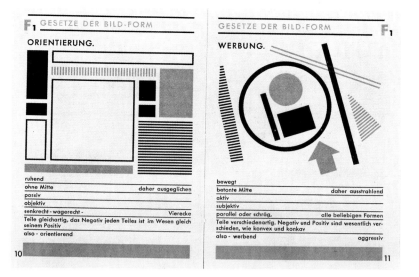

83. Kurt Schwitters. Double-page spread from the pamphlet *Die neue Gestaltung in der Typographie.* c. 1925. Printed, 5⅞ × 8½" (14.9 × 21.6 cm). The Museum of Modern Art, New York. Jan Tschichold Collection, Gift of Philip Johnson

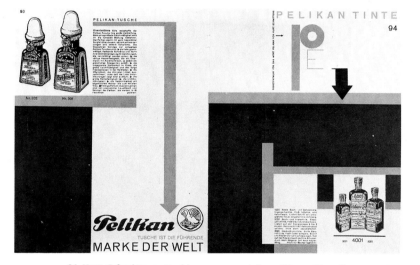

84. Kurt Schwitters. Double-page spread from "Typoreklame" issue of *Merz*, 1924. Printed, 11⅜ × 17¼" (29 × 44 cm). Collection Merrill C. Berman

carefully preserved snippets of ephemera also suggested a new way that personal fantasy, nostalgia, and intimate psychic complexities could build their own nests with threads from the fabric of a mass commercial society.

The simultaneities of Schwitters's early life take place, however, and Agha's wheel turns, wholly within the circle of the *printed* word. In this cycle of modern artists engaged with the products of the modern world, we never seem to step outside the world of words that are pre-processed by social functions such as journalism, advertising, and packaging. We might well expect that the relation between artists and their sources in urban culture would change if the language at issue were still further outside the domain of art—not on up-to-date posters and newsprint, but in the raw, immemorial vernacular of the streets. And that scarred and obscure field of writing is our next concern.

1. **Giacomo Balla.** *Bankruptcy*. 1902. Oil on canvas, 46⅛ × 63⅛″ (116 × 160 cm). Museum Ludwig, Cologne

hen Picasso and Braque stopped on the boulevard to look up at the possibilities in newsprint and billboards, they felt the winds of modernity's springtime in their faces. But in 1902, when Giacomo Balla looked down at tangled chalk marks closer to the gutter (figs. 1, 2), he inhaled another atmosphere, vented from the underside of society in a form that seemed stagnantly invariant. In opposition to the snappy, upbeat look of the new publicity, here was a kind of public "writing" that was clumsy, untutored, willfully destructive, and ignorant of pretense to commercial utility. Across the shiny surface of progress's *yes*, it scrawled a stubbornly atavistic *no*.

Yet this kind of scrawl has now become an inevitable, inescapable fixture of modern experience. As the tide-line left by an irrepressible social current, it has in the past quarter century flowed down every city street in the Western world, over concrete roadway barriers, brimming to the top of subway cars, coating park benches, toilet stalls, and monuments alike. And an equally unavoidable counterflow of opinion has tried to press it on our minds as the authentic signature of our overenergized but rotting cities. It has been praised and damned as the telling upsurge of the "primitive" into the present, and has

GRAFFITI

been embraced as the last authentic domain of a "natural" expressive art. In an age of processed information, this guerrilla channel gives us raw news from society's margins: the writings on public walls appear to manifest libido without limits; an urge to defile, triumphant over respect for property or fear of law; and the shrieking, antisocial assertion of "me" against all civic constraint. Like crime, poverty, and other intractable features of human society, it seems to take on a new intensity and range of meaning in the present, as its very persistence mocks proud hopes for a modernity nobly different from the past.

Anyone who has lived through these past twenty-five years knows that this kind of writing has a sharply defined contemporary history, marked by the advent of new media, an ebb and flow of styles, moments of invention, strands of development, and periods of exhaustion. But in longer-range terms, it has had no recorded history: we know precious little about it, because apparently no one but we, and our immediate ancestors in Western culture, have ever cared to know. We blithely think of inscribing and drawing on public walls as a universal part of human nature, familiar in varying guises to all societies from the Pleistocene to Pompeii. Yet, while we can show that ancient Egyptians and Romans commonly scratched names and messages onto monuments, there is no sign that anyone, until the eighteenth and especially the nineteenth century, thought this was a separate, special category of activity worthy of any notice. And the distinctions we now make between licit and illicit markings, or between adornment and defacement, involve ex-post-facto categories that ill accommodate a range of instances stretching from commissioned votive prayers on Nubian temples to pictograms scratched on Mayan stelae and explorers' marks in the American deserts (fig. 3). To lump all these marks from the past together, and relate them to the walls around us, we have settled on a blanket term of convenience, originally adopted by nineteenth-century archeologists: *graffiti*. And in every sense of its meaning to us, graffiti is a recent discovery.

We will never be able to write a full history, back through the ages, of what graffiti has been: for one thing, practitioners and enemies alike have effaced the evidence a thousand times over. But we can sketch the history, over the past two centuries, of what we have thought it to be, and of how we came to think about it at all. The story of that discovery is intertwined with the story of modern art's origins and development. Yet for anyone prone to global generalizations about the relationship between easel art and street art, it is a cautionary tale. Unlike the history of words and typefaces, which centered on the innovative phenomena of modern publicity, this is a history of how new attitudes came to embrace something very old—how fresh possibilities and modern poetics came to be found where only immemorial, unregenerate vandalism seemed to lie. And the story advances with an altogether different, surprising rhythm, as an intellectual prelude in the last century sets up a special combination of prepared expectations and postponed conclusions in this one.

Bankruptcy (fig. 1) seems to be the first painting ever to give center stage to graffiti. But by the time Balla painted it, archeologists, linguists, and sociologists had been thinking seriously about the subject for more than a century—and studiously ignoring it for at least half a century more than that. There had been rare mentions of graffiti in literature before the mid-eighteenth century, and even curiosities like the jocular compendium of "bog-house" messages (bathroom

2. Giacomo Balla. Study for *Bankruptcy*. 1902. Crayon on paper, 3⅞ × 3⅛″ (9.5 × 8.2 cm). Private collection, Rome

mind. But equally new with Romanticism was a heightened admiration for popular-cultural features, such as folk song, that had formerly been thought merely debased and inferior. And as this sentiment developed, simple documentary attention to graffiti was gradually supplanted by a special appreciation for unofficial inscriptions as a singular class of evidence, that afforded a particular insight into the mores of past cultures—including, after this long delay, Pompeii's.

English visitors of the early 1830s remarked on the graffiti, and one of them, the Rev. Christopher Wordsworth, devoted a book-length study to the *Inscriptiones Pompeianae*.[4] But these early notices[5] disclaimed any regard for the aesthetic quality of what they saw, and bridled at discussing the numerous obscenities (which were evidence, Wordsworth sniffed, of the moral depravity underlying the beauty of the ancient city's décor). In the ensuing years, not just the textual evidence but the look of the walls themselves became more thoroughly documented. The Italian scholar F. M. Avellino published engraved reproductions of some of the inscriptions in 1841 (fig. 4),[6] and

epigrams, also known as "latrinalia") published in London in 1731.[1] The excavation of Pompeii that began in 1748, however, opened a fresh set of possibilities for this subject's entry into recorded history. Vesuvius's eruption in A.D. 79 had preserved in Pompeii a unique, freeze-frame record of antiquity; and when it was uncovered, modern eyes saw pristine evidence of everyday chalked and scratched wall inscriptions, preserved from the overlays and effacements that had long since covered their like in exposed sites. On these walls as nowhere else, a wealth of oaths and imprecations, drawings and historical references, prayers and obscenities, put the flesh (sometimes all too weak and human) of daily life back onto the noble skeleton of an idealized ancient culture.

Yet, in an early demonstration of a rule that has shaped the whole history of graffiti's "discovery," all this was largely ignored until observers were prepared to make something of it. The Pompeian graffiti apparently had nothing to say to those who looked at it with tastes informed by nascent neoclassicism. Though the inscriptions were recorded in the reports of the excavations, and mentioned briefly in at least two late eighteenth-century studies, more than eighty years elapsed between the start of digging and the publication of the first serious remarks on their content.[2]

Serious historical documentation of graffiti began only in the early years of the nineteenth century, at the time of the Napoleonic incursions into Egypt, when French scholars, such as Jacques-Joseph and Jean-François Champollion (the latter was decoder of the Rosetta stone), resolved to base their study of the exotic and ancient on a diligent notation of all the textual evidence inscribed on monuments and ruins.[3] Such objective scrutiny of previously uncharted phenomena was characteristic of the emerging Romantic frame of

3. Timothy O'Sullivan. *Historic Spanish Record of the Conquest, Inscription Rock*. 1873. Albumen print. National Archives, Washington, D.C.

in 1856 Raphael Garrucci brought out a larger study that became widely known (figs. 5–7).[7] Garrucci, whose book is the most important early treatment of the subject, extended the meaning of *graffiti*, till then a paleographer's term, to include popular wall drawings as well as discursive inscriptions. Subsequent archeology of antique and Christian Rome uncovered more pockets of such unofficial markings (fig. 8).[8]

These ancient "demotic" or "cursive" inscriptions interested historians for what they said about those who inscribed them; but others began speculating on what such marks revealed about human nature in general, and about art in particular. In an 1848 treatise,

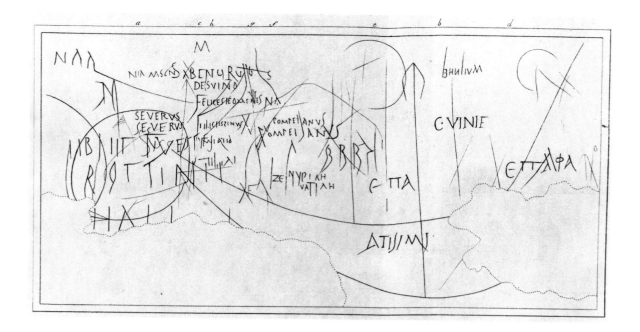

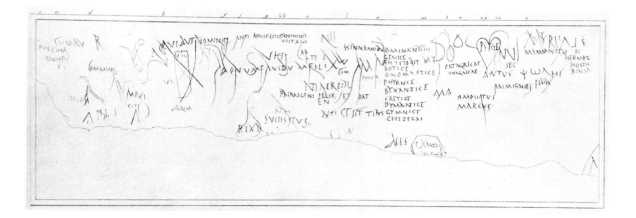

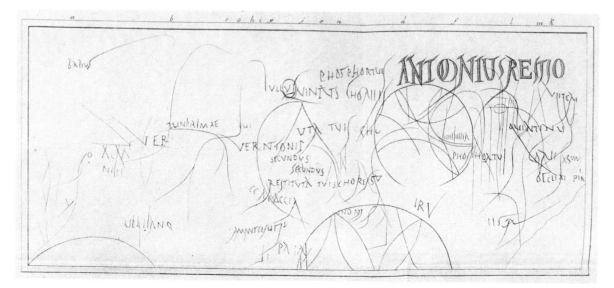

4. Pompeian wall inscriptions, from Cav. F. M. Avellino, *Osservazioni sopra alcune iscrizioni e disegni graffiti sulle mura di Pompei* (Naples: Stamperia Reale, 1841), figs. 2, 3, 1

the Swiss artist Rodolphe Töpffer expressed delight at learning that the wall drawings of Pompeii and Herculaneum (which apparently he knew only by reports) resembled the drawings of children and the art of "savages." He took all these things as evidence for a common, universal point of origin for all art and all ideas of beauty. That origin lay, Töpffer asserted, not in the instinct to imitate appearances, but in an urge to give material form to mental conceptions. And he felt the rude, schematic nature of the excavated wall drawings bore witness to this unchanging, innate dominance of invention over imitation in all human expression.[9]

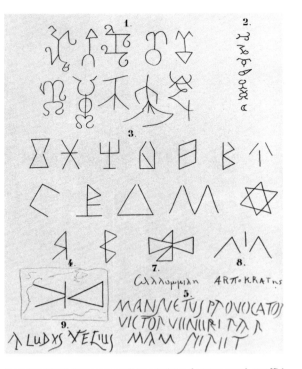

7. Unidentified Pompeian wall inscriptions, from Garrucci, *Graffiti de Pompéi*, pl. 29, nos. 1–4, 7, 8

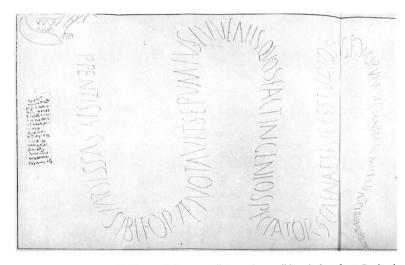

5. "Serpentis lusus. . . . " Pompeian wall inscription, from Raphael Garrucci, *Graffiti de Pompéi*, 2nd ed. (Paris: Benjamin Duprat, 1856), pl. 6, no. 1

6. "Psyce." Pompeian wall inscription, from Garrucci, *Graffiti de Pompéi*, pl. 16, no. 8

In his 1865 study of caricature, the French champion of folk song Champfleury followed the same line of thinking, and took the crucial step of seeing one of the most famous of Pompeian graffiti (fig. 9) in aesthetic terms. He argued that it was a painter's first idea for a composition, with the same traits of impetuous brevity he admired in Delacroix's initial sketches.[10] If the general thrust of graffiti study was toward a new knowledge of the lower orders, Champfleury, more explicitly than Töpffer, linked this to a notion of genius: the essential fire of an artist, he felt, already appeared in those rare older expressions that were urgent, unpremeditated delineations of ideas.

8. Inscriptions over a wall painting of Saint Cornelius, from Abbé Martigny, *Dictionnaire des antiquités chrétiennes*, 3rd ed. (Paris: Librairie Hachette, 1889), p. 336

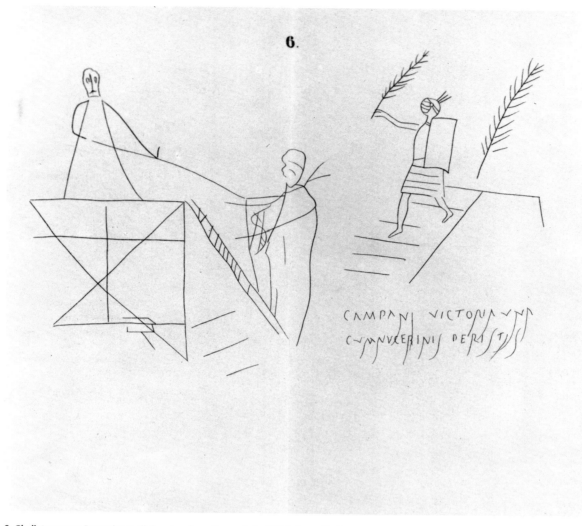

9. Gladiator scene. Pompeian wall drawing, from Garrucci, *Graffiti de Pompéi*, pl. 29, no. 6

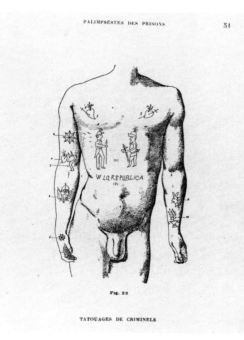

10. Tattoos of criminals, from Cesare Lombroso, *Les Palimpsestes des prisons* (Lyon: A. Storck; Paris: G. Masson, 1894), fig. 23

These first responses to graffiti were based on a positive idea of primitivism, which saw in all untutored drawings a valuable residue of the primary urge to create. But decades later, amid pseudo-Darwinian concepts of evolutionary progress, the idea that graffiti was essentially a primitive form took on a less appealing coloration. At the end of the nineteenth century, when sociologists finally directed serious study toward modern Western society's own wall inscriptions, they focused exclusively on the graffiti in prison cells—recording and classifying it, in the same way they examined the slang of low-life types, in order to discern the distinctive states of mind of thieves, murderers, and their ilk. Less formal compendiums of folkways like the Rev. J. W. Horsley's *Jottings from Jail* (1887) gave way to such "scientifically" serious tomes as Dr. Émile Laurent's *Les Habitués des prisons de Paris* (1890) and Cesare Lombroso's *Les Palimpsestes des prisons* (1894), and the study of graffiti became associated with theories of criminality as atavism (fig. 10).[11]

Lombroso might be taken as a harbinger of today's rogue-chromosome theories of criminal behavior; he was best known for his general notion that criminality was hereditary, and that criminals were throwbacks to earlier evolutionary states. Along these lines, he saw graffiti as the recurrence of an original form of language, which he linked both to the infantile desire to scribble and to the revelation of the unconscious in the unguarded drawings of geniuses. Havelock Ellis followed this same reasoning in *The Criminal* (1890, rev. 1903), when he saw the human tendency to make graffiti as "scarcely distinguishable from the instinct which leads to the production of heroic works of art."[12] In each case, graffiti was taken seriously, only to be stigmatized as the unevolved, regressive behavior of the socially dysfunctional.

These psychologically oriented studies were finally extended beyond the sphere of pathology in the series of articles on graffiti published by G. H. Luquet, beginning in 1910. Luquet gathered his evidence from the walls along Parisian streets, from barracks

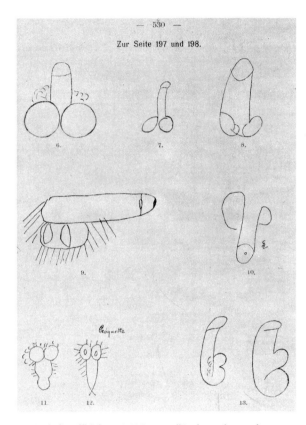

11. Genital graffiti, from G. H. Luquet, "Sur la survivance des caractères du dessin enfantin dans des graffiti à indications sexuelles," *Anthropophyteia*, 7 (1910), p. 530

and toilet stalls. For him, exactly the kind of obscene drawings which had seemed so base and unworthy to early writers on Pompeii were of special interest, as markers of universally shared preoccupations (figs. 11–14). Luquet sought to make specific, structural connections between the manners of rendering in primitive art, children's art, and the graffiti of adults. All of these, he felt, showed the innate predominance of what he called "logical realism." This way of drawing stressed the depiction of attributes thought important, whether they were visible or not: when male genitals were drawn, for example, the testicles would appear as circles inside the scrotum (figs. 11, 14). Luquet felt the evidence showed that this conceptual mode of representation was innate, while "visual realism," which only rendered appearances, had to be learned.[13] By World War I,

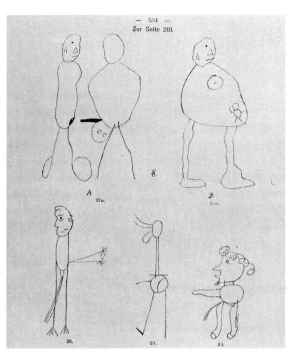

12. Urinating figures, from Luquet, "Sur la survivance des caractères du dessin enfantin," p. 534

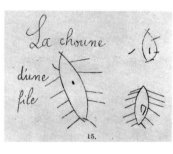

13. Genital graffiti, from Luquet, "Sur la survivance des caractères du dessin enfantin," p. 531, fig. 15

14. Genital graffiti, from G. H. Luquet, "Sur un cas d'homonymie graphique: Sexe et visage humain," *Anthropophyteia*, 7 (1910), p. 536

then, Töpffer's initial intuition about the universal origins of "childish" and "savage" art in basic mental processes of creative conception had been codified in modern psychology and anthropology; and both the criminality and sexuality of graffiti had become established parts of its appeal to science.

Well before such writers on graffiti had become interested in the ways children and criminals might be like artists, however, there had already been a modest echoing tradition, in which artists seem to have enjoyed thinking of themselves as children and criminals. In the seventeenth century Pieter Saenredam and Gerard Houckgeest, Dutch painters who depicted the spare interiors of Protestant churches, painted in their signatures as if scratched on the church piers, along with the other childish drawings they recorded on these columns—a gently self-humbling idea of the artist as scribbler, with some

15. **Charles-Joseph Traviès.** "La Poire est devenue populaire!," from *Le Charivari*, April 28, 1833. The Metropolitan Museum of Art, New York. Gift of Arthur Sachs, 1923 (23.92.1)

overtone of a *vanitas* marking by a passing actor on a permanent stage.[14] Their contemporary colleague in Rome, Pieter van Laer, showed his rowdy fellows in a more secular setting and earthier mood, scrawling their names and various farcical caricatures on a tavern wall.[15] And in an exceptional journal made between 1780 and 1787, *Mes inscripcions*, the French writer Restif de La Bretonne evoked himself as graffiti-maker in still more complex terms.[16] Despite the mockery of urchins who often defaced his work, Restif took a bittersweet pleasure from inscribing various spots in Paris with the record (solemnly rendered in Latin) of telling moments in his life, and then periodically returning to see how his marks were faring. (Recent art-world language would class this as a "process piece.") Restif's work was a kind of diary, in which the graffiti served as a stimulus for meditations on mortality and the passage of time—a way to map the author's private existence on the public fabric of Paris, and vice versa.

16. **J. J. Grandville.** Artist drawing his name on a graffiti-covered wall, from *Cent Proverbes* (Paris: H. Fournier, 1845), p. 354

Such rare early documents linked the creator's activity with that of innocents, or of lovers who mark their trysting spots. But nineteenth-century instances are more explicit about the criminality of graffiti, and the artist's identification with that outlaw aspect. Daumier's contemporary Charles-Joseph Traviès imagined street urchins propagating his colleague Philipon's insulting caricature of King Louis-Philippe as a pear (*poire* means something like "fathead" in French slang), and implicitly associated the outsider aggression of his trade, political satire, with the irreverent and irrepressible crudities of street art (fig. 15). The caricaturist J. J. Grandville showed himself, with a furtive glance over the shoulder, adding his signature to the roster of graffiti on an oft-marred wall (fig. 16). In each case, the satirist implicitly adopted

17. **James Ensor.** *The Pisser*. 1887. Etching, 6 × 4¼" (14.9 × 10.8 cm). Private collection, Brussels

18. Vittorio Corcos. *Portrait of Yorick*. **1889. Oil on canvas,   6′6⅝″ × 55½″ (200 × 141 cm). Museo Civico Giovanni Fattori, Livorno**

the urban scrawler's marginal role as antiauthoritarian bad boy—and perhaps fantasized about a form of art that could communicate the most aggressive impulses directly to the public without censorship or compromise. In a less romanticized vision, the Belgian painter James Ensor "inscribed" imprecations against himself (ENSOR EST UN FOU ["Ensor is a madman"] appears just over the graffiti drawing in fig. 17), and then had his surrogate figure defame the

defamation, by urinating against the offending wall. And in a final, Realist instance from 1889 that brings us back, close to the milieu of Balla's *Bankruptcy*, the Italian painter Vittorio Corcos showed the critic Pietro Ferrigni against a graffiti-decked wall, on which a crude, potbellied figure seems both a mocking echo of the subject himself and a good-humored homage by the artist to the more pungent immediacy of another style of rendering (figs. 18, 19).[17]

19. Vittorio Corcos. *Portrait of Yorick* (detail)

In both intellectual and visual terms, then, the chronicle of early interest in graffiti is one that we might imagine was approaching its logical conclusion, around the time of World War I, in the emergence of these markings and drawings on public walls as a source of inspiration for modern artists. We can see that all the elements were available for this renegade form to take its place among other kinds of low art and non-art—folk broadsides, children's drawings, tribal art, and others—whose styles would be embraced by the avant-garde as antinaturalistic antidotes to established standards, and as affronts to common notions of trained technique.

Yet the story does not have that expected result; for, while those other forms of "untutored" expression came to have a sharp impact on early modern artists, graffiti did not. Tribal art helped catalyze some of Picasso's most impressive innovations, folk painting influenced Vasily Kandinsky's abstraction, and children's drawings affected the work of Paul Klee; but, as measured both by the record of statements and manifestoes and by the visual evidence, graffiti remained almost entirely beyond the pale.

It is tricky to speculate on why something did *not* happen, but it would seem fair to venture some guesses. Graffiti as a whole is a composite phenomenon, part childish prank, part adult insult. It is whimsical and political, amused and angry, witty and obscene, often tending toward the palimpsest, and made up of elements of imagery, writing, and simple marking. One part of that mix, caricatural drawing, was taken into modern art from other sources (examined in the next chapter). For the rest, Guillaume Apollinaire may have had graffiti's peculiar combinations of words and images in mind when he made his experimental poem-pictures of 1913–16, the *Calligrammes,* published in 1918 (fig. 20); such imagistic arrangements can be found as far back as the serpent from Pompeii (fig. 5). And the words inscribed across several paintings by the Russian avant-garde artists Mikhail Larionov and Aleksandr Shevchenko around 1911–12 may also count graffiti among their sources of inspiration.[18] But in general graffiti was perhaps perceived, despite the elements of atavism many claimed to see in it, as an urban and street-smart phenomenon, barren of the connotations of exotic liberty from Western knowledge, or of unspoiled purity, that made folk or tribal art attractive. Also, the typical aleatory and additive look of graffiti lacked the concision of form that was inspiring in, say, African sculpture; and, finally, the associations it carried were perhaps more strongly those of wear and tear, decay and degradation, than of primordial originality.

Two exceptions, early works that do take notice of graffiti, tend to confirm such suspicions. Balla's *Bankruptcy* stems from a period of his painting that charts the gritty working life of the modern city. The random handwriting of the down-and-out, which he studied in a preparatory drawing (fig. 2), was wholly at odds with the misty residue of "scientific" pointillism in the painting. Unlike the typical Futurist celebrations of things to come, the picture bears impassive witness to what is ending, and what remains unreformed: the casualties of modern capitalism and the crude impulse to deface. A mordant bit of social reporting on the look of failure and abuse, it has little to do with the chronophotographic dynamism of Balla's later Futurist canvases, and still less to do with his later ventures into a geometrically based abstraction.[19]

The other early modern work obliquely related to graffiti, a whimsical piece of smut by a Frenchman bent on renouncing painting altogether, was even further from Havelock Ellis's "instinct which leads

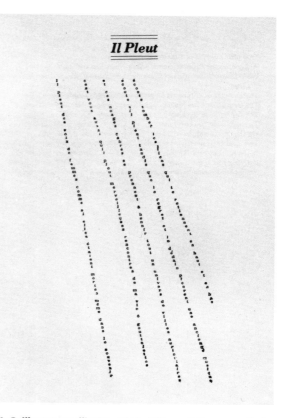

20. Guillaume Apollinaire. "Il pleut," from *Calligrammes* (Paris, 1918)

to the production of heroic works of art." In 1919 Marcel Duchamp produced a small "rectified Readymade" in the form of a photomechanical reproduction of the Mona Lisa, to which he added a pencil mustache and the letters L.H.O.O.Q. (fig. 21; as every French schoolboy knew then, and as every American art history student knows now, these letters pronounced in French yield something very like "*Elle a chaud au cul,*" or roughly, "She's got a hot ass"). Since Balla's painting is still essentially a piece of Realist reportage, this little card is arguably the first fully modern work to incorporate graffiti into its strategies. But it does so in a way directly contrary to the high-minded estimations by Lombroso, Ellis, and Luquet of the raw atavism expressed in such markings. Duchamp's little defacement identifies graffiti-writing as a reactive rather than creative activity,

L.H.O.O.Q.

21. Marcel Duchamp. *L.H.O.O.Q.* **1919. Rectified Readymade: pencil on a reproduction, 7¾ × 4⅞″ (19.7 × 12.4 cm). Private collection**

absorbed in criticizing or commenting on what others have done, rather than in direct self-expression. The supposed sanctity of the high tradition (made freshly accessible to "street-level" response by photoreproduction) finds its debunking antagonist in the parasitic graffito "adjustment"—positioning graffiti not as the ancestral cousin of high painting, but as its incorrigibly *méchant* juvenile sibling. If Duchamp is suggesting that the two are alike, it is at the expense of a former ideal of art, not to the credit of a new ideal of graffiti. The proposal here is that the modern artist may act like the street artist, not in the recuperation of some preverbal barbaric force, but in

a cynical, knowing irreverence, and in the sniping use of crudely barbed wit against established shibboleths.

This gesture suited Duchamp's ideas perfectly. His notion of a modern art at the service of the mind made Töpffer's and Luquet's concerns beside the point: it concerned itself neither with imitation (which the postcard suggests has become outmoded by technology) nor with innate conceptualization, but with transformation, transposition, critique, and subversion. By using the same kind of commonplace, off-color wordplay that Picasso and Braque had made from newspaper mastheads and headlines,

L.H.O.O.Q. smirks with a specifically Duchampian, urbanely self-conscious perversity. The mustached Mona Lisa involved a sophisticated in-joke about the model's (and Leonardo's) ambivalent sexuality, as well as Duchamp's own interests (he later created a transvestite alter ego, Rrose Sélavy).[20] Although common and public, the joke is thus at the same time inbred and personal. And the piece as a whole has nothing to do with the sprawling, messy vitality sometimes associated with wall scribblings; instead, its studied parsimony is consistent with Duchamp's particular idea of economy, producing big perturbations by an elegant little gesture and a minute expenditure of energy. The graffito here enters modern art not, as might be expected, as the sign of the outsider's impulsive, raw expressiveness, but as a vehicle for a bit of in-house gamesmanship—a matter, like so much else in Duchamp's art, of knowing and violating specific decorums, rather than simply being asocial or antisocial.

History would of course not care a whit for this little *jeu d'esprit* were it not from Duchamp's hand, and if it did not resonate within a complex career of contrariness and provocation. The gesture of the mustache made in that context has carried an altogether different weight and set of meanings from similar mustaches made by countless others before and since. And within the development of modern art, what might seem a trifling one-time stunt is actually a tart foretaste of some of the complexities of what is to come—an anomaly that unsettles some clichéd expectations, and points to some larger rules.

We might suppose, for example, that modern artists bring graffiti into art like a rap musician into a cotillion, to bust up stale conventions and put us back in touch with what is really happening on the street. This would dovetail with the general idea that forms of low or mass art are a collectively generated "reality" of twentieth-century life which art must constantly break conventions to accommodate—or indeed which provides (in the face of exhausted or inadequate resources within artistic tradition) the new forms that allow artists to confront life more directly.

In fact, though, the story of graffiti has more to do with changes that first occur within art, changes that then permit artists to see new possibilities in what was previously ignored—and ultimately to derive a complex range of individual poetics from forms that had once seemed too trivial, too limited, or too anarchic for anything other than restricted, immediate purposes. The result was not to shine the light of art on some fixed, given thing that graffiti was, but to make available to artists a broad set of expressive possibilities encompassing many of the widely different things graffiti might be: brutally simple or complexly tangled, clever and witty or raw and impassioned, and viciously ugly or tender and playful. None of this really began to happen, however, until the century was nearly half over.

The crucial artistic impetus for a reassessment of graffiti came from Surrealism in the 1920s and 1930s, and the major consequences were not visible until the 1940s and 1950s. The first steps, literary and intellectual rather than formal and artistic, involved a new devotion to the unconscious as a source for art, and a related elevation of the grotesque as its characteristic expression. Surprisingly perhaps, in light of their will to provoke and their *nostalgie de la boue* (only partially translatable, involving a yearning to wallow in what is seen as low and filthy), the Surrealists were notably silent on the subject of graffiti itself. But their veneration of the unconscious carried with it the implication that the true, best sources of creativity were precisely those impulses which had been repressed and censored by Western civilization, and which escaped along the unclean margins where society's control was slackened, and where its bourgeois premises were vulnerable to attack.

Out of this milieu came one focused appreciation of graffiti as a form of art, in the photographs and brief remarks published by the photographer Brassaï in the Surrealist organ *Minotaure* in 1933 (fig. 22).[21] Brassaï's vision of crusty, long-abused old walls in Paris was informed by his belief that graffiti drawings were akin to cave art, as well as by a familiar Surrealist association between the glamorously "dangerous" mysteries of urban lowlife and the marvels of the deeper psyche. The legacy of Baudelaire's nostalgic love for the piss-stained corners of Paris, as well as the spirit of the figural deformations of Picasso, Klee, and Joan Miró, lurk in these dark images of crudely hacked-out skulls and hearts and heads (figs. 23–25).

Exactly a century after the first writers noted the cursive inscriptions of Pompeii, Brassaï's attention brought contemporary wall markings into the circle of avant-garde art, but with a sharp change in attributed meaning. Brassaï saw the linkage, which virtually all writers since Töpffer had noticed, between graffiti and children's drawings. For Brassaï, however, graffiti was "childish" in its vehemence, rather than in any innocence or naïveté. His text (expanded and clarified when he published a later version in the 1950s)[22] insisted that true children's creations were not just sunny and playful. When juveniles wielded knife against stone on public walls, as opposed to crayon on paper in supervised playrooms, an authentic ferocity emerged. These street drawings were not lifelines back to an innocence we all once shared, but marks of the common torments of the human condition, experienced all the more painfully in youth. Brassaï valued graffiti drawings precisely in the ways they were *unlike* more casual infantile scribblings, because they were realized with an intensity more closely related to the darker side of the psyche, and thus were in closer touch with the powerful figurations of mythology. He still felt, as others had before him, that graffiti revealed the funda-

22. **Brassaï.** *Graffiti parisiens.* **Photographs from** *Minotaure*, 1, nos. 3, 4 (1933), p. 7

ments of artistic conception in the mind. But now the mind was seen as an emotionally charged battleground of psychic forces, and the lines of graffiti as traces of inner trauma.

Curiously, the other major adept of graffiti between the two wars, the psychologist and champion of the art of the insane, Hans Prinzhorn, had evoked a wholly different mode of creation in 1926, by stressing the boredom and the passive, dreamlike mood that he felt led prisoners to mark their cell walls.[23] And while the markings Brassaï selected had an obvious resonance with the contemporary art he knew, the drawing practices of Brassaï's Surrealist

contemporaries were actually closer to Prinzhorn's notion of chance inspiration and reverie, rather than gouging, as the avenue to the unconscious. The Surrealist artists favored more labile techniques of self-surprise, with pliant materials: collaborative drawings, inkblots, and especially automatic writing, the random scribbling designed to coax elemental forms from areas of the mind beyond the reach of conscious intent.

Again, we are left to speculate on an absence— for, despite their interest in various kinds of unsanctioned art made by outsiders to the Western tradition, including tribal wall drawings,[24] the Surrealists apparently paid little attention to the urban graffiti around them. Beyond their general encouragement to wrest meaning from "mindless" scrawling, the Surrealist exercises in automatic writing translated into a specific distaste for compositions organized along Cubist lines, and a preference for biomorphic forms and looping, continuous contours that conjured a fluid, rambling stream of thought. And this fostered free-form styles of abstraction, as well as scrawling, simplified figurations such as those of Klee and Miró, which seemed to refer to primitive pictographs. But while they were intent on conjuring imagery of the marvelous and magic from the unconscious, the artists associated with Surrealism apparently had little affection for the brusque, crude, and often scurrilous forms by which graffiti seemed to express hostility and frustration. It was only through the inheritors of Surrealism, in the 1940s, that the markings on public walls came to develop their most pointed connections with modern art.

24. Brassaï. Photograph (1932–58) from Brassaï, *Graffiti,* **p. 57**

23. Brassaï. Photograph (1932–58) from Brassaï, *Graffiti: Zwei Gespräche mit Picasso* **(Stuttgart, Berlin, and Zurich: Chr. Belser Verlag, 1960), p. 26**

Following on the lead of André Masson and others in developing experimental doodling and the rambling lines of automatic writing into improvisational paintings, American artists such as Jackson Pollock and Willem de Kooning developed, in the late 1940s, a new manner of abstraction that suggested a new way of looking at graffiti sharply different from that of Brassaï. This new painting valued the energy of gesture, dispersed throughout the field of the canvas, over any discernible figural content; and made the act of marking itself—not the imagery it might dredge up—a primary vehicle of picture-making. Pollock especially, in the works he made around 1950 (fig. 26), showed how painterly "rambling" without a preset goal, and with the entertain-

ment of chance, could go beyond the Surrealists' exhumation of stock symbols from the psyche, and yield possibilities for the expression of a new lyricism, on a scale that stretched the limits of the personal gesture toward an encompassing, mural-like field. Also, Pollock and the other Abstract Expressionists showed a willingness to work with chance in their engagement with their materials. The more agitated nature of the surfaces of their canvases—with prominent splatters and drips, or an emphasis on the resistance of thick paint to the thrusts of the brush—opened an avenue of appreciation for the look of rough walls with layered textures of haphazardly accumulated marks.

25. Brassaï. Photograph (c. 1933) from Brassaï, *Graffiti,* **p. 95**

26. **Jackson Pollock.** Untitled. 1950. Ink on paper, 17½ × 22¼″ (44.4 × 56.5 cm). The Museum of Modern Art, New York. Gift of Mr. and Mrs. Ronald Lauder in honor of Eliza Parkinson Cobb

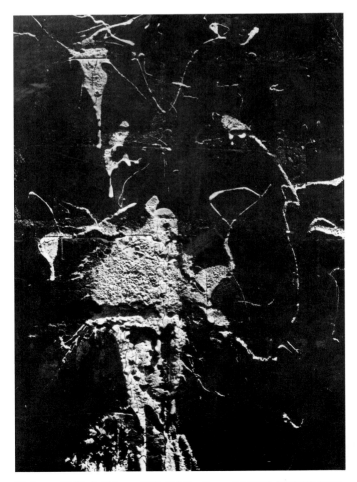

27. **Aaron Siskind.** *Chicago.* 1948. Gelatin-silver print, 19¹³⁄₁₆ × 14″ (50.3 × 36 cm). The Museum of Modern Art, New York. Gift of the photographer

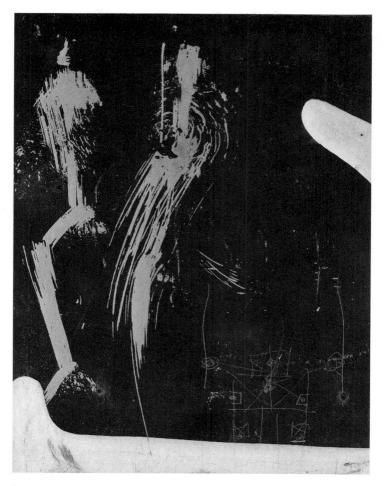

28. Aaron Siskind. *Hoboken, New Jersey.* **1948. Gelatin-silver print, 9½ × 7″ (24.2 × 17.8 cm). Collection of the photographer**

Aaron Siskind's photographs of the later 1940s and early 1950s (figs. 27–29) present an imagery of public walls in accord with the formal lessons of such paintings, and especially with the work of Franz Kline and Clyfford Still (artists Siskind knew well). In marked contrast to Brassaï in the previous decade, Siskind dealt not with layered carvings, nor with venerable symbolic imagery, but with the broader sweep of paint, or the impersonal patterns of things torn and peeled, on public walls. He cropped the original messages and imagery to yield abstracted compositions in which elements of the ground and figure interlock, finding the calligraphic, gestural energies within the possibilities of graffiti.

In Europe, the postwar abstract painting known as *tachisme* took a similar interest in calligraphic "writing," and in experiments with the active manipulation of rough, painterly surfaces. The Spanish artist Antoni Tàpies began to push this style toward direct references to graffiti in the mid-1950s, and

29. Aaron Siskind. *Bronx I.* **1950 (printed later). Gelatin-silver print, 8⅝ × 12¹¹/₁₆″ (22 × 32 cm). The Museum of Modern Art, New York. Gift of Frances F. L. Beatty**

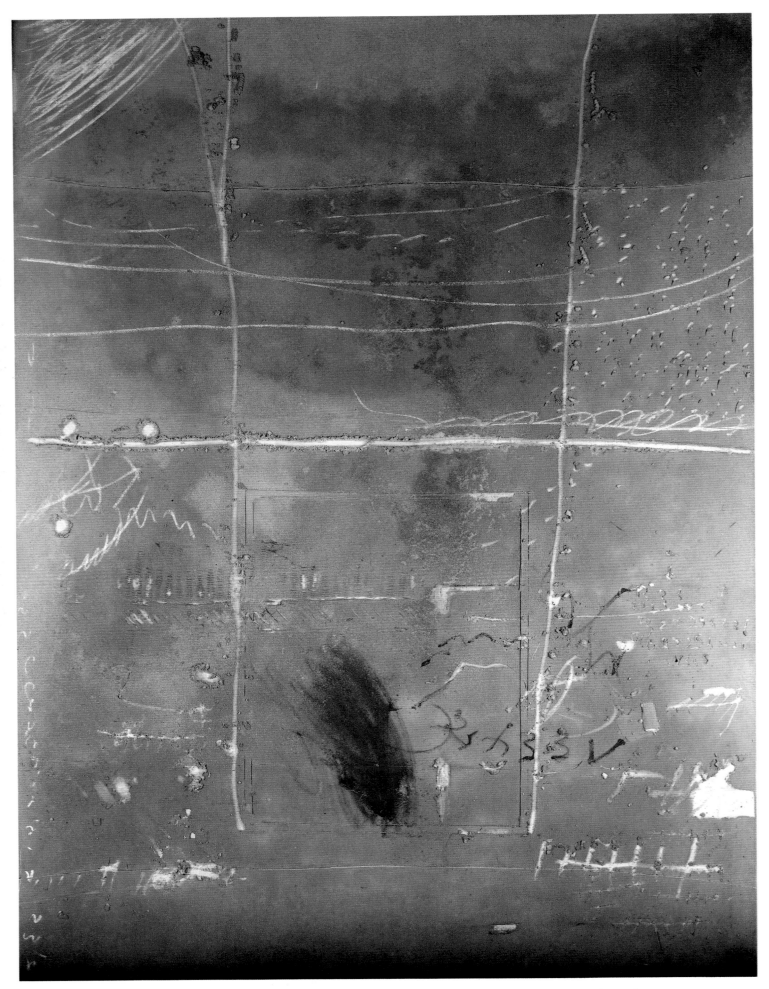

30. **Antoni Tàpies.** *Writing on the Walls.* 1971. Mixed media on canvas, 8′10¼″ × 6′6¾″ (270 × 200 cm). Collection Beyeler, Basel

31. **Jean Dubuffet.** *The Lost Traveler.* 1950. Oil on canvas, 51¼″ × 6′4¾″ (130 × 195 cm). Collection Beyeler, Basel

has continued to experiment with a combination of coarsened materials and lyric gestural drawing that purposefully evokes the look of markings made on coruscated walls (fig. 30).

The shift from the 1930s to the late 1940s involved, however, more than aesthetic evolutions and different tastes in formal patterns. When artists turned their attention to graffiti in the years following World War II, it was certainly with a fresh set of concerns for gestural abstraction—but also with an altered idea of the nature of the unconscious mind, and of the way individual creativity interacted with the order of society. The double-edged nature of graffiti as a fusion of personal style and political statement became newly apparent and important: untutored markings on public walls seemed to insist on the rights of the private imagination at the same time that they embodied rebellion against the re-

pressions of civic discipline, and an urgent will to communicate with an audience beyond the sophisticated confines of the world of art.

Jean Dubuffet—the most obvious hero in the story of modern art's attention to graffiti—is a prime case in point. Graffiti was among the "outsider" manifestations of *art brut*—art of the insane, children's drawings, naïve art, tribal art—that Dubuffet championed, from the later 1940s onward, as superior to the debilitated, inauthentic art of the European tradition (figs. 31–35).[25] The terms in which he glorified this kind of imagery (arguing for its unmediated access to elemental powers of the deep psyche) were rationales that had been in place since the time of Lombroso and Luquet. The difference lay in the intensity with which Dubuffet valued criminal expressions such as graffiti, precisely for being criminal. Even more emphatically than Brassaï, Dubuffet identified the "childish" element of such untutored work

32. **Jean Dubuffet.** *Wall with Inscriptions.* **1945. Oil on canvas, 39⅜ × 31⅞" (99.7 × 81 cm). The Museum of Modern Art, New York. Nina and Gordon Bunshaft Fund**

not with charming simplicity, but with a street-toughened air of tortured conflict and angry rebellion. And this insistence that true art is born from violent personal resistance to culture seems particularly conditioned and catalyzed by the experience of Europe in the late 1930s and 1940s.

The Nazi program had cast a deep pall over all notions of the unifying power of elemental myth, and on the romance of a healthy, integrated folk culture in general. Dubuffet rejected that tainted vision of social solidarity, with its nostalgia for a harmonious past. His interests were grittily urban and cosmopolitan at base. They valued the work of the rogue individual, and of isolated and alienated figures,

including madmen. Tribal art, too, was valued for its uncensored "savagery," and its traffic in harsh forms of the grotesque. Recoiling from a forced diet of propaganda which had extolled collective "health" over decadence, Dubuffet's art of the postwar years insisted that the saving grace of the culture was precisely to be found where incompetence or depravity seemed most apparent, and where the deforming marks of maladjustment were most vivid. Connotations of graffiti that were marginal or negative for those who studied it at the turn of the century seemed, in this altered framework of understanding, its most distinctive, powerful attributes.

The unconscious in Dubuffet's art is not peopled

33. **Jean Dubuffet.** *Life in the Country*. 1949. Oil on canvas, 49⅝ × 35″ (116 × 89 cm). Private collection

34. **Jean Dubuffet.** *Man Caught in the Walls*. 1945. Lithograph, 14¼ × 11¼″ (36 × 28.5 cm). The Museum of Modern Art, New York. Gift of Mr. and Mrs. Ralph F. Colin

35. **Jean Dubuffet.** *Aztec Profile*. 1945. Oil on canvas, 25¾ × 21½″ (65 × 54 cm). Collection Dieter Hauert, Berlin

36. Raymond Hains. *The Gypsy Woman.* 1960–68. Torn posters on canvas; four panels, overall 6'6¾" × 12'4½" (200 × 402 cm). Musée d'Art Moderne de la Ville de Paris

by lubricious or seductive erotic phantoms, but haunted by the specter of the concentration camps. In place of labile biomorphic form and free-flowing calligraphy, it favors violent, push-and-shove encounters between a clawing will to give form to the ugly and a set of materials that are resistant, abrasive, or congealed. Often nightmarish, it also has no lingering Surrealist fancy for the dreamlike, and is instead earthy to the extreme—instead of privileging receptive states of divination or the courtship of precarious chance, it attacks.

Dubuffet's art also transforms the role ascribed to wit in popular culture, from an amusing game to a weapon of salutary cruelty. Art should employ wit not like the surgeon's probe but like the mugger's shiv, and reckon pain an essential part of its task. In this belief Dubuffet follows an openness to the lacerations of gutter life that is a particular part of the French tradition of urban imagery, from Baudelaire to Jean Genet and Louis-Ferdinand Céline; he also rubs shoulders with the aesthetic of his compatriot and contemporary Antonin Artaud. To these ends,

37. Jacques de la Villeglé. *Sèvres-Montparnasse Intersection, July 1961.* 1961. Torn posters on canvas, 11 × 27' (319 × 810 cm). Courtesy Galerie Reckermann, Cologne

38. **Mimmo Rotella.** *Mythology.* 1962. Torn posters on canvas, 64″ × 6′2″ (164 × 190 cm). Courtesy Studio Marconi, Milan

39. **Raymond Hains and Jacques de la Villeglé.** *Ach Alma Manetro.* 1949. Torn posters on canvas, 22⅞″ × 8′4⅞″ (58 × 256 cm). Musée National d'Art Moderne, Centre Georges Pompidou, Paris

Dubuffet's general revivification of the strategies of caricature as the tools of highly nuanced individual portraiture is remarkable enough. More striking still is his ability to find the elements for a general physiognomy of the age of Auschwitz, the A-bomb, and Existentialism, graven on latrine stalls and alley walls. He formulated an artistic language capable of conveying an unprecedented, specifically contemporary vision of the human condition, working from a source—graffiti—that had long been either neglected, or thought of principally in terms of an ageless, prehistoric atavism.

Shortly after Dubuffet's searing imagery of the later 1940s, however, there emerged at two points in a rebuilding Europe, and in America as well, a much more depersonalized mode of attention to the look of public walls—an art of assemblage or collage, strongly conditioned by aesthetic reactions to postwar abstract painting, and more concerned with the evidences of social commerce than with the romance of isolated alienation. In this work, by the Europeans known as the *affichistes* and by Robert Rauschenberg in New York, the look of the street was conjured by mass-produced ephemera, and graffiti was evoked by the evidences of defacement and painterly overlays. In different ways, each of these approaches to art brought into collaboration two previously separate veins of modernist interest in graffiti: on the one hand, the notion, announced in Duchamp's *L.H.O.O.Q.*, of a vandal art, criticizing the givens of culture; and on the other, the Surrealist

40. Jacques de la Villeglé. *122, rue du Temple.* **1968. Torn posters on linen, 62⅝" × 6'10¾" (159.7 × 210.2 cm). The Museum of Modern Art, New York. Gift of Joachim Aberbach (by exchange)**

idea of a ''primitive'' art of aggressive gesture and confrontation with chance.

Two Frenchmen, Raymond Hains and Jacques de la Villeglé, and the Italian Mimmo Rotella, began in the late 1940s and early 1950s to base their work on layered and torn paper agglomerations. These collage-style works were found on public walls, and consisted of posters that had been glued one on top of the other and then subjected to decay or vandal-

ism (figs. 36–41).[26] But, aside from Villeglé's notion that the serendipitous syntax of these stuck-together poster fragments constituted a way to articulate a ''collective unconscious'' of the society,[27] their aims and motivations seem to have been wholly at odds with the psychological emphases of both the Surrealists and Dubuffet. The *affichistes*, as these three and some later practitioners of a similar method came to be called, were not a self-conscious movement (the Frenchmen did not show their poster work until 1957, and did not learn of Rotella, who had first shown torn posters in 1954, until 1958),[28] but they shared certain interests, notably in phonetic poetry and linguistic experiment. Hains's point of departure in the torn-poster work, for example, involved ''exploding'' texts into illegibility by photographing them through a special shatter-effect lens.[29] And, to varying degrees, their work seems to reflect a shared love/hate relationship with postwar abstract painting: rejecting the trace of a personal touch and the studio's isolation in favor of a more Dada-like stance, they nonetheless followed an aesthetic of full-field gestural energy in the sections of torn-poster groups they appropriated (and sometimes ''assisted'' by further, selective tearing).

41. Mimmo Rotella. *Cinemascope.* **1962. Torn posters on canvas, 68⅛ × 52⅜" (173 × 133 cm). Museum Ludwig, Cologne**

Most important, for all of them the writing on the wall did not consist of gouged-in markings that harked back to Pompeii and the caves, but of the daily accretion of mass-produced contemporary ephemera—bold and sensationally up-to-the-minute, but at the same time thin, fragile, and almost instantly tattered and replaced. These poster-tearers became annexed to Pop art after 1960, and were touted for their precocious embrace of popular culture. But seen in the context of the 1950s, their interleaving of paper dreams of abundance with physical realities of transience and decay seems less

42. Asger Jorn. Untitled. 1964. Torn posters on canvas, 25¼ × 19⅜″ (64 × 49.1 cm). Silkeborg Kunstmuseum, Denmark

than wholeheartedly optimistic—as close in some ways to the postwar neo-realism of a filmmaker like Vittorio De Sica as to the post-1960 *nouveau realisme* of their early promoter Pierre Restany.

The sociopolitical thrust of Dubuffet's glorification of "outlaw" art had remained on a general, residually Romantic level of antibourgeois offenses to taste. The incorporation of the commercial dimension of contemporary street life by the *affichistes* opened up onto a more specifically contemporary realm of politics, grounded in the antagonism between the European left and the accelerated rise, in the 1950s, of a mass culture driven by a resurgent postwar capitalism and perceived as imposing American values. Hains, Villeglé, and Rotella made no strong political claims for their work; but the specific issue of vandalism as a form of activist art was raised by the later, related work with torn posters of the Dane Asger Jorn (and to a lesser extent by that of François Dufrêne).[30]

Villeglé had been associated at the outset of his work with the politicized Lettrist group in France; and that had in turn been one of the origins for the

radical-thinking Situationist International movement, of which Jorn was an important member from 1957 to 1961.[31] Though Jorn resigned from the group in 1961, his torn-poster work (from 1964 to 1969) and other defacements of found imagery —*détournements*, to use a term he adopted—were self-conscious acts of plagiarism and subversion that he saw as consistent with its program of anti-capitalist critique (figs. 42, 43). He edited a book (to which he contributed a major essay) on the graffiti of medieval churches in Normandy; and according to Anne-Charlotte Weinmarck, he honored such vandalism against institutions of authority as corresponding to the spirit of popular liberation he found in Nordic folk art, and he saw it as a source for a new communitarian fellowship of the oppressed.[32]

Aside from this exceptional instance of primitivism, the work of the *affichistes* abandoned the idea of "raw" street culture that had surrounded previous approaches to graffiti. The walls from which they extracted their work were not shaped by isolated "street artists" but by an anonymous collective of

43. Asger Jorn. *The Avant-Garde Doesn't Give Up.* 1962. Oil on canvas, 28¾ × 23⅝″ (73 × 60 cm). Collection Micky and Pierre Alechinsky, Bougival, France

forces, including chance. The artist, in turn, acted as a collector or commentator rather than as an individual generator of meaning. The model of linguistic activity within which graffiti was seen as operating had shifted from one emphasizing innate creativity to one emphasizing social interaction and the manipulation of culturally determined conventions. These artists wanted to disrupt established language, rather than revert, as the Surrealists hoped to do, to preverbal "handwriting." Dubuffet stands at the end of a lineage that reaches back through Brassaï to Luquet; but it is Duchamp's notion of the graffito—as

44. Joan Miró. *May 1968.* 1973. Synthetic polymer paint on canvas, 6'6¾" × 6'6¾" (200 × 200 cm). Fundació Joan Miró, Barcelona. Gift of Pilar Juncosa de Miró, 1986

an act that appropriates and rearranges the terms of a dominant culture—that finds an unexpected expansion here. No longer solely an art-world strategy, it even becomes, in the case of Jorn, the grounding for a utopian countercultural scheme.

The Situationist ideas Jorn and others supported had their most direct engagement with graffiti during the uprisings in Paris in May 1968, when students from the École des Beaux-Arts and elsewhere waged an intensive campaign of postering and sloganeering on walls throughout Paris. With simply conceived silk-screened images and painted aphorisms such as *"Sous les pavés, la plage!"* ("Beneath the paving stones, the beach!"), these students tried to reawaken the power of writing on public walls as something immediate and instrumental, rather than

immemorial and merely self-indulgent—to construct on the model of graffiti a renewed public art that, with a knowing eye to the power of advertising's catchphrases, would define a binding, antiauthoritarian language of the oppressed. For this moment, it seemed that a true civic art form, politically effective yet consecrated to the expanded reign of play and imagination, had come alive through a new merger between the art studio and the street. It was doubtless that sense of possibility that the aging Joan Miró honored, and recognized as consonant with his own ideals, in his *May 1968* (fig. 44), painted in 1973. In this work, Miró pushed familiar features of his art—scrawling, pictographic figuration, mural scale, and an impulsive attack on the surface —back toward a kinship with graffiti.

Robert Rauschenberg. *Rebus.* 1955. , pencil, paper, and fabric on canvas, × 10'10½" × 1¾" (243.9 × 331.4 × 4.5 cm). llection Hans Thulin

The European torn-poster artists were contending with aesthetic and social forces—a new mode of abstract painting based on heroic individualism and an increasingly aggressive mass culture—that inevitably had a very different effect on young artists such as Robert Rauschenberg and Cy Twombly in New York in the 1950s.

In a way that recalls the double life of Kurt Schwitters, Rauschenberg designed midtown store windows for a living while he scavenged downtown streets for the elements of his art.[33] The personal, sometimes diaristic aspect of his work did not have to do with a "signature" brush style, but emerged from the idiosyncratic associations he made between these found images, phrases, and objects. The Europeans who worked with public printed matter favored the poetry of decomposed and run-together word fragments. But Rauschenberg worked to build up a different kind of language, almost narrative in its stringing together of interpolated images and words. A work like *Rebus* (fig. 45) continually challenges the viewer to construct a coherent reading that will resolve the "puzzle" and bring together the various levels of commercial material, art-historical reproductions, and handmade additions like the tiny, graffito-like drawing affixed at the lower left (in fact executed by Rauschenberg's friend Twombly).[34]

In an image such as this, however, the artist as rag-picker and riddler is joined with the artist as defacer. The element of paint is itself double-edged in *Rebus*. The inclusion of strips of color samples refers both to the commercial, pre-prepared nature of the medium of painting itself and, in a subversive and deflating way, to the notion of purely abstract art; while the prominent, seemingly spontaneous and gestural brushwork, like the improvisatory nature of the work as a whole, honors the lessons of Abstract Expressionist painting. But here as in other related Rauschenberg works, the painterly gestures of the artist have connotations of an assault on the legibility and integrity of the assembled materials—a kind of vandalism. That use of painted marks and scumbled lines as cancellations or negations was intentionally contrary to the Abstract Expressionists' will to invest the calligraphy of brushstrokes with autonomous meaning; and it was entirely consistent with Rauschenberg's earlier, infamous stunt of erasing a drawing by Willem de Kooning.

Rebus evokes the look of a posted urban wall, and involves somewhat the same combination seen in the *affichistes*, of an interest in dealing with impersonal, found material and an aesthetic attuned to the full-field, painterly abstraction of the postwar years. The picture is, among other things, a montaged summation of the different things modern art-

46. Cy Twombly. Untitled. 1955–56. Oil and graphite on canvas, 45⅛ × 53¼″ (114.7 × 135.4 cm). **Courtesy Galerie Karsten Greve, Cologne**

47. Cy Twombly. Untitled. 1955–56. Oil and graphite on canvas, 45⅛ × 53¼″ (114.7 × 135.4 cm). Collection the artist

ists had seen in graffiti: the reproductions of Botticelli and Dürer recall Duchamp's idea of an art that appropriated and worked over souvenirs of the Renaissance tradition; the gestural scribbling and seemingly infantile drawings hark back to the concerns of Töpffer, Champfleury, and Luquet, and even recall the early painters and caricaturists who included imagery of such alternative modes of creating; and the fabric of comics, newspapers, and posters connects to the *affichiste* imagery of the wall as the field of chance on which the overlord forces of commercial ephemera meet the anonymous interventions of random decay and active defacement.

Cy Twombly, in the same years of the mid-1950s, was forming an art that would incorporate many of these same models. He staked everything on the language of painting and drawing, without reference to the found material Rauschenberg and other artists addressed. Yet his work has been, in its internal complexity as well as in its focused, long-term consistency, the most comprehensive personal reconcili-

ation in modern painting of all the different strands of the story we have chronicled. No modern painter invites, as consistently as Twombly does, association with the traditional language of graffiti. But no art could be less limited by the reference. Because Twombly's work is so steeped in the high modern tradition that extends through Abstract Expressionism back to Surrealism, his painting thoroughly belies any simplistic notion that such art merely "borrows from" or "copies" outside models of form. And, because Twombly moved from New York in 1957 to live in Rome, the trajectory of his career as an artist brings us back to the chalked-upon and incised ancient walls with which this story began.[35]

If Rauschenberg seems to have been moved by a desire to clutter up the mural look of Abstract Expressionism with the stuff of daily life, Twombly moved instead to empty it out—especially in a series of small canvases, of about 1955–57 (figs. 46, 47), with creamy surfaces of off-white house paint that were drawn into with a pencil or a stylus. The house paint yielded surfaces that were thickly viscous but

48. Cy Twombly. *Leda and the Swan.* **1961. Oil, oilstick, and crayon on canvas, 6'2¾" × 6'6¾" (190 × 200 cm). Collection the artist**

wholly without the fat lusciousness of, say, de Kooning's; and the pictures were at once ghostly pure and scrofulous. Twombly here transformed the declarative brushstroke of painters like de Kooning and Kline, which Rauschenberg had made into a looser and more episodic manner, back into an unexpected form of "automatic writing." The "signature" of these works was a thinned-down and colorless running scrawl, following an apparently uncomposed and unstructured repetition of cursive gestures. This handwriting spiked the vaunted spontaneity of gestural abstraction through the heart, but brought forth in its place another complex form of individuality that melded the apparently casual and the apparently obsessive.

In the broad variety of Twombly's subsequent work, that consistent opposition between a mural-like field of paint and a linear "written" overlay has sustained the basic affinity with the look of drawn-upon public walls (fig. 51). The images vary from airy tumbleweeds of tracery to monumental rhetoric, and often achieve the kind of enveloping intimacy

that has marked a particular strain of modern larger-than-easel painting, from Monet's *Water Lilies* decorations to Pollock's large dripped canvases. And the drawing, alternately innocent and expressive, follows a deceptively "untutored" course between the pitfalls of the merely brittle or the merely fluid, in lines that loop, pause, and run on, at paces that are by turns ambling, ruminative, and impulsive, through skeins, knots, and thicket-like clusters (figs. 48, 51). The surfaces and the emotional impact of Twombly's paintings are enriched, too, by a duality: they seem to show both the basic urge to scribble and, simultaneously, the compulsion to deface. He often appears engaged in constant self-vandalism, as if he were editing while he wrote, making marks with one hand and covering them or emending them with the other. Impulse and erasure, or confession and repression, lock together in a work like *The Italians* (fig. 51), as every area of the canvas seems subject to revision, separate cancellation, and reintegration. Yet the end results, while rife with scattershot diversity and moments of frenzy and frustration, often have an ardent lyricism. From a purposefully limited palette and set of formal strategies, Twombly has coaxed an astonishingly broad range of aesthetic reference and emotion, from a dark-alley impassioned urgency to the ethereal, decorative feel of cloud-spotted skies by Tiepolo.

The impact of the work and its connection to graffiti are not however limited to abstract, formal properties. The merger of handwriting, drawing, and painting in Twombly's art is matched by an interlocking of the verbal and pictorial levels of reference, in a variety of random notations—numbers, geometric forms, archi-

low artifacts or ironic quotations, but as models of feeling to be reimagined and absorbed into a personal, original sensibility. And in an act of compression without diminishment, he brings these high traditions into contemporary art through the apparently lowest portal of form.

When Twombly began as an artist, the most prestigious theory of modern art's progress suggested that, as part of its impulse toward the quality of absolute flatness, painting aspired to the condition of a wall. To this formalist idea, he has added a sharp personal

49. Cy Twombly. *Dionysus.* 1975. Crayon, oil, and pencil on paper, 39⅛ × 27¾″ (99.5 × 70.4 cm). Collection Dorothy Schramm, Burlington, Iowa

tectural references, penises, hearts, simple scrawls—that, individually and often by their general manner of free-floating placement in the field, evoke the sense of a profusely marked wall. Moreover, the figuration is frequently explicitly sexual, even specifically ejaculatory (figs. 49, 50), and evokes memories of centuries of scurrilous ''bog-house'' messages. Yet this graphology is recurrently yoked to a high, monumental ambition, and applied to the recuperation of grand themes, from Romantic poetry or Greek myth (figs. 48, 49). Duchamp played on the antagonism between the great traditions of the past and the minor, marginal languages of the present; Twombly reconciles the two. His art shows how Aeschylus and Keats and Raphael can be taken up within modernism, not simply as hol-

twist: his art has internalized the structure of the public walls that shape his Roman life. The distinctive conjunctions and overlays in Twombly's art—of private obscenities and noble literature, or ancient heroism and urchin-like, spontaneous impulse—bring Pompeii back to us, whole. They resuscitate in one artistic personality the collective compilations of sentimental confessions, scurrilous accusations, odes, and oaths that the Romantic generation first addressed on ancient walls as evidence for the diversity of a whole society. And the result is unmistakably a record of present-tense experience, of the light and landscape and texture of Twombly's Italy, a modern life lived among the ruins: the sense of the mighty and venerable seamlessly coexisting with the lowly, private, and scatological

50. **Cy Twombly.** *Wilder Shores of Love.* 1985. Oil, crayon, colored pencil, and pencil on wood, 55⅛ × 47¼" (140 × 120 cm). Collection the artist

—and of the personal mark made into a memorial of past heroes and visitors.

Twombly's art has absolutely nothing to do with appropriating, or still less copying, graffiti. Yet it brings together a nearly comprehensive array of the themes that the modern imagination has found in the writing on the public walls: scribbling that, as in Balla's painting, seems to rise from the underside of a collective mentality; uncensored sexuality, such as interested Luquet; idle doodling and automatic writing, which Prinzhorn and the Surrealists saw as a window onto the unconscious; defacing, erasure, and cancellation, of the kind that Duchamp and the *affichistes* both thought central to modern art's response to the givens of tradition and society. Ultimately neither his art nor the story we have traced is about graffiti as any one of these, but about the modern imagination's encounter with graffiti as all of them, and more. One of the messages Twombly's art conveys is that seemingly base, trivial things can become in art the vehicle for complex and lofty issues of our collective tradition. Another, the converse, is that forms which seem to be anonymous, collective, and immemorial can be reformulated into the vehicle of individual contemporary experience. But a still further lesson is that artists can, in the varied threads of their personal experience, find a way to bind together the contradictory pluralities of high and low that define the richness and contradictions of any human community, ancient or modern. No less complex than a wall with the marks of centuries, no less

encompassing than the city that holds that wall, are the potentials that may coexist within the life of one person.

As particular and personal as Twombly's achievement has been, it embodies a pattern we will see again, in which a powerful but apparently static high tradition—in this case, not simply the distant classical heritage denoted by Twombly's written references to ancient myth and Renaissance painting, but also the immediate stylistic legacy of Abstract Expressionist painting—is revivified by hybridization with forms drawn from popular culture. Yet, because Twombly looked to the language of graffiti with a sensibility so specifically shaped by the calligraphic and painterly idiom of de Kooning and Pollock, he left aside one of the forms most closely associated with graffiti in the studies of scholars such as Luquet, and in the popular imagination as well: the irreverently and often scabrously distorted or recomposed human form, and especially the face. We might easily assume that satirically reinventing an individual's features was an integral, immemorial part of graffiti (as it seemed to be in the age of Daumier and the pear-headed king [fig. 15]). But we would be wrong. True caricature has a wholly other origin, more recent in history and more firmly within the high tradition; and it has had an almost opposite rhythm of engagement with modern art, which will require a special and separate examination in the next chapter.

51. **Cy Twombly.** *The Italians.* 1961. Oil, pencil, and crayon on canvas, 6'6⅝" × 8'6¼" (199.5 × 259.6 cm). The Museum of Modern Art, New York. Blanchette Rockefeller Fund

1. Jean Dubuffet. *Fautrier with* Spidered Brow. 1947. Oil emulsion on canvas, 45⅝ × 35⅛″ (116 × 89 cm). Collection Dorothea and Natasha Elkon, New York

Modern art is full of funny faces. Women with both eyes on the same side of their nose; men with ears where their mouths should be; ordinary families with the eyes of desert rodents and the skulls of apes—a mixed-up face is the heraldic emblem of modern art in the same way that the beautiful nude is the emblem of antiquity, or the receding-perspective checkerboard the emblem of the Renaissance.

Some of these strange faces, like the ones that Paul Klee called, pugnaciously, *Vulgar Comedy* (fig. 2), seem to reflect a gleeful urge toward violent symbolic animation, a desire to bring invented faces to life by making them look funny. Others seem more narrowly purposeful. Some, like the Edvard Munch figure with the bleeding scream (fig. 3), have become masks of a century's anxiety; others, like Dubuffet's 1947 portrait of the painter Fautrier (fig. 1), seem to sum up in a single scowl not just an individual but a whole city and climate of opinion— the moral rot and nervous energy, the catacomb chic, of Parisian intellectual life after the German occupation. Still others, like Picasso's 1910 portrait of his friend D.-H. Kahnweiler (fig. 4), are small, miraculous passports, fixing their subject's essential features with an imperturbable detachment and then stamping on them the seal of an invented world, so that the sitter can pass like a bewitched hero from his normal identity in the world outside, to his second citizenship in the closed country of the artist's imagination.

Often, these funny faces sit on top of weird bodies. There are women with the lower halves of dolphins, men made up like Oz's Tin Man from mechanical parts, department-store mannequins acting out the lives of demigods. Sometimes, these funny faces are themselves made out of weird bodies or erotic body parts, as in Magritte's *The Rape* (fig. 5) or in Picasso's phallic head of 1932 (fig. 88). Some of these bodies, too, seem merely fanciful and purposefully absurd; others seem to give permanent symbolic form to the demons of human desire.

The abundance of funny faces and weird bodies in modern art represents an assault on the decorum of style that modern art inherited from the past. For what's striking in art before our century is not that there are no funny faces or weird bodies in it, but that they can be found only in the cheap seats, segregated from serious art in the tradition of satiric metamorphosis that we call caricature. One of the achievements of twentieth-century art has been to make the exaggerations, stylizations, and indulgences that once were permitted only in popular imagery part of the language of serious visual expression. As an ironic consequence, "caricature" for many twentieth-century people no longer defines a genre with a history so much as it seems to refer to one among all those generalized processes in modern art that the Mock Turtle would have called "uglification." We're now liable to see caricature, like graffiti, as just another raw form that modern art has digested.

Yet even Dubuffet's willfully crude, scrawled portrait of Fautrier represents—in contrast to the stereotyped, unvarying faces that actually appear in the graffiti on Parisian walls—a sophisticated transformation that is as unique to Western art as linear perspective: the adaptation of grotesque form to the ends of epigrammatic portraiture. For all its ferocious intensity, Dubuffet's portrait of Fautrier involves a refined orchestration of visual puns and condensed observations—the self-assured head metamorphosing into a spider's arms, the mad, asymmetrical scowl belied by the oddly delicate and feminine grasp of the cigarette—that is in every way more like an expansion of the game the seventeenth-century Italian sculptor Gian Lorenzo Bernini was playing when he mockingly rendered Pope Innocent XI as an immense grasshopper (fig. 6)[1] than like anything that one might actually find scrawled on a pissoir.

The story of this dialogue between modern art and popular culture is therefore different from those we have told before. The story of the word in art was a story of a positive, original response in the studio to the call of something new and perplexing in the world. The story of graffiti and modern art was a chronicle of artists seeing the potential for poetic expression in something as old as writing itself, but always previously thought to lack any significant form. The history of caricature and modern painting and sculpture is a story of evolutionary transformation: a sophisticated and fully developed art form which had previously been allowed to do only one thing was made to do another, and a new kind of social institution grew up around that newly altered form.

"After Courbet, after Manet—the caricature! What could be more logical!" a critic named Maurice du Seigneur wrote in disgust in 1888, after seeing an exhibition of cartoons at the École des Beaux-Arts.[2] You could see his point. By the end of the nineteenth century in France, the relationship of the stylizations of the

2. **Paul Klee.** *Vulgar Comedy.* 1922. Lithograph, 9¼ × 11¼" (23.5 × 28.5 cm). The Museum of Modern Art, New York. Gift of Victor S. Riesenfeld

new modern art to the experiments first tried out in the free zone of humor was already apparent. But the nature of the logical relationship that the conservative critic recognized between the new high art and the old low jokes is still mostly undefined. Since the pioneering scholarship of Meyer Schapiro and E. H. Gombrich first drew attention to this relationship, half a century ago,

the role of popular imagery in making art modern has been emphasized by historians again and again.[3] To understand the "logic" that modern art took over from satiric imagery, we need to understand the long history of the low style's evolution and see exactly what it offered. It's not that modern artists were conscious of any or all of this history when they drew a

3. **Edvard Munch.** *The Shriek.* 1895 (signed 1896). Lithograph, 13¹⁵⁄₁₆ × 10" (35.5 × 25.4 cm). The Museum of Modern Art, New York. Matthew T. Mellon Fund

4. **Pablo Picasso.** *Portrait of Daniel-Henry Kahnweiler* (detail). 1910. (See fig. 73)

5. **René Magritte.** *The Rape.* 1934. Oil on canvas, 29 × 21¼" (74 × 54 cm). The Menil Collection, Houston

funny face or strange body—it's that the act of drawing itself is a kind of shortcut through history. Each purposefully funny face in art is always bound about by the ghosts of every other funny face that artists have drawn before; a seemingly simple practice—a moment's touch—is made possible only by a long tradition of individual contributions and inventions.

Caricature is often seen as a primal scream, or a long

Bronx cheer: a product of the childhood of art and part of the common inheritance of all cultures. In fact, though, we first see deformed faces apparently used to define individual characters only at the end of the fifteenth century in Florence, in the grotesque heads attributed to Leonardo. Of course, there are a lot of strange faces in ancient and medieval art, but so far as we can tell they were never meant to be taken as like-

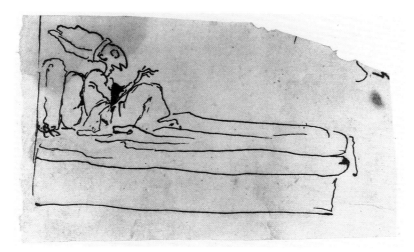

6. **Gian Lorenzo Bernini.** *Caricature of Innocent XI.* c. 1676–80. Ink on paper, 4½ × 7⅛" (11.4 × 18 cm). Museum der Bildende Künste, Leipzig

7. **Artist unknown.** *Four Heads* (after Leonardo). n.d. Red chalk on paper, 7⅝ × 5¾" (19.5 × 14.6 cm). Windsor Castle, Royal Library. 12493

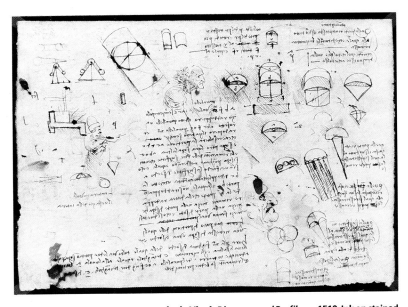

8. **Leonardo da Vinci.** *Diagrams and Profiles.* c. 1510. Ink on stained paper, 8¼ × 11¼" (21 × 28.5 cm). Windsor Castle, Royal Library. 12669R

their origin as purely imaginary as the gargoyles on Notre-Dame. His grotesques appear originally only as quick, automatic drawings, hardly more than doodles, filling the margins of his scientific notebooks (fig. 8). They are generic hieroglyphs of ugliness. The most familiar Leonardesque grotesques are really copies packaged by his followers after their master's death. (One of Leonardo's inept but well-meaning apprentices cut the heads out of Leonardo's codices and pasted them down on sheets of paper [fig. 9], apparently convinced

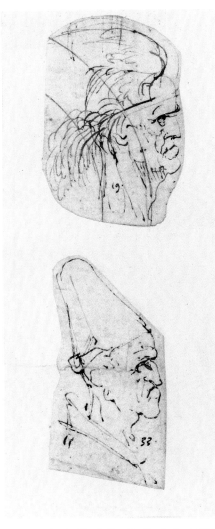

9. **Leonardo da Vinci.** *Two Profiles* (cutouts from the *Codex Atlanticus*). c. 1485. Ink on paper; top 2½ × 1⅝" (6.3 × 4.2 cm), bottom 2⅝ × 1⅜" (6.6 × 3.4 cm). Windsor Castle, Royal Library. 12461R, 12462R

nesses. Ancient art is full of funny faces, too—but it's almost always the same funny face.[4] They are stereotyped grotesques, representing generic, otherworldly demons or comic buffoons—types, rather than individuals.[5]

The sketches, always associated with Leonardo, in which the deformed, the toothless, the distended, and the just plain ugly are lined up in lists like faces on "wanted" posters (fig. 7), look like the first instance in art of an enterprise that seems truly "caricatural"—at once aggressively grotesque and recognizably individual.[6] But in fact, Leonardo's grotesque profiles are in

that the old man had some large, mysterious purpose in mind; another copied them out [fig. 10], his hard, unvarying touch belying the original welter of sketched ambiguities.)[7]

Even so, it's not completely wrong to see in these gargoyles some kind of individual life. The most common of these grotesque heads, the toothless old man with a nutcracker jaw (fig. 11), occasionally appears in larger drawings, paired with an idealized head of a beautiful youth (fig. 12). Gombrich has argued persuasively that this alpha-and-omega juxtaposition invested the old man's head with particular meaning for Leon-

10. Leonardo da Vinci (attrib.). *Five Grotesque Heads*. n.d. Brown ink on paper, 7¹⁄₁₆ × 4¹¹⁄₁₆″ (18 × 12 cm). Galleria dell'Accademia, Gabinetto Disegni (Drawing 227), Venice

ardo: the heads symbolized the artist himself as the exceptionally beautiful youth we know he was and then as the old man he knew he would become. The grotesque doodles became terms in a private language of brooding internal fear, tools for introspective analysis, beads in an abacus of the self.[8]

When Leonardo's disciples cut out these heads and copied them, they, too, seem to have been trying to find a rationale for the old man's reveries, in this case satiric rather than confessional; copied and compiled, the grotesques looked encyclopedic, like an attempt to define individuals by recording profiles as unique as the cut edge of a key. The simple acts of cutting and copying became ways of bringing private faces into a public space. These acts brought the forms of Leonardo's imagination into the common inheritance of art.[9]

It was only at the end of the sixteenth century that some of the masters of the early Baroque—most prominently Annibale and Agostino Carracci, and then later Bernini—began to draw "true" caricature, "loaded" or "charged" portraits. When they did, they began to search grotesque forms for the faces of particular friends (figs. 13, 14). The language of mocking portraiture for the Carracci, as we see when we look at the big sheets of improvised profiles that are the proving ground of so much early caricature (fig. 15), obviously derives from a composite of the gro-

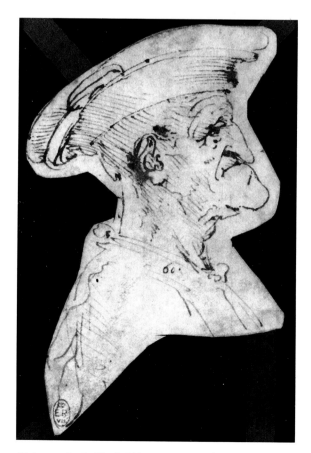

11. Leonardo da Vinci. *Old Man*. c. 1496. Ink on paper; cutout, 3½ × 2⅛″ (9 × 5.5 cm). Windsor Castle, Royal Library. 12475R

12. Leonardo da Vinci. *Two Profiles* (detail). n.d. Brown ink on paper; sheet, 7⅞ × 10½″ (20.1 × 26.7 cm). Gabinetto Disegni e Stampe degli Uffizi, Florence

14. Gian Lorenzo Bernini. *Portrait of the Captain of the Papal Guard of Pope Urban VIII.* Before 1644. Ink on paper; sheet, 7⅜ × 10¹⁄₁₆″ (18.8 × 25.6 cm). Instituto Nazionale per la Grafica, Rome. Fondo Corsini 127521 (579)

tesque heads of Leonardo, along with the masks of the commedia dell'arte, the comic tradition exemplified by Callot (figs. 16, 17), and the physiognomic comparisons of della Porta (fig. 18).[10] Although the revolution of caricature may just look like the consequence of an all-purpose new license for satire, the growth of purposeful caricatural distortion depended on the previous creation of a grotesque vocabulary. Caricature for Bernini and the Carracci isn't just distortion; it's distortion within the constraints of an already developed

13. Gian Lorenzo Bernini. *Caricature of Cardinal Scipione Borghese.* 1632. Ink on paper, 10³⁄₁₆ × 7⅞″ (27.4 × 20 cm). Biblioteca Apostolica Vaticana, Vatican. Ms Chigi P.VI.4, fol.15

15. Agostino Carracci. *Sheet of Caricature Heads.* 1594. Ink on paper, 8 × 10″ (20.3 × 27.9 cm). Private collection, Great Britain

16. Jacques Callot. *Dancers with a Lute.* 1617. Etching, 6⅛ × 7⅛″ (5.5 × 8 cm). The Metropolitan Museum of Art, New York. Harris Brisbane Dick Fund, 1953 (53.600.3736)

18. Giovanni Battista della Porta. Physiognomic comparison, from *De humana physiognomonia* (from a revised edition; first edition published Vico Equense, 1586)

style. If Bernini had drawn big noses or one-line eyes on Cardinal Borghese in the style of his "high" drawings (fig. 19), they would have just looked horrific. It was an already evolved grotesque style that supplied Bernini with a developed language of simplified, non-illusionistic form that made the distortions of his caricatures meaningful. Bernini didn't just draw a face with exaggerated features; he drew a face in a style that already permitted exaggerations, and then took advantage of that permission to make a new kind of portrait, rearticulating the stereotyped distortions of a joke to make them define individual elements.

Part of the unmatched wit and gaiety of the Bernini caricatures lies in the way they search out the most improbable and resistant languages of abstract form in which to render familiar faces. As Irving Lavin has

shown, the Pope is supposed to look like himself, and he is also supposed to look like a cricket.[11] The game resides in searching the most peculiar and improbable representational vocabularies for surprising matches. Leonardo saw himself in his own doodles; Bernini sees his patron's face in a cabinet of curiosities.

Composite bodies—strange human forms made out of fruit or fish or the emblems of an occupation—are obviously different in purpose from portrait caricature. Until the nineteenth century, composite bodies were not for the most part used to represent particular people; they were made to be enjoyed as fantasies, perhaps with an allegorical subtext. But they eventually came to play so large a role in the popular comic traditions which influenced modern art that their origin is

17. Jacques Callot. *Sheet of Studies.* n.d. Ink and chalk on white paper, 9⅞ × 7″ (25.2 × 17.8 cm). Gabinetto Disegni e Stampe degli Uffizi, Florence

19. Gian Lorenzo Bernini. *Portrait of Cardinal Scipione Borghese.* 1632. Red chalk and graphite on paper, 9⅞ × 7¼″ (25.2 × 18.4 cm). The Pierpont Morgan Library, New York. IV, 176

20. **Giuseppe Arcimboldo.** *The Vegetable Gardener.* c. 1590. Oil on wood, 13¾ × 9½" (35 × 24 cm). Museo Civico ala Ponzone, Cremona

worth exploring—for it, too, demonstrates the same process of imaginative rethinking of familiar form that occurred in the invention of particularized funny faces. The composite head or body first appears at the end of the sixteenth century, in the work of a single artist, Giuseppe Arcimboldo (fig. 20). After centuries of neglect, the composite heads that Arcimboldo made at the Habsburg court have been used in our time as contemplative material by everyone from Dalí to Roland Barthes. The desire to make them modern, or at least profound, has obscured their origins in the local sixteenth-century vocabulary of grotesque ornament. From the time of the rediscovery of the Domus Aurea at the end of the fifteenth century, grotesque decorations that looked like faces had been widely circulated (figs. 21–23). What was new in Arcimboldo was the recognition that the game of composing human heads from inanimate objects could be extended beyond the normal boundaries of garden ornament.

Arcimboldo was interested in form rather than in physiognomy—in heads rather than in faces—and his followers, like the Italian Giovanni Battista Braccelli (fig. 24), soon learned to play Arcimboldo's game with full-length human figures. Braccelli saw, for instance, that bodies made out of geometric parts could be made

21. Grotesque mask with drooping mouth, from *10 Engravings of Grotesque Masks in the Manner of Arcimboldo* (17th century). Etching, 4⅛ × 3¼" (10.5 × 8.3 cm). The New York Public Library. Print Collection, Miriam and Ira D. Wallach Division of Art, Prints and Photographs

22. Drawing after the Volta delle Civette in the Domus Aurea, from *Codex Escurialensis*, **fol. 12v. El Escorial, Spain**

23. Giovanni Antonio da Brescia. Panel of ornament with grotesque figures. c. 1509–17. Engraving, 11⅛ × 6¾″ (28.2 × 17.1 cm). Bibliothèque Nationale, Paris

subject to the language of rhetorical movement, and that heroic pose could be divorced from human anatomy.[12]

There is nothing hallucinatory or visionary about Braccelli's figures; the origins of Braccelli's mechanical men in perspective training manuals is apparent (figs. 25, 26). It had been known for a long time that one could comprehend human anatomy more easily if it was first reduced to a language of geometric solids; Braccelli asks what would happen if we treated those diagrams not as didactic examples, but as personages with passions and desires of their own. By treating the foot soldiers of the grand manner as though they were themselves heroes, by looking at the first step as though it were the final outcome, Braccelli could make images that might at once look wonderfully bizarre and also supply pointed and poetic images of the reduction of a man to an occupational type, geometers made out of geometry (fig. 27). If there is an "Arcimboldo effect" in Western art that extends to our own time, it depends less on mysterious allegories about the duality of nature and man than on the discovery of small jokes buried in descriptive form.[13] If that effect looks modern, it may be in part because it depends for its discoveries on the mechanical reproduction of imagery. Grotesque ornaments, scientific texts, didactic manuals, theatrical encyclopedias, popular prints— the ribbon of utilitarian illustration that had just begun to flourish could be scoured for oddities and puns. The little world of caricatured faces and composite bodies emerged as a pleasure garden in an empire of rhetoric.[14]

The comic tradition that begins with Leonardo and extends to Bernini and the Carracci and then in a dif-

ferent way to Arcimboldo and his followers is therefore not a tradition of "looking at" but one of "looking into": the artist begins to search the fantastic, unnatural, and grotesque for reflections of this world. The birth of mocking portraits and composite bodies involves the invention not of a new kind of grotesque but of a new way of looking at the grotesque. From its birth caricature is not a formal, mathematical invention, like perspective, with rules and models that tell an artist how to construct an artifact; it is instead an exhortation to search for likeness in the seemingly abstract, to look for the individual in the generic, to

24. Giovanni Battista Braccelli. Figures on the ground, from *Bizzarie* (1624; facsimile 1963). The New York Public Library. Print Collection, Miriam and Ira D. Wallach Division of Art, Prints and Photographs

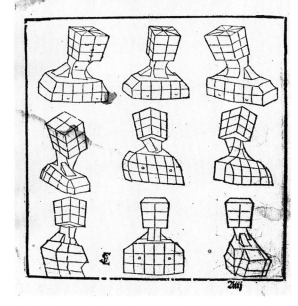

Die ander vigur.

Die angesicht wil ich Vleinerla weys anzaigenn vntersich nebenn sich fürsich vnnd vbersich wie du sibe dann vor augen sicht.

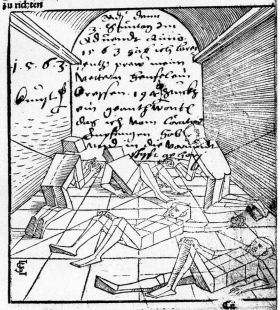

Die zehennd vigur.

Die zehennd Figur zaygt an von Fünf possen / in einem Gehews / vo dreyen ligenden / vnd zweyen knieenden / mit Jren dreyen beweglichen gelidert wie sie in der vierung begriesen sind / so wayst du dich darnach zu richten

25. Erhard Schön. Series of busts, from *Unterweissung der Proportion und Stellung der Bosse* (Nuremberg, c. 1538–40)

26. Erhard Schön. Reclining figures, from *Unterweissung der Proportion und Stellung der Bosse*

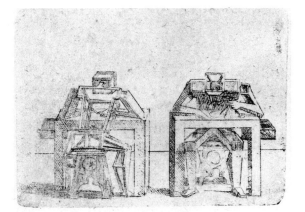

27. Giovanni Battista Braccelli. Two geometers, from *Bizzarie* (1624; facsimile 1963). The New York Public Library. Print Collection, Miriam and Ira D. Wallach Division of Art, Prints and Photographs

examine depictions of the alien for images of one-self—to search the signs of fantasy for signs of life.

For almost another century these kinds of humorous imagery continued to belong to the world of aristocratic wit: refined and a little decadent. The first step into modern political cartooning, in mid-eighteenth-century England, depended, paradoxically, on a revolt against caricature. When Hogarth denounced caricature in his famous print *Characters and Caricaturas* (fig. 28), it was because of the caricature's aristocratic origins and snobbish pretensions. Caricature, Hogarth suggests, is a decadent, elite game played in ignorance of the grander and truer tradition of Raphael, with its emphasis on clear stories and rounded characters. Hogarth's polemic is a little like the attacks of the Social Realists in the 1930s on "advanced" art with a Cubist basis; he thought that caricature substituted a rich

man's game for a responsible engagement with the world. Far from providing the basis for a low, popular art, caricature until the end of the eighteenth century seemed one of the things that stood in the way of such an art—it belonged to the world of the salon rather than the soapbox.[15]

The reconciliation of caricatural form and satirical comment takes place only at the end of the eighteenth century, and then almost entirely through the genius of a single gifted artist. Art historians talk easily about the influence of "English political caricature" on neoclassical and Romantic style, in both England and the Continent. Yet most of these discussions end up with their key examples taken almost entirely from the work of a single caricaturist—James Gillray. And when we analyze Gillray's style, what we find is high art looking back at its own slightly distorted reflection.

Gillray was, above all, a parodist, with an exception-

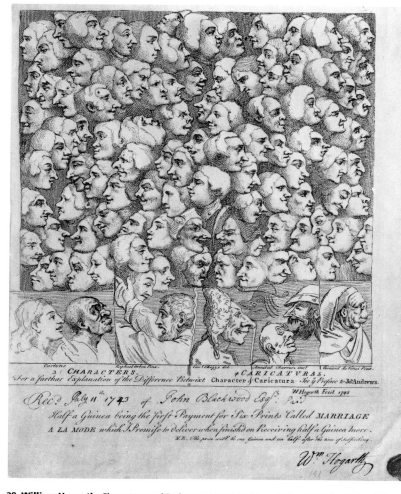

28. **William Hogarth.** *Characters and Caricaturas.* 1743. Etching, 10¹⁄₁₆ × 8″ (25.5 × 20.3 cm). The Metropolitan Museum of Art, New York. Harris Brisbane Dick Fund, 1932 [32.35 (152)]

ally subtle feeling for the avant-garde art of his day. Where others saw in the gothic phantasmagorias of Fuseli and Tibaldi a world of fantastic dreams, Gillray saw an armature for political satire (figs. 29, 30).[16] The melodramatic juxtapositions of English Romantic painting provided a model for Gillray through which the most grotesque conglomerations of symbols, allegorical figures, and visual oddities could be brought together in a single, binding dramatic pattern. The apparent disconnections and weird juxtapositions of Romanticism could be rationalized as satiric metaphor. Gillray (as in fig. 31) could borrow compositions like Fuseli's *Three Witches* or his *Satan and Death with Sin Intervening* (fig. 32) and make them into allegories of the shifting alliances and suspicions of English politics during the Napoleonic wars. Leonardo had seen

29. **John Henry Fuseli.** *The Three Witches.* 1783. Oil on canvas, 25⅝ × 36″ (65 × 91.5 cm). Kunsthaus Zürich

30. **James Gillray.** *Weird-Sisters; Ministers of Darkness; Minions of the Moon.* 1791. Hand-colored etching and aquatint, 9 × 13″ (22.9 × 33 cm). The New York Public Library. Print Collection, Miriam and Ira D. Wallach Division of Art, Prints and Photographs

31. **James Gillray.** *Sin, Death, and the Devil.* 1792. Hand-colored etching, 11¾ × 15⅜" (29.9 × 39 cm). The New York Public Library. Print Collection, Miriam and Ira D. Wallach Division of Art, Prints and Photographs

his own face in the margins of his notebooks, and Bernini had seen the faces of those around him in the language of the Leonardesque grotesque; Gillray discovered the figure of the feverish alliances and realignments of contemporary politics in the melodramas of Fuseli. If Bernini had begun the tradition of satiric art by taking something low, like commedia dell'arte masks and grotesque ornament, and making them high, Gillray made caricature into a popular form by taking high material and making it low. Yet the distinctive creative process is the same: an artist looks at a form thought to be fantastic or dreamlike, and shows that it provides a model for organizing real experience.

Gillray's burlesques of high art were essentially, if brilliantly, opportunistic; they provided a convenient vessel into which he could pour his satiric visions. But they rebounded back into high art with immensely serious effect. Gillray's prints supplied a model for artists as apparently opposite as William Blake and Jacques-Louis David, transmitting to Blake (fig. 33) a screen of bizarre form onto which Blake could project his private mythology,[17] and at the same time supplying for David a mannered Hellenism, intensified beyond anything he could have found in Gillray's own sources, that would, startlingly, eventually enliven a neoclassical machine like *The Sabine Women* (fig. 34).[18] The circling movement that has characterized modern art, from high to low and back again—Dr. Agha's wheel, as we encountered it in the history of typography—begins with

32. **John Henry Fuseli.** *Satan and Death with Sin Intervening.* 1799–1800. Oil on canvas, 26½ × 23" (67.3 × 58.4 cm). Los Angeles County Museum of Art. Gift of Mr. and Mrs. Frederick M. Nicholas, Mr. and Mrs. Harry B. Swerdlow, and Mr. and Mrs. William K. Glikbarg

Gillray's appropriation of Romantic style in order to serve the enlarged popular audience for humorous imagery, and the quick return of those parodic intensifications back into high art. Not for the last time, political reaction (Gillray's allegiances, or at any rate his

33. William Blake. *Satan, Sin, and Death: Satan Comes to the Gates of Hell.* **1806–07. Ink and watercolor with liquid gold, 19½ × 15⅞" (49.6 × 40.3 cm). Henry E. Huntington Library and Art Gallery, San Marino**

original and type of a vanguard art. It has no essence; its evolution tracks only the growth of extreme self-consciousness about style, and the proliferation of styles through mechanical reproduction. Its emergence as a popular style depended not on its sudden awakening to social responsibility but on a shrewd and essentially conservative parody of high art. Its history shows a fever chart of shifts in social uses, whose one continuous theme is the rationalization of the seemingly irrational. From Leonardo to Gillray, the story of caricature is like a variant of the Narcissus myth: an artist stares into a stream of form that seems completely independent of his own experience, and cries out as he discovers there the face of something familiar staring back at him. With each advancing generation, his descendants see more faces in the stream and the artists' cries are heard by more people: Leonardo sees in the grotesque the form of his own fear, Bernini sees a social circle, and Gillray sees the form of social life itself.

By the 1840s, caricature belonged to Paris, even though French caricaturists suffered from constant and often arbitrary censorship of a sort no longer found in England. It was there that caricatural political satire took the form that we still are inclined to think was somehow always natural to it—it became the expression of the indignant eye. Its triumphs opened up a new channel for high artistic invention and at the same time dammed up other channels, creating a barrier between high and low that was more extreme than anything that had come before. Modern art got inspiration both from proceeding down those newly opened courses and from exploding through the barriers.

That French caricature had this power is largely

patrons, were all essentially conservative) produced radical art. As much as any one artist could, James Gillray (who went mad before he was fifty and died in dire poverty) set the wheel of modern invention in motion.

What caricature bequeathed to the early modern era is therefore not at all the expected inheritance—a tradition of satiric realism and social protest which finds a larger and larger audience in the emerging world of mass urban culture. Far from being in its "essence" a low, popular form, a slang, caricature is the

34. Jacques-Louis David. *The Sabine Women.* **1799. Oil on canvas, 12'7½" × 17'1½" (385 × 522 cm). Musée du Louvre, Paris**

35. **Honoré Daumier.** "Combat des écoles: L'Idéalisme et le Réalisme," from *Le Charivari*, April 24, 1855

owing to the combined efforts of a great poet and a remarkable entrepreneur, and, above all, to the gifts of probably the greatest caricaturist who has ever lived. Almost forty years after Gillray's death, when a by now familiar motif passed into the hands of Honoré Daumier (fig. 35),[19] the image of infernal conflict became a satiric metaphor for the emerging battle of styles between realists and idealizing artists. Yet what is new and overwhelming in Daumier's version is the severe and, in its way, oddly classical authority of his drawing. Gillray's figures had been mere marionettes and stick-insects; Daumier seized on this rudimentary, anticlassical caricatural convention of satiric drawing, and really used it to create a conscious language of truthful form in images that protested against the idealized academic vision of the human body. Daumier's figures, for all their comic awkwardness, have an authority of line, an immediate grasp of weight and of contour, that none of his contemporaries, high or low, could equal. And then how dark most of Daumier's drawings are. Their evocation of an envelope of gloom—at once a gas-lit city and a dim, gray battlefield—became a kind of permanent twilight that passed into the hand and manner of artists as different as Millet and Charles Addams. It was this darkness, literal and metaphoric, that Daumier added to the language of popular imagery; and it gave to caricature, in his hands, an almost tragic high seriousness.

This seriousness was in part the consequence of a new intensity of commitment. (Gillray's political prints assumed a façade of measured cynicism; "The world's

a charade," he drank in a toast with Rowlandson. Daumier takes sides, passionately.)[20] But it is also in part the consequence of a new attitude toward the purposes of parody. The high-art parodies that Gillray had used to give dramatic structure to political caricature became in Daumier's hands the foundation of a powerful, alternative vision of classicism (fig. 36). As Lorenz Eitner puts it: "The serious intention that guided Daumier's parodistic invasions of high art was not to de-

36. **Honoré Daumier.** "Ménélas vainqueur," from *Le Charivari*, December 22, 1841

37. Honoré Daumier. Headpiece for *Le Charivari*, November 26, 1833

value the great traditions, but to give them new life by freeing them from the preciousness of a mandarin culture, reanimating them with genuine feeling and bringing them into the reality of modern experience."[21] It isn't surprising that other, younger artists—Degas most prominent among them—saw that these parodies cut through an unreal visual rhetoric to provide a style that was more authentically classical than all the waxworks of the academy. Though Gillray's parodies had rebounded back into high art, that process had been largely haphazard and unintentional; with Daumier, parody for the first time became serious—an authentic, self-conscious source of innovation, a way of reclaiming the tradition while seeming to kid it, a new process of invention that began in mockery and ended in rediscovery.

Daumier's working space was largely created through the shrewd business sense and progressive idealism of one of the great men of the nineteenth century, the publisher and occasional caricaturist Charles Philipon. Philipon's journal *Le Charivari* (figs. 35–38) seems to have begun as a commercial enterprise without an overriding political ambition. The vagaries of the July Monarchy, however, made Philipon a leader among the radicals, and the author of the most famous and influential caricature of the first half of the nineteenth century, in which, almost for the first time, an Arcimboldesque transformation was identified with an individual and given a political point—the reduction of Louis-Philippe to a *poire*, the French slang for "fathead" (fig. 38). The transformation spread irresistibly, like a contagion (fig. 39).[22]

Philipon is almost single-handedly responsible for our sense of caricature as an art of indignation and as a champion of the oppressed. Yet he created a new space for progressive imagery through an unprecedentedly aggressive "commodification" of art. He financed his political journals through a subscription series, both of comic art and, more often, of reproductions of old and new painted masterpieces, sold to an emerging audience of middle-class patrons. Within the orbit of Philipon, however, many different styles, social

attitudes, and ideas about the range and function of caricature were possible. J. J. Grandville, Daumier's immediate predecessor as Philipon's leading artist, soon left his work as a caricaturist, and began the series of illustrated fantasies on which his fame depends today, and which led both to John Tenniel and to Odilon Redon.[23]

The caricature sculptor Jean-Pierre Dantan, on the other hand, another artist who was occasionally involved with Philipon, made a series of small sculptures eventually called, half mockingly and half not, the "Musée Dantan," which employed the tradition of the composite body less for political satire than to make rebuses—punning riddles on their subjects' names. (Those that have survived are startling enough; apparently a whole second set of obscene ones filled the back room of the Musée Dantan and were even more extreme.) These rebuses began as simple inscriptions on the bases of his figurines, and then evolved into more complicated and bizarre transformations: actors and men of letters made into coatracks or into bugs (figs. 40, 41) in ways that punned on their given names and, occasionally, suggested something about their métier.[24] Though Dantan's work belongs less on the barricades than in the smoking room, he was, more than anyone else, responsible for joining the tradition of caricatured faces to the tradition of composite bodies in a way that, by the middle of the century, made both of them seem part of an organic genre called "caricature."

But what relationship did all this new imagery have to the art that hung in the Louvre? One line of thought—exemplified by the work of the historian Champfleury, and seconded by the English historian Thomas Wright, who wrote a multivolume history of caricature—linked it to the ancient stream of grotesque form, and insisted that caricature was so vital because it was the oldest of all the arts, the primal vocabulary of visual expression.[25] Champfleury and Wright wanted to elevate the low satiric form by attaching it to universal, common properties of the human mind. But Champfleury had a poet friend who

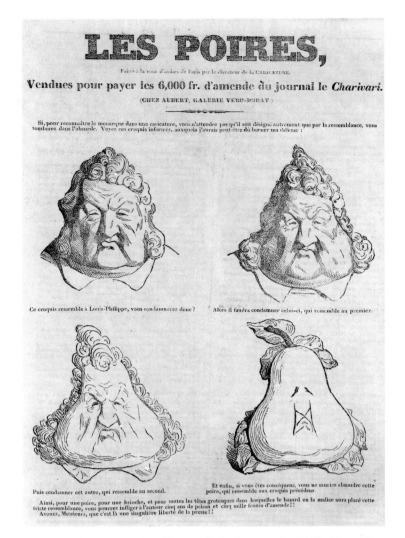

38. **Charles Philipon.** "Les Poires," from *Le Charivari,* January 17, 1834. The Metropolitan Museum of Art, New York. Gift of Arthur Sachs, 1923 (23.92.3)

39. "Voici Messieurs, ce que nous avons l'honneur d'exposer journellement," from *La Caricature,* March 6, 1834

40. Jean-Pierre Dantan. *Neuville*. 1843. Plaster and terra-cotta, 16⅛" (41 cm) high. Musée Carnavalet, Paris

41. Jean-Pierre Dantan. *Romieu*. 1835. Plaster and terra-cotta, 11" (28 cm) high. Musée Carnavalet, Paris

was interested in caricature, too; the friend even drew a caricature of himself and Champfleury together (fig. 42). He was Charles Baudelaire, who became the first writer to cut caricature off from an imagined inheritance in primitive form. In 1844 Baudelaire's small income had been placed in the hands of a trustee, who, in effect, condemned the poet to a life of small rooms and sad hotels. Filled with self-loathing and a masochistic desire for degradation, Baudelaire decided to become an art critic. In 1846, he wrote an essay on caricature: "On the Essence of Laughter."[26]

Caricature for Baudelaire is the sophisticated, urban art par excellence, not just in its choice of subjects but in its intrinsic style. "Primitive nations," he wrote, "cannot conceive of caricature.... When it comes to the grotesque figures that have been left to us by antiquity—the masks, figurines, the muscular Hercules, the little Priapuses with their tongues curved into air—...all these things are fully serious. We laugh after the coming of Jesus.... The idols of India and China do not know that they are ridiculous; it is we, Christians, who know that they are comic." Caricature for Baudelaire is also "Satanic"—that is (in Baudelaire's idiosyncratic sense), profoundly human. "In effect, as laughter is essentially human, it is essentially contradictory, that is, it signifies at the same time an infinite grandeur and an infinite misery—infinite misery relative to the absolute being of which man was possessed at conception; infinite grandeur relative to beasts. It is in the perpetual

shock of these two infinities that laughter takes place.... A sign of superiority relative to the beasts, laughter is the sign of inferiority relative to the sages, who by the contemplative innocence of their spirit approach childhood."[27]

42. Charles Baudelaire. *Caricature of Champfleury and Self-Portrait*. c. 1850. Pencil on paper. Present whereabouts unknown

Baudelaire thought of caricature not as the lingua franca of primal consciousness but as the *argot plastique*, the plastic slang, of civilized life, and of the city,[28] possessed of a quicksilver intelligence and mysterious double nature that allowed it to capture the perplexing ambiguities of modern life in a way that the stilted formal language of academic art could not. The caricature, for Baudelaire, is the symbol of a self-consciously contradictory existence, of man poised between another world and this one. When we look at Daumier, he argues, what we are seeing reminds us of the grotesque absurdity of this fallen and chaotic world; at the same time, that we laugh rather than turn in revulsion suggests our memory of order. Our response to caricature is a measure of our sophistication, and it is possible only in a civilization that is at once Christian and corrupt, dreaming of a lost innocent unity and conscious of its own departure from it.

For Baudelaire one kind of comedy, which he called "absolute" comedy, is the comedy of joy. This kind of comedy—that of E.T.A. Hoffmann or, in a different way, Rabelais—aspires to re-create, for a moment, the innocent, Edenic condition from which we have fallen. But another kind of comedy—"significant" comedy, of which caricature is the best example—departs from appearances only to make the truth of life plainer, leaves the world only to return to it. Absolute comedy uses abstract forms—grotesque faces and odd bodies and elegantly resolved plots—for abstract effects; "its only test is laughter,"[29] and it is, in this sense, abstract and musical. Significant comedy puts those ideal forms at the service of a moral idea.

Baudelaire grasped intuitively that the history of caricature depended on the tension between the creation of an "absolute" otherworldly realm and the decision to enter that realm to find the familiar within it. What Baudelaire changed was the sense of how the moral pluses and minuses ought to be scored. In the past, it had been the otherworldly, the unnatural, and the fantastic that had been domesticated by caricature, and part of the pleasure of the form lay in seeing the threatening made humane; for Baudelaire, the grotesque represented a lost world of uncircumscribed feeling, and every time we laughed at any caricature we memorialized our own entry into consciousness and guilt. The world of demons is our own. What Baudelaire admired about Daumier was, in a sense, that he was *not* of his time: that looking past the trivia of contemporary politics, his grim welter of grotesque faces marked the space between the rational animals we would like to be and the fantastic beings we really are. Like Dickens, Daumier shows us the monsters of affectation that are our true selves.

Baudelaire saw that Daumier was really astonishing not for what he pinned down but for what he left open. When we look at Daumier, despite the connection of his art to encyclopedic programs of physiognomic identification, what strikes us is how mysterious the expressions of his people really are; they appeal to our fascination with the double edge of things, and mark the fine line between comedy and tragedy, between anxiety and vanity.[30] The drama in Daumier lies in the tension between the definition of social roles, indicated in his figures' mime-like gestures and as-

43. Honoré Daumier. *Study of Heads.* c. 1850. Ink over charcoal and black chalk on paper, 5⅛ × 7″ (13 × 17.7 cm). The Brooklyn Museum, New York. Carl H. De Silver Fund

44. **Honoré Daumier.** *The Drinking Song*. c. 1860–65. Black chalk, ink, and watercolor on paper, 10¼ × 13⅜" (26 × 34 cm). Private collection

sumed postures—the whole world of social imprints on a human body that would become the basis for Sherlock Holmes's deduction—and the multivalent ambiguity of their expression. Far from anatomizing the set poses of modernity, Daumier's figures remain compelling for their invocation of moments of doubt, doubleness, and emotional complexity (figs. 43, 44): people in reverie, introspection, uncertainty; people caught in the margins of expression rather than at its center. For Daumier, even such a seemingly straight-forward satiric target as M. d'Argo (fig. 45), the gov-ernment minister, can become a pathetic monster, at once self-satisfied but strangely conscious of his ab-surdity. Such images, for Baudelaire, were the deepest moment of caricature—the moment when the mask has just slipped on the face, and its wearer hardly knows whether to be delighted at his performance or appalled at his imposture.

Even the most brutally satiric comedy had, before Baudelaire, usually been explained as a form of ther-apy. Showing us the grotesques of life, comedy taught us discrimination and good manners; we enjoy satire because we are reminded (or learn) that it is better not to be like that. In a way that anticipates Beckett and Kafka as much as Dubuffet, Baudelaire saw in his con-templation of caricature that comedy need not be un-derstood simply as a dream of conflicts resolved, with happy endings all around; through Daumier's exam-ple, he saw that comedy could register profound am-bivalences and permanent doubts. It is not, as is sometimes said, that Baudelaire and Daumier emanci-

pated caricature from the reflex of laughter; it is that they emancipated laughter from the reflex of joy.

When Baudelaire's essay on laughter was finally published in 1857, it confirmed an intuition that artists had already begun to make part of their practice. The plastic slang of the city was already on its way to be-coming one of the primary alphabets of avant-garde art. From the ardent affection of Manet for the popu-lar print[31] to Gauguin's cult of caricatural imagery, French art of the second half of the nineteenth century was marked by almost innumerable borrowings—some overt and some surreptitious—of vanguard art from popular satire. The old order of art came under siege from a new alliance of wise guys. But people still argued about what this relationship really demonstrat-ed. Through the opposed models of Champfleury and Baudelaire, caricature could be understood as both very old and very new. Some people emphasized the place of caricature as a psychologically primitive form, and thought that modern artists ought to use carica-tural form because it was basic and uncorrupted, a kind of living fossil. Others thought that caricature was useful to modern art because it was a model of sophis-tication, the measure of our rueful knowledge of our own absurdity. Translated into the practice of picture-making, this ambivalence proved fruitful and form-creating. In pictures like the *Vision after the Sermon*, Gauguin could join Daumier's outline to the hard, de-terminate form of folk art, aligning *Le Charivari* with the world of the Breton peasant. Caricature for Gau-guin offered the distilled essence of all art-making:

Pl. 292

Mᴿ D'ARGO . . .

45. Honoré Daumier. "M. d'Argo . . ," from *La Caricature,* **July 11, 1833**

"Drawing honestly," he wrote, "does not mean affirming a thing which is true in nature, but, instead, using pictorial idioms that do not disguise one's thoughts."[32] Yet Degas could also use Daumier's anticlassical burlesque figures as inspiration for his courtesan bathers. The intellectual quarrel between Champfleury and Baudelaire took shape in art as a fruitful tension that allowed artists to use popular form both as a symbol of "primitive" honesty and as a way of engaging modern life.

Yet if the figure style and draftsmanship of popular imagery were allowed in art, their distortions of the face on the whole were not. Funny faces in art were still only good for a laugh, even though serious artists loved to draw them. By the end of the nineteenth century, *everybody* drew portrait caricatures. Wonderful caricatures have come down to us from such unlikely academic artists as Frédéric Bartholdi, Thomas Couture, and Horace Vernet (fig. 46).[33] A flair for caricature was one of the marks of a genuinely distinguished artist; and, as the critic du Seigneur's complaint ("After Courbet, after Manet—the caricature!") reminds us,

46. Horace Vernet. *Desnoyer Reading a Report.* **n.d. Ink on paper, 8⅞ × 3¹⁵/₁₆" (22.5 × 10 cm). Bibliothèque de l'Institut de France, Paris**

47. Pierre Puvis de Chavannes. *Young Girls at the Edge of the Sea.* 1879. Oil on canvas, 6'8¾" × 60¾" (205 × 154 cm). Musée d'Orsay, Paris. Gift of Robert Gérard

even shows of caricature by academic artists were part of the landscape. Yet there were understood rules about what was acceptable as game and what was acceptable as art, and artists adhered to these rules with a fanaticism that seems to us in retrospect almost a little schizophrenic. Puvis de Chavannes (fig. 47), for instance, whose columnar figures and chaste sub-Piero reticence inspired even Seurat, also drew caricatures of an intensity and meticulousness that would have delighted Baudelaire (fig. 48). But no sign of his

48. Pierre Puvis de Chavannes. *Expressive Head: Concierge.* n.d. Drawing. Present whereabouts unknown

caricatural flair was ever allowed to enliven the poised balance of Puvis's tranquil pictures.[34]

The art world in Paris, so far from being one where all the rules were in the air, was more like the salons described in Proust, where the rules of conduct, the boundaries of the permissible and forbidden, were at once infinitely subtle and perfectly plain. Of course, some art in late nineteenth-century Paris—Lautrec's is an obvious example—was full of caricatural elements, and even startling simplifications of faces (fig. 49). But this art, like the subjects it most often depicts, belonged to a kind of demimonde, neither high nor low, vanguard nor popular. The split between caricature and serious painting, exemplified by Puvis, looks to us now like a "crisis" that had to be "resolved." Yet the same split also forced the creation of a kind of "middle kingdom" for caricature, found in the caricature journals—*L'Assiette au beurre*, *Le Journal amusant*, and, in Germany, *Simplicissimus*—that enriched city life at

49. Henri de Toulouse-Lautrec. *Yvette Guilbert*, from the *Café-concert* series. 1893. Lithograph, 17¹¹⁄₃₂ × 12½" (44 × 31.7 cm). The Metropolitan Museum of Art, New York. Harris Brisbane Dick Fund, 1923 [23.30.3(2)]

the end of the last century. Artists who chose to live in this demimonde created a tradition that was, by itself, the progenitor of much that remained stirring in the next century's art.[35]

The Daumier tradition went north. Passing from Ensor into German Expressionism, the multivalent ambiguity of those faces, divorced from their specific satiric uses, was seen as a material for art. The foggy faces of Daumier initiated a line of imagery that runs beyond Realism into Symbolism and Expressionism, and connects the painterly indignation of Goya with the graphic distortions of Munch and of Max Beckmann.

Even well into the modern era, the tradition of the caricature journal still could be enlivening. The politicized art of Berlin Dada depends on the already soured and bitter satiric tradition present in the great German caricature journal *Simplicissimus,* whose roster of artists included the savage Olaf Gulbransson (fig. 50). What gives the work of George Grosz and John Heartfield its razor edge is the forceful combination of the non sequiturs of Dada imagery with the emphatic stresses of an already developed language of political cartoons. In Grosz's early work, like the *Republican Automatons* (fig. 51), the reduction of a social class to a mechanical type—bourgeois into robot—obviously has its roots in the quick-cutting imagery of the political cartoon, only now Grosz adapts the private languages of the School of Paris to popular satiric form: the melancholy perspectives and wan streets of de Chirico, the tubular men of Léger, the stencils of Cubism, are parodied for satiric effect. It is no disrespect to Grosz—just the opposite—to see that his most successful work belongs to another and different (though not lesser) history than that which descends from Manet to Cézanne and beyond; his art belongs to the history of modernist invention rebounding back into popular imagery. Grosz became the Gillray of Weimar, parodying the high art of his time and finding in it a cutting edge of political truth.[36]

Other, less directly engaged art, too, could continue to find energy and inspiration in the caricature journal. Paul Klee's grotesque heads of the teens and twenties (fig. 52), with their apparent throwaway inconse-

50. Olaf Gulbransson. "How can we poke the fire any longer? We have no more charcoal" (1915?), reprinted in *Arts et métiers graphiques*, 31 (September 15, 1932)

quence, are in part a self-conscious attempt to substitute the humane tabletalk of the caricature journal for the big declamatory stuff of either academic or sol-

51. George Grosz. *Republican Automatons.* 1920. Watercolor on paper, 23⅝ × 18⅝" (60 × 47.3 cm). The Museum of Modern Art, New York. Advisory Committee Fund

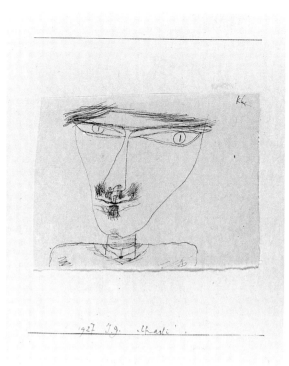

52. Paul Klee. *Charli.* 1927. Ink on paper, mounted on cardboard, 3⅞ × 4⅞" (9.9 × 12.3 cm). Kunstmuseum Bern. Paul Klee Stiftung

emnly "advanced" art. The tradition in modern art that runs from Klee to Alexander Calder to Saul Steinberg, and has as its end a conversational directness and simple punning flair, begins in the middle kingdom of caricature at the end of the last century.[37]

One man's decorum is another man's intolerable hierarchy. If it was possible to see the caste system of French art—with the Beaux Arts in one place, the avant-garde in another, and the caricature journals someplace in between—as an essentially happy division of labor, it was also possible to see it as a neurotic segregation of the organic elements of art. For the full potential of the comic tradition to be released into serious painting, it was necessary for an artist to have a natural gift for funny drawing, to have a deep emotional dissatisfaction with the accepted decorum, and finally to find some new and unexpected catalyst that could unlock the repressed energies of satiric imagery in a way that would allow them to enter, and even annex, high art.

This was achieved in about eighteen months in the middle of the first decade of this century by Pablo Picasso. The transformation in Picasso's art from 1905 to 1907 is still perhaps the most astonishing transformation in art history, and it has often been described and diagnosed, usually in terms of the impact of new influences or as the logical working out of possibilities implicit in his earlier paintings. But it is also possible to see this transformation as the resolution—happily, to the Devil's advantage—of the entire late nineteenth-century psychomachia between notebook jokes and easel pieties.

Caricature was Picasso's mother tongue.[38] His first recorded drawings are all caricatures. (In this case, the codices are textbooks that he doodled in during dull hours at school [fig. 53].) The notebooks of his early years in Barcelona are filled, alive, with caricature. A single sheet (fig. 54) chosen more or less at random from a notebook of 1900 displays childlike scrawls, hollow-eyed, emaciated, tonal heads (a kind of mock-Symbolist agony), crisp, quasi-quattrocento profiles, and a kind of proto–Farmer Alfalfa figure, rendered in one serpentine line complete with dialogue balloon. What is finally most impressive in these early notebooks is less the gift for likeness, remarkable as it is, than the *horror vacui* that leads Picasso to crowd page after page with every kind of distorted physiognomy. Picasso had an apparent compulsion not simply to record faces in a virtuoso shorthand but to reinvent faces, and to push caricature toward new extremes of simplification.[39]

In Picasso's early work as a caricaturist, two clearly distinct styles still stand out among all the variety. One style is sophisticated, and descends from Lautrec. It involves an allusive reduction of features to a telegraphic code of dots and dashes, suavely placed against blank white faces (fig. 55). Another style involves changing the relation of features to face, in an almost graffiti-like distortion that enlarges the subject's eyes and makes them part of a geometric, simplified design—an original style someplace between Fayum funeral portraits and Thomas Keane's moppets. In this second caricature style, Picasso often uses the curious device of

53. Pablo Picasso. *Various Sketches.* 1893–94. Lead pencil on printed page, 10⅝ × 5⅛" (20.7 × 13 cm). Museu Picasso, Barcelona

54. Pablo Picasso. *Sketches with Pierrot Figures.* 1900. Ink, conté crayon, and colored pencil on paper, 8⅝ × 12½″ (22 × 31.8 cm). Museu Picasso, Barcelona

55. Pablo Picasso. *Caricatures and Portraits: Guillaume Apollinaire, Paul Fort, Jean Moréas, Fernande Olivier, André Salmon, Henri Delormel.* 1905. India ink on paper, 10 × 12⅞″ (25.5 × 32.7 cm). Musée Picasso, Paris

56. Pablo Picasso. *Head of a Man.* 1899–1900. Ink and red pencil on paper, 2¾ × 3½" (6.9 × 8.9 cm). Museu Picasso, Barcelona

of the mature portraits—the scabrous insights, the extravagant physiognomic rearrangements, the fearless combinations and recombinations of borrowed styles—in a way that Picasso's painted portraits of the same years, and even of the next decade, with their calculated wistfulness and tepid Symbolist effects, do not (fig. 66).

This split between Picasso's notebook caricatures and his easel portraits is, as we've seen, common at the end of the nineteenth century. Yet for Picasso this split seems to have been especially disturbing, in part perhaps because in the context of the art of the Barcelona renaissance, with its heavy linear designs and sim-

treating an unnaturally enlarged eye as a circle within a geometric lozenge (fig. 56). Some of Picasso's Barcelona caricatures in this second style have an aggressive simplicity, an extreme insistence on symmetry and abstraction, that is still genuinely startling, as in a series of studies he made of his friend Jaime Sabartés (figs. 57, 58).

In these early caricature pages, too, a couple of persistent themes—obsessions—also appear. Picasso, like Leonardo (whose grotesque heads he knew and admired),[40] was fascinated by imagining the ravages of time. His notebooks are filled with pages where old age descends like a disease on odd little faces (fig. 59). In one strange drawing, he seems to imagine his own face as an old man (fig. 60); and a later group from 1906 shows Josep Fontdevila (fig. 61) suddenly undergoing the horrors of age in a series of animated drawings. Caricature for Picasso was a kind of cruel, substitute magic, in which a few bags and sags and lines around the mouth could conjure up in a scribble all the horrors of mortality and time. Where old age suggests a kind of wan bathos in Picasso's painted pictures of this time, in his caricatures it is imagined as a mocking rash, an unavoidable plague.

Another obsession of Picasso's, evident in his notebooks long before it was evident in his finished pictures, involved the possibilities for portraiture in marginal and unfamiliar styles. On several occasions in the years from 1895 until 1900, Picasso would first absorb an exotic new language of form and then immediately explore its possibilities as a new code of identification. In one series of drawings from 1899–1900, he plays with the resemblances between passersby seen from a café and the El Greco portraits he had recently come to admire (figs. 62, 63). On another occasion, he assimilated a friend's face to the forms of an Egyptian figure he had just seen (figs. 64, 65). His extraordinary virtuosity as a caricaturist seems to have given Picasso a natural tendency to see an individual in terms of a highly stylized manner, and to see in a highly stylized manner the surprising possibility of defining an individual.

Throughout the first decade of his work, it is in these notebook drawings alone that we see intimations of the artist Picasso will become. They have the qualities

57. Pablo Picasso. *Caricatures.* c. 1899–1900. Conté crayon on paper, 3½ × 4⅜" (8.9 × 11 cm). Museu Picasso, Barcelona

58. Pablo Picasso. *Caricature.* c. 1899–1900. Conté crayon on paper, 3½ × 4⅜" (8.9 × 11 cm). Museu Picasso, Barcelona

59. Pablo Picasso. *Sketch: Heads (Père Romeu).* 1899. Ink on paper, 8 × 5⅛" (20.5 × 13 cm). Musée Picasso, Paris

60. Pablo Picasso. *Self-Portrait.* 1898. Lead pencil on paper, 7¹¹⁄₁₆ × 4¾" (19.5 × 12 cm). Museu Picasso, Barcelona

plified patterns, the space between caricature and serious art must have seemed especially arbitrary. Catalan art journals were full of caricature, which often sat side by side with reproductions of French vanguard art; and that high art itself, when reproduced, looked more graphic and linear than in fact it was. The absolute division between what you were allowed to do in a notebook and what you were allowed to do on an easel must have seemed to Picasso genuinely peculiar. What's more, the enforced decorum seems to

61. Pablo Picasso. *Portrait of Josep Fontdevila and Sketch of a Nude with Raised Arms.* **1906. Conté crayon on paper, 10⅛ × 7⅞"** (25.7 × 20 cm). Musée Picasso, Paris

have left him blocked emotionally. It's as though he could only draw his true, demonic, gleeful self in caricature (fig. 67), while for portraiture he had to put on the uneasy, self-conscious face of Romantic longing.

But these low strategies could not be released into Picasso's high art until a new and more dignified costume, a different mask, had been placed on them—literally a mask, for it was Picasso's discovery of archaic and primitive art that allowed him to release the energy of his notebooks into the world of his big finished portraits. Picasso's deeply idiosyncratic use of primitive art—for he alone turns the schematized codes of primitive art into a language of likeness, a language used to define particular individuals—was in one respect a way of bringing the latent potential of the caricature into vanguard art. The search for likeness in the grotesque and unfamiliar that had long been embed-

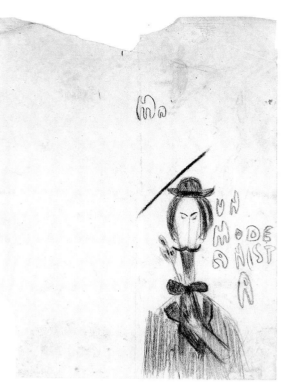

62. Pablo Picasso. *Five Sketches of Greek Personages.* c. 1899. Conté crayon and pencil on paper, 14⅛ × 8⅝″ (30.6 × 22 cm). Museu Picasso, Barcelona

63. Pablo Picasso. *Modernist.* 1899–1900. Conté crayon on paper, 8⅝ × 6¼″ (22 × 15.9 cm). Museu Picasso, Barcelona

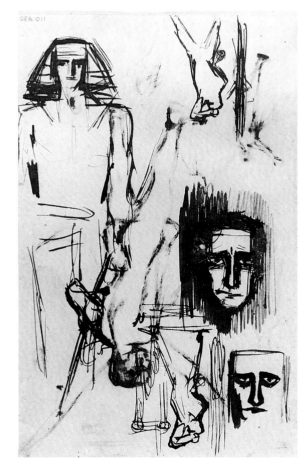

64. Pablo Picasso. *Egyptian and Other Sketches.* c. 1900. Ink on paper, 8⅛ × 5⅛″ (20.8 × 13.1 cm). Museu Picasso, Barcelona

65. Pablo Picasso. *Various Sketches.* c. 1900. Ink on paper, 8⅛ × 5⅛″ (20.6 × 13 cm). Museu Picasso, Barcelona

66. **Pablo Picasso.** *Self-Portrait.* 1899–1900. Charcoal on paper, 8⅞ × 6½" (22.5 × 16.5 cm). Museu Picasso, Barcelona

ded in the caricature tradition could be integrated into Picasso's finished portraits only after it had first been reimagined as primitivism.

As William Rubin has written, "Not surprisingly, one discovers that the 'low art' of Picasso's caricature starts fusing with his 'high art' at precisely the moment his primitivism begins, with the repainting of Gertrude Stein's face in the Iberian manner on his return from Gósol [in the fall of 1906]."[41] Picasso's portrait of Gertrude Stein (fig. 68) is one of the monuments of modern painting, yet its formal structure has never really been sorted out. While the painting is accepted as an extraordinary, magic likeness, the archaic forms of Iberian sculpture which the artist used to recast the sitter's face are consistently described as "monumental," "timeless," and even "inexpressive." That Picasso was able to wrest likeness from such resistant material is still seen as a formidable achievement; that the game of wresting likeness from resistant material has a history of its own within the Western tradition has been largely overlooked. The unfamiliar vocabulary of form blinded people to the familiar underlying grammar.

In the Stein portrait, a likeness that began as a study in physiognomic ambiguity, in the grand manner, is transformed through the use of primitive form into a

study in physiognomic identification through distortion: the low went high in the disguise of the exotic. Even the particular forms Picasso selects from the vocabulary of Iberian art—the oversize eyes, the mag-

67. **Pablo Picasso.** *Self-Portrait and Other Sketches.* 1903. Ink on paper, 4⅝ × 4¼" (11.8 × 10.7 cm). Museu Picasso, Barcelona

68. Pablo Picasso. *Portrait of Gertrude Stein.* 1906. Oil on canvas, 39¼ × 32″ (99.6 × 81.3 cm). The Metropolitan Museum of Art, New York. Bequest of Gertrude Stein

nified and thrust-out brows—are precisely those that, ever since Bernini, artists had been taking from the language of the grotesque and using to identify individuals. The key device that Picasso is supposed to have taken from "Iberian" sculpture is the eyes, which are suddenly treated as a geometric, faceted element. Yet as we've seen, it is precisely this stylization that is a commonplace of Picasso's caricature sketches of the

previous decade. The Stein portrait is the first of those breakthrough works of Picasso's in which he discovered that some exotic feature of primitive art bore a punning or rhyming relationship to a mannerism that already existed in his notebooks. Just as the "African" scarifications in the *Demoiselles d'Avignon* are the serendipitous children of idle shadings and crosshatching that existed in Picasso's carnets independent of African

69. Pablo Picasso. *Self-Portrait.* **1907. Oil on canvas, 19¾ × 18⅛″ (50 × 46 cm). National Gallery, Prague**

influence, so the Iberian eyes of Gertrude Stein are at once an exotic "timeless" form and a familiar caricatural mannerism. The move from low to high, the victory of the sketchbook over the easel, is accomplished through the Trojan horse of primitivism.[42]

For the next three years, we can recognize a steady and recurring pattern of this kind in Picasso's art. A vocabulary of primitive form is first absorbed and then transformed into a new language of likeness. In a masterpiece like the self-portrait of 1907 (fig. 69), Picasso created a new kind of monumental caricature in which the firm contours and quick sure insights of the notebook jokes are given a new weight and unforgettable plastic intensity.

The caricatural element in Picasso's "primitivism" was recognized at once in his circle. The critic Félix Féneón, looking at no less "primitivized" a picture than

the *Demoiselles*, told Picasso that he probably had a future as a caricaturist.[43] And Picasso himself saw clearly the route he had traveled from caricature to vanguard portraiture by way of primitivism; the path from sketchbook to easel went by way of Africa. In a group of drawings from late 1907, variations on a caricature of André Salmon, who had been the first writer to associate Picasso with primitive art,[44] we can see Picasso retracing his steps, unmistakably and purposefully assimilating the vocabulary of primitive and archaic art to the grammar of the caricature. Picasso begins with a wonderfully jaunty full-length caricature of Salmon (as William Rubin has pointed out, this is the first Picasso caricature executed on large-scale drawing paper):[45] half-smiling, a folio volume held in his relaxed clasp—the imperturbable evangelist of primitivism (fig. 70). But then Picasso turns the collection on

70. Pablo Picasso. *Portrait of André Salmon.* **1907. Charcoal on paper, 23⅝ × 15¾" (60 × 40 cm). Private collection, France**

the collector; Salmon is caricatured as a primitive object. In one extraordinary sheet—the art-historical equivalent of the intermediate fossil which is the dream and despair of the paleontologist—the caricature of Salmon is caught forever in transition from caricature to primitivized image (fig. 71). The passage between primitive art and caricature is made the explicit subject of the image. First, in the upper left, Picasso further simplifies the queer, fin-like, and already somewhat Africanized arrangement of the clasped hands from the original drawing. Then, in an inspired visual pun, Picasso sees that the suave, cursive shading of the original can, with only a slight change in rhythm and direction, become a striated pattern that echoes the scarification of African art: Salmon's body now bears the scars of his own obsession. Once again, Picasso discovers a punning relationship between the distant and exotic and the informal and near at hand.[46]

Next, the great jutting chin and lantern jaw put Picasso in mind of Pharaonic art, and the head is wrenched into full profile and distended into a likeness of an old-dynasty Egyptian king. Salmon's high forehead is turned into a headdress, his spiffy middle part into a bony ridge. On the far left of the sheet, the figure (attitude carried over intact from the original caricature) is inspected from the rear and then—the

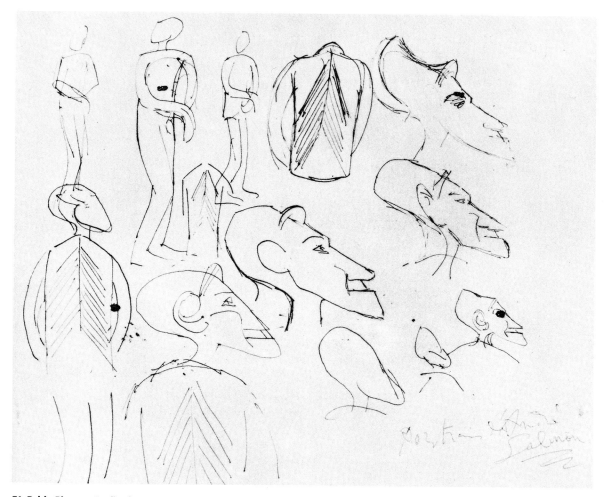

71. Pablo Picasso. Studies for *Portrait of André Salmon.* **1907. Ink on paper, 12¾ × 15¾" (32.5 × 40 cm). Private collection, France**

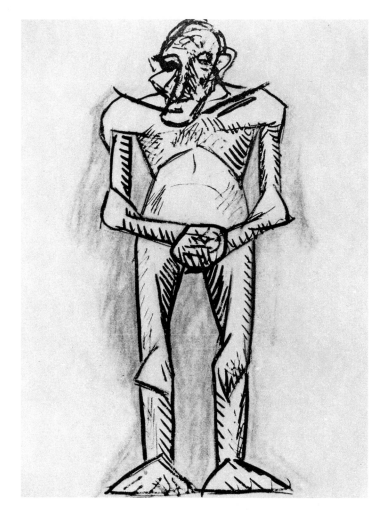

72. **Pablo Picasso.** *Portrait of André Salmon* (final state). 1907–08. India ink on paper, 24¾ × 19⅞″ (63 × 48 cm). Private collection, France

climax of this parody rite of passage—the Pharaonic profile is mounted on the scarified torso. Salmon has been inducted into the hybrid tribe: the barbarian alliance of caricature and primitive art, of the lowbrow and the alien, that will conquer the Western portrait. Eventually, in a later drawing in this series (fig. 72), Salmon becomes a flat-footed, hunched-over, and, above all, aged nude—an old man—with the same schematic face as Picasso's other friends who had also been maliciously "aged" in his caricatures.

In a way, Picasso was just rejuvenating the tradition that Braccelli had begun three hundred years before as a joke. Through the examination of strange form, the artist creates an image where the emblems of his subject's trade or preoccupation are made part of his appearance.[47] Picasso's Salmon is the great-great-grandson of Braccelli's geometric geometers; here, the primitive fetishist is made into a primitive fetish.

And in all of these portraits from 1906–07—those of Stein, of himself, and of Salmon—what Picasso was doing was in one sense simply a brilliant extension of the tradition that we have chronicled: searching an unfamiliar vocabulary of seemingly non-mimetic form, he found a new and startling kind of mimesis. What Picasso found in his own notebooks wasn't a style so much as a way of proceeding, an instruction to look at stylized, exotic form and make it real. That instruction,

as we've seen again and again, that way of proceeding, is exactly what the caricature tradition has always insisted on—that process, that injunction is, in a sense, all that caricature is.

Yet Picasso's achievement is larger and more powerful because it involves more than the creation of a new subdialect. It involves uneasy alliances of existing idioms as well as surprising puns between them. For, once we have seen how much their structure depends on the kinds of things Picasso was already doing in his notebook jokes, the question still remains, Why aren't any of these pictures funny? The answer at one level is obvious: they don't *look* funny. The hulking monumental body of Gertrude Stein as she presses forward to the picture plane, like a child pressing its nose against a window; her set mouth and heavy, Michelangelesque hands—all of these elements are employed by Picasso to counterpoise the element of charged portraiture. The play between bravura likeness and monumental weight in the Stein portrait is matched in intensity by the tension between graphic simplicity and illusionistic lighting in the 1907 self-portrait. That picture draws on the "big-eyed" caricature style which had before been present only in Picasso's sketchbooks, now remade in the image of tribal art, but adds to it a sobering overlay of a carefully recorded screen of highlights and shadows, climaxing in the odd, bright white circle that rests in the artist's right eye.

It isn't, though, that these pictures are in any sense failed or tentative. They are authoritative reorchestrations of many different codes of likeness, and they remind us of how much our sense of the comic depends not on a fixed psychological structure, but on a mutable context of expectations. Almost everyone who has theorized about caricature, from Henri Bergson to Freud to Rudolf Arnheim to the contemporary cognitive psychologist David Perkins, has insisted that caricature is funny because it is in some sense "economical"; that its simplifications in some way satisfy the permanently tendentious organization of the mind. The gestalt psychologist may theorize that caricatures work because they represent an extreme, simple-to-grasp demonstration of the deviations from the norms of perception that make all expression possible;[48] the psychoanalyst may suggest that it works because "the claims of instinctual life are satisfied by its content, the objections of the superego by the manner of its disguise";[49] and the cognitive psychologist may suggest that caricature mirrors the schematized imagery of cognition.[50] But all of them agree that the caricature is, in some sense, parsimonious, primitive, elemental, a "saving of mental energy"; that the "mind's eye" in some sense already sees caricatures, prefers caricatures, and that the artist pleases the viewer by satisfying this preference. The artist overcharges his portrait so that the viewer doesn't have to overcharge his mind.

But of course most kinds of serious learning and serious art are, in this sense, "economical" too—they help us to organize seemingly unconnected concepts into a simpler pattern. What distinguishes jokes from other kinds of surprising structures—from scientific theories, for example—is that the jokes propose a manifestly false economy. For a joke or a picture to be funny, it has to propose a new way of organizing the world that is completely logical and at the same time obviously provisional. It isn't that the mind's eye sees caricatures. It's that the mind's eye can recognize in a caricature a process of simplification and tendentious classification similar to that which allows us to function in the world at all; only now the process is used not to posit an enduring, permanent category but instead to draw our attention to a peculiar structural resemblance between two unrelated things—between a pope and an insect, or a king and a pear, or an American writer and an Iberian mask. This coincidental likeness, for a moment, seems at once to parody all our fixed and "natural" categories and (in a way that can be maddening if you are the king who looks like the pear), for a little while, anyway, to take on some of their authority.[51]

The apparent "economy" of caricature had in this sense always depended not on its intrinsic structure but on its fixed place within the secure decorum of art. Here psychology, of whatever school, is subsumed in a history of social order—of prejudices. The basic equiv-

alence between what the caricaturist did and what the artist of the grand manner did had, after all, been apparent since the first appearance of the comic form—both kinds of work used a conventional set of formulae to "see the lasting truth beneath the surface of mere outward appearance," as Annibale Carracci put it, and in this sense the caricaturist's task was, as Annibale also said, candidly, "exactly the same as the classical artist's."[52] But before Picasso, one of those practices of stylization had always been designated as a norm, a true report about the world and the other, caricature, as an exception, an extreme case, a peculiar structural trick—a joke.

With Picasso's portrait of Gertrude Stein and with his own 1907 self-portrait, however, the decorum of norms and exceptions is not just stood on its head (that had been done before) but completely rearticulated, in a way that denies any secure sense of hierarchy, and therefore any simple, closed, response. By orchestrating a very complicated set of effects—by taking up totally unfamiliar stylizations, like those of "Iberian" art, that were exotic but also in some ways oddly classical; by infusing graphic caricatural elements into otherwise "painterly" pictures—Picasso showed that you could take up the strategies of caricature without being forced into the "marginal case" logic of humor. Are these faces or masks? "Platonic" truths about the sitters, or journalistic ones? Aggressive or generous gestures? Caricature had in the past really been a two-beat process: first, surprise at the strange equivalence, then reintegrating laughter as we put it in its provisional place—the strange equivalences discovered on the margins of art at once expanding our horizons and reaffirming the normality of the center. "Laughter," Bergson once wrote, "appears to stand in need of an echo....It can travel within as wide a circle as you please; the circle nonetheless remains a closed one."[53] For Picasso there is no fixed center; the circle never closes, and the second beat is never struck.

In the high Cubist portraits of the following years the dialogue of previously irreconcilable styles reaches a climax of poetic intensity. Picasso's ultimate achievement in the portraits of his high Analytic Cubist period is the fusion of the two seemingly irreconcilable portrait styles descended from the time of Leonardo. The portraits of 1906–08 involved the reuse of the staring, big-eyed style present in Picasso's early caricature; the language of simplification in the great high Cubist portraits, on the other hand, appropriately for its dandified milieu, involves instead an adaptation of the elegant, dots-and-dashes style of the Parisian caricatures.[54]

Yet the tiny set of physiognomic clues in each portrait is merged into an envelope of light which is at once beautifully specific—the silver and gray light of a Paris winter—and resonantly metaphysical. In the high Analytic Cubist portraits, and above all in the Kahnweiler portrait (fig. 73), the visual metaphor is much like that of Leonardo or Rembrandt, perceptual uncertainty made into a metaphor for the unresolvable mys-

73. **Pablo Picasso.** *Portrait of Daniel-Henry Kahnweiler*. 1910. Oil on canvas, 39½ × 28⅝″ (100.6 × 72.8 cm). The Art Institute of Chicago. Gift of Mrs. Gilbert W. Chapman in memory of Charles B. Goodspeed

74. **Kees van Dongen.** "Cocotte," from *L'Assiette au beurre*, October 26, 1901

75. **Juan Gris.** Cover of *L'Assiette au beurre*, May 29, 1909

tery of human personality. At the same time, these likenesses retain the self-conscious wit and compression of the caricature, the schematic likeness that recalls the mind's constant search for provisional order.

In the high Cubist portraits, Picasso combines the enigmatic poetry of the Rembrandtesque portrait with the epigrammatic precision of the caricature.

Picasso's revolution in face-making blurred forever

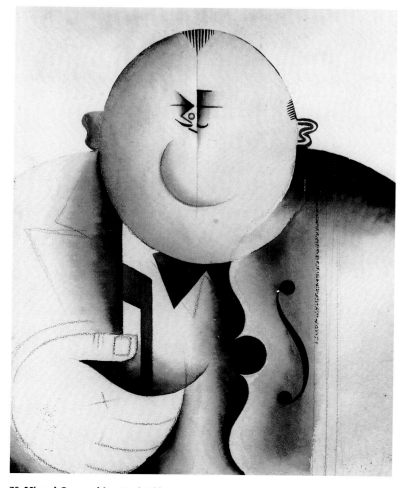

76. **Miguel Covarrubias.** *Paul Whiteman.* c.1924. Watercolor and charcoal on cut paper, 11½ × 9⅝" (29.2 × 24.4 cm). Prints and Photographs Division, Library of Congress, Washington, D.C. Gift of Caroline and Erwin Swann

the line between caricature and conventional portraiture. The most obvious evidence of the evaporation of this distinction becomes apparent in catalogues of Picasso's own work. Before 1907, "caricature" pages appear again and again in his notebooks, as a distinct, identifiable genre; after that, there is virtually not a single page in all the archives of the Musée Picasso in Paris that can be classified separately from the rest of Picasso's drawings as a caricature. The line between caricature and portrait has been so thoroughly annihilated that the distinction has become meaningless.

In the wake of Picasso's revolutionary realignment of face-making, a line of caricaturists emerged who now had a new license to present the imagery of the caricature journals as a form of vanguard art (fig. 74). Many of the second generation of Cubist artists, from Juan Gris (fig. 75) to Jules Pascin, who helped turn

77. Miguel Covarrubias. *Clark Gable vs. Edward, Prince of Wales.* **1932. Tempera on paper, 14 × 11" (35.6 × 27.9 cm). Iconography Collection, Harry Ransom Humanities Research Center, The University of Texas at Austin**

Cubism from a private, two-man code into a popular language, had received their training not in the halls of the École des Beaux-Arts but as caricaturists in the pages of *L'Assiette au beurre*.[55]

Other artists who remained within the world of the humor magazines took up the new language of caricature as it had been invented by Picasso. Perhaps the most gifted of these post-Cubist caricaturists was the Mexican-born Miguel Covarrubias. His work relied on reinterpreting faces into a system of interlocking planes (fig. 76, 77) that depended obviously and self-consciously on the style of Picasso's Cubist portraits. Covarrubias is the Gershwin to Picasso's Stravinsky, taking up new rhythms (whose not-so-distant origins lay in "low" art) and making them brightly syncopated. His skill as a caricaturist seems to have led him to an increasing fascination with a particular branch of art

history. He eventually gave up his career in New York to return to Mexico City—where he spent the rest of his life as the curator of the National Museum's Department of Primitive Art.[56]

Caricature died so that modern art might live. Just as it becomes impossible, after the work of 1908–10, to distinguish in Picasso's own work between "caricature" and high drawing, it soon became impossible to distinguish between modern art that self-consciously drew on the caricature tradition and modern art that just looked like other modern art. The conceptual leap that saw large-scale possibilities in the recycling of little jokes simply became part of the modern tradition; artists did it without thinking about where it came from.

Yet, as we have seen, the same process of rethinking the possibilities for individual jokes in generic form that had produced charged portraits had, since the first exhortations of the satiric tradition in the seventeenth century, produced other kinds of visual jokes and puns, too. Men remade in the shape of the emblems of their trade or preoccupation (a transformation that Picasso had only hinted at in the private drawing of Salmon), in the tradition of Arcimboldo and Braccelli; punning, "rebus" portraits in the tradition of Dantan—the tradition of the composite body was available to the modern imagination, too. The revolution in portraiture that Picasso began just by paying attention to his own notebooks also suggested other revolutions that might result from paying attention to the big, serious potentials latent in old, small jokes. After 1912, part of the creative logic of modern art involved taking a comic or satiric motif and using it in a new context of ideas and associations. If caricature had been born as a new way of looking at the grotesque, a vein of modern art was rooted in a new way of looking at caricature, in which distortion, stylization, and the marriage of the demonic and the near at hand were no longer seen as jokes but as mysterious, irrational visions. A tradition that passed from Baudelaire to Picasso and into Surrealism (like the parallel literary tradition that passed from Baudelaire to Kafka) transformed vulgar comedy by turning its vision from the surface absurdities of social life to the deeper irrationalities of death and desire.

Consider the history of one peculiar motif in the tradition of the composite body: the "body/face transformation." Vanguard art between the two world wars is full of such transformations, faces made in the shape of human bodies, or in the form of phalluses and vaginas. When we look at such transformations—at Picasso's head of Marie-Thérèse Walter, from 1932 (fig. 88), or at Magritte's *The Rape*—we seem to be seeing images that bypass the old order of art altogether to come into direct contact with the primal, pre-rational, symbolic vision of the unconscious. Yet although we might expect this motif to have a long history in sacred art—in Greek herms and "primitive" art—in fact it appears most often in a stereotyped kind of graffiti and in a rich, though narrow vein of the low tradition of

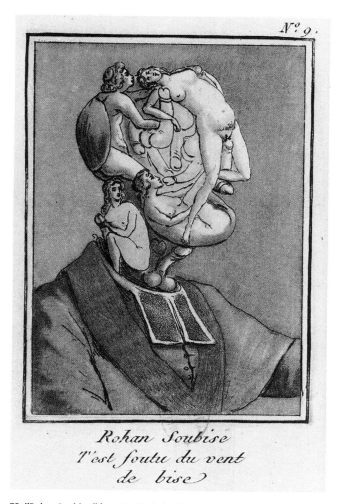

Rohan Soubise
T'est foutu du vent
de bise

78. "Rohan Soubise," from *Les Fouteries chantantes, ou les récréations priapi-ques des aristocrates en vie par la muse libertine* **(A Couillardinos, 1791)**

M. de Polignac. N.º 29.

Ah! ah! voila mon Portrait

79. "Ah! ah! voilà mon portrait," from *Les Fouteries chantantes*

weird, composite bodies. Surprisingly, the erotic extension of this transformation first appears in popular imagery around the time of the French Revolution.[57] In a set of remarkable images, from the time of the Revolution, an anonymous artist had joined satiric depiction of the circles of aristocratic and ecclesiastical power to obsessive, intricately wrought obscenity (figs. 78–80). A little later, such body/face transformations became protest art, as when a German artist named Johann Michael Voltz designed a grim protest caricature of Napoleon with his face composed of naked corpses (fig. 81).[58] This kind of metamorphosis had by then become a commonplace smutty joke of nineteenth-century French postcards.[59]

When similar imagery began to appear in vanguard art, it was apparent to some observers that these transformations had their origins in popular caricatural imagery. In the 1933 *Minotaure*, for instance, Paul Éluard reproduced old, pre–World War I comic postcards showing this kind of erotic transformation (fig. 82) precisely in order to show that naughty postcards might be the bearers of demonic visions; these images were, Éluard said, only "the small change of art and of poetry. But this small change sometimes gives an idea of gold."[60]

For Éluard, at least, the connection of these images to the repressed and neglected language of comic

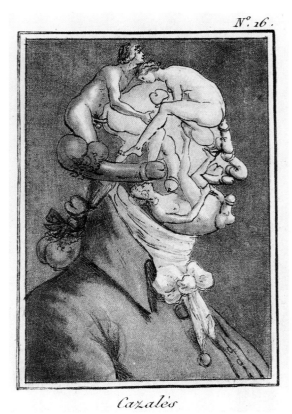

Cazalès

80. "Cazalès," from *Les Fouteries chantantes*

81. **Johann Michael Voltz.** *True Portrait of the Conqueror.* 1814. Engraving. Collection Arthur Brincombe, Exeter

drawings and smutty postcards was part of their radicalism. In these images, the social and revolutionary aspects of Surrealism are allied, the inward- and outward-turning sides come together. The repressed image of the psyche turns out to be the devalued coin of the social world.

In Surrealist pictures like Magritte's *The Rape* (fig. 5), or any number of early Dalís, however, the move from low to high involves only the mechanical reversal of the emotion that the motif is expected to evoke—dread and wonder instead of a nudge and a wink. These pictures are simply smutty postcards presented straight, without the need of a rationalization. The tradition that had begun with a mocking re-read of the otherworldly became otherworldly again through a solemn re-read of the satiric, and one may have the sense in these images of a simple change in decorum trying to do the work of original imagination.

More telling than these simple restatements of the body/face pun by Magritte and Dalí are the contemporary restrikes of the same tradition by Picasso and Brancusi. Although we are accustomed to seeing Brancusi only in terms of a search for pure essences, a move toward perfect surface and the ultimate reduction, nonetheless it was Brancusi who, in his pre—World War I sculpture, first made the conceptual leap which allowed a structure that had always before been confined to the most vulgar kind of humor to achieve the complexity of high art. From 1913 on, Brancusi took up the low tradition of dissolving a face into an object or body and showed how it could be associated with the perfect, streamlined forms of modern engineering. (Indeed, the same issue of *Minotaure* in which Éluard reproduced his obscene postcards includes an article by Maurice Raynal on the emancipation of sculpture, showing "how the plastic sensibility has finally been liberated by a sort of freedom that permits a lyricism of overflowing danger and necessity"[61]— and Raynal's article is accompanied by quotes from Brancusi, and photographs of his atelier.)

This Surrealist attempt to annex Brancusi to itself had its own politics. Nonetheless the sense that the polished surface of his art is the outward shell of a witty, multireferential internal life—that his work sits between Cycladic sculpture and a dirty joke—provides a real insight into the way Brancusi's art actually works. The quasi-theosophical search for the underlying geometric order of the universe is joined in Brancusi's work to a love of double and triple meanings, and it is this that makes him more than merely pious. It isn't that Brancusi's works in any sense look like caricature in any simple way—they don't—or that his formal language can be reduced to a tradition found on latrine walls and dirty postcards. It's that their aesthetic involves a new freedom, and invites a particular kind of punning scrutiny that had previously been allowed in art only when the image was clearly designated as a joke.

His first mature plastic statement, *The Kiss* (fig. 83), is, after all, a pun as direct and crude as anything in Dantan or Philipon: the chunky block bodies of the two fused lovers form into a single Cyclops face with an absurd Al Jolson smile. This simple body/face trans-

82. Postcards, from *Minotaure*, nos. 3, 4 (1933)

83. Constantin Brancusi. *The Kiss.* c. 1912. Limestone, 23 × 13 × 10″ (58.4 × 33 × 25.4 cm). Philadelphia Museum of Art. Louise and Walter Arensberg Collection

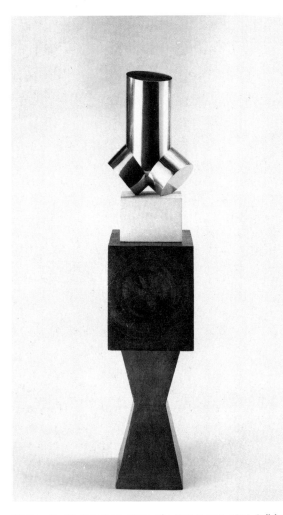

84. Constantin Brancusi. *Torso of a Young Man.* **1924. Polished bronze on stone and wood base, 18 × 11 × 7″ (45.7 × 27.9 × 17.8 cm). Hirshhorn Museum and Sculpture Garden, Smithsonian Institution, Washington, D.C. Gift of Joseph H. Hirshhorn**

formation is given new life and a touching naïveté in *The Kiss* because it is made part of a language of apparently resistant, folk-art block form. Like Picasso's *Portrait of Gertrude Stein,* Brancusi's *Kiss* joins archaic form to a caricatural transformation.

Brancusi's plastic simplifications depend on metaphoric complications, on precisely the invitation to "look into" that had been kept alive in the past by the tradition of comic imagery. When we look at an apparently "essential" Brancusi like the *Torso of a Young Man* or *The Beginning of the World* (figs. 84, 85), our response rests not on a passive acknowledgment of wholeness and finality, but on our creative ability to project into simplified form a whole tradition of illusion; the *Torso of a Young Man* is the stenographic form of Rubens, and depends for its power on a "conceptual set" which makes us ready to see as, rather than look at. In the *Princess X* (fig. 86), the elegant swan-necked girl of Brancusi's ideal doubles as a phal-

85. Constantin Brancusi. *The Beginning of the World.* **c. 1924. Bronze, 7½ × 11¼ × 6⅞″ (19 × 28.6 × 17.5 cm). Musée National d'Art Moderne, Centre Georges Pompidou, Paris. Bequest of the artist**

lus, and the image of a dream girl, a dirty joke, and a profound fertility symbol are all made inseparable aspects of a single streamlined form. Brancusi's repositories of polish and reduction are really echo chambers of multiple reference: the exotic and the near at hand, the conceptual and the accidental, the muse and Mlle Pogany (fig. 87), streamlined Bugattis and Cycladic sculpture, all brought together. His purity, his distilled platonic abstraction, rests on a deeper life of playful impurity beneath the perfect surface, the fetal heartbeat within the egg.

Brancusi elevated the low tradition in his search for a symbol of androgyny, fusing male and female into a single erotic hieroglyph: fertility as a pansexual fact. Yet even the *Princess X* may seem to have something chilly and deco about it; a touch of the erotic frigidaire. When Picasso took up an apparently similar body/face metamorphosis at the end of the 1920s, it expressed

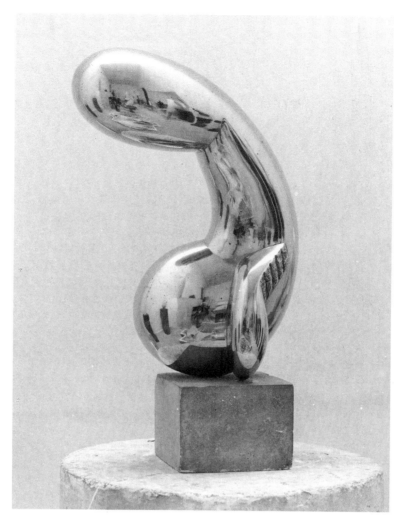

86. **Constantin Brancusi.** *Princess X.* 1916. Bronze, 22¼ × 16½ × 9½″ (56.5 × 42 × 24 cm). Musée National d'Art Moderne, Centre Georges Pompidou, Paris. Bequest of the artist

not a dream but an appetite, a direct fact of projected desire. Picasso's insistence on remaking the image of his mistress of the twenties and thirties, Marie-Thérèse Walter, has about it the spirit of Pygmalion in reverse, taking a real woman and forcing her back into an artwork. Where Brancusi fuses multiple levels of reference into a seamless form, Picasso uses the old joke as an image of sexual conquest. Picasso's fantastic metamorphoses are entirely narcissistic; his own erection projected onto his lover's body like an image on a screen, her body re-formed in the shape of his lust (figs. 88–90).

Where Brancusi's heads belong formally to the world of submarines and deco objects, Picasso's Boisgeloup heads are situated, at once parodically and caressingly, within the classical, Mediterranean tradition; surely Picasso, crowding his studio with these transformed phalluses, was thinking in part of the antique tradition of the herm. These are, in fact, herms for modern times, dedicated to the cult of the *folie à deux*, an Olympus populated by a single mutable goddess and scaled by one's self. As much as the contemporary Vollard Suite, these heads are invocations of the classical past. That connection, at once longing and mocking, provides the iconographic force of Picasso's helmeted warrior (fig. 91), who combines Etruscan

87. **Constantin Brancusi.** *Mlle Pogany.* 1913 (after a marble of 1912). Bronze, 17¼ × 8⅛ × 12″ (43.8 × 20.5 × 30.5 cm), including base. The Museum of Modern Art, New York. Acquired through the Lillie P. Bliss Bequest

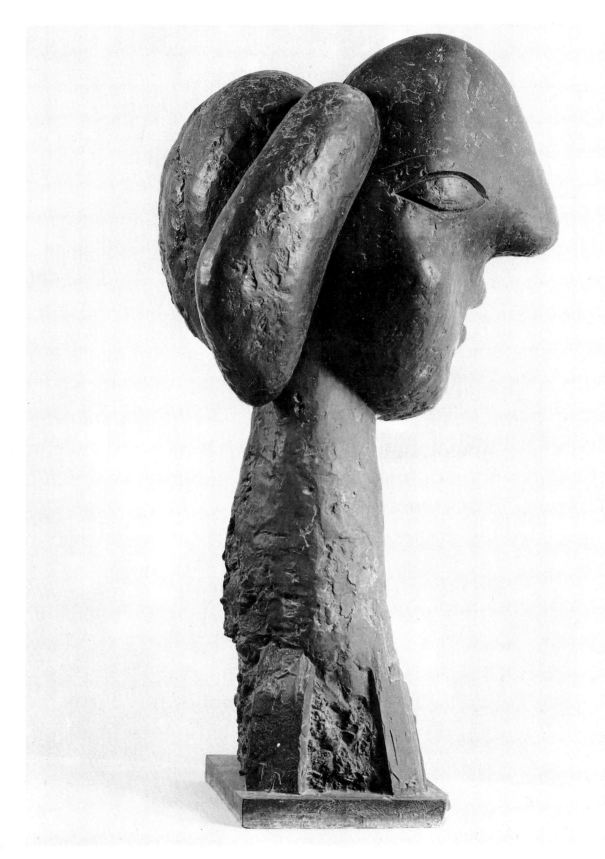

88. **Pablo Picasso.** *Head of a Woman (Marie-Thérèse Walter)*. 1932. Bronze, 50⅝ × 21½ × 24⅝″ (128.5 × 54.5 × 62.5 cm). Musée Picasso, Paris

89. **Pablo Picasso.** *Head of a Woman (Marie-Thérèse Walter).* 1932. Plaster, 52½ × 25⅝ × 28″ (133.4 × 65 × 71.1 cm). The Museum of Modern Art, New York. Gift of Jacqueline Picasso in honor of the Museum's continuous commitment to Pablo Picasso's art

élan and early Greek aplomb with erotic obscenity. The theme of metamorphosis is, of course, a classical one, the great Ovidian subject. Yet by taking up as the basis for a classical art the low, comic, anticlassical tradition of overloading double and triple and even quadruple meanings in a single form—by seeing in a girlfriend's face the possibility of a mushroom, a classical profile, an Etruscan warrior, and an erection—sexual metamorphosis becomes a human fact rather than a heightened process, psychology rather than myth.

There's no sense in which what Brancusi and Picasso are doing can be reduced to a satiric or comic tradition. But in these less immediately apparent cases, as much as in Picasso's earlier portraiture, the new language of modern art expanded by taking advantage of the expressive possibilities latent in a transformation previously restricted to the precincts of low humor. "But this small change sometimes gives an idea of gold." The specific precedents for Picasso's and Brancusi's sculpture all lie in low art, in graffiti, and in the developed comic language of the rebus and the punningly transformed body, of the kind one finds in Éluard's postcard collection. Picasso's and Brancusi's body/face transformations reclaim the Mediterranean tradition for us in the same way that Daumier had reclaimed it for his time: the recuperation of classical form takes

90. **Pablo Picasso.** *Bust of a Woman.* 1931. Bronze, 24⅝ × 11 × 16⅜″ (62.5 × 28 × 41.5 cm). Musée Picasso, Paris

91. Pablo Picasso. *Head of a Warrior.* 1933. Plaster, metal, and wood, 47½ × 9¾ × 27″ (120.7 × 24.9 × 68.8 cm). The Museum of Modern Art, New York. Gift of Jacqueline Picasso in honor of the Museum's continuous commitment to Pablo Picasso's art

place through its apparent parody. Though Brancusi seems to us to recapture the purity of Cycladic art, and Picasso to rejuvenate the tradition of arcadian pleasure, these ambitions were, after all, in themselves commonplaces of their time, and most often produced dead, surface eclecticism. The genius came in seeing that what had always before looked like the low alternative to classical purity could become the source of its renewal.

If it was still possible to remake tradition through a sculptural marriage of classical form and its parody, by the end of the 1930s the reimagining of the caricatural likeness had become so common that it had lost all power to disturb. The funny face had become simply the heraldic emblem of modernism. It required some great crisis to make a mixed-up face seem again like

something more than syncopated décor, and that was achieved just after World War II by Jean Dubuffet. Dubuffet's aggressive, graffiti-style caricatural portraits of 1946–47 (figs. 92–96) are in part caricature in the simplest sense, a mocking variant on the pantheons of artists that had become sober clichés of even "radical" French art, as in Surrealist group portraits. But Dubuffet's portraits manifest the revolt, and revulsion, of intellectuals: mental energy and will are now all that matter, and the body can (indeed, must, as a Savonarola-style demonstration of adherence to a new anti-faith) go to hell. His writers and intellectuals are pathetic monsters, their features reduced to pop-eyed scrawls, their aplomb prodded into jumping-jack spasms. Yet, since grotesque harshness and imbalanced disturbance are in Dubuffet's view tokens of authenticity, to be portrayed by him with scar-like

92. **Jean Dubuffet.** *Monsieur Dhotel.* 1947. Oil and sand on canvas, 46½ × 35⅛″ (118 × 89.1 cm). Collection Hans Thulin, Stockholm

contours and inept anatomy is, perversely, to be made glamorous. A rich and peculiar underlying conservatism can be found in Dubuffet's portraits, one that is expressed in their choice of subjects. Léautaud (fig. 97), for instance, was not an outsider of any kind. He was a theater critic who set himself against the dying traditions of the Comédie-Française and the seventeenth-century tragic tradition, to insist on the supreme value, for modernity, of farce, music hall, and boulevard comedy. Dubuffet's portraits, far from purposely lying outside the realm of cultural debate, choose up sides and manners from deep within it.[62]

Like Giacometti's gaunt walking figures, these portraits are, of course, self-conscious visual metaphors of Existentialist man. But if for Giacometti that condition was expressed in the play between leaden-footed movement and immense solitude, for Dubuffet the same angst could be captured through the play of the spastic figure within compressed space. His intellectuals are like pinned insects, leaping and writhing as they are pierced and labeled. Yet even these inadequate, absurd, incongruous leaps and claps and bounds have some baseline heroism about them: they are images (in every sense) of survival, even if they show the will reduced to a nervous spasm and the smile of reason reduced to a reflexive grimace.

Where Picasso had integrated caricatural style into

93. **Jean Dubuffet.** *Jules Supervielle, Large Myth Portrait (Supervielle, Large Banner Portrait).* 1947. Oil on canvas, 51½ × 38½″ (130.8 × 97.8 cm). The Art Institute of Chicago. Gift of Mr. and Mrs. Maurice E. Culberg

94. **Jean Dubuffet.** *Joë Bousquet in Bed.* 1947. Oil emulsion in water on canvas, 57⅝ × 44⅞″
(146.3 × 114 cm). The Museum of Modern Art, New York. Mrs. Simon Guggenheim Fund

poetic portraiture, and where the Surrealists had found in jokes the stuff of dreams, Dubuffet's portraits obstinately insist that caricatural wit (and the social life it belongs to) is itself a kind of mania. As much as in his transformation of the meaning of graffiti imagery in art, in these portraits Dubuffet was also out to change our sense of the role of wit in art. For Freud, jokes and dreams had been complementary "primary processes"; wit and dreams were parallel because both derived from the operation of unconscious associations and connections, though one had to contrast "wit as a consummately social product with dreams as a consummately asocial one."[63] The Surrealists thought that the consummately unsocial product was the thing to pay attention to, and they were interested in low jokes only in as much as they could be made to look like dreams. Dubuffet reversed this process. The line between constructive, healthily "socialized" outward life and dangerous (if arrestingly rich) mental life—the line that had in the past been the distinction between wit and dreams—was for Dubuffet an illusion. You didn't have to look past the caricature for the craziness; the caricature itself showed you all the craziness you needed to see. Look into the caricature, the

Surrealists had suggested, and you may see there a little piece of the intricate psyche of modern man; look into the psyche of postwar man, Dubuffet's portraits insist, and all that remains is a caricature. The change from what Picasso did with caricature to what Dubuffet does with it is, in a way, like the difference between James Joyce's and Samuel Beckett's reuse of low verbal comedy. In each case, the older artist finds in comic form—the caricature for Picasso, the pun for Joyce— the possibility of a kind of pregnant reduction that, by focusing down on what in the past had seemed merely coincidental resemblances of form or language, simultaneously opens his art to a dazzling multiplicity of reference. Graphic satire allows us to enter the mysteries of African art; Irish wordplay revives the Greek epic. For Dubuffet, however, as for Beckett or Antonin Artaud, comic form was made serious not by transforming it but by insisting on it: by making caricatural drawing and slapstick routines so intense and unrelenting that the emotion they provoked, from sheer overload, would spill back over into the grotesque.

Dubuffet's portraits show the last gasp of the power of caricature to create even a symbolic disturbance. At the same time as Dubuffet's portraits were being

95. **Jean Dubuffet**. *Dhotel Shaded with Apricot*. 1947. Oil on canvas, 45⅝ × 35″ (116 × 89). Musée National d'Art Moderne, Centre Georges Pompidou, Paris

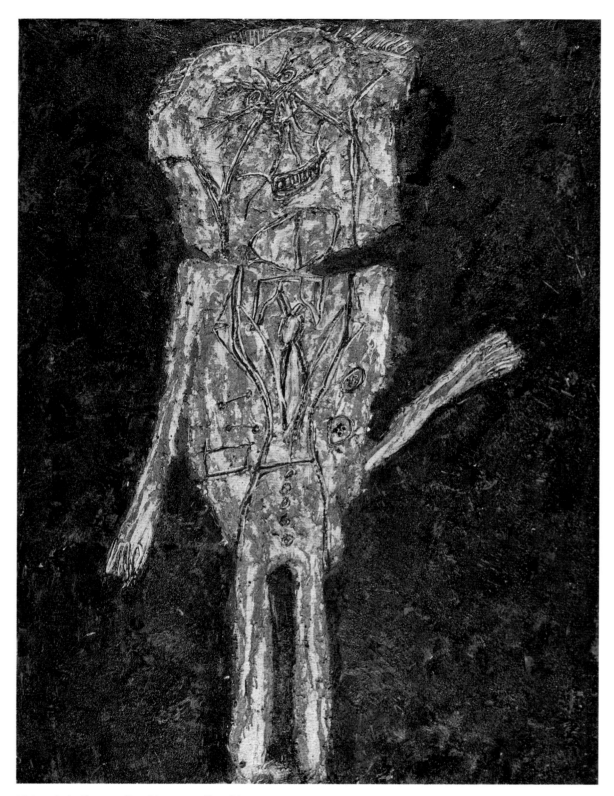

96. **Jean Dubuffet.** *Bertelé, Wildcat.* 1946. Oil emulsion on canvas, 51¼ × 38¼" (130 × 97 cm). Collection Stephen Hahn, New York

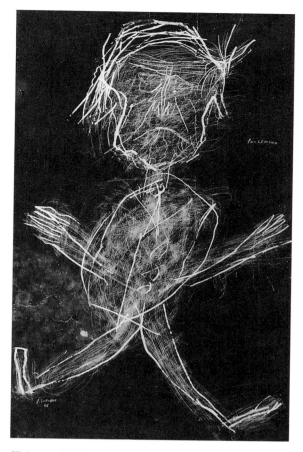

97. Jean Dubuffet. *Léautaud, White Scratchings.* 1946. Ink on paper, 19¾ × 12¼" (50 × 31 cm). Present whereabouts unknown

painted, in the aftermath of war, the popular cartoon shook off the last vestiges of its allegiance to the caricature tradition. Saul Steinberg and James Thurber—the one working from a surfeit of kitsch modernism, the other working "naïvely" from a comic tension between sophisticated mind and awkward hand—began to replace the old, mutable faces of Daumier with cool, unvarying comic masks. The new humor of the cartoon lay in watching unchanging masks confront the perplexities of modern urban life. Caricature became sophisticated again by returning to the purposefully stereotyped and repetitive language of the grotesque. If we look at an early Steinberg sheet of "caricature" heads, for instance (fig. 98), though it may seem at first to be a straightforward descendant of the old, crowded sheets that passed, as an improvisatory laboratory of form, from Agostino Carracci to Picasso, a closer look shows that where those drawings were about the power of small changes to create the illusion of individuality, Steinberg's heads are about the inability of cosmetic changes—the moustaches and inscriptions—to alter the essential monotony of modern types. Like the mock-italic inscriptions which accompany them, these heads provide the illusion of meaningful difference only to reveal an absolute sameness. They are finally as unvarying as the Gorgons of Greek art. Steinberg's heads close a cycle; caricature had begun by representing monsters as

98. Saul Steinberg. Page from an unpublished sketchbook. c. 1950. Collection the artist

99. Pablo Picasso. *Young Girl Seated.* 1970. Oil on plywood, 51¼ × 31⅝″ (130.3 × 80.3 cm). Musée Picasso, Paris

people, and ends by representing people as monsters: the gargoyles' revenge on Leonardo.

Kenneth Tynan wrote once that the central story of modern expression was the "steady annexation by comedy of territories that once belonged to the empire of tragedy."[64] The story of caricature and modern painting was an episode—in many ways, the very first chapter—in the story of how this tragic century has revolted against the old forms of tragedy, and reassembled new memorial styles from the language of incongruity, exaggeration, and extravagant conceit that once belonged to comedy. These annexations of tragedy by comedy have a familiar double movement: play, fantasy, and free invention enter high art, and at the same time the predictable order that once made the stable responses of comedy and tragedy possible ends. Without that fixed order—without gods or fates or moral principles or just an accepted decorum of style—we may seem to lose the possibility of a hierarchy by which art can be measured and judged.

But from Leonardo on, the tradition of caricature had always been to take the timeless and otherworldly and make it enter time; and in this way the comic tradition had always had implicit within it the beat of the most basic kind of human order—it had, muffled inside it, an immutable clock. Not just Leonardo's simple opposition of youth and age, but all the subsequent strange translations of real people into abstract form suggested a discrepancy between the ideals of invented order and the fact of human fragility. Perhaps turning the caricatural vision away from the ephemeral absurdities of social life, and returning it to the deeper absurdities of identity, desire, and mortality, allowed modern art to amplify that beat, and find in it a new kind of elegiac music.

Picasso ended his life as a caricaturist. After sixty years of extravagant rearrangements of faces, at the very end Picasso returned to his oldest manner. Instead of the wild and seemingly unconstrained reinterpretations of the human face that had, with increasing mannerism, dominated his painting for the previous quarter century, he began to make images of himself and his intimates that had a legible, pointed clarity, uncannily close to his first likenesses of all (fig. 99).[65]

In his last years, Picasso became obsessed with his own image as an old man. He painted his bald head and ravaged face, with a weak monkey jaw, and with age expressed as a rash, a disease, a spreading contagion (fig. 101). We have seen this face before; it is the face out of his early Barcelona sketchbooks, the faces of the old men whom Picasso mocked and into whose form he liked to change the faces of his dependent friends (fig. 100). The same sunken chest, the same incised lines cutting the face apart from mouth to chin, the same absurd slump, as though the old man's head were presented on the platter of his shoulders. Picasso's last self-portrait is a double image; it is both the truest of self-portraits, and the final presentation of a lifelong symbolic image. The old man had been a schema, a token for aging, and then he became Picasso himself. In his last self-portrait Picasso took the generic form of a derisive fantasy—invented to show the power of the young artist to impose the processes of age on his subjects, to make time itself subject to his will—and discovered that in it he had, long ago, been shown the image of his own last face.

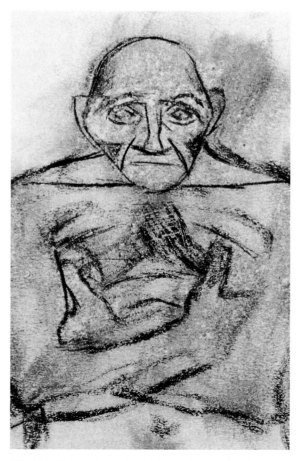

100. Pablo Picasso. *Josep Fontdevila* (detail). 1906. (See fig. 61)

101. **Pablo Picasso**. *Self-Portrait*. 1972. Crayon on paper, 25½ × 20″ (65.7 × 50.5 cm). Collection Fuji Television Gallery, Tokyo

1. **Ed Ruscha.** *OOF.* 1962. Oil on canvas, 71½ × 67″ (181.5 × 170.2 cm). The Museum of Modern Art, New York. Gift of Agnes Gund, the Louis and Bessie Adler Foundation, Inc., Robert and Meryl Meltzer, Jerry I. Speyer, Robert F. and Anna Marie Shapiro, Emily and Jerry Spiegel, an anonymous donor, and purchase

Open the funny pages of the New York newspapers in the last decade of the twentieth century and you see a coral reef of modernity, a slowly accumulated deposit of the century's styles and preoccupations and properties. Here is the art-deco duplex of a blonde flapper and her wistful husband; the Depression-era mansion of a wide-eyed street waif and her gleaming millionaire sugar daddy; the melodramatic lighting and hatchet-faced detectives of a forties film noir; the dusty expanses and two-story houses of a suburban tract development after World War II, with pensive children worrying on bare curbs. If the comics page is a mirror of modern life, it is a mirror of a curiously retentive kind, in which a reflection lingers in the glass long after its original has vanished from the world. Old comic strips, by now often in the hands of second- and even third-generation makers, have persisted long after their parallel forms in the other popular arts have become small-minority enthusiasms. It's as though Mack Sennett two-reelers and Warner Brothers crime melodramas and Paramount social comedies were still being turned out every day on a discreet back lot in Los Angeles. The comic strip has endured by inventing complete, self-sustaining secondary worlds, where evil and suffering are either banished altogether or else are represented in an unambiguously simplified and comprehensible form—so stylized and heightened that they transcend the moral muddle of caricature to attain the timeless clarity of myth or folk tale.

That satiric caricature might give birth to its own opposite, that from the stylizations of James Gillray a new form might emerge—warm where caricature is cold, and reconciling where caricature is divisive, and clear where caricature is ambivalent—is an old and surprisingly self-conscious dream. It begins not at the time of the newspaper barons, at the turn of the last century, but before then, in the Romantic dream of a rejuvenated folk culture. It is a dream that begins in the age of Goethe, who, as an old man in Weimar, worried about the disappearance of a collective popular culture in Europe.[1] To Goethe, it seemed that the old, unifying culture of folk songs and folk tales had been replaced by a culture of celebrity and contempt, produced by the spread of the English tradition of political caricature. Goethe thought that Napoleon, in particular, had been reduced by caricature into what we would think of now as the first truly Warholian celebrity. Political cartooning had made the Emperor familiar across Europe not as a distant, fixed figure of authority but as a household demon or household idol—the imp and the Emperor, Bonaparte and Boney; it had robbed him of his aura even as he was built up as a popular legend. What seemed particularly chilling about political caricature to Goethe was that it was so casually cruel, less apt to crusade for an ideal than to represent social life as a hysterical chorus of ambitions, lusts, and schemes. It wasn't that Goethe thought that caricature was too radical—the kind he objected to most was in its origins profoundly reactionary—but that it had no respect for anything. Caricature was the enemy of that sense of community, with people united by a love of something other than themselves, which the elderly Goethe had come to feel was the real unifying force of civil society. Could any new art form, Goethe wondered, emerge in the cosmopolitan world and become an effective cultural glue?

When he saw the picture novels of Rodolphe Töppfer, Goethe decided that one of the few things that might work to unify modern culture was the comic strip. The picture novels that Töppfer, a Swiss educator and art theorist, drew from 1815 to 1834 (figs. 2, 3) seemed to have begun an entirely new popular form by marrying the old folk form of the broadsheet picture story to the incandescent style of English caricature. As Friedrich Vischer, another German critic, said about Töppfer's hybrid form: "The malice, the bitterness associated with caricature is volatized in the light champagne of humor."[2] Goethe thought that Töppfer's invention might spread out from the small circle of initiates it had already charmed and become a new mode of cultural reconciliation—a popular form that could make a big, anonymous society feel like a family.

Caricature, as we have seen, takes place in time and, in a sense is *about* time; it offers a relentless series of mocking comparisons between grotesque, otherworldly form and ephemeral events and faces. The comic strip has, from its first appearance, been in many ways outside time. It has at moments fulfilled in low, commercial form Baudelaire's vision of an innocent or absolute comedy, constructing secondary worlds that return us to common feelings.

The comic strip's connection to a Romantic dream of a universal language may remind us that the comic strip is in many ways not a precursor of modern art but another kind of modern art, and shares many of the same motives, forms, and dreams. This is true in one straightforward sense: the comics have been the chosen medium of a handful of remarkable artists whose work, in its aggressive, individual stylization, its eccentric graphic simplification—its entrance into worlds of fantasy that are touched by an undertow of strangeness, disorder, or unease—seems to belong to the modern tradition. In the same way that our sense of the achievement of nineteenth-century art is incomplete without an appreciation of Honoré Daumier and J. J. Grandville, our sense of the achievement of twentieth-century art is incomplete without an appreciation of the work of Winsor McCay, George Herriman, and Robert Crumb.

But the relationship between the comics and modern art transcends the presence of a few outstanding figures who bridge both worlds, crucial and irreducible though that presence is. For the dream of a universal language of common form is the optimist's dream in modern art, checking and complementing the vision of an art that would testify to modernity's fragmentation, anxiety, and alienation. And just as the pessimist's vision drew powerfully on the reservoir of caricature, the optimist's vision has drawn regularly from the comic strip for jokes, puns, and inspiration.

In Ed Ruscha's *OOF*, for instance, the huge enlargement of a comic-strip exclamation (fig. 1) puns on the resemblance between the hard-edge geometric Minimalism of Kenneth Noland and Frank Stella—in 1962, the latest and most trumpeted installment of pure, high, immediately communicative abstraction—and the simplified, stereotyped properties of the comics. The enormous, graphic O's and angles of Ruscha's *OOF* are at once an affectionate parody of the avant-garde search for the clean, universal sign (touched in this case by a certain cool, West Coast bemusement at all the self-righteous "struggling" and huffing—the big, self-conscious "oofs"—that emanated from New York art as it arrived at this simple place) and a testament to the way that search can be seconded and enlivened by the forms of popular culture.

Yet the optimist's dream that art can be comprehensible and universal need not decay into the fatuous notion that everything imagined in it is for the best. Creating heightened and dramatically simplified worlds, the stylizations of the comic strip have provided a model for many kinds of mythmaking in modern art; the low, popular form of the comic strip has supplied for modern artists not only paradisiacal but also infernal imagery, pictures of heaven and hell alike. The comics have served sometimes as a meta-language of modernism, a fixed point of reference outside modern painting to which artists could refer in order to make puns and ironic jokes. But the comics have also served as a safe house for representational schemas and symbolic imagery, in which simplified illusionistic constructions and symbolic forms have been kept alive, to be called on again as needed. If, by offering an unpretentious, ready-made tradition of stylization, caricature offered a shortcut into abstraction, the comic strip eventually offered a shortcut back out again.

The story of caricature and modern art is a story of ambiguities recognized and embraced. The story of the comic strip and modern painting, however, is a story of convergent development rooted in a common ambition: to make art a serious game. If you stood back far enough from the history of modern visual expression, it might almost seem as if, sometime in the Romantic era, two similar dreams of a new, universal language for art came into existence, and each began to work out its own possibilities. The low, popular form of the comics tried to arrive at a unifying common language by telling stories; the high form of what would become modern art tried to get there by completely eliminating storytelling. These two tracks, however—narrative and antinarrative—turned out to be less like two streets that lead off from a fork in the road, in opposed directions, than like two paths that lead into a maze from opposite sides. For long periods the two parties of wayfarers on the paths are completely unaware of each other; then at times they become obsessed with the noises they can just make out coming from the other side of a hedge; and at times they stumble right over each other. When we look back at the history of these two journeys now, it may even seem that they have finally ended up, if not together at last in the center, then at least wandering around in more or less the same corner of the labyrinth.

When did the comics begin? Some scholars, hoping to attach the "low" twentieth-century commercial tradition to authentic folk traditions of protest and indignation, choose an early date, the Protestant propaganda panel-narrative of the 1490s, for example. Others settle for Töppfer's comic novels of the 1820s; still others, for Wilhelm Busch's *Max und Moritz* illustrated children's books of the late 1880s. Most often, historians of the American comic strip have insisted on a primary date of 1896, the year of the first appearance of Richard Outcault's Yellow Kid, when new color-printing technologies, unprecedentedly aggressive subscription wars between Hearst and Pulitzer, and a new, immense (and, it is often said, largely illiterate) urban audience all came together to turn a bit of European whimsy into an American mass phenomenon.[3]

Yet the comics emerged at the beginning of this century not as the efflorescence of one coherent popular tradition, but as bits and pieces of a lot of popular traditions. The art historian David Kunzle has shown that the comic strip—a burlesque told in narrative panels—so far from having been "invented" at the turn of the century in the United States, existed as a popular tradition throughout the nineteenth century in Europe, although it was not often clearly differentiated from a general soup of humorous illustration and caricature. What seems genuinely new in the most interesting early American comic strips, however, is not only their extension of this storytelling tradition but also their simultaneous popularization of a refined form of illustration.[4] The early comics brought together at least three separately nourished low manners: Töppfer's and Busch's literary experiments, the broadsheet folk tradi-

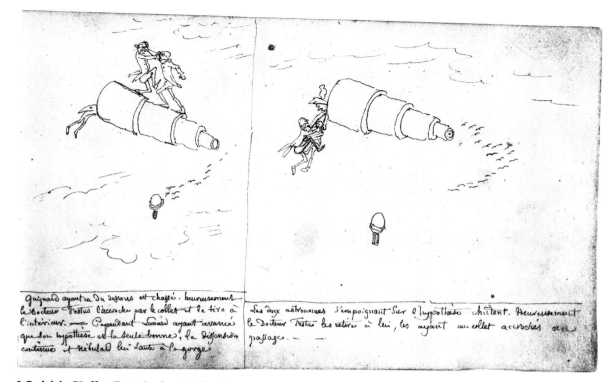

2. **Rodolphe Töpffer.** Illustration from Töpffer, *Voyages et aventures de Docteur Festus* (Geneva, 1829)

tion of narrative panels, and a sophisticated tradition of fantastic illustration—the tradition of "nonsense" in the Carrollian sense—that had been the companion and alternative to caricature throughout the nineteenth century.

From the point of view of style, therefore, and especially from the point of view of modernist style, a genesis moment for the transformation of caricature into comic strip occurred in 1834, when Jean-Ignace-Isidore Gérard, under the pen name J. J. Grandville, quit his job as the lead caricaturist of Philipon's *La Caricature* and began to draw picture stories that seemed to make no sense at all. Grandville had been the primary caricaturist for *La Caricature* throughout its first embattled years. He left it abruptly, perhaps because he was afraid of violence from Philipon's enemies. Yet

3. **Rodolphe Töpffer.** Illustration from *Voyages et aventures de Docteur Festus*

there must have been deeper currents at work, too; Grandville's portrait of his own political enemies, the print called *Oh! Les Vilaines Mouches!!* (fig. 4), has an edge of the maniacal, a desire not to mock or deflect his own demons but to insist on their hallucinatory power; it suggests an interest in pure nightmare form more fundamental to his character than mere political prudence alone could have produced.[5]

Whatever his motives, Grandville did not simply abandon one form; he fled to invent another. In a series of remarkable books begun in the 1830s, Grandville emancipated fantasy from folk art, and caricature from satire, and began to construct parallel universes out of parts of this one (figs. 5–7). His congresses of animals are based on an almost improbably rigorous core of empirical observation—he was, in his own way, as gifted an observer of animals as Audubon. Yet instead of merging his animal heads with human faces

4. **J. J. Grandville.** *Oh! Les Vilaines Mouches!!* 1831. Lithograph, 10⅝ × 14⅝" (27 × 37 cm). Bibliothèque Nationale, Paris

CONCERT A LA VAPEUR.

5. J. J. Grandville. "Concert à la vapeur," from Grandville, *Un Autre Monde* (Paris, 1844)

ville begins with pure grotesque, free and unhindered invention, and then leaves it to us to discover where and how it fits familiar experience. In Grandville, as later in Lewis Carroll, we miss the meaning entirely if we try to discover coded satire in individual scenes; the point instead is that the apparent absurdity of the scene or image will allow us later to recognize the equivalent absurdity of common life when we encounter it. (It works, too. Just as there is hardly any philosopher's conceit that cannot be summed up by a passage from *Alice's Adventures in Wonderland*, there is—as the editors of *The New York Review of Books* have shown for many years—hardly any social issue or intellectual debate of modern life so absurd that it cannot be evoked by a scene from Grandville's fantasies.)

In some demonologies of popular imagery this makes Grandville into a villain, and the tradition of fantastic illustration he began into one merely of escape; the larger transition from caricature to comic strip is therefore imagined simply as a transition away from courageous protest into craven collaboration, "harmless" whimsy. Yet this dismissive account oversimplifies a complicated art and a complicated larger historical

6. J. J. Grandville. "Au jardin des plantes," from *Un Autre Monde*

7. J. J. Grandville. "Les Grands et les petits," from *Un Autre Monde*

in a caricatural manner, or using them as symbolic images of virtues and vices, in the tradition that extends from the Greeks to Goya, Grandville displays them as autonomous, invented beings whose satiric commentary on our experience is both disturbingly plain and nightmarishly elliptical. What seemed haunting about Grandville's work even to his contemporaries was not the way it dramatized explicit allegorical ideas, but instead the way his fantastic bestiary reenacted the clamor and fretfulness and hysteria and intellectual preening of human life in the familiar world. It is satire that works, so to speak, from the top down. Where a Daumier caricature meditates on the relationship between temporal folly and timeless grotesque, Grand-

situation. The historical transformation of the tradition of caricatural satire into one of humor rooted in imaginative fantasy is part of a larger transformation in comic style in the 1840s, one that often led to more, not less, "radical" comedy.[6] The fantasies of Grandville, far from providing a mere template of meaninglessness, involved an imaginative interrogation of the logic of representation itself: not a flight into mere fantasy but an exploration of the dialogue between imagination and observation. Grandville's art became a kind of encyclopedia of alternative style, providing artists from Odilon Redon on with a repertoire of fantastic form—a vehicle of revolution which proved at least as potent for modern art as Daumier's noble humanism.[7]

8. **John Tenniel.** "The Jabberwock," from Lewis Carroll, *Through the Looking Glass* (London, 1871)

9. (Above) **Edouard Riou.** "Skeleton of the Mammoth," from Louis Figuier, *The World Before the Deluge* (London, 1865)

10. (Right) **George Du Maurier.** "A Little Christmas Dream," from *Punch*, 26 (December 1868)

A LITTLE CHRISTMAS DREAM.

If Grandville's fantasies are one source for the stylizations of the early American comic strip, John Tenniel's illustrations to *Alice's Adventures in Wonderland* and *Through the Looking Glass* are perhaps even more influential. Where caricature had always taken fantastic and unreal parts and molded them into a convincing whole, the new tradition of Tenniel or Grandville took fanatically literal drawing and used it to illustrate the extravagantly illogical. The terrifying Jabberwock, for instance (fig. 8), a variation on a George Du Maurier parody of an engraving in a natural-history book for children (figs. 9, 10), is a trophy of Victorian order turned into a monster of disorder.[8] Tenniel and Grandville together invented what is for us the way dreams look: rigorously logical in all their parts, but gibbering and disorienting as a whole.

The insertion of this Grandville/Tenniel tradition of fantastic illustration into the Töppfer and Busch tradition of satiric comic narrative was the special accomplishment and glory of the first genius of the modern comic strip, Winsor McCay. McCay made his early reputation as a virtuoso sign and décor painter in Cincinnati (he made a living for a while by a kind of vaudeville, painting outdoors high above a paying crowd).[9]

While McCay was performing in the Midwest, a new hybrid form was growing up on the two coasts of the United States. Popular myth sees the comics as the turn-of-the-century urban invention par excellence—an expression of the world created by the great immigrations that changed American cities, and New York in particular, before World War I. And this is not entirely false, since the first high period of the comics would center in New York. But the oddities of invention are irreducible, and the comics in fact began in San Francisco, where William Randolph Hearst, who had vague, happy, childhood memories of Wilhelm Busch's *Max und Moritz* picture stories (fig. 11), found in Jimmy Swinnerton an artist who he thought might do something similar in the Hearst papers.[10] As the new form prospered, it became a key element in the subscription wars between the Pulitzer and Hearst newspapers (which came to be called "yellow journalism" because of the presence of the amiable Yellow Kid in Richard Outcault's first comic strip [fig. 12]). Winsor

Das Pusterohr

Pop—from his hand the crust is flying,
Old Bartelmann of fright's near dying.

Und – witsch – getroffen ist die Brezen,
Herrn Bartelmann erfaßt Entsetzen.

Then at his eye Frank aimed a dart;
Which made it sorely ache and smart.

Und – witsch – jetzt trifft die Kugel gar
Das Aug', das sehr empfindlich war.

11. Wilhelm Busch. Illustrations from Busch, *Max und Moritz* (Munich, 1871)

THE OPEN-AIR SCHOOL IN HOGAN'S ALLEY.

12. *Hogan's Alley*, October 18, 1896. Drawn by George B. Luks, continuing the comic strip created by Richard Felton Outcault

McCay was soon called to New York, to draw cartoons for the *New York Herald*.

McCay was a provincial, and the feeling of an outsider lost in the delirious metropolis is the emotion at the heart of his sober poetic style. The real city he found was itself delirious: he went to work every day in a building on Herald Square modeled after the campanile in the Piazza San Marco, only radically stretched and flattened out; when he left to go home every night, he looked up at the little stone owls which bordered that same building's parapet. Their electric lightbulb eyes blinked on and off all night.

His provincial origins affected his style in other and more surprising ways, too. His early work in the Cincinnati newspapers had been single panels in the manner of Grandville and Tenniel, but he was rooted as well in the vaudeville house and world's fair (a world to which he dreamed of returning even after his fame was made as a comic-strip artist) and, perhaps most important, he had early on been exposed to an academic "high art" curriculum that, absorbed in debased form out in the provinces, he alone practiced in the metropolis with a stubborn, anachronistic faith. Although McCay's snaking, hypnotic line has often and rightly been compared to that of international art nouveau, what separates McCay's style from that of all the other gifted illustrators of his time was its use of art-nouveau linearism within insistently wooden, rigorous, and, by 1908, totally outdated perspective constructions. McCay's carefully elaborated architectural scenes are, in their origins, a bit of Ohio art school showing off that would have seemed embarrassingly backward to anyone at the *Yellow Book* or *Revue blanche*. (McCay had been taught true perspective at art school back

home, an experience so intense that years later, when he was the most famous cartoonist in America, he still incongruously insisted on "the cone, the sphere, the cylinder and the cube" as the basis of his art.)[11]

It is not much of an exaggeration to say that the whole aim of the kind of academic art instruction that shaped McCay's style was to teach you how not to draw comic strips; the student was taught a set of formulae, evolved over centuries, that would make a single memorable image convey all the narrative information you needed. Torn between the pleasures of the new storytelling form and the demand for overall, unified design, McCay's art brought high-art style down into the comic strip just as the comic strip was getting off the ground. The forward, storytelling propulsion of the comics was overthrown by McCay before those storytelling conventions had quite crystalized. He thought in terms of whole pages and overall designs, and, in order to achieve that kind of graphic unity, he had to inject an element of fantasy and dissociation that upset the momentum of all those little panels. Almost from its birth the comic strip started sending up its own conventions even as they were being set down.

Instead of the slapstick movement and slang energy most often associated with the early comic strip, McCay's spectacular style barely concealed an atmosphere of sexual disturbance. McCay's first, and in some ways best, strip was the *Dream of the Rarebit Fiend*, which ran in the *Herald* from 1904 to 1911. The *Dream* was a Bintel Brief of twentieth-century hysteria—an almanac of dreams sent in by McCay's readers. It is almost always structured by a tension between intricate patterning and incipient violence: ink blots

13. Winsor McCay. *Dream of the Rarebit Fiend*, April 7, 1907. © Ray Moniz

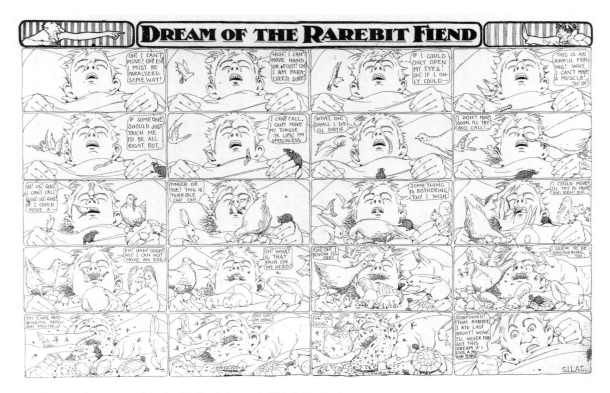

14. **Winsor McCay.** *Dream of the Rarebit Fiend,* August 4, 1907. © Ray Moniz

15. **Winsor McCay.** *Dream of the Rarebit Fiend,* August 14, 1908. © Ray Moniz

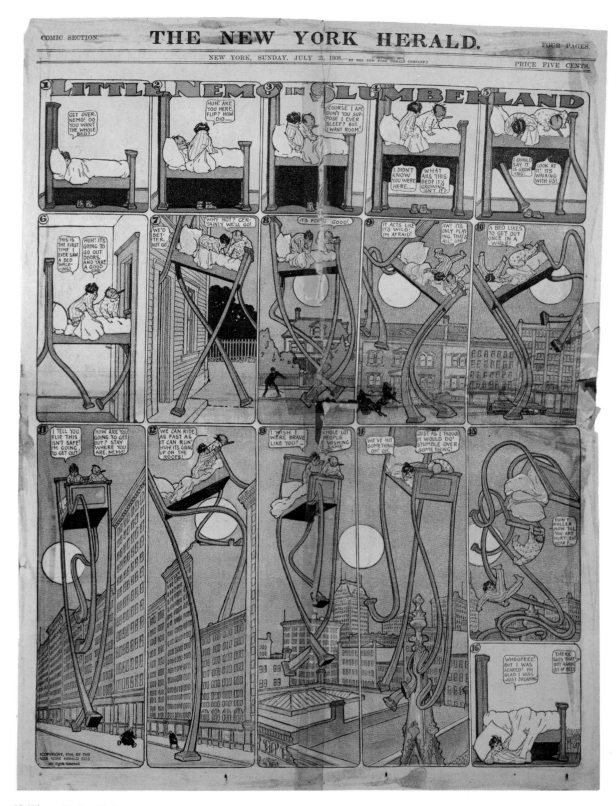

16. **Winsor McCay.** *Little Nemo in Slumberland,* July 26, 1908. © Ray Moniz

that eat the world, or men who burst into art-nouveau flames (figs. 13–15). Many of them are also explicitly and almost frighteningly erotic, for instance the *Dream* (fig. 14) in which a man fantasizes that small animals stuff themselves into his mouth as he sleeps.

In 1905, McCay began what is still one of the most completely successful works of pure fantasy in twentieth-century art—the comic strip *Little Nemo in Slumberland* (figs. 16–18). Many of McCay's devices, like

his love of stretching and pulling human form into elongated taffy (fig. 18), derive from Grandville. But on the whole, *Little Nemo* is obviously Carrollian. Its tone and mood are those of the trial of the Knave of Hearts or the banquet at which Alice is made a Queen: those climactic last chapters during which Alice totters on the edge of sleep, and the dream begins to collapse in on itself. (Tenniel's uncharacteristically animated illustrations for these chapters, drawings themselves in-

17. **Winsor McCay.** Original ink drawing for *Little Nemo in Slumberland*. c. 1908. Collection Mr. and Mrs. S. I. Newhouse, Jr. © Ray Moniz

spired by Grandville designs, supply an obvious model for many of McCay's *Little Nemo* drawings.) Whole blocks of tenements rise to life; a bed the size of the Woolworth Building races on rubber legs across a city at night; newsprint comes to life and yammers away at the characters. What is perhaps most striking about all of the extraordinary metamorphoses in *Little Nemo* is that they seem to just happen; the underlying logic of an alternative universe, which in the past had always been necessary to justify the fantastic and unreal, is largely left out. The usual slow-footed mechanisms of children's fantasy—the justifications and rationales—are eliminated; we are in the middle of the dream before we know we are dreaming.

Little Nemo's dreams, like those of the Rarebit Fiends, are insistently hostile and disturbing. Yet their threatening dislocations are oddly tranquilized both by the wedding-cake precision of the architecture and by the lulling tinted color that the *Herald*'s craftsmen added to McCay's drawings. The coloring in *Little Nemo*, for all it is made with the same Benday-dot technique later associated with the lurid polychromes of the superhero comic books, regularly achieved a delicate watercolor effect, like the hand-tinted color of early silent films. The overwhelming success of *Little Nemo* suggests that the translation of the old languages of aristocratic idyll into popular form—the sudden appearance of Beaux-Arts architectural phantasmagorias and

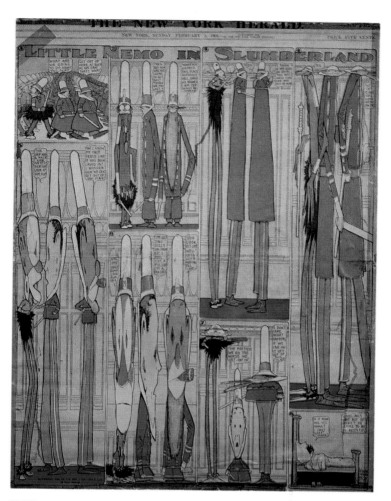

18. **Winsor McCay.** *Little Nemo in Slumberland,* February 2, 1908. © Ray Moniz

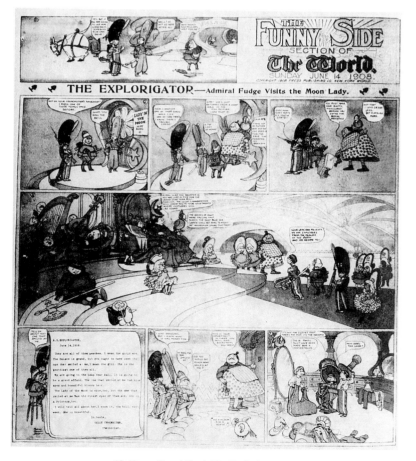

19. **Harry Grant Dart.** *The Explorigator,* June 21, 1908. © King Features Syndicate

delicate Watteau-like washes in the Pulitzer press— was at least as important to their success as the creation of a new visual slang. In McCay's hands the comics became, above all, spectacular.

After *Little Nemo*, McCay's story is tragic. He had drawn *Nemo* for only four years before he allowed himself to be lured away by the Hearst organization, whose peon he remained for the rest of his life. Hearst, who would later be capriciously generous in his stubborn patronage of George Herriman's unpopular *Krazy Kat*, was just as capriciously destructive to McCay, forcing him to give up comic strips for editorial cartooning and relentlessly, even sadistically, thwarting McCay's ambitions both to be an animator and to return to vaudeville.[12]

Comparing McCay to his immediate successors, the animator Chuck Jones once said that it was "as though the first creature to emerge from the primeval slime was Albert Einstein; and the second was an amoeba."[13] *Little Nemo* immediately inspired a huge host of imitations, like Harry Grant Dart's *Explorigator* (fig. 19),[14] none nearly so good as McCay's original but all accepting his premise that the comic strip was a theater of dissociated fantasy—a tradition that, passing on into worlds as different as Herriman's Coconino County and Alex Raymond's Planet Mongo, nonetheless made the comics, very much against the grain of the farcical and moralizing tradition of Busch and

20. **Tad.** Panels from *Silk Hat Harry's Divorce Suit,* 1910. © King Features Syndicate

21. **Cliff Sterrett.** Panels from *Polly and Her Pals,* November 28, 1926. © King Features Syndicate

22. **Cliff Sterrett.** Panels from *Polly and Her Pals,* June 2, 1927. © King Features Syndicate

23. **James Swinnerton.** Panels from *Little Jimmy,* December 11, 1904. © King Features Syndicate

Töpffer, a template of dreams for the modern imagination.

While McCay was conceiving the comic strip as a form of imaginative escape, several comic-strip artists grouped around the *New York Journal* were inventing a very different, slapstick comic-strip style of their own, a park-bench, hot-dog stand, cop-on-the-beat world that was the necessary counterpart to McCay's high style. The greatest of these artists, George Herriman, would become such a remarkable figure that it has been easy in the past to see him as the exclusive author of this second comic-strip style.[15] Yet in fact this is not

the case. The comic-strip world around 1913 divides into McCay and his lesser imitators in fantastic art, and a second group of almost interchangeably gifted comic-strip artists, Herriman among them, practicing a common style. This group included Bud Fisher (*Mutt and Jeff*), the sports cartoonist Thomas A. Dorgan, (called Tad [fig. 20]), Cliff Sterrett (*Polly and Her Pals* [figs. 21, 22]), Rube Goldberg (who began *Boob McNutt* in 1918), and Jimmy Swinnerton (*Little Jimmy* [fig. 23]).[16] Together, they invented the style that still seems to us generic, just what the comics look like.

What are the elements of that style? There is, first, a basic rearticulation of the standard anatomical distortion of nineteenth-century caricature drawing. Daumier's people have big heads and little, tapering bodies; the people of the early comic strip have little heads and big feet. The big heads of the caricature tradition had a simple purpose; they were the place where mocking portraiture happened. The bodies of the second comic-strip style, of Fisher's *Mutt* or Herriman's *Baron Bean*, are not the forms of men whose character is written on their faces; they suggest figures in a state of parodically exaggerated adulthood, possessed of a dignified self-importance constantly undercut by the world's indignities. They are drawn in a thin, nervous, agitated pen line—a world away from the greasy, accentuated curves that would later become the signature style of the comics, under the influence of Disney—and presented against backgrounds that suggest a condensed, poetic reduction of the lower-middle-class apartment, the racetrack, or the vaudeville stage. It is a style that accepts the conditions of mass reproduction as givens and then really uses them, instead of pretending that they don't exist. Where even Tenniel attempted to give his crosshatchings the appearance of rich, painterly chiaroscuro, the comic strip treats crosshatching as a symbolic shorthand. A quick tic-tac-toe scratched on the side of a face suggests at once stubble, shadow, and *sprezzatura* scribble.

Where did this style begin? The simplest and in some way the truest answer is: in the ballpark. Or, more precisely: on the sports page. Almost all the artists who belonged to the *Journal* group, including Goldberg, had begun as sports cartoonists, and their world is one immediately recognizable from the writing of Damon Runyon, Ring Lardner, and A. J. Liebling. The early comic-strip artists were also, like early ballplayers, the serfs of their owners. The cartoonist drew under contract and could not keep the copyright to his creation. To move from one paper to another was to give up one's signature strip; although artists could, and often did, attempt to re-create the strip in a slightly different form or under a slightly different title— McCay tried this after he moved to Hearst and began a self-plagiarizing strip called *In the Land of Wonderful Dreams*—the old strip would still be continued by another artist. (Bud Fisher, who suffered particularly from his inability to move to a new paper for more money, helped finish off this reserve clause in an incongruously epic legal battle over the rights to *Mutt and Jeff*.)[17] Despite all that, the world they lived in and imagined still communicates an almost paradisiacal sense of nascent possibility. The *Journal* cartoonists were conscious of themselves as an almost-brotherhood of almost-artists. Looking at photographs or comic drawings of the *Journal* ''bullpen'' before World War I, one com-

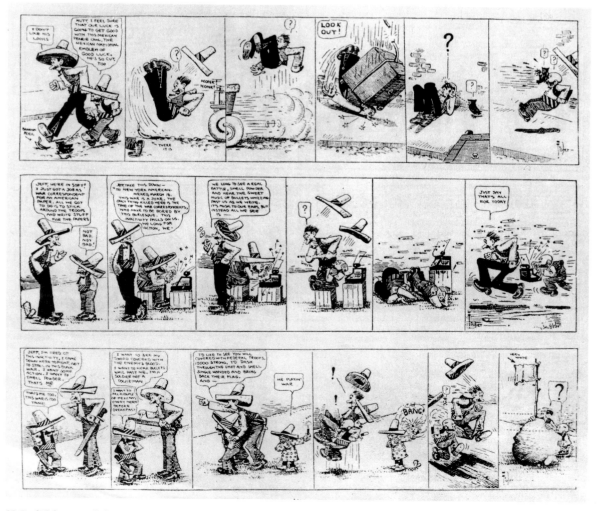

24. Bud Fisher. Panels from *Mutt and Jeff*, c. 1914. © H. C. Fisher

pares this circle immediately to the artists on the masthead of *La Caricature*. Where the generation of French artists almost a century before looked like a determined band of freedom fighters, keen-eyed and filled with rectitude, the comic-strip artists who clustered around the *Journal* seem suffused with the joy of city life. So far from suggesting that they saw themselves enslaved to a low world of illustration, their memoirs and occasional letters suggest an arcadian world of new popular leisure—the world of the ballpark, the movies, the musical comedy, the tabloid press—to which the cartoonist not only had entry, but in which he was the central, the all-purpose figure: a free man.

Bud Fisher, who invented *Mutt and Jeff*, and who began, like Herriman and Swinnerton, in San Francisco, is an exemplary figure of this generation. He came east, drew his comic strip, became enormously wealthy—a ladies', or anyway chorus girls', man—and by 1914 was hungry for a larger adventure. He ended up in Mexico with his friend John Wheeler, fighting alongside Pancho Villa. (Wheeler was the journalist who ghostwrote the first classic baseball book, *Pitching in a Pinch,* for Christy Mathewson.) The friendship between Villa and Fisher blossomed, and Fisher introduced Mutt and Jeff to Mexico, where they are shown fighting (poorly) as mercenaries (fig. 24). Fisher finally offered Villa a deal: if Villa would eventually hand over half of Mexico, Bud Fisher would use *Mutt and Jeff* to popularize Villa in America. Villa at least thought it over. As a grim gesture of good faith, he had a prisoner executed and gave Fisher the prisoner's ivory-handled pistol.[18] ("R. Mutt," partly after Fisher's creation, was of course the name that Marcel Duchamp signed on his *Fountain* in 1917. So a single orbit of the imagination gives us Duchamp, Pancho Villa, and *Mutt and Jeff*, all together—a modern historical romance waiting to be written.)

The comics on the one hand were practiced as a simple money-making activity, but on the other they could be perceived as the vessel of a new freedom, and this enduring ambiguity is beautifully embodied in the work and career of a single artist, the German-American cartoonist and painter Lyonel Feininger. Born in the United States (his father was a refugee from the revolution of 1848), Feininger lived in New York as a child. There, he absorbed a series of impressions of the burgeoning industrial landscape—images of bridges and viaducts, of the girders of the Third Avenue El, "extending as far as the eye could reach, downtown in a terrific row"—that remained the permanent skeleton of all his later luminous art. In 1887, only sixteen, he left for Hamburg, intending to study music, and later drifted into art school. He assimilated the styles of the more decorative advanced painting of the day, Whistler and art nouveau. At the same time, he quickly became a successful popular artist, working at once for the German caricature journals, as a political satirist, and for various American magazines as an illustrator of children's stories—practicing simulta-

neously, and as a happy personal accident, the two European traditions that were already, across the ocean, combining in the new American form of the comic strip.

In 1906, a representative of the *Chicago Tribune* came to Germany searching for cartoonists able to adapt their style to the demands of the new comic strips, and discovered Feininger. Agreeing to try to draw a comic strip in the American style, Feininger insisted on remaining in Paris, where he had by then

25. **Lyonel Feininger.** *The Kin-der-Kids' Narrow Escape from Auntie JimJam,* September 2, 1906. Newsprint halftone, 23⅜ × 17¹³/₁₆" (59.4 × 45.3 cm). The Museum of Modern Art, New York. Gift of the artist

gone to live, while mailing in his cartoons to his publishers. Within a few months he had begun to produce two comic strips for the American papers: *The Kin-der-Kids* (fig. 25), a competitive response to Rudolf Dirk's immensely successful *Katzenjammer Kids* (which had in turn originally been inspired by Busch's demonic children), and *Wee Willie Winkie*, a comic whose interest depended on the stately animation of landscape and the metamorphoses of dead objects—an obvious, though inspired, response to McCay. Feininger drew both of these comic strips in a studio on the boulevard Raspail, all the while simultaneously absorbing, and sending back in simplified and slightly deflected form, the burgeoning manners of Cézannist faceting and

26. **Lyonel Feininger.** *Uprising.* 1910. Oil on canvas, 41⅛ × 37⅝″ (104.4 × 95.4 cm). The Museum of Modern Art, New York. Gift of Julia Feininger

Fauvist simplification—the look of pop culture in America daily being remade from within the citadel of the avant-garde in Europe.

Drawing comic strips released Feininger's own high style. He had always dreamed of an art of "pure humor," untraditional nonsense expressed in a personal language. Before he began *The Kin-der-Kids* and *Wee Willie Winkie,* however, his imagination had been forced to choose between either the standard "pointed" gag cartoons of the caricature journals, or the sensitive, vague art of the *fin de siècle.* In his comic strips, with their mix of gothic angularity and American machine-age poetry—half Hansel and Gretel, half Rube Goldberg—Feininger found his own language for the first time. What Feininger called "crystallization," a kind of simplified conceptual drawing in which figures could have the immediate clarity of cheap signboards or of the figures in shooting galleries, was fully achieved for the first time in his comics, and quickly rebounded into his paintings. In a picture like the *Uprising* (fig. 26) of 1910, characters who possess the marionette-like articulation and jaunty, heavy-footed angularity of his comic-strip characters are painted with a lurid coloristic intensity, and shown as participants in some fantastic Middle-European, festive, an-

archist apocalypse. Fauvist hedonism meets Futurist millennialism through the mediation of the comic strip. In this picture, revolution is imagined as a comic subject—as a carnival. Feininger recognized that he had found this imagery and this joy only through his work as a popular cartoonist, writing to a friend that "I was invariably berated and threatened with loss of position for the very traits which make me an artist of original power."[19]

Similarly, we know that Picasso adored the early comics—especially *The Katzenjammer Kids* and Swinnerton's *Little Jimmy*—and though there may be some relation between the simplified outline drawing of Synthetic Cubism and the style of the early comics, we need not insist on a formal affinity in order to detect the affinity of spirit. The comic strip, like silent comedy, was seen as something not just unthreatening to vanguard values but as a pleasing and unpretentious embodiment of those values, sharing the spirit of *blague*—of mischief and metaphysics combined—that was the guiding principle of the Cubist revolution.

When art in the later teens and twenties began to include images taken from the comics, it was informed by this sense of the comic strip as the popular embodiment of avant-garde values. When Stuart Davis, for in-

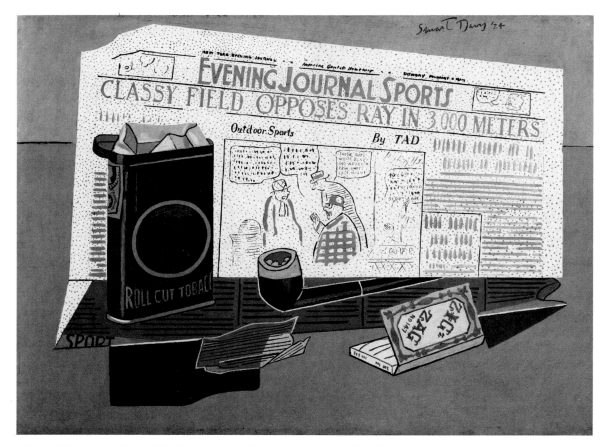

27. **Stuart Davis.** *Lucky Strike.* 1924. Oil on paperboard, 18 × 24″ (45.6 × 60.9 cm). Hirshhorn Museum and Sculpture Garden, Smithsonian Institution, Washington, D.C. Museum purchase

stance, included one of Tad's comic strips in his *Lucky Strike* (fig. 27), for instance, he did it in the same spirit in which Léger drew images of Charles Chaplin—as a devotional icon of the democratic spectacle. The comics played the same role for Davis that cabaret culture had played for Braque and Picasso: at once a bit of fresh popular lingo and also a reservoir of stylization. With their hard, declarative drawing and direct, slangy address, the comics fulfilled Davis's dream of an art made exclusively from a counterpoint of urban dialects.

This strain in Davis's painting was given systematic expression in one of the most original critical essays of the twenties, Gilbert Seldes's *Seven Lively Arts*.[20] *Il faut d'être de son temps*, and the time for Seldes was one not of a cult of images that had to be collected in secret and displayed in private, but of joyful common spectacle, to which the highbrow critic could nod his own slightly bemused assent. And of all the popular artists of his time, two stood out for Seldes above all the others as heroes, and even saints of a sort: Chaplin and George Herriman.

Alone among comic-strip artists, George Herriman has never lacked for admirers.[21] From the first appearance of his comic strip *Krazy Kat* before World War I, it was widely recognized that Herriman had achieved something at once entrancing and uncannily modernist, with a deep affinity to the spirit and form of vanguard art. Herriman has been for so long the single okay figure among comic-strip artists—the figure, like Cha-

plin or Duke Ellington in their realms, whose apparent atypicality made him acceptable—that comic-strip historians today are occasionally inclined to debunk him. It's certainly true that Herriman's exceptional gifts would not have been apparent to anyone who was looking at the comics in 1910, before *Krazy Kat*: Fisher is funnier, Goldberg stranger, Tad a more vigorous draftsman. Herriman is rooted in the common style of his generation—but once Herriman had shifted his characters outdoors, and fused the quick slapstick style of his friends with the kind of large-scale fantasy inspired by McCay, something amazing happened: in his own small realm, Herriman played a crucial part in this century's emancipation of the tradition of the sublime landscape from the decorum of high seriousness.

Born in New Orleans in 1880, Herriman began drawing comics in San Francisco, where he first made roustabout picaresque comics in the manner of Bud Fisher, and soon thereafter began a much more original bestiary strip, *Gooseberry Sprig*, in which some of the characters and themes of *Krazy Kat* were introduced.[22] Herriman arrived in New York from the West Coast in 1907, and his first comic strip for the *Journal* was *The Family Upstairs*, the tale of the monomaniacal attempts of a New York family, the Dingbats, to somehow obtain a glimpse of the bohemian family that lives one flight above them. Perhaps the most beautiful and original thing about *The Family Upstairs* (fig. 28) is Herriman's drawing of the Dingbats' apartment, a spare world of white walls, geometric moldings, bare hanging bulbs, and gridded windows—the desert of the

28. George Herriman. Panels from *The Family Upstairs*, November 22, 1910

lower-middle-class apartment, whose emptiness becomes a screen for paranoia. Soon Herriman added another secondary comic strip to the main story (a common device at the time; most of Rube Goldberg's most famous works, the mechanical contraptions, were introduced as sidebars to less memorable "continuity" strips—that is, strips which told a story that unfolded over weeks or even months). One of these sidebars to the Dingbat family involved the adventures of a neurotically inverted cat and mouse: the mouse chased the cat. Before long they had become more interesting than their human neighbors, and Herriman decided to make a strip for them alone.

Sometime around 1910, Herriman had visited Monument Valley, in Arizona, with its sublime western landscape of jagged rock and limitless horizons. In its combination of geometry and whimsy, it seemed made for the artist's newly evolved style—God's answer to the Dingbats' apartment. The reductive urban slang of right angles and emptied-out shallow space could be perfectly adapted to this otherworldly terrain, where nature appeared to have been shaped by the acts of an immense, eccentric sculptor. Herriman loved the long expanse of mesa, the lunar crags and neolithic needles, as well as the art of the Zuni and Hopi who lived in the valley, and whose geometrized textiles

seemed to him already a stylization of the landscape. Herriman moved the cat and mouse out of the Dingbats' apartment into the enchanted mesa of Monument Valley and began the strip we know now as *Krazy Kat* (figs. 29–36). (It was never really popular. For a long time, in fact, its Sunday page appeared only in one American paper—the remote *Seattle Sun Times* —and then only at the insistence of Hearst himself, to whose gloomy and elephantine imagination it had a peculiar appeal.)

The tension between city and country, between urban rhythm and the Arcadian subject, is central to *Krazy Kat*. Herriman's landscapes (figs. 29, 30, 32–34, 36), with their constant ambiguity about what in the scene is natural and what manmade, seem to mediate between Rockefeller Center and Arizona. In the same way, the pidgin that all of the animals speak is an urban melting-pot pidgin. The dialect is not really a dialect joke; like Chico Marx's "Italian," it floats free from any ethnic origin.

The essential, endlessly repeated and just as endlessly varied story of *Krazy Kat* involves a three-way dance between Krazy, Ignatz, and the dog called Offissa Pupp. It is a little bit like what would have happened had there never been a Fall, and Adam and Eve (poetically represented in their presexual state as the sexually

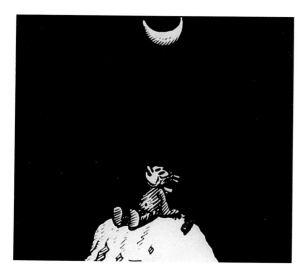

29. George Herriman. Panel from *Krazy Kat*, August 19, 1917.
© King Features Syndicate

30. George Herriman. Panel from *Krazy Kat*, August 14, 1918.
© King Features Syndicate

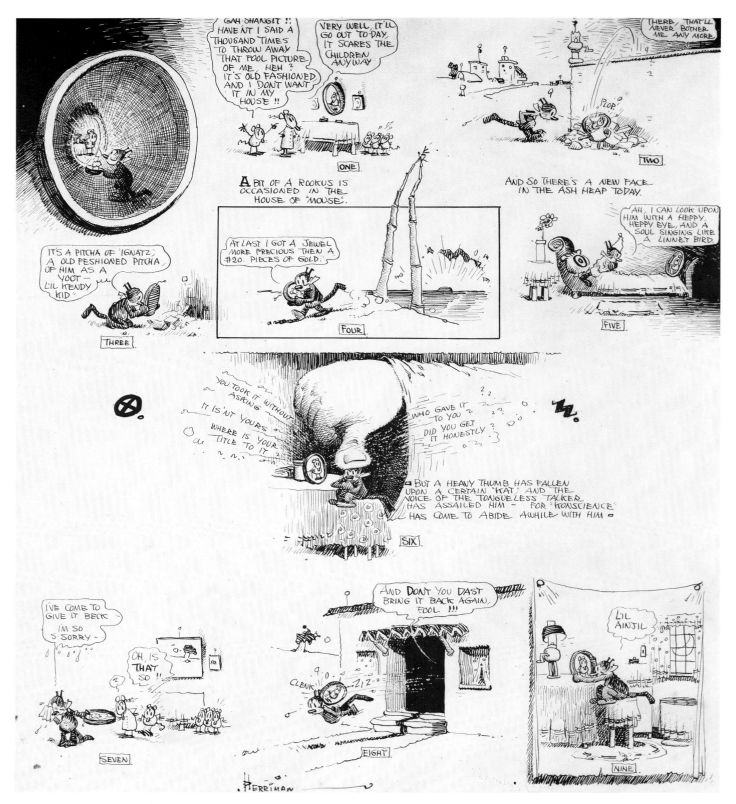

31. **George Herriman**. Original ink drawing for *Krazy Kat*. n.d. © King Features Syndicate

32. **George Herriman.** Original ink and colored pencil drawing for *Krazy Kat*. n.d. © King Features Syndicate

33. George Herriman. Panels from *Krazy Kat,* January 20, 1918. © King Features Syndicate

double Krazy), the serpent (Ignatz), and the Archangel Michael (Offissa Pupp) had been left alone in Paradise. Ignatz, who came out of Herriman's pen as a malignant little tangle of barbed wire, with the gaunt form and gimlet eyes of a sewer rat, isn't "mischievous" like his cousin, Mickey. Ignatz is wicked. He embodies every cruel and destructive human impulse, and his obsessive and unmotivated anger finds its outlet in his desire to throw bricks at the dreaming and innocent Krazy—who chooses to see Ignatz's relentless nastiness as an expression of love. Herriman's recurrent image of the instant after Krazy has been hit by Ignatz's brick (fig. 34) has the symmetry of a photograph of a subatomic collision: at the same moment as the brick bounces harmlessly off Krazy's head at one angle, a little heart, symbolizing Krazy's love for Ignatz, shoots off at a right angle—a complementary particle produced by the balanced moral physics of Herriman's world.

If Ignatz's brick represents evil, in its original state, as pure energy, then Offissa Pupp represents Law as pure form. Offissa Pupp, who ends almost every strip by throwing Ignatz into a little one-mouse jail, really has no need to enforce the law: Krazy likes being hit by bricks and Ignatz likes throwing them. Offissa Pupp's

obligation is to the abstract concept of justice as a pleasing formal arrangement: he puts Ignatz in jail for aesthetic reasons. (Offissa Pupp loves Krazy himself, but his allegiance to the web of order in his world prevents him from ever declaring his feelings.)

Krazy Kat is an imaginary vision of a perfectly happy and harmonious place. As much as any artifact of the twentieth century, it seems to have achieved the status of the joyful unifying popular comedy that criticism struggles to name—the form that Baudelaire, looking at E. T. A. Hoffmann, called "absolute" comedy; that Auden, looking at P. G. Wodehouse, called "Edenic comedy";[23] and that the Russian literary historian Mikhaïl Bakhtin, looking at Rabelais, called "carnival comedy."[24] It is arcadia without nostalgia; the visual language in Herriman looks "modern" in a way that, say, McCay's and Fisher's invented worlds do not. Yet mutual incomprehension between high and low still afflicts discussion of Herriman's place as a modern artist. Just as the high tradition either excludes Herriman, or sees him as a peculiar special case, the admirers of the low tradition treat the provisional categories of art history as though they were timeless descriptive terms. So, for instance, a recent admirer of Herriman's could say, loftily, that though Herriman uses "Surrealist devices," he is not a Surrealist,[25] when the point of course is that Herriman's style was fully evolved before Surrealism existed, and that it is closer to the truth to say Surrealism employed some of Herriman's devices. The problematic affinity can't be wished away by taking it out of history.

When we talk about surreal elements in *Krazy Kat,* we don't mean that the landscape looks strange or that the action is incongruous; it is something much more specific than that. Herriman responds to the same mixture of places, myths, and ambitions that would move Surrealism properly so called a decade after Herriman began his art: the same fascination with aboriginal art, the same love of anthropomorphic bestiaries, the same love for desert landscape. If we search for a real visual parallel that unites *Krazy Kat* and European

34. George Herriman. Panel from *Krazy Kat,* October 6, 1940. © King Features Syndicate

35. George Herriman. Original ink drawing for *Krazy Kat*. n.d. Collection Mr. and Mrs. S. I. Newhouse, Jr.

Surrealism, however, it can be found in some of Miró's paintings of the mid-1920s. In Miró's *Dog Barking at the Moon* (fig. 37), or his *Harlequin's Carnival*, or *Landscape with Rooster* (fig. 38), or *Dialogue of Insects* (fig. 43), there is a positive affinity with Herriman's comic strip, rooted in a shared and previously unknown system of form: an imaginary anthropomorphic bestiary, drawn with dancing grace and wiry life, poetically juxtaposed against an infinite and numinous landscape. Like Herriman, Miró places his animal characters against a limitless space. It is not the uneasy void of de Chirico or Tanguy, or the barren plain of Dalí, but an expanse that suggests tranquil, oceanic stillness. Like Herriman's strips, Miró's paintings of the mid-twenties are shaped by the play between terse indoor and expansive outdoor form. *The Harlequin's Carnival* takes place in a stripped-down indoor space (the insects, Miró said, should seem to have crawled out of the cracks in the plaster)[26] that is the analogue and starting point for the endless imaginary dream space of the *Dog Barking at the Moon*. The squiggled needle and monoliths glimpsed in Miró's paintings could have come right out of a *Krazy* Sunday page (fig. 36), while Miró's soaring ladders have their counterpart in Herriman's great stone fingers. Both devices suggest an enchanted universe where heaven and earth still adjoin, like tenement apartments connected by a fire escape. Even Miró's most succinct statement of his artistic ends and means could easily have come from Herriman: "In my pictures, there are tiny forms in vast empty spaces. Empty space, empty horizons, empty plains, everything that is stripped has always impressed me."[27]

36. **George Herriman.** *Krazy Kat,* April 11, 1943. © King Features Syndicate

37. **Joan Miró.** *Dog Barking at the Moon.* 1926. Oil on canvas, 28⅞ × 36½" (73.4 × 92.7 cm). Philadelphia Museum of Art. A. E. Gallatin Collection

What has the Kat staring at the stars to do with the dog barking at the moon? One answer is nothing. Such affinities, we are told, wrench imagery out of its social context and create false resemblances based only on superficial matches between essentially different art-making activities. Yet a look-alike this complex and singular is as meaningful for the history of visual expression as a similarly far-reaching analogy of form is to natural history. An assemblage of styles and imagery that had never been seen before suddenly appears in two different places at the same moment in the history of Western art; whether we believe that art is only an epiphenomenon of a material foundation, or that it is a transcendent product of uniquely gifted individuals, this homology needs to be explained. If we insist on seeing art only as a thing evolved in an environment, we would still have to cut off the boundaries of that environment in an arbitrary and irrational way in order to avoid looking at this resemblance, and thinking about what it says about the visual culture of the

twentieth century. But *how* to look at it?

The problem moves toward a simple, positive resolution if we begin to look in detail at the source of this affinity. Not only is the resemblance highly specific and local—not Surrealism but Miró—it can also be traced to a single moment, and even a single sketchbook, from the winter of 1923–24. Here we see the origins of the language of the *Dog* and the *Rooster*. These drawings are full of references to popular form: drawings divided into panels, figures whose exclamations float above them, all assembled from a mélange of Cubist puns, Catalan ornament, and popular imagery (figs. 39–42, 45). In a study for what would eventually become the painting called *The Somersault* (figs. 44, 45), the little kinetic stick figures declare "Ah!!" and "Oooh!," while a newspaper headed JOUR materializes beside them; Cubist and comic-strip conventions are set free from their original moorings into an expanse of fantasy. The emblematic Cubist JOU is treated throughout this sketchbook by Miró as a pure universal excla-

38. Joan Miró. *Landscape with Rooster.* **1927. Oil on canvas, 51⅛ × 76¾″ (129.6 × 195 cm). Collection Stephen Hahn, New York**

mation, not something broken off from a headline but something floating free as an integral universal motto.

Using this new style which mixed popular, vanguard, and folk form, Miró eventually drew a first study for a painting of a dog barking at the moon (fig. 39). In the original drawing, both dog and moon have dialogue balloons rising from their mouths. "Boub, boub," barks the dog. "*Je m'en fous tu sais,*" the moon replies ("I don't give a damn, you know"). Miró said that he was "making a sort of comic strip."[28]

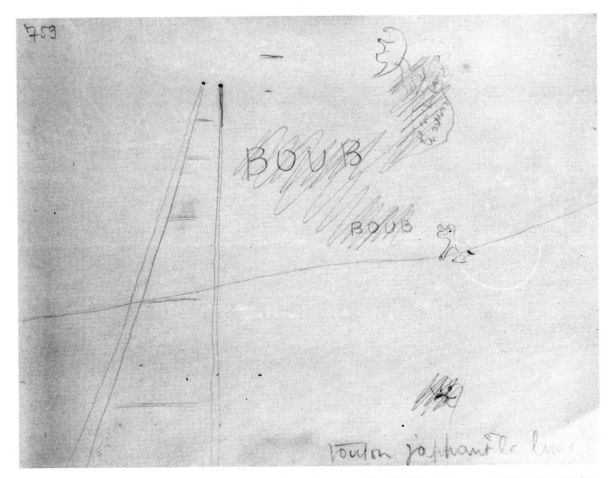

39. Joan Miró. Study for *Dog Barking at the Moon.* **1926. Graphite pencil on paper, 5⅞ × 7⅜″ (14.9 × 18.6 cm). Fundació Joan Miró, Barcelona. Gift of the artist, 1976**

40. (Above left) Joan Miró. Studies for *Terra llaurada* and *Pastoral*, with other studies. 1923–24. Graphite pencil on paper, 6½ × 7½" (16.5 × 19.1 cm). Fundació Joan Miró, Barcelona. Gift of the artist, 1976

41. (Above) Joan Miró. Study for a composition. 1924. Graphite pencil on paper, 6½ × 7½" (16.5 × 19.1 cm). Fundació Joan Miró, Barcelona. Gift of the artist, 1976

42. (Left) Joan Miró. Study for *Dialogue of Insects*. 1924–25. Graphite pencil on paper, 6½ × 7½" (16.5 × 19.1 cm). Fundació Joan Miró, Barcelona. Gift of the artist, 1976

The discovery of a positive, inarguable relationship between *Dog* and *Kat* opens as much as it resolves. When Miró said that he was "making a sort of comic strip," could he have meant that he wanted it to look like a Herriman? For there are no other comic strips of the time, in Europe or America, in which this assem-

43. Joan Miró. *Dialogue of Insects.* 1924–25. Oil on canvas, 25⅝ × 36¼" (65 × 92 cm). Collection Berggruen, Geneva

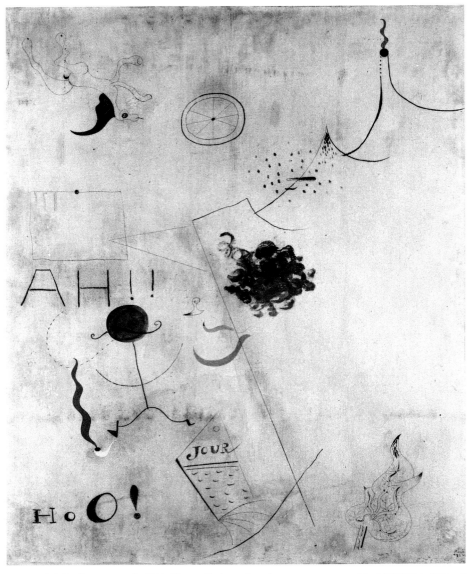

44. Joan Miró. *The Somersault.* 1924. Oil, pencil, charcoal, and tempera on canvas, 36 × 28½″ (91.5 × 72.3 cm). Yale University Art Gallery, New Haven, Connecticut. Gift of Collection Société Anonyme

45. Joan Miró. Study for *The Somersault.* 1924. Graphite pencil on paper, 7½ × 6½″ (19.1 × 16.5 cm). Fundació Joan Miró, Barcelona. Gift of the artist, 1976

blage of styles occurs. But even if we didn't have positive evidence about the relationship between these two styles, what would remain striking is the way that Herriman and Miró turn to similar sources to make something new.

It's not just that a comic strip can be like a Miró, it's that a Miró is, as he declared, a little like a comic strip. Both Miró and Herriman were in revolt against the idea of the sublime landscape as an icon of solemnity; both sought to make instead a landscape that was musical and free. Both Herriman and Miró wanted to draw sublime landscapes that would be an uncanny delight to look at, and this unpretentious ambition was more revolutionary than it may sound. In literature, of course, as Baudelaire had recognized, the comic and pastoral traditions, the traditions of farce and of the landscape of pleasure, had often been spliced together, from the Forest of Arden to Dingley Dell. But the comic tradition in Western art before 1900 is almost exclusively satiric, the tradition of caricature—of "significant" comedy. The pastoral, on the other hand— the landscape of pleasure we find from Giorgione to

Seurat—is essentially serious.

One explanation of this oddity was offered by Johan Huizinga in his profound essay *Homo Ludens*.[29] Huizinga was the first to notice the absence of a tradition of festive or Edenic or pastoral comedy in the plastic arts, and believed that this had happened because they had been denied, in their cultural infancy, the gift of high-spirited improvisation basic to music, drama, dance, and poetry. He wrote: "The very fact of their being bound to matter and to the limitations of form inherent in it is enough to forbid [the visual arts] absolutely free play and deny them that flight into the ethereal spaces open to music and poetry. . . . However much the plastic artist may be possessed by his creative impulse he has to work like a craftsman, serious and intent . . . where there is no visible action, there can be no play."[30]

The dream of play is one that is deeply embodied in all of this century's art, and we are, of course, familiar with the various attempts to gain the possibility of free play for painting and drawing. One way, of course, is to cut the knot and make "visible action" the whole subject of the painting. Yet another way to fly into "ethereal spaces" involves not the splatter and splash of paint, but the creation of interrupted stories, through narratives that bear no moral or allegorical freight beyond their own implied joy in action.

The elements that Miró assembled from the peripheral traditions at hand to fulfill this ambition were in many ways the same as those that had been cobbled together to make *Krazy Kat*. For Miró and Herriman alike, originality lay in taking already existing idioms, popular and peripheral—the anthropomorphic bestiary of Grandville, the zigzag rhythm of folk art—and putting them together in a new way. The two lines of descent in the history of fantastic illustration, flowing from Grandville on the one hand and Redon on the other, at this moment move together again. Miró and Herriman are not twin expressions of the zeitgeist but common inventors, drawing on and transforming common sources. Splicing together odd and previously unattached traditions, Miró was primed to recognize in a new popular contraption an assemblage of styles similar to his own; what he was doing already looked sort of like a comic strip. In this sense, Herriman isn't a wistful imitator of Miró, or an accidental look-alike. Nor is Miró a mere appropriator of Herriman's low art. Their relation isn't like that of the dog to the moon, aspiring to a distant place, but like that among the insects in the dialogue, reveling amiably in a common condition.

If the comic strip in the twenties could be a partner in absurdist comedy and poetic nocturne, from Seldes's and Davis's streetwise art to Miró's and Herriman's dream worlds, in another set of circumstances the heightened symbolic language of the low form could produce infernal imagery, too. The language of the early comic strip assisted Picasso in making the two most important images of suffering of pre–World War

46. Pablo Picasso. *Dream and Lie of Franco.* 1937. Etching and aquatint, 12½ × 16⅝″ (31.7 × 42.3 cm). The Museum of Modern Art, New York. Purchase Fund

47. Pablo Picasso. *Horse's Head* (study for *Guernica*). 1937. Graphite and gouache on paper, 11½ × 9⅛″ (29 × 23.1 cm). Cason del Buen Retira, Museo del Prado, Madrid

48. René Dubosc. "Le Petit Chaperon rouge," in *L'Humanité*, January 9, 1937

49. José Robledano. "El suero maravilloso," in *Infancia*, April 2, 1911

the *Dream and Lie* has a source in Catalan folk narratives. Yet the *Dream and Lie* seems haunted, too, even more than Miró's comic imagery, by the tradition of the strange, indigenous Catalan comics. With the spread of the comics before World War I, Catalan artists had begun to draw their own responses to the strips emerging from America, ranging from crude imitations of *Little Nemo* (fig. 49) to much more peculiar local inventions, where the comic-strip style was pursued with a deliberate primitivism more aggressive than found anywhere else in Europe—a world away from the vaudeville jauntiness of their American models.[33] The scrawled, child-like figures and empty, cursive outlines of these images seem to have affected Picasso more deeply than the suave crosshatchings of the American comics.

But an even more telling source for *Dream and Lie of Franco* can be found in the wealth of propaganda comic strips that are one of the most peculiar artifacts of the Spanish Civil War (figs. 50–52). Produced by both sides in the conflict, they are shaped by a coalition between knockabout parodic comedy and tragic subject. If their taste for popular sources is similar, the difference between what the two greatest Spanish masters of the last two centuries made of popular "cartoon" imagery is in its way exemplary of the difference between what caricature offered to the nineteenth century and what the comic strip has offered to the twentieth. Goya loved political caricature because in it he found a fully developed language of anticlassi-

II art: *Guernica* and *Dream and Lie of Franco*.

Miró made his comic-strip images in an atmosphere of paradisiacal possibility; when Picasso, his fellow Catalan, who shared his love for the comics, turned to the comics ten years later, it was in a world gone mad. The genesis of *Guernica*, as the art historian Phyllis Tuchman has shown, involved Picasso's assimilation and transformation of imagery and style taken from anti-fascist cartooning in the popular Parisian press (figs. 47, 48).[31] (The analogy often drawn between the Picasso of *Guernica* and Goya runs deep, for Goya too had used the popular imagery of atrocity, and of crude caricature during the Napoleonic period, as the armature for his *Disasters of War*.)[32]

The panel story of the *Dream and Lie of Franco* is a kind of comic strip, too (fig. 46); the parody adventures of an anti-superhero, the grotesque polyp Franco. In its squared-off panels and symmetrical layout,

cal form—a way of imagining horror that passed beyond the rhetorical clichés of the classical battle, and pointed at a new kind of truth. Popular imagery offered him the mold for an almost unbelievably horrific truth. If Goya found in caricature a way of making the horrors of war look more immediate, Picasso found in the stylizations of the comic strips a myth-like shapeliness that was still outside the domain of ''art.'' Goya found in the cartoon a way past the received rhetoric

50. **Altimara.** *Auca del moro feixista.* 1937

51. **Juez.** *Auca del Treball a Catalunya.* 1937

of war; Picasso found in the comic strip a way of stylizing horror without aestheticizing it.

By the middle of the 1930s, much of the energy in the comics had passed from the comic strip to its stepchild, the comic book.[34] Although publishers had often previously assembled popular strips into independent collections, the comic book as an independent form is generally thought to begin with what remains its most famous example: Siegel and Shuster's *Superman* (fig. 53). At once too crude and too urgent for the urbane newspaper pages, *Superman* established a new genre, the superhero, and pointed the way toward the emancipation of comic-strip style from humor, or to put it another way, its degradation into illustration.[35] This was a process already under way in the comic-strip pages, with the work of ''adventure'' strip artists like Alex Raymond (*Flash Gordon*) and Hal Foster, who drew *Tarzan*. But in these instances, the relationship of the adventure and ''serious'' comic strips to traditions of magazine illustration was much more straightforward. Hal Foster is essentially a descendant of Howard Pyle. The low-rent, underbelly quality of early comic

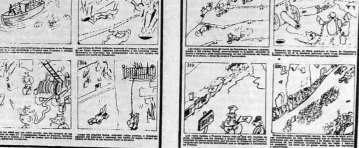

52. **Artist unknown.** *Historia del movimiento nacional,* May 2, 1937

53. **Joe Shuster**. Panel from "Superman," in *Action Comics*, 1 (June 1938). © D.C. Comics

books from the thirties makes them much more peculiar and much rawer.

Comic strips, like the movies, were a public and ceremonial form. They were part of the larger experience of the newspaper, integrated into a ribbon of wars and sports and society. They had a place in a hierarchy. A comic book, on the other hand, was something you had to walk into a store and buy; it was in its very nature outside parental control—and it had overtones, always, of the secretive, the menacing, and the faintly masturbatory. That familiar scene of late twentieth-century life—the twelve-year-old raptly absorbed in some pop-culture narcotic—first appeared with the comic book. The comic book presupposed, as a condition for its existence, the fragmentation of the genuinely mass or folk audience that had embraced the comic strip.

As the comics were transformed from an after-dinner to an after-school medium, their makers came to have a very different place on the totem pole of popular entertainment. The difference in social status and apparent self-esteem between the generation of Fisher and Herriman and the generation of Siegel and Shuster is like the difference between the experience of Chaplin or Keaton and that of Abbott and Costello. Fisher and Tad and Herriman and Goldberg were gents, popular figures, men about town who had a lot of money and a surprising social cachet. But Siegel and Shuster, even after their success, remained Depression-era drudges, working for ten dollars a strip, their copyright long since sold away. The comic strips had been the court jesters in the empires of Hearst and Pulitzer; the comic book was the pornography of the prepubescent. The comic book was typically put out by a marginal publisher, and never entirely escaped a depressing air of the illicit, of life lived at the baseboards of culture. Within the seemingly unvariegated world of cartooning, a hierarchy almost as strict as that of the museum set in; the comic strip passed down stylized form, and the comic book vulgarized it in a way that had a compelling rawness.

The first *Batman* strips of Robert Kane, for instance, obviously derive from the wonderfully mannered black-and-white stenography of Chester Gould's *Dick Tracy* (figs. 54, 55).[36] But where *Dick Tracy* was always drawn with a residue of irony, *Batman* had the sincere

self-absorption of adolescent fantasy. The comic-strip artists on the whole had contempt for the comic-book artists; and the comic-book artists themselves wished they were doing something else. The comic strip, as Seldes had recognized, was a genuinely innovative form; the comic book was increasingly a pendant, even a parasitical, form, feeding, above all, on the movies, the undisputed dominant form of American popular entertainment. Once, the traffic between the comics and the movies had run both ways, so that the first steps in the art of animation were made by Winsor McCay, and the narrative structure of the early two-reeler absorbed something from *Mutt and Jeff* and *Krazy Kat*. By the 1930s, the traffic ran largely in one direction, from the movies down into the comic book. Disney's triumphs as an animator had, on the whole, a disastrous effect on the popular cartoon, making the impersonal Disney house-style—bright colors, infantile features, thick, accentuated curves—the dominant style of cartoons, comic strips, and comic books alike (fig. 56).[37]

If this dependency reduced comic books to a minor-league mass entertainment, the comic books at this moment also began to include a surreptitious element of the grotesque, a crude, exhausted simplicity of style, that began to have a power of its own. A kind of double helix of development takes place in the comic book for the next twenty years, and each strand played a role in modern painting. The comic book evolved a narrowly stereotyped vocabulary to represent heightened states of heroism and romantic ardor, and at the same time it began to take up taboo areas of lurid horror and crude humor. Both these models—popular drama stylized to an almost Kabuki-like extreme on the one hand, and cartoon style turning in on itself in an extreme of mordant, self-annihilating grotesquerie on the other—would have profound effects on what happened in modern painting. The same Edenic and infernal possibilities that Miró and Picasso drew from popular imagery would continue, but with the difference that one could no longer take up comic style without a guilty or defensive knowledge of its degeneration into kitsch.

By the 1940s the comics had begun to be seen not as the vital bearer of democratic promise but as a virus of leveling decay. Clement Greenberg's "Avant-Garde

54. Robert Kane. Panel from "The Batman," in *Detective Comics*, 27 (May 1939). © D.C. Comics

55. Chester Gould. Panels from *Dick Tracy*, September 16, 1944. © Tribune Company Syndicate

and Kitsch''[38] includes the comics, without comment or argument, as one of the obvious sources of mass-cult banality. In some cases, this new rejection of the comics involved simple amnesia about the past enthusiasm; in other cases, it involved a larger self-conscious

56. Poster for Walt Disney's *Wild Waves*. 1929. **Ub Iwerks**, artist.
© Walt Disney Productions

sense of decline. The twenties, the heroic age of the comics, came to seem to some American intellectuals of the forties—to James Agee, Manny Farber, and Otis Ferguson, for instance—the last golden period of what was then called "folk art," that is, unpolluted pop culture. Greenberg's attack on kitsch was the battle hymn of abstraction. His reduction of the complex dialogue between modern art and popular styles into a story of simple threatening contamination, though undertaken largely in ignorance of the way that modernist history had really happened, was designed to establish the principle that real art had to have no imagery at all.

When the comic book began to return to modern art, at the end of the 1940s, its meanings had altered. The intense personal styles of the generation of Herriman and Tad had either been remade into a melodramatic, cinematic style, most notably by Milton Caniff in *Terry and the Pirates* (fig. 57), or else been dissipated into a common schlock style. Comic-book imagery was valuable to art now not as a passport into another world but as a *lingua franca* of clichés, one-dimensional types: the Superhero, the Lovelorn Girl, the Teenager. The comics became to postwar imagery what the headline had been to Cubist collage—a neutral, found, public code that could be kidnapped and "turned."

Perhaps not surprisingly, it was the greatest connoisseur of detritus that the century had produced, Kurt Schwitters, who was the very first to recognize this new possibility. Schwitters saw that if the comics had become a form of kitsch, they had also become a form

57. **Milton Caniff.** Panels from *Terry and the Pirates,* 1940. © Tribune Company Syndicate

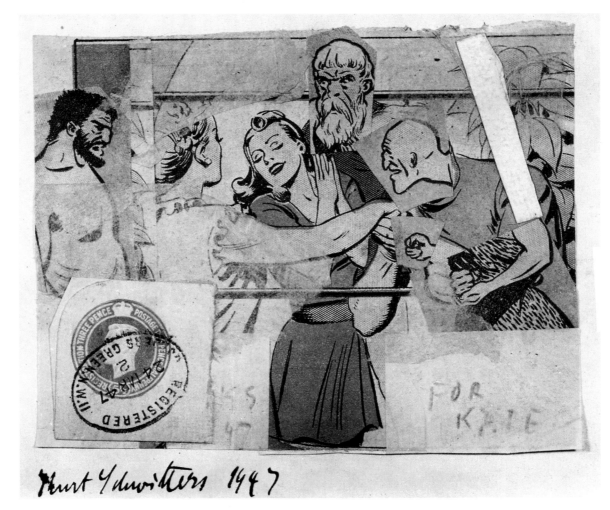

58. **Kurt Schwitters.** Untitled (For Kate). 1947. Collage, 4⅛ × 5⅛" (10 × 13 cm). Private collection

of Merz—one more element in the common language of modern life that could be woven into the artist's enveloping nest. In a 1947 collage (fig. 58), Schwitters uncannily anticipates the comic-book art of the next decade. The prewar collages of Schwitters had conveyed the darkling melancholy of decaying Middle Europe, structured by an uneasy truce between the last remnants of the confident nineteenth century and the austere utopian geometry of modern style. In a single collage one has a sense both of the little café and the alarming newspaper read inside it, the hard edges of modern events and the soft, surrounding upholstery of European culture. But in 1947, the elements of Merz are no longer little snippets from an economy of scarcity, nuggets of information and records of commerce tidily saved like cigarette butts; they are now big chunks of bright fatuous color, a souvenir from the land of the lotus-eaters.

For the rest of the century the comics as a subject for art would remain inseparable from the matter of America. Seen from a distance especially, the comics, good, bad, and indifferent, were an emblem of the triumph of American popular culture, a flood of songs and rhythms and bright images that was to the American empire what hot water had been to the Roman. By the middle of the 1950s, this triumphant (or devouring) pop culture had become, by attraction and repulsion, one of the central events and issues of European culture. For Miró and Picasso, the comic strip had still some of the universality that Goethe had hoped to invest it with; after the war, the comics just said America.

It was not that there were no comic strips produced in Europe. On the contrary, the postwar years in Europe saw a renaissance in the comic strip, and the invention of a new form that came close to Töpffer's original invention: the *bande dessinée*, or hardbound picture novel. The best of these, particularly Herge's *Tin-Tin* and Goscinny and Uderzo's peerless *Astérix* stories, were as charming and pleasing works as the form would ever produce. (*Astérix*, in particular, with its mock-epic vision of French life, imagining the origins of the culture in order to deflate its enduring pretensions, probably came as close to fulfilling Goethe's dream of a made folk culture as any comic strip could.) But these works were really a form of children's literature and rarely broke out into the debates and strategies of serious art.

Among European artists after the war, a quotation from the comics became either a guerilla protest against the American empire, or else the expression of a wistful longing for a life lived in the Circus Maximus. The Situationists in France, casting themselves as Astérix to the Americans' idiot Romans, thought that the comics could provoke only a subversive jeer. For the English artist Richard Hamilton, on the other hand, the comic book was tantalizing not for the style it offered but for the abundance it symbolized. The romance comic that appears on the wall in Hamilton's collage *Just What Is It That Makes Today's Homes So Different,*

59. **Richard Hamilton.** *Just What Is It That Makes Today's Homes So Different, So Appealing?* 1956. **Collage on paper, 9⅞ × 10¼" (25 × 26 cm). Kunsthalle Tübingen. Collection Professor Dr. George Zundel**

So Appealing? (fig. 59) is an exotic orchid from a real paradise of innocent plenty, potently artificial.

Yet in America itself, comic-strip style in art had become profoundly ambivalent. By the mid-fifties, the cultural meaning of the comics in America had changed, radically. From London or Paris, the comics looked like the insignia of a confident, voraciously leveling society; closer to home, they looked riven and troubled. Even in the newspaper strips, a decline had set in, exemplified by the forced disappearance of the humorous "continuity" strip, which had been replaced either by "serious" detective stories modeled on television serials or else by what comic-book artists still call, a little contemptuously, "gag-a-day" strips, like Mort Walker's *Beetle Bailey* and *Hi and Lois*. What good new work could be done was essentially satiric, expanded editorial cartooning: the line that passes from *Peanuts* and *Pogo* through to *Doonesbury* and *Bloom County,* and may have found its apex in Al Capp's mid-to-late forties *Li'l Abner*. But the renaissance of satire in the comic strip in the fifties got its energy from the reader's sense of surprise at seeing unexpected issues—the epistles to the Corinthians, anti-McCarthy satire, a knowledge of psychoanalysis and Existentialism—brought down into an unexpected place. Even the most familiar images that come to mind from the comics of the fifties—the *Peanuts* children sitting on the curb; the eclogue in Okefenokee Swamp—resemble less the self-sustaining world of Herriman's Coconino than they do the older tradition of allegorical fable used to comment on contemporary politics and thought. However rich this tradition has turned out to be, ultimately rejuvenating an editorial-cartoon tradition that had exhausted its vocabulary (too many Seas of Public Indignation and too many little taxpayers in barrels), it was no longer possible to see the comic strip as a home of the mythmaking imagination.

For comic-book artists and publishers, this decline was more like a free-fall. The drop in comic-book readership will probably be elegantly explained someday in simple demographic terms; within the confines of the comic-book world, it is always explained in terms of the great morality tale of American culture in the early fifties: the rise and fall of E.C. Comics.[39] E.C. (the initials stood, originally, for "Educational Comics") was begun by the publisher M. C. Gaines in the mid-forties.

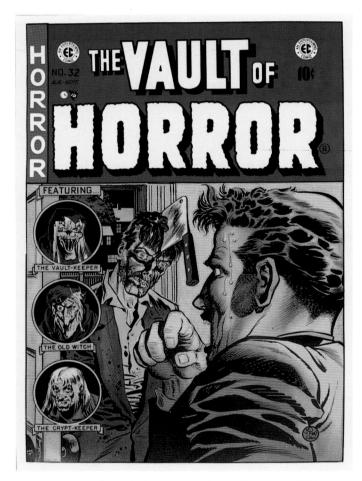

60. **Johnny Craig.** Cover of *The Vault of Horror*, 32 (August–September 1953). © 1953, 1981 William M. Gaines

Gaines, whose original intention was to publish magazines that would provide children with stories taken from biblical and Western history, died shortly after beginning E.C. and left the business to his son William Gaines. William, an interesting mixture of Philipon, Roger Corman, and Larry Flynt, had the insight (or the desperation) to see that money could be made by driving the already low-rent world of the comics further and further into the margins of the lurid, the grotesque, and the horrific. He also had extremely good judgment about which artists could delineate this sordid vision, and added to the mix a genuinely "enlightened" Stevensonian liberalism. (This last trait ultimately expressed itself in a line of "advanced," high-minded

comic books, including one called *Psychoanalysis*.) In prime E.C. comics, social consciousness, cynical exploitation, shameless Grand Guignol, and attentive, documentary realism all sit together. Although their reputation now is for sheer gore (and considering their covers [fig. 60], no wonder), E.C. comics in fact were touchingly "well-researched," and seen at the time as "realistic." They addressed subjects—the Korean War, the Holocaust—that were largely out of the way of more prudent comic-book enterprises. The ultimate story for an E.C. comic book was one, like the famous *Undercover!,* in which D-cups, flagellation, Klansmen, liberal piety ("Look, Ed! They've kidnapped and flogged innocent people—guilty of nothing more than practicing democracy!"), hideous grimaces, and an O. Henry ending could all be blended.

The success of the horror and crime comics led in 1954 to Fredric Wertham's infamous *Seduction of the Innocent*, which asserted that the growth of what was then still quaintly called "juvenile delinquency" was the consequence of the proliferation of crime and horror comic books.[40] Wertham's book in turn led to the Kefauver hearings on the comic books and the self-censorship of the "Comics Code."

Among comic-book aficionados, Wertham remains, to this day, a demon. "We hate him, despise him. He and he alone virtually brought about the collapse of the comic book industry during the 1950s . . . even the younger of us know the legend well, for it is repeated among us like some tribal myth," comics historian Catherine Yronwode wrote in a 1983 column in *The Comic Buyer's Guide*.[41] As the story is told in comic-book fan mythology, Wertham was a McCarthyite killjoy, a censorious reactionary who, frightened by the existence of a potentially subversive subculture outside the control of parents and schools, used pseudoscientific scare techniques to intimidate the marginal publishers.

In fact, however, Wertham was a pioneering liberal psychoanalyst, born and trained in Vienna, with a long and courageous history of commitment to progressive causes. Before *The Seduction of the Innocent,* Wertham had been most famous for his work in behalf of the American civil-rights movement. In 1946 he had established a free psychiatric clinic in Harlem called the Laforgue Clinic, after Karl Marx's son-in-law. His studies there of the psychological effects of discrimination on children led to his testifying at the key desegregation trials of the early fifties; his research became a crucial part of the legal argument used in Brown v. Board of Education. He also testified on behalf of the Rosenbergs (and helped arrange the adoption of their children). He often spoke out against the censorship of modern literature, and edited an anthology of modern writing, including works by Kafka, Faulkner, and Dostoyevsky, seen from a psychoanalytic perspective. What's more, Wertham was a passionate and discriminating collector of modern art. His collection included work by Archipenko, van Doesburg, Feininger, Goya, George Grosz, and John Heartfield. Its centerpiece was a collection of thirty-four works by El Lissitzky, and it also included African and Indonesian art, Wertham's own abstract collages, and drawings and watercolors made by Zelda Fitzgerald after she had been confined to the Phipps Clinic.[42]

Wertham's attack on the comics, therefore, far from being a hysterical extension of "watch-the-skies" paranoia into the world of pop culture, in fact represented almost its opposite: a paternalistic puritanism of the left, rather than a conformist paranoia of the right. Wertham's view of the comics was rooted in a European leftist critique of the culture industry: he thought that the comics represented a false, exploitative consciousness cynically imposed by a greedy culture industry on its most vulnerable consumers. The ideal of modern communication that Wertham would have opposed to the comics was not the *Saturday Evening Post* cover but the Lissitzky Proun.

Yet Wertham seems to have been puzzlingly unaware of how much his own attack on the comics unconsciously mimicked and recapitulated the by now familiar form of the reactionary attacks on modern art, with their insistence that modern art offered only corrupting, macabre sensualism. Many of the works in Wertham's collection depicted violence in a fashion not that dissimilar to the kind Wertham attacked when he saw it in the comics. Wertham owned, for instance, a Grosz engraving of a hanged man dangling from a scaffold that is not only as disturbing as anything in E.C., but which was typical of the kind of modernist imagery that had in its own day been subject to the same charges Wertham leveled at the comics: that it offered lurid, debasing sensationalism in the guise of social comment.

This odd double vision seems in part explicable in terms of Wertham's ideas about the meanings of modern art. Wertham, who was most active as a collector in the forties, seems to have been one of those violence-hating people who, during and just after World War II, came to see modern art not as a purposefully disruptive, "subversive" enterprise, but as the last repository of humanism. For Wertham, modern paintings, and particularly the abstractions he loved, "reveal to us the elements of general principles of order of an implicitly social character."[43] Like Greenberg's attack on "kitsch," Wertham's attack on the comics was the product of a peculiar kind of amnesia, in which the origins of modern art in an engagement with popular culture were forgotten, and the future of the pure values it supported was assured only by the quarantine or suppression of its low "opposite."

In another sense, of course, the Wertham dispute was really a dispute over style, and a kind of comedy of manners. Just about the only comic-book figure who would have shared Wertham's politics, after all, was William Gaines of E.C., who even extended, in his comic books, a privileged role to the psychoanalyst as the sage of modern life. What Gaines and Wertham could not have shared, though, was a common sense of the rules of interpretation. Wertham obviously had

an extremely sophisticated grasp of the decorum of interpretation in high modernism. He understood that an image of seemingly random horror, à la Grosz, could be a vessel of powerful social protest, or that a couple of circles and a diagonal line could suggest utopian dreams of harmony. But he couldn't see that the comics might have implicit stylistic conventions of their own. Wertham took it for granted that, while the graphic violence depicted in his Goya and Grosz prints —or for that matter in "The Penal Colony" or *Light in August*—could be understood as either realist protest against violence or as a powerful probe into unconscious desires and fantasies, the violence depicted in the E.C. comics could only be taken straight. He assumed that the comic-book audience had no kind of distance from the material it loved, or even any simple knowledge of the conventions of the form and its distant relation to any real experience. As subsequent research demonstrated, however—and as common sense in any case always suggested—the kids who read the horror comics always understood that what they were looking at were horror comics: Grand Guignol melodramas that provided particular kinds of lurid frissons but that were no more to be taken at (mutilated) face value than was a Frankenstein movie or, for that matter, a Grimm Brothers folk tale. The innocent seduced by the imagery of violence seems, in this case, to have been the decent but literal-minded psychoanalyst, too easily persuaded to take as documentary fact what a knowing adolescent might have helped him to recognize as stylized fiction.

Wertham and his followers were effective propagandists for their cause, however, and the Comics Code, which soon curtailed E.C.'s output, has continued in force to this day. The Code insists that not only must crime not pay, but it must be *seen* not to pay, and it must be seen not to pay through the actions of heroines with demure proportions and heroes with a lofty, disinterested desire for abstract justice.

All of these elements—the censoring impulse that insisted the comics were a virus of corruption and of kitsch, the gradual decline in the comics themselves, an inevitable poetic preference for the elegiac over the fatuously affirmative—came together to change the meaning of comic-book form in American art. To invoke the comics now was no longer to invoke the promising Damon Runyon outlook that Stuart Davis had memorialized; it was to invoke a neglected, even repressed, undercurrent in American experience. By the fifties, the comics looked sinister, or touching. Above all, they could now look old: the toy found in the attic, a forgotten artifact of the century's bright beginnings.

The appearance of comic imagery in the art of Jasper Johns and Robert Rauschenberg is often explained in narrow, historicist terms as the first breathings of Pop—the real object's tentative answer to the transcendent painterly gesture. But if the fragmentary appearance of comic imagery in the work of Johns and Rauschenberg involved in part a bit of nose-thumbing

61. **Jasper Johns.** *Alley Oop.* 1958. Oil and collage on composition board, 22⅞ × 18⅛″ (58.1 × 46 cm). Collection Mr. and Mrs. S. I. Newhouse, Jr.

directed against the lofty disapproval of Abstract Expressionism, with Clement Greenberg cast as a kind of highbrow Wertham, their art offers a complex poetics that transcends the oppositions of avant-garde art politics.

Jasper Johns's *Alley Oop* (fig. 61) of 1958, for instance, in which the artist pasted a comic strip to his canvas and then overlaid it with veils of paint, reduced the comic strip to its most basic, familiar pattern—the sequence of adjoining panels. V. T. Hamlin's comic strip *Alley Oop* (fig. 62) was by 1958 an old chestnut in the comic-page treasury.[44] It was a comic strip that

was about age—the story of a caveman and his family who slip easily back and forth between modernity and the antediluvian past. To Johns, the comic strip was another of the found, timeless, low formats—flags, targets, maps—that are the ground of his painting. Yet his subject, in *Alley Oop*, as so often elsewhere, is the way that private signatures emerge from public signs. For Davis and Miró, popular imagery had still held the old Goethean promise: the divisive hierarchies of public and private seemed about to dissolve in a shared, universal language. For Johns, disabused of that utopian dream, popular secondhand imagery could none-

62. **V. T. Hamlin.** *Alley Oop*, April 16, 1930. © N.E.A. Service

theless still play for art a role like that of the inherited formats of still-life painting: the standard, received forms make the small, exquisite touch meaningful, the sounding board that gives resonance to the stubborn, small treble of the individual voice. Beyond its place in a narrowly conceived battle of gestures, *Alley Oop* establishes an attitude toward pop culture at once detached and unthreatened. Maybe it was because the comic strip already had an inexpungible element of the personal signature—unlike a map or a flag, it was a particular thing made by a particular person—that Johns finally found it resistant to his purposes. *Alley Oop* remains an anomaly in his art.

In this new environment of small, measured marks and scruples, however, borrowed, individual styles could still take on new meanings; even Herriman's *Krazy Kat*, the undisputed exemplar of the lost golden age, began to appear as part of an iconography of quizzical hesitation. Johns's and Rauschenberg's friend Öyvind Fahlström,[45] for instance, liked to scramble, chop up, and reassemble Herriman's masterpiece in a way that is a kind of homage and also adds a disturbing element of Dada non sequitur to the intricately balanced machinery of Coconino (figs. 63, 64). What began to seem important about the comics was not their content but their form, which one suddenly saw with a new clarity as the narratives were broken up; the secondary machinery of the comics—the panels and balloons and onomatopoeia—began to have an iconic force greater than any image they might contain.

In the work of Saul Steinberg, this same spirit took a turn at once drier and more generous. Steinberg's style had been formed in the thirties in the still thriving

63. **Öyvind Fahlström.** *Performing K.K. No. 11 (Sunday Edition)*. 1962. Tempera on board, 35⅜ × 21⅝" (90 × 55 cm). Collection Mr. and Mrs. S. I. Newhouse, Jr.

64. **Öyvind Fahlström.** *Performing K.K. No. 3.* 1965. Oil and collage on canvas, with four movable magnetized parts, 54⅜ × 36⅝ × 2″ (138 × 93 × 5 cm). Collection Robert Rauschenberg, New York

world of the European caricature journal. For him, "cartooning" even in the thirties had meant the tradition of Klee and Grosz. Yet Steinberg's interest had from the beginning of his career been less in the style of modern politics than in the politics of modern style. Arriving in America in 1942, he found his great subject: the collision of the irresistible force of a triumphant pop culture with the immovable objects of modernist rectitude, and he has spent the last forty years recording the aftermath of their violent encounters with absorbed detachment. Steinberg's 1958 *Comic Strip* (fig. 65) has some of the quality of Max Beerbohm's drawings of the old and young selves of a single person—the aristocratic European eye of the high caricaturist inspects its alarming and overfed New World progeny. Steinberg was among the first to recognize that the properties and machinery of the comics—the onomatopoeic exclamation, the dialogue balloon, the bubbled line that symbolizes thought—had become a modern decorative order. Beginning in the mid-fifties, he used the machinery of the comics

for his own ends. His favorite device was the balloon, especially the thought balloon. The simple oval outline was transformed into a variety of shapes and substances that surveyed the décor of modern art: out of the mouths of ephemeral persons came complex art-deco façades, while society matrons dreamed in Bauhaus design; freehand cubes imagined life as geometric cubes, while geometric cubes imagined being free; dogs barked in *art brut*, and cats dreamed in Cubism. Steinberg saw that modern style was increasingly becoming, especially in New York, a folk style, a common inheritance, and he expressed this realization through the seamless fusion of the machinery of the comics and the machinery of the museum. In *Comic Strip*—a drawing that resembles an eighteenth-century Egyptian Revivalist's rapt copy of a wall of undeciphered hieroglyphs—Steinberg presents a tender abstract encyclopedia of comic-strip clichés, robbed of any symbolic or narrative urgency. In a way that was prescient of much Pop art, Steinberg sensed that the props and symbols that indicated energy in the com-

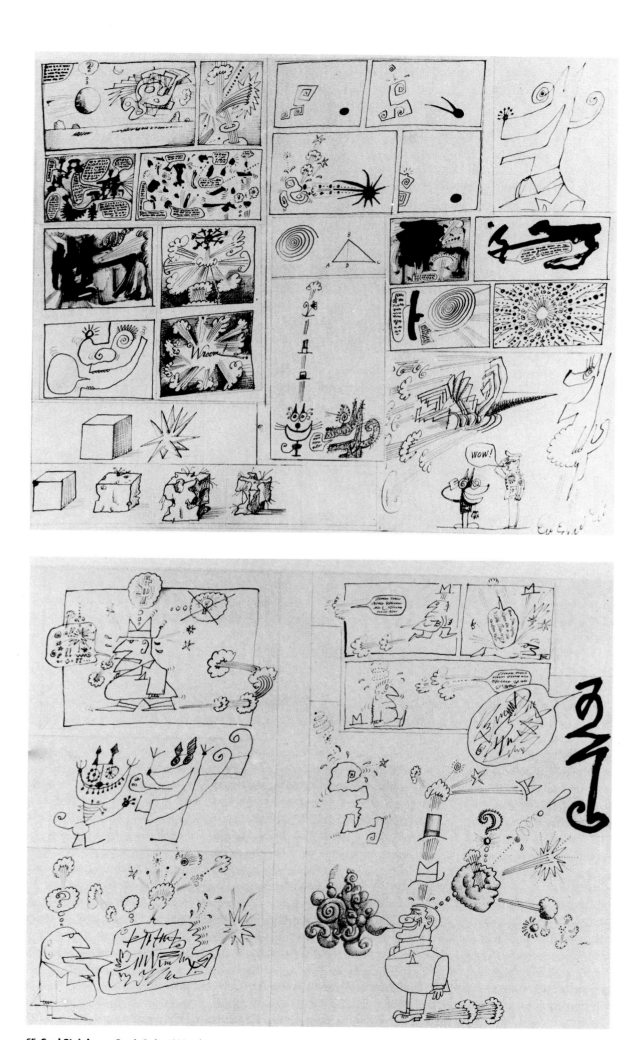

65. Saul Steinberg. *Comic Strip*. 1958. Ink on paper; two sheets, each 23 × 29″ (58.4 × 73.7 cm). Collection the artist

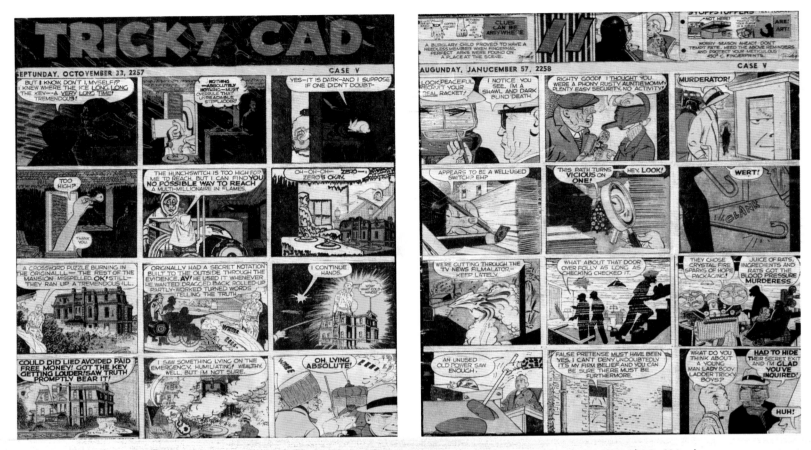

66. Jess. *Tricky Cad: Case V*. 1958. Collage of colored newspaper, clear plastic wrap, and black tape on board, 13¼ × 24⁵⁄₁₆″ (33.7 × 64.1 cm). Hirshhorn Museum and Sculpture Garden, Smithsonian Institution, Washington, D.C. Joseph H. Hirshhorn Purchase Fund

ics—the lines of force, the star-burst explosion, the puff of smoke as a character races away—had become as standardized and formal as the cryptic images on the back of the dollar bill. If the comics could supply social adhesion, it was not through the invention of kitsch heroes and villains, a manufactured mythology, but through the solemn, shared heraldry of their secondary signs.[46]

Steinberg is usually seen as an "outsider," yet his sense that the comics were intrinsically strange, that their elaborate conventions and properties, far from offering a "natural" or "folk" order, in fact turned on a sinister secret code of bizarre hieroglyphs, was an intuition that helped shape a moment in art; as the comics retreated from the center ring of the circus of popular culture, a buried and censored strangeness began to emerge from their forms. Artists could stand Wertham on his head, finding in the comics the same kind of secret, sinister forces that he insisted were latent there, and then come to value the comics precisely because they did seduce the innocent. Even the most seemingly innocuous and conventional strip

might be shown to hold a hidden passage to the repressed underside of a complacent bulwark culture. For the isolated San Francisco artist named Jess, the sense that comic books were a kind of genetic code of popular imagery, one that could be recombined and split up and forced to produce mutants, achieved an extraordinary expression in a series of collages begun in 1958: the *Tricky Cad* pictures (figs. 66, 67).[47] An anagram of *Dick Tracy*, Chester Gould's expressionistic comic strip of the 1930s, Jess's *Tricky Cad* collages rearranged words and images from *Dick Tracy* in apparent non sequiturs, so that the stereotyped exclamations and imagery of Gould's comic strip suddenly became scenes from a nightmare. "But I know, don't I myself!!?? I knew where the ice long long the key—a very long long time! Tremendous," says one silhouette to another. These two collages were from a series of images that Jess referred to as Paste-Ups and Assemblies, filled with popular images ranging from nineteenth-century engravings to bubble-gum cards of the Beatles. Similar in spirit to the collections of Joseph Cornell, most of Jess's Paste-Ups and Assemblies

67. Jess. *Tricky Cad.* c. 1959. Newsprint collage, 29 × 7" (73.7 × 17.8 cm). Los Angeles County Museum of Art. Gift of Mr. and Mrs. Bruce Conner

have a small-scale, Surrealist dreaminess and an obvious dose of "poetic" transformation. What makes the *Tricky Cad* collages so radical and disturbing, and gives them a found Expressionist urgency that recalls Hannah Höch or John Heartfield, is the way the nightmarish art image sits only one short half-step away from its apparently banal pop source. Jess recognized that beneath the simple cops-and-robbers narratives of Gould's strips there was already an element of melodramatic weirdness, a love of the freakish, misshapen, and forbidden. Tracy himself, the square-jawed detective whose eyes never open and whose expression

never changes, seems less the sympathetic G-man of the movies than an embodiment of single-minded, amused vengefulness. The overwrought stylization of Gould's strip, so at odds with its overt rhetoric of conventional morality and high-tech detection, made *Dick Tracy*, as Jess saw, already a kind of crack in the façade of pop cheerfulness.

Andy Warhol's comic-strip and comic-book paintings of the early sixties, though we associate them sentimentally with the burgeoning of the florid and spectacular pop culture of that period, really belong to this nostalgic and backward-looking strain of imagery, long shadows cast at twilight. When Warhol filled a department-store window in 1961 with stark, single images taken from pulp ads and the comics—*Dick Tracy*, *Popeye*, *Superman*, and *Nancy* (figs. 68, 69)— he chose images from the comic books of his childhood. Yet the graphic intensity with which he viewed them is different in spirit from the work of Rauschenberg and Johns that had preceded and inspired his. What makes Warhol original is the isolation of his comic images: the detective and the little girl and the superhero are not fragments shifting within the kaleidoscope of mass culture but icons, fixed and staring. What's original in Warhol is not that he painted Dick Tracy, but that he *just* painted Dick Tracy.

Warhol's comic paintings are formally much closer to the floor-to-ceiling assertions of Abstract Expressionism than they are to the palimpsests of fifties neo-Dada. For Johns and Rauschenberg, the inclusion of comic-book imagery in the midst of a painterly rhetoric borrowed with genuine reverence from de Kooning and Pollock still had about it an air of muted protest and debunking. They share a sense, as strong as Schwitters's, of the world breaking in on the studio, insistently and surely, and share also an infinite hesitation to choose only one or the other. It was Warhol's wicked and demoralizing intuition to see that the choice was in any case unnecessary, that the very highest and very lowest visual elements in the culture— Mondrian and a crossword, a Newman zip and comic-book panels—had already a punning similarity. Part of the joke in Warhol's *Dick Tracy* lies in its deflation of the old, transcendent pretensions of American abstraction, but part of the joke also lies in its translation of pictorial absolutism into the vernacular.

Yet Warhol's real genius was for the off-register print; for the lag moments in culture, for the thing just on its way out: the tabloid headline in the age of television, the movie star in the age of rock. He had an unerring instinct for those occasions when the iconic image was just beginning to disconnect from its audience. His great subject was celebrity as it sat uneasily on the San Andreas Fault of media culture, and by the 1960s the comics had long since been toppled; one had to look back not five years but thirty to find comics with anything more than a subculture resonance. The comics had been bound up for so many years with their Kabuki-like internal decorum and storytelling codes that they had none of the apparent art-

68. **Andy Warhol.** *Popeye.* 1960. Synthetic polymer paint on canvas, 68¼ × 58½" (173 × 150 cm). Collection Mr. and Mrs. S. I. Newhouse, Jr.

lessness, the seeming codelessness, of Warhol's favorite subjects, the news photo or the publicity still. If Depression-era comic-strip imagery had the graphic finality of high abstraction, the comics had become by the early 1960s as formalized, as ritualized, as inbred and minor a form as second-generation Abstract Expressionism. It would require a painter with a dry feeling for the potencies of even the smallest formal gestures to rescue them as art.

In 1947, Irv Novick, an officer at an Army boot camp, was asked to take a look at drawings by a young private with an interest in art. Novick saw that the private had some talent—not a particularly good draftsman, he thought, but a good colorist—and arranged to

have this young man transferred to his unit, where, Novick felt, he would be more useful helping to make posters and signs than he had ever been swabbing out officers' latrines.[48] Soon after, both men left the service. Irv Novick became a D.C. cartoonist, and Private Roy Lichtenstein became a vanguard painter.

From a purely worldly point of view, it was soon clear who had made the better career move. The imposition of the Comics Code had led to a desperate, full-scale depression in the comic-book business. In the deep trough of the late fifties, D.C. comics, with its still profitable line in superhero comics, was by far the largest and most effective of the comic-book publishers. But within D.C. itself there was a strict and recognized hierarchy, with the superhero comic books at the

69. **Andy Warhol.** *Dick Tracy*. 1960. Synthetic polymer paint on canvas, 6'7" × 45" (201 × 114 cm). Collection Mr. and Mrs. S. I. Newhouse, Jr.

top—*Superman* and *Batman* at the very top of those —and, near the bottom, the profitable but unprestigious romance comic books; beneath that was a line of war comics meant largely for boys. *Heart Throbs, Secret Hearts, All-American Men of War, Our Fighting Forces, Our Army at War*—the already archaic titles of these comics in the world of Brando and Elvis suggest their enormous distance from any larger pop-culture universe. Such comics spent their time endlessly spinning out the same one or two stories, to which, increasingly, only the young and ignorant would still listen. The romance comics, for their part, were less moralizing than lachrymose. Far from inculcating a shrewd or get-your-man morality, their heroines seem to drift, wide-eyed, from one weeping embrace to an-

other.[49] The last page of a typical story ends with the heroine losing one cleft-chinned prince at the top of the page and, five panels later, floating off in the arms of another one: anonymous, impersonal romance, the habits of Joe Orton in the manner of Mary Worth. The emotional climaxes tend not to be those of soap opera or women's-magazine fiction, on which the stories so obviously depend—the Big Fight, the Discovery—but reside in isolated panels of unanchored emotion: the girl in extreme close-up, crying vaguely for love.

D.C. war comics were almost exclusively devoted to World War II stories (it had been one of the innovations of E.C. to tell stories about the Korean War), with the old imagery of Milton Caniff endlessly recurring against a remote, forgotten background of the Euro-

70. **Roy Lichtenstein.** *Blonde Waiting.* 1964. Magna on canvas, 48 × 48″ (121.9 × 121.9 cm). Courtesy Gagosian Gallery, New York

71. **Roy Lichtenstein.** *Look Mickey.* 1961. Oil on canvas, 48½ × 34¾″ (123.2 × 88.3 cm). Collection the artist

72. Panel from "Give Me an Hour," in *Girls' Romances*, 81 (January 1962). **Tony Abruzzo and Bernard Sachs,** artists; **Ira Schnapp,** lettering. © D.C. Comics

pean theater of 1944. By the late fifties, the old Bili Mauldin foot soldiers—the G.I. with his helmet strap loose, chin covered in three-day-old beard, and eyes filling with the thousand-yard stare, the surrounding platoon an array of ethnic types—had been recruited for a new, "cinematic" ballet of aerial combat.

War comics showed faces in close-up only in moments of extreme duress or rage; the climax of the story almost always is seen at a god-like distance, the hero's exclamations rising from within his airship as some haunting memory is expunged through the therapy of mass destruction. In this world, the incessant onomatopoeia—WHAAM!, RATATATA!, BLAAM!—is less a simple symbolism of noise than a kind of Greek chorus, linking separated events, joining panels, and acting as a unifying design device.

Yet, for all their formulae, the romance and war comics were made not by inert institutions but by young staff artists, and these artists had of course ambitions of their own—if not for their "art form" or the genre, then at least for their own careers. Basically, their ambition was to demonstrate enough talent to get a job doing something else. One route up and out lay, particularly for the war-comics cartoonist, in eventually being allowed to draw superheroes. For the artist condemned to the delusive mine of the lovelorn, a

more plausible escape lay not in the comics at all, but in magazine illustration. The artists drew comics in order to show that they could draw for *Redbook*.

The ambitious, upwardly mobile illustrators who drew romance comics at D.C. particularly admired and imitated an artist and illustrator named Tony Abruzzo, both the Chuck Yeager and the Utamaro of the lovelorn.[50] Abruzzo had invented—or at any rate was given credit among other illustrators at D.C. for having invented—the Heartbreak Face: the girl with parted lips, head tilted at a slight angle, possessed of a surprisingly strong and even masculine jaw, and having enormous, unnatural, liquid eyes. Abruzzo also discovered that while slightly parted lips are pleasing, teeth are not, and he helped codify the solution—the aesthetic cuirass of the love comic—by which teeth are represented by a streak of unvariegated white. Above all, Abruzzo taught that expression didn't have to be coherent to be moving; you could add beautifully shaped tears—illustrators called them "popcorn tears"—to a face that showed no other signs of emotion, and still get an effect. The other romance artists copied Abruzzo's faces whenever the script they were handed let them. In part, these extreme close-ups were showcase drawings, designed to demonstrate to anyone who might happen to see them that the artist who drew

73. **Roy Lichtenstein.** *Drowning Girl.* 1963. Oil and synthetic polymer paint on canvas, 67⅝ × 66¾″ (171.6 × 169.5 cm). The Museum of Modern Art, New York. Philip Johnson Fund and gift of Mr. and Mrs. Bagley Wright

them was not quite the hack he might be taken for. "We thought that every day at work would be our last," recalls one of these Abruzzites, John Romita, now an art director of Marvel Comics.[51]

If the sign of a "good," that is, a painstaking and ambitious, artist in the love comics was that he got the close-ups right, and displayed an Abruzzo-like attention to moments of enigmatic or in-between expression, then the sign of an ambitious or skilled artist in the war comics was in what was called "characterization." A good war comic was one that put a new and surprising spin on the old stories, producing, for instance, not just jet pilots, but American Indian jet pilots. Their "realism," expressed in sudden cutaways to the sweating faces of cowards and the noble faces of reluctant warriors, indicated their ambition and skill, especially if joined to a flair for large-scale action. The meticulous realism of E.C., which sat so oddly with its equal insistence on the horrific, had been replaced by a realism of "characterization" and complex storytelling.

Almost without exception, Lichtenstein's comics paintings from the early 1960s (as Lichtenstein, of course, could not have known; all of the romance and war comics were unsigned) were adapted from the work of a small handful of ambitious comic-book artists. The styles of these artists were distinct enough that, thirty years later, their work can still be picked out immediately by the Berensons and Offners of the comics. Lichtenstein's romance images are adapted almost entirely from the works of Tony Abruzzo, John Romita, and Bernard Sachs; his war images almost entirely from the work of Russ Heath—and Irv Novick. High art on the way down to the bottom met, without quite knowing it, low art struggling to find its way back up.

Lichtenstein recast his found images in complicated ways.[52] Ironically, he had to aggressively alter and recompose them to bring them closer to a platonic ideal of simple comic-book style—he had to work hard to make them look more like comics. The effects that make Lichtenstein into Lichtenstein involved not the aestheticizing of a consistent style through mechanical displacements, but the careful, artificial construction of what appears to be a generic, whole, "true-folk" cultural style from a real world of comics that was by then far more "fallen" and fragmented. His early pictures work by making the comic images more like the comics than the comics were themselves.

Lichtenstein was often taken with the Abruzzo-like close-ups of girls caught, lips parted, in states of clichéd emotion: tension, anxiety, misery. But he consistently simplified and isolated these images, translating what was essentially an illustration style into a comic-book style. Compare Lichtenstein's *Blonde Waiting* (fig. 70), for instance, to the image from which it derives, a panel by Abruzzo in "Give Me an Hour" (fig. 72), and one sees how intently and ingeniously Lichtenstein had to work to eliminate all the anecdotal detailing Abruzzo had so painstakingly included. Lichtenstein edited out all the realistic freehand shading and loose-limbed crosshatching that

Abruzzo scribbled on the back of the alarm clock, and on the bedstead behind the girl's head. Instead, Lichtenstein borrowed a bit of atypically simple diagonal shading from the bedpost on the far left of the original image and applied it to the back of the alarm clock, dramatically changing the purposefully showy vocabulary of modeling into a much simpler graphic pattern. The girl becomes a blonde rather than a brunette, and her gaze is turned away from the alarm clock on which it rests in the original. The whole complicated plot of the original story, which turns on the passing of the hour, is tossed away in the interests of an iconic look of lovelorn poignancy.

74. Panel from "Run For Love!," in *Secret Hearts*, 83 (November 1962). **Tony Abruzzo**, artist; **Ira Schnapp**, lettering. © D.C. Comics

The style that Lichtenstein uses in *Blonde Waiting* to indicate that this image belongs to the world of the comics is really adapted from the style of the Disney cartoons meant for children—a style whose woodcut-like contrasts and serpentine, emphatic outlines Lichtenstein had inspected before, in his earlier *Look Mickey* (fig. 71)—rather than taken over from the more restrained, illustrational style of the love comics: not found imagery in a deadpan appropriation, but two found styles combined.

Sometimes, Lichtenstein can seem like the perfect Abruzzite. Intuitively recognizing that the girls' faces had a kind of strange intensity that the other elements in the comics lacked, Lichtenstein would pull them out of context, until today the Abruzzo girls have become immortalized, through Lichtenstein, as pop clichés. In *Drowning Girl* (fig. 73), he changes a hero's name from what was, for his purposes, the wrong cliché (fig.

75. **Roy Lichtenstein.** *Hopeless.* 1963. Oil on canvas, 44 × 44" (112 × 112 cm). Kunstmuseum Basel, Ludwig Collection

74)—the peculiar "Mal"—to the right cliché, the nifty "Brad." But the girl's face and the swirling, Beardsley-like, high-contrast liquid patterning of the background are lifted from the original almost entirely intact.

In *Hopeless* (fig. 75), Lichtenstein again simplifies Abruzzo's stylized pupils and lips and again magnifies and emphasizes the relatively restrained stress pattern of the original lettering (fig. 76). And again, he changes her from a brunette to a blonde. (Lichtenstein presumably wasn't aware that the comic-book artists liked to use big, unvarying areas of dark tone in order to protect themselves from their "inkers," the artists who transferred the designs from the drawings to mechanicals, and who could ruin the intended effect of a page if they were allowed enough white space.) Throughout these transpositions, Lichtenstein emphasizes his constant imposition upon his cartoon figures

of Benday dots which, surprising as it may seem to those of us who have learned to see romance comics through Lichtenstein, are hardly visible in the original (figs. 77, 78).

Lichtenstein's culling and splicing together of images borrowed from war comics is even more enterprising. In *Whaam!*, for instance (fig. 79), he paraphrases a horizontal panel drawn by Irv Novick in *All-American Men of War* (fig. 80). The original onomatopoeic "Whaam!" seems to tremble in the heat of the explosion; Lichtenstein makes it a much more stately and inevitable WHAAM!, with a Rodchenko exclamation point in place of the stubby rectangle and blob of the original, so that the image now has a blank, disassociated finality. All of the "story line" and "characterization" which were so crucial to the original comic book have been eliminated. In the original

76. Panel from "Run for Love!," in *Secret Hearts,* 83 (November 1962). **Tony Abruzzo,** artist; **Ira Schnapp,** lettering. © D.C. Comics

comic of which *Whaam!* is a paraphrase, this scene of jet-fighting is a fantasy of the future imagined by a World War II American Indian pilot, Johnny Cloud. In the original, Johnny Cloud's fantasy rocket hits home and he announces, "The enemy has become a flaming star!" Lichtenstein edits this out and replaces the real cliché of the comic book with a much simpler, yet more ominous cliché: the jet pilot with ice water in his veins, the man with his cool finger on the button. Lichtenstein also edits out the two attending planes of the squadron—one of those realistic details on which artists like Novick so prided themselves—in order to make the image seem flat, candid, and schematic, and invents a Hiroshige-like pattern of curvaceous flame—more poured paint than gasoline—in place of the jagged projectile burst of flame which Novick had taken such pains to draw with careful, asymmetrical vio-

lence. The ironies here are much more intricate than those involved in a deadpan displacement of low object to high context. In order to invent a non-art object, an image that looked utterly low—popular, mass-produced, and anonymous—Lichtenstein had to reject from his sources anything that seemed merely narrative, anecdotal, or illustrative, enforcing one set of old high-modern prohibitions in order to undermine another.

It's not that the comic books Lichtenstein was looking at weren't simply compendiums of clichés. They were. But the clichés they anatomized were more intricate, more "original"—wistfully touched with the desperate attempt to wring one last varied drop from familiar material—than the confident, blank clichés that were his platonic image of Pop style. This translation of detailed storytelling into simplified icons distin-

77. Panel from "Give Me an Hour," in *Girls' Romances*, 81 (January 1962). **Tony Abruzzo and Bernard Sachs**, artists; **Ira Schnapp**, lettering. © D.C. Comics

guishes all of Lichtenstein's paintings of the early sixties, as when, simply by turning a gun turret from a near horizontal to an emphatic, double-banded diagonal, he flattens out the space, and creates the imposing *As I Opened Fire*, taken from panels drawn by Jerry Grandinetti in *All-American Men of War* (figs. 86, 87).

The funniest and most complex of all these transpositions and editorial rearrangements appears in the 1963 *Okay, Hot-Shot* (fig. 85). Lichtenstein spliced together elements from three different stories to produce this picture: the general idea and the dialogue are taken from a panel in a story called "Aces Wild," drawn by Russ Heath in *All-American Men of War* (fig. 81); the background airplane and the VOOMP! are borrowed from two panels in another story drawn by Irv Novick (figs. 82, 83); and the pilot's face is taken from the D.C. title *G.I. Combat* (fig. 84) (This face, oddly

enough, was also drawn by Russ Heath.) The big face, seen in extreme close-up, derives from a very different set of clichés than those of the air-battle comics he liked best, with their cool, wisecracking pilots. This pilot's face has been implausibly plucked out of the grim interior of a Sherman tank. (Enraged faces in the war comics are most often associated with infantry action; the pilots are either invisible inside their aircraft, or else they are utterly cool, quite unlike the sweating, unshaven men who fight tank battles in small Italian towns and ruined German cities.) The VOOMP! in the original comic book accompanies an explosion which has no resemblance to the Morris Louis Aleph that Lichtenstein creates. (The dialogue that provides the painting's title is an obvious in-joke on the insistent and, by 1963, itself stereotyped cult of the poured painting.) *Okay, Hot-Shot* culls out a set of independent clichés

78. **Roy Lichtenstein.** *Tension*. 1964. Oil and magna on canvas, 68 ×68″ (172.7 ×172.7 cm). Private collection

from the comics and assembles them into a kind of super-cliché which looks more like a comic than the comics. The picture, though it is often taken to be only a joke about the decorum of museums, actually depends for its force on another and less studied joke about the internal decorum of the comics.

What looks in Lichtenstein like an appropriated mass style is in fact a homogenized assemblage of personal styles; what look like pop clichés appropriated deadpan are in fact invented pop clichés, spliced together from bits and pieces of individual manners. The style that now says "pop culture" to us is not a common style to which Roy Lichtenstein drew our attention; it is to a very considerable degree a style that Roy Lichtenstein made up. Or, more precisely, it was a style made up in a complicated lobster quadrille, with

79. **Roy Lichtenstein.** *Whaam!* 1963. Magna on canvas; two panels, overall 68 × 160″ (172.7 × 406.4 cm). The Trustees of the Tate Gallery, London

Abruzzo and Romita and Novick and Heath on one side, pursuing their dreams, and Lichtenstein on the other, pursuing his. Lichtenstein isolated and emphasized some of those artists' pet stylizations, added other elements, like the enlarged dots, that they would not have seen as stylization at all, and edited and refined all those elements in a way that came to permanently symbolize what the comics look like. The Benday dots, Tony Abruzzo's "popcorn tears," the slanted shading—from a rich language of existing individual stylizations, Lichtenstein picked out a small subset, and made them say "Pop."

At the same time, Lichtenstein discovered in the comics a whole set of representational clichés and compositional schemata that he was already inclined to recognize as art. If he had to recompose the art of the "good" comic-book artists to make them look

more like comics, he still recognized in their work the debased style of *fin-de-siècle* narrative painting. The platonic ideal of the comics that Lichtenstein struggled to realize from his low sources was, in its origins, inseparable from memories of the museum, Gauguin's imagination gone to earth in the manner of Irv Novick.

The scaffolding of history that made *Okay, Hot-Shot* possible is far more complex than the simple inversion of categories that is usually assumed to support it. Gauguin, in pictures like the *Vision after the Sermon*, had paraphrased Degas in the light of Daumier, creating a cartoon version of a favorite Impressionist compositional device: the big, looming foreground counterposed to the sudden whistling recession. This kind of dramatic close-up juxtaposed with action in depth was then, in turn, taken up as an avant-garde device by the cinema—by Eisenstein, for instance, in

204

80. Panel from "Star Jockey," in *All-American Men of War*, 89 (January–February 1962). **Irv Novick**, artist; **Gaspar Saladino**, lettering. © D.C. Comics

81. Panel from "Aces Wild," in *All-American Men of War,* 89 (January–February 1962). **Russ Heath,** artist; **Gaspar Saladino,** lettering. © D.C. Comics

82. Panels from "Star Jockey," in *All-American Men of War,* 89 (January–February 1962). **Irv Novick,** artist; **Gaspar Saladino,** lettering. © D.C. Comics

83. Panel from "Star Jockey," in *All-American Men of War,* 89 (January–February 1962). **Irv Novick,** artist; **Gaspar Saladino,** lettering. © D.C. Comics

84. Panel from "Haunted Tank vs. Killer Tank," in *G.I. Combat,* 94 (June–July 1962). **Russ Heath,** artist; **Gaspar Saladino,** lettering. © D.C. Comics

85. **Roy Lichtenstein.** *Okay, Hot-Shot.* 1963. Oil and magna on canvas, 80 × 68" (203.2 × 172.7 cm). Collection Mr. and Mrs. S. I. Newhouse, Jr.

Ivan the Terrible. From there, it went on to become a cliché of the movies; then Milton Caniff filched it for his war comics in the forties, and the whole long chain of invention eventually came to settle in the unassuming pocket of Irv Novick—which Roy Lichtenstein then neatly picked in order to produce paintings that would come to be seen as the latest step in the long chain of avant-garde invention that descended from Degas and Gauguin. What looks like a simple ironic inversion of values, a ladder stood on its head, is, in pictures like *Okay, Hot-Shot*, really the consequence of a much more complex chain of borrowings that snake back and forth from high to low and back again: a ring, not a ladder.

The effect of Pop in general and Lichtenstein in particular on the comic books was intense and immediate. Pop art saved the comics. The most successful comic books in the stunning and unlooked-for comic-book boom of the sixties, those produced under the editorship of Stan Lee at Marvel, enthusiastically took up the elements of Lichtenstein's style—its rejection of ''realistic'' detail, the emphasis on undulating black curves, the whistling, plunging spaces, the irony—and began to apply them to the mass-culture objects as they were being made. Lee, for instance, soon would instruct his artists (who before long included many of the more talented members of the D.C. stable, among them John Romita) to draw pages of action without any plot—the Fantastic Four tearing apart a space station, say, with no plot in mind or purpose in sight—to which Lee would only later add dialogue that was deliberately, ironically at odds with the action.[53] (''Hey Strecho, didja remember to turn the stove off?,'' the Thing might cry as he pitched a villain in Plastic Man's direction.) The ironic disassociations of tone that Lichtenstein had achieved through his arsenal of transformations were quickly incorporated into the style of the comics themselves. Marvel even produced a line of ''Pop'' comics.

The conventional story insists on Lichtenstein's as the archetypal Pop surrender to the forces of anonymous mass-cult style, with the individual imagination capable only of a few mechanical ironies of scale, and a few helpless aestheticizing gestures, in the face of the big, irresistible media machine. The truth is almost the direct reverse: ''mass culture'' in this instance turns out to be a handful of young artists hanging on for life; it was high art that had the live ammo, and it recreated popular culture in its own image.

Lichtenstein took as his subject the very lowest of comics, those that had hit bottom but that nonetheless could be shown to still possess the accents and rituals of a higher past. What interested Claes Oldenburg were not the comics that had sunk down to the bottom and become almost invisible, but those comic images that had become so familiar that they had, so to speak, come loose from their moorings and now looked down on American life, like superintending Macy's Parade balloons. Oldenburg's great subject is

metamorphosis, and the already myth-like creations of the comic strip have on the whole been less congenial subjects for him than the mute order of primary objects: plugs and ironing boards and clothespins. Yet one comic-book (and strip and movie) icon had, Oldenburg recognized, become so ubiquitous in American life that by the end of the 1950s it had already in fact left its origins in the comics and entered the realm of objects with multiple secret lives, and that was Mickey Mouse.[54]

First drawn by Ub Iwerks as the subject for the animated silent *Plane Crazy*, Mickey Mouse in his initial appearance was a ragged, scrawny troublemaker.[55] He soon became a common property of the stable of Disney artists. Mickey, as we know him, is very much a mouse made by a committee; and what that treatment at the hands of the (then anonymous) Disney cartoonists did was to reduce his face to a standard and, when you think about it, entirely unmouselike form: three interlocking circles. (Disney artists recall what a pleasure it was to draw Mickey after all the painstakingly ''lifelike'' characters of the animated movies; three turns of the wrist and the emblem of the kingdom was there.)[56] Mickey for the next twenty-five years was less familiar through his (increasingly rare) appearances in the movies than through the daily comic strip drawn by Floyd Gottfredson (fig. 88). Gottfredson's strip was made more or less independent of Disney, an extension of the empire that was too trivial for close direction. Gottfredson's Mickey is neither the imp of *Plane Crazy* nor the bland theme-park greeter, the corporate mouse, he would later become; he is more like Harold Lloyd, an essentially gallant mouse who stoically suffers through a series of adventures. What is strange and a little disquieting in Gottfredson's Mickey is the lower-middle-class background. Far from being a creature of an enchanted kingdom, Gottfredson's Mickey lives in a claustrophobic, uncarpeted world of walk-up apartments, and his tormentors are not witches or dapper foxes but, more often than not, big, thuggish dogs in cloth caps.[57]

By the early sixties, when Oldenburg first took him as a subject, Mickey had largely disappeared from the fabric of everyday life, leaving behind, like a vanished god, only his sign: the two perfectly round ears, the emblems on the cap of the kids inside the Mickey Mouse clubhouse. Mickey by 1960 had a double nature: he was familiar both as the half-remembered low hero of old comics and cartoons and as the omnipresent image of Disneyland culture. Oldenburg's first use of Mickey, in the poster for his first show at the Dwan Gallery (fig. 89), seems designed to reanimate the mouse—to take a fixed, hieratic image and reinvest it with lust and glee. This Mickey derives formally from Gottfredson's strip, but Oldenburg supplies Gottfredson's virginal, upright Mickey with an evil, conspiratorial leer. The joke—that the repressed libidinal underside of Disneyland culture could be expressed by showing the ''real'' Mickey—was a common one at the time. The cartoonists at *Mad*, a few years before,

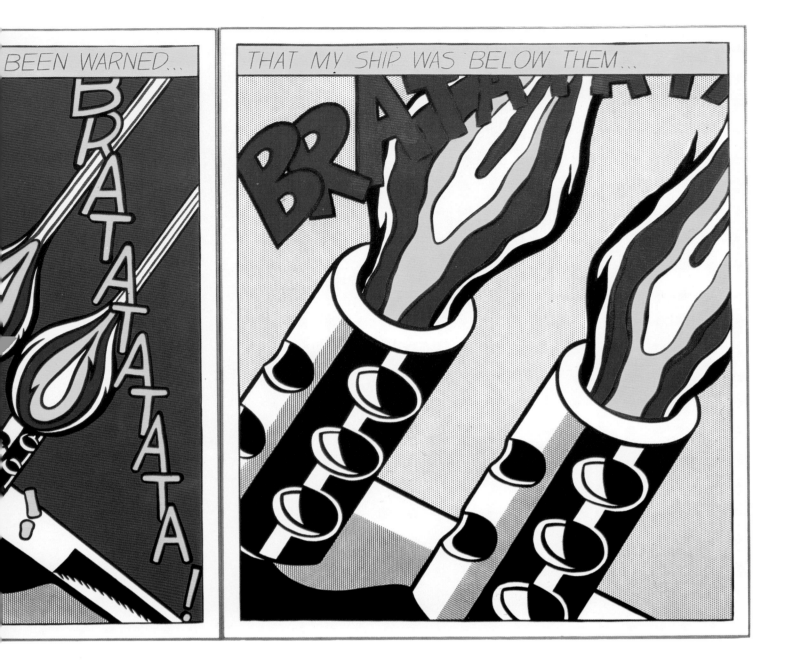

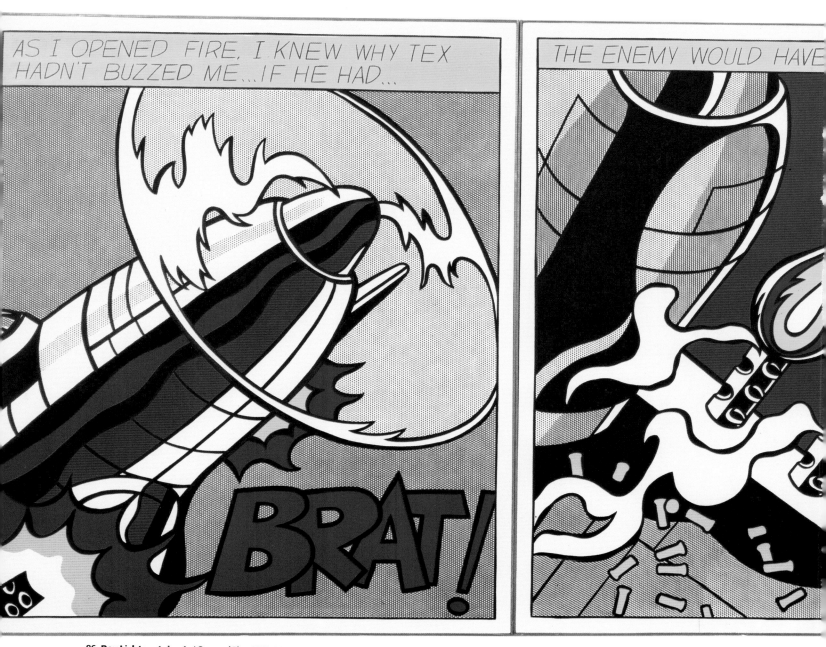

86. **Roy Lichtenstein.** *As I Opened Fire*. 1963. Magna on canvas; three panels, each 68 × 56″ (172.7 × 142.2 cm). Stedelijk Museum, Amsterdam

87. Panels from "Wingmate of Doom," in *All-American Men of War*, 90 (March–April 1962). **Jerry Grandinetti,** artist; **Gaspar Saladino,** lettering. © D.C. Comics

88. Floyd Gottfredson. Panels from *Mickey Mouse*, April 22, 1948. © Walt Disney Productions

89. Claes Oldenburg. Poster for the artist's exhibition at the Dwan Gallery, Los Angeles, October 1963. Color offset, 22 × 17" (56 × 43 cm). Courtesy of the artist

denburg drew plans and on a couple of occasions actually constructed a walk-through museum in the shape of a geometrized Mickey head (fig. 92). Inside, Oldenburg displayed his precious catalogue of found pop objects—toys and novelty items that he had bought in five-and-ten stores. The Maus Museum was a hallucinatory parody of what was becoming the pyramid of American culture: the modern museum, the stern International Style building with its prized transformed detritus stored inside. And then the joke turned back in on itself, for Oldenburg insisted the container and the thing contained were more or less the same thing. The enclosing high-art context into which pop artifacts could be ironically displaced—the Maus Museum—was just a humorless version of the pop artifacts. Like Warhol's comic-book images, Ol-

90. Will Elder. Panels from "Mickey Rodent," in *Mad*, 19 (January 1955). © 1955, 1981 E.C. Publications

had also liked to show the "real" off-screen Mickey as a ratty, prurient wise guy (fig. 90).

But soon Oldenburg began to play with a drier and more complicated metamorphosis for Mickey. He recognized what the animators at the Disney studios had known years before; that the three-ring face was less a caricatural simplification than a willfully antinatural geometric reduction. He saw that the familiar simplification of Mickey's face, imagined on a large architectural scale, oddly resembled and repeated the grave simplifications of high-modernist Bauhaus design. This joke first appears in a proposal for a new façade for the Museum of Contemporary Art, in Chicago (fig. 91); it then became the basis for a much larger joke, the Maus Museum. Beginning in the early seventies, Ol-

denburg's Maus Museum suggests not so much that the line between modern art and pop culture might be violated as that it had only a delusional existence in the first place: that each high-modernist urge has its companion echoing urge in pop culture, and that in America everybody in the long run ends up with mouse ears on. In Oldenburg's vision, the Maus Museum soon became symbolic of one of two complementary poles in modern life. On the one side the Mouse with its museums, an American Athena; on the other the darker, invented pop deity whom Oldenburg (with a genuinely scary prescience) called Ray-Gun. Ray-Gun has his own temple—the Ray-Gun wing of the Maus Museum, filled with Oldenburg's own "ray guns," pieces of trash in the familiar shape of Buck Rogers's stream-

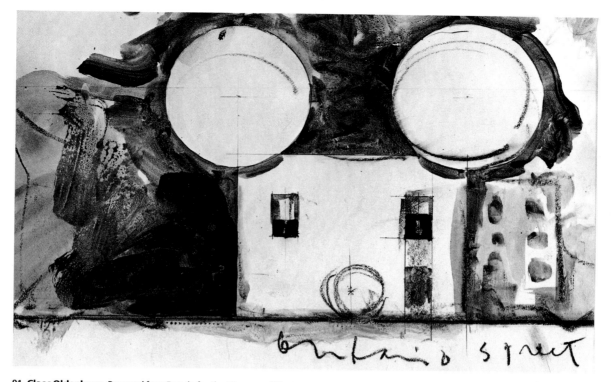

91. Claes Oldenburg. *Proposal for a Façade for the Museum of Contemporary Art, Chicago, in the Shape of a Geometric Mouse.* 1967. Crayon and watercolor on paper, 10½ × 16¼″ (26.7 × 41.3 cm). Collection Claes Oldenburg and Coosje van Bruggen, New York

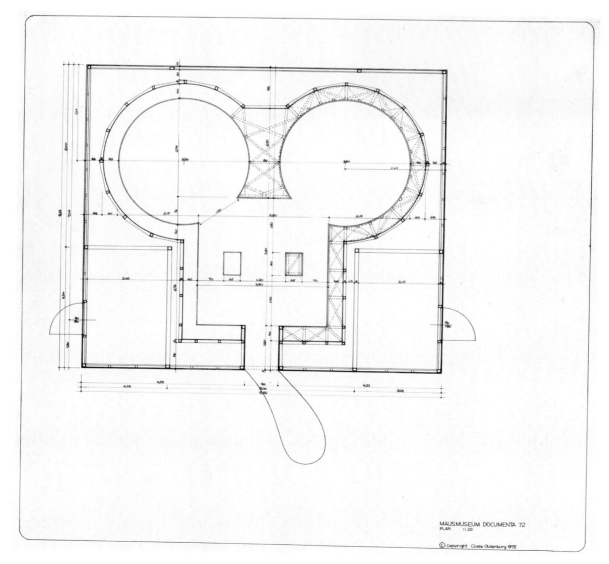

92. Claes Oldenberg. *Architect's Plan for the Maus Museum at Documenta 5.* 1972. Ink on paper, 29⅞ × 30⅞″ (75.9 × 78.4 cm). Drawing prepared by Bernhard Leitner and Heidi Bechinie. Collection Claes Oldenburg and Coosje van Bruggen

lined, high-tech weapon—found things rather than bought things. Where the Mouse represents the self-caressing urge of American consumer culture, and is the deity of Woolworth's and Macy's, Ray-Gun represents its complementary urge toward self-annihilating violence, and he is the god of Fourteenth Street. This battle between the Mouse and the Ray-Gun, consumer culture and gutter culture (which had an earlier version in Oldenburg's art as the struggle between the Store and the Street, and also had resonance for him with another found myth—the battle between Ignatz and Mickey),[58] has become for Oldenburg the symbolic struggle of American culture: violent energy against knowing complacency.

Both Lichtenstein and Oldenburg shared the century-old dream of finding a modern mythology in the comic strip. But the mythology that Lichtenstein found and assembled in the failed comics was in a sense still paradisiacal: an imaginary folk culture, a coherent world of stereotyped action that seemed at once to echo and second the apparently sophisticated world of avant-garde gestures. Oldenburg's pop mythology is, by comparison, almost Hindu in its multiplicity, and sinister in its effect. His Mickey is, by turns, lecherous, benevolent, frightening, and distant, the benevolent overseeing presence in the temple of shopping and the hard, impassive, sacrifice-demanding deity of the museum—a mouse whose three circles suggest a thousand faces.

The decline and relative fragmentation of the comics after World War II changed the way avant-garde artists saw them. But they also changed the way the comics saw themselves. In 1952, Harvey Kurtzman, who had been, with Al Feldstein, one of the two chief editors at E.C., decided to give up war comics and begin a new satiric comic book.[59] The new comic book, Mad (fig. 93), would anticipate and even lend a tone to the flowering of American satire, particularly in the work of Lenny Bruce (a figure Kurtzman in many ways resembles). Like Bruce, Kurtzman was a creature of popular entertainment—the movies and comics and now television—and at the same time had a city wise guy's disintoxicated sense of their utter artificiality. Mad is perhaps the first American satiric magazine that got its effects almost entirely from the parody of other popular entertainment. There was an implicit knowledge in Mad that the golden age of comics as a true mass or folk form—a fixed point of reference for a huge audience—had passed, and that another role for the comics might lie in creating a small, unified subculture of wise guys and shriptzers. Mad became, as Paul Goodman once wrote, the Bible of eleven-year-olds.[60] Mad seized on the comic books' aura of the illicit, the forbidden and, instead of apologizing, made it the magazine's raison d'être. Mad was hardly an underground comic book, but Kurtzman was perhaps the first to insist that the borderline zone that the comics had inescapably come to inhabit was itself a good place to be—a place outside the consensus culture. Reading

Mad, one always has a sense of the sensibility of bright (and largely Jewish) New York boys torn between their infatuation with pop culture and their knowledge of a grimmer reality—Siegel and Shuster's revenge on Superman.

None of that would have mattered had Kurtzman not also found a genuinely disturbing style for Mad, one made up in large part of the grotesque crudities that had always before lurked only on the fringes and in the lower depths of comic-book art. Superman flat out on his back (fig. 94), a hole in the boot of his costume, inhabits a world of grimy, cracking walls and bandaged foreheads—a world of cruel and disturbing children, galumphing men, and idiotic women. Mad's grotesques mostly derived from the infantile world of cheaper comics, and in particular from the work of Basil Wolverton. Wolverton had been drawing the lowest

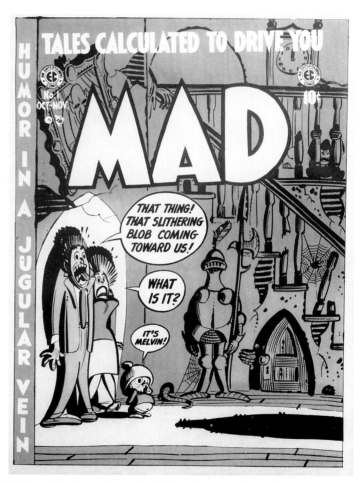

93. **Harvey Kurtzman.** Cover of Mad, 1 (October–November 1952). © 1952, 1980 E.C. Publications

kind of comics for years—he was most famous for a cowboy character called Powerhouse Pepper (fig. 95)—in a style that took the slapstick of Fisher and Herriman and reduced it to a burlesque-house rawness. In Mad, Wolverton's grotesques, with their bandaged faces and dewlapped, unshaven mugs, suddenly had a new satiric edge. They were no longer merely the grungy poor relations of the comic-strip heroes, but symbols of a truth repressed by the cosmetic, smooth surface of television and the movies. In the

94. **Wally Wood.** Panels from "Superduperman," in *Mad*, 4 (April–May 1953). © 1953, 1981 E.C. Publications

context of *Mad*, Wolverton's grotesques were no longer just the pop forms *Hi and Lois* sprang from; they were the people Hi and Lois were trying to keep out of the neighborhood. The odd, almost unintentional glimpses of lower-middle-class truth that had always filled Wolverton's drawing—raw plank floors, mugs with cigarettes clamped between their teeth—suddenly became in the context of *Mad* the bearers of a larger message: that the carnival of pop culture was essentially a slick, dispiriting fraud.

By the mid-1960s, however, this style, popularized in *Mad*'s clones, cheapened in *Mad* itself, had become the common style of rat-fink figurines and gimmick greeting cards. And it is there, in the racks of wise-guy birthday cards (fig. 96), that one first finds the work of the most singular and original comic artist since Herriman: Robert Crumb.[61]

There was a moment in the late sixties when Crumb's imagery was so omnipresent that, for many, it still remains difficult to separate his art from his moment: a generation found its bliss listening to the Grateful Dead's *Workingman's Dead* and *American Beauty* while reading Crumb "comix." Crumb's signature imagery belongs not to the high happy point of San Francisco culture but to a moment just after that, to 1968 and 1969, to the retrenchment of rock music in its country "roots," and the glum recognition by the counterculture of its future in urban squalor and rural drudgery. Crumb anatomized the counterculture at a moment when it had come to recognize itself as fundamentally unserious, or at least essentially impotent, torn between a nostalgia for American rural and ethnic styles, particularly the Delta and Chicago blues, and some undefined apocalyptic dream of social revolution. Crumb's comics delineated this moment so perfectly that many of his old admirers probably find it surprising that he has gone on drawing, and that, on the whole, his best work has been made in the past five years.

Crumb is one of the most relentless nay-sayers in American art, as convinced as any neoconservative of

95. **Basil Wolverton.** Panels from "Powerhouse Pepper," in *Tessie the Typist*, 8 (January 1947). © 1947 Twentieth Century Comics Corp.

96. **Robert Crumb.** *I'd Like to Go Out with You* (from Monster Greetings Cards). 1965

97. **Robert Crumb.** Drawing for "The Old Songs Are the Best Songs." 1977. Ink on paper, 14 × 17⅛" (35.5 × 43.5 cm). Collection Michael Wolff, Paris

the waste and dreck of American popular culture; but instead of a renewed authoritarian culture he dreams of an imaginary county in which the lower-middle-class neighborhood of Cleveland or Detroit in the forties backs onto a few acres of the Mississippi Delta; a world of sober folk musicians and defeated men in hats. Plans for mass resettlement occur, and only half jokingly, in his notebooks:

Move large masses of people from all sectors and classes of society out of cities & suburbs, away from useless jobs back to the farm lands.... Simultaneously shut down all mass media, including television networks and stations, all newspapers, all magazines.... Entertainment industry will be severely curtailed. All amplification of sound will be outlawed....[62]

The Crumb country is located irretrievably in the American pop-culture past—early jazz, country blues, suits as thick as carpets and faces as stoic as masks—a vision out of James Agee and Walker Evans. It is far too melancholy to be taken as a picture of a good or happy place; but it is, for Crumb, at least a picture of a real place.

Next to old styles, Crumb's favorite subject is his own lechery. The disturbing element of misogyny in

Crumb's work is never complacently preening, but always placed in a context of misanthropy, frustrated desire, and self-reproach. Crumb has an eye for truth as relentless in its way as Daumier's and made all the more incongruous by its insistence on expressing itself in the language of Wolverton and Fisher. A realist impulse as glum as any in Chicago Depression literature is at the heart of Crumb's work, and remains in tension with his deliberately secondhand and archaic comic style. That style is valuable to Crumb not just as a vehicle for disillusionment but because it is in itself worn. "The Old Songs Are the Best Songs" is the motto of one of his strangest and funniest comic strips (fig. 97). His deepest hatreds are reserved for Broadway shows, art-deco marquees, Swing bands, even rock music— all of the "sophisticated" or acceptably stylish parts of pop culture. Like all puritans in art, he is a relentless tastemaker, and many of his comic strips are simply moralizing lists of what is decent and what is fake in American pop culture. He is convinced that all matters of taste are matters of principle. The comedy of his work derives from its monomaniacal dependence on a wistful, secondhand, already defunct comic-strip style to express this fervent impulse to truth. He loves to make ranting lists of cautious, warning queries for his potential readers—"Are you constantly complaining about this that and the other thing? Are you frequently horrified by reality? Do you find happy people intensely irritating? Are you barely able to stand being alive?"—Phillip Larkin lost in the country of Basil Wolverton.

Robert Crumb was born in 1943 and grew up in Cleveland. He has described his home life, variously, as sordid, psychotic, and bitter, and the characters of the family drama—cold unyielding father, drugged and apathetic mother, hysterically vivacious sister, thwarted, cruel, and gifted brother—recur again and again in his work. "We could always retreat into the wonderful, wacky world of comic books,"[63] he recalls glumly; what Crumb saw in the comics, in those dead picket fences and Joe Palooka inanities, was an unintentionally truthful vision of respectable squalor. "In the old days the cartoons just came out of the soup," he has said. "You can smell the stale bread and boiled cabbage as you read."[64] The artists who seem to have affected Crumb's later style most were Gene Ahern, E. C. Segar, and Al Capp. Many of Crumb's creations, from *Mr. Natural* (who is rooted in a character drawn by Ahern) to the little cyclops who descends from Capp's Bald Iggle (figs. 98, 99), derive from these comics. But he discovered this grotesque comic style through Wolverton's work, particularly through its second home in *Mad*, to which Crumb recalls being obsessively devoted. Eventually, Crumb was offered a job in New York by Kurtzman, who had long since left *Mad* and was then working for Hugh Hefner. (Crumb was offered a job doing backgrounds for *Little Annie Fanny*.) Crumb was distressed to find Kurtzman turned into Hefner's clown; in a 1985 notebook Crumb would scribble to himself: "Don't let what happened to Harvey Kurtzman happen to you!!"[65] The alliance

99. **Robert Crumb.** Drawing for "What Gives." 1974. Ink on paper, 11 × 13¾" (28 × 35 cm). Collection Michael Wolff, Paris

98. **Al Capp.** Panel from *Li'l Abner*, November 16, 1955. © Capp Enterprises, Inc. All rights reserved

between progressive satire and rapacious sexual license, which had for so long seemed a natural alliance, suddenly looked to the puritanical Crumb merely pathetic, and he returned, defeated, to Cleveland.

Then, in the middle of 1966 Crumb began to take hallucinogens, and the drugs that had for Aldous Huxley unlocked the gates of Eden, unlocked for Crumb visions of the little domestic circuits of hell. His vision was filled with the recapitulated comic imagery of his childhood, only this time seen as nightmare rather than dulling anaesthetic.

[I experienced] a sort of hearkening back, a calling up of what G. Legman had called the horror-squinky forces lurking in American comics of the 1940s. I had no control over it . . . a grotesque kaleidoscope, a tawdry carnival of disassociated images kept sputtering to the surface. . . . [Once] we found a drab unnamed store which was filled with remaindered old magazines and comics with the covers torn off. The comics were all Brand X, low-grade stuff from the Post-War era . . . a nickel apiece. . . . I studied these funny books closely. . . . Lurid funny animals that tried to look cute but weren't lived in a callous savage world of cold violence and bad jokes, exactly as Fredric Wertham and G. Legman had said. They were very much akin to the nightmare visions spinning out of my fevered brain.[66]

Crumb also recalls that "it was during this fuzzy period that I recorded in my sketchbook all the main characters I would be using in my comics for the next ten years: Mr. Natural, Flakey Foont, Schuman the Human, the Snoid, Eggs Ackley, the Vulture Demonesses, Shabno the Shoe Horn Dog. It was a once in a lifetime experience, like a religious vision that changes someone's life, but in my case it was the psychotic manifestation of some grimy part of America's collective unconscious."[67]

Crumb's characters are rarely memorable or even particularly individualized, beyond the funny names. They are interesting not as invented personalities but as projections of his own fears. Crumb's genius is for imagery, voicing a Depression realism in the hallucinatory language of the cheap comics. In his pages the moment of vision that he had found in 1966 was relentlessly laid out and repeatedly elaborated; a genre of drawing that had before been seen simply as part of an undifferentiated mass of harmless pap entertainment got played back as urban blues, absurdist nightmare, direct confession (figs. 100–103).

The element of conscious protest in Crumb's comics is addressed less to the social system, which is always imagined as unavoidably malignant (its opponents are imagined as insanely naïve), than at the previous style of comics. Crumb's style is clearly a protest against the florid banalities of the superhero comic book. The same set of clichés that Lichtenstein had celebrated as a whole folk style only a few years before were now seen as just part of a larger culture of lies.

Crumb is an uncanny caricaturist in the most old-fashioned sense, and uses the same intently cross-hatched, dark manner to draw straightforward, subdued images of lost rural rectitude, as in his portraits of old bluesmen. Crumb's drawing is built around a constant tension between his chronicle of the grotesque and his search for the authentic. The Basil Wolverton line in Crumb is turned to realist melancholy, which works best when it is applied to secondhand imagery, as in his copies of figures from Krafft-Ebing's *Psychopathia Sexualis* (fig. 105). In his best drawing, old, fantastic comic styles are reimagined as descriptive styles. In an extraordinary drawing from 1970, Crumb adapted one of the central fantastic images of Romantic art, Fuseli's *Nightmare*, and used it as the armature for a mocking image of his girlfriend and his own libido perching above her (fig. 106). Fuseli's style, which had served so often as the basis for Gillray's leap into imaginative cartooning, here returns as the parodic basis for a new kind of ironic, confessional realism.

Crumb's drawings are a fan's notes, a peculiarly intense and personal extension of the general new spirit of comic-book connoisseurship that grew up in the seventies. A new comic-book culture came into being

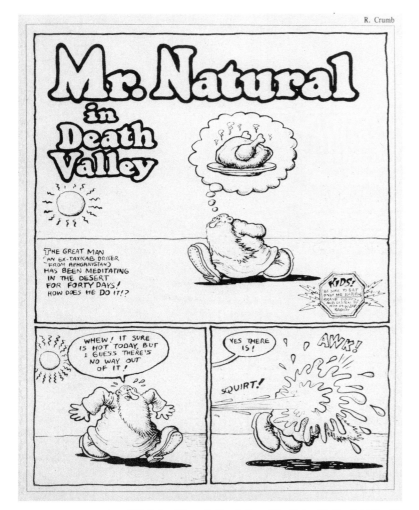

100. Robert Crumb. Panels from "Mr. Natural in Death Valley," in *Zap,* 1 (November 1967). © 1983 R. Crumb

101. Robert Crumb. Panels from "Schuman the Human," in *Zap,* 1 (November 1967). © 1983 R. Crumb

102. Robert Crumb. Cover of *Uneeda Comix* (July 1970). © 1983 R. Crumb

that, far from passively consuming whatever new products the D.C. and Marvel assembly lines turned out, instead showed an obsessive, tender concern for old comic-book styles and history. This new subculture—the subculture of the fanzines, and comic-book conventions—was often, ironically, granted by liberal-minded people, and particularly by committed leftists, an authenticity that had always been denied to the objects of its attention. To many people, it seemed that the real folk culture lay in the informal celebration of the ersatz, manufactured pop culture. One formidable student of popular culture wrote, in praise of this new subculture, that the kind of attention it gave to its objects was "essentially unpolluted by the greed, the arrogance, and the hypocrisy of so much of our intellectual life," and was also "certainly outside the stream of our computerized conformity, and unmanipulated from above."[68] These lines occurred in a 1973 book called *The Fanzines*; their author was Fredric Wertham.

It was only in the early eighties, when he began to publish the magazine *Weirdo*, the semi-official news agency of the Crumb family, that Crumb found a way to make this style work consistently for his storytelling; the hallucinatory imagery he had first envisioned in 1966 became domesticated, depressed, slowed down

103. Robert Crumb. Panels from "Mr. Natural Visits the City," in *Zap*, 1 (November 1967). © 1983 R. Crumb

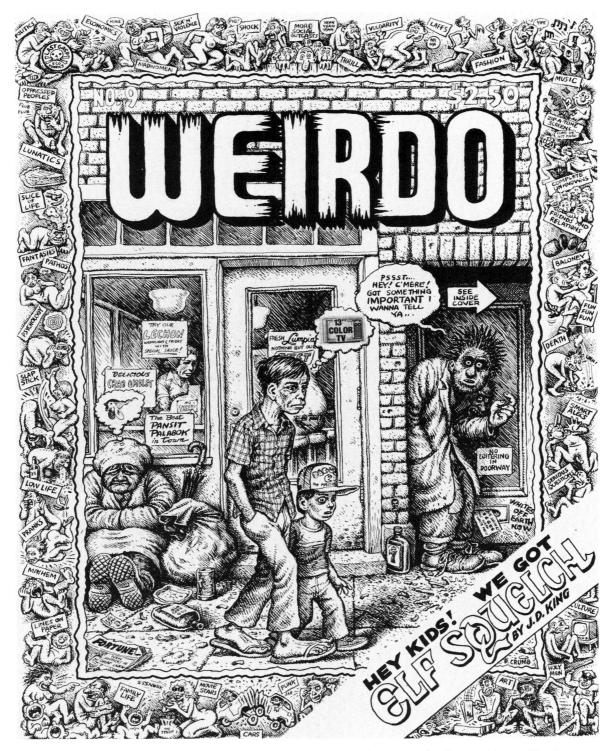

104. **Robert Crumb.** Drawing for cover of *Weirdo*, 9. 1983. Ink on paper, 14 × 17⅛″ (35.5 × 43.5 cm). Collection Michael Wolff, Paris

into a series of confessional memoirs—the *homme moyen sensuel* at home in California with a new wife and a queasy purchase on respectability. In the past decade, Crumb has been writing a series of stories and covers for *Weirdo* that are the most complicated and interesting things he has ever done (figs. 104, 105). One strain in this new work is grimly, relentlessly realist; a series of pseudo-documentary recountings of life with the Crumb family; his wife Aline, and his daughter Sophie, whose childhood Crumb is recording in a style at once tender and suspicious. He has even illustrated Boswell's *London Journal*. The connection to Boswell, however improbable, was touched with gen-

ius, for Boswell's artistic problem and Crumb's are alike: how to convert self-absorption into a comedy of egoism that will seem universal. Crumb's answer was to present his own story as folk tale, popular narrative, burlesque humor—as a comic strip.

The tradition of rethinking grotesque and fantastic styles as models of truth is a long and noble one; as we have seen, it is the great theme of the caricature tradition. What is distinctive in Crumb is that the grotesque style is treated so matter-of-factly. Crumb shows us a world that looks as if it had been made in the imagination of Basil Wolverton, yet presents it as a simple, stubborn, inarguable truth. Crumb identifies not with

105. Robert Crumb. Drawing for cover of *Weirdo*, 13. 1985. Ink on paper, 14 × 17⅛″ (35.5 × 43.5 cm). Collection Michael Wolff, Paris

106. Robert Crumb. *The Nightmare.* 1970. Ink on paper, 14¼ × 18⅜″ (35.7 × 46.6 cm). Collection Kathy Goodell, New York

the urbane and self-consciously stylish caricature tradition but with older traditions of peasant art, in which archaic folk form and close observation are inextricably mixed. In one of his notebooks from the 1980s he copied out a passage from a book about Bruegel which he obviously applied to himself. "Although Bruegel was famous in his own lifetime, the archaic tone of his imagery and his refusal to adopt the idealized figure style evolved by Italian Renaissance artists had, in sophisticated circles, an adverse effect on his reputation."[69] The pervasive depression that is the overwhelming emotion in Crumb's art is alleviated by a strangely tender regard for the rectitude of cartooning.

Although he is the grandfather and the leading figure of the underground comics, very few of his followers have ever attempted to take his backward-looking style seriously. The underground cartoonist essentially accepts the post-Disney cartoon; its speed, its impatience, the cheerfulness of its quick, graphic enthusiasm. Crumb transformed comic style into a slow, dragging net in which all the navel lint and dust of the world is caught and scrutinized. Insistently banal, his art protests all the enforced cheerfulness of American official style. He despises the cleaned-up,

perfect surface that is the *beau ideal* of all American popular culture. And yet he has a deep and touching faith in the truthfulness of the low, grotesque style that evolved in the margins of that culture.

Crumb, as much as any appropriation artist, uses a style as borrowed and secondhand as an old hat; yet he believes that his is the one true and authentic hat, and he wears it not with a dandy's flair but with a Mennonite's stubborn faith. It is the improbable passion and fervor that Crumb brings to his archaic style that gives his work both its intense conviction and (as he knows very well himself) its monomaniacal absurdity. As passionately as Blake convincing himself that the cheap neoclassical prints on which his imagination fed could picture eternal cosmic forces, Crumb regards the carnival of comic-book grotesques that he saw in his moment of vision in 1966 as a permanent legation of the American collective unconscious. Recasting a grotesque style as a realist style, Crumb has also been trying to remake a decrepit pop style into an authentic folk style, with the underlying melancholy knowledge that what he would achieve in the end could be only a private and poetic—that is, a modern—style.

107. **Philip Guston.** *Head and Bottle.* 1975. Oil on canvas, 65½ × 68½″ (166.4 × 174 cm). Private collection

108. **Philip Guston.** *Strong Light*. 1976. Oil on canvas, 80½ × 69″ (204.5 × 175.3 cm). Collection Mr. and Mrs. Harry Macklowe, New York

In 1966, at the same time Crumb was experiencing his moment of vision and revolt, another and larger revolt against an entrenched and cheerful lie of art had just begun, larger than Crumb's revolt in its scale and ultimate achievement and yet oddly similar in its visionary intensity and in the formal language of protest it would choose. In 1966 Philip Guston gave up abstract painting. Guston, who was born in 1913, had belonged to the generation of American painters who invented Abstract Expressionism, but he had found his style and fame a few years after Kline and de Kooning and Pollock had found theirs. For a long time that seemed part of his good luck. He belonged to the fifties, not to the forties—to a time when the fight for abstraction had been won and American abstract painting could begin to become placid and luxurious and even a little complacent. He was a slow-motion action painter, with a hesitant, watery, aquatic touch: reaching for analogies, people saw reeds and clouds and pond lilies in his pictures. He was a famous and inspiring teacher, and even those people who privately thought that he belonged to the second string of American abstraction recognized something fastidious and incorruptible in his work.

Then, in 1966, Guston began an agonized, violent repudiation of his own art. "American abstract art is a lie, a sham, a cover-up for a poverty of spirit," he wrote, "a mask to mask the fear of revealing oneself. ... It is laughable this lie. Anything but this."[70] He began to draw and paint a repentant catalogue of all the mundane objects that had been excluded from his art for the past quarter century: old shoes, rusted nails, mended rags, brick walls, cigarette butts, empty windows, naked light bulbs, wooden floors, faces with

109. Philip Guston. *Chair.* 1976. Oil on canvas, 68 × 80½″ (174 × 204.5 cm). Private collection

day-old stubble. His fluent style became halting, and soon the figures in his once high-minded drawings and paintings came to look like the characters in those same comic strips of the thirties and forties—the guys at *Our Boarding House,* the bums in *Powerhouse Pepper*—that Crumb was devouring and reimagining in his psychedelic ecstasy.

Guston came by this style, in part, as genuine recollection. He had begun his career as an artist, a quarter century before, with a series of heavy-handed and oddly ineffective protest cartoons that featured hooded Klansmen improbably placed in de Chirico-like plazas. Yet these odd figures remained stubbornly fixed in

Guston's imagination, and he searched to invest them with meaning throughout his life. His moment of crisis in the mid-sixties is often interpreted as a desire to reattach art to life—a move toward "realism" and the "figure" over "abstraction," but the truth seems very different. What Guston needed, like so many damaged and visionary old men, was above all a private style. And by then abstraction had become irrevocably public: the official style of a staggeringly successful art culture. What is most striking in the series of drawings that Guston made in 1966–67, and that are generally held to herald his decisive repudiation of abstraction, is not how real they look, but how uncrowded.

110. **Philip Guston.** *Mesa.* 1976. Oil on canvas, 64 × 115″ (162.5 × 292.1 cm). Courtesy David McKee Gallery, New York

The hooded figures returned, but now as Beckett tramps rather than W.P.A. villains. The Klansmen go for trips in old convertibles, smoke cigars over breakfast, paint their own portraits, engage in finger-pointing arguments, lie awake in bed at night. Busyness and enterprise and hopelessness are inextricably bound up together. Their pathos, like that of Goya's monsters, lies in not knowing that they are monsters.

As time went on, the storytelling was refined out of Guston's work. He gave up the Klansmen, and his protagonist became a stubbled, balding, disembodied male head with a single, visor-like eye (fig. 107). The Cyclops is Guston's self-portrait, but it seems to derive from a motif from the comics of the forties: Al Capp's Bald Iggle. (Who has in fact two eyes, but is almost always shown in profile, with one large, questioning eye. In *Li'l Abner* it is the Iggle who leaves people unable to speak anything but the truth.)

By the last years of Guston's life, even the Cyclops had been eliminated. Immobile knots of legs and pipes and ladders are laid out against an infinite, promising horizon which may be a melancholy recollection of Herriman's paradisiacal desert. Two motifs in particular came to be of supreme importance for Guston: the naked light bulb, dangling from its segmented metal chain—a light and a noose at once—and the insect-like assemblage of naked, hairy legs with oversized feet turned up to reveal the cobbled, nailed sole (figs. 108, 109, 111).

While Guston's late work remained embattled, his admirers understandably played down the origin of his imagery in the comics, afraid, perhaps, that the pictures might be seen merely as an exercise in painterly Pop. (They were also rightly afraid of seeming reductive.) But now that Guston's greatness is taken for granted, one can see how much not just his touch but his iconography derive from memories of popular imagery.[71] Almost all of the catalogue of symbols that possessed him in that last decade—the light bulb, the big, upturned sole, the hairy leg—derive from comic-book sources; the oversize, upturned cobbled sole first appears in Fisher's comics, the bare bulb and the stubbled faces each with a cigarette butt planted dumbly in the mouth appear regularly in the work of Ahern and Wolverton; the Cyclops, as we have seen, derives from Capp, while, as Robert Storr has observed, the clown-like gloved hands and skinny legs with big shoes derive from Gottfredson's version of Mickey Mouse.[72]

Guston would even make these references insistent, as in his homage to Herriman's endless space called *Mesa* (fig. 110). Yet all of this iconography is used straight; not as a comment on the popular style but as an extrapolation of its repressed intimations of pain. Guston put on the mask of Bud Fisher for the same reason that Beckett put on the deadpan of Buster Keaton. Both artists had the insight to see in a popular style an undercurrent of dread which could be magnified, cultivated, reimagined, and expanded, and still remain strangely comic, tender, and unpretentious.

In this sense, Guston's work is closer in spirit to the Johns of *Alley Oop* than it is to anything in Lichtenstein or Oldenburg. The language of American comics be-

111. **Philip Guston.** *Sleeping.* 1977. Oil on canvas, 84 × 69″ (213 × 175 cm). Private collection, New York

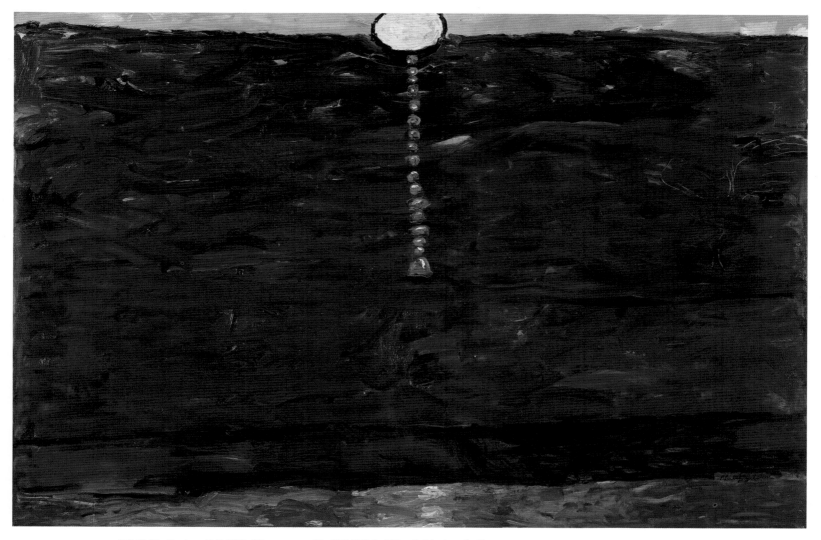

112. **Philip Guston.** *Pull.* 1979. Oil on canvas, 60 × 100″ (152.4 × 254 cm). Private collection

comes a diction for private poetry. Johns and Guston both emerge in the aftermath of achievement, from an acute consciousness of the greatness, at once liberating and imprisoning, of American abstract painting. Yet the dialogue between private and public which Johns expressed as a muted *koan* becomes in Guston an absurd expressionist tragedy. Guston never forsook his gift for pure painting, or his control over "epic" size canvases. In fact, his late paintings, far from having the flat or impersonal surfaces of Pop, have an impassioned richness of surface, a mix of butter-cream and blood, as luxurious as anything in his delicate abstract pictures. For all the suggestive relationship between Crumb and Guston, it is here that they are most different. In Crumb's art, the tension is between Kurtzman

and Superman. Guston's art is built around an argument between Ahern and Goya. (And, in this way, Guston's art resembles Goya's; for Goya's art, after all, was structured by a dialogue between Gillray and Velázquez.) In paintings like the late *Pull* (fig. 112), the comic-book images have been isolated, reduced, purified, and made into heralds of death. They display at once a death-knell feeling for the pathos of the small, repeated, and segmented stroke—the nails on the sole, the links in the light-bulb chain struck like a tolling bell—and also for the grand organ peal, the big, melodramatic gesture. Very little art in this century has been so intensely polarized, but few modern pictures have made so operatic a case that painting, as Guston put it prophetically, long before he abandoned abstraction,

113. **Robert Crumb.** Cover of *Weirdo*, 7 (1983). © R. Crumb

"is impure. It is the adjustment of impurities which forces its continuity."[73] Lichtenstein and Warhol had still had an odd residual and not quite conscious faith in a kind of purity, and had invented imaginary pop universes of clean, unmediated gestures. The intensity of Guston's faith in the power of impurity produced paintings that have some of the concentration of great religious art. Looking at Guston's work, as Robert Storr has written, "We confront them now with the same puzzlement that Guston himself felt each morning looking at the accomplishment of the night before, seeing both an image of the familiar, and a vision of the unknown."[74]

Guston's work, which at first was seen as simply a little insane, had by the time of his death in 1980 become for many young painters something like what Cézanne's had been for painters of the generation of 1906: a lost second-stringer of the defunct old school turned out to be the prophet of a new vision. But Guston was no more an "eighties" painter than Cézanne was a Cubist. Guston's thoughts and problems and obsessions always remained rooted in the feelings that created New York abstraction. Guston remained loyal to the primary attitudes and beliefs that produced Abstract Expressionism—all of those attitudes and beliefs, compounded of Kafka and Kierkegaard and Beckett and Sartre, that now seem as distant and (in an era of poststructuralism) as reassuringly humanist a

faith as that of Matthew Arnold. It was Guston's conviction that the absurdity and shame of modern life obliged the artist to search for an authentic style in the refuse heaps of the old official culture. Truth in the twentieth century could only be made from spatter cloths and vaudeville skits and unposted letters. Guston, alone among his contemporaries, at the end chose the vaudeville skit rather than the spatter cloth—chose to express his faith in a cycle of muted and ambiguous parables rather than in a set of defiant painterly gestures. The greatness of Pollock and de Kooning had lain in the dialogue in their art between existential angst and decorative luxuriance. Guston rejected the decorative swoon altogether. Only by pushing his essentially literal gift all the way into the most banal kind of illustration could he find an original style. His last paintings and drawings—particularly the monumental, heart-breakingly direct *Pull*, where sepulchral abstraction and four-in-the-morning realism are inextricably joined—are the improbable, appropriate end of the pilgrimage of the New York School.

Sometime in the early seventies, someone showed Crumb's work to Guston, and he immediately recognized a mordant companion.[75] Later, in the early eighties, Crumb saw Guston's work. "It was as though we had both tapped into this great grungy unconsciousness, all the unconscious imagery of the lower-middle-class America," Crumb said.[76] On the cover of

114. **Robert Crumb.** Back cover of *Weirdo*, 7 (1983). © R. Crumb

Weirdo in 1983 (figs. 113, 114), Crumb faithfully copied Guston's stubbled Cyclops head, which he had already drawn years before (fig. 99), and added a Herriman-derived cityscape in the background. Coming from one of the heads is a dialogue balloon. "Oh, what a fool I've been," Crumb has Guston saying, "and will continue to be." ("And *must* continue to be," Guston would perhaps have added.) Crumb called the image "A Fine Art Piece of Business."

For the past twenty years, the comics as a popular form have been in what seems to be an inexorable decline. The reasons for this are complex: comic-book fans put it down to the greed and cupidity of the big syndicates, who have entirely eliminated the full-page Sunday comics that were the prize exhibit of the comics through the 1960s. At the end of this century the comics are crowded, three or four to a page, even on Sunday. The big syndicates have also campaigned against "continuity" strips in favor of what is called, contemptuously, gag-a-day.

If the comics, as old as the century, are passing with it, what have we made of them and what have they made of us? If Goethe returned and wanted to know how fully his hope for the new form had been realized, what would we tell him? What kind of social cement have the comics provided for modernity? The artists who have taken up imagery from the comics have, in effect, each answered, differently, "I made a sort of comic strip." For Miró, this meant an escape into Eden; for Lichtenstein, it meant the subtle assemblage of a formal metalanguage; for Guston, it meant the assertion of existential truth against the transcendent lie of formalism. If there is any larger binding pattern in all this, perhaps we see it best not in a big generalization about history but in the history of a tiny motif: the little dot.

The comics depend on little dots. The revolution in printing and color reproduction that took place at the end of the nineteenth century and that made the comics possible depended on the discovery that cheap matrices of primary colored dots, laid one on top of the other, could reproduce a rainbow of colors. The American illustrator Benjamin Day was, shortly after the Civil War, primarily responsible for this advance, and since then, those little dots have borne his name.

In the 1880s, these mechanical dots existed as a kind of commercial parallel to Georges Seurat's mosaic construction of pictures. Seurat's little dots became at once a classicizing response to Impressionist brushwork—evoking symmetry, order, and solemn drumbeat rhythm—and a half-embracing, half-parodic reference to popular reproduction. This kind of pointillism eventually became part of the seasoning of luxury art, its reference to mechanical technology mostly forgotten as it enriched Cubism and Fauvism alike.

But the same Benday dots went on doing drudge work as the drones of cheap color printing, and it was only when Roy Lichtenstein picked them out from comic books in the early sixties, and made them so aggressively evident that they began to play a separate formal role of their own, that they once again entered art as a self-consciously "low" form. As Lichtenstein's work developed, the circle closed, and the artist began to use his enlarged Benday dots as an independent formal element, a bit of found abstraction with which to parody and inspect the solemnities of Op Art and post-painterly abstraction (fig. 116).

Then, Lichtenstein's Benday dots escaped even from their liberator, and returned to popular imagery in their newly enlarged form. They began to take on a permanent symbolic significance. Now they are the sign that says "pop culture" to the world; any magazine cover or advertisement that includes a visible screen of little dots is meant to be understood as a Lichtenstein—the little dots instruct us, all by themselves, to treat the image we are looking at as an episode from a pop epic (fig. 115). What was invisible to the eye thirty years ago has now become a conventional form as immediately understood as a dialogue balloon.

The pun in Lichtenstein's parodies involves a now familiar joke about the likeness of two dreams of a com-

mon language. Only now we understand that the parody *is* the achieved common language. The dream of recovering a common folk culture is futile, and the comics won't fulfill it; neither will modernist art. But the joke in the little dot lies in the way that a long history of cultural fragmentation can be condensed into epigrammatic form and still be meaningful. To call this simply "irony" is to miss its reach, and its peculiar equanimity. The common language we have is the common knowledge that we don't have one, and that we don't need one to still make sense.

The paradise of form that Goethe thought the comics might provide was, like the paradise promised by modern art itself, long ago lost, broken into the many little intractably individual pieces with which this chapter began. What Lichtenstein saw when he looked closely at the little dots is what we see when we look closely at the comics themselves: not a fixed, repetitive, imprisoning structure, but a mosaic of adaptable elements, an array of possibilities. If the comics provide a language, it is a language like any other: an all-purpose code kept in play to say different things at different moments. Perhaps our sense of the modernity of the poetry which can be made from that language lies in our knowledge of its sudden mutability, of the way that its elements—the little dots, the long, bare horizon—can be made to shift in a moment from drudgery to comedy, or from a landscape of pleasure to an interior of dread.

The little dots, like the comics they have come to symbolize, are not the atoms of a new folk art. But they're not a deadening full stop at the end of an authentic common culture, either. Like the comics themselves, the little dots are more like an ellipsis within modern culture, an elusive link between high and low, whose meanings we will have to continue to complete for ourselves.

115. Gary Hallgren. Cover illustration for *New York* magazine, **March 5, 1990.** © 1990 New York Magazine

Though the comics are in many ways the low art form of our century par excellence, they nonetheless remain an escape, a diversion, a pleasure, made by identifiable people for complicated purposes. The comics entertain. Yet their history as mass-produced imagery touches the edge of that other modern invention whose purpose is not to give pleasure but to create behavior, to persuade and seduce and even control. And what modern artists have thought and made of that invention, advertising, is the next, and the most complex and demanding, of the stories we have to tell.

116. **Roy Lichtenstein.** *Magnifying Glass.* 1963. Oil on canvas, 16 × 16″ (40.6 × 40.6 cm). Private collection

1. Lucien Boucher. *La Publicité moderne.* **Photomontage from** *L'Art vivant*, **January 1927, p. 193**

olding out the reproduction, near the end of this chapter, of James Rosenquist's eighty-six-foot-long painting *F-111* (fig. 213), we seem to be confronted with the visual equivalent of this century's primal scream—a "yowling discharge," as Robert Hughes called it,[1] that spews forth all the totems and bogeymen of our time. Leisure and amusements are run on with death and destruction, and smiling, peroxide youth is encased beneath gleaming chrome, assaulted by a colossal engine of doom, and overlapped with the trivia and confected nourishment of consumer life. And all this is arrayed in the unmistakable vocabulary of advertising, the great shaper of consciousness and fabricator of myth in the Western nations in our century. The lurid colors, glamorized rendering, bizarre juxtapositions, and drastic transformations of scale all seem components of the capitalist economy's dream machine, here gone haywire.

How did we get to such an image? The same vernacular of advertising, in the less disembodied phenomena of shop windows, electric signs, and posters, was already the happy slang of the 1920s, celebrated by an art magazine in a montage of comedy, excitement, and urban pleasures (fig. 1). It was the same mother tongue of commerce Georges Seurat felt gave Paris its particular accent in the 1890s, and that the Cubists saw as a lexicon for puns and other wordplay in the early teens—the come-on carnival cry of publicity that writers such as Guillaume Apollinaire and Blaise Cendrars hailed as the poetry of the age. And advertising has spoken in a broad variety of dialects, not just waxing grandiloquent, but also offering the laconic propositions of object displays, the tiny, crowded chatter of mail-order catalogues, and the sly persuasions of magazine pictorials. Where did that pervasive, multifaceted language come from, what has it had to do with art—and, above all, how have we moved through the kaleidoscopic dizziness of the 1920s montage to Rosenquist's hallucinatory billboard? These questions require a consideration different from any we've given to other aspects of popular culture, because advertising has had such a singular role in constituting modern society.

Advertising, after all, is not an upstart poor neighbor of painting and sculpture, one that annoys like graffiti or amuses like comics. It is a powerful rival intent on controlling the ground. Supplied with lots of money and abetted by a steady stream of crossover collaborators, advertising aspires to capture the power of the image, which art had thought its own most basic ally.

And that hostage knows too much: taken away from the ideal realm of disinterested contemplation, the images of advertising threaten to enslave people to artificial desires, and transform even the most sacrosanct and intimate aspects of our experience into commodities. Or so one version of the story goes. In modern art, many of the most inventive wielders of images have seen the situation differently—believing in advertising as a liberating power, for example, or seeing in it a wealth of techniques and materials artists could draw upon with profit. But in any and all its versions, the story of modern artists' responses to advertising, and vice versa, is the most complex and tendentious of the various histories this book addresses. This gives us even more reason to treat it as a series of stories about individual artists, from Seurat to Duchamp to Rosenquist, with many others in between, and about specific kinds of posters, billboards, and displays. Advertising has no more been a monolithic, unchanging presence in modern life than modern artists have been an organized lot with a common purpose. In order to understand the ways advertising has interacted with modern art, we will have to chart some of the different things it has been—to see the different forms it can take in any one period, and examine the shifting assumptions and intentions that have governed its changing appearances across the decades.

A part of this story has already been told, when we dealt with logos and slogans in the chapter titled "Words." Now we will concentrate primarily on imagery and objects. Especially since the advent of new technologies of photomechanical reproduction in the later nineteenth century, advertising has yielded an overwhelming flood of imagery, in posters, billboards, catalogues, and newspaper and magazine pages, that has attempted to make things—light bulbs, tires, automobiles, clothing, and so on—arresting, memorable, and desirable. But it has also altered, or asked us to reconsider, the forms of the things themselves; by strategies of display and transformation—changes in scale, patterns of arrangement, or devices of packaging—advertising has acted to change our apprehension of the real objects we acquire and use. This story of images and objects is a composite woven from different strands, involving the tiniest snippets of printed matter and the showiest spectacles of mass communication; violent intrusions of color into the vistas of the city and the landscape, and quiet catalogues in cozy parlors; or lowly hardware in shop windows, and chrome-decked machines exported internationally. It runs the length of the century, paralleling and often crossing the path of modern art's development, to create a tandem history of great hopes and profound suspicions, high spirits and abject cynicism, that puts the independence of the individual imagination itself in play against a shifting array of strategies designed to intrigue and seduce the modern mind.

Before 1900

Apologists like to argue that advertising is universal and ageless—that the Christian cross, for example, was essentially a forerunner of the corporate logo, and that the Olympian gods were products of the same strategy of personification that brought us Speedy Alka-Seltzer and the Frito Bandito. But in fact modern art and modern advertising were born together in the late nineteenth century. In the 1870s and 1880s, at the same time that Impressionist and Post-Impressionist painters in Paris began to break away from the official Salon exhibitions, new laws and altered economic forces made posters, billboards, and newspapers freshly obtrusive presences in their city. And almost immediately, in the late 1880s and early 1890s, advertising began to be involved in the development of modern painting, when Georges Seurat developed a fascination for a particular kind of illustrated poster.

If we ask, Why Paris?, the answer is relatively simple. Many other cities experienced a similar expansion of advertising, in this same period or even earlier. But few

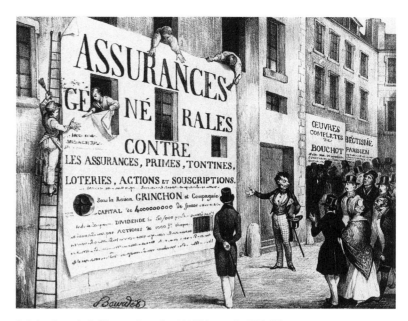

2. **Jules-Joseph-Guillaume Bourdet.** *L'Affichomanie.* 1836. Lithograph. Bibliothèque Nationale, Paris

were so marked by the illustrated poster, and none had such a contingent of avant-garde painters, bent on capturing the look of modern life. If we ask, Why around 1890?, the answer is more complex, and requires a little historical background. It's not that advertising didn't exist in Paris before the second half of the nineteenth century. By 1700 the first newspaper ad had appeared, shop signs were already a crowding problem, and posting was on its way to being one.[2]

3. **P. Edmonds.** *Rue de la Colombe.* c. 1870. Photograph. Bibliothèque Historique de la Ville de Paris

4. **Charles Marville.** *Rue Tirechapps.* c. 1865. Photograph. Bibliothèque Historique de la Ville de Paris

5. **Eugène Atget.** *Rue Saint-Jacques.* 1906. Photograph. Bibliothèque Historique de la Ville de Paris

Moreover, this story, like most stories about modern society, picks up decisive momentum with the French Revolution. The rights of citizens to post and publish, opened up in 1789, were soon made subject to government regulation and then (when private enterprise began vigorously posting ads in the early nineteenth century) to taxation.[3] These first steps established a complex choreography of contending interests that shaped the development of advertising down to Seurat's day, and that continues to shape it now. Governments typically maintained an interest in controlling the publication of information, both in newspapers and in posters. But as capitalism and industrialization accelerated their transformation of the European economies, a broadening array of citizens engaged in commerce wanted to attract customers and expand their affairs through advertising. And officials both local and national not only shared this general desire to foster business, but held a particular interest in encouraging those activities likely—as posting and publishing were—to provide substantial tax revenue.[4]

These contending forces engaged in a dance of ex-

pansion and restraint that was well practiced by the 1850s (fig. 2). But it was the changes of the next half century—the changes that differentiate walls photographed in Paris in the mid-century decades (figs. 3, 4) from those we see in other views around 1900 (figs. 5–8)—which modernized the business of advertising and set it on a course to intersect with the development of modern painting. The earlier photographs show both the architectural fabric of old Paris, in the narrow streets and small squares of self-enclosed neighborhoods, and the commercial fabric, in the painted notices for shops and enterprises in these buildings or the immediate area. In the later images, such notices still exist, but they have been bracketed by different kinds of ads, big (as for LU biscuits [fig. 5]) and small (the rash of posters collaged on the wall [figs. 6–8]), that are signs of the way the city, the nation, and its businesses had been transformed since 1850.

The big ad for a small product was a distinctive sign of the times. The business-minded Napoleon III boosted the growth of the railroads and mandated a system

dise, and innovated by publicizing limited-time or seasonal promotions and special discounts. Along with rivals like the Samaritaine, it created a larger superstructure of sales above the small, neighborhood shops as surely as the expanded metropolis invaded and superseded the old "city of a hundred villages."[7]

The clustering of smaller posters in these later photographs, however, tells another tale about the economy of advertising itself, more specifically germane to Seurat's eventual interest. The Second Empire wanted to encourage business, but also to control commerce in all things, including the flow of information and opinion. Accordingly, it censored the press and obliged all those who posted notices of any kind to register themselves and submit their work to the authorities for advance approval. These restrictions discouraged the entry of small posting firms into the field, and favored the domination of public advertising by larger companies (the head of one such firm boasted in 1880 that he could have a given advertisement posted in 35,937 municipalities within five days).[8] It was the lifting of these obligations for licensing and review, under the ensuing Third Republic, that opened the floodgates for the more widespread, heterogeneous advertising Seurat saw on Parisian walls at the end of the century.

It took nearly a decade for the Third Republic to come to terms with the consequences of the Empire-ending defeat by the Prussians in the war of 1870, and the uprising and suppression of the Paris Commune in 1871. But when the Republic's parliament finally voted amnesty for the Communards, it also voted in close concurrence the important liberalization of publishing

6. Rue de Viaigues, Paris, 1907. Bibliothèque Historique de la Ville de Paris

of new boulevards in Paris. And as these made both goods and people more mobile, the business of selling one to the other changed: no longer an affair of habitual clients and immediate passersby, solicitation had to reach beyond a particular neighborhood or city to a widely dispersed population of potential buyers. This was the dawn of citywide and national publicity for things that were "on sale everywhere," especially candy, liqueurs, and other products aimed at a general clientele. The notion of a nationwide cookie with a brand name—like LU, which was the brainchild of a baker from Nantes, in 1860[5]—and the appearance of huge ads for it in every city are symptomatic of the new merchandising. In 1866, recognizing these commercial circumstances and the advent of more large-format ads, the government markedly reduced the taxes on posters and made these tariffs proportional with size.[6]

The mid-century years were also the era of the first large department stores, and the special styles of consumption they promoted. Just off one of the new Parisian arteries, the master merchant Aristide Boucicaut established Au Bon Marché, the store that was the inspiration for Emile Zola's *Au bonheur des dames* (1883), and the trial ground for commingling several new approaches in salesmanship. The Bon Marché stocked an unprecedentedly broad variety of merchan-

7. **Eugène Atget.** *Rue des Petits Pères.* c. 1900. Photograph. Bibliothèque Historique de la Ville de Paris

8. **Eugène Atget.** *Impasse des Bourdounnais.* 1908. Photograph. Bibliothèque Historique de la Ville de Paris

9. Painted notice, Paris, 1989

10. Painted notice, Paris, 1989

rights that we discussed (in the chapter "Words") in connection with the newspapers the Cubists used in their *papiers collés.* More literally than any other, that law left its mark on Paris: the painted notice DÉFENSE D'AFFICHER, LOI DU 29 JUILLET 1881 ("Posting Forbidden, Law of 29 July 1881") is still the commonplace inscription on walls all over the city (figs. 9, 10). From this evidence we might assume that the law barred posting, but the reverse is true. While its primary purpose was to lift censorship from the press, it also eliminated registration and prior-approval requirements for posting, made it a crime to tear down or deface posters, and gave both building proprietors and municipalities clearer control—for banishment or for sale of rights— over posting on their walls.[9] Not for the first, and certainly not for the last, time, the issues of civic liberty

and commercial expansion were knotted together in this liberalization.

The timing was propitious: new freedom for advertising coincided with a new rash of things to advertise, and new technologies with which to do it. Not just in France, but in every country with an expanding industrial economy (especially the United States), the last few decades of the nineteenth century saw a sharp swing from the traditional method of selling certain basic commodities as bulk goods, via the bins of local merchants, toward the sale of brand-name packaged goods—a move by manufacturers to market directly to purchasers in controlled units, without the vagaries of middlemen. The change from the proverbial cracker barrel to the Uneeda biscuit box (the American equivalent of LU's brand approach, launched by Adolphus

Green of the National Biscuit Company in 1886), and the advent of Ivory Soap (1879) and Quaker Oats (1877), are symptomatic examples; but there were countless more every year in the 1880s and 1890s, each requiring a name, stylized logo, and campaign of publicity that would attract the customer's preference.[10]

In this field of opportunity, advertising deployed new advances in printing. The first great boon to the industry of public advertising had been the invention of lithography in the early nineteenth century, which allowed easier experimentation with type styles and weights and swifter production. But printers only started producing successful multicolor lithographs in the 1830s, by overprinting with separate stones. Innovations in this use of color, and advances in the photographic adaptation of images to gravure and lithography processes, yielded a huge boom in illustrated posters in the 1880s and 1890s. This kind of color-image poster was popular throughout Europe, but it became an especially central staple of the French advertising business, and remained so well into the twentieth century. Extensive use of such posters established the French as the leading proponents of a style of commercial persuasion that stressed image over text, and paid serious attention to questions of artistic merit.[11] The proliferation of these posters in Paris also fostered the first crossovers between modern art and advertising.[12]

Though academic circles continued to regard color printing as a corruption of the graphic arts until the turn of the century,[13] independent painters and enterprising dealers saw the potential here for a new kind of art, with an expanded market. Chromolithography seemed made to order for the numerous Post-Impressionist artists who admired Japanese woodblock prints and favored flattened, silhouetted planes of unmodulated hue. And by the 1890s artists such as Toulouse-Lautrec and Bonnard (fig. 11) had elevated the artistic status of the poster format, while dealers such as Ambroise Vollard had begun to promote "original print" art posters that passed directly into connoisseurs' hands via limited-edition portfolios.[14]

For the later history of modern art, though, the more germane questions are not about these fine-art productions, but about the way commercial posters changed the look and feel of the city at large. Street advertising had been a part of Paris for generations, in painted walls, shop signs, and wooden palisades. Yet, as a host of pre-1880 city views by Monet, Manet, Degas, and others attest, it had been something a painter of the city could readily ignore. By the 1890s, however, the changes in commerce, the law, and the technology of the poster had conspired to make poster advertising a much more prominent, indeed virtually inescapable, aspect of Paris. In an article on "The Age of the Poster" written in 1896, the conservative writer Maurice Talmeyr argued that this "media blitz" was in fact the visual signature of the epoch. "Nothing is really of a more violent modernity, nothing dates so insolently from today," he said, "[as] the illustrated poster, with its combative color, its mad drawing, and fantastic character, announcing everywhere, in thousands of papers that other thousands of papers will have covered over tomorrow, an oil, a bouillon, a fuel, a polish or a new chocolate."[15]

The unprecedented speed with which the paper images appeared, became faded and vandalized, and then disappeared to be replaced by new ones, seemed to Talmeyr to reflect all that was accelerated and uncertain in modern life, "in the way the instability of water reproduces, and adds something to, the trembling of leaves." Exaggerated mirror of a deformed world, the garish color poster absorbed, he said, "not only the rapidity, but also the acuity and the cruelty" of contemporary existence, "in order to play them back like bizarre cries with phonographic distortions." Other epochs, with a slower, more ordered social life, had their architecture; fin-de-siècle France had its posters—alas! And as to the messages this torrent of paper conveyed, Talmeyr penned an indictment whose echoes would be heard down through a long lineage of complaints against the insidious force of advertising:

[The poster] does not say to us: "Pray, obey, sacrifice yourself, adore God, fear the master, respect the king...." It whispers to us: "Amuse yourself, preen yourself, feed yourself, go to the theater, to the ball, to the concert, read novels, drink good beer, buy good bouillon, smoke good cigars, eat good chocolate, go to your carnival, keep yourself fresh, handsome, strong, cheerful, please women, take care of yourself, comb yourself, purge yourself, look after your underwear, your clothes, your teeth, your hands, and take lozenges if you catch cold!"... And isn't that, in effect, the natural and logical art of an epoch of individualism and extreme egotism? Isn't that just the modern monument, the paper castle, the cathedral of sensuality, where all our culture and aesthetic sense doesn't find anything better to do than to work for the exaltation of well-being and the tickling of the instincts? Architects can keep building churches, just as rhetoric professors can keep making Latin verse! They're working, both of them, with dead languages, and the true architecture today, the one that grows from palpitating ambient life, is the poster, the swarming of colors under which the stone monument disappears like ruins under teeming nature.... Triumphant, exultant, brushed, posted, torn up in a few hours, and continually sapping our heart and soul by its vibrant futility, the poster is really the art, and almost the only art, of this age of fever and laughter, of struggle, of ruin, of electricity and oblivion.[16]

Talmeyr, a right-wing Catholic, saw the seductions of these posters as destined to erode the discipline that kept the masses in their place. The beckoning women of modern advertising were to him only the resurgence, in newly vulgar and excessive form, of the spirit of the gargoyles and grotesques of older art. But where such older forms had been limited and avoidable, advertising assaulted without respite and overrode one's will to resist. All Parisians, without asking for it, thus came to have a perpetual Moulin Rouge cancanning away in their minds. And this constant incitement to self-concern and pleasure would, our au-

11. Pierre Bonnard. *La Revue blanche.* **1894. Lithograph, 31¾ × 24⅜" (80.7 × 62 cm). The Museum of Modern Art, New York. Abby Aldrich Rockefeller Fund**

thor felt, wave a red flag before the "beast" of the weak-minded lower classes. Reaching back twenty years for a still-fearsome memory, Talmeyr warned: "Paul Bourget tells the story of a barmaid, a certain 'Nini-Petrole,' who got herself made a nurse under the Commune, and wound up shooting the priests on the rue Cujas [a notorious massacre of hostages]. The poster is like that girl. She's at the beer hall; we'll see her on the rue Cujas."[17]

Talmeyr was in no doubt as to the evil genius who had let loose this malign force: "The creator of the poster—of that kind of poster—is Chéret, and never has there been a creator more exclusive than he. He did not renew or perfect a genre, he invented it. The poster, such as it gladdens or scandalizes our streets now, did not exist before him, and nothing even foretold it."[18] Yet this is the same fountainhead of modern depravity—Jules Chéret, the reigning originator as both designer and technician of the color poster of the *fin de siècle*—who was the object of Georges Seurat's admiration. Seurat's friend Émile Verhaeren wrote that the painter "adored" the "genius" of Chéret, and was "charmed . . . by the joy and gaiety of his compositions. He studied them, hoping to decipher Chéret's expressive methods and to ferret out his aesthetic secrets."[19] Seurat was so taken, in fact, that he persuaded his mother to collect these posters.[20] His contemporaries recognized an affinity between Seurat's later paintings of city life and Chéret's imagery (figs. 12, 13); and, as Robert Herbert has shown in convincing detail, these later paintings, *Le Chahut* of 1889–90 (fig. 14) and *The Circus* of 1890–91 (fig. 15), in fact borrow directly from Chéret. The high-stepping chorus dancers of *Le Chahut*, and the spritely acrobats and clowns of *The*

12. Jules Chéret. *Folies-Bergère: La Loïe Fuller.* **1893. Lithograph, 48½ × 34½"
(123.2 × 87.6 cm). The Museum of Modern Art, New York. Acquired by exchange**

Circus, have near direct sources in Chéret posters, and both paintings show a general debt to his distinctive manner of articulating postures and evoking agile dynamism.[21]

Such borrowings are logical given Seurat's new-found concentration, after 1888, on the areas of urban entertainment Chéret's posters often advertised; and Chéret was in many senses an obvious choice. By the end of the 1880s there was nothing unusual about thinking of him as an artist—and, by dint of his technical skills with new printing processes, a particularly modern one at that. Chéret was the king of poster-makers, a Chevalier of the Légion d'Honneur whose studio was frequented by connoisseurs such as Edmond de Goncourt and artists like Rodin. Long before, in the 1850s, he had begun as apprentice to a printer in England, where he may have absorbed influences as diverse as those of the vaporous landscapes of Turner and the bold, crudely colored posters of touring circuses. His move back to Paris and the establishment of his own shop, in 1866, had been the crucial starting point for the expansion of poster advertising in France.

Beginning in the later 1860s, he had developed a special process for producing complex sheens of color from the three-stone separation process that allowed chromolithography to expand its range of subtlety enormously. This success, and his gradual elimination of black from his posters of the 1880s, were achievements very much in line with Seurat's aesthetic.

Nonetheless, Chéret remained an odd choice for Seurat in several respects. As opposed to the popular broadsides Seurat, like Courbet and others before him, had previously admired, Chéret's posters were a sophisticated, urban, manufactured form, with no hint of the rude naïveté of folk art about them. And by focusing on them, Seurat bypassed a whole politically motivated realm of poster-making and graphics that we might suppose would have been more consonant with his anarchist ideals.[22] In the eighties and nineties, Théophile Steinlen, Willette, and others associated with the artistic circle around Aristide Bruant in Montmartre embraced the slang and mannerisms of Paris lowlife as the natural vocabulary of bohemian dissidence, and practiced a graphic art whose caricatural

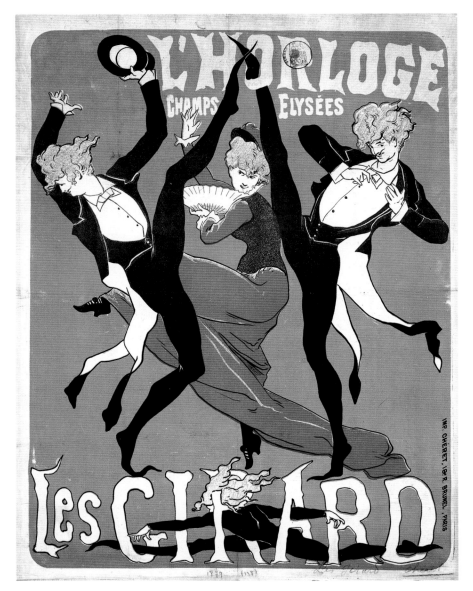

13. Jules Chéret. *Les Girard: L'Horloge Champs-Élysées.* **1879. Lithograph, 22⅝ × 17" (57.4 × 43.1 cm). The Museum of Modern Art, New York. Acquired by exchange**

14. **Georges Seurat.** *Le Chahut*. 1889–90. Oil on canvas, 67⅛ × 55¼" (171.5 × 140.5 cm). Rijksmuseum Kröller-Müller, Otterlo

harshness was part of its critical tenor. That art was grounded in an apparent devotion to an authentic working-class culture. Chéret's work on the other hand was not just commercial, but giddily so. From the 1870s on, his posters for soaps, oils, cough drops, circuses, concerts, and so on were all variations on his signature motif, of figures with animated contours and butterfly-wing colors in situations of levitating, pleasurable excitement. His elongated female figures, the so-called *chérettes* who apparently set a fashion for working-class women in Paris, gave rise to countless imitators and were instrumental in fostering the romance of the fun-loving, perpetually flirtatious *parisienne* who was and still is a staple of the tourist-brochure Montmartre.[23]

Seurat had never ignored the frivolous, fashionable aspects of his day; but his earlier ambition had been to freeze such manners into gravely static permanence—to make a woman in a bustle, for example, take on the columnar geometry of a caryatid. When he painted *Bathing, Asnières* in 1884 and *Sunday Afternoon on the Island of the Grande Jatte* (fig. 16) in 1886, he looked back to Renaissance masters such as Piero della Francesca, and beyond them to the measured rhythms of the Parthenon frieze, for the proper models by which to embody a mixture of arcadian calm and stiff ennui. But Chéret had a wholly different pantheon of admired masters. His greatest love was for Tiepolo, especially in the aerial dream worlds of the Venetian master's ceiling paintings, and Chéret's path through the Louvre veered toward the elegant and amorous canvases of Watteau and Fragonard. From these

15. **Georges Seurat.** *The Circus.* 1890–91. Oil on canvas, 6'1" × 59⅛" (185.5 × 152.5 cm).
Musée d'Orsay, Paris

sources he drew a vision of modernity that was rococo, and concerned with the gossamer rustle of evanescent, shot-silk pleasures—but from which the courtly wistfulness of the eighteenth century had been banished in favor of a permanent carnival frivolity.

On the evidence of *Le Chahut* and *The Circus*, it was precisely these "lightweight" qualities, in a double sense, that Seurat wanted to draw from the poster master. Chéret's feel for a "floating world" of upturned line and airborne leaps provided a formula for the levity of entertainment. But more than that, his relentlessly animated, shadowless, nonstop pep—what Verhaeren called "the joy and gaiety of his compositions"—held a note Seurat wanted to work with. In

17. **Georges Seurat.** *Invitation to the Sideshow (La Parade de cirque).* 1887–88. Oil on canvas, 39¼ × 59" (99.7 × 149.9 cm). The Metropolitan Museum of Art, New York. Bequest of Stephen C. Clark

this cheery superficiality, Seurat saw the seed of something profoundly true of his epoch.

What Chéret's vision lacked, and what Seurat instilled in his paintings, was linear discipline and organizing tempo. In those last images of city life, Seurat was bent on banishing the still composure, and with it the bittersweet melancholy of afternoon boredom, that marked the *Grande Jatte* and *Bathing*. In their place he devised a new mixture of dynamism and distraction that dwells on the expressiveness of willfully artificial gestures, painted-on smiles, and staged performance. The *Invitation to the Sideshow* of 1887–88 (fig. 17) had also dealt with the promotional come-on of entertainers, but it was about the half-light of show

16. **Georges Seurat.** *Sunday Afternoon on the Island of the Grande Jatte.* 1884–86. Oil on canvas, 6'9" × 10'3⅜" (205.7 × 305.8 cm). The Art Institute of Chicago. Collection Helen Birch Bartlett Memorial

18. Posted wall, Paris, c. 1908

business's tattered fringes, with reminiscences of Daumier's sad clowns and lonely saltimbanques.[24] *Le Chahut* and *The Circus* present more brightly lit visions of mercilessly upbeat performances.

These pictures transform Chéret's lessons into hard-edged caricature, imparting a sense of overwound mechanical drive that seems alternately comic and grotesque—Offenbach's *Gaieté parisienne* played one turntable speed too fast. We can easily convince ourselves that Seurat intended—in the doll-like rictus of the circus spectators, the well-drilled gaiety of the lock-stepped dancers, and the cretinous leer of the customer below—a critique of the world of paid pleasures Chéret's posters so often touted. Yet Seurat seems to have been resolved that these pictures should produce a happy feeling in the viewer. The consistent rising lines and upturned angles in *Le Chahut* particularly are demonstration-piece applications of the psychological theories of Charles Henry with which Seurat was fascinated; and by those formulae, the picture should be irresistibly exciting and pleasurable.[25] As the *Grande Jatte* is both idyllic and sad, ennobling and indicting at

once, so these later pictures deal with staged artificialities that are both enervating and energizing, madly false and cloying, yet wholly alive with a specifically modern vitality.

Talmeyr saw poster advertising as an essential part of the age, because it had a febrile ephemerality that reflected the instability of the modern world in the way water reflected a quaking leaf. But Seurat expressed the world of posters in terms of a wholly other kind of modernity, hard, electric, and mechanical. This machine beat, so evident in the dancers of *Le Chahut*, is nowhere within any single Chéret poster, but was a feature of the way posters—especially those for commodities, as opposed to performances—were regularly displayed, in repetitious groups that vividly spoke of mass production (figs. 18, 19). Seurat translates this new, aggressive structure of repeat-hit advertising into the style of the individual image.[26] Where Talmeyr saw modern chaos and feared an incitement to anarchy, Seurat found the terms for a vision of insistent, fast-stepping modern order, edging over into grinning rigidity. And by applying Henry's lessons and adding this repetitive rhythm, Seurat transformed the givens of Chéret into something more prophetic for modern advertising than was Chéret himself. *Le Chahut* is much closer to the notions of programmed emotive response in the self-styled "scientific" advertising of the twentieth century than is anything in the original posters.[27]

It is commonplace to associate Seurat's system of little dots with the machine age, and Norma Broude has shown how those dots may in fact have a direct relation to the color-printing processes of his day.[28] But there is another level of connection with modernity, and with advertising particularly, that is implicit in the profit drawn from Chéret. It involves the appeal of vulgarity. There was something crass and vulgar that Seurat found singular, interesting, and original in the performances he painted in the last two works—a stagey kind of vibrancy that, especially in *Le Chahut* with its exaggerated style of chorus dancing, seemed peculiar to the new urban temperament of the moment. Chéret's work was closely in tune with that energy. It was, by the classic definition, kitsch: a degraded form of the high art of the past, coarsened and mass-reproduced to serve the world of popular entertainment in an explicitly commercial way. But Seurat, one of the most discerning eyes of his day, liked these posters, collected them, and encouraged others to admire them. Moreover, he found them not merely appealing in a trivial sense, but useful and instructive for his art. Seurat seems to have liked Tiepolo's lessons as translated by Chéret more than he ever liked Tiepolo's own art—perhaps precisely because the reductive,

cartoon translation of that aesthetic had a feel of the moment, and a rightness for the world it belonged to that was Chéret's original contribution. Such corruptions have their own special qualities. They can schematize or make more vivid a property only dimly latent in the original item; and by making that aspect, like a freed atom, available for bonding to other things, they can spur the creation of new, unexpected syntheses.

Van Gogh, in exactly the same years, also found something worth using in the "defects" of mass-production images. Trying to portray a woman of Arles as a secular madonna who would comfort sailors on the sea (fig. 20), he described the colors he had chosen ("...discordant sharps of crude pink, crude orange, and crude green...softened by flats of red and green") as making the work "like a chromolithograph from a cheap shop."[29] In another corner of the same domain of public, commercial imagery where Seurat found the seed of something specifically urban, frivolous, and mechanistic, van Gogh found a useful analogy for the look he was seeking, of the rural, pious, and irrational. And where Seurat responded to an individual commercial talent as bearing the spirit of the city and the age, van Gogh saw the general, anonymous character of a mass-production process as appropriate to his efforts to express the quality of an individual. But in both cases, they saw vulgarity and kitsch—simplified sentiments or crude means that were outside the decorums of painting—as routes to embodying new kinds of emotional power in their work.

The relationship between Seurat and Chéret inaugurates the specific dialogue between the imagery of

19. Posted wall, Paris, c. 1910

20. **Vincent van Gogh.** *La Berceuse (Madame Roulin).* 1889. Oil on canvas, 35⅞ × 28⅛″ (91 × 70.5 cm). Stedelijk Museum, Amsterdam

advertising and the development of modern painting; and, with the story of van Gogh's colors, it also belongs to a broader history, in which advertising has been a prime participant, of the effects of modern mechanical reproduction on art in our era. In that larger field of inquiry, this first case of the poster-maker and the painter stands witness to an interesting principle of give and take. We can easily see how the advent of mechanical reproduction can coarsen our view of the high tradition of painting, and put modern commerce into a parasitic relationship with the individual creativity of the past. But Seurat's and van Gogh's initial brushes with chromolithography suggest two quite different lessons: that modern reproductive techniques may open up, by individual innovations as well as inadvertent side effects, an independent gamut of possibilities; and that these may nourish the new in exactly the same ways that they betray the familiar.

1900–1920

The development of advertising as a specialized trade had proceeded at an uneven pace in Europe and America throughout the latter half of the nineteenth century. In France, when the first firm concerned with newspaper advertising, the Compagnie Générale des Annonces, had been established in 1845, its owner cited "the example of England and the United States, where this development [of advertising] has attained

gigantic proportions."[30] But far from being a prototype of what we now think of as an ad agency, the Compagnie Générale simply leased and brokered page space; and French firms made on its model, which tended to monopolize this corner of the trade, were considered an outmoded impediment to development by the turn of the century.[31] Ad agencies formed and prospered more swiftly in America in the last decades of the nineteenth century and were more active in cleaning up the image of a business that had traditionally been dominated by the snake-oil trade. In the U.S., the false claims and flimflams grouped under the bland rubric of "abuse" of advertising prompted government reform (such as the Pure Food and Drug Act of 1906) and the early formation of professional associations to monitor standards and ethics in the trade. The English formed a society "for checking the abuses of public advertising" in 1893 and passed an advertisements regulation act in 1907.[32] French advertisers were slow to follow, in part because, well into the twentieth century, their ads were still heavily dependent on selling nostrums for baldness, flagging virility, female complaints, and so on.[33] (When several American states passed laws to control false advertising around 1915, a French cynic remarked that such action would cut the local business by fifty percent.)[34] Huckstering put the whole enterprise in bad odor, and many established manufacturers saw it only as a refuge for charlatans.[35]

Whether or not outsiders scorned it, however, advertising in Europe and America began to take itself seriously as a profession around the turn of the century: associations formed, journals began publication (*Printers' Ink* in 1888, *La Publicité* in 1903), and "how-to" books began to be more intently "scientific." Nineteenth-century writers on advertising commonly held that the way to win the customer was to appeal to his reasoning faculties: a potential buyer wanted to see a "reason why" to prompt his or her purchase, and the ad simply provided information and addressed common sense. At the same time, few claimed (and most openly doubted) that such appeals could ever be made to operate in a sure-fire or systematic way. The conventional wisdom held that the consumer was rational, but advertising was not.[36]

After 1900, though, books like Walter Dill Scott's *The Theory and Practice of Advertising* (1903) and *The Psychology of Advertising* (1908), made into serious doctrine what had already become a strong minority view in the business: that people were really a bundle of irrational hankerings and habits, and that the way to their pocketbooks was through their suggestibility rather than their calculating faculties. That point of view had earlier been confirmed by the success of P. T. Barnum and his ilk. Scott based his arguments, though, on more prestigious psychological science, in the theories of William James's *Principles of Psychology*, and in the statistical studies of behavior associated with the positivism of Wilhelm Wundt. James's key notions of the stream of consciousness, the fixation of attention, and the relation of repetition to habits seemed to confirm skepticism about the role of will and reason in human affairs, while the emphasis on experiment and statistics promised to set the business of persuasion on a base of verifiable, proven method. In the new view, advertising was rational, and the consumer was not.

This claim for advertising as a science, with its related view of human nature as a manipulable entity, would endure and transform itself in many guises in the course of the century, and occasion considerable paranoia along the way. In the immediate context of pre–World War I advertising, as it cribbed from the late nineteenth-century thought of James and others, such progressive thinking tended to mean recourse to some form of perceptual psychology tinged with nascent behaviorism. And, with an emphasis on irrational suggestion that privileged images over words, it yielded a lingering dependence on a late nineteenth-century, essentially Post-Impressionist, notion of the way pictures communicated. Posters with a clear, dominant patch of color, or ads with images and texts of reductive simplicity, were touted as the sure-fire means to arrest attention and penetrate consciousness. Offering such prescriptions about the most efficient relation of an image to the sensorium and spirit of an individual, admen prided themselves on exemplifying the modern scientific spirit and on following the lessons of what they saw as worthy modern art.[37]

The rogue successes of early advertising, though—the tricks that were made up by manufacturers as they went along, without benefit of expert counsel—often have an interest for modernism far surpassing that of, say, posters by Cappiello, and other venerated instances of properly arty appeal. The advent of modern publicity involved a great deal more than vividly colored paper; and its relationship to early twentieth-century vanguard art is not simply a matter of borrowed imagery or shared styles, though these abound. The growth of advertising in the early twentieth century depended on a constellation of strategies for making certain objects or products take on vivid lives in the public imagination; and these efforts had, as artists realized, affinities with modern art's insistence that the world be seen anew, as well as with its general spirit of invention and demand for change. These commercial strategies for attracting attention, fixing memory, or generally eliciting a desire for novelties were often arrived at by wholly "unscientific" or ad hoc means. And yet, in their disregard for tradition, their wholehearted embrace of the materials of industrial production, and their glamorizing of certain promises of modern life,

Bibendum par Bibendum.

21. Illustrations from the catalogue *Le Joyeux Bibendum* (Clermont-Ferrand, 1923), pp. 6, 9

these improvised public solicitations—in billboards, in shop windows, in imaginative avatars that stood for companies, or in prize contests—could seem among the most potent agents for social change.

Let one such idiosyncratic invention exemplify these energies and their impact. We now know the Michelin tire man, Bibendum, as a chubby-cheeked tourist and itinerant gourmet. But this fellow has a shady past in the raw, early years of modern advertising, when he was an aristocratic rake with Rabelaisian appetites, and a mercilessly competitive sportsman: he abducted women, taunted weaker rivals, and, as an adept of kick-boxing, donned leopard-skin trunks to punch forward his non-skid cleated treads (figs. 21, 22, 24). The circumstances of his birth are so unlikely and contrary to rule that they bear recalling.

The tire man's origins date to the 1890s, early in an age when countless related representative figures were also spawned (the RCA dog, Nipper, of "His Master's Voice," for example, first portrayed in 1902 on the basis of a real pet and an actual incident; or the White Rock girl, devised in 1894; Mr. Peanut came later, in 1916).[38] His conception began with a phrase, de-

22. **Hindre.** *Pneu vélo Michelin.* 1911. Poster, 31½ × 23⅝" (80 × 60 cm). Courtesy Michelin, Clermont-Ferrand

23. "La Pile de pneus dont Bibendum est sorti," from the catalogue *Le Joyeux Bibendum,* p. 3

24. **O'Galop.** *Le Coup de la semelle Bibendum.* 1910–11 (from a design of 1905); reconstructed, 1987. Stained glass, 9'8⅛" × 7'11½" (295 × 242.5 cm). The Conran Shop, London; formerly the Michelin Building

vised by André Michelin to sum up the inflated tire's smoother ride over bumps and stones: "the [pneumatic] tire," André said in 1893, "drinks up the obstacle."[39] The next piece in the puzzle came when André and his brother Édouard visited their company display at a fair in Lyon in 1897. Édouard, an artistically inclined man and former student of the academic painter Adolphe Bouguereau, remarked of a stack of tires that, with the simple addition of arms, it might resemble a man (fig. 23). These two disconnected elements then cross-pollinated in the brothers' work with a poster artist who drew under the name O'Galop. Apparently modeling their concept on a beer-hall ad, they commissioned the image of a man made from tires preparing to drink a glass full of "obstacles" (broken glass, nails, and so on). And to complete what then must have had the character of a private joke, they gave their man pince-nez glasses in caricatural reference to André, and titled the image with a Latin post-

25. **O'Galop.** *Nunc est Bibendum.* 1898. Poster, 17⅞ × 14⅛" (45 × 36 cm). Courtesy Michelin, Clermont-Ferrand

victory exhortation from Horace's ode on the Battle of Actium, *Nunc est bibendum* ("Now is the time to drink") (fig. 25).[40]

A pet phrase, a chance fantasy about a rubber snowman, and an esoteric toast in a dead language—hardly a recipe for scientific selling. Yet it caught on, especially after a race driver at an auto rally hailed André, in apparent ignorance of the word's meaning on that first poster, by the nickname "Bibendum," and thus gave the tire man a name. At nearly a century's remove and millions of Bibendums later, we can see how this idea took life. Instead of working with a watered-down version of recent high art, the makers of the Michelin man operated in a way that was independently modern. They tapped into long-standing

26. Bibendum figures at Carnival, Nice, c. 1912

minor traditions of playful symbolization by object-attributes (such as images of pan vendors in which the figure is made out of pans) and into marginal realms like children's illustrations (such as the Tin Man in *The Wizard of Oz*, conceived from funnels and tubes and drawn by W. W. Denslow in 1900), to come up with a figure that in a literal sense embodied a new product. Working with "found objects" and exploiting these old strategies in a new way, they concocted a "Tubism" well before Fernand Léger's tubular metal figures of the teens, and made a true "machine man" to symbolize the spirit of a new age. (An age, though, when girth still spoke for unashamed appetite and conquering pride: Bibendum was, as per French slang, *gonflé*—inflated, or full of himself—without apology.)

Bibendum, made of carriage or bicycle tires before there were automobiles, came to be the very model of a motor-age man, at a time when owners of motorcars were more likely to read Latin. Eventually, when car ownership became available to a wider public, he discreetly shed his gold cufflinks and traded in his pince-nez for driving goggles, to be a more popular sort. But he was a thoroughly modern advertising form from the outset, not just in the way he looked, but above all in the way he was used. The Michelin brothers were early masters of publicity in the broadest sense, with a keen sense of how they might promote their products in the public consciousness in a variety of newsworthy ways. And the memorable figure of Bibendum became a key adjunct of these campaigns of public relations. The early "science" of the ad's effect on the individual viewer's sensorium, irrelevant to an understanding of Bibendum's origins, was even less in touch with these promotions and sponsored events, by which the Michelin company, more than simply selling tires directly, expanded its market by increasing the general allure of automobile travel and reinforcing the prominence of the firm. Those kinds of promotional campaigns are crucial to understanding advertising's role in emergent modern society, and some key artistic responses to advertising's impact.

In the guise of its newfound avatar, the Michelin company presided over Carnival parades (fig. 26),

sponsored auto rallies, and offered prizes for aviation feats, including aerial-bombing contests.[41] It also lobbied for road improvement, established the first consistent network of highway markers in France, and distributed the first serious guides to motor travel.[42] In all these activities, the goal was not simply to sell a product to a waiting market, but to create that market—to hasten the arrival of a world where people drove cars regularly, aviation developed broadly, and where, inevitably, Michelin products would be more in demand. This involved a social process more complex than just the stimulation, or fabrication, of new desires. It entailed the encouragement of a world of events in which the lines between puffery and progress—between what was hype and what was really happening—became difficult to fix. Car rallies, air

27. Gamy. *Grand Prix Michelin de l'aviation.* **1911, commemorating a competition held in 1908. Lithograph, 29½ × 14¾″ (75 × 37 cm). Courtesy Michelin, Clermont-Ferrand**

races, and the like were certainly pseudo-events, intended to exploit a dubious notion of made-to-order "news" that had itself been fostered by a competitive press in quest of sensation to sell. Yet these were real events as well. The competition they fostered, the money they injected into the process, and the attention they drew to themselves gave crucial boosts to the

28. **Robert Delaunay.** *The Cardiff Team.* 1912–13. Oil on canvas, 10'8⅜" × 6'9⅞" (326 × 208 cm). Musée d'Art Moderne de la Ville de Paris

progress of the car and the airplane which in turn, to use a trite phrase that here is true, transformed the world.

One item that stands for a host of these activities is the poster of 1911 (fig. 27) that celebrates the winning of a grand aviation prize at Clermont-Ferrand (the town was Michelin's headquarters, and André had offered the prize money that made this feat worth attempting). With the spire, the plane above, and the wall with ads below, the image is structurally similar to Robert Delaunay's *The Cardiff Team* of 1912–13 (fig. 28). And the echo is more than superficial, since De-

29. Blériot monoplane on display at *Le Matin* newspaper office, Paris, c. 1910

launay's picture similarly glorifies aviation, in the airplane above, at the same time it also honors advertising. By setting the painted palisades as bold planes of color in the background, Delaunay made clear the way billboards matched his interest in immediate, vividly untraditional communication. Moreover, the idea of advertising as a modern symbolic language tied to primordial human aspirations is honored in the emphasis on the name ASTRA. (Here it proclaims an airplane-construction business, but the primary import of the enlarged word is its Latin meaning, "stars," as in *ad astra*, or "toward the stars," suggesting a reach for the heavens appropriate to the picture's exaltation of flight.)[43]

Billboards are joined with the Eiffel Tower, the giant Ferris wheel on the Champ-de-Mars, upsurging rugby players, and the airplane as parallel expressions of modernity; and the artist "posts" his own identity by emblazoning his name in sign-painter's letters along the background wall. Delaunay seems to have liked the fantasy of his fame reaching a broad public, as a part of the visual array of the city, in the same way Picasso enjoyed seeing KUB proclaimed on the sides of buildings. Just as the French aviator Louis Blériot's flight across the English Channel in 1909 had heralded a new era in which national boundaries were more easily superseded, and the rugby game spoke for athletic engagement between France and Britain, so the inscription NEW YORK. PARIS . . . below the artist's name suggests the notion of an international "trade" in this "brand."[44]

The Cardiff Team, like the Michelin poster, celebrates things that were part performance and part promotion. The foreground event was fresh from the current sports pages:[45] rugby, a notably rough and unfamiliar British game, was being transplanted to France to foster international sports competition, in the same spirit of vitalist health-and-fitness awareness, and stopwatch standardization of athletics, that had not long before informed the creation of the Olympics.[46] The Eiffel Tower behind had been a "sport" of another kind, constructed only as a giant signboard for

the 1889 World's Fair; and the Ferris wheel beside it was an even more evident example of advanced engineering at the service of crowd-pleasing sensation. Even France's triumphs in aviation had been a matter of achievements that, like the Clermont-Ferrand arrival and Blériot's feat as well, were the direct result of prize promotions or sponsorship. (The flight over the Channel had been spurred by a prize offered by the London *Daily Mail*, though the Parisian daily *Le Matin* wound up promoting Blériot as a hero in France [fig. 29].)[47] In sum, the picture posits a coalition among adventurism, athletics, technology, publicity, and art. And the whole composite alliance is suffused with the glow of a fairground modernity based on the creation of new thrills, spectacles, or amusements—things produced either for their own sake or in hope for profits, but with no excuse in practicality or necessity.

In this and other pictures, Delaunay sought to convey a transcendent, even mystical, spirit of his epoch (in another version his name is replaced on the sign by the word MAGIC).[48] But he seems to have felt no conflict—on the contrary, a real partnership—between these ideals and showy publicity. His general enthusiasm for the sensational aspects of modern life reflects in part his contact with the Italian Futurists, led by F. T. Marinetti. Those impatient champions of the world to come identified progress not only with propellers and crankshafts, but with the thrill of speed and the glamor of novelty. And they wanted their art to incorporate the new forms of power, including those of arresting mass attention. Marinetti clearly understood the role of charged symbolism and spectacular gestures in attracting adherents. For him as for others of his epoch, art was a form of propaganda or advertising, a means to alter consciousness and promote the triumph of new social forces. And parallel to the way Bibendum's rallies and road signs made motor travel happen, the Futurist program, with its press-conscious trappings of staged provocations and intransigent rhetoric, had an inestimable role in getting modern art rolling, especially in remote venues like Russia. (One astute Russian observer sneered in 1913 that Futurist experiments were "mere American advertisement.")[49] The pitch became part of the product in such cases, where the distinctions between a genuine modernity and a promotional one, between real innovation and mere show, seem problematic at best.

The Cardiff Team is more specifically linked, though, to the vision of commercial "spectacle" expressed by Delaunay's close associate Léger. Writing in 1924, Léger cited the Eiffel Tower and the Ferris wheel beside it as examples of the modern "object-spectacle" which dominated Paris. He recognized that "industry and commerce" had first seized on these forms of attraction, in making a "spectacle" of shop windows and department stores by "creating an enveloping, pressing atmosphere, using only the objects at their disposition." For Léger, these powerful strategies for capturing the imagination challenged the painter to rise to their level. Confronted with the enormity of modern life, the artist had only one choice if he were to survive: taking everything around him as raw material for art, he had to "choose in the turbulence that rolls under his eyes the possible plastic and scenic values, [and] interpret them in the sense of a spectacle." And he had to *invent*, to match the pace of innovation around him. Mere adaptation to the new forces was not enough, for "life today never adapts, it creates every morning, well or badly, but it invents. If adaptation is defensible from the point of view of theater, it is not from the point of view of spectacle."[50]

Whether this spectacular, promotional aspect of modern life leads ultimately to social good or social evil is a separate question. In the 1990s any honest answer as to whether items of progress that were nurtured by such promotion—like the department store, the automobile, or the airplane—have been more pluses than problems is bound to be at least qualified, if not fraught with the most deeply felt contradictions. But in the Western industrialized nations the expansion of material life along capitalist lines has been a central, defining factor in the experience of modernity, for better and worse; and the hype has been as consistent and essential a part of that experience as the hardware. Contemporary writers have in fact recently reaffirmed how central the commercial notion of the "spectacle" has been to modernity. But they have seen it as the displacement of truth by empty falsehood, and as the mounting of deceptive distractions from realities better confronted head-on.[51] For Léger, as apparently for Delaunay, spectacular promotions, from department stores to billboards to fairground towers, were an arena of invention from which art could learn, a way to shake off the old, fix the mind on the present, and summon the imagination of the future.

Their response was not a simple, naïve assent, but a choice among conflicting options. New things, after all, can displace or destroy old things, and a characteristic dilemma of modernity from the outset has been that of the need to choose between having better roads and keeping more tranquil fields, or between the brightly colored promises of commercial expansion—including billboards—and the preexisting beauties of old buildings and agrarian landscapes. That latter choice was a matter of acute debate just at the time of the conception of Delaunay's painting, as a long-running battle against outdoor advertising mounted to a special pitch of intensity.

In Paris, the desire to control and delimit public posting of ads had followed almost immediately on the liberalizations of the law of July 29, 1881.[52] By the early 1900s, battle lines had already been drawn between the business-minded advocates of progress and the defenders of historic preservation in the capital, and between advertisers (or people who liked to lease their land or wall space to advertisers) and defenders of the pastorale in the provinces. (In 1906, at the moment of Fauve visions like Matisse's *Bonheur de vivre*, the first law establishing nature preserves was passed; and the national law of April 20, 1910, was particularly concerned to exclude posting on such classified sites and monuments.)[53]

By 1911, an advertising commentator saw a nationwide "posterphobia" against outdoor signs, brought on by the fact that the poster—far from being the here-today, gone-tomorrow phenomenon of the city that Talmeyr observed—had followed the new motoring public into every corner of the countryside, and had set itself there permanently. "The principal fault of the modern poster," the writer said, "is above all its dimensions, more and more enormous, and also its permanence, its immutability. If it was formerly a transitional thing, something fugitive and almost discreet, it has become, by the force of natural laws, the obsessing vision our gaze can't ever shake the habit of, which pursues the poor traveler in his every move, in all his innocent pleasures, ever bigger—because of the competition—ever redder or bluer, following the whim of its author, like the inept refrain that everyone hums, or the *leit motiv* of a Wagner opera."[54]

An angry debate, centered on a proposal to ban all freestanding signs in the countryside, was waged in the legislature and in the Parisian press during the spring of 1912. Rural prohibition, it was recognized, would make billboard advertising almost exclusively an urban phenomenon, and accelerate the rush for appropriate space in Paris.[55] And indeed, in July, when prohibitive taxes on rural signs were finally passed, the city of Paris turned its attention to mounting similar restrictions on its own billboard excesses.[56] In August 1913, a prefectural ordinance sharply hiked the fines for poster violations set by a 1910 law and extended the area it covered.[57] Even more severe taxation measures were being pressed in 1914, aimed at posters in general and especially at large billboards.[58]

Such reaction in Paris was especially well supported by a long-established community of preservationist interests (the Commission for Old Paris, known as a major patron of the photographer Eugène Atget, was founded in 1897). But the tide was turning against outdoor advertising in England and Germany as well.[59] And though in America posters were consid-

30. Fifth Avenue and 108th Street, New York. Photograph from *The Mayor's Billboard Advertising Commission* (New York, 1913)

ered a less dominant part of advertising, the companies concerned with them were massive, and their
effect, aided by railroad distribution and electric-light
visibility, was pervasive. (In 1912, American advertisers
spent thirty million dollars on posters, and the American Tobacco Company alone used five million poster
sheets annually.)[60] And there, too, recoil against this
force showed up in strength in the years just before
World War I. In September 1911 the state of New York
passed a law prohibiting roadside signs that blocked
the view of official signage or natural beauty,[61] and in
1913 New York City sharply curtailed street-level
signs.[62] The mayor of New York appointed a special
commission in 1912 to make recommendations on the
excesses of billboards, and its documents (figs. 30, 31)

show that signboards were a far more aggressive presence in the cityscape during the first decades of the
century than at any time since.[63]

During the years 1911–14, advertising was seen, internationally, as having grown into something monstrous that threatened the quality of life. Delaunay's
and Picasso's decision to pull billboards into their pictures (fig. 32) at precisely this time seems implicitly to
bring their artistic enterprises into at least a limited
partnership with those business- and progress-minded
types who scorned the lovers of *vieux Paris*, and opted
for the new world of paint and paper—"ever bigger
. . . ever redder or bluer"—over that of picturesque old
streets and unadorned architecture. In Picasso's painting, the city fades away to a pale, uniform backdrop

31. Fifth Avenue and 98th Street, New York. Photograph from *The Mayor's Billboard Advertising Commission*

for the floating planes of color, the variety of graphics, and the gigantism of the enormous bottle. And the young Léger, speaking in 1914 in the immediate aftermath of the restrictive laws, specifically derided the societies formed to protect the landscape, sneered at the boring municipal walls labeled DÉFENSE D'AFFICHER, and identified the billboard—"imposed by commercial necessities," he said, and "brutally cutting off a landscape"—as one of the elements of shock and contrast by which modernity was defining itself. He asserted that "this yellow or red poster, screaming in this timid landscape, is the most beautiful new pictorial motive there can be: it knocks down the whole sentimental, literary concept and announces the advent of plastic contrast." And, while he allowed that something so radically unfamiliar could only be appreciated by advanced visual sensibilities, he related the new force of posters and illuminated signs to those of the car and the train, as elements of progress that were relentlessly

Not just the bright colors of the posters, but also the effect of their contrast with existing landscapes and architecture, was a fact of modern life, not to be ignored or quashed. Better such contradictions as the price of dynamism, he felt, than the narrow monotony of a compromised status quo. In such conflicts an artist could find the elements of a new form of beauty, with the particular raw violence and dynamism of the age.

Delaunay and the Futurists raised anthems to what they saw as the heroism of modern life, and explicitly or implicitly subsumed advertising in that music. But there were many other ways to respond, in part because, as an all-pervasive aspect of economic modernization, advertising was encountered in so many different forms—not just as color in the landscape, but as a new look in shop windows, or as catalogue and newspaper illustrations. The Cubists, for example, working in exactly the same years, favored commercial

32. **Pablo Picasso.** *Landscape with Posters*. 1912. Oil and enamel on canvas, 18⅛ × 24″ (46 × 61 cm). The National Museum of Art, Osaka

casting old ideas of harmony into the dustbin of history.[64]

Léger's words bring back memories of an alliance, since grown less easy, between modern commercial expansion and hopes for liberating social change. For him, bourgeois taste connoted a blind unwillingness to see the world as it was, and a stultifying desire to maintain everything—the city, the home, painting, life—in a static, banal, middle-tone balance. In that sense the forces of outdoor advertising seemed powerfully antibourgeois. The growth of billboards appeared, like the advent of the machine, tied to "commercial necessities," and part of an evolution toward a new society free from the penuries and prejudices of the old order. Léger welcomed these aspects of modernity as others of his generation looked forward to war, in deep frustration with what they saw as the inertia and unjust hierarchies of the belle époque, and with commitment to a life lived more intensely.

notices that spoke of the domain of private consumption and amusement, not grand stunts and public energies. Picasso's *Landscape with Posters* (fig. 32) is the unique exception in this regard. More typical in their focus on smaller ad sources are Picasso's *Au Bon Marché* (fig. 33) or Braque's *Glass and Bottle* (fig. 35). As Rosenblum and others have noticed, Picasso seems to have been concocting a sly little tableau in *Au Bon Marché*, with the quaint illustration taken from an announcement of a lingerie sale at the Samaritaine (fig. 34), a package label from its crosstown rival, and truncated letters reading TROU ICI in the wedge of open space below.[65] Among all of the Cubists' *papiers collés*, *Au Bon Marché* is one of the boldest direct appropriations of a commercial logo; Picasso was apparently pleased to contrast its florid, cursive style with the blunter typeface of the Samaritaine's sale announcement. This is also one of the very rare instances of a figure appearing amid Picasso's clippings from the

33. **Pablo Picasso.** *Au Bon Marché.* 1913. Oil and pasted paper on cardboard, 9¼ × 12¼" (23.5 × 31 cm). Ludwig Collection, Aachen

34. Advertisement for the Samaritaine department store, from *Le Journal*, January 25, 1913, p. 9

35. **Georges Braque.** *Glass and Bottle.* 1913–14. Charcoal and pasted paper on paper, 18⅞ × 24⅜" (48 × 62 cm). Private collection

press; Braque's inclusion of a large, undisturbed portion of a furrier's ad is equally exceptional. Yet even the ad images in these two works, gaudily declarative in the context of Cubism, are fairly banal stereotypes of small-time commerce, trifling and quaintly nostalgic when compared to the homages to innovative spectacles that Léger espoused. They seem to point in another direction altogether, toward Kurt Schwitters's fascination with the bland, empty smiles of the women in fashion advertisements—an impersonal pleasantness that Schwitters lovingly lampooned by setting it up as a Raphaelesque ideal of a modern madonna (fig. 36). Delaunay and Léger seem to have felt great excitement over the power of advertising to generate things that were bolder and bigger than the forms of traditional life; and they felt challenged to compress that force into the compass of a painting. These two Cubist selections, and Schwitters's art more generally, re-

sponded on the contrary to advertising's production of tiny, minutely particularized worlds to which art gave a larger life by strategies of isolation or unexpected juxtaposition.

The adoption of commercial material by other Dada artists in the same years offers an even sharper contrast with the rhetorical monumentality of Delaunay. The rugby players of *The Cardiff Team* are a long way, for example, from the nine "malic molds" (fig. 37) that eventually became part of Marcel Duchamp's *Large Glass (The Bride Stripped Bare by Her Bachelors, Even).* Yet Duchamp's motif also has a point of origin in the turn-of-the-century vogue for new sports. These "molds" are derived in part from images of sporting attire, and for them Duchamp took a page from advertising. The source outfits were apparently lifted from a mail-order catalogue of the bicycle and automobile division of the Manufacture Française d'Armes et Cycles

36. **Kurt Schwitters.** *Knave Child.* 1921. Collage, 6¾ × 5⅛″ (17.1 × 12.9 cm). Sprengel Museum, Hannover

de Saint-Étienne, a publication devoted to feeding the mania for bicycling that had sprung up in the last part of the nineteenth century (fig. 38).[66]

Growing up in a well-to-do family in the provinces, Duchamp must have felt the fascination of such children around the industrialized world for this kind of merchandising device, of which the Sears Roebuck catalogue was perhaps the grand example (fig. 39); later, when describing the book of notes for the making of the *Large Glass,* Duchamp referred to the document as "a kind of Sears and Roebuck catalogue."[67] These densely printed and copiously illustrated surrogate show windows arrived in countless living rooms from points beyond the horizon, with a cornucopia of strange objects and prim figures (fig. 40). Running together page after page of corseted ladies, potions for intimate malaises, odd cleaning devices, underwear and hardware, a Sears-style catalogue of the date might solicit from an adolescent browser fantasies that

mingled material cupidity and sexual desire. These intimations needed only to be preserved and transferred into adult expression to yield a peculiarly Duchampian mixture of the inert and the eroticized. The empty but puffed-out sports suits, for example, without heads or gestures, provided perfect generic dummies to suggest the collectively faceless, onanistic bachelor types who pine in vain for the unattainable bride above, in the complex mechano-sexual allegory of the *Large Glass.*[68]

These books were dreams in waiting, full of stories that asked to be told. Especially when woodblock or steel engraving still dominated as illustration techniques, sales catalogues hardened into one fastidiously bland style, amazing arrays of things prosaic and exotic, in a way that begged the active mind to construct narratives from their overload of disconnected information. The British writer E. V. Lucas and his collaborator George Morris said just that in the opening

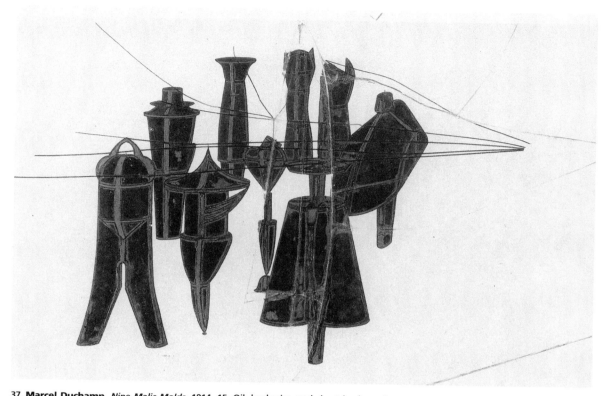

37. Marcel Duchamp. *Nine Malic Molds.* 1914–15. Oil, lead wire, and sheet lead on glass, mounted between glass plates, 26 × 39¹³⁄₁₆″ (66 × 101.2 cm). Private collection, Paris

38. Page from *Manufacture Française d'Armes et Cycles de Saint-Étienne* **(Saint-Étienne, 1913)**

note to the collage "autobiography" *What a Life!*, which they created from cutouts of a department-store catalogue in 1911: "As adventures are to the adventurous," their note ran, "so is romance to the romantic. One man searching the pages of Whiteley's general catalogue will find only facts and prices; another will find what we think we have found—a deeply-moving human drama."[69]

They found swans in candlesnuffers, zoo beasts in long-handled flatirons, floor plans in luggage-compartment diagrams, and hats and monuments in jelly molds. They then brought these animated objects into untoward conjunction with stereotyped gents and ladies, all smugly impassive whether in greatcoats, gowns, or long johns. What the authors applied to the catalogue imagery was not so much an eye of fantasy as one with a preternatural innocence, which by reading all too literally could find the bizarre peeking through the cracks of convention: an empty dress became a phantom (fig. 41), glove ribs were horrid veins on the hand, and isolated accessories of fashion evoked the horror of severed body parts (fig. 43). The humor comes not from exaggeration, but from the forced dislocation of one set of banalities into the company of another: the stereotypical linecuts are spliced,

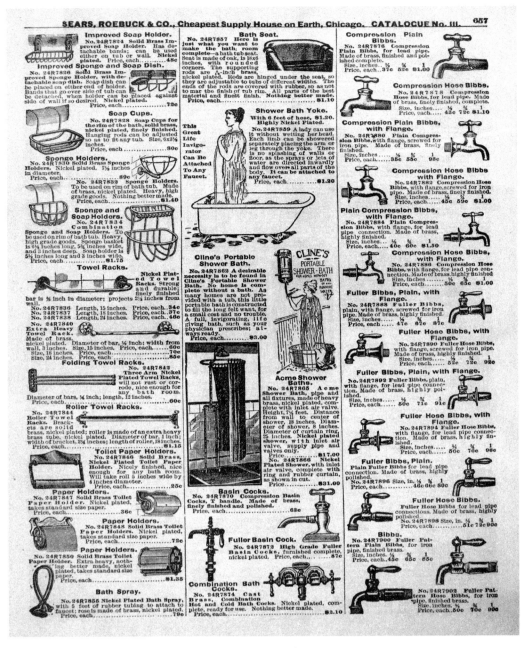

39. Page from *Sears, Roebuck & Co.: Catalogue No. III* (Chicago, 1902)

40. Pages from *Whiteley's Catalogue* (London, 1915)

But at this moment the detective returned, in a disguise calculated to baffle the keenest observer.

The contents of the mysterious bag having been analysed,

he showed us that the ring was movable,

and drew our attention to the fact that there were signs of a struggle.

He then showed us the print of a blood-stained hand on the wall,

41. Double-page spread from E. V. Lucas and George Morris, *What a Life!* (London, 1911)

than a headless apparition was seen to move slowly across the moonlit hall.

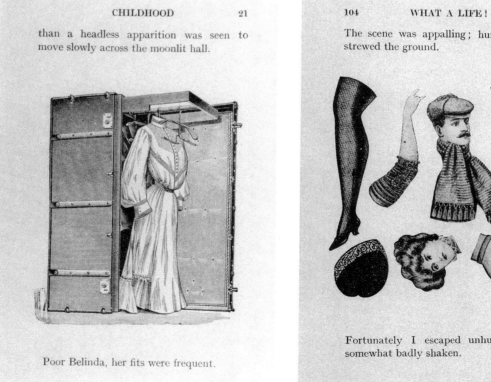

Poor Belinda, her fits were frequent.

42. Page from *What a Life!*

The scene was appalling; human remains strewed the ground.

Fortunately I escaped unhurt, although somewhat badly shaken.

43. Page from *What a Life!*

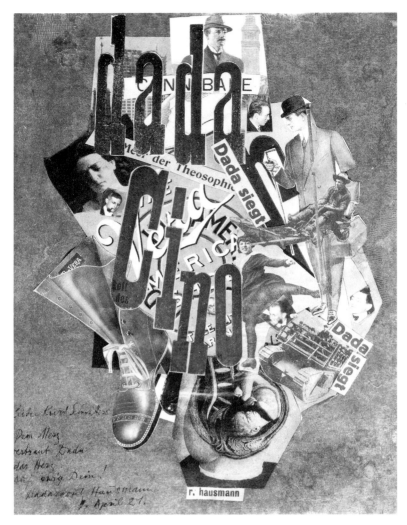

44. **Raoul Hausmann.** *Dada-Cino*. 1921. Photomontage, 12½ × 8⅞" (31.7 × 22.5 cm). **Private collection, Switzerland**

all too "logically," with the ludicrously conventional manner of the storytelling (chapter titles include "School Days," "Travel and Adventure," and "A Tender Passion"), which was "clipped" in its own way from the standard fabric of Victorian tales of the "deeply-moving human drama" of the comfortable classes.[70]

Lucas and Morris (a frequent illustrator for *Punch*) intended their "shilling nonsense" to strike a popular audience for cheap illustrated books. Instead it gained a small cult following and has since, with obvious justice, been assimilated into the history of Dada and Surrealism.[71] *What a Life!* is an early instance of the recognition, crucial to so many artists of the teens and twenties, that bourgeois society was producing in great volume precisely the petards on which it could most neatly be hoisted. The vast compendium of desires—for health, for beauty, for style, for diversion—in catalogues like those of Whiteley's or Harrods or Sears added up to a panorama of cheerily philistine materialism, latently replete with the very things it least thought to include: absurdity, self-satire, and deranged logic. Especially in the later teens, as the fashions in old catalogues became outmoded and the engraving style a relic of the past, overtones of a de-

parted naïveté made these volumes inviting prey to artists with a critical eye for burgher folly.

Catalogues, brochures, and illustrated magazines were godsends to the Dada avant-garde. Ephemeral, dispensable, and dismemberable, they rendered questions of draftsmanship moot, and allowed artists so inclined to put the emphasis where many of that generation felt it should be: solely on the ideas in the art. This was particularly true for the Dada artists of Germany, such as Raoul Hausmann (figs. 44, 45) and Hannah Höch (figs. 46, 47). In the context of their politically minded critique of bourgeois society, the avoidance of "touch" and personality in art was as imperative as the disruption of pictorial logic and of scale consistency. The availability of a steady supply of pre-formed photographic images, from ads themselves or from the ad-supported press and illustrated journals, provided them with the ingredients they needed—generic types of wealth, poverty, glamor, misery, and stupidity, portraits of friends and enemies, and ancillary items such as disconnected machines large and small, corsets, cows, grimacing dogs, overstuffed ottomans and speeding motorcycles, and so on ad infinitum.

The Dada artists well understood that this stream of

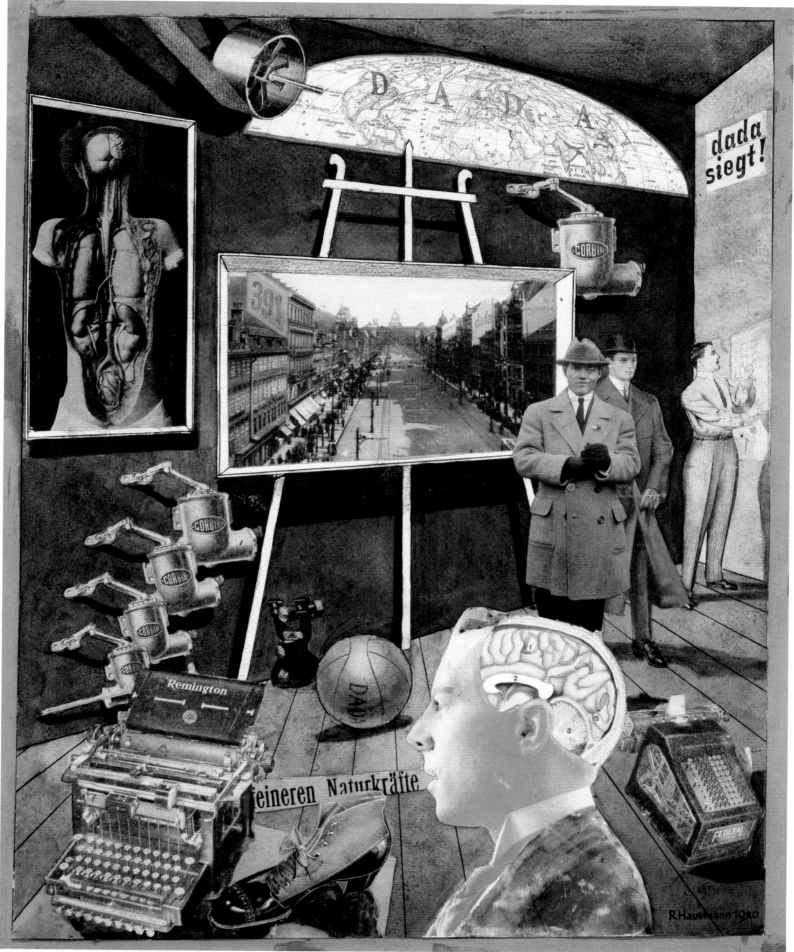

45. Raoul Hausmann. *Dada Siegt*. 1920. Watercolor and collage on paper, mounted on board, 23⅝ × 17¾″ (60 × 45 cm). Private collection

46. Hannah Höch. *The Lovely Maiden.* **1920. Photomontage, 13¼ × 11⁷/₁₆″ (35 × 29 cm). Private collection**

imagery was being aimed at their consciousness by the engine of capitalist commerce, and this lent extra appeal to the exercise of redirecting it toward the unsettling of that system. Their magazines were full of self-mocking slogans and promotions ("Subscribe to Dada: The Only Loan That Brings No Return," or "Opening of the Great DADA Season").[72] And the techniques they often used—especially photomontage, and the cutout masking of photo forms—were established tricks of the press and advertising.[73] They delighted in turning such strategies, designed to make communication attractive and efficiently intelligible, to the exactly opposite end of willful confusion. These techniques allowed them to combine the disrupting fragmentation they liked in Cubism with the narrative, socially oriented content they found lacking in such hermetic painting—and thus use business tools to subvert the order of art at the same time they aimed their art to subvert the normal order of business.[74]

The Cologne Dadaist Max Ernst drew on catalogue material, however, in a markedly different manner. The commercial methods and materials that were a way into the mechanical rush of disrupted modernity for others, for him offered bridging devices back to the dreams and nightmares of childhood. Where Hausmann and Höch gravitated to current photographic

imagery and lived in the jumble of the chaotic present, Ernst looked backward—both to a more artisanal style of commercial rendering, and to the didactic clarity of schoolroom instructional charts. And where other collagists were active in dismemberment and reformulation, Ernst used a passive, enchanted receptivity as a way to see the marvelous in the banal: he intervened only enough to coax out of found imagery its potential for the fantastic and bizarre. In a famous text published in 1936, Ernst remembered happening upon the catalogue of his dreams:

One New Year's day, 1919, finding myself in rainy weather in a town beside the Rhine, I was struck by the obsession worked on my irritated gaze by the pages of an illustrated catalogue in which figured objects for anthropological, microscopic, psychological, mineralogical and paleontological demonstration. I found brought together there elements of figuration so distant from each other that the very absurdity of this assemblage provoked in me a hallucinatory succession of contradictory images, double, triple, and multiple images, superimposing themselves one over the other with the persistence and the rapidity proper to amorous memories and half-asleep visions. . . .

Ernst felt that he needed to add to these pages only small indications in paint or by drawing—a horizon

47. **Hannah Höch.** *Cut with the Kitchen Knife.* 1919–20. Photomontage, 44⁷/₈ × 35⁷/₁₆″ (114 × 90 cm). Nationalgalerie, Berlin

line, a color, the suggestion of an alien landscape—to fix the images of his hallucinations, and to "transform into dramas revealing my most secret *desires*, what were previously only banal pages of advertising."[75]

Werner Spies has convincingly shown that Ernst's account of the rainy-day revelation repeats the classic trope of the "epiphany" moment, found in the writings of James Joyce, as well as in those of Giorgio de Chirico and members of the Surrealist group.[76] But the book—the *Kölner Lehrmittel-Anstalt*, a catalogue of teaching aids from alphabets to anatomical charts—was real, and a frequent basis for Ernst's work of the early 1920s. It contained an astonishing array of material, dispersed throughout the full-page plates and sometimes crowded together on one page (fig. 48). If the department-store catalogue was a universe of commodities, this was a universe proper, or at least the ideal mental universe of a positivist academic imagination, embracing cultural and natural phenomena in a leveling rationality of encyclopedic knowledge.

The didactic purposes of the charts required that they render all lessons with an equally idealized clarity, in disturbingly concrete form. The initial "surreal" work of forced conjunction—of suspending things of wildly different kinds and scales in one representational matrix—had already been done in the *Lehrmittel-*

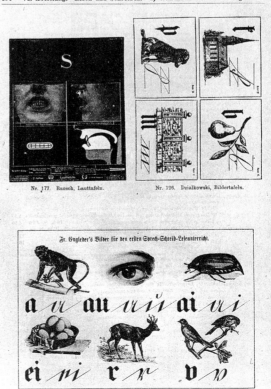

48. Pedagogical charts from *Kölner Lehrmittel-Anstalt* (Cologne, 1914), p. 194

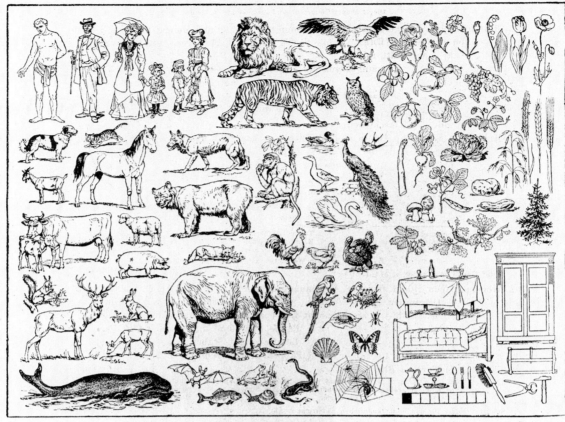

Nr. 160. Schreiber, Sprach- und Anschauungsunterricht.

49. Pedagogical chart from *Kölner Lehrmittel-Anstalt*, p. 142

50. **Max Ernst.** *The Master Bedroom—The Bedroom of Max Ernst*. 1920. Gouache and collage over reproduction, 6⁷/₁₆ × 8¹¹/₁₆″ (16.3 × 22 cm).
Private collection

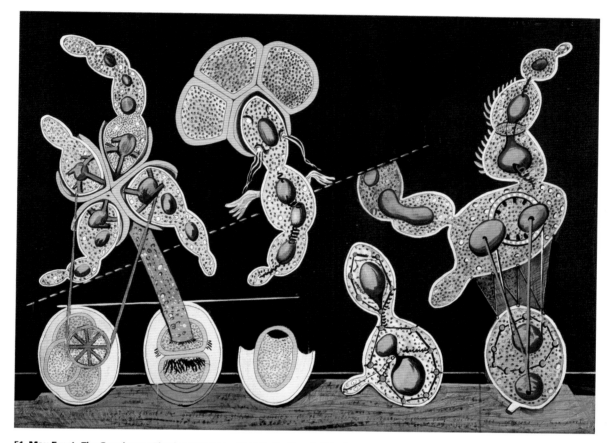

51. Max Ernst. *The Gramineous Bicycle Garnished with Bells the Dappled Fire Damps and the Echinoderms Bending the Spine to Look for Caresses.* 1920–21. Botanical chart altered with gouache, 29¼ × 39¼" (74.3 × 99.7 cm). The Museum of Modern Art, New York. Purchase

Anstalt. Like Lucas and Morris in *What a Life!*, Ernst made narrative "sense" out of things that had been juxtaposed but never intended to cohabit. Out of the crowded menagerie of a page (fig. 49), he could isolate a bed to make a bedroom, and then create a forced-perspective "space" to allow an oversize bear, and an equally undersize whale, to be his bedtime companions (fig. 50). A group of abstract forms for geometrical instruction (fig. 52) could be given a similarly untoward materiality as a kind of pseudo-Cubist sculpture (and doubtless as an intentional satire of Cubism itself; fig. 53). In these instances, he acted not to take material reality and bend it to his ideas, but to take images that were intended to elucidate ideal concepts such as those of geometry, and treat them as if they were descriptions of material reality.

From Odilon Redon in Symbolism through Mark Rothko in the 1940s, artists have found forms to picture the world beneath consciousness in scientific illus- trations of things below the threshold of vision. Ernst seems to have recognized that scaleless images of mi- croscopic fauna, or cross-sectional analyses of unrec- ognizable organisms and geologies, could, if simply turned upside down or slightly adjusted, become crea- tures of another mental order (figs. 51, 54–57). Where a more prosaically minded student might have asked, What is this?, Ernst asked, What might this be? His imagination acted similarly on the more humdrum giv- ens of fashion illustrations. An array of men's hats, selectively isolated and joined by colored tubular forms, became an adman's Bibendum-style dream of commodity-figures, a wittily literal concretization of the cliché that is the title (*The Hat Makes the Man*), and perhaps (as Werner Spies suggests) a sly dig at the colors and "Tubism" of Léger's Contrast of Forms paintings of the teens (fig. 58).[77] And in an extreme of fetishism gone awry, a milliner's line-up of ladies' hats was transplanted to the desert and transformed into a

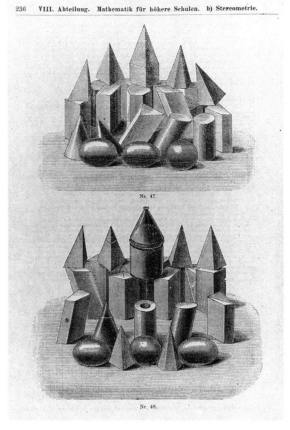

Nr. 47.

Nr. 48.

52. Pedagogical illustrations from *Kölner Lehrmittel-Anstalt,* p. 236

53. **Max Ernst.** *Sheep.* 1921. Collage on paper, 4⁷⁄₁₆ × 6⁵⁄₁₆″ (11.2 × 16 cm). Musée National d'Art Moderne, Centre Georges Pompidou, Paris

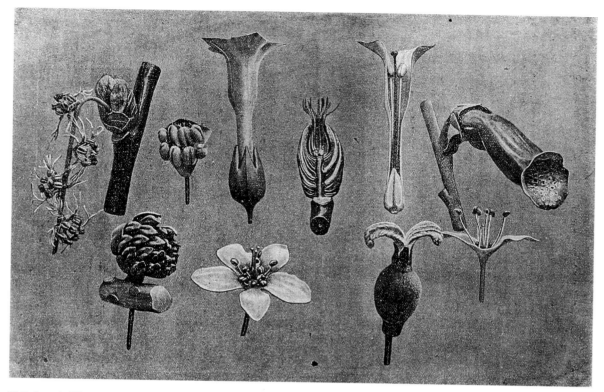

54. Pedagogical illustration from *Kölner Lehrmittel-Anstalt*, p. 624

55. **Max Ernst.** *The Enigma of Central Europe—Always the Best Man Wins.* 1920. Gouache, watercolor, and pencil over reproduction, 5⅞ × 8⅝" (15 × 22 cm). Private collection

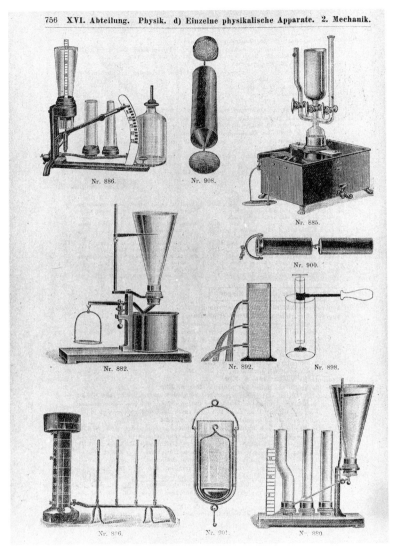

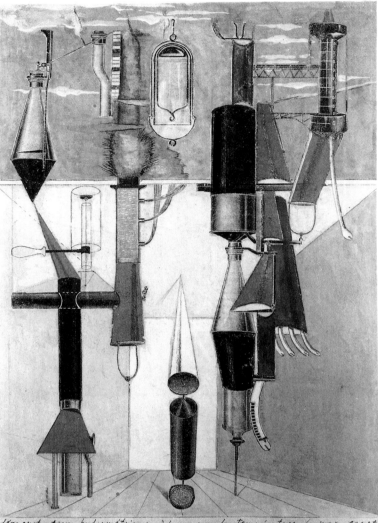

56. Pedagogical illustration from *Kölner Lehrmittel-Anstalt*, p. 756

57. **Max Ernst.** *Démonstration hydrométrique à tuer par la température.* 1920. Collage, gouache, watercolor, and pencil over reproduction, 9½ × 6⅝″ (24 × 17 cm). Private collection

58. Max Ernst. *The Hat Makes the Man.* 1920. Cut and pasted paper, pencil, ink, and watercolor on paper, 14 × 18″ (35.6 × 45.7 cm). The Museum of Modern Art, New York. Purchase

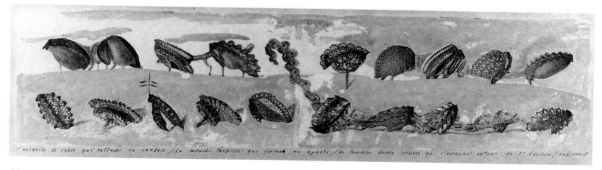

59. Max Ernst. *The Sandworm Attaches Its Sandal.* 1920. Gouache and watercolor over reproduction, 4⅝ × 19⅞″ (11.8 × 50.5 cm). Private collection, England

60. Max Ernst and Louise Ernst-Straus. *Augustine Thomas and Otto Flake.* **1920. Photomontage and collage on paper, 9¹/₁₆ × 5¹/₁₆″ (23 × 13.5 cm). Sprengel Museum, Hannover**

segmented sandworm, a fly, or "terrible solar lips" (fig. 59). Even an imaginary, incongruously domestic shop window could be constructed to advertise the appeal of strange dislocations (fig. 60).

As became even clearer in later collage novels by Ernst (which, based on illustrated journals rather than advertising, are beyond our present scope), there were florid, gothic possibilities lurking in the kind of line-engraved plates that had been a staple of Victorian popular publishing. But contemporary low-grade commercial illustration was also the source for a whole vein of Dada work concerned with a more deadpan, sardonic humor. The leading practitioner of such work, around World War I, was Francis Picabia.

Picabia's object-portraits (figs. 61, 63, 65, 66) are commonly associated with Duchamp's interest in mechanomorphic imagery, and practice a similar debunking association of personality, and sexuality, with impersonal machine elements (especially auto parts, such as sparkplugs, carburetors, and windshields).[78] Picabia's source here is not the machine objects themselves, though, but ads for them. Three plausible source advertisements can be found, for example, in *The Saturday Evening Post* for June and July of 1915 (figs. 62, 64, 67). And the style in which Picabia presents them is crucial for their baldly anti-artistic feel. Both he and Duchamp liked non-virtuoso ways of rendering, such as the schemas of engineering and mechanical diagrams[79]—and, in the case of the object-portraits, an *Ur*-language of commercial graphics that persists in cheap ads and inventory-type catalogues down to the present. This style was not just "found," however, but selected and imposed: comparison with the source images shows how Picabia leveled them to a common, coarser level of simplicity.[80]

This is the opposite end of the stylistic spectrum from the loud glamor of outdoor advertising and lacks even the quaint, dated fascination of steel-engraved plates; but for certain aspects of early modern expres-

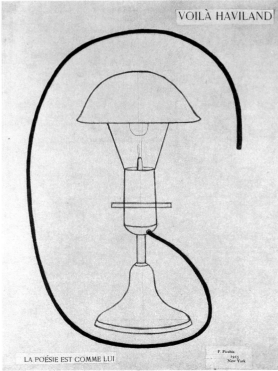

61. (Left) Francis Picabia. *La Poésie est comme lui (Voilà Haviland).* **1915. Tempera and collage on paper, 25⅞ × 18⅞″ (65.5 × 47.7 cm). Kunsthaus Zürich**

62. (Below) Advertisement for Wallace Portable Electric Lamp, 1915

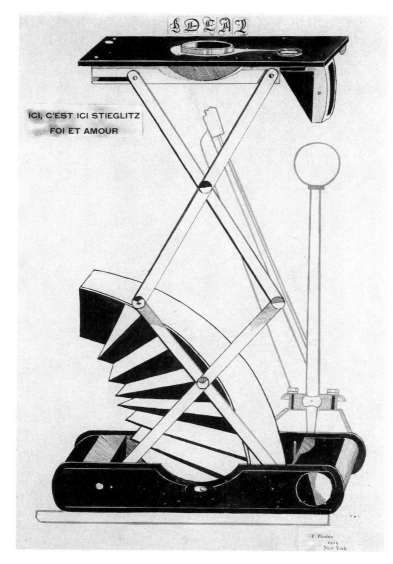

ICI, C'EST ICI STIEGLITZ
FOI ET AMOUR

63. **Francis Picabia.** *Ici, c'est ici Stieglitz.* 1915. Pen and ink on paper, 29⅞ × 20″ (75.9 × 50.8 cm). The Metropolitan Museum of Art, New York. The Alfred Stieglitz Collection

As right as a full jeweled watch

The Vest Pocket Autographic Kodak

with Kodak Anastigmat lens, *f. 7.7.*

64. **Advertisement for The Vest Pocket Autographic Kodak camera, 1915**

sion it was a more inspirational model. Marketing of mass-produced products often used such manner of bland, generic idealization, and artists of a certain temperament responded to that non-style as perfectly suited for satiric critique of the inertia of bourgeois mindlessness, or even as a metaphor for the hollowness of the larger human condition. (The most obvious instance of this, though it does not involve a form new in itself, is the shop-window mannequin. After de Chirico used mannequins and lay figures in his paintings around World War I, they became widely favored human surrogates. The shop dummy allowed for a human presence that was explicitly dehumanized, and for the appearance of the figure without the bother of anatomy or modeling that usually went with it; and it also had a profitably unstable combination of smooth ideality and impotent passivity that seemed appropriate for diverse kinds of imagery of machine-age humanity, serving pessimists, cynics, idealists, and pranksters alike.)[81]

Part of the joke involved in the Picabia "portraits" is the forced incongruity between the inert objects drawn in this generic manner and the titles conferring

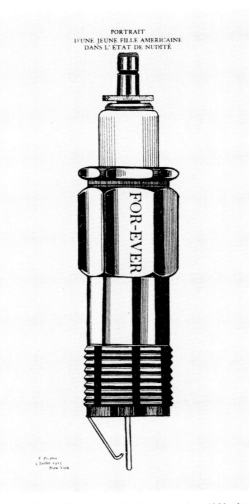

65. **Francis Picabia.** *Portrait of a Young American Girl in the State of Nudity.* **1915. Ink on paper. Present whereabouts unknown**

individual personality, emotion, or sexuality. By reducing to an absurd extreme the basic notion of the animated object or the anthropomorphized machine—the principle by which Léger made metal men or the Michelin brothers made Bibendum, and by which Rodchenko would later make a figure from watches (fig. 68)—Picabia produced an ironic, disaffected, and debunking wit that is the opposite of heroic. But his "portraits," too, involve a partial parallel between art strategy and ad strategy. By the time of Picabia's object-portraits the practice of making objects sell themselves was yielding, in ads for auto accessories precisely, incongruities that are just a slight ratchet-shift away from his. Michelin, for example, published a "Theater of the Tire" brochure, in which tales of horror and woe were associated with the vicissitudes of tire wear, and in which each page featured a tire with an incongruously dramatizing title, such as "The Martyrdom of St. Sebastian" or "The Half-Virgins" (figs. 69, 70). Modern advertisers were aggressively engaged in such efforts to transform and dramatize objects of everyday life. And their efforts provided models of strategy that became especially relevant when Dada artists, Duchamp prime among them, seized on the idea of making an art of altered or merely displaced functional objects. Duchamp is the crucial figure through whom modern art's progress becomes entwined not just with commercial modes of representation, but with advertising's attempts to affect people's immediate relation to the objects themselves, by strategies of display or changes in context and scale.

66. **Francis Picabia.** *Portrait of Max Jacob.* **1915. Ink on paper. Present whereabouts unknown**

67. (Right) Advertisement for Eveready flashlights, 1915

68. Aleksandr Rodchenko, text by **Vladimir Mayakovsky.** Advertisement for Mozer watches at Gum, the State Department Store, Moscow. 1923. Printed, 7 × 6" (18 × 15.2 cm). Private collection

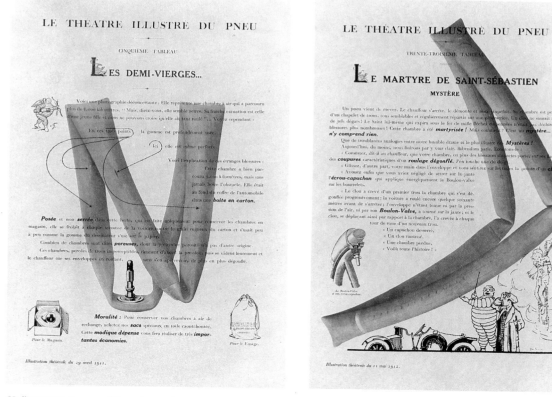

69. "Les Demi-vierges...," from the catalogue *Le Théâtre illustré du pneu par Bibendum* (Clermont-Ferrand, 1912)

70. "Le Martyre de Saint-Sébastien: Mystère," from *Le Théâtre illustré du pneu par Bibendum*

71. **Marcel Duchamp.** *Readymade Girl with Bedstead (Apolinère enameled).* 1916–17. Painted tin advertisement, 9¼ × 13¼" (23.5 × 33.7 cm). Philadelphia Museum of Art. The Louise and Walter Arensberg Collection

Duchamp worked in various ways with the material and methods of commerce. In 1913 he altered a plaque for Sapolin paint (fig. 71) by adding a small "reflection" in the mirror of the scene, selectively blacking out parts of the lower text to yield a new non-sense sentence, and altering the brand name to make a sound-alike reference to his friend Guillaume Apollinaire. That sense of the "private advertisement" later yielded Duchamp's own "house brand": having concocted an alternative feminine identity with the punning name Rrose Sélavy, he fabricated a perfume label bearing the vamping likeness of his alter ego and put

72. **Marcel Duchamp.** *Belle Haleine, Eau de Voilette.* 1921. Assisted Readymade: perfume bottle with label, in oval box, 6⁷⁄₁₆ × 4⁷⁄₁₆" (16.3 × 11.2 cm). Private collection, Paris

73. **Marcel Duchamp.** *Box in a Valise*. 1935–41. Leather valise containing miniature replicas, photographs, and color reproductions of works by Duchamp, 16 × 15 × 4″ (40.7 × 38.1 × 10.2 cm). The Museum of Modern Art, New York. James Thrall Soby Fund

together a package-and-bottle presentation for this scent, which he called *Belle Haleine, Eau de Voilette* (fig. 72). He later produced a *Box in a Valise* (fig. 73) that was likely modeled on a salesman's sample kit and

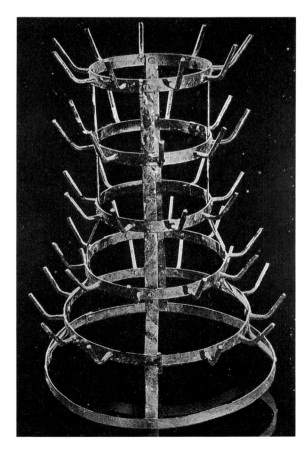

74. **Marcel Duchamp.** *Bottle Rack (Bottle Dryer)*. 2nd version, c. 1921 (after lost original of 1914). Readymade: galvanized-iron bottle dryer, 23¼ × 14½″ (59.1 × 36.8 cm). Private collection, Paris

carried miniature replicas of his whole "line." Duchamp was also in demand as a promoter when it came to the innovative design of exhibitions and journal covers, and on one occasion in 1944 he and André Breton collaborated to produce a window display, complete with mannequin, at the Gotham Book Mart in New York.[82]

His most enduringly disruptive works, though, were those that consisted of displaying functional objects as art. These "Readymades" (his term was itself derived from merchandising)[83] included prosaic things of relatively general utility: a snow shovel and racks for drying bottles (fig. 74) or hanging hats; the more esoteric item of a partially disassembled cattle comb (figs. 75, 76); and an accessory of more recent invention, a cover for one of the newly popular typing machines (fig. 77). For years, these amusements were only known to those who frequented his studio, and in most cases the originals have disappeared, leaving us with only the artist's later recollections, a few photographs, and a smattering of reproductive editions to verify this exceptionally influential activity. The first Readymade, for example, of a bicycle wheel fastened to a stool (as if it were a wheel-centering mechanism of the kind he had doubtless seen in catalogues, if not in person [figs. 78–80]), is known to us only through a photograph of what was apparently its *re*-creation in New York, and through later authorized facsimiles. And the one object which was placed on public view, a urinal dubbed *Fountain* and submitted to the 1917 Society of Independent Artists' exhibition in New York with the signature "R. Mutt" (fig. 81), raises no less vexing questions —which William Camfield has recently examined in an

75. **Marcel Duchamp.** *Readymade Comb.* **1916. Steel comb, 1¼ × 6½″ (3.2 × 16.5 cm). Philadelphia Museum of Art. The Louise and Walter Arensberg Collection**

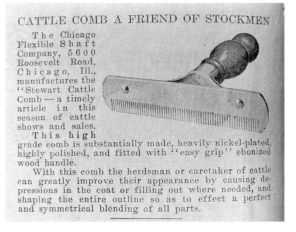

CATTLE COMB A FRIEND OF STOCKMEN

The Chicago Flexible Shaft Company, 5600 Roosevelt Road, Chicago, Ill., manufactures the "Stewart Cattle Comb — a timely article in this season of cattle shows and sales.

This high grade comb is substantially made, heavily nickel-plated, highly polished, and fitted with "easy grip" ebonized wood handle.

With this comb the herdsman or caretaker of cattle can greatly improve their appearance by causing depressions in the coat or filling out where needed, and shaping the entire outline so as to effect a perfect and symmetrical blending of all parts.

76. Cattle comb, from *Hardware World*, November 15, 1920, p. 184

77. **Marcel Duchamp.** *Traveler's Folding Item.* **1964 (replica of 1916 original). Readymade: Underwood typewriter cover, 9¹⁄₁₆″ (23 cm) high. The Ringling Museum of Art, Sarasota, Florida. Gift of the Mary Sisler Foundation/Mrs. William Sisler**

excellent analysis of *Fountain*'s selection, non-display, and consequences in later modern art.[84]

One of the nicer twists of history's perversity is that, while the Duchamp *Fountain* exists in numerous replica versions, a surviving example of the original type of urinal has proven impossible to locate. If it exists at all, it is now an item of exquisite rarity. Still, we can clearly define this Readymade's forgotten place in the commercial context from which it was taken. In 1917, this urinal was to plumbing fixtures what Picabia's ads were to commercial illustration: the bottom end of the line. Urinals were of course primarily for institutional use, and hence not part of the "designer" aspect of a plumbing company's offerings. But within their group

there were distinct grades, and Duchamp went for the least prestigious. His selection was a porcelain flat-back Bedfordshire urinal, with lip (figs. 82, 83); and on the scale which started at the top with full-length porcelain wall units, only the porcelain flat-back Bedfordshire urinal *without* lip and the tiny, corner units used in prisons held a lesser place. This model was cheap (eight to fifteen dollars at the time), light, and easy to install; but it was hard to clean, had no water reservoir, and tended to be unhygienic and malodorous.

If the piece was plebeian, though, the ostensible manufacturer was aristocratic. Duchamp later explained that the pseudonym R[ichard] Mutt was taken both from the character in the *Mutt and Jeff* comic

78. **Marcel Duchamp.** *Bicycle Wheel.* 1951 (third version, after lost original of 1913). Assemblage: metal wheel mounted on painted wood stool, overall 50½ × 25½ × 16⅝" (128.3 × 63.8 × 42 cm). The Museum of Modern Art, New York. The Sidney and Harriet Janis Collection

Fig. 9.—Wheel Jack

79. (Left) Bicycle jack, from S. DeVere Burr, *Bicycle and Automotive Repair* (New York: David Williams, 1912), p. 133

80. (Above) Illustration from *Bicycle News,* 4 (October 1915), p. 16

strip, and from the plumbing company J. L. Mott Ironworks.[85] That company fancied its wares the Cadillacs of the bathroom trade, advertised on the basis of snob appeal in places like *Vanity Fair*, and maintained a showroom on Fifth Avenue at Seventeenth Street for its finer retail clientele. But it is improbable that Du-

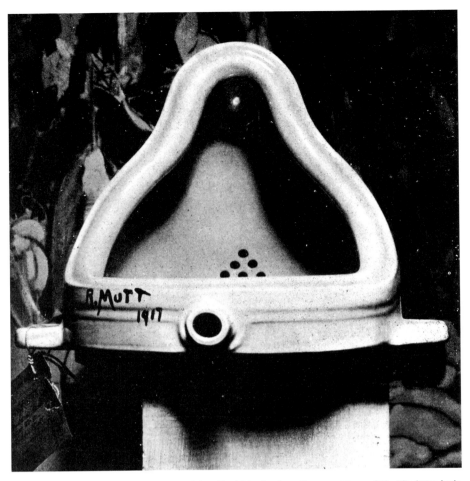

81. **Marcel Duchamp.** *Fountain.* Photograph by Alfred Stieglitz, from the second issue of *The Blind Man* (published May 1917 by Duchamp, Beatrice Wood, and H.-P. Rouche)

82. (Left) Porcelain flat-back Bedfordshire urinal, with lip; plate 6592-A from *Mott's Plumbing Fixtures: Catalogue A* (New York: J. L. Mott Ironworks, 1908), p. 418

83. (Below) Porcelain flat-back Bedfordshire urinal, with lip, from *A. Y. MacDonald Catalogue A* (Dubuque, Iowa: A. Y. MacDonald Mfg. Co., 1912), p. 380

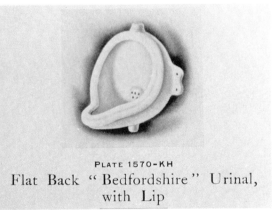

champ saw any urinal in that display, much less a flat-back Bedfordshire. Even when such a piece was (rarely) reproduced in Mott catalogues, it was consigned to the very back pages. Moreover the first *Fountain* may not have been a Mott product at all. We can count the drain holes, visible in photographs of the original item, and their number and pattern do not match anything in the Mott line; so we are licensed to speculate that Duchamp bought from a lesser source (the holes match perfectly with those in the flat-back Bedford-

84. Constantin Brancusi. *Cup II.* 1917–18. Wood, 5⅞ × 11 × 9¾″ (15 × 28 × 24.7 cm). Brancusi Studio, Musée National d'Art Moderne, Centre Georges Pompidou, Paris

Duchamp also insisted at the time that it was in no way absurd to consider plumbing as art. In the avant-garde journal *The Blind Man*, he published (anonymously) a protest against the refusal to display the piece at the exhibition to which it had been submitted. There he opined that "the only works of art America has given are her plumbing and her bridges"[90]—a predictable affirmation of a proper modernist admiration for the raw virtues of engineering. (Duchamp may have covertly stressed that engineering aspect of the piece, in the way he signed it and had it photographed [fig. 81]: this top-first view is the one used to show the fixture in architectural notation [fig. 85].)

But his statement also has a curious parallelism with the way the merchandisers of plumbing promoted their wares. The front page of the Trenton Potteries

shire of the A. Y. MacDonald Company) and illegitimately ennobled the object with the classier brand-name association.

Duchamp was later at pains to insist that the Readymades were carefully chosen so that they would have absolutely no aesthetic appeal;[86] but Camfield has shown that those in Duchamp's immediate circle found something quite appealing—even reminiscent of the flowing forms of a seated Buddha figure—in the white porcelain form of *Fountain*.[87] There also seemed to be a kinship between the kind of pure, streamlined forms espoused by modernists such as Constantin Brancusi or Léger and the unselfconsciously functional shapes of such banal objects.[88] Brancusi himself produced a semi-Dada object along these lines, in his several versions of a geometrically purified *Cup* (fig. 84). And Edward Weston's photographs of his toilet, from the 1920s, prove how directly one could transpose admiration for Brancusi into appreciation of plumbing.[89]

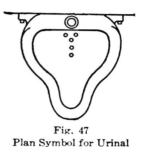

Fig. 47
Plan Symbol for Urinal

85. Notation for urinal, from J.J. Cosgrove, *Plumbing Plans and Specifications* (Pittsburgh: Standard Sanitary Mfg., 1910), p. 20

Company publication of May 1915 remarked: "Someone has said that, so far, the great contribution of America to Art is the pure white American bathroom. Certainly one of the chief contributions of America to health and comfort is her sanitary pottery."[91] The display of sanitary fixtures was moreover a developing, studied craft by this time. Trade journals admonished that "Artistic Display of Sanitary Plumbing Facilities is Promotive of Increased Sales,"[92] and the Mott company boasted that its showrooms were "artistic and

86. Trenton Potteries Company exhibition, from *Sanitary Pottery*, 7 (July 1915), p. 8

87. J. L. Mott plumbing exhibition, from *The Plumbers' Trade Journal*, August 1, 1915, p. 172

Fountain, Duchamp noted that the urinal, like the bathtub, was "a fixture you see every day in plumbers' show windows." And explaining Mr. Mutt's artistry, he said he "took an ordinary article of life, placed it so that its useful significance disappeared under the new title and point of view—created a new thought for that object."[96] But the little comedy of parallelism between his idea of display and that of the plumbing manufacturers shows that the notion of the "ordinary article of life" may be just as problematic as the notion of "art." This "ordinary" thing that Duchamp selected had in fact a very specific place in a specialized hierarchy of style and judgment. In this case as in countless others, the idea of an inert and undifferentiated "low" world, which often serves as foil to a notion of high art as a uniquely complex and dynamic world of discriminations, is clearly false. Duchamp did not reach down into the clutter of artless functionality and wrest this toilet up into another realm where people bothered about aesthetics and decorums of display. The world of the plumbing fixture was one with developed, self-consciously modern notions of display, which were concerned precisely with the notion of giving an object a new appeal over and above its "functional significance" (fig. 88). Thinking about toilets as art was an already existing practice, but till then it had led only to show ribbons and hardware-trade critique; Duchamp saw that the same practice could work to make people think about art as toilets, and made it into a vehicle for some of the most tendentious and longest-burning intellectual debates in this society.

beautiful."[93] Booths at trade conventions were judged "from an artistic viewpoint,"[94] and prizes were awarded for presentation (figs. 86, 87). Remarked one such review of a sanitary-pottery show, flatly: "This display is a work of art."[95]

In his mock-protest article about the rejection of

88. **Wolcott.** Cartoon: "In the slum district of New York City I saw a lavatory as the entire window exhibit, but it was a puller, for the denizens of that quarter stopped by the scores to look at it." *The Plumbers' Trade Journal*, September 1, 1917, p. 282

Duchamp's found-object sculptures emerged from within a dense network of avant-garde thinking about the relationship between things for use and things for show, and about the intrusion of commonplace objects into the category of sculpture. Picasso had early on broached the notion of making art from ready-made commercial products, in his incorporation of printed oilcloth, imitating chair caning, in a still-life painting of 1912. And he continued these experiments of overlap between handmade representations and appropriated actual objects in the playful sculpture he assembled in his studio in 1912–13, involving a paper figure and a real guitar, and a table with a still-life arrangement of a bottle, pipe, cup, and newspaper (fig. 89). In thinking about the possibilities of hybrid forms in his modeled sculpture as well, Picasso seems to have been intrigued simultaneously by the game of conflating painting and sculpture on the one hand, and found things and surrogates on the other, often in the same work—as for example in the *Glass of Absinth* of 1914, with its ersatz sugar cube and actual strainer (fig. 90). In the same line of thought, he seems to have had a particular affection for making the illusions of art more

89. View of Picasso's studio, early 1913

90. Pablo Picasso. *Glass of Absinth.* **1914. Painted bronze with perforated absinth spoon, 8½ × 6½ × 3⅜" (21.6 × 16.4 × 8.5 cm). The Museum of Modern Art, New York. Gift of Mrs. Bertram Smith**

clunkily handmade and evident when he opposed them to the prosaic "artistry" of cheap decorative or illusionistic devices of non-art manufacture. The impeccable illusionism of the photoreproduced chair caning has this effect in conjunction with the painted still life, as does the rope frame around that picture, which echoes a cheap framer's notion of imitating the relief of a carved-wood frame.

A similar role is played by the add-on strip of ball fringe that decorates the table edge in the wood *Still Life* construction of 1914 (fig. 91). The fringe, the chair caning, the ornately decorative strainer, and the rope frame are all degraded commercial imitations of materials and techniques that had belonged to a preindustrial tradition of craftsmanship. They are mass-produced items of show replacing artisanal items of substance, and Picasso seems to have liked them precisely because of that. An obvious intent of a piece like the 1914 *Still Life* was to confuse the codes of illusion and reality—to put an actually projecting table surface under obviously fake food and attach a fully projecting blade to an ungraspable knife handle, against a wall with real but conventionally trompe-l'oeil molding. And for someone with that mischievous intent, the elements of modern décor—wallpaper, ball fringe, fake wood, fake marble, and fake cane weaving or wood-carving—offered not just useful shortcuts to representation but elements of an enriching ambi-

guity. The dilemma of the thing itself and its overlap and interpenetration by the thing made "just for show" was the occasion for a new form of originality, and the teasing gambit in a whole new game of code and convention in art.

The idea of "creating a new thought" for functional objects was, however, also very much on the minds of those who sold such commodities, and whose livelihood depended on the way they displayed them. In the period immediately after World War I, trade journals frequently featured new thinking about store-window display, dealing with what H. Glévéo called the "power of suggestion by the object."[97] Glévéo, an accomplished shop stylist and writer on techniques of window arrangements, described the "provincial" style of presentation, which he still found in older quarters of Paris, as a more or less permanent, crowded array of a mixed lot of the things available in the store (fig. 92). And he contrasted this to the modern, "Parisian" way, which consisted of isolating an object or type of object for a dramatized, regularly changing window arrangement.[98] The object thus isolated and featured would take on "a little magnetism, and convincing force; it is somehow suggestive, silently but surely, to the brain of the public drawn to the window."[99]

Pre–World War I documentation is slim, but it seems safe to assume that, in the numberless passing

92. Eugène Atget. *Naturaliste, rue de l'École de Médecine.* 1926–27. Albumen-silver print by Chicago Albumen Works (c. 1984), 8⅞ × 6¹¹⁄₁₆″ (22.5 × 17 cm). The Museum of Modern Art, New York

strategies window designers devised to give "a new thought" to commercial objects, from pots and pans and tennis rackets to clothes (figs. 93, 98), the kind of tableau Picasso constructed in his studio, where objects took on a new life as props in an implied story,

was a staple of show-window technique. And certainly the seductive and/or disturbing objects given contradictory life by the Surrealists following Duchamp's lead—Man Ray's *Gift* and Meret Oppenheim's fur-lined teacup are among the classic instances (figs. 95,

93. Department-store window, Paris. c. 1926. Plate from *Présentation 1927: Le Décor de la rue* (Paris, 1927), p. 165

94. Plate from A. Manera, *Étalages* (Paris, n.d.), n.pag.

95. **Man Ray.** *Gift.* c. 1958 (replica of 1921 original). Painted flatiron with row of thirteen tacks, heads glued to the bottom, 6⅛ × 3⅝ × 4½″ (15.3 × 9 × 11.4 cm). The Museum of Modern Art, New York. James Thrall Soby Fund

96. **Meret Oppenheim.** *Object.* 1936. Fur-covered cup, saucer, and spoon, overall height 2⅞″ (7.3 cm). The Museum of Modern Art, New York. Purchase

96)—were made against a daily backdrop of shop-window play, with the notion of the mind-arresting isolation, transformation, and dramatization of similar-ly banal items (figs. 94, 97). We know that by 1907, major stores in Paris employed professional window designers; and in that year one writer on the subject offered advice that seems artistically ahead of its time:

In many cases [of displaying merchandise], the most *risqué* contrast gives a very certain effect, even when it finds itself in opposition with artistic harmony. It can seem strange to ex-hibit, for example, a vulgar leather boot on a cushion of richly brocaded satin. But the inherent contrast between these two objects establishes its own attraction.

In the same way, it could seem in doubtful taste to put a magnificent rosewood piano in a decor representing a wood-

97. Department-store window, Paris. c. 1925

98. Department-store window, Paris. c. 1926. The Cooper-Hewitt Picture Library, Bonney Collection

chopper's hut. But if the lighting is well disposed, the rudimentary character of the hut will, by contrast, put more in value the luxurious appearance of the piano....

The hat-maker ... displays his waterproof hats right in the water of a miniature waterfall installed right in his window.... The maker of special shoes for winter had the idea, by way of a refrigeration device, to preserve a block of ice in his shop window. Two enormous shoes are placed on the block, and a thermometer placed inside one of the shoes to indicate that the interior temperature is not influenced by the ice.

A thousand other examples of this kind remain to be cited.... A lot of merchants, especially abroad, have recourse to the pun or the historical word. Someone told us they saw in London, in the window of a butcher, a huge piece of meat on which a plaque was placed reproducing the famous phrase of Shakespeare: "Upon what meat does this our Caesar feed that he hath grown so great." And a second panel said "This is the meat." The crowd laughed ... and bought.[100]

The advent of professional window designers, many of them would-be artists, led by the 1920s to self-conscious emulations of the look of avant-garde art; and artists like Dalí later did windows for stores such as Bonwit Teller, directly in the line of the provocative stunts arranged for a more limited public in Dada and Surrealist manifestations. (When Bonwit's altered Dalí's display, the artist rammed a fur-covered bathtub through the glass.)[101] The majority of such later, art-conscious displays were simply derivative. More important, they were, in effect, only fancy homecomings for now-glamorous notions that had their humble beginnings in similar windows long before. The spirit of

Dada and Surrealist work with the secret life of objects shared with such commercial formats, from the outset, a search for ways to take inert things and make them surprising, memorable, and seductive.

The objects represented, selected, or incorporated by Picasso, Duchamp, and others were the props of a long-running joke about mores, codes, and conventions. They manifested the uncomfortable idea that art is not predetermined by its subject, or by where or in what material one finds it, but is a matter of incessantly problematic judgment. This simple "revelation" of something that had in fact been true all along is parallel to other twentieth-century revisions (such as Ferdinand de Saussure's rethinking of language, for example) which insisted that meanings the previous century had taken for granted as "natural" and fixed were, in fact, only matters of mutable convention. As a premise for making or viewing art, this truism admits a variety of responses, as we will see shortly. But it needs stressing, in regard to Duchamp's way of pointing up this aspect of art, that not just the Readymades themselves, but also the notions of display he and subsequent modern artists used to present such objects, had an independent, parallel life in the show business of everyday modern commerce. If we ignore that comedy of parallelism, then we misconstrue the punch line, and short-circuit the power of his joke.

The 1920s

Léger also paid attention to shop windows, but in a wholly different spirit. He admired the change from

99. **Fernand Léger.** *Umbrella and Bowler.* 1926. Oil on canvas, 50¼ × 38¾″ (130.1 × 98.2 cm). The Museum of Modern Art, New York. A. Conger Goodyear Fund

what Glévéo called the "provincial" to the "Parisian" style of window display, in which he felt "quality replaced quantity" as fewer items were highlighted in special arrangements. For him this new, "spectacular" order along the vista of the street was "a very important event . . . the beginning of a new popular art."[102] By 1928, he felt that poster advertising had been eclipsed, and that modern stores, working with the direct appeal of their objects, were providing not just raw material for the artist but accomplished, finished works.[103] The ability to recognize the art in such artisanal arrangements required an unprejudiced eye,

which would in turn be the harbinger of a new social order. He wrote in 1924 that: "My goal is to impose this: that there is no catalogued, hierarchically ordered Beauty; that this is the heaviest error there can be. Beauty is everywhere, in the order of your casseroles, on the white wall of your kitchen, more perhaps than in your eighteenth-century salon or in the official museums. . . ." He continued,

The art of storefronts . . . has taken on a great importance for several years now. The street has become a permanent spectacle of an always mounting intensity.

The window-spectacle has become a major concern in the

business of the merchant. A frenetic competition presides there: *to be seen more than one's neighbor is the violent desire that animates our streets.* Do you doubt the extreme care that governs this work?

…Among these artisans, there is an incontestable art, linked directly to the commercial goal, a plastic fact of a new order and the equivalent of any artistic manifestations existing, whatever they may be.

We find ourselves before a completely admirable Renaissance, of the world of creative artisans who provide joy for our eyes and transform the street into a permanent spectacle, infinitely variable. I see the show halls emptying out and disappearing, and people living out-of-doors as if the prejudices of the *hierarchy of art* did not exist. The day when the work of the whole world of workers will be understood and felt by people exempt from prejudices, who will have eyes to see, we will truly witness a surprising revolution. The false great men will fall from their pedestal and values will finally be in their place. *I repeat, there is no* hierarchy of art. A work is worth what it is worth in itself and a criterion is impossible to establish, it is a matter of taste and individual emotive capacity.

…The plastic life is terribly dangerous, equivocation is perpetual there. No criterion is possible, no tribunal of arbitration exists to settle the dispute over Beauty.[104]

That last phrase could seem Duchampian, but the spirit is completely different. Duchamp, in an aristocratic and dandyish spirit, used the display of functional objects to highlight contradictions, demoralize the notion of high art, and point up the conventions of taste that layer and divide society. Léger, working from a socialist viewpoint, focused on functional objects as elements of labor and beauty combined, and saw their artful display as the way to new conciliations, and a liberating elevation of ignored quality. He believed that, if working people could remove the blinders of prejudice faulty education had given them and learn to see the inventive beauty of the new objects, machines, and displays that they were making every day, they would not need the alcohol and pandering music-hall spectacles that they sought as distractions from the hard temper of modern times.[105] The artist's role was to organize such new forms of beauty and make them more visible. And it seems certain that the monumentalized arrangements of hats, umbrellas, and other everyday items in shallow spaces in several of Léger's canvases (figs. 99, 100) were consciously conceived as a homage to the new styles of display he saw in the storefront windows of Paris.

His isolated and aggrandized soda syphon (fig. 101) was similarly drawn from the world of advertising. Those in circles close to Léger, such as Le Corbusier and Amedée Ozenfant, held that such objects of everyday use could embody the true modern spirit of spare, functional necessity.[106] That outlook could well have prompted contempt for the art of embellishment, or for attempts to provoke new desires and render things seductive for consumers. Yet Léger modeled this image on a newspaper ad (fig. 102), of the kind advertisers praised for its effective clarity and immediate comprehensibility (fig. 103).[107] Like the syphon itself, this image had no novel or original qualities in 1924; as Léger saw, it was stereotypical.[108] But after 1920 he had developed a hard-edge, geometrically simplified realism; and this change, along with the socialist interests that helped motivate it, made him alert to effective forms of mass-audience communication. An ad that spoke clearly *to* the people seemed *of* the people, possessed of a frankness that made it a kind of urban popular art. (Léger was fond of saying that "the people are poetic," citing slang as an example of authentic poetry, and saying "our painting, that's also a slang.")[109] As the merchant did in the shop window, he needed only to isolate this fragment of poetry from the lower ranks of commercial imagery and give it a larger life on the canvas, in order to show its intrinsic value. *The Syphon* is one of the earliest instances in which modern artists paid homage to something they liked in advertising imagery by using one of advertising's favorite devices—the marked enlargement of scale, to focus attention on the latent power of an everyday thing that might otherwise pass unnoticed.

In *The Syphon*, as increasingly in all of Léger's art after World War I, the insistence on impersonality is striking. Léger felt that the beauty of modern life came from machines and objects, and that the most telling forms of modern expression—in the circus and in the new ballet as well as in shop windows—were those in which individuality was suppressed, and the human presence integrated on more equal terms with the décor. The artist's role, too, was not to be a star performer, but a kind of choreographer, who would direct the advent of the *objet-spectacle* as a modern form.[110] The generic, everyman-style impersonality he admired, and painted recurrently—in the robotic forms of the worker amid poster hoardings in *Bargeman* (fig. 104), the *Typographer* (fig. 105), or in the blank-faced cylinder-figures of *The City* (fig. 106), for example—was both his equivalent for the masked personae of antique theater and a socialist ideal for a rationally run, machine-age society.[111]

In *The Syphon*, *Bargeman*, and *The City*, the conjunction of advertising with this ideal of generalized standardization is exactly contrary to Picasso and Braque's affection, only a few years earlier, for the quirky variety of logotypes and brand designs. But the difference corresponds to historical changes in conceptions of what the aims and methods of advertising might be, catalyzed by the wartime experience of 1914–18, and by the eagerness for rational rebuilding after that trauma.

Beginning around 1920, French advertising literature sounds two notes of change: first, a desire, partly a consequence of the war, to appeal to the masses rather than the individual; and second, a greater insistence on behavioral science as a key to success. In *La Publicité* in 1921, the inopportunely named Jules Lallemand (to French ears it sounds like "Jules the German") argued that the era of mass society had arrived, and that the war had shown propaganda to be the necessary tool for binding this new polity together.[112]

100. **Fernand Léger.** *Composition with Four Hats.* 1927. Oil on canvas, 8'3¾" × 6'1¼" (248 × 185 cm). Musée National d'Art Moderne, Centre Georges Pompidou, Paris

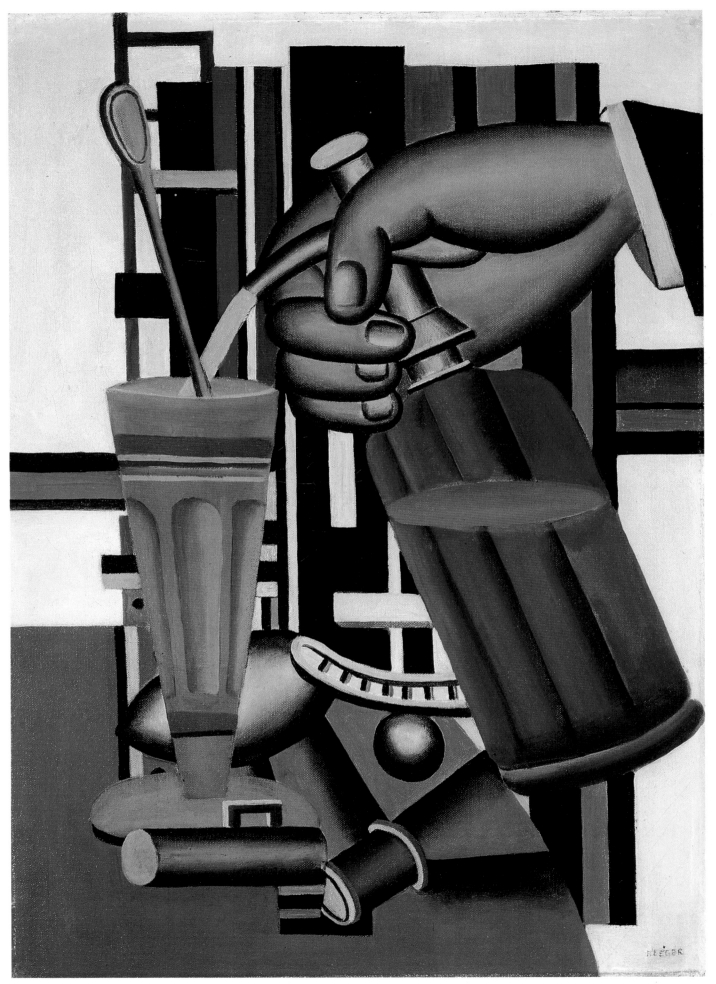

101. Fernand Léger. *The Syphon.* 1924. Oil on canvas, 25⅝ × 18⅛″ (65.1 × 46.3 cm). Albright-Knox Art Gallery, Buffalo, New York. Gift of Mr. and Mrs. Gordon Bunshaft

102. Advertisement for Campari aperitif; from *Le Matin,* September 12, 1924, p. 3.

103. Advertisement for Kneipp coffee; from *La Publicité,* January 1914, p. 35

He followed with articles on "Propaganda and Advertising,"[113] and further articles by other authors appeared on "National Propaganda and Advertising" and "The Organization of Propaganda" in the same journal in 1923 and 1924.[114] All stressed that lessons learned from advertising's studies could be applied to solidifying the integrity of the nation. The important thing was to address one's appeal to the mass of citizens rather than the private psyche. Lallemand called for a "commercial sociopsychology" that communicated with people in the way the cinema did, in groups, as social animals.[115]

In this task, advertising would need to depend more closely on science, and proven technique; and the source for these new methods was often reckoned to lie across the Atlantic. America had long been looked to as the country where the techniques of industry, and of modern business, were developing most impressively; and, in the period of reconstruction following World War I, those who sought to make the French economy more efficient and productive often studied the American system, including advertising practices. Observing those practices, a foreigner would have noticed that, beginning around 1910 (and continuing through the twenties), American advertisers embraced the terminology and techniques of applied science more openly and consistently.[116] The champion of behaviorist psychology John B. Watson was even made a vice president of the J. Walter Thompson agency in 1924.[117] The same developments were pronounced in postwar France; and, though some French admen traced the scientific heritage of their profession in a lineage from Descartes to Auguste Comte,[118] the

changes in their conception of the trade, around 1920, seem part of a broader thrust toward forms of social engineering that had originated in America, especially the time-motion methods of labor management developed by Frederick Winslow Taylor and Henry Ford. Articles in *La Publicité* made a direct association between these methods and new efforts to make the effect of an advertisement optimally efficient.[119] The same enthusiasm for these organizational techniques gripped Russia following the Revolution; and the ultimate ideal in both cases was not simply that better methods of persuasion would make the nation think as one, but that, in breaking old habits and forming new ones, publicity could help base the economy on a more efficient correspondence between demand and supply. The efforts of Rodchenko and Mayakovsky, which we looked at in our earlier chapter on "Words," were very much a part of that effort of rationalization.

Advertising, the very process of public persuasion that Talmeyr looked on in the 1890s as base seduction, and suspected of sowing anarchy in the land, was now looked to by some as a means to establish national solidarity. In the law of July 29, 1881, the Third Republic had unleashed social liberties and the forces of commercial advertising together, in a spirit of laissez-faire. Now, three decades later, the hope was that the worker and the factory owner would join in the benefits of a technocrat-run efficiency, and that publicity could be yoked to ideals of mass solidarity. It is impossible to associate Léger specifically with any of this thinking about advertising; but his Purist associates, such as Corbusier, were explicit in their insistence that Taylorism was a key to human happiness in the machine age.[120] And Léger's idealized, rationalized vision of advertising images, colors, and letters, in conjunction with a depersonalized type of humanity, suggests parallel aspirations toward a collective unity linked to the discipline of standardization.

This was basically an optimist's vision, but Léger was no pollyanna celebrant of mass culture. He wanted his art to contend with forces that he recognized as potentially oppressive, even devastating, and the positive aspects of his outlook in the 1920s were wrested from his experience of the condition of war. World War I had revealed the conditions not simply of modern chaos, but also of a ruthless efficiency, and rule of pragmatic necessity, that broke the stranglehold of stifling traditions. The war had laid bare and revised all moral and material values, he felt:[121] the experience of times when a nail or a shoelace could cost the lives of a regiment had taught that there was no such thing as a negligible object or person, and had set a standard of judgment by hard efficacy which pitilessly ignored all niceties of convention.[122] The commercial competition that followed the war was equally merciless; but it, too, created extreme pressures that destroyed prejudices and old hierarchies, and brought people to focus with new intensity on every aspect of life. "I place myself face-forward to life, with all its possibilities," Léger said in 1925.

I love what they choose to call the state of war, which is nothing other than *life at an accelerated rhythm*. The state of peace being life at a slowed rhythm, it's a braking situation, behind venetian blinds, when everything is happening in the street where the *creator* ought to be. Life reveals itself there accelerated and profound and tragic. There, men and things are seen in all their intensity, examined in their every aspect, stretched to the breaking point....

Life today is a state of war, that's why I profoundly admire my epoch, hard, acute, but which, with its large glasses, sees clear and always wants to see clearer, whatever that brings. The fog is finished, gone the half-light, this is the coming of the state of light. Too bad for weak eyes.[123]

A crucial part of that new era of light, for Léger, was the advent of a more brightly colored world; and outdoor advertising, a preeminent expression of the wars of commercial competition, was a key source for that intensification. "It was after the war that suddenly walls, roads, objects became violently colored," he wrote in 1937.

...An unleashing of life forces filled the world...by the open window the facing wall, violently colored, enters our home. Enormous letters, figures four meters tall are projected into the apartment. Color takes its position...economic struggles will replace the battles on the front. Industrialists and merchants confront each other brandishing color like an advertising weapon. A debauchery without precedent, a disorder

104. Fernand Léger. *Bargeman.* **1918. Oil on canvas, 18⅛ × 21⅞" (45.8 × 55.5 cm). The Museum of Modern Art, New York. The Sidney and Harriet Janis Collection**

105. Fernand Léger. *The Typographer.* 1919. Oil on canvas, 32 × 25½" (81.2 × 64.7 cm). Staatsgalerie Moderner Kunst, Munich

makes the walls explode. No brake, no law comes to temper this overheated atmosphere that shatters the retina, destroys the wall.... Can we perhaps put order in this?[124]

Léger's most encompassing vision of an order for that world of colors without chiaroscuro was the monumental *The City* of 1919 (fig. 106). In a later conversation with his friend the poet Blaise Cendrars, Léger recalled how the place de Clichy, the locale of some of the largest and most aggressive billboards in Paris, had been the site of "the birth of advertising," and a key source for his imagery in *The City*.[125] The memory of those giant panels lives on in the picture's inclusion of large letters and broad planes of unmodulated color, as well as in its mural scale (seven and a half feet tall and almost ten feet long);[126] the more compressed versions of the same motif (fig. 107) share this powerful combination of monumental form, bold hues, and clear evocation of advertising's impact. Yet, though the picture has a pronounced element of dy-

namism in the cinematic overlapping of fragmentary views of differing scales,[127] it lacks entirely the exhilarated, skyward uplift of Delaunay's *Cardiff Team*. Leaping, athletic heroism has been supplanted by the descent of robotic figures with a measured tread. Team effort has given way to uniformity, and the corresponding billboard representations of human torsos do not speak of individuality and aspiration, but (in gingerbread-man silhouettes that seem premonitory of computer-age signage) of generic, unisex anonymity.

Something of Seurat reemerges in *The City*, but not the Seurat of Chéret and *Le Chahut*. The manic intensity is gone, along with the insistent smiles, and we recover some of the dignity of the *Grande Jatte*. Seurat's willingness to see a nobler condition in the grittier and less prestigious areas of Paris is here, for the place de Clichy was the raw heart of a quarter of tawdry nightlife and working-class residences. But Seurat's feel for afternoon half-light and melancholy, and his carica-

106. **Fernand Léger.** *The City.* 1919. Oil on canvas, 7'6¾" × 9'9¼" (230.5 × 297.8 cm). Philadelphia Museum of Art. A. E. Gallatin Collection

tural appreciation for the quirky physiognomies of so-cial style, have been burnished off this utopian billboard for machine-age urban life.

The boldness and variety of this vision are immensely impressive, but its cinematic syncopation is accompanied by an underlying tone that is sober, if not solemn. Even the stenciled letters, which in Cubism had appeared as an appreciation for the do-it-yourself unpretentiousness of low-grade commercial signs, here have been purified into more perfectly geometric forms. The typeface, like the picture in general, looks to the future; nothing like this lettering appeared on the billboards of the place de Clichy in these years. *The City* is not an appreciation of mass advertising as the explosive and unregulated force it had been before 1918, but a vision of the new, ordered presence in life it could become.

Léger painted *The City* with a prophet's eye. Delaunay's vision of the modern spirit, by contrast, had been put together from the recent past (the Eiffel Tower

was almost a quarter century old at the time of *The Cardiff Team*). But in neither case was there a simple equation between the dominant facts of the society that surrounded the artist and the world created on the canvas. France in 1920 was still relatively underdeveloped as a society of industry and urban centers. But Paris was at the forefront of artistic innovation, and had been for decades; and from this vantage, the future was visible, or at least depictable, as it was not from others. In their ability to represent what they thought of as the spirit of modern life, French artists depended at least as much on models of artistic construction and color that were wholly un-urban and unconcerned with the iconography of popular culture—the landscape paintings of Cézanne or van Gogh in Provence, for example—as on the data of daily experience. In America, however, the trappings of modern material life came earlier and were more dominant in the major cities, but no new manner of painting provided an appropriate way to take them on.

Léger and his Purist associates were drawn to Amer-

ica as a model for modernity, in the power of its industrial forms (grain silos as well as skyscrapers) and in the promise of a more rational production and distribution of goods. The United States had also long been regarded as the homeland of advertising, the society most attuned to everything commercial. (In Picasso's costumes for the 1917 ballet *Parade*, while the "French manager" holds a clay pipe of the type which so often stood for the pleasures of idle reflection in his café still lifes, the "American manager" holds a megaphone, as a relentlessly loud carnival barker calling up the crowd.) American modernists, though, largely learned to see this through outsiders' eyes. They were drawn to the work of their European contemporaries as a model for assimilating and representing the look of their own society, especially in advertising.

The two central exemplars of this connection, Stuart Davis and Gerald Murphy, absorbed Léger's geometrized planes of color and monumentalizing simplicity. But they combined the café table and the billboard by joining that style to a Cubist iconography of the more private pleasures offered by modern mass production and packaging—cigarettes, newspapers, safety matches, and shaving razors (figs. 108, 109, 111, 115)—and to a Cubist appreciation for the look of in-

107. Fernand Léger. Study for *The City*. 1919. Oil on canvas laid down on board, 31⅞ × 25⅝" (81 × 65 cm). The Swid Collection

108. Stuart Davis. *Sweet Caporal*. 1922. Oil and watercolor on canvasboard, 20⅛ × 18½" (51 × 47 cm). Thyssen-Bornemisza Collection, Lugano, Switzerland

109. **Stuart Davis.** *Cigarette Papers.* 1921. Oil, bronze paint, and pencil on canvas, 19 × 14"
(48.3 × 35.6 cm). The Menil Collection, Houston

dividual logos. Davis's *Odol* (fig. 110) or Murphy's *Razor* (fig. 115), for example, would never be mistaken for European art of the period. A comparison with the Léger *Syphon* makes it clear that the American works are less interested in the classic, generic item of popular use, or in a standardized form of communication, than in the varied look of product design and brand identity. *Odol* has a head-on acceptance of the package design that seems flat-footed on the one hand, and on the other possessed of a bald power that looks ahead to later Pop painting.

Davis's early homages to cigarette packs (figs. 108, 109) offer an enlarged, simplified updating of Braque's and Picasso's play with bits of the same kind of material. And the slightly later *Lucky Strike* pulls together a knot of European and American sensibilities (fig. 111). The attention to newspapers has its obvious models in prewar Paris, but the focus here on *The Sporting News*, and particularly on its cartoon, adds a layer of timely appreciation for the worlds of athletics and amusement combined, celebrating the popular appeal of both the paper and the comic style;[128] the result is a jocular American conjunction of the same forces of games and publicity that Delaunay had celebrated in a more epic, internationalized vein. Davis's casual layout and celebration of the immediate pleasures of

sports and brightly colored packaging also make a telling contrast with Kurt Schwitters's incorporation of cigarette wrappers, just a year before (fig. 112). Schwitters's work combines a meticulously balanced composition, whose architectural rigidity and coloristic austerity are influenced by Constructivist design, with an affection for the romance of the imaginary "Miss Blanche," and for the refined exoticism of the Egyptian trappings on the label. The garrulous, masculine, and populist associations of *Lucky Strike* suggest an entirely different temperament; and the choice of the particular cigarette package in the foreground adds an important element with specifically American connotations.

The Lucky Strike brand had been launched by the American Tobacco Company in 1917. Its name had been revived from that of a cut-plug tobacco firm the company had bought out in 1905. The thought was that this name's evocation of the forty-niners gold rush would have a popular, specifically American appeal which would counter the pseudo-aristocracy of Chesterfield, and the exotic overtones of Camel. And the target-like design, punchy and no-nonsense, was arrived at by translating into a new language of contrasting complementaries the simple red disk that had been a background element on the former chewing-tobacco can (figs. 113, 114).[129] Like the poster typefaces Pi-

110. **Stuart Davis.** *Odol.* 1924. Oil on canvasboard, 24 × 18″ (60.9 × 45.6 cm). The Crispo Collection, New York

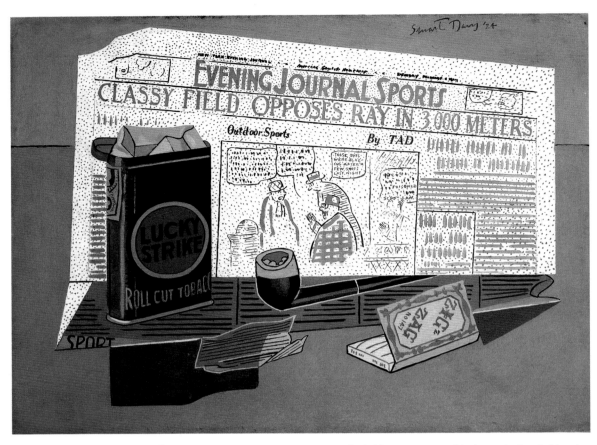

111. **Stuart Davis.** *Lucky Strike.* 1924. Oil on paperboard, 18 × 24″ (45.6 × 60.9 cm). Hirshhorn Museum and Sculpture Garden, Smithsonian Institution, Washington, D.C. Museum purchase

112. **Kurt Schwitters.** *Miss Blanche.* 1923. Collage, 6¼ × 5″ (15.9 × 12.7 cm). Collection Prof. Dr. Werner Schmalenbach, Düsseldorf

113. Lucky Strike cigarette pack. c. 1920

114. Lucky Strike cut plug. c. 1900. Printed tin, 2½ × 4½″ (6.7 × 11.7 cm). Manufactured by R. A. Patterson Tobacco Co.

casso and Braque selected, or the simple Campari ad of Léger, this was an instance of old-fashioned, baldly simple commercial design being isolated and revived as the appropriate look for an era of new democracy and machine production; but in this case the process of refinement and modernization had taken place within the making of the commercial design itself, with the appeal to a mass market as motivation.

The period in which Davis and Murphy painted these jazz-age images of modern commercial life has been regarded by many as a kind of golden age for advertising, when public mistrust abated and ads seemed a natural part of the spreading prosperity in many of the Western nations.[130] It is the same epoch, for example, when the Parisian magazine *L'Art vivant* published the upbeat montage we saw at the chapter's beginning (fig. 1). And two of the most salient characteristics of the field in these years were the increasing penetration of European markets by American ad agencies and American techniques on the one hand, and the increasing influence of European modernism on American advertising on the other.

The European-American exchange was marked by mutual mistrust and misunderstanding. In stereotypes both sides fostered, the Europeans were thought to be too devoted to the poster and to the idea of arty, but ineffective, ad imagery; while the Americans, more given to editorial-style texts in their ads, were thought to be, for better or worse, the masters of market research and planned campaigns.[131] Inexorably, however, and especially after the Universal Exposition of

Decorative Arts in Paris in 1925, advertisers on both sides of the Atlantic began to pay far more attention to the lessons that might be learned from the innovations in modern art they had formerly derided.

At the time of the Armory Show of European modernism in New York in 1913, all but the most adventurous advertisers had found the new art aberrant and useless. The progress from the smug derision of *The Century* at that time (fig. 116) to the eager brochure on "Going Modern" offered by an advertising firm in 1929 (fig. 117) was piecemeal at first, then headlong in the last years before the Great Depression. In 1925, *Printers' Ink* announced that "Futuristic Monstrosities Are All the Rage," but the article stressed that modern art was simply being used as a stunt, to attract attention by its very strangeness. The trend was attributed primarily to the importance of younger consumers, and women; but even manufacturers who detested the style used it, because it sold the goods.[132]

By 1928, when *Advertising and Selling* announced that "Modernism Emerges Full-Fledged," it became increasingly clear that "even the bitter-enders among the conservatives are feeling the modern influence." Reading between the lines, however, it is equally clear that the modernism in question was an indiscriminate mix of Bauhaus-influenced graphics, French art deco, and Wiener Werkstätte stylizations.[133] If a seller felt that the "emotion of modern drawing can give a small car new dignity and make us covet one . . . [or] glorify so prosaic an article as the kitchen range," the "modernist" result in an ad might be the "cartoon simplicity" commissioned from an artist like Rockwell Kent.[134] The showiest and least interesting applications of European lessons came in illustrations with gratuitous "moonbeam" diagonals in the background or "zigzag" inflections. The most pervasive and serious absorptions were in typography and layout, where art directors with a taste for European modernism (such as M. F. Agha of Condé Nast, whom we discussed in relation to sans-serif typefaces, in the chapter on "Words") imposed lessons learned from the graphic designers of the Russian and German avant-garde.[135]

Still more telling, though less immediately remarked in the literature of advertising itself, was the extension of versions of modernism into the design of products, in order to make them advertisements for themselves. A decorative version of modern architectural design now came back to take over the original sources—unpretentious machine products and items of everyday use—from which some modern architects had originally drawn inspiration.[136] Those in marketing who saw this development as forward-looking promoted it with rhetoric that distantly echoed some of the founding manifestoes of modernism. Earnest Elmo Calkins, for example, president of the firm of Calkins & Holden, held that "An exotic art cloistered in museums can never be a vital factor in modern life compared with that which springs from the daily interests of the people. . . . If we are to have beauty it must grow out of our modern industrial civilization. . . . A really beautiful fac-

115. Gerald Murphy. *Razor.* 1924. Oil on canvas, 32⅝ × 36½" (82.9 × 92.7 cm). Dallas Museum of Art. Foundation for the Arts Collection. Gift of the artist

tory building is worth more, has more influence on us today, than a museum full of the choicest art of antiquity." Calkins expressed these sentiments in an article titled "Beauty in the Machine Age," with the subhead "The New Concern with Esthetics That Is Dominating Advertising Is Having an Influence on Manufactured Goods." Discussing the "new merchandising device known as 'styling the goods,'" he explained:

Until recently style was confined to strictly fashion goods, things to wear mostly, "ruffs and scuffs and farthingales and things." Now the idea of style is extended to include nearly every article of human use, towels, telephones, typewriters, fountain pens, bathrooms and refrigerators, as well as furniture, draperies, motor cars and radios. These articles are rede-

signed and colored in the modern spirit, something entirely apart from any mechanical improvement, to make them markedly new, and encourage new buying, exactly as the fashion designers make skirts longer so you can no longer be happy with your short ones.

. . . The influence that is at work making over so many kinds of manufactured goods is the new concern with esthetics that is dominating advertising. The men called in to redesign the product are the very artists who have been creating new techniques for the representation of goods. Many a color scheme put forward tentatively in an advertisement has been adopted at the factory. Production is living up to its advertising. . . . Gradually a new field is developing. The artist . . . is combining the work of making advertisements to sell goods with that of making goods more saleable.[137]

116. Advertisement for *The Century*, 1913

Calkins's article signals a new overlapping of two of the tracks we have been following: the representations in advertising of everyday objects of commerce; and the physical presentation of these objects themselves. This conjunction would strongly affect the modern artist's sense of the commercial world. Artists like Léger and Duchamp had looked to the world of hardware—syphons and urinals—as a world shaped by relatively "unconscious," uncorrupted forces of functional design, which advertising and display then devised means to dramatize. Now utilitarian objects of this sort, including especially consumer items such as appliances, might begin to have the dramatizations of advertising built into their form from the outset—so that, far from representing an independent world of changeless simplicity as the syphon did for Léger and his friends, these new appliances would come to represent a changing array of derivative stylizations, often echoing in a distorted fashion the look of modern styles of painting, sculpture, or architecture. Increasingly, a modern artist looking to the imagery of advertising or to the world of hardware was likely to find there some mark—usually trivialized, but also sometimes interestingly transformed—of the repertoire of modern styles that made up his own tradition.

In these same years, while advertisers and designers reached out to incorporate what they saw as modern art, modernists increasingly celebrated advertising as art. Writers such as Apollinaire had long before referred to advertising as a form of urban poetry, and this kind of appreciation now became a familiar refrain. One devoted champion of the art of the street, Louis Chéronnet, waxed rhapsodic on "Advertising, the Art of the Twentieth Century," in *L'Art vivant* in 1927:

The composition of the air has changed. To the oxygen and nitrogen we breathe we have to add Advertising. Advertising is in some way an elastic gas, diffuse, perceptible to all our organs.... Technicians and "engineers" have certainly codified it and dominated it. But we have not been aware enough of its beauty, latent, profound, scattered, spontaneous.... The first domain of Advertising was the street.... Now it surrounds us, envelops us, it is intimately mingled with our every step, in our activities, in our relaxation, and its "atmospheric pressure" is so necessary to us that we no longer feel it.[138]

Cendrars, the poet friend of Delaunay and Léger, went further, classing advertising among the seven wonders of the modern world. He wrote in 1927 that "Advertising is the flower of contemporary life, it is an affirmation of optimism and gaiety; it distracts the eye and the spirit."[139] And finding that ads constituted an art—by their fusion of punchy, economical words and quick-impact images—he sought to praise them on their own terms. He adopted the address, terseness, and rhythm of slogans at the end of one part of a text titled "Advertising = Poetry":

Yes, really, advertising is the most beautiful expression of our epoch, the greatest novelty of the day, an Art.

An art that calls on internationalism, on polyglotism, on the psychology of crowds, and that overturns all the known static or dynamic techniques, by making intense use, incessantly renewed and efficient, of new materials and fresh procedures.

What characterizes the ensemble of worldwide advertising is its lyricism.

And here publicity touches on poetry.... Poetry makes known [in the way advertising does a product] the image of the spirit that conceives it....

That's why I call here on all poets: Friends, advertising is your domain.

It speaks your language.

It realizes your poetics.[140]

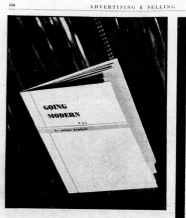

117. Illustration from *Advertising and Selling,* September 4, 1929, p. 104

118. Billboards, Paris. c. 1925

For many, the most exalted form of publicity remained the city billboard, whose monumental scale seemed the stuff of dreams, myths, and vast cults. Maurice Talmeyr had lamented that, replacing sacred architecture, the poster had become the "cathedral of sensuality" for a decadent age; Chéronnet, in unconscious echo, genuflected before the billboard as the shrine of a dynamic modernity: "Excessive, hallucinatory, the billboard imposes itself everywhere, whatever the speed of the passerby or the thoughts that absorb him. It surges like a cathedral. Its frescoes come out of the ground, its vertical masses and planes run together in the assault on story-heights and its spires thrust themselves into the heavens it has conquered. It is in the image of our existence: multiple and simultaneous."[141]

This same sense of the mythic, oneiric power of modern billboards appears in literature as well. One of the most inescapable French advertising figures of the twenties and thirties was the huge, grinning baby used to promote Cadum soap (figs. 118, 119). The Bébé Cadum, who even makes a cameo appearance in René Clair's 1924 film *Entr'acte*,[142] was referred to repeatedly when ads were discussed. Writing to a friend in 1923 that "It's the century of advertising," Picasso's friend the poet Max Jacob questioned, "Will we do less for Art and Faith than Cadum does for its soap?"[143] Even Léger, who felt billboards could no longer compete with the *objets-spectacle* in stores, allowed that "Only the Bébé Cadum, that enormous object, persists."[144] The gigantesque infant became one of the epic protagonists in a novel by Robert Desnos, *La Liberté ou l'amour!* of 1927, in which advertising personages come down from billboards and walk the city streets performing miracles appropriate to their roles. In the guise of the "new redeemer," transformed later into the Christ Child, is the monstrously clean Cadum baby. As a symbolic embodiment of good, he triumphs in a battle with a rotund figure of evil, Bibendum, the Michelin man. (This titanic struggle

119. Billboards, Paris. c. 1925. Photograph from *L'Art vivant*, August 1926, p. 619

ends, however, with the baby done in by an attack of bouncing tires spawned by his defeated nemesis.)[145] The private caprice Kurt Schwitters essayed, when he fused divinity and religious ideals with the dreamy fantasies of the world of advertising personae in one irreverent exercise (fig. 36), here attains the scale of epic spectacle.

Yet amid this fascination with big, spectacular urban advertising, and in this epoch of ads made over with lessons from modern art, the artist who was perhaps most directly connected with advertising, René Magritte, made art by appropriating a style right-thinking merchants had long since left behind. Advertising agents were more and more interested by the way a diluted version of a modern style such as Cubism could serve as a mind-arresting gimmick in the presentation of an object for sale; they urged their clients to see that a degree of abstraction would still allow an item to be recognized, with a little salutary effort on the part of the intrigued viewer. One such agency instructed its audience, in regard to a composition of circles and curves, that IT'S A PIPE! (fig. 120). But at the same time those advertisers were learning to see that familiar things could profitably be represented in strange new ways, Magritte was demonstrating that entirely traditional ways of representing things could, with minute alterations, arrest the mind with more enduringly discomfiting effect. THIS, he advised, in perhaps his most succinct and memorable epigram on the problematic nature of all representation, IS NOT A PIPE (fig. 121).

IT'S A PIPE!

IT'S NO TRICK to smoke up a yarn about quality, service and price. But, somehow, today, the wiser buyers aren't satisfied listening to the golden tongue. Mere words, they know, are like the blue-gray puffs from a jimmy pipe, that soon disappear in the surrounding air . . . When you talk to a representative of McGrath, notice the meat in what he has to say. He knows engraving, as well as how to sell. He'll give you a new light on some facts about your engraving problems.

McGRATH ENGRAVING CORPORATION
PHOTO ENGRAVERS • ELECTROLYTIC HALFTONES • 509 S. FRANKLIN ST., CHICAGO

120. Advertisement for McGrath Engraving Corporation, 1931

121. René Magritte. *The Treachery of Images (This Is Not a Pipe).* **1928. Oil on canvas, 21½ × 28½" (62.2 × 81 cm). Los Angeles County Museum of Art. Purchased with Funds Provided by the Mr. and Mrs. William Preston Harrison Collection**

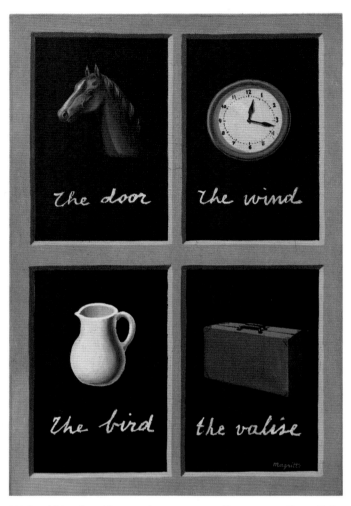

122. René Magritte. *The Key of Dreams*. **1936. Oil on canvas, 16¼ × 10¾″ (41.3 × 27.3 cm). Collection Jasper Johns**

Magritte had himself been employed in the advertising business, as a window designer among other things; and he continued to make part of his living by designing packaging and ads. But, as in the case of Schwitters, there seems to have been no conflict, and little overlap, between the day job serving commerce and the studio role of a professional subversive. Some early Magritte paintings reflect a window-dresser's idea of arrangement, and some of the lesser graphics he produced for advertising in turn use familiar props, like the *bilboquet*, from his personal repertoire.[146] But his mature vision—of impossible situations rendered eerily plausible, or of word-and-image conundrums (fig. 122)—had little to do with his own ads or with the billboards of the day. Instead, these memorable images recuperated the style of antiquated catalogues and charts. The layout in a single work of a series of disparate images — horses, gloves, eggs, and so on— has precedents in the little rebus puzzles frequently printed in popular almanacs; and the isolation and framing of one named object, aggrandized but devoid of scale reference, was a staple of certain kinds of turn-of-the-century catalogues.

One of the most suggestive parallels for Magritte's unblinking, daylight Surrealism, though, lies in the same domain as Ernst's *Lehrmittel-Anstalt*, among the paraphernalia of childhood instruction. The handwriting in *The Treachery of Images* is that of a grade-school primer on penmanship: a script not infantile but mindlessly impersonal, devoid of the quirks that distinguish individual penmanship. And the word-and-image presentation of the pipe, like the similar pairings in *The Key of Dreams*, strongly recalls schoolroom charts such as those produced by the Deyrolle firm in Paris before 1900 (figs. 123, 124). The wan palette of these charts, the evenly shaded modeling of each image, and the manner of rendering—objective but in no sense mechanical, without a trace of photographic intervention—all anticipate the look of Magritte's counterlogical "lessons." Elements of widely different reference and scale, including lamp bulbs and light-houses if not umbrellas and sewing machines, are as-

123. Pedagogical chart (Paris: Deyrolle & Fils), c. 1890

sembled in ordered rows within these antiseptic and wholly consistent non-spaces, in a series of unselfconscious incongruities that require only slight adjustment to release their quotient of the absurd.

Magritte was out to make swampy the very ground that the school charts sought to solidify. But the subversive principle he used had analogues in the workaday world. Any subscriber to the mail-order botanical business would have been as undisturbed by seeing pictures of pears called KING OF PRUSSIA, or of roses crowned DUCHESS OF KENT, as we are to see a photograph of a horse inscribed SEA BISCUIT, or tomatoes labeled BEEFSTEAK. And the new business of ordering things by telegraph had prompted the invention of codes with even odder conjunctions. The Michelin company, for example, issued books in which every spare part they sold—various size tire irons, valves, tubes, and so on—was given a specific, wholly arbitrary name which would make an order by wire unmistakably precise. As manifest in rosters of tire irons christened ''forum,'' ''rifle,'' or ''film'' (fig. 125), such foolproof communication needs only the eye of a sufficiently shrewd fool to mutate into a daft poetry.

Magritte made conundrums and logic games from

124. **Pedagogical chart (Paris: Deyrolle & Fils), c. 1890**

125. **Francisque Poulbot. Advertisement for Michelin automotive repair tools, 1913 (detail)**

the simplest readjustment of presentations that were more about telling than selling. But when new convictions about the irrationality of human motivation came to the fore in advertising of the 1950s and 1960s, these formats of bland, "self-explanatory" communication, revealed as part instructive and part seductive by his paintings, came to play an important role in progressive advertising. The trick of making familiar things unforgettably odd by changing their scale and context, which his work began to feature after World War II, was similarly a conduit by which some very old ideas—like the rosewood piano in the logger's hut of 1907—reentered modern advertising's efforts to arrest the mind by images. By now, thanks to Magritte, the schoolboy instructional style has moved from grade school to graduate school, as the painting that admonishes THIS IS NOT A PIPE has become the standard visual

aid of the followers of Michel Foucault.[147] And the bland, calmly viewed impossibility which seemed archaic in the 1920s has come to be a cliché quote for any advertiser who wishes to sell, not simply by irrational associations, but by associations with the particular irrationality of modern art.

The 1930s

The mutual infatuation between modern art and advertising chilled quickly after 1930. The Great Depression brought capitalism under fire, and the rise of the dictators threw a different light on methods of mass persuasion. Those who still needed such methods, whether to rally the *Volk*, consolidate the workers' paradise, or just make a sale in hard times, looked at modern stylization as either a luxury or an outright corruption, unsuited to the tasks at hand.

American advertisers who had used modern design inflections to entice prosperous consumers now felt impelled to make a harder sell to a broader audience with less money to spend. Rationalizing a change to a more prosaic manner, writers in *Printers' Ink* argued that the consumer had once again become a more reasonable creature, who wanted facts rather than fantasies.[148] But this posture was part of a broader attempt to justify advertising's utility in the face of widespread accusations that it contributed to economic disorder. The visible result was not clear information aimed at a reasoning audience, but a hard-sell look, devoid of subtlety, that the advertisers called "buckeye" style, tailored for an audience presumed dumb. In a way, advertising underwent its own "Pop" episode here, as it turned away from European modernism, to borrow instead the devices of the tabloid newspaper and the comic strip, for more effective communication to a broader audience.[149] The champion of "styling the goods," E. E. Calkins, was still maintaining as late as 1933 that "beauty pays."[150] But by 1934 he ruefully recognized that there had been a "turning back from modernism to the more obvious style of illustration we call realism," and that "advertising is beginning to make its appeal to a lower intellectual stratum . . . now when every square inch of advertising space must carry its load, we turn back to a simpler, more familiar and probably safer technique, and the result is art that leaves little to the imagination because of its diagrammatic simplicity. . . . It is now going on the theory . . . that if you reach the dullest mind you reach them all."[151]

The lowest-common-denominator approach carried with it a populist rhetoric, and a measure of exultant anti-intellectual pleasure in the collapse of modernist pretensions. "This is no time for noble experiments in the name of art, culture or good taste," an advertising writer opined in February 1932, allowing sarcastically that "of course, illustrations made for the sole purpose of calling to public attention the merits of a certain vacuum cleaner or a tooth paste are possibly more restricted in concept than the brainstorms of absinth sippers who live a sketchy life in Montmartre."[152] In the same vein, a writer from Young & Rubicam chastised "The Disloyal Art Director" in August 1932, arguing that admen should read *True Story* and *Motion Picture* more than literary journals, and that "If he wishes to become more proficient in his work a trip to the movies will teach him more than a trip to the Modern Museum."[153]

Michael Schudson's term for American advertising, "capitalist realism,"[154] is a particularly apt description of the ads developed in the thirties, at the same time that Nazi Germany and the Soviet Union were developing a national propaganda based on a return to heroicized forms of realism. The basic purposes, of moving the broadest audience with styles that were reassuringly legible and impervious to ambiguity, were parallel. And those in the capitalist countries kept casting a wary eye at the practice of other systems, especially that of Goebbels in Germany, who was alternatively proposed as an object lesson for, or an apt student of, American advertising techniques. The old analogies between propaganda and advertising begged to be drawn again as they had been in the early twenties, but this time less under the sign of hope than that of fear. The power of capitalist seduction to heat up individual self-indulgence had proved dangerous, and the ability of mass emotional appeal to effect

an opposite, regressive embrace of racial solidarity was demonstrated more disturbingly every day. The dream of Léger and Cendrars and others, that the spectacle of advertising was opening a new world of social fulfillment and liberated poetry, went sour, and such voices fell silent against the tinkling of beggars' cups and the rhythmic fall of jackboots.

This was a time for polarizations, with forceful populism and the call for an authentic proletarian culture meeting academic recoil against any idea of pandering to the "popular." From several sides, insistences were heard that modern art was by nature difficult of access, and therefore—for better and worse—wholly incompatible with the culture of the masses. But the pragmatic dialogue and interaction between modern art and advertising went on, in smaller corners. Men like Agha at Condé Nast, or Alexey Brodovitch at *Harper's*, carried on training younger designers and photographers who would have a powerful impact on the resurgence of European modernist influences in American advertising after World War II. And two remarkable instances of engagement with the material of advertising, on opposite sides of the Atlantic, kept alive in the domain of private fantasy what had been, and would be again, one of modern art's primary linkages to the broad public forces at work in the society around it.

By the 1930s, Joan Miró was already a well-established master of empty dream spaces; and he seems to have felt the need to be crowded by things material and prosaic. He made several drawing-collages with photographs and postcards, and sculptures from found objects, in an established format of irrational assemblage. In 1933, in order to provoke his imagination with points of sharp resistance—as a grain of sand irritates an oyster into making a pearl—Miró cut out from ads and sales catalogues a roster of images of silverware, household objects, combs, machines, and the like, and arranged them in an unpredictable variety of ways on eighteen large sheets of paper. From these, by dint of scrutiny with a willfully hallucinating eye, he conjured the compositions of eighteen paintings. The final results of this exercise seem to move to the primordial rhythms of the unconscious, with echoes from the underground bestiaries of Lascaux and Altamira (figs. 127, 129, 131, 133). But the starting points dance to the tune of the Bon Marché and Sears (figs. 126, 128, 130, 132).[155]

The collages themselves are remarkable specimen boards. Miró took lowly drones from the world of advertising, of the kind that Léger might have seen as latently heroic and Picabia exposed as irredeemably inert, and plucked them from the swarming hive of the catalogue to unaccustomed individuality on the scaleless expanse of these large sheets. The oddity of some of these images needed only this room to declare itself, and under the heat of his gaze the colanders and combs mutated into fabulous creatures by fast-forward evolution. Prominent masses withered to vestigiality, minor appendages metamorphosed into

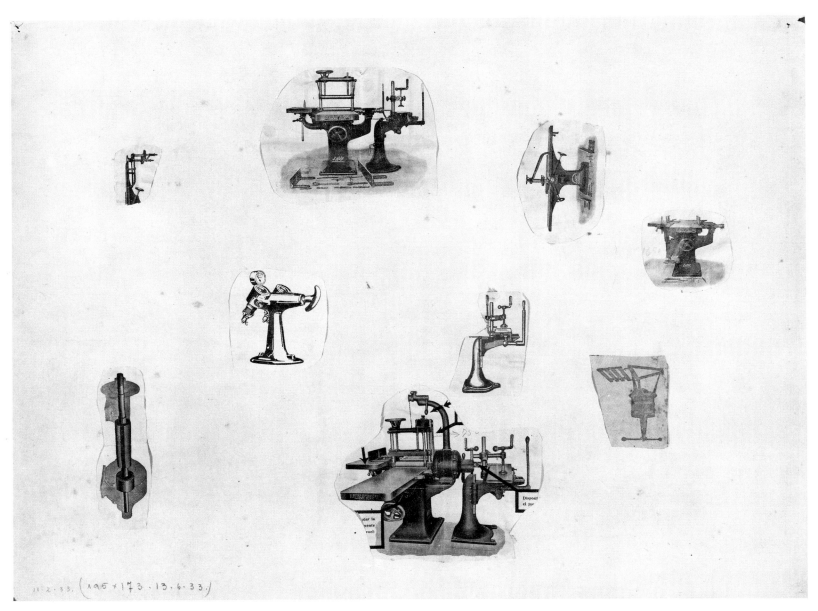

126. **Joan Miró.** *Collage* (study for *Painting*, 1933). 1933. Cut-and-pasted photomechanical reproductions and pencil on paper, 18⅛ × 24⅞″ (46.8 × 63 cm). The Museum of Modern Art, New York. Gift of the artist

unexpected dominance, and eventually the figural elements in the paintings—while still carrying in uncanny ways the physiology of combs and forks and so on—shed the carapace of their origin, to become soft-bodied creatures populating nocturnal, aqueous environments altogether different from the clinically white isolation of their paste-up pages.

Both Picabia and Ernst had made fine artistic capital out of a posture of enlightened passivity before the products of commercial reproduction. But Miró conjured a world like Ernst's from material like Picabia's, by imaginative staring. He wanted to find out what the unconscious looked like—the grail quest of all the Surrealists—and he intuited that the way in led through the hardware department. The standard spur for the

imagination, since Leonardo, had been to study natural accidents—moss on trees, veins in marble. Surrealist devotees of automatic writing pursued something similar, making their own free-form "accidents" and finding the representations hidden in them. Miró reversed the process, finding the nature of thoughts by looking hard at things that had been purposefully designed and thoroughly processed as images.

Miró understood that nothing may be so limiting, and so prone to merely reproducing itself in standardized form, as fantasy with no flint to strike against—and that the realization of what is uniquely personal, or original, may emerge from dialogue with what is external and not under one's control. Opening up to seemingly petty irritations, choosing to devote an extra

127. **Joan Miró.** *Painting.* 1933. Oil on canvas, 68½" × 6'5¼" (174 × 196.2 cm). The Museum of Modern Art, New York. Loula D. Lasker Bequest (by exchange)

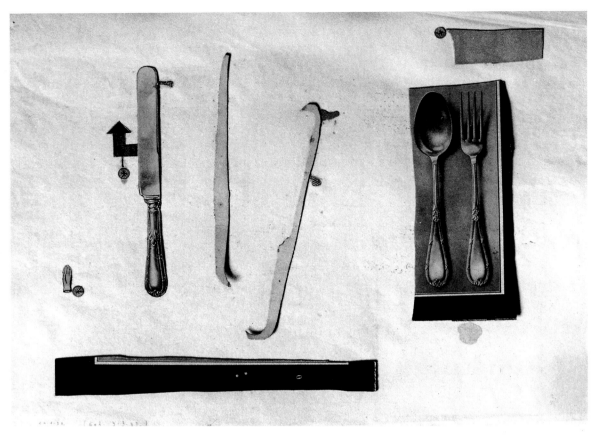

128. **Joan Miró.** *Preparatory Collage for Painting.* 1933. Graphite pencil and collage on paper, 18⅝ × 24⅞″ (47.1 × 63 cm). Fundació Joan Miró, Barcelona. Gift of the artist, 1976

129. **Joan Miró.** *Painting.* 1933. Oil on canvas, 51⅛ × 38⅛″ (130 × 97 cm). Musée d'Art Moderne, Villeneuve d'Ascq

130. **Joan Miró.** *Preparatory Collage for Painting.* 1933. Graphite pencil and collage on paper, 18⅝ × 24⅞″ (47.1 × 63.1 cm). Fundació Joan Miró, Barcelona. Gift of the artist, 1976

131. **Joan Miró.** *Painting.* 1933. Oil on canvas, 51⅛ × 63¾″ (130 × 162 cm). Kunstmuseum Bern

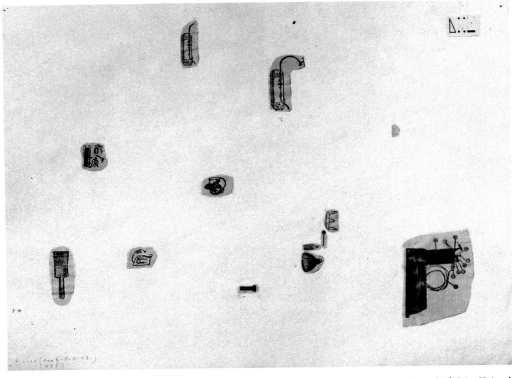

132. **Joan Miró.** *Preparatory Collage for Painting*. 1933. Graphite pencil and collage on paper, 18⅝ × 24⅞″ (47.1 × 63.1 cm). Fundació Joan Miró, Barcelona. Gift of the artist, 1976

133. **Joan Miró.** *Painting*. 1933. Oil on canvas, 51⅛ × 63¾″ (130 × 162 cm). Collection Arnold and Milly Glimcher

measure of attention precisely to dime-a-dozen things others regard as useless or merely functional, can sometimes be the crucial step in making powerfully original art. More specifically, though, his remarkable experiment belies the familiar notion that the world of commercial reproduction is hostile territory for the artistic imagination. Miró saw that the dreams of retail produce monsters—that the obscene fecundity of commercial image production can serve as a giant gene pool in which, if one keeps an attentive enough eye, bizarre prototypes of potential new life forms are constantly, carelessly spawned.

For Miró in Paris, those little printers' slugs were stepping stones toward a world outside of time and away from public subjects. But for a man on Utopia Parkway in Queens, New York, advertisements were tickets into a social, cosmopolitan world he would otherwise never know. Joseph Cornell's boxes collapse one of advertising's standard distinctions, for in them notices that are straightforward informational prose are also fetishes of longing and dream association. Cornell made a Europe of the mind, from hotel ads and chocolate labels (figs. 134–136), in boxes that were part coffin and part cradle.[156]

Coffin, because here the world of Cubist collage has been interred and memorialized. Newspapers, notices, and wrappers that for Picasso and Braque were chips in the game of urban life become the tarot of a stately solitaire in Cornell. Formerly low and scattered fragments, they now have gained the patina of a high world of art: they evoke the world of Cubism itself, become prestigious and almost antique, as much as the Grand Tour voyages the hotel names conjure. These relics—*Chocolat Menier* (fig. 134), *Le Journal*— were by then drenched in nostalgia, souvenirs of a world Cornell had never known: the daybook of the *flâneur* become the historical romance of the shut-in. Nor is this Schwitters's world of things soiled and torn with use, but one of pristine fragments handled with a collector's tweezers. The Cubist and Dada artists had put the little things in life under a magnifying glass and found energy, amusement, and lyric sentimentality in what was close to hand. Cornell puts those things behind a pane that separates, and exacerbates the voyeur's longing: he looks at their world through a telescope, from the wrong end.

Coffins, yet cradles too. Cornell made these elements of European low culture, now standing for European high culture, collide with the local vernacular of

134. **Joseph Cornell.** *Chocolat Menier.* 1952. Construction: wood box with mixed media, 17 × 12 × 4" (43.2 × 30.5 × 12.1 cm). Grey Art Gallery and Study Center, New York University Art Collection. Anonymous gift

Among his simplest and most memorable productions, a series of Pharmacies (fig. 138) show an eye for the structures of store display that looks backward to the crowded, unstyled vernacular of an archaic era of commerce, and at the same time forward to the interests of the artists of the 1960s in repetition, as an artifact of showing and selling in the world of mass production. The Pharmacies, and a great deal else in Cornell's work, follow the interests of Magritte, Léger, and many other modern artists in the poetics to be found in systems of classification, instruction, and utilitarian presentation. There are metaphors lurking on store racks and in school charts, of an unprejudiced evenhandedness in dealing with the things there are to learn, to know, or to use in the world's multifarious production. For Cornell these grid structures of identical units, of potion bottles or Bronzino portraits, are conditions of the mind at work and of affection in play simultaneously, the common attribute of the naturalist, the merchant, and the game board. Inventory is poetry to the eye that will see and frame it.

135. **Joseph Cornell.** Untitled (Hôtel Beau-Séjour). 1954. Construction: wood box with pastel on pasted papers, mirror, metal rod and ring, paper cut-out (cockatoo) mounted on wood, branch, cork ball, piece of wood, and drawer containing patterned papers, 17¾ × 12¼ × 4½″ (45.2 × 31.1 × 11.5 cm). The Museum of Modern Art, New York. Promised gift of an anonymous donor

the penny arcade, in a way that sounds premonitory notes. Cornell took genuine delight in the design of penny-arcade devices, studied them, and took friends to see special new models, like Monet rushing afternoon visitors to see his water lilies before they closed.[157] The happy notion of bringing together the Uffizi and the pinball parlor, and using the matrix of such cheap amusements to render homage to Mannerist portraits (fig. 137)—or conversely, of using postcard princesses as the avatars of private games—looks forward to aspects of the work of Robert Rauschenberg. (And one of its side effects is to let these grave little nobles become children again, in a world of urban amusements they never knew.) Cornell's affection for unobtainable women embraced without irony or cynicism the common elements that made movie stars, Russian ballerinas, and ladies of the long-dead Italian nobility into equal subjects for admiration. This notion of celebrity, and the multiplication of identical reproduced images, are minuet rehearsals for some of the disco productions of Pop.

136. **Joseph Cornell.** Untitled (Parrot Collage: Grand Hôtel de la Pomme d'Or). 1954–55. Construction: wood box with mixed media, 18¹⁵⁄₁₆ × 10¹¹⁄₁₆ × 3³⁄₁₆″ (48.1 × 27.1 × 8.1 cm). The Joseph and Robert Cornell Memorial Foundation

137. Joseph Cornell. Untitled (Medici Princess). c. 1948. Construction: wood box with mixed media, 17⅝ × 11⅛ × 4⅜″ (44.8 × 28.3 × 11.1 cm). Private collection, New York

138. **Joseph Cornell.** Untitled (Pharmacy). 1952. Construction: wood box with glass, mirror, shells, sand, printed papers, coral, cork, feather, metal, and liquid, 14¼ × 13¼ × 5¼″ (36.2 × 33.7 × 13.3 cm). Collection Muriel Kallis Newman

By the time Cornell began showing these boxes in New York, the cosmopolitan popular culture of France, which figured so strongly in many of them, was not far from being swallowed up by the *Volk* of thatched roofs and National Socialism, and a crucial bend in our story was about to be turned. In a strict sense, nothing new happened between the fields of modern art and advertising during the war years. But a polarity that had been a central aspect of that story collapsed. In the twenties and thirties, commercial advertising and the culture around it was often thought of, hated or loved, as something associated with American culture, while modern art was a part of Europe. After World War II, however, while advertising and the consumer values it promoted were even more exclusively associated with the tendentious issue of Americanization in Europe, modern art gained a much firmer foothold in the United States, both in the avant-garde of painting and sculpture and in the day-to-day business of advertising.

The fallout from these changes—as well as from the cautionary experience of the fascist appeal to the masses, and from the trauma of the war itself—established new stakes for the confrontation between a transplanted European modernism and a newly energetic and sophisticated American advertising industry.

The 1950s

Advertising often pretends to traffic in "timeless values," "ageless beauty," and "enduring quality," but the culture that it spends a great deal of its time selling us—the culture of cars, clothes, music, and other items of fashion—is insistently time-bound, and geared to planned obsolescence, continual novelty, and instant nostalgia. To the extent this peculiar historical sense allows for a belle époque, we have had it drummed into us—largely through movies, television, music, books, and advertising for them—that the great era was the "happy days" of the 1950s, the endless summer vacation of Marilyn, Marlon, and Elvis, before drugs, before the sexual revolution, before Vietnam, when tail fins were tall, chrome gleamed bright, and black leather was for real thugs only.

Yet even clichés can be complex. The fifties are a golden isle of the pop-culture imagination, and like all such isles they stand as much for vulnerability and potential loss as they do for fulfillment. The oldies effect arrived a nanosecond after the Top Ten, and rock and roll was not just hedonistic, but also morbid and nostalgic, from the outset. The *vanitas* figures of James Dean and Buddy Holly haunt the imagination of the epoch; and later, with the years rolling on since John Kennedy's assassination, it has become clear that the fifties are the era that can never grow up. As the imagined high-water mark of philistine consumer pleasures, but simultaneously as a period that epitomizes foolhardy naïveté and political lethargy, this decade seems to knot together many of the ambivalences inherent in any assessment of the seductions and betrayals of a modern, pervasively materialistic, and insistently commercial culture. Like Marilyn and Elvis, without a capacity to cope gracefully with growth and change, the epoch seems fated for eclipse in bloated corruption—or, more generally, hangs around in our mind like some pouty juvenile delinquent on the soda-fountain stool, full of troubles, promises, and portents that can't ever seem to get resolved.

This is not just a phenomenon of retrospective vision. Critics, historians, and politicians of the fifties all debated the goods and evils of its mass culture, particularly the American version, which seemed headed toward becoming a global model. Was this the dawn of a new era of democracy and human hope, or the onset of degraded, hollow values and superficial amusements? And what place was to be found within this transformed world for the previously marginal, minority culture of modern art?

Frequently in these debates, advertising appeared as the primary vehicle of the suspect new values and new desires. But very little art of the period chose to incorporate this all-pervasive, highly visible force, or any other aspect of the new commercial culture America was producing. In fact, critics who defended the dominant new art of the early 1950s, Abstract Expressionist painting, did so in terms that insisted on lofty detachment from the concerns of the herd, and on the adversary position of the artist as existential hero, vis-à-vis anything resembling mass communication. Clement Greenberg had said in *Partisan Review* in 1948 that "Isolation, or rather the alienation that is its cause, is the truth—isolation, alienation, naked and revealed unto itself, is the condition under which the true reality of our age is experienced. And the experience of this true reality is indispensable to any ambitious art."[158]

Greenberg's pronouncement reflected a deep pessimism about the possibilities for human fulfillment within the context of a modern mass culture, and called for art to pull as far away as possible, in order to preserve a domain of uncorrupted individual values. This appeal set itself against all those who, for reasons of politics or simple philistinism, wanted an art that would be more easily accessible and reassuring to the common citizen. Yet in the mid-1950s, when paintings appeared that broke from the isolation Greenberg encouraged and incorporated elements from advertising, they turned out to have a character that pleased the populists no more than the isolationists.

The story of that new art begins with debate and discussion in London and then centers on two artists in New York. But the backdrop to the tale is the developing nature of advertising itself; because advertising in the 1950s was no longer an affair of local billboards and posters, nor was it simply involved in selling products. It had become, on an international scale, an industry concerned with promoting a broad set of values about the way life might be lived. And that industry was concerned to learn and apply the lessons of modernism to achieve its ends. When modern artists looked at advertising of the fifties, they were not looking at a force that was merely independent or simply hostile, but often at parts of their own tradition, absorbed, transformed, and become both newly effective and newly problematic.

In 1954, a writer from the research department of Young & Rubicam said, "If we were to eliminate, in any one issue of *Life*, all advertisements that bear the influence of Miró, Mondrian, and the Bauhaus, we would cut out a sizable proportion of that issue's linage."[159] After the retrenchment of the 1930s, American advertising of the 1950s clearly embraced the look of European modern art. Arp-like blobs, vaguely Léger-like figuration, and Constructivist-inspired layouts and type designs became pervasive. What had seemed a novelty attraction after World War I, then an ideological cause and class marker in the later twenties, and a suspect pretension in the Depression, was absorbed after the war as standard "good design"—much as Miró devolved into kidney-shaped swimming pools, and modernism in general, beginning with figures like Picasso and Henry Moore and Jackson Pollock, began its turnaround from a clubby minority culture to the linchpin of a new humanism, and eventually to part of popular culture itself.

In advertising, these changes can often be traced to small circles of influential people who worked to make them happen. The geometric abstraction of the CBS eye (fig. 139), for example, was designed in 1952 by William Golden, as part of a plan to package the newly television-conscious broadcasting network in a "corporate identity"—a concept Golden is credited with pioneering.[160] Golden had been trained in the offices of Condé Nast in the 1930s, under the tutelage of M. F. Agha.[161] Along with Constructivist-influenced typefaces and layout, part of Agha's innovative approach had involved the conception of a coherent modernized "look" that would work with editorial policy.[162] He and his younger cohorts seem to have moved, by a system of ascending linkages, from an interest in modern type style as a meaningful new "signature," to magazine design as "personality," to the design of abstracted logos as memorable marks, to the packaging of a "corporate identity."

The most important assimilations of European modernist ideas happened on this level of conception rather than in the adoption of particular design elements. "The truth is," a commentator wrote in *Printers' Ink* in 1953, "that the more modern an advertisement is, the less its modernism is likely to be expressed by mechanical means."

When we call modernism a *spirit*, or an *attitude*, we have given the best definition available. It has, indeed, some of the quality of humor; is even a bit light-hearted in its willingness to romp a little with the subject—and with the reader—if a sufficiently striking and memorable expression of the appeal may be found.

Hence no formal rules can be laid down for producing

139. William Golden. *CBS Symbol.* **Illustration from** *The Visual Craft of William Golden* **(New York: George Braziller, 1962)**

such advertisements. We can, however, isolate some of the elements that enter into modern creative design. First of all comes a firm conviction that it is possible to take things that already exist, give them new shapes, use them in new combinations, and apply them in expressing ideas with which they have no commonplace associations. This is just what the modernists seek to do.[163]

The ubiquitous codeword for this kind of thinking in the world of fifties advertising was "creativity," and its main spokesman was William Bernbach. Bernbach formed the firm of Doyle Dane Bernbach in 1949, after he had already forged an alliance with the designer Paul Rand, a senior statesman among American designers appreciative of European modern art and graphic design. The campaign they did for Ohrbach's department store in that year set the tone for which Bernbach would become famous: aside from the new unity of copy, image, and layout in their stripped-down, eye-catching design (fig. 140), these ads were irreverent and humorous. They made fun of other ads (one spread featured a mock-serious discussion of the medical need for SNIAGRAB ["bargains" spelled backwards] in a lampoon of the laxative brand SERUTAN ["natures"]), and they played with visual and verbal

gimmicks (a cat with a hat and cigarette holder to embody cattiness). And it worked: Bernbach "repositioned" Ohrbach's with a new clientele who now found its lower-priced line of clothes not just cheap but smart, in the double sense of the word.[164]

These ads showed the influence of modernism, but not in the form of the decorative "moonbeams" and zigzags of the late 1920s, and not as derived from machine-age rhetoric. The interest in incongruity, humor, and surprise that had been essential to so much early modern art here found its way back into alliance with modern graphic design. And since there seemed to be no formula or quantifiable rationale for these ads (Bernbach was fond of saying, "Persuasion is not a science, but an art"),[165] their success made the word

140. Advertisement for Ohrbach's department store, 1953

"creative" a synonym in advertising literature for imaginative campaigns that called attention to their cleverness as they violated conventional wisdom.

Not everyone was a believer in creativity, however. Bernbach's approach was suspected of appealing only to a limited audience of sophisticates, and of being too quirky to succeed consistently. Advertising moguls in search of more systematic forms of improvement bowed to a rival shibboleth, often referred to simply as M.R.: Motivational Research. If the modern spirit was thought to be part imagination and part science, Bernbach's approach stood for the imagination, and that of Dr. Ernest Dichter for the science—a new wave of advertising science, no longer concerned, as Walter Dill Scott had been, with the neural connections between perception and habit, but with the more ineffable realms of unconscious drives and interpersonal feelings. As president of the Institute for Motivational Research, Inc., Dichter became an oracle for those who believed that human desires could be charted and shaped by a combination of sociological investigation and applied psychology. He rejected the cruder behaviorism that had previously been favored in advertising circles and favored inquiry into matters of affect and emotion—"the social and personal forces [that] direct . . . life goals and ambitions"—over the traditional market research that simply charted statistics of income and acquisitions.[166] Some people, however, had ethical or moral problems with this approach. M.R. was often linked with S.A. (for Sex Appeal), and dealing with unconscious motivation was seen by many as just a new, more insidious way of selling things with sex.[167]

The "creative" and M.R. camps had little time for each other (Bernbach said, "I consider research the major culprit in the advertising picture. . . . It has done more to perpetuate creative mediocrity than any other factor").[168] But they seem to have shared some basic assumptions. First among these was the idea that an ad should convey an "image," an "identity," or a "personality." This is what Golden did for CBS, or what Bernbach did for Ohrbach's; and Dichter said in 1956 that the prime question research should address was, "Does a product have the right personality?"[169] A second shared assumption was that the advertisement worked by indirection, through symbolism, to conjure a mood or set of associations with the product or manufacturer. The eye patch that the advertising magnate David Ogilvy put on a Hathaway shirt model in 1951 was one of the landmark instances of this approach, prefiguring "the Marlboro man" and countless other symbolic figures.[170]

Since M.R. people believed in appeal by irrational association, and the creative side loved high-impact images, ads of the mid-fifties had less text and bigger, more independent pictures, predominantly supplied by color photography.[171] (Ironically, this new focus on style and illustration brought American advertisers closer to the traditional European poster idea, which they had criticized as soft-headed in earlier decades. The promotion of a product by association with an attractively styled and appealing figure was in essence the formula of Chéret, which even the French themselves had long dismissed as outmoded.) By 1957, a writer in Printers' Ink bewailed this triumph of "imagism" as a power play by art directors, signaling the end of any aspiration for ads to do more than make a "vague, over-all impression."[172]

This critic had a point. In the age of "total marketing," complex apparatuses of research and strategy were put at the service of achieving broad, generalized goals of orienting the image of a manufacturer, and coloring the consumer's feelings. Fascism and the war had fostered new notions of modern man as deeply irrational and prone to conform to group pressures; and the postwar rise in prestige of the social sciences, notably anthropology, reflected a new tendency to rethink behavior in Terre Haute and Tupelo in terms that had formerly been applied to Bali and Bora-Bora. For advertisers, thinking in those social-science terms encouraged the devaluation of words and an emphasis on symbols, and provided the broader concept of a socially shaped "personality" that was applied both to consumers and to corporate entities.[173] Virtually all pretense to providing information about a product or appealing straightforwardly for a sale had been abandoned. Dichter-style consumer interviews, from which many advertisers tried to divine a working notion of the people they were targeting, were typically nondirected, stream-of-consciousness confessionals; and just as the sociologists tended to examine the P.T.A. as if it were a tribal council, Dichter's agents applied lessons from psychoanalysis to people's remarks about soap powders and shoe polish. Ideas from psychotherapy bolstered, for example, the notion of "creating a friendly, sincere, and understanding atmosphere which shows the benefits of the product without direct intention to sell."[174]

A mirror-effect arose between these beliefs within the trade and those of outside commentators and critics. Vance Packard raised tremendous paranoia about the power of advertising in The Hidden Persuaders of 1957,[175] by taking in deadly earnest M.R.'s claims for its powers to tap the involuntary mechanisms of desire (and by publishing as evidence selections from inhouse M.R. documents). Not for the first time, people who thought they practiced witchcraft brought forth people disposed to hunt witches: wishful thinking about irresistible power on the part of advertisers found a match in a muckraking effort to convince the public it was prey to a plot.

An adventurous wing of academia and belles lettres, though, was more studiously tolerant, and even appreciative, of what Madison Avenue was doing. Looking at contemporary society anthropologically meant disregarding normal hierarchies of value, and redefining "culture" to include all social phenomena. Books like Marshall McLuhan's The Mechanical Bride: Folklore of Industrial Man of 1951, or essays on popular culture like those that Roland Barthes began publishing in 1952 (collected in Mythologies, 1957), set about applying to the artifacts of advertising the methods of cultural anthropology (in Barthes's case, a semiotic approach based in lingustics-derived methodology that had also fostered structural anthropology). Some of the fun of their exercises—willfully outré though ultimately earnest for McLuhan, epicurean if contemptuous for Barthes—involved the mind-opening incongruity between subjects from the local newsstand and the kind of language and analytic techniques normally let loose only on great texts and faraway tribes. Barthes's first essay, for example, was on pro wrestling, which he deemed diacritical, and similar to Balzac's novels in being a semiosis, as opposed to a mimesis.[176] In plainer terms (and in contrast to, say, Delaunay's enthusiasm for sport as modern organized energy), Barthes chose a "sport" that was built wholly on the sham acting-out of conventional roles. And he found that this empty dumb-show aspect best indicated both wrestling's relation to art and its function within popular culture. He appreciated the absolute falsity of all such diversions, but found advertising's "myths" more noxious. Barthes felt that ads acted through secondary, covert signals, to make the order of the bourgeoisie seem like the natural order of the world; and he unmasked such devices by virtuoso explanations of the hidden meanings in manipulative devices such as the language used to sell facial moisturizers.[177]

Much of the intellectual pleasure in these studies derived from watching an agile mind extract structured systems of meaning from what seemed anonymous, mindless artifacts of commerce—rather like a wine connoisseur holding forth on varieties of Kool-Aid. The larger comedy, though, is that the people putting out the ads were often working from similar, anthropologically based intellectual models. This was an era when American advertisers gave unprecedented attention precisely to the impact of associations generated by imprecise symbols, and set great store by the premise that the ad worked through its style more than its literal content—a pragmatic guideline that contained in germ McLuhan's more global postulate that the message is ultimately less important than the means by which it is communicated.[178] What the agile mind managed to find in ads—myth-like presence, unconscious symbolism, the play on complex social desires, a densely structured "language" of nonverbal communication—was what Madison Avenue strove self-consciously to put into them. As to whether the broader consuming public saw ads this way, or responded in the appropriately manipulated manner if they did, the answer is far less clear.

The fantasy Desnos had essayed in his imagination of the Bébé Cadum as redeemer, of ads as totems peopling the dream life of modern society, now became institutionalized both on the side of the makers of advertising, and on the side of their critics. And Barthes, against his intention (since he later avowed that popular culture nauseated him),[179] wound up resembling what he beheld. One of his best-known remarks from *Mythologies* was a response to the advent of the hot new DS-model Citröen in 1955: "I think that cars today are almost exactly the equivalent of the great Gothic cathedrals: I mean the supreme creation of an era, conceived with passion by unknown artists, and consumed in image if not in usage by a whole population which appropriates in them a wholly magical object." To which a reviewer in the *Times* of London replied in only partial irony, "What a copywriter."[180]

For many people, the part-serious, part-bemused approbation of the professors made it acceptable, even chic, to affirm an interest in aspects of mass society such as advertising. But others were not at all bemused. The uneasy relationship between liberal politics and advertising, for example, which went back

at least as far as the French press law of 1881, turned antagonistic in the 1950s. Madison Avenue became for the liberal left, unhappy with the passing of the New Deal, what communists were for Senator McCarthy: an insidious conspiracy out to subvert cherished national values. With John Kenneth Galbraith as its most prominent spokesman, this viewpoint argued that where needs were answered, wants should not be provoked—that in an affluent society the stimulation of superfluous desire by ads would not only cause havoc in the economy, but encourage wasteful self-indulgence at the expense of civic-minded behavior.[181]

Packard had tapped one fear that was associated with the specter of communism and exacerbated by the talk of "brainwashing" that surrounded the Korean War: the fear that the men on Madison Avenue were turning citizens into sheep. This anxiety about forced conformity, prevalent in contemporaneous movies about body-snatchers and brain-eaters, was also nurtured by books like *The Organization Man*.[182] Galbraith expressed the complementary worry, that unbridled capitalism led to an atomized society of spoiled, alienated egotists. Mass seduction, or the war of all against all waged with barbecue forks on suburban lawns—whichever poison one dreaded, it was said to be in preparation in ad-agency boardrooms.

If these writers were afraid advertising would destroy American values, their European counterparts were at the same time even more fearful that advertising would disseminate and promote American values. They perceived advertising as the sinister advance guard of a rampant Americanization which, importuning weak citizens with the lure of consumer comforts, threatened to erode or eclipse local traditions, and leave in their place only an inauthentic culture of hollow symbols propped up solely by cash. Where Galbraith saw ads as inimicable to the interests of the good liberal bourgeoisie, Barthes saw them as securing those same people's hold on the world. (An observer with sufficient distance from the situation might have spotted an irony here. American advertising of the day was, after all, drawing much of its power—particularly in its emphasis on seduction by style and symbolism— from the "Europeanization" of Madison Avenue. What Europeans such as Barthes were deploring as American corruption was actually a transmuted form of some of the lessons, and talents, that Europe had sent to New York in the 1930s and 1940s.)

In Britain, however, a small group of artists and critics both recognized the impact of this new commercial force, and saw in it a positive challenge to which art had to respond. "Ordinary life is receiving powerful impulses from a new source," the young London architects Alison and Peter Smithson argued in 1956. "Where thirty years ago architects found in the field of popular arts, techniques and formal stimuli, today we are being edged out of our traditional role by the new phenomenon of the popular arts—advertising. Mass

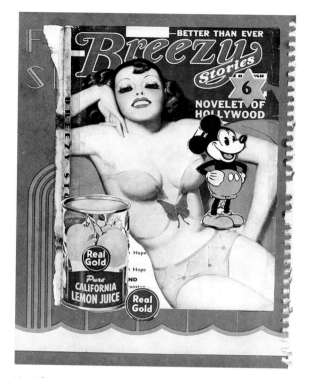

141. Eduardo Paolozzi. *Real Gold.* **1948. Mixed media on paper, 14 × 9¼" (35.6 × 23.5 cm). The Trustees of the Tate Gallery, London**

production advertising is establishing our whole pattern of life—principles, morals, aims, aspirations, and standard of living. We must somehow get the measure of this intervention if we are to match its powerful and exciting impulses with our own." In boldface type, like a poem, they set down a credo of change within continuity:

> Gropius wrote a book on grain silos
> Le Corbusier one on aeroplanes,
> And Charlotte Periand brought a new object
> to the office every morning;
> But today we collect ads.[183]

The Smithsons had been founding members of the Independent Group, a small circle of artists, critics, and architects who formed a splinter association of the Institute for Contemporary Art. Operating on the premise that they would make better and more original art if they knew more about the world around them, the group devoted itself to lecture series and group discussions that featured, along with considerations of science and philosophy, material from a wide range of popular culture. The kind of popular culture that most excited them, though, had little to do with the British working-class traditions that were close at hand; instead, the members of the I.G. were fascinated by the more colorful, sexier, and gaudier exotica of consumer life that they saw, at a distance, as the imagery of postwar American society. One of the group's definitive moments came at the very first meeting in 1952, when the sculptor Eduardo Paolozzi presented a lecture-demonstration that included projections of some of the material, often lurid and trashy, that he had been collecting from American magazines (fig. 141).[184] From that moment forward, and well into the later 1950s after the official meetings ceased, the circle associated with the I.G. kept the matter of art's role vis-à-vis advertising—meaning, most specifically, American advertising—more or less constantly in the forefront of their concerns.

Some of the principals went on to stage memorable exhibitions—notably "Parallel of Life and Art" in 1953, "Man, Machine, and Motion" in 1955, and "This Is Tomorrow" (fig. 142) in 1956.[185] But the one moment that most saliently focused the issues the I.G.'s discussions had raised about American advertising was the great tail-fin debate of the mid-fifties. The architectural historian Reyner Banham, a founding member of the I.G., wrote later that this dispute was considered "the Vietnam of product design," as it split people radically along lines of politics and attitudes toward Americanization, as well as on issues of aesthetics: "More than chrome, more than the implications of sex, etc., the tail fin in the end, which means 1955/56, focussed the whole issue."[186]

As Banham remembered, the argument was global in implications and couched in the language of barricade politics. But it included at its core an argument about styling as advertising; and a key aspect of this debate, which was apparently waged over questions of high art and popular culture, was actually an in-house tussle between rival claims to the legacy of modernism. The Institute for Contemporary Art, led by

142. Installation by Richard Hamilton and John McHale, exhibition "This is Tomorrow," The Institute for Contemporary Art, London, 1956

143. Richard Hamilton. *Just What Is It That Makes Today's Homes So Different, So Appealing?* 1956. Collage on paper, 9⅞ × 10¼" (25 × 26 cm). Kunsthalle Tübingen. Collection Prof. Dr. Georg Zundel

the established evangelist for modernism, Herbert Read, considered itself as headquarters for the modern tradition that the London-based magazine *Architectural Design* defined as the meeting of "science and free aesthetic fantasy"[187]—Constructivism (in the manner of, say, Ben Nicolson) being the form of the first and Surrealism (as in Henry Moore) the embodiment of the latter. And, like modernism elsewhere, this British version was just becoming accepted in the fifties as compatible with good human and national values. Its concerns with consumer culture were principally manifest in the judgments of the Council on Industrial Design on the correctness of new functional-object designs.

Tail fins were the apex of the incorrect. They were an egregious instance of Borax, the term of convenience for style features that were put on just for show and sales appeal, with no functional excuse for being. Detroit cars of the mid-1950s were the space-age inheritors of the machine-age notion Elmo Calkins had heralded in 1930, of "styling the goods"; and their resemblance to jet fighters seemed as gratuitous and objectionable to pure-minded modernists of the fifties as streamlined toasters had seemed to their forebears. Some key members of the I.G., however, not only liked these cars (at a distance; there were precious few of them in Britain), but felt that such admiration was perfectly consistent with the modernist tradition as they understood it.

First of all, they reckoned that what had made modernism important was not its ability to enshrine itself, but its ability to keep itself open to an unprejudiced engagement with diverse aspects of the life of its time. When the Smithsons looked at the heritage of Corbusier, for example, they saw less the dictates of the Modular formulae than his practice of absorbing elements from café life, factory buildings, and airplane design. The logic of that practice in contemporary terms was, they felt, self-evident. Did the lesson about liking automobiles only apply to vintage Bugattis?

Banham was meanwhile pursuing a separate vision of what modernism had been. His thesis, which later became *Theory and Design in the First Machine Age*, was centered on an appreciative reestimation of the driving role of Futurism in modernist thought; and Banham was the first to publish a complete English translation of the founding Futurist Manifesto of 1909 (in 1959, in London's *Architectural Review*).[188] Reviving this branch of early modernism meant not just encouraging an openness to simple vernacular in the mode of Corbusier or Léger, but rekindling an emotional investment in the sex appeal of a fantasy future, more closely allied to Marinetti's lust for speed and dynamism. After Mussolini, Futurism was in somewhat the same bad odor as was Wagner after Hitler. But, despite the dangers of its militarism and irrational devotion to power, and despite the sad proportion of production to promise in its history, Banham saw that the Futurist imagination—with its sense of the future as technological myth and dream, as well as its keen appetite for the gaudy energy of the present—was a vital part of modernism's story, without which the heritage could too easily be condensed into desiccated canons. He further held that, for those who were eager to confront the real world of machines and mass production, the acutely time-conscious Futurist aesthetic—closely attuned to the remorseless cycle of youthful innovation and swift obsolescence—might provide a better guide than what he saw as the classicizing tastes of Corbusier and the Purist artists.[189]

Banham and others in the I.G. saw that symbolic/visionary aspects of modernism censored out of the high tradition had taken refuge in unlikely places: in the science-fiction movies of Hollywood, for example

144. Kurt Schwitters. *Green over Yellow.* 1947. Collage, 6½ × 5¼" (16.5 × 13.5 cm). Courtesy Marlborough Fine Art, London

(Robby the Robot of *Forbidden Planet*, Hollywood's most Freudian vision of outer space, was the greeting figure in the part of the "This Is Tomorrow" exhibition that Hamilton helped install; fig. 142); and especially in the American automobiles of the mid-1950s, whose wrap-around windshields, bullet-nosed bumpers and air scoops—and tail fins—conjured associations of jet planes and space flight. For them, this bad-boy, ersatz version of a proper modern machine aesthetic was the place where a key element of the original faith was being kept alive. These machines attracted Banham (*pace* Corbusier) precisely because they were *not* strictly functional, mechanical designs, but instead new hybrids of advertisement and object, designed as much for sales appeal and symbolic satisfactions as for practical use. Moreover, Banham's enthusiasm was not a literary appreciation, on the model of Barthes's nod to the Citröen as the modern analogue of the cathedral. He had a genuine, and informed, fascination with the particulars of these cars, which he regarded as remarkable objects of industrial design. As impatient with academics who assessed without understanding as with purists who scorned without looking, Banham turned to automobile magazines for writing that criticized from a base in both observation and facts.[190]

Richard Hamilton, meanwhile, had still other interests in mind. Earlier, as one of the organizers of "This Is

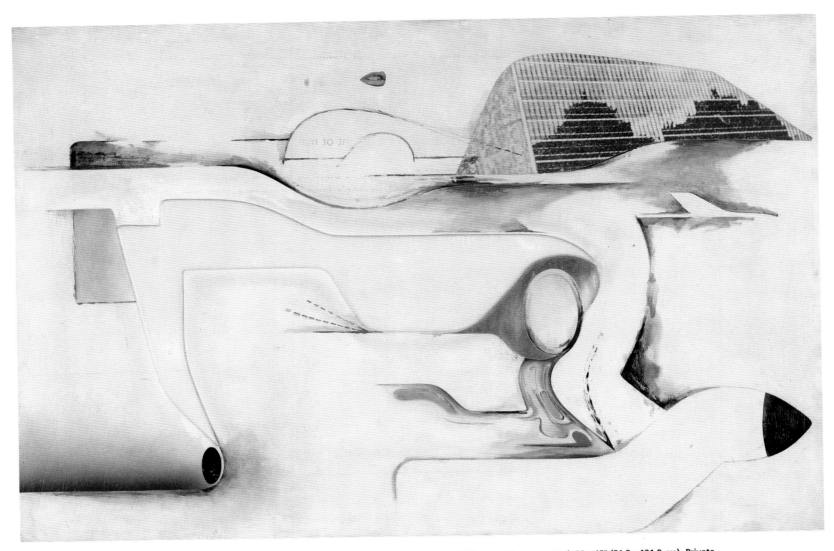

145. Richard Hamilton. *Hers Is a Lush Situation.* 1958. Oil, cellulose, metal foil, and collage on panel, 32 × 48″ (81.3 × 121.9 cm). Private collection

Tomorrow,'' he had made a collage for the exhibition poster, titled *Just What Is It That Makes Today's Homes So Different, So Appealing?*, which gloried in the cheap glamor of overmuscled men and oversexed women in a décor of appliances, movies, and oversize candy (fig. 143). As Thomas Lawson points out, despite the looming planet on the ceiling, this whole ensemble manages somehow to be airlessly cozy in a specifically British way;[191] yet a comparison with the amiable vision Kurt Schwitters constructed of commercial culture in Britain less than a decade before (fig. 144) points up a sharp change. For Schwitters, as a foreign visitor, what was attractive about British commercial imagery were the reassuring trappings of a frugal domesticity, having to do with tea and jam. For Hamilton's generation of native Britons—frustrated with the austerity of the postwar period—the taste for Tootsie Pops was part of a more expansive desire for the faster-paced public pleasures of consumerism, touted by American advertisers. The show this poster heralded was, like the image, a crowded effort at multimedia simultaneity, in which the culture of American magazine advertising played a central role. If Cornell had looked at Europe through a distancing lens, Hamil-

ton now stood on a stack of pulp arrivals (and on a legacy of Hausmann-style montage) and looked back across the Atlantic with a telephoto vision that piled up every magazine fantasy available into a drastically compressed and luridly fun America of the mind.

By the time Hamilton made a painting that memorialized the tail-fin era, however, he had come to see America in terms of an altogether different kind of Dada. *Hers Is a Lush Situation* of 1958 (fig. 145) caresses the hollows and curves of the 1957 Cadillac and accentuates its protrusions and orifices, in a cool, meticulous way that is part engineer, part fetishist—in short, Duchampian. Absorbed by and informed on questions of industrial design since the earliest days of the I.G.,[192] Hamilton also developed a fascination for the (then much neglected) work of Duchamp, especially in the complex mechano-sexual allegory of the *Large Glass*. (Just as Banham got the Futurist Manifesto back into circulation, Hamilton played a key role in the first English publication of Duchamp's notes for the *Glass*.) Under this influence, the collaged media panoramas in the earlier exhibitions fell away in favor of a far more oblique and nuanced approach to the voluptuousness of consumer culture—and an argument about industrial design became the matter of an idiosyncratic art of private references.

The immediate source for *Hers Is a Lush Situation* was Cadillac's 1957 ad for "the greatest advancements it has ever achieved in motor car styling and engineering" (fig. 146). Though Hamilton could not resist adding the tail exhaust and the fin (for reasons similar to those that brought Picasso to show the breasts and buttocks of Marie-Thérèse Walter simultaneously), he primarily responded to the cropping by which the advertisers had emphasized the decorative chrome parts of the car, which signaled bullets, breasts, or anything but the functional nature of an automobile.

Hamilton recognized, as Banham had, that American cars embodied an altered kind of "functional" design. They were working within a new economy of abundance, which counted on relatively brief life spans and continual new versions for consumer machines—in short, an interdependence of staged novelty and planned obsolescence. If this pattern of selling made the economy work (and postwar American prosperity seemed to be proving it could), then the function of the stylist was at least as important as that of the traditional engineer/designer. The stylist made the product sell, and this meant knowing more about sexual sym-bolism than about drive trains or airflow engineering.[193] To Hamilton, this manipulation of devices of show and symbolism was not a simple betrayal of more truthful values of narrowly defined "utility" and "function," but a modern skill richly deserving of serious attention, as one of the keys to the functioning of a new mass society and to a potentially broad-based improvement of material life. The title *Hers Is a Lush Situation* was taken from an *Industrial Design* review of the 1955 Buick by Deborah Allan, a favorite writer of Hamilton's (and of Banham's, who had cited this same review in a 1955 article).[194] Her witty, shrewd commentary—appreciative, yet critical and attentively analytic of the particulars—epitomized the kind of study of popular culture he respected; and the reference to her text confirms that the picture was made neither in a spirit of ironic condescension nor in one of simple dewy-eyed celebration. *Hers Is a Lush Situation* embodies a more complex response—cerebral, libidinal, and aesthetic—to a world of design and criticism, outside the accepted art world, that Hamilton recognized as powerful and original. Like Banham, Hamilton saw an informed grasp of this sphere of advertising and styling both as essential to an artist's reckoning with the society of his time, and as perfectly compatible with the effort to recover personal heroes from the margins of the established modernist canon.[195]

146. Advertisement for 1957 Cadillac, 1956

The tail-fin debate, and paintings like this one, are often cited as the first tremors in a coming upheaval—the advance drum-roll for the Pop art of the 1960s. But the idiosyncratic combination of critical design scholarship and self-conscious modernist revivalism in Banham's writing or in Hamilton's work has no successor in later Pop art. And the tricky part about drawing lessons from the tail-fin episode lies not just in the individuality of the artists involved, but also in the singularity of the popular culture they focused upon. The moment preserved in Banham's debates about Borax and Hamilton's painting is specifically 1955–57, and the subject is a few Detroit automobiles. Add a year or two, or swap French toasters for American cars, and the dialogue between art and popular culture would not have had anything like the same tenor or implications.

Lemon.

This Volkswagen missed the boat.
The chrome strip on the glove compartment is blemished and must be replaced. Chances are you wouldn't have noticed it; Inspector Kurt Kroner did.
There are 3,389 men at our Wolfsburg factory with only one job; to inspect Volkswagens at each stage of production. (3000 Volkswagens are produced daily; there are more inspectors

than cars.)
Every shock absorber is tested (spot checking won't do), every windshield is scanned. VWs have been rejected for surface scratches barely visible to the eye.
Final inspection is really something! VW inspectors run each car off the line onto the Funktionsprüfstand (car test stand), tote up 189 check points, gun ahead to the automatic

brake stand, and say "no" to one VW out of fifty.
This preoccupation with detail means the VW lasts longer and requires less maintenance, by and large, than other cars. (It also means a used VW depreciates less than any other car.)
We pluck the lemons; you get the plums.

147. Advertisement for Volkswagen, 1960

American automobiles occupied a unique, top-level niche in consumer manufacturing, as dreams that only big money could buy. And the cars made by the top Detroit firms reached unprecedented, never-to-be-repeated apogees of symbolic design just in these years. As Banham saw, consumer imagination had been sparked by the various "dream cars of the future" that companies had commissioned their stylists to devise from science-fiction fantasy as a promotional device. And in a fiercely competitive push to make each year's new model more "progressive" than the last, the Detroit designers began in 1956 to lift certain motifs, like the fin, from the "dream cars" and push them further and further, trying to make the product in next year's showroom have the allure of an imagined 1973 model.[196] A writer at the time called 1956 "the first Baroque year in half a century of car styling."[197] And Madison Avenue matched Detroit in overreach. *Advertising Agency* called the introduction

of the new models in late 1957 "the most lavish and splendiferous displays of money-spending our industry has ever seen," citing record amounts of space purchases (Chrysler took as many as thirteen consecutive pages in leading magazines) as the culmination of a postwar trend to ever more costly "spectaculars and spreads and saturation techniques."[198]

This was however the last grand moment for the tail fin, and for all it symbolized. The launch of the Russian satellite Sputnik in 1957 may have made rocket styling less appealing for U.S. buyers. More concretely, in 1958 the Nash Rambler surged from twelfth to seventh place in U.S. car sales, and accelerated the move to more compact and efficient cars that would be the dominant trend by 1960.[199] Auto makers who were conscious, in Dichter's terms, of "identification between the personality of the car and the personality of the buyer" were told by motivation researchers in 1958 that, in an increasingly suburbanized America, the big Detroit companies had been building futures of the recent past. Dichter argued that the 1957 models, the paragons of excess "which set off the recent anti-Detroit campaign," had actually been made to suit 1955 tastes. "It is only within the past year or two that consumers have shown a heightened desire for more subtle design," he wrote in November of 1958; "...the symbols of status have changed...[and] it becomes ostentatious to have the more obvious symbols of status—those with too much chrome." His researchers reported that interviewees now wanted "a car that is 'more honest,' 'more real'—a *truer* car."[200] Finally, the *coup de grâce* for the baroque epoch was the fiasco of the Edsel in 1957–58, which shook the assumptions of makers and advertisers alike. The mightiest styling investment of one of the most powerful corporations in the world, pushed to the maximum by a heavy advertising effort, flopped.

If we see 1957–58 as years in which artists of the postwar era began to come to terms with American advertising's campaign to shape the minds of the world, then we also have to recognize a heavy irony. For this was precisely the moment when that ad industry, having gotten caught up in a fierce spree of competitive spending by a couple of big automobile manufacturers, stumbled and fell on its face. It was also the period in which it became progressively clearer that the anthropological models of mass society both the industry and its critics had believed in were seriously flawed. Instead, the plural, unpredictable nature of consumer society became painfully apparent in the matter of automobile purchases; and the battle of competing ideas within the industry itself was also highlighted. In 1958, the advertising agency in charge of Peugeot for the U.S. said that their ads were being made "purposely cold" as a counter to the "sugary" copy in Detroit advertisements.[201] The next year, Doyle Dane Bernbach took over the advertising for Volkswagen and pushed a similarly laconic style, with its appeal to wit and reason more than sex and glamor (fig. 147). And with Detroit looking on in some dismay, the

Volkswagen's beetle-like design, which had remained essentially unchanged since Hitler had promoted it in the thirties, began to enjoy runaway success. One shadow version of modernism, the sexy Futurism of the mid-1950s cars, seemed outmaneuvered by another: the cool, joke-oriented recycling of familiar things in surprising presentations. This pushed the product stylists into the back seat, and suggested that advertising which was sufficiently creative and attuned to one particular segment of a fragmented constellation of markets—rather than to a putative mass consciousness—could make anything seem newly meaningful.

By the time *Hers Is a Lush Situation* appeared, and "British Pop" began to be a recognized phenomenon, the 1957 Cadillac and the advertising ethos that went with it were looking like dinosaurs caught in a fatal climatic shift. As when Picasso clipped older typefaces and smaller ads at the moment when newspapers were modernizing, or Lichtenstein chose romance comics in the last flicker before they went under, Hamilton seems to have trapped in the amber of his art a moment in popular culture that had just passed by. That combination of participation in the present and incipient nostalgia for the just-departing past is endemic to the experience of popular culture in this century, and especially evident in the late 1950s. And an appropriately mixed image of mass advertising—the world of visionary myth, but also the domain of fickle ephemerality—appears reflected in both the forward bumper and the rear-view mirror of the tail-fin episode.

In the year Hamilton painted the 1957 Cadillac, Jasper Johns and Robert Rauschenberg had their first one-man shows at the Leo Castelli gallery in New York. Those events are frequently cited as the crucial next step toward fulfilling, in the American Pop art of the 1960s, the promise of an engagement with popular culture that had been heralded by the British. But Johns and Rauschenberg had virtually nothing in common with what had been going on in London. Banham, Hamilton, and the others looked at America from afar and were drawn to areas of futuristic fantasy in its popular culture—missiles, chrome, sex appeal, and high-gloss color. Johns and Rauschenberg lived in the very belly of the beast. And from a vantage in the metropolitan center of the dominant capitalist culture in the Western world, in the heyday of its power as an exporter of the consumer ethos, they looked on this culture and saw beer cans, old neckties, torn newspapers, and re-used coffee containers with paint drips.

Early British Pop was a matter of ideas, while the Americans were dealing with experience, but the differences are more complex than that tidy distinction implies. Faced with what they saw as a moribund modernist establishment, the British used the gaudy fantasies of a foreign culture to heat things up. The two American artists, confronted with the expansive success of Abstract Expressionism, used banal local

148. Stuart Davis. *Visa.* 1951. Oil on canvas, 40 × 52" (101.6 × 132.1 cm). The Museum of Modern Art, New York. Gift of Mrs. Gertrud A. Mellon

material to cool things down—to introduce notes of impersonality, irony, and mundane reality into the act of painting. In the early 1950s, Stuart Davis could find that the language of American advertising still had an organized rhythm and upbeat color that could connect with the tradition of high modern decorative painting, and that seemed to speak of optimism and pleasurable energy (fig. 148). But a work such as Rauschenberg's *Rebus* (fig. 149) takes on a more anonymous mélange of commercial printed matter, in a decidedly different mood, as detritus.

In Hamilton's *Just What Is It...*, the big comic on the wall is the exotic arrival, crowding out the old portrait that stands for fusty local conventions. In *Rebus*, the foreign visitors are (as they were for Cornell) the high European tradition, represented by reproductions of Botticelli's *Venus* and a Dürer self-portrait; it is the line-up of comics, newspapers, and posters that constitutes the local vernacular. More important, while Rauschenberg's hoardings of scrap may have precedents in European art such as that of Schwitters, the mural scale and disregard for niceties of craft in *Rebus*, and the rambling way the found material sprawls across the canvas, also involve an aesthetic found close to hand. The picture embodies a conception of the artist's unpremeditated relation to his process and to his material that supposes an immediate contact with New York School painting of the early 1950s.

Yet the two big brushstrokes in the center, which at first seem to mime the energetic calligraphy of Abstract Expressionism and extend the directional verve of the two runners in the photographs at either end,

finally sag downward as much as they move forward: their lethargic drips are realist rebuttals to the romanticism of action painting's trademark splatters. And the culture of ephemera is similarly shown as seedy, scrawled-on, and stained. The "media" here—nondescript tabloid sports photos, long-running Sunday comic strips, and a hack election poster for a forgotten lieutenant governor's race—have the same deflating relation to high-gloss advertising and big-time "I Like Ike" productions as the turgid brushstrokes do to the fine flourishes of second-generation Pollock-school painting.

This is American life seen from street level in Lower Manhattan, not in imperial plenitude but patched together with scraps. *Rebus* is a picture that is personal and impulsive without being private or decisive, and it is full of contradictions—energy and irony, fresh and faded, eternity's icons and yesterday's papers. Commercial imagery is just one part of the incoherent patchwork of daily experience, assimilated into the diaristic activity of picture-making, through an unpredictable, reflexive openness to illogical simultaneity. The same character marks the statement Rauschenberg wrote in 1963, peppered with the clichés of advertising as if written while driving down an American highway; a typical sentence reads: "My fascination with images open 24 hrs. is based on the complex interlocking of disparate visual facts heated pool that have no respect for grammar...."[202]

Though *Rebus* has little to do with the brighter-than-life advertising that Hamilton had parodied in *Just What Is It...*, Rauschenberg's *Coca-Cola Plan* of 1958

149. Robert Rauschenberg. *Rebus.* **1955. Oil, pencil, paper, fabric on canvas, 8′ × 10′10″ × 1¾″ (243.9 × 331.4 × 4.5 cm). Collection Hans Thulin**

150. **Robert Rauschenberg.** *Coca-Cola Plan.* 1958. Combine painting, 26¾ × 25¼ × 4¾" (67.9 × 64.1 × 12.1 cm). The Museum of Contemporary Art, Los Angeles. The Panza Collection

directly engages the rhetoric of product promotion (fig. 150). But this winged altar enshrines three lowly Coke bottles. Not the king-size version, not the can—and in 1958 mercifully not yet "classic"—this shape from the pre–World War I era had the unnoticed status of a reassuring cliché (and again, the artist caught it just before it passed out of this state of grace). The sculpture takes a pomposity associated with the packaging of high-status new products and plays it off against a shelf of empties that represent the steadily available, unchanging staples of consumer life: it's a hood-ornament treatment for brake linings. The combination ironizes the rhetoric, but also elevates the familiar and mundane.[203]

Implicitly in *Coca-Cola Plan*, and explicitly in *Gloria* (fig. 151), Rauschenberg took on the aspect of com-

mercial culture—steady, every-unit-the-same repetition—that was opposite to the singular, always-changing, spectacular designs the British loved. In *Gloria*, given the subject (Gloria Vanderbilt's third marriage, heralded in the headline), and the use of the word fragments BI and CO that suggest prefixes for terms of duality and mutuality, the multiple images may have been a commentary on the celebrity's sequential mates. The repetition of the photo seems to prefigure Warhol's fascination with the mechanical production of celebrity images, but it also looks back, through earlier Rauschenberg images such as *Mona Lisa* of 1953 (fig. 152) to the lessons Rauschenberg learned from Cornell's little pinball Uffizis of recurrent portraits (fig. 137). And *Gloria*'s focus is not on America as dream machine and fabricator of glamor; the

151. Robert Rauschenberg. *Gloria.* 1956. Oil, paper, and fabric on canvas, 66¼ × 63¼″ (168.3 × 160.7 cm). The Cleveland Museum of Art. Gift of the Cleveland Society for Contemporary Art

subject is the cheapening of old values, in the descent of blueblood American aristocracy into tabloid copy. Vanderbilt's picture appears in the work as a literal embodiment of the steady-beat replication that marks mass production, and as a figurative representation of the fickle, inconstant mobility that is just as certainly a sign of modern American times.

Rauschenberg's most focused treatment of repetition came in the two paintings, *Factum I* and *Factum II* (figs. 154, 155), which constitute a complex meditation on the relation of variety to sameness, or more precisely on the play between uniqueness and doubling—in nature (the trees), in time (the twin calendars, and the sequential photos of the burning building), and in mass-produced imagery (the side-by-side portraits of President Dwight D. Eisenhower). Within each individual picture, these instances of doubling stand in contrast to the "unique" and "accidental" brushstrokes; but when the two pictures are seen together, the matching painted passages themselves become another element in the play between singularity and replication, in a way that calls into question matters of "accident" and spontaneity

152. Robert Rauschenberg. *Mona Lisa.* 1953. Collage, 9½ × 7½″ (24.1 × 19 cm). Collection Adele Bishop Callaway

153. **Robert Rauschenberg.** *Mainspring.* 1965. Frottage on paper, 32 × 62½" (81.3 × 158.8 cm). Collection Donald B. Marron

154. **Robert Rauschenberg.** *Factum I.* 1957. Combine painting, 61½ × 35¾" (156.2 × 90.8 cm). The Museum of Contemporary Art, Los Angeles. The Panza Collection

155. **Robert Rauschenberg.** *Factum II.* 1957. Combine painting, 62 × 35½" (157.5 × 90.2 cm). The Morton G. Neumann Family Collection

in art, as opposed to intention and planning.

The two *Factum* paintings work, appropriately, as a double-edged sword. They debunk the notion of unique individuality in calligraphic action painting, by showing how the signs of chance and inspiration can be planned and fairly replicated. But they also make evident the leeway that exists, for variation and change, within the acceptance of strictly similar formats, and even within the intention to do the same thing twice. This unusually didactic demonstration fits with the more general idea Rauschenberg's techniques embody—that artistic originality is a matter of dialogue and negotiation, not conjured from pure inspiration, but left to emerge from the practice of accumulating, and lending personal order to, the materials society provides. Rauschenberg's "touch," or "signature" stroke, for example, becomes less and less an arbitrary intervention (as it still is in *Rebus* or the *Factum* paintings) and more a purposive mark having to do with task-oriented rubbing, in the transfer drawings (made by pressing solvent-soaked printed matter onto paper, and thus transferring an inked residue of the original printed image) and in the silkscreen paintings. The stroke in a transfer drawing such as *Mainspring* (fig. 153) subsumes all the disparate advertisements and photos under one handmade look, as the process bleeds their colors into a more uniformly veiled paleness, consistent with the artist's love for translucent or faded and bleached fabrics. The rag-picker's heritage of Schwitters combines with the panoramic reach and the insistence on gestural engagement of New York School painting; but the precise and concrete miniaturism of Schwitters gives way to something more blowsy and disorganized, while the gestural language is purposefully more episodic and workaday than spontaneous or rhetorical.

In all these works, the response to the givens of American advertising is directly contrary to that of Hamilton and his cohorts: instead of power and calculated high style, the material is that of standardization, coarse production, and leftover tatters, assimilated not as a strategy for the masses but as the attributes of individual idiosyncracy. Imperial Rome may look like aqueducts and legionnaires from outside, but at home it's experienced as a chaos of private matters, competing interests, and cats in the sewers.

The same confrontations we see in Rauschenberg's painting and assemblages—between the personal mark and the found image, or between the public givens of commerce and the construction of a personal style—occur in a more muted and laconic way in Jasper Johns's works of the same period. *Painted Bronze II* of 1960 (fig. 156), for example, restates the kind of incongruously formal presentation Rauschenberg essayed in *Coca-Cola Plan*; but in Johns's hands the irony is deadpan and terse, as opposed to Rauschenberg's garrulous mock heroics. The familiar story behind this sculpture of ale cans, that it was conceived in response to Willem de Kooning's bitterly admiring remark that

156. **Jasper Johns.** *Painted Bronze II*. 1960. Painted bronze, 5½ × 8 × 4¾" (14 × 20.3 × 12.1 cm). Collection the artist

Leo Castelli could sell beer cans if that were what he was given,[204] affirms that these items were seen as utterly lacking in distinction. They were motifs of the kind Johns favored, static and familiar to the point of being visually inert. And he put them on a pedestal in a formal fashion that has to do neither with one-at-a-time consumption, nor with six-pack packaging, nor with the repetition of shelving. This twin presentation has only to do with art, or with the artificial orders of advertising imagery—and, indeed, virtually the same front-and-center pairing can be found in Ballantine ads from Johns's childhood (fig. 157).

Painted Bronze II translated Duchamp into contemporary American terms, leaving behind the deft elegance and chilly eroticism Hamilton had admired. For Duchamp, taking an object from everyday life and putting it on a pedestal involved a punctilious economy of effort, that used faceless objects to insist on an art of the mind rather than mere manual skill. Johns pointedly chose brand-name objects and turned them into a pretext for hand labor of a painstaking kind. The can forms and the pedestal were modeled from scratch and cast in bronze with all the clumsy imperfections preserved; then the labels were hand-rendered with a studied blend of earnest diligence and slurred approximation. The final result, which seems made up in part of the sophistication of French modernism and in part of the straightforwardness of bronzed baby booties, is fast and slow at once: the initial sense of an immediate, iconic legibility is coupled with the evidence of an imperturbably slow facture.

Johns's work with objects stands contrary to the notion, commonly advanced by Harold Rosenberg and other advocates of Abstract Expressionism, that an original, personal art can only be summoned up by freewheeling gestures, out of the unknown depths of the soul. The ''touch'' in these sculptures emerges as the opposite of spontaneity, from a cumulative overlay of labor on impersonal formats, in a stubbornly plodding praxis. At one level, objects like the *Flashlight* (figs. 158, 159) or *Light Bulb* (figs. 160, 161) are simply contrary, period: the artist works to deaden an object of energy, make the clear opaque, and the delicate heavy. But metalicizing a light bulb and laying it on a pedestal also coaxes from it some unexpected references. The difference between the bulb ''emerging'' from its loosely modeled ''bed'' (fig. 161) and the bulb as autonomous form (fig. 160) may even reflect the then current opposition between a Rodinesque tradition of ''unfinished'' surface, much favored in 1950s sculpture, and a more Brancusi-like smoothness of separate forms, returning to greater favor among younger artists around 1960. The light bulb takes on the air of a Brancusi head, and its horizontality is made to suggest sleep and pensiveness, or even the violence of a severed throat.

Just as the *Factum* paintings are Rauschenberg's meditation on his activity as an artist, *Painted Bronze (Savarin Can)* (fig. 162) is Johns's emblem of his art. Traditionally, the palette is the emblem of painting, laying out the array of neutral matter with which the artist begins, as implicit testimony to his craft in conjuring a world from the base and unformed. Johns instead chose as his sign the motif of the end of the day: the solvent can into which all the brushes are stuffed to await another session. This constricted, bristling array of handles stresses the fixed and inexpressive ''working'' part of the brush, over its supple, expressive end, and throws the housepainter's broad tool in with the artist's fine instruments. The Savarin coffee can, its label repainted with a care that extends to re-creating an accidental drip of overflown paint, also appears as an item of personal recycling. It is adapted to new use, just as the sculpture as a whole is about taking something familiar and unpromising and making it do a different kind of work. In this sculpture—part downturned wrecking pile of the painter's labor, part rising bouquet of exclamations—the point where the handwork of the individual artist meets the stream of replicating commercial design is not a crisis of identity, but a situation of unprejudiced, improvised adaptation. The banal item is seized on to serve the purpose of the moment, first as an accessory to the making of art, then as art's substance.

British interest in American mass production in the 1950s had to do with its capacity to produce things that were constantly new, and just as constantly obsolete. The fevered advertising culture of high design, and its determination to produce the exaggerated semblance of differentiation and choice, were the

157. ''J. Walter Thompson Company / P. Ballantine & Sons. Gold Award in Metal-Container Division of 1935, All-American Package Competition,'' in *Printers' Ink* (February 27, 1936), p. 9

158. **Jasper Johns.** *Flashlight I*. 1958. Sculp-metal over flashlight and wood, 5¼ × 9⅛ × 3⅞″ (13.3 × 23.2 × 9.8 cm). The Ileana and Michael Sonnabend Collection

159. **Jasper Johns.** *Flashlight II*. 1958. Papier-mâché and glass, 3 × 8¾ × 4″ (7.6 × 22.2 × 10.1 cm). Collection Robert Rauschenberg

subject of fascination, and also of fear. One of the great fears of the advertising-driven consumer market that arose in the 1950s concerned the overstimulation of false desires, and Hamilton and Banham were ready to face that demon. Johns, however, seems to adopt an altogether different part of consumer culture, where steady banality reigns. Here the accompanying fear was for the numbed passivity of those who only consumed, without real choice; and this too seems

closer to the terrain on which Johns moves. The two *Painted Bronze* sculptures are passivity enshrined, consumer items lovingly turned to solemn objects of contemplation. But they seem to have less of the feared impotence of the sheep-like consumer mentality than of a personal attitude both more mundane and more exalted: matter-of-fact and pragmatic, in the use of common things for unexpected purposes; and Zen-like, along the lines of John Cage's insistence on open-

160. **Jasper Johns.** *Light Bulb I.* 1958. Sculp-metal, 3⅛ × 8 × 5″ (7.9 × 20.3 × 12.7 cm). Collection the artist

161. **Jasper Johns.** *Light Bulb II.* 1958. Sculp-metal, 4½ × 6¾ × 4½″ (11.5 × 17.1 × 11.5 cm). Collection Dr. and Mrs. Jack Farris

ness to the potential of the unconstructed givens of life. And within the framework of Johns's stubborn American version of Oriental surrender to contingency, we have a thankless task if we attempt to decide to what degree this art is ironic, or critical, or simply stoic. Is the passivity of these sculptures, in relation to the world of mass advertising they include, a contemplation like that of a monk meditating upon a rock, or a strategic acquiescence, like the judo adept who ac-cepts the oncoming blow only in order to use the pow-er of his adversary as a weapon? Seen from the vantage of the Abstract Expressionist aesthetic, these works seemed deflatingly inert, negative, and destruc-tive: they appeared to be using the stuff of commerce to counter art. But from the viewpoint of younger art-ists in the next decade, they seemed like a liberation, and an incitement to use art as a means of coming to grips with the larger world.

162. **Jasper Johns.** *Painted Bronze (Savarin Can).* 1960. Painted bronze, 13½″ (34.3 cm) high × 8″ (20.3 cm) diam. Collection the artist

The 1960s

American Pop art of the 1960s has become, more swiftly and perhaps more widely than any other kind of modern art, genuinely popular. Andy Warhol, for example, achieved the fame usually reserved for entertainment stars, and his style, like that of Roy Lichtenstein, has had a broad impact on graphic design of all kinds. But back in the towers of the art world itself, doubts persist, and battles still are waged. There are people who have long since come to terms with the presence of material from the world of commerce and advertising in modern art—who revere Cubist collage, think Duchamp's Readymades profound, find Schwitters poetic and Léger noble, cherish Stuart Davis as all-American and Johns as wonderfully enigmatic—but who still draw the line at Pop. And among those who are convinced this art is enduring and important, there is no agreement as to why.

There has even been a basic argument about what Pop looks like. For some, this art is simply trash blown up large: the subjects are everything, and the look—Warhol's repetition, or Lichtenstein's dot screens—just came along in the bargain when artists decided to make big things out of cheap commercial products. (This lack of style is a sign, either of these artists' craven unoriginality, or of their Duchampian cleverness, depending on one's point of view.) But others, first among them Robert Rosenblum in 1964,[205] have argued that we should look beyond the diverse subjects and see that Pop has an aesthetic of its own—that, as a close twin of the hard-edge abstract art of the same period, it was conceived as a formal statement in self-conscious opposition to the painterly looseness of Abstract Expressionism.

The larger argument, though, has been about what Pop means, as an expression of its makers and the society around them. In 1962 Max Kozloff bewailed the invasion of the art galleries by the "New Vulgarians," to whom he ascribed (with a perfect ear for cultural clichés of the previous decade) "the pin-headed and contemptible style of gum-chewers, bobby-soxers, and, worse, delinquents."[206] Countless others have since agreed with this indignation over Pop as the triumph of the yahoos and philistines: a repellent farce foisted on us by sham artists, conniving dealers, and nouveau riche collectors. But another faction argues that it was really those social-climber collectors that were duped—that true Pop art, underneath its apparently swinging look, was chewing nails, not gum. In this view, the art drips with irony and contains a scathing critique of the failures and phony values of a society in deep trouble. And still more radical views in turn insist that it is those who believe in such critical content who are fooling themselves, since deep down Pop's protest is a palace rebellion, and the art is impotent because it is implicated in the very capitalist values it presumes to comment on. All these points, and hybrid variations on them, are still being belabored today.

The two debates, over form and over content, need to be addressed together. Their seemingly separate questions—of what this gaudily image-oriented art has to do with the purities of abstract form, and of what it says about America in the 1960s—are in fact intertwined. The Pop artists staged confrontations between cheap commercial figuration and the tradition of modernist abstract art, not just to pose an either/or choice, but to produce both/and situations, in works that seemed, irritatingly, to speak in the two contradictory languages at once. These odd aesthetic conjunctions, often initiated as parodies, proved able to serve as the vehicle for a similarly mixed array of personal responses—not classifiable as simple assent or dissent—to the society these artists experienced. In Pop art, where style *was* meaning, the favored arena of styles was that of advertising. And in an art much concerned with irony, one enduring irony is that artists who, more than any others of the century, embraced that public language, with its high-definition, mass-appeal formulae for communication, wound up giving us an art that stays so stubbornly ambiguous.

Pop art did not blur the line between art and advertising; that line was already impossibly muddy by 1960. Instead, early Pop art such as that of Andy Warhol was concerned to redraw the division more aggressively, by turning to the meaner depths of the advertising world, where art had not penetrated. By the 1960s, when high-level mass advertising had adopted many of the strategies and inflections of modern art and was operating at an extraordinary level of sophistication, artists had to dig deeper to find motifs and styles that would distance their work both from the romance of art and from the slick visual cleverness of contemporary ads. This is a partial explanation for the streak of nostalgia that permeates Pop, and that drew these artists to motifs dating back to the decade just past, or to the longer-enduring commercial culture of their childhood. Warhol's transformation from commercial artist to painter involved this key move downward and backward, in which the *entente cordiale* between art and popular culture that made him a successful advertising draftsman had to be changed to a polarized opposition that could make him an artist.

In 1955 the shoe merchants I. Miller & Sons had decided to organize their advertising on the timely premise that "every company has to find its personality."[207] And since they felt that the most profitable personality would be one with prestige appeal, they had cut ninety-five percent of their small weekday ads and cast their fortune with Sunday editions, big-time fashion magazines, and an artist. The art director of I. Miller stressed that his goal was not to advertise the product per se, but to conjure a set of favorable associations for it, in what *Printers' Ink* called "idea art": "We try to stir the woman's imagination," he said, "...to make her think of shoes without giving her the details. The artist, Andy Warhol, is allowed a certain amount of freedom. We believe this contributes to the ad. We're trying to sell fashion in the most contemporary way we can."[208]

The fay, spiky-line renderings Warhol gave the firm had the stamp of individual style and "sensitivity" all over them, and an "arty" look that echoed the drawings William Golden had commissioned from Ben Shahn for the classier CBS ads.

Within Warhol the songbird of advertising, however, lurked a would-be diva of art; and, in order to get where he wanted to be, Warhol had to play different sides of the commercial-art/fine-art divide against each other in a complex process of liberation and constraint. Liberation came first, in the familiar territory of the shop window. For all the "certain amount of freedom" afforded by the people who paid him to draw shoes, that kind of print advertising—the couture accessory and Playhouse-90 end of the business—was bound by strict decorums, centered on building a consistently sophisticated image for the client on a wan, narrow notion of what read properly as "art." The shop window on the other hand encouraged theatricality—a swiftly changing series of purposefully *outré* tableaux to arrest the passerby today, and be gone next week. Léger had once looked to the store window as a model for modern aesthetics, in the merchants' intense, competitive efforts to highlight the goods themselves. But at fashionable emporia such as Bonwit Teller (fig. 163), where Warhol (like Johns and Rauschenberg before him) worked, the window had long since become the venue for what seemed an ongoing Beaux-Arts ball—a playground at the fringes of the art world, frequently trading in derivative references to current shows and styles. Display here had no decorum of consistency and encouraged anything that was, in a trivially "surrealist" way, surprising and a little sensational.

The costumes Warhol chose to try for himself in this masquerade were drawn from comics, and from the

163. Andy Warhol. Window display, Bonwit Teller department store, New York, 1961

164. Andy Warhol. *Before and After.* 1960. Synthetic polymer paint on canvas, 54 × 70" (137.2 × 177.8 cm). Private Collection

low end of advertising, beneath even the daily tabloids I. Miller had deserted. The crude *Before and After* come-on for a beautifying nose job (fig. 164) was typical, and doubtless used in part as a foil for the confident, urbane fashionableness of the clothes. But

165. Advertisement for Bell Telephone Company, 1928. The New York Public Library Picture Collection

enlarging these bits of printed matter to stage-prop size made something quite different of them, and the joke suggested serious possibilities. Passing through the free zone of the shop window, en route from the Sunday fashion supplement to the hardware section of supermarket fliers, Warhol had come upon a fright mask that emboldened him: these crude ad images gave him a way to obliterate the facility that had determined his appeal as a commercial artist, and take on a wholly insensitive toughness that could be an entrée into the world of modernist painting. After some hesitation with brushiness and drips that retained a residue

of arty touch, Warhol made the crucial decision to present the advertisements in an absolutely flat-footed graphic style.

Again, as with Picabia's willfully banal hardware ads, this was a matter of imposed regression. Warhol's goal, though, was not numbed illustrational neutrality, but large-scale affront. The telephone he painted (fig. 166) was derived from an image that had elegantly blended a modern spatial composition and archaizing engraving technique decades before (fig. 165). Warhol took from it only the baldly frontal foreground, and reduced the Rockwell Kent style of halftone rendering to

166. Andy Warhol. *Telephone.* 1961. Oil on canvas, 69¾ × 54″ (177.2 × 137.2 cm). The Estate and Foundation of Andy Warhol

167. **Andy Warhol.** *Storm Window.* 1961. Synthetic polymer paint on canvas, 6′ × 60″ (182.9 × 152.4 cm). Collection Robert and Meryl Meltzer

a blunter, simplified play of black and white. The icily sharp *Storm Window* has the same uncompromising impact (fig. 167). These raw blow-ups of dated or generic ads were intended to be obnoxious; but they also were invested with a drop-dead flatness of both space and emotional tone that was set up to rival by perverse mimicry some of the qualities of the dominant abstract painting they blasphemed. The *Telephone* has a scale, format, and absolute immediacy that echo Barnett Newman.

From these first beginnings, Pop was not involved with either a simple copying of commercial sources or a simple rejection of the look of abstract art; instead, Warhol set up more or less obviously parodic situations of uncomfortable similarity between the two. On a smaller scale, but in even more pointed fashion, Roy Lichtenstein did the same. He delighted in finding, amid the crude graphics of cheap black-and-white ads, patterns that mimed the styles of various abstract painters. Both the soles of the *Keds* (fig. 169) and the tread of the *Tire* (fig. 170), for example, were simplified in a way that brought them recognizably close to the geometric abstractions of the European painter

168. **Victor Vasarely.** *Mizzar.* c. 1956–60. Oil on canvas, 6′4″ × 44⅞″ (195.3 × 114 cm). Hirshhorn Museum and Sculpture Garden, Smithsonian Institution, Washington, D.C. Gift of Joseph H. Hirshhorn

169. Roy Lichtenstein. *Keds.* 1961. Oil and pencil on canvas, 48½ × 38¼" (123.2 × 97.5 cm). The Robert B. Mayer Family Collection, Chicago

Victor Vasarely (fig. 168). This little joke poked fun at such ''scientific'' abstract art, which touted itself in the late 1950s as a ''universal language'' of democratic appeal to the basis of human perception. Against this, Lichtenstein holds up the drudge language of commodity capitalism, as if to say, as Léger did when he clipped the Campari ad, that what we really have in common is what is most common—that the workaday style of ad stereotypes can have a direct forthrightness more profitable for art, and more binding for society, than utopian ambitions for invented absolutes.

Lichtenstein's Pop was, however, never a simple

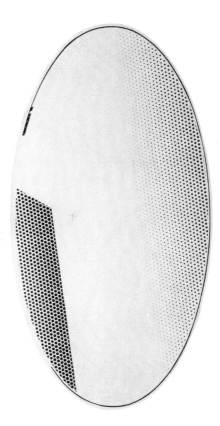

170. **Roy Lichtenstein.** *Tire.* 1962. Oil on canvas, 68 × 58" (172.7 × 147.3 cm). Private collection, Italy

171. (Right) **Roy Lichtenstein.** *Mirror #1.* 1971. Oil and magna on canvas (oval), 6' × 36" (182.9 × 91.4 cm). Collection the artist

plea for realism or refutation of abstraction. Walking the edge was what gave him his art. He liked poking fun at his contemporaries, by showing how seemingly anonymous and conventional stylizations could brush close to their signature styles—the feathering vertical highlight on the fighter pilot's face in *Okay, Hot-Shot* ("Comics," fig. 85) plays on Morris Louis's Unfurled paintings as certainly as the sneaker sole looks like a Vasarely. But it was precisely because he was also devoted to the high modern tradition of painting that Lichtenstein seems to have had a genuine fascination for the latent abstraction in the conventions of dots and dashes and bars used as descriptive codes in com-

ics and cheap ad images. Such minimal formulae of rendering "effects" would, for example, be the impetus behind his play with the "reflections" in his later Mirror series (fig. 171), which were based on catalogue ads. He loved to convert the mottled grays and faded hues of cheap printing into oppositions of buzzing dot fields and flat planes of primary and high-keyed secondary hues, and to distill from the crude codes that suggested light, modeling, and atmosphere an authority of abstract shapes that mimed the vocabularies of both Surrealist organicism and Op geometry (figs. 172–174). In the reductive, conventional styles of these workaday representations, Lichtenstein

172. **Roy Lichtenstein.** *Spray.* 1962. Oil on canvas, 36 × 68" (91.4 × 172.7 cm). Staatsgalerie Stuttgart

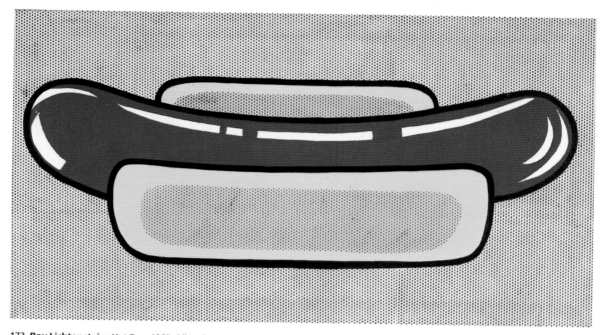

173. **Roy Lichtenstein.** *Hot Dog.* 1963. Oil and magna on canvas, 20 × 36″ (50.8 × 91.4 cm). Collection Anne and Martin Z. Margulies, Miami

174. **Roy Lichtenstein.** *Duridium.* 1964. Magna on canvas, 26 × 36″ (66 × 91.5 cm). Collection Mr. and Mrs. S. I. Newhouse, Jr.

saw the unlikely prodigal twin of modernism's effort to condense experience into a vocabulary of purified form.

Part of what the sneaker and the tire have to say is that, given the range of manmade forms and the mind's irrepressible capacity for analogy, pure abstraction—an art that looks like nothing else—is an impossible dream. But the other part of their message is that, given the same conditions, art is served by open-ended possibilities, abstracting new meanings from unlikely forms that seem inert or crudely functional. The little puns contain a dissenting view of what modernism is about—not just the steady exclusion of reference to the world and the search for forms of purity, but also the constant attentiveness to the ignored forms the world provides, which can be adapted to the purposes of art. The artist's eye sees analogies between the most disparate worlds of form, and this allows him to unite zones of meaning and status others would keep strictly separate—so that a tire tread can conjure not only a

175. **Claes Oldenburg.** *Notebook Page, Clipping #302: Close-Up of Tire Tread with Ice.* 1965. Clipping with ink on paper, 11 × 8½" (28 × 21.6 cm). Collection of Claes Oldenburg and Coosje van Bruggen, New York

geometric painting but also, as it did for Claes Oldenburg in an ad he clipped for his notebook, the decorative language of another civilization (fig. 175). And the inadvertent oddities of the reductive schemas used in cheap catalogue ads could conversely suggest improbable systems of abstract form, as in the lumpy biomorphism of the wig ads that caught the eye of both Oldenburg and Warhol (figs. 176, 177). By being open to the rogue possibilities of these neglected, contemptible things, the artist broadens the range of new possibilities both for style and for expression.

In the way that van Gogh had been taken with the colors of cheap chromolithographs, and Picasso and Braque had adopted Ripolin paint and expeditious decorators' techniques, Warhol and Lichtenstein were both drawn to the mechanical and accidental residues of cheap printing processes—such as coarse dot screens, out-of-register color separations, and the slur of silkscreen—as a means of injecting a new set of possibilities, alien but thereby invigorating, into their painting. They saw that in isolating and exaggerating these side effects of mass reproduction they could find elements for an individual style. Some modern equivalent of Goya's biting, nocturnal aquatint could be found in grainy news photos of horrific scenes, and

comic dots could give back either hard Op Art effects or Seurat-like scintillations, depending on how one pushed them. These Pop painters replayed the wheel-like story of sans-serif type. They began with mechanical, impersonal bits of background noise that were the marginal and least artful aspects of the world of sixties printing—a world dominated by high cosmetic styling and slick color photography. But after the artists pulled them up onto canvas and made them over as the components of personal styles, these mistakes and milling-marks became the distinguishing stylistic traits of the time, and have come now to stand not just for the sixties, but for "modern" and for "art," as quasi-independent languages of form. When the Michelin company wanted to remake Bibendum into a symbol that would "say tire in 300 languages" to the age of multinational corporations, they not only infantilized him in the big-eyed, cheerily androgynous manner of Mickey Mouse, but had him printed in Warholian off-register colors (fig. 178).

The implacable passivity and acceptance of standardization that first made their tentative appearance in Johns's works could rightly be called the hallmarks of American Pop art's response to commercial culture.

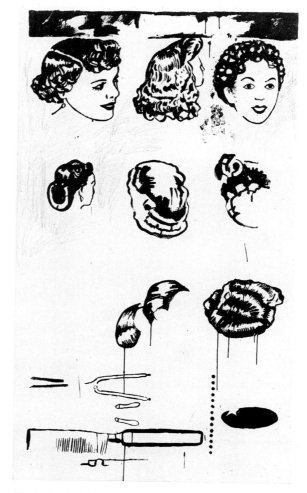

176. **Claes Oldenburg.** *Notebook Page, Clipping #44: Advertisement for Hairpieces.* 1963. Clipping outlined with ink solvent on paper, 11 × 8½″ (28 × 21.6 cm). Collection Claes Oldenburg and Coosje van Bruggen, New York

177. **Andy Warhol.** *Wigs.* 1960. Oil and wax crayon on canvas, 70⅛ × 40″ (178.1 × 101.6 cm). Dia Art Foundation, New York

178. **Boulet Dru Dupuy Petit.** *Ça dit pneu dans 300 langues.* 1986. Postcard. Courtesy Michelin, Clermont-Ferrand

179. **Andy Warhol.** *Campbell's Soup Cans.* 1962. Synthetic polymer paint on canvas; thirty-two panels, each 20 × 16″ (50.8 × 40.6 cm). Collection Irving Blum, New York

But to different artists in different circumstances, the same damned thing again and again can have widely different meanings. For Warhol, a response to mass-produced uniformity translated into a use of repetitive modules, alternately jumpy and hectoring, or steady and monotonous. The series of Campbell's Soup Cans he first showed in Los Angeles in 1962 (fig. 179) is a prime example of this apparent surrender to the mechanistic facts of an assembly-line consumerism. But this art was hardly a simple reflection of some condition of production specific to his time; if anything, the Soup Cans are archaic, and nostalgic in both their form and subject. The device of drumming an image into the consumer's mind by constant repetition had,

after all, been familiar in advertising since at least Chéret's day (fig. 180). By the time Warhol formed his style, such reiteration was in fact regarded in some marketing circles as an old-fashioned strategy, expensive and unimaginative. (A dominant dispute in early 1960s advertising pitted against each other the competing philosophies of Rosser Reeves and David Ogilvy, with Reeves advocating massive repetition of a single idea as the prime instrument of selling, and Ogilvy standing for the new wave of a more inventive, varied approach.)[209]

The Soup Cans, in any event, have more to do with the supermarket shelf than with the ad page, and with the devolution of old devices of show into frozen hab-

180. Posters for Dunlop tires on the railroad bridge at Eu, 1907

LABELS WITH SALES FORCE: THE FIRST TWO ILLUSTRATE THE ARTICLE ITSELF IN A SIMPLE WAY AGAINST AN UNINVOLVED BACKGROUND; THE OTHERS ARE EXCELLENT EXAMPLES OF THE TIE-UP OF NATIONAL ADVERTISING WITH THE CONTAINER LABEL

181. Illustration from *Printers' Ink*, July 10, 1915, p. 28

its of inventory. The repetition of objects that in Léger's day had been admired as a spectacle born of fierce urban competition (figs. 93, 98) appears here as the signature format of complacent suburban abundance. And the object Warhol chose was, like the Coca-Cola bottle Rauschenberg had used, a prime example of consumer culture as a static reservoir of invariance. In 1961, Campbell's ads trumpeted the fact that the price of this can had not changed in thirty-nine years;[210] and the label design was a perennial survivor, having remained the same for more than fifty years. In 1912, *Printers' Ink* cited the Campbell's label as an example of effective packaging, good for display purposes,[211] and another article in 1915 on "Designing the Label with the Sales 'Punch'" included the Campbell's can as an item with "sales force" and an "excellent example" of coordination between advertising and packaging (fig. 181).[212] By the time Warhol looked at it, though, this was no longer Picasso's kind of motif but Johns's—not an attention-grabber and sign of commercial variety, but a form so well known it had become completely banal. The rows of different soups—tomato, asparagus, chicken noodle—stress the leveling production of standard varieties that allow choice only within near-identical similarity. Warhol's dead-handed evenness sets forward a structure that is made up of equal parts efficient, enduring stability and numbing monotony. These soups and the stacked Brillo Boxes of 1964 (fig. 182) are Johns's Zen *koan* of double objects become mind-numbing incantation.

182. **Andy Warhol.** *Various Boxes.* 1964. Silkscreen ink on wood, dimensions variable. The Estate and Foundation of Andy Warhol

183. **Ed Ruscha.** *Standard Station, Amarillo, Texas.* 1963. Oil on canvas, 64⅞" × 10'1¾" (164.8 × 309.2 cm). Hood Museum of Art, Dartmouth College, Hanover, New Hampshire. Gift of James J. Meeker, Class of 1958, in memory of Lee English

The Brillo and Ketchup Boxes were also obvious parodies of the modular structures of Minimalist sculptors such as Carl Andre and Donald Judd. In finding the aesthetic of the avant-garde in the dated banalities of the storeroom, Warhol made somewhat the same point Lichtenstein had made with the sneaker sole, about the futility of trying to quarantine pure form and crass reference from each other. But the Minimalist aesthetic was not just a generic form of abstraction; it involved a specific range of manmade materials, and a sensibility of materialist austerity, that separated it from the idealizing abstract art of earlier modernism. Moreover, in paintings such as Frank Stella's black-stripe canvases, and in sculptures as diverse as Dan Flavin's fluorescent tubes or Carl Andre's metal plaques, Minimalism permitted a variable range of feelings (pristinely clinical rationality, or brute, raw power, or imposing theatricality, or brash opulence, to cite only a few); and its use of clarified, impersonal standardization could serve an artist as an adjustable lens rather than just an immovable template. Ed Ruscha's *Standard Station, Amarillo, Texas* (fig. 183), for example, was—no less than the Soup Cans and Brillo Boxes—knowingly fixed on the reductivist aesthetics of its day, and involved in partial parody of hard-edge abstract painting. Yet its emotional response to the encounter of that aesthetic with the look of mass society is wholly different.

Where Warhol and Lichtenstein made a salutary regression into the world of cheap, coarse printing, Ruscha effected a smoother segue between basic art-school graphic technique and a personal poetics. When he included material similar to that of New York Pop, such as a comic or a Spam can, he isolated these things in fields of color, enlarging the detached logos to assume a classic rectitude, while leaving the trashy querulousness of the object itself to plead against the cool, clean silence (fig. 184). Like others before him, Ruscha found a landscape that made him a painter; in his case it involved an interlock between the expanse of the Western deserts or the Pacific vista and the blandness of "modernized" commercial design. In works like *Standard Station*, Ruscha finds his Minimalism not along the K-Mart shelves, but out where the commercial template of clean, neat invariance falls into synchronization with a landscape of endless anonymity—primary-colored plastic evenly illuminated against empty sky. The modular, mechanical rhythm of Warhol is here translated into an extended, imperturbable continuity, and repetitious crowding is replaced by remote loneliness. Here also the fake promotional rhetoric of colossal grandeur—the plunging forced perspective of the gas station image—meets the reality of the country's scale. The odd alchemy that Ruscha sees and conveys is that a specificity arises from the meeting of two seemingly generic absolutes: a set of

346

184. **Ed Ruscha.** *Actual Size*. 1962. Oil on canvas, 6′ × 67″ (182.9 × 170.2 cm). Los Angeles County Museum of Art. Anonymous gift through the Contemporary Art Council

impersonal commercial conventions, plus the intractable nature of Western space, yield a distinctive sense of place—and a peculiarly American poetry of absence to match Warhol's run-on rhymes of monotonous abundance.

Lichtenstein, Warhol, and Ruscha all took their cues from elements of graphics and printing in commercial imagery. But Claes Oldenburg, beginning with a sculp-

tor's feel for tactile values and form, made very different use of many of the same sources. Oldenburg is the Courbet to Warhol's Manet—an artist out to grip the power of fleshy matter, rather than a connoisseur of surfaces. Warhol responded to Johns's ale cans with his cooler but brighter and more brittle *Soup Cans*; Oldenburg's riposte to the same model was his *Dual Hamburgers* (fig. 185)—emblems of an appetite veering toward disgust rather than of acceptance border-

185. **Claes Oldenburg.** *Two Cheeseburgers with Everything (Dual Hamburgers).* 1962. Burlap soaked in plaster, painted with enamel, 7 × 14¾ × 8⅝″ (17.8 × 37.5 × 21.8 cm). The Museum of Modern Art, New York. Philip Johnson Fund

186. **Claes Oldenburg.** *39 Cents (Fragment of a Sign).* 1961. Muslin soaked in plaster over wire frame, painted with enamel, 29 × 38 × 4″ (73.6 × 96.5 × 10.1 cm). Collection Anne and William J. Hokin, Chicago

187. **Claes Oldenburg.** Installation, *The Store*, 107 East Second Street, New York City, December 1961–January 1962

188. **Claes Oldenburg.** *Auto Tire with Price.* 1961. Muslin soaked in plaster over wire frame, painted with enamel, 49 × 48 × 7″ (124.5 × 121.9 × 58.3 cm). Collection Jean-Christophe Castelli

ing on anomie. This is an art in touch with the flabby paunch behind the hard commercial façades of American culture, and its stock-in-trade is not transpositions of style but transformations of state—from hard to soft, from mechanical to corporeal, and above all from small to large. In that realm of mutability—between the certainties of the machine and the weaknesses of the flesh, or between the tiny banalities of private life

and the overweening ambitions of public symbolism—Oldenburg found his way to deal with the peculiar complexities of his society.

Oldenburg's early work, marked by the influence of Dubuffet, found a repugnant vitality in the gritty margins of urban life. But when he opened his studio on the Lower East Side of New York as *The Store* (figs. 186–189), he swapped grit for garishness, and decided to deal with the energies of selling rather than only with the look of the worn and abused. Delaunay's and Picasso's old fantasy of avant-garde art as a publicized business in the stream of urban commerce was

189. Claes Oldenburg in *The Store*, December 1961 or January 1962

190. Installation of works by Claes Oldenburg at the Green Gallery, New York, September–October 1962

brought down to street level here, as *The Store* (and the "happenings" that took place there) dealt head-on with the notion of art as a business among others in the community, where customers are served and commodities bought.[213] After the pieties that had surrounded the painting of the Abstract Expressionists and the accompanying model of the lonely, suffering creator, American artists of Oldenburg's generation adopted the guise of the small entrepreneur, or in Warhol's case the manager of the loft-factory, as a way of debunking Romantic notions of bohemian gen-

ius, and getting back to the reality of a life lived in contemporary society.[214] Oldenburg's well-known litany, in which each line begins "I am for an art...," embraces a world where commerce and advertising add a crazy, hyped-up slang to the rotting, funny, appalling fullness of daily experience. Screeds of brand names and come-ons alternate here with passages of quieter wonder, pain, and sentiment:

I am for Kool-art, 7-UP art, Pepsi-art, Sunshine art, 39 cents art, 15 cents art, Vatronol art, Dro-bomb art, Vam art, Menthol art, L & M art, Ex-lax art, Venida art, Heaven Hill art,

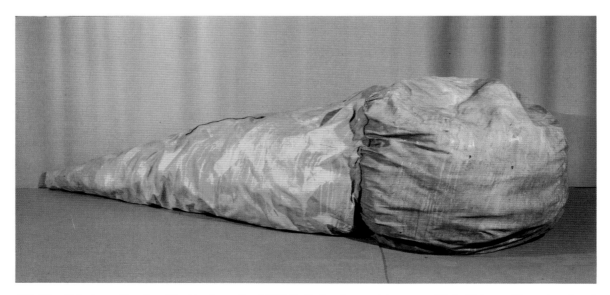

191. **Claes Oldenburg.** *Floor Cone (Giant Ice-Cream Cone)*. 1962. Synthetic polymer paint on canvas filled with foam rubber and cardboard boxes, 53¾″ × 11′4″ × 56″ (136.5 × 345.4 × 142 cm). The Museum of Modern Art, New York. Gift of Philip Johnson

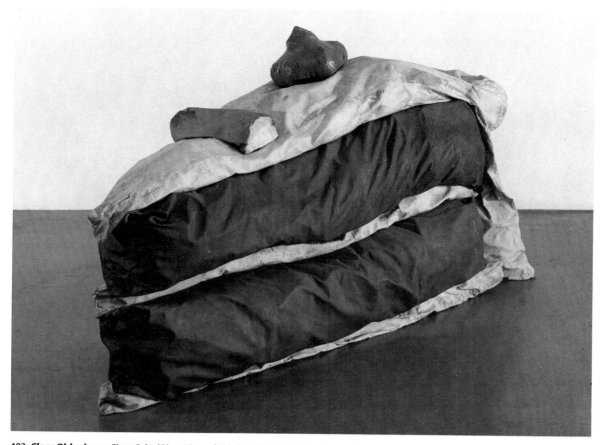

192. **Claes Oldenburg.** *Floor Cake (Giant Piece of Cake).* **1962. Synthetic polymer paint and latex on canvas filled with foam rubber and cardboard boxes, 58⅜″ × 9′6¼″ × 58⅜″ (148.2 × 290.2 × 148.2 cm). The Museum of Modern Art, New York. Gift of Philip Johnson**

Pamryl art, San-o-med art, Rx art, 9.99 art. . . .

I am for an art of things lost or thrown away, on the way home from school. I am for the art of cock-and-ball trees and flying cows and the noise of rectangles and squares. I am for the art of crayons and weak grey pencil-lead, and grainy wash and sticky oil paint, and the art of windshield wipers and the art of finger on a cold window, on dusty steel or in the bubbles on the sides of a bathtub. . . .

I am for U.S. Government Inspected Art, Grade A art, Regular Price art, Yellow Ripe art, Extra Fancy art, Ready-to-eat art, Fully cleaned art, Spend less art, Eat better art, Ham art, pork art, chicken art, tomato art, banana art, apple art, turkey art, cake art, cookie art. . . .[215]

Oldenburg's initial model of commerce was that of the overstuffed shops of immigrant neighborhoods, and *The Store* reverted back to what Glévéo had long before called the "provincial" style of merchandising: food and tires and clothes all together, treated alike. Immediately afterward, however, the artist reversed field for an uptown exhibition at the Green Gallery and adopted the format of the "spectacular" display of giant, isolated things. As opposed to the residually painterly look of items from *The Store*, these oversized items of food and clothing (figs. 190–192) brought out Oldenburg's feel for the basic geometry of forms, and for the relation of art to the body. These grossly physical objects also invited with a special baldness the accusation leveled against Warhol and Lichtenstein, that Pop art was simply a one-joke style based on inflating the trivial. Scale—the relation between minor things and major formats—was central to almost everything Pop

art explored. But for no artist was it a more important consideration than Oldenburg; beginning with the larger-than-life objects in the Green Gallery show, it became his signature, and the major device by which he expanded the concerns of his art from the realm of the body and the studio to those of the city and the society at large. Enlargement as a single issue brought into his sculpture all the conjunctions of hype and humility, and the complexities of sprawling, omnivorous vitality, both farcical and menacing, that he saw as the epoch's character and his art's subject. And nothing in Pop brought the attendant questions into clearer focus than his proposals to turn everyday objects into vast civic monuments (figs. 193–195, 197–199). These colossal absurdities spoke directly to issues that seemed to haunt all of Pop art, of the relation between the power of advertising, and the artist's private imagination. These *were* jokes; that was part of what was so serious and original about them.

The device of the architectural-scale object is one that Oldenburg shares with a venerable mode of spectacular advertising. The Baltimore skyline was formerly dominated by the Bromo-Seltzer building, for example, which was a rough copy of the Palazzo Vecchio in Florence, with the tower culminating in a giant, illuminated Bromo bottle; and the Heinz Corporation installed an eighty-foot pickle at the intersection of Fifth Avenue and Broadway in 1906. But this strategy has had a much longer life in the human imagination, and the advertisers are just part of a complex genealogy that runs back and forth from sophisticated fictions to

193. **Claes Oldenburg.** *Late Submission to the Chicago Tribune Architectural Competition of 1922: Clothespin (Version Two).* 1967. Pencil, crayon, and watercolor on paper, 22 × 27" (183.3 × 68.6 cm). Des Moines Art Center. Gift of Gardner Cowles by exchange and partial gift of Charles Cowles

cheap popular humor, with at least two serious strains of intent. In Jonathan Swift's *Gulliver's Travels* or in Lewis Carroll's *Alice's Adventures in Wonderland*, vast changes in scale were a way to transform the world we take for granted into a wholly unfamiliar, disorienting place that had to be re-addressed part by separate part—from cavernous nostrils to towering furniture. These authors intended to change the way people looked at the world and its hierarchies by a willful use of confusion and disorientation. But eighteenth-century visionary architects such as Étienne-Louis Boullée and Jean-Jacques Lequeu, associated with the Enlightenment's program of radical reason, had the opposite purpose in mind when they proposed to make cattle barns in the form of giant cows, or brothels in the form of male genitals:[216] they wanted a utopian clarity, in which the manmade world appeared as an array of immediately apprehensible signage that made the order and hierarchy of things crystal clear. Oldenburg eventually spliced the genes from both these ancestries, but the basic device of enlargement had been living an active life in popular culture and the advertising world in the interim.

The philosophical desire for clear, legible signs had its pragmatic and commercial progeny in the giant objects such as scissors or shoes or wine bottles that were familiar devices of urban shop signage long before 1900. And when photography became a manipulable part of printing in the late nineteenth century, the disorienting effects of fictional gigantism slipped down from the realm of political critique to the more folksy tasks of making "tall tales" concrete: whale-size fish caught in the Catskills, or the prodigious vegetables of the Midwest soil (fig. 196). Then around the time of World War I, when print advertising became more organized as a competitive profession, advertisers began to look on the natural discrepancies in scale that commonly appeared in a page's array of ads—hotels and shoes side by side at the same size—as something that could be manipulated to make products more vividly impressive. A 1921 article in *Printers' Ink* on "'Jumbo' Display That Dominates" responded, for example, to an ad in which a watch had been enlarged many times to fill a large page. The innovation was (like the borrowing of tabloid style and comics for the thirties "buckeye" look) a pre-Pop appropriation within adver-

194. Claes Oldenburg. *Proposed Colossal Monument for Park Avenue, New York City: Good Humor Bar.* 1965. Crayon and watercolor on paper, 23½ × 17½" (59.7 × 44.4 cm). Collection Carroll Janis

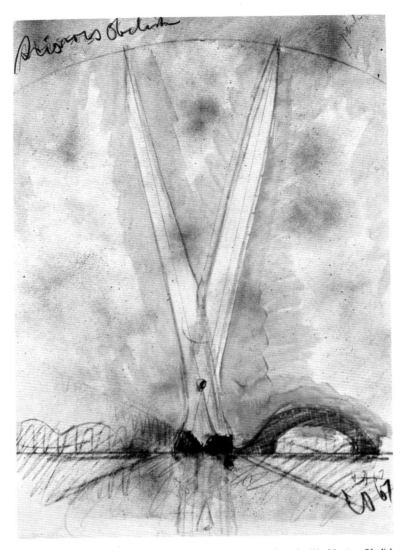

195. **Claes Oldenburg.** *Proposed Colossal Monument to Replace the Washington Obelisk, Washington, D.C.: Scissors in Motion.* 1967. Crayon and watercolor on paper, 30 × 19¾" (76.2 × 50.2 cm). Collection David Whitney

tising itself, which involved moving a poster format into the newspaper world. ''Now that showing the goods has become almost an advertising fad,'' the author reasoned, ''these freak layouts are worthy of analysis.'' And, while he worried that the public might find such scale shifts strange, he took comfort in the way audiences were accepting the innovative close-ups of faces in movies. The trick was to get Boullée without Swift—to obtain the impressive, memorable force of the deformation without letting its bizarre or repellent potential take over. The huge watch succeeded, he reckoned, because it was ''to the reader, no more than

196. Postcard. c. 1909. Charles C. Stack & Company, Sioux Falls, South Dakota. Collection Andreas Brown, Gotham Book Mart, New York

197. Claes Oldenburg. *Proposed Colossal Monument for Thames River: Thames Ball.* 1967. Crayon, pen, and watercolor on postcard, 3½ × 5½″ (8.9 × 14 cm). Collection Mrs. Edwin Janss, Thousand Oaks, California

198. Claes Oldenburg. *Proposed Colossal Monument for Thames River: Thames Ball.* 1967. Crayon, pen, and watercolor on postcard, 3½ × 5½″ (8.9 × 14 cm). Collection Carroll Janis

Inverted plug as Skyscraper

CO69

199. Claes Oldenburg. _Proposal for a Skyscraper in the Form of a Chicago Fireplug: Inverted Version._ 1969. Pencil, crayon, and watercolor on paper, 17½ × 12″ (44.5 × 30.5 cm). Collection Dr. and Mrs. Phillip T. George

200. Constantin Brancusi. *Torso of a Young Man.* 1924. Polished bronze on stone and wood base, 18 × 11 × 7" (45.7 × 28 × 17.8 cm). Hirshhorn Museum and Sculpture Garden, Smithsonian Institution, Washington, D.C. Gift of Joseph H. Hirshhorn

a literal translation of a well-known timepiece. It commands attention because, in all memory, the average person has never seen so large a watch in picture form.'' But to control that reaction required considerable artistry in the simplification of effects, tricks of forced perspective, and extensive retouching of any photo used; and unless one chose the right kind of item, and used the right blend of generalization and specificity, the results became disturbing or potentially monstrous. '' 'Jumbo' Display...'' is a remarkable document of the way in which competitive sales pressure first brought advertisers to confront, Janus-fashion, both the problems of Gulliver and the potentials of Pop:

201. René Magritte. *Personal Values*. 1952. Oil on canvas, 31⅝ × 39½" (80.3 × 100.3 cm). Collection Harry Torczyner, Lake Mohegan

People are impressed by size.... For almost a year the campaign for Champion spark plugs has been guided by this principle. The plugs are shown as large as they can be worked into full pages, and most cleverly retouched to bring out not only their detail, but the various qualities of metal and porcelain, by means of expert poster retouching.

Thus when a magazine is unfolded, a great spark plug greets the reader, so impressive in size and so complete in its form and mechanism that the man not altogether familiar with them is in a position to study every separate part.

On the other hand, to show that it may not always work out successfully, an advertiser hit on the idea of showing enlargements in a line of various crackers, cookies, breadstuffs, doughnuts, etc. The eye refused to accept them in this dilated form. They were ugly, not at all palatable.

Another advertiser reproduced his cigar at least five times its real size. And here again no smoker could look upon the result with zest. For some reason, although the form and texture were faithfully reproduced, these drawings did not look like cigars....

It is always possible to secure most unusual illustrative ef-

fects by enlarging the product, and then introducing other units in normal size.

Thus we find a Life Saver mint display, with an enormous mint placed in juxtaposition to tiny figures, grouped around and about it, examining its good points. The mint seems as big as a planet yet it is always the advertised product, unmistakably....

One of the strongest advertisements we have observed was a double spread in newspapers used in the South some years ago, when an advertiser, weary of little, tight, cramped reproductions of his product, had an immense coarse-screen half-tone made of a fruit beverage in a glass.

The tumbler reached from the top of the paper to the bottom and simply "flabbergasted" the reader when the paper was opened.

To get attention, it is sometimes necessary to have the "Biggest Show on Earth."[217]

By the early 1950s, within the legacy of Surrealism, this amplification by image had once again become a device of the sophisticated and philosophical imagination, in works by Magritte such as *Personal Values* (fig. 201) or *The Listening Room* (fig. 202), which induced odd Romantic comminglings of unease and exhilaration by setting small, routine possessions against beckoning skies of freedom, or imprisoning monstrous vegetable life in the confines of a domestic chamber. In science-fiction movies of the same period, meanwhile, scale change became the curse of a world thrown out of balance by the mad dreams of atomic science: giant ants and spiders stalked the earth as radiation mutants. And on planes both popular and more prestigious, radical size shifts returned to their function of demolishing conventional ways of thinking about human society and its values. The 1957 movie *The Incredible Shrinking Man* related, with the aid of oversize-object props, a Kafka-with-popcorn fable for the Existential age; continual shrinkage forces the movie's hero to face his ultimate inconsequence as an atomized soul in a vast world. And in 1968 the designer Charles Eames produced *The Powers of Ten*, a remarkable sequence of scale-multiplied images, from the microscopically minute to the telescopically galactic in swift hops, as a way of encouraging a humbling sense of proportion in an over-proud technological era.

Finally in Oldenburg's day, the long-traveled strategy of gigantism resurfaced as a "new" technique in print advertising. Realized with technicolor photography, the "jumbo" object of the 1920s became, in the early 1960s, the antidote to the vague indirection of 1950s advertising, which had grown routine. The influence of market research, the ad executive Walter Weir wrote in 1962, had led to a reliance on "tested" formulae that brought laziness, and a tendency to fall back on the feel-good associations of "the smiling, prancing housewife, the triumphant-looking husband and the excessively buoyant and deliriously happy family group." But he noted approvingly that the "latest school...rebels....It attempts instead a sheer, stark presentation of the product—not in the lower right-hand margin where it was formerly relegated, but right smack up where the big illustration used to be, and BIG...." And the revolution came, Weir saw, from a forced marriage of genres within the trade. His "look of the sixties" in advertising was the (Warholian) combination of *Vogue* plus the supermarket magazine, the stylishly spare techniques of glamor fused with the straight-up factuality of commodity ads.[218]

When Oldenburg clipped a close-up, enlarged, sixties ad for coffee creamer and noted next to it "rainstorm at sea" (fig. 203), he was thus both responding to a stylization of the advertising of his particular time, and recovering from it a fundamental device of the human imagination, a device which had been passed up and down through the commercial and artistic imagery of the century (just as Lichtenstein had found in Irv Novick's comics the residue of compositional ideas that had left the world of prints and paintings to live in

202. René Magritte. *The Listening Room.* 1952. Oil on canvas, 17⅝ × 21⅝" (44.8 × 54.9 cm). The Menil Collection, Houston

rainstorm at sea

203. Claes Oldenburg. *Notebook Page, Clipping #500: Rainstorm at Sea.* 1966. Clipping with ballpoint pen on paper, 11 × 8½" (28 × 21.6 cm). Collection Claes Oldenburg and Coosje van Bruggen, New York

movies and then return to illustration). Oldenburg's paste-up notebooks attest that he saw advertising as a rich repository of such potentials, which only needed to be coaxed to reveal an untoward power. The extraordinary image he clipped of women cowering before rolls of carpet, for example (fig. 204), did not just harmonize with the scale joke in projects like that for sculptures of colossal cigarettes (fig. 205); it suggested a play with the same basic symbolism of phallic menace. The fallen-down woman added at the right stood for the result of the confrontation, and the little head of Daniel Boone, with its admonition to LEARN THE FOR-

EST'S SECRET, suggested to Oldenburg the larger notion of confrontation with the "savage" or "wild" side of consciousness.[219] Ad imagery strung together in this way yielded an unexpected Freudian narrative. But this was no longer the situation of Victorian catalogues, where, as Lucas and Morrow said, one man will find mere facts and another drama; advertising itself had become routinely full of drama. Influenced strongly by the success of Doyle Dane Bernbach's campaigns in the 1950s, sixties advertising was obsessed with "creativity," and the injunction to make imagery surprising and dramatic had perked down to broad strata of the

204. Claes Oldenburg. *Notebook Page, Clipping #560: Tumbling Carpet Rolls.* 1967. Clippings on paper, 11 × 8½" (28 × 21.6 cm). Collection Claes Oldenburg and Coosje van Bruggen, New York

205. Claes Oldenburg. *Colossal Fagends in Park Setting with Man.* 1961. Pencil and watercolor on paper, 30 × 22" (76.2 × 55.9 cm). Collection Mrs. Rene d'Harnoncourt

trade.[220] For Oldenburg, the most interesting results obtained not at the high, "Cadillac" (or now, more properly, "Volkswagen") end of such styling, but in its mutation in the unexpected domain of the killer carpets and the isolated, aggrandized hamburger and fries (fig. 206).

The processes of retouching, enlarging, and printing ad photographs could exaggerate textures, or make evanescent things concrete, in ways that attracted the sculptor's eye for form and tactile values. The crinkly texture of a French bra, for example, highlighted by the crude lights and darks of an ad, could spur a Surrealist body/food analogy (fig. 207); and the lighting patterns on french fries or water drops could become, if nudged just a bit further by an outline, an independent vocabulary of form, involving a transformation of states—liquid to solid, soft to hard—that interested Oldenburg.

The project drawings for monuments bring these rich constellations of possibilities—Enlightenment ideals of communication, Freudian analogy, and monumental pickles—to bear on a singular blend of personal memory and futuristic public fantasy. Items like the clothespin (fig. 193) and the ice bag were artifacts of the pre-1950s past, and the fireplug was specifically the Chicago model of the artist's childhood (fig. 199). Yet these monuments were conceived as engaging directly with the conditions of the present. Long before the notion of specific "site-relation" in sculpture, these colossal signposts were often intended to be immediately symbolic of their sites (for example, giant knees for miniskirted London) or to respond to the specific environment around them: the toilet-tank floats in the Thames turned the movement of the tides into a "spectacular" civic occurrence (figs. 197, 198). And the monuments spoke truth about cities: the proposal for bowling balls on Park Avenue, or wiper blades by Lake Ontario, or scissors for the Washington Monument (fig. 195) involved potential threats that were designed to teach constant, fast-stepping alertness to danger amid the amusement. These visions echo less Duchamp's urbane strategies than Léger's vision of modern urbanity—a hard, congested, competitive environment where liberating joy might consist of recognizing and elevating the grandeur of the commonplace, and where the scale of giant advertising sets the tone to be rivaled.

As with Lichtenstein's little jabs at Vasarely, there is an implicit aesthetic-cum-social argument here—directly against the afflatus of commemorative sculpture, but implicitly against ideals of social and cultural unity being vested in an abstruse, hypocritically lofty symbolic language. To ask whether these proposals are ironic or heroic is to miss the point: they use irony as a vehicle of heroism in the way Philip Guston's paintings take comedy as a vehicle for tragedy. The radical idea of satire is uppermost here, in the Swiftian sense that by making familiar things alien, we get outside our conventions and achieve a critical objectivity about our society. And certainly the projects were per-

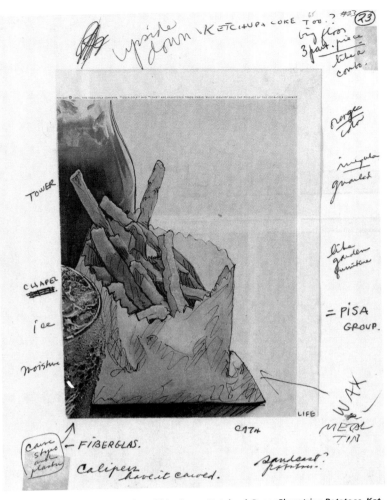

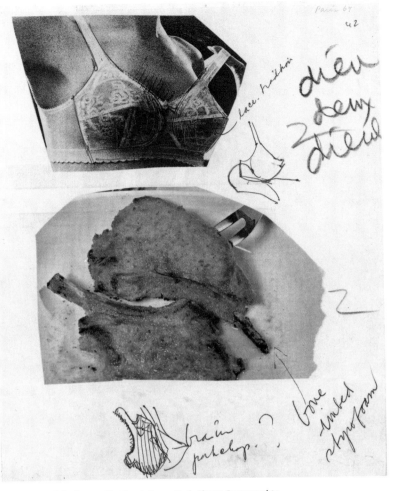

206. **Claes Oldenburg.** *Notebook Page: Shoestring Potatoes, Ketchup Bottle and Coke Glass*. 1965. Ballpoint pen and clipping on paper, 11 × 8½" (28 × 21.6 cm). Collection Claes Oldenburg and Coosje van Bruggen, New York

207. **Claes Oldenburg.** *Notebook Page: Pork Chops Compared to Breasts in Brassiere*. 1964. Ballpoint pen, crayon, and two clippings on paper, 11 × 8½" (28 × 21.6 cm). Collection Claes Oldenburg and Coosje van Bruggen, New York

ceived as radically critical: the Marxist theorist Herbert Marcuse felt certain that if such things could ever be erected, it would signal that the whole enterprise of modern capitalist society had collapsed.[221] But the monuments also translate into modernist terms the eighteenth-century ideal of a public landscape full of form-signs instantly understood by all citizens, by making something big out of common, ignored resources. Unlike the architect making the cow stable in the form of a cow, or the barrel-maker's house out of rings, Oldenburg inverts rather than codifies the existing order of things, and rifles the kit-bag of his personal experience—clothespins, fireplugs, and toilet balls—for objects that will say "me" and "you" and "us" all at once. The harmonious certainty of social niches is dethroned by the bumptious volatility of individual play as the embodiment—or objectification—of civic good. The smile of reason has become the guffaw of a huge, absurd, and quite serious joke, which Marcuse only half got.

Again and again, we have seen how popular culture has served modern artists as a point of recovery for certain aspects of the high-art tradition. The proposals for colossal objects are yet another instance, for they included some references by Oldenburg to Brancusi (the

inverted fireplug, for example [fig. 199], echoes *Torso of a Young Man* [fig. 200]), which were part of a broader reassessment of Brancusi that was also being pursued by contemporary Minimalist sculptors such as Carl Andre and Robert Morris. The Minimalists, however, revered the Rumanian master as a prophet of systems of pure geometric forms. Oldenburg recovered a different heritage from the same source, by making his fireplug reaffirm the phallic nature of Brancusi's *Torso*, and by conceiving the symmetry of a clothespin as the analogue of the passionate couple in Brancusi's early *Kiss*. His Brancusi was an artist in whose work a basic shape could evoke multiple references to the body, and to social and erotic life. It was this simultaneous engagement with condensed forms and enlarged meanings that Oldenburg sought to expand, by carrying both Brancusi's eye for formal analogy and his feel for the eroticized object into the broader range of manmade things. Brancusi helped him see new possibilities for fireplugs, and looking at fireplugs helped him rethink what Brancusi could mean for the future of art.

Similarly, when Oldenburg looked back, as the Minimalists did, to the art of the Russian Revolution, he was less drawn to the pure Suprematist forms of Kasimir Malevich than to publicity, in the broadest sense: the

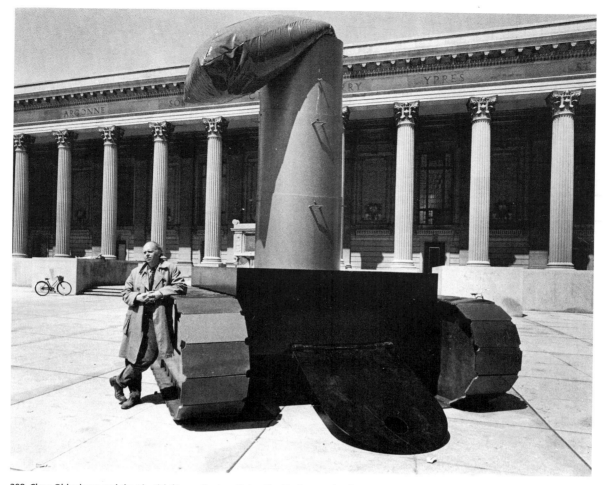

208. Claes Oldenburg and the *Lipstick (Ascending) on Caterpillar Tracks*, at Beinecke Plaza, Yale University, 1969

visionary radio towers, kiosks, and monuments in which Russian avant-garde artists set themselves the task of informing and inspiring the citizens of the new society. The clearest homage to this ideal was the only one of the early monuments to be realized, the *Lipstick* made for and donated to Oldenburg's alma mater, Yale University, in the spring of 1968 (figs. 208–210). When the *Lipstick* was brought to Yale as a part of the protests against the war in Vietnam, one of the precedents Oldenburg thought to evoke was the visionary project conceived in 1920 by the Russian revolutionary

artist Vladimir Tatlin, for a *Monument to the Third International*. Tatlin's giant, spiraling tower would have been a point of dissemination for news and information, and a symbol for a new world order; Oldenburg's monument was intended to provide a rallying point for protest gatherings, and a platform for speakers.

The *Lipstick* also attempted to recover the alliance Rodchenko and Mayakovsky had tried to forge between consumer advertising and social reform, and to renew the promise that Léger had seen in the commercial *objet-spectacle* as a focus for a new conscious-

209. Installation of Claes Oldenburg's *Lipstick (Ascending) on Caterpillar Tracks* at Beinecke Plaza, Yale University, May 15, 1969

210. Claes Oldenburg. *Lipstick (Ascending) on Caterpillar Tracks.* 1969, reworked 1974. Painted fiberglass tip, aluminum tube, and steel body. Tip, 10′ (304.8 cm) high × 48″ (121.9 cm) diam.; tube, 7′ (213.4 cm) high × 48″ (121.9 cm) diam.; body, 5″ × 8′ × 11′ (12.7 × 243.8 × 335.3 cm). Yale University Art Gallery, New Haven, Connecticut. Gift of the Colossal Keepsake Corporation

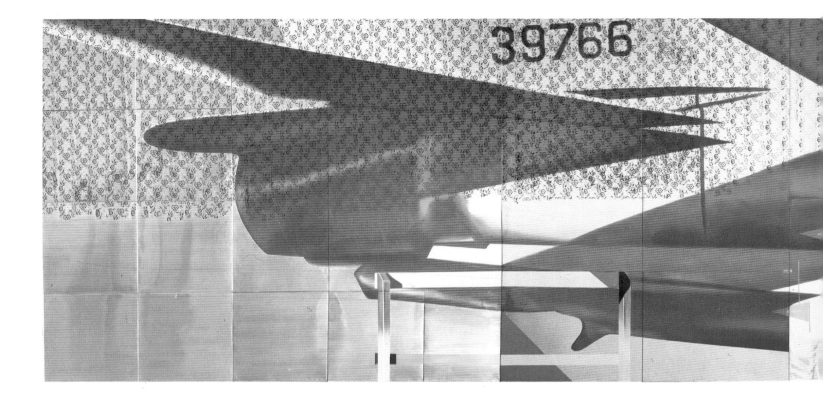

As opposed to the visionary projects for monuments, which imagined small things as enormously grand, the *Lipstick* recaptured and reduced to human, interactive scale the apparatus of grandiose corporate advertising. When Léger took something small and forthright from the little world of newsprint announcements and blew it up, he intended to celebrate the no-nonsense directness of commerce's appeals (figs. 101, 102); Oldenburg instead humbles an item made over-large by glossy pictorials, in order to point out the equivocal nature of advertising's seductions. This is a sculpture that speaks the language of glamor magazines, billboards, and television; but it does so in a format of communication more appropriate for town criers, and the Speaker's Corner of Hyde Park in London. It is both monumental and toy-like. Hence its strengths and weaknesses, as a memento of a time when it seemed that small communities of privileged university students could steal the consciousness of the world away from the power of mass media, by using that same power to better ends, and by staging more memorable spectacles, within the smaller world they controlled. At a moment when it was thought "the whole world is watching," this sculpture lifted the none-too-subtle gesture of a vertical middle finger toward the larger field of exploitative sexual imagery in mass advertising. Yet even in its ironizing antagonism, the *Lipstick* also represents one of the singular moments when—as with Delaunay, Léger, and Rodchenko before—it seemed that the artist might seal a partnership with the forces modern publicity had

tapped, and leave the role of café consumer or small entrepreneur to join the ranks of the professional movers of mass imagination.

A half century before the *Lipstick*, Léger had asserted that the state of war had determined the tenor of modern times; but in his view, that tenor had to do with an intensity of competition that stripped away complacency and favored the inventive spirit. The Vietnam War, by contrast, linked commerce and militarism in an entirely different way: it seemed to epitomize the bloated excesses of overextended corporate production, and the way it was "sold" by the government seemed a natural extension of the feel-good rhetoric by which consumer spending was promoted. American dreams and American lies seemed, like passive comfort at home and active aggression abroad, inextricably enmeshed.

James Rosenquist's *F-111* (fig. 213) was one of the most direct and memorable responses to this situation, yet it had its origins in an unlikely, outmoded corner of sixties advertising. When he first came to New York, Rosenquist joined the venerable line of modern artists who have earned part of their living in some form of commercial art (Magritte, Schwitters, Warhol, and Ruscha are only a few of the obvious examples). But the job he took was the blue-collar labor of painting huge billboards, in Times Square and elsewhere. As he recognized, this employment put one part of his existence back in touch with the Mexican muralists of the thirties, while his work as an artist was dealing with the

213. **James Rosenquist.** *F-111*. 1964–65. Oil on canvas with aluminum; overall, 10 × 86' (304.8 × 2621.3 cm). Collection Richard E. Jacobs

effects of Abstract Expressionism.[222]

In an age of television, the billboard was no longer the menace it had appeared to be around World War I. It seemed more like an endangered species, or at least a white elephant, while the hot-eyed young creators on Madison Avenue focused their best efforts on making playlets for the small screen. Rosenquist saw, however, that his day job could, beyond just paying the bills, offer something to his art. At first, as an abstract painter, he tried expanding his color selection by taking the exaggerated palette of the giant signs—Man-Tan orange, Franco-American spaghetti orange—back to the studio.[223] Then he saw that the "non-style" he used in executing hundreds of square yards of enlarged photographic imagery could give his work a look of infuriating neutrality, which would allow him special artistic room within which to maneuver. The dead-handed, evenly modeled look of billboard renderings led backwards, toward the cool impersonality Magritte had first adopted from utilitarian instructional imagery, and seemed appropriate to the dated material—ten-year-old cars, out-of-style hats, and other items remote from contemporary stylishness—Rosenquist favored as subject matter.[224]

Rosenquist sought to adopt these dated techniques and images, however, to deal with the impact of advertising in his own time; for he saw ads both as the stuff of his daily existence and as a pillar of the society he lived in—the source of a tremendous power that art might emulate. He told an interviewer in 1964, the year he conceived *F-111*, that he was "excited and fas-

cinated" by the way modern communications used "things larger than life" to attack sensibilities with a speed and force that made traditional painting seem old-fashioned. And he saw advertising as the crucial model to adopt if art hoped to have a voice in such an age. "I think we have a free society," he said, "and the action that goes on in this free society allows encroachments, as a commercial society. So I geared myself, like an advertiser or a large company, to this visual inflation—in commercial advertising which is one of the foundations of our society." Stressing that advertising had "such impact and excitement in its means and imagery," he continued:

Painting is probably much more exciting than advertising—so why shouldn't it be done with that power and gusto, with that impact. . . . My metaphor, if that is what you can call it, is my relations to the power of commercial advertising which is in turn related to our free society, the visual inflation which accompanies the money that produces box tops and space cadets. . . .[225]

In choosing the F-111 fighter-bomber as the subject for an immense painting, Rosenquist understood that the object itself, as well as the advertising style in which it would be shown, were linked to the basic structure of the American economy. This was the newest, most technologically advanced weapon in the Air Force arsenal. And Rosenquist saw, as Hamilton had seen in regard to mid-fifties cars, that such items of accelerated progress were manifestations of a system of rapid turnover between invention and obsolescence. For Hamilton this system held broad promise in

generation. The speed with which advertisers and manufacturers adopted the trappings of this sexual liberation and turned them into a "new look" for the purposes of sales, proved (depending on one's point of view) either the extraordinary resiliency and capacity for adaption within Western societies, or the voracious power of the established economy to assimilate and thus render impotent all rebellions. In any event, the situation made overheated images of sexuality in mid-sixties advertising into charged zones of contradiction between the forces of change in society and the blatant machinations of the familiar dream machine of economic seduction. (The artist clipped a particularly egregious, sexist example for his notebook in 1965 [fig. 212].) The *Lipstick* was in no way dependent on such ads, but it played on their form of gigantesque Freudian imagery. The priapic authority of the monument's shaft was undermined by its sagging tip: this red protrusion was originally made purposefully limp, so that each speaker, on mounting the platform base, could pump it into erection, as a call for attention. A leaking valve allowed it to deflate each time, leaving this symbol of triumphant potency in chagrined relaxation until the next stimulus. The pretensions of grandeur were displayed, in other words, only to mock them; and the power of sexuality was reclaimed by leavening it with humor.

211. Claes Oldenburg. *Lipsticks in Piccadilly Circus, London.* **1966. Clipping on postcard, 10 × 8″ (25.4 × 20.3 cm). The Trustees of the Tate Gallery**

ness. Oldenburg set out to do this by stealing back the language of symbolic spectacle American business had been using in its mass advertising, and by then turning it against the ideals of armed belligerency that seemed supported by that same corporate establishment. The combination of symbolism in the *Lipstick*, of sexuality and military hardware, is the same formula for consumer seduction that had been at work in the bumpers and fins of the 1957 Cadillac. Here, however, the usage is critical and satirical, rather than mythifying. The erect phallic symbol that moves on tank treads insists on the link between male sexuality and America's military aggression, and highlights the sinister aspect of the commingling of glamor, sex, and power in American fantasies.

Oldenburg had previously imagined a retractable lipstick as a monument to replace the statue of Eros in London's Piccadilly Circus (fig. 211), recognizing the combination of fashionable glamor and sexuality in the "swinging London" of the early 1960s. This conjunction between cosmetics and sex was self-evident, and advertisers had long played upon it as a staple of their trade. In the early sixties, however, a more overt insistence on eroticism, as embodied in the miniskirt and exaggerated facial make-up, had an element of social defiance as well, exemplifying youthful openness in revolt against the more straightlaced mores of an older

212. Claes Oldenburg. *Notebook Page, Clipping #322: Lipstick Advertisement, in a British Publication.* **1965. Clipping on paper, 11 × 8½″ (28 × 21.6 cm). Collection Claes Oldenburg and Coosje van Bruggen, New York**

1. Jeff Koons. *Rabbit*. 1986. Stainless steel, 41 × 19 × 12″ (104.1 × 48.3 × 30.5 cm). Private collection

the domain of material life, and in the creation of modern fantasies. But for Rosenquist the dilemma was more acute, as the surplus of economic energy seemed vented, not into chrome surrogates for space flight, but into real-life militarism. The 1957 Cadillac had been a jet-styled dream that a person could own; the bomber's styling was deadly functional, and destined solely for national-security purposes. The relation between that governmental scale of reality and the smaller objects of personal, material consumption—or between collective obsessions and private fantasies—is among the subjects the painting treats. And where Lichtenstein's comics-based images had just a few years before ironized the cowboy myth of the air ace, this picture treats both the engine of warfare and the language of advertising in terms that are more ominous, ghostly in their smoothly modeled anonymity, and overpowering. The vast shape of the bomber weaves its way through the array of more domesticated advertising images, as Robert Hughes said, "like a shark threading a reef."[226]

Scattered throughout this painting is a mini-history of the motifs we have followed not only in this chapter, but throughout the book till now. The painted flower pattern at the left end, a device Rosenquist had seen used in lobbies as a simulation of wallpaper, is a decorator's shortcut that recalls the *faux bois* technique Braque and Picasso used. In the Cubists' hands, such a device had been a jaunty little joke about the pretensions of the decorative; here, where the painter wanted it to evoke an atmosphere "solid with radioac-

tivity and other undesirable elements," it has been elevated into a symbolic language for concerns of life and death. The tire, constituent of the Michelin man and point of interest for Lichtenstein and Oldenburg as well, serves as a colossal, geometrically abstracted "crown" over the flag-decked angel-food cake, rhyming the air-filled confection of sugar with the inflated piece of rubber hardware.[227] And the light bulb, ironic surrogate of the human head for Picabia or Johns, and emblem of lonely nights for Guston, here embodies a peculiar dialogue of colors, in which subtly nuanced hues in painterly oils emit a glow against the sharper rhetoric of the commercial, fluorescent paints behind them.[228] The grinning little girl, descendant of the inescapable Bébé Cadum and countless other symbols of cleanliness and innocence, is now dwarfed by the adult-scaled, massive chrome hairdryer whose bullet-like styling ties it to the plane. And in the rhyming juxtaposition of the bubbling discharge of an aqualung with a mushroom cloud from a nuclear explosion, we have both a minor restatement of the painting's major theme—the interrelation between private consumer amusements and massive societal malfeasance—and a terrible echo of the optimism of such earlier juxtapositions as the biplane, the Ferris wheel, and the rugby game (fig. 28). Finally, all of this comes to a conclusion with the erect nipple of the jet's nose cone laid over the tangled skeins of a mass of spaghetti. Drawn directly from Rosenquist's former billboard repertory of Franco-American foods, it here suggests visceral gore as well, a culminating field of gruesome internal or-

ganicism against the hard metals and surface glamor that dominate the imagery.

Recapitulating the major and minor themes of modern art's engagement with advertising, *F-111* is also a narcissistic *Guernica* for the sixties, concentrating on the psychosocial life of those who do the bombing, rather than on the traumas of the bombed. But attempts to wrest from it some clear political "message" may be even more futile than the many attempts to decode Picasso's mural. This painting was, in very real ways, never meant to be seen whole. Conceived at a scale that would cover all the walls of one relatively small room in Leo Castelli's gallery, the picture was to engulf the viewer, and be all around at once. This is, of course, the opposite of the billboard's intended effect. *F-111* presents the billboard as Rosenquist experienced it while painting one. And by using long-distance techniques in intimate quarters, and the devices of instant, clarified impact in a broken-up, wrap-around format, Rosenquist turned advertising's devices and imagery to art's purposes. From the stuff of easy recognition and hard sell, he created an experience with no one category of association, difficult to absorb, and without clear mandate. Oldenburg had used enlargement to gain distance, to make the monumental ironic, and upset decorums of proportion. But by pushing the viewer deeper into colossally scaled images, Rosenquist encouraged an opposite response, of confusion. He forced the antiquated techniques and scale conventions of sign painting to yield an equivalent for the jumpy, disjointed perceptions of an electronic age:[229]

the painting was purposefully conceived as an assemblage of separate panels and was intended to be sold off piecemeal.[230]

One of the quintessential movies of the sixties was Michelangelo Antonioni's *Blow-Up*, and one of its themes was the premise that the more we push our technology toward what we take to be certainties, and the more we enlarge the images in which we put our faith, the more profound will be the grainy uncertainty, moral as well as optical, we are obliged to confront. When Seurat, or Delaunay, or Léger looked to advertising, they saw a power to focus the mind, arrest the imagination, and convey immediate excitement. Rosenquist, however, in blowing things up, and in borrowing directly from the techniques and imagery of advertising, searches a modern form of dispersed attention and moral doubt, amid a paradoxical overlay of pleasure and fear, triviality and power. And in this regard, the *F-111*—on a grand, intently serious, and panoramic scale—also descends from the intuitions of Picasso, Braque, and Gris, when they abutted the headlines of war with little ads for light bulbs or underwear and snippets from current songs. The sounds of a century—the lilt of the Cubists' popular refrains, the clamor in the competitive shop window, the lyrics of countless slogans, and the crash of billboards "screaming . . . in the timid landscape"[231]—here coalesce in a stunning crescendo, where the devices of high-impact certainty conspire to yield an encompassing, disorienting experience of ambiguity and contradiction, compellingly unresolved.

First time farce, second time tragedy.[1] This reversal of Marx's aphorism about the way history repeats itself is true for the history of modern art. If there's a pattern that connects all the contingent, individual histories we have chronicled, it's that things which began in modern culture as jokes, come-ons, and sideshows—comic-strip conventions and Edwardian humor books and shop-window arrangements—have been transformed by modern artists into mysteries, lyrics, and elegies. Miró found the form of the unconscious in a catalogue for hair combs; Picasso found a Mallarméan poetry of the modern city in the accidents of a newspaper-kiosk display; Guston found a tragic grandeur in the unshaded light bulbs and bare plank floors of Depression comic strips.

In the past twenty years, though, the pattern by which jokes have been repeated as elegies has taken on a new and unexpected intensity. However complicated the play of attraction and repulsion between modern art and popular culture may have been in the past, the low world outside the studio had remained for a century—from Seurat's mad mechanical dance through Picasso's syncopated found poetry to Warhol's bright, incantatory repetitions and Rosenquist's overload of images—a source of irreverent energy. Pop culture, good or bad, was almost always hot.

In contemporary art, however, the meaning of the invocation of popular culture in art seems to have changed dramatically. Instead of evoking humanity in motion, either racing ahead to utopia or dashing lemming-like off a cliff, the forms of popular culture as they are reflected in contemporary art seem glacial—the fixed heraldry of a humorless, monolithic, ceremonial civilization. Pass in imagination from Rosenquist's *F-111* ("Advertising," fig. 213) to the calm, impersonal electric display boards of Jenny Holzer, with reports of human suffering streaming by as if they were emphemeral news, or from a room of the metamorphosed soft objects of Claes Oldenburg to the paralyzed and armored metal objects of Jeff Koons (fig. 1), and you feel a deliberate drop in temperature—a sense of having entered a new Ice Age of pop imagery. The shift from the Pop art of the sixties to this world of the eighties is like the moment at the end of the Beatles' "A Day in the Life"—the mounting and increasingly incoherent orchestral scream subsiding into the big, endlessly sustained funereal chord. Extend the histories we have chronicled to their current incarnations, and, again and again, you

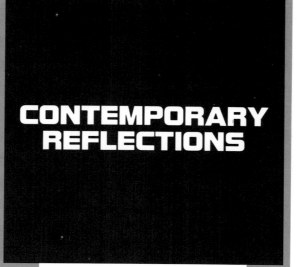

CONTEMPORARY REFLECTIONS

encounter old forms reincarnated in a new and calmly embittered spirit: word art that insists on the impossibility of any private language remade from public speech; graffiti art that declares its own inability to make an authentically personal mark; cartoon art that can only repeat, rather than reimagine, popular form; ad art as icy and cynical as anything from Madison Avenue. If in the past the jokes of pop culture had been the templates for the elegies of modern art, now the jokes of modern art have become the templates for a new despairing mannerism. No period in modern history has seen so many artists involved with so many kinds of popular culture as has the last decade—and in no period has it been so difficult to discriminate between mere ideological parroting and art of real feeling and genuine intensity.

The mercury had already begun to fall at the start of the seventies, when two elements that had first emerged as the heralds of a new openness to pop culture in London in the fifties—serious attention to vulgar commercial design, and fascination with science-fiction fantasies—reappeared as portents of a darker sensibility, in the work of Robert Venturi and Robert Smithson. The architect and the sculptor both went west, to the region associated with freedom and renewal in American life, and both found there not vast possibility but a prophetic glimpse of a fixed and unvarying cultural order.

Venturi's *Learning from Las Vegas* appeared in 1972,[2] after the triumph of Pop, and for a little while its message was confused with that of Pop. Venturi seemed to reformulate the affections of artists such as Oldenburg—the love of colossal ducks and hot-dog stands that looked like hot dogs—into an official program for a new landscape of irreverently energetic architecture. But something crucial was lost in the translation. Venturi's seemingly warm embrace of pop culture in fact laid a chilly hand on its subject, and its spirit finally had less in common with the ardent gaze of Pop than with the benumbed, leveling stare of the Photo-Realist painting that followed Pop. Back in 1955, the creative spirits of the Independent Group—Reyner Banham, Richard Hamilton, and Peter and Allison Smithson—had singled out what they saw as the best in a globe-devouring wave of new commercial design, and had argued that its vitality might be a purposeful force in remaking contemporary society. Venturi focused, though, on peculiar backwaters of pop invention—the neon boomerangs of motel and casino signs—and reveled in their afunctional showiness much as Roland Barthes had delighted in professional

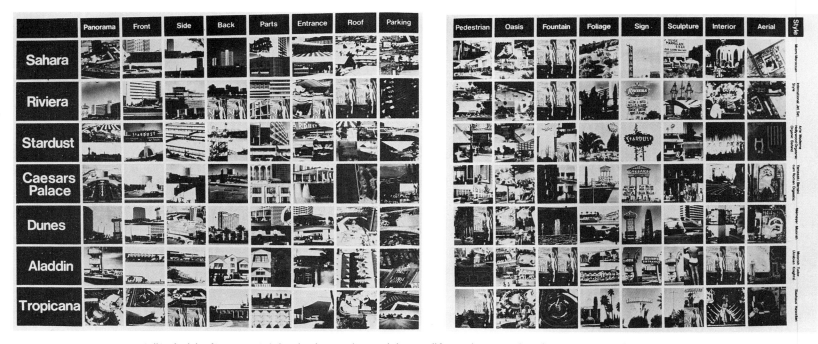

2. "A schedule of Las Vegas Strip hotels: plans, sections, and elements," from Robert Venturi, Denise Scott Brown, and Steven Izenour, *Learning from Las Vegas* (Cambridge, Mass., and London: MIT Press, 1972), pp. 38–39

wrestling: as a stereotyped dumbshow of signage to be clinically dissected (fig. 2). Venturi's *Learning from Las Vegas* was perhaps the first important book to champion pop culture in a spirit less of rebellion than of stoical resignation. It was the put-down of the Borscht Belt comedian offered as a philosophy of art: Hey, folks, these are the jokes. This strip, these bright lights, these signs, these big, decorated sheds and buildings shaped like ducks are ours, the real forms of American life as it is lived. One might use such forms—the pathetic colonnade of the "Monticello" house, the brick and stucco façade of a fire station—between clenched teeth, in a mode of vengeful irony, but they were in any case all there was to take the place of a delusional utopianism.

Where others had looked to low culture as a way to revivify the modern tradition, Venturi saw pop culture as modernism's polar alternative. Banham looked at Las Vegas in order to revive the root energies of Corbusier; Venturi looked at Las Vegas as a club with which to beat Corbusier to death. With the absolute displacement of the vernacular into a mode of irony came a new distance from it. A smoothed-out, academicized catalogue of interchangeable secondhand icons—today an arch, tomorrow a lawn jockey—began to take the place of the intense dialogue with the particulars of popular culture that had been the inheritance of Pop and the Independents.

If a newly pessimistic sensibility was coming into focus around the history of pop form, it required a visionary intensity to recast the heroic spirit of Minimalism and Pop as a form of nihilism. This was achieved in large part by the American sculptor Robert Smithson. Smithson's big, grim earthworks might seem to have been conceived at the farthest possible remove from the predicaments of popular culture. His *Spiral Jetty* (fig. 3) in the Great Salt Lake, made in 1969–70,

seemed to mark a total departure from the world of urban culture of any kind—that of the gallery and museum as well as that of the newsstand and billboard—and announced an oncoming decade of art that would be shaped by an apocalyptic primitivism, or by the austere antimaterialist attitudes of Conceptual art. But in fact Smithson explicitly linked his vision of cosmic collapse to his disaffected experience of pop culture. Minimalism for Smithson was not the style of standardized abundance that it had seemed to be for artists as diverse as Warhol and Ruscha. The impersonal severity of the "new monuments" of late sixties art was, Smithson thought, rooted in the dead zones of the city, and in bleak afternoons spent at seedy cinemas watching B-movies. Like the members of the Independent Group, Smithson loved lurid science fiction; but where Hamilton and his friends had loved these fantasies for their power-happy and sex-charged prophecies of the future, Smithson preferred another, gloomier vein of sci-fi, full of visions of apocalyptic desolation. Ironically, one of his favorite authors in this vein, J. G. Ballard, had been involved with the I.G. in the fifties. In Ballard's novels, the sign of an exhausted culture was not anarchic disorder but a gloomy and oppressive hyper-order.[3]

Smithson summed up his vision of modern life in a single word: *entropy*. The law of thermodynamics which insists that all physical systems devolve inexorably from organization into chaos, from states of heat and energy into cold immobility, seemed to him to apply to civilizations, too. The world grew cold, inanimate matter triumphing over the busy irregularities of life. For Smithson, the triumph of entropy was as certain a destiny for culture as it was for nature. The fate of the galaxy, it was also, by the early seventies, a fact about the rust-belt industrial New Jersey cities where Smithson had grown up. You didn't have to look at the edge of the universe to glimpse the god of entropy; you could see him already triumphant in Passaic. The commercial and industrial culture that had made modernity was, Smithson thought, running down. And he thought that the ruins of those factories and furnaces looked less pathetic, like the ruined monasteries of Romantic stage properties, than oddly majestic and timeless—Egyptian in their ceremonial solidity. Modernity, Smithson thought, having reached its apex of progress, was now moving backwards, and the monuments it would leave behind would be vast and charmless—blast furnaces that had turned into palaces of ice.

"Running out of gas...the fucking world is running out of gas." Thus begins John Updike's *Rabbit Is Rich*, his peerless evocation of the late 1970s. Smithson's melodramatic imagination seemed oddly to capture some general shared intuition about the evolution of American life in what seemed to be a new age of limits. For a generation of American artists who went to art school and began to do their own work in the sev-

3. **Robert Smithson.** *Spiral Jetty.* Rozel Point, Great Salt Lake, Utah, 1970. Mud, precipitated salt crystals, rocks, and water; coil 1,500' (457.2 m) long, 15' (457.2 cm) wide. Now submerged

enties, the poetic vision of Smithson's entropic art seemed affirmed by a general sense that all of American commercial culture had long passed its apex, and that the future promised largely scarcity, austerity, limits.[4]

Yet the moment Updike caught in amber turned out to be less an expiring exhalation than a deep breath before the next big rush. The next decade offered for the commercial life of America and Western Europe, and particularly for its art-making subculture, a period of prosperity and extravagance that had few precedents in modern history. And it was here that the rhetoric of entropy met the culture of overload. In the

past, the booms of commercial culture had played a crucial part in the cyclical inventions of modern art—a prod to keep the wheel in motion. The artist looked at a blossoming popular culture and then borrowed from it whatever he wanted for whatever private purpose he might have. But by the early eighties it was plain that this was no longer possible on the same terms that it had most often been in the past. The wheel in some ways was stuck. For it became apparent that a historical change, in process for several decades, had by the early eighties become an institutional fact. Modern art had become a kind of popular culture.

It was not that the boundary between high and low had been newly "blurred," in the sense of being muddied or obscured. That boundary had been blurred long ago—blurred because it was always in motion, and impossible to fix. It was precisely the blurring of the boundary, in fact, the constant, aggressive redefinition of where that line ought to fall, the endless series of purposeful transgressions and rescue operations and redefinitions, which had, from Goya to Guston, been one of the crucial acts that made modern art modern. Now, for the first time, modern art had become so institutionalized as a tradition and a practice—so entrenched and so popular, so sure of its moves and so inclined to repeat them, so confident in its audience and of its own continued triumphs in making modernity look Modern—that its engagement with the world around it would apparently no longer allow for the uncharted complexity, the immediacy, the individual eccentricity usually possible before. Relations between high and low became formalized, ponderous, and self-conscious, like the relations between two wary, heavily armed courts.

Though the list of important modern artists who had throughout the century been engaged in some way with popular culture is long and distinguished, hardly a single artist on that list had been engaged with pop culture in a way that depended on a self-conscious sense of "modern art" and "mass media," conceived as abstract terms. Léger, looking at the billboards in the place de Clichy, was involved not in a boundary dispute but in a land grab. He didn't think of the billboard as something outside modern art because he didn't have a fixed idea about what the boundaries of modern art were. This is ours, his art announced. Picasso looking at the newsstand and revue, Miró staring at the silverware catalogue, Lichtenstein looking at the comic book—that the things they absorbed belonged to popular culture was of course part of their significance, but the artists were drawn above all to the particular possibilities in these particular forms. Even Duchamp's jokes depended for their punch lines, as we've seen, on the singularities buried within what might have seemed, at first, to be generic objects—on the peculiar positioning of plumbing fixtures, for example, within an emerging tradition of window displays. And Pop art, for all of its digs at a solemn priestly caste of high seriousness, found its own mundane salvation in an almost absurdly obsessive engagement with the specific: Lichtenstein with his romance comics, Oldenburg looking at Mickey, Warhol and his little Olympus of Jackie and Marilyn and Liz.

Since ordinary life, at least as it was lived in the large urban centers where most American art got made and seen, now seemed in so many ways centered on the modern museum, it became hard to find a place for these singular imaginative transformations. It seemed increasingly that the life of American culture had become polarized into two rival citadels that, like medieval fortresses in wartime, pulled all their former dependencies inside—on one side, the devouring television cable box; on the other, the museum. And in the barren plain in between there was not much of anything. There might be a small independent subculture eking out life in a ditch or trench—comics culture or revival-house movie culture or the equivalent. But these things existed only as inheritors and unconscious parodists of the vanished life of the avant-garde. Robert Crumb writing and self-publishing the comic book *Weirdo* for a tiny, devoted audience was closer to the old spirit of the Bateau-Lavoir (however much this thought would have dismayed him) than was anyone in SoHo. For the most part, you chose between the little box or the big one, and it seemed at times that even the struggle between these two towers was a bit of a sham. As perhaps in all cold wars, the ideology of hostility increased in inverse proportion to the plain fact of coexistence.

By the early eighties, a new art had appeared which took up the old pop icons and methods in a new spirit of disaffection, and this art was supported by a rhetoric as vengeful and suspicious as any that modern art had previously directed at commercial culture. Something was conjured into being for the purposes of allowing artists to dissect and condemn it, and this was the "media image," an undifferentiated ribbon of undifferentiated imagery set down with purposeful affectlessness; Venturi's unmodulated strip seen through Smithson's entropic eye.

For one artist at least, David Salle, this vein of imagery seemed invested with a real core of feeling. Salle's subject was the leveling of experience. His art was in fact what Warhol's had been only in theory: a translation of television experience into paint. Warhol's art, for all the talk about its remote-control indifference, had nonetheless looked for its structure not to the television image, which sees each thing for a moment and passes on, but to the older reiterations of posters and pop songs and fan magazines. Salle depicted life as though the whole world had been programmed onto cable television at two in the morning. He showed a world where eroticism had become pornography, the vernacular had become banal, the painterly had become rote, and each one of these debased things sat equally beside all the others (figs. 4, 5). Girls with their panties around their knees shared diptychs with screwball rabbits; ghostly faces sat beside generic geometric abstractions; Jack Ruby's gun next to the glistening eyes of a Charles Keane child. Aside from the voyeuristic images of punk striptease sex that frequently recur like unfulfilled aches, there is no real esoteric private symbolism as there had been in the Rauschenberg combines from which the grammar of these paintings ultimately derived. Salle's purpose was not to kid the high or to champion the low, but to insist on their absolute equality. He was the first artist to paint T.V. experience in T.V. light—the life of the deep blue bedroom lit by the light of the dark blue box.

It seemed that one could find a life inside pop culture now only as a voyeur—or perhaps as a spy. Cindy Sherman took as her subject the secondary apparatus of celebrity culture—the movie still and the fan-magazine publicity shot—but instead of floating disembodied above it, like Salle, she sunk deep into it,

4. David Salle. *Muscular Paper.* 1985. Synthetic polymer paint and oil on canvas and printed fabric, 8′2″ × 15′7½″ (248.9 × 476.32 cm). Douglas S. Cramer Foundation

5. **David Salle.** *The Tulip Mania of Holland*. 1985. Oil on canvas, 11′ × 17′½″ (335.3 × 519.4 cm). The Carnegie Museum of Art, Pittsburgh; A. W. Mellon Acquisition Endowment Fund, 1986

until her own identity was lost in the set poses of secondhand life (figs. 6, 7). In some ways, Sherman's disguised self-portrait seemed to descend from Lichtenstein's ardent girls. Sherman had as subtle an eye as Lichtenstein for clichés that one had never before been conscious of—the first-day-in-the-big-city look, the smolderingly-sensual look, the full-of-trepidation-yet-still-determined look. She cast herself in these roles with a conviction that was a little frightening.

But where Lichtenstein had taken the little overlooked pop artifact and made it big and public, Sherman took the enlarged, overwhelming wide-screen image and made it little and fragile. She recognized that the stereotyped images in the fan magazine were empty vessels into which an uncertain self could constantly be poured and remade. Her work suggested, in its constant, mercurial redefinitions, the life of the celebrity, with its constant "stretches" and new beginnings. Where the taking on of a fake identity in the vanguard art of the past had, from Duchamp and Pica-

bia on, been a form of high style, or of camp, in Sherman's work it had a wistful tone that seemed to define the fan's life as much as the star's. The new sense that one could find one's own self only by losing it in the language of public spectacle, was, however melodramatic in its import and dubious in its truth, genuinely and chillingly felt in all of her early work. Yet the affectingly moody and melancholic art of Salle and Sherman and their lesser satellites was supported by a rhetoric totally out of proportion to its real core of feeling: a rhetoric that insisted not that this art could participate in and poeticize cable-box culture from a secure position of authority within another part of "media culture," but on its supposedly heroic ability to resist and "deconstruct" media culture altogether, in a spirit of beleaguered opposition. "Only by embracing the intensity of empty value at the core of mass-media representation and the fierce recycling of styles used to twist and pervert every intention," one curator wrote in explication of Salle's paintings, "only then can the

6. **Cindy Sherman.** Untitled Film Still #21. 1978. Black-and-white photograph, 8 × 10″ (20.3 × 25.4 cm), Courtesy Metro Pictures, New York

perennial challenge be met of finding and constructing significant meanings in the midst of declining values for images and words."[5]

Yet what was this mass-media image? Where was it? It didn't seem to include the poses and imagery of pop music—the album covers and promotional videos—on which artists drew for inspiration and as a model of life; it couldn't really be found in the movies, which by 1980 provided for most educated people a tradition of artistic heroism at least as potent and complex as that of the vanguard art tradition. It certainly couldn't be found in the enormous world of reproductions and museum catalogues and glossy magazines

and books through which this new art was made public.

If you actually looked at the work of Salle or Sherman (or of Robert Longo or Richard Prince), it became plain that the "media imagery" in their work derived from those marginal parts of popular culture which the museum had not yet annexed. The intensely empty mass-media representation which only art could repel turned out to be, for all the belligerent rhetoric, a handful of television cartoons, some old images of soft-core porn, the memory of television sitcoms of the fifties, and some movie stills. In the galleries of the eighties, one sometimes had the sense of seeing the

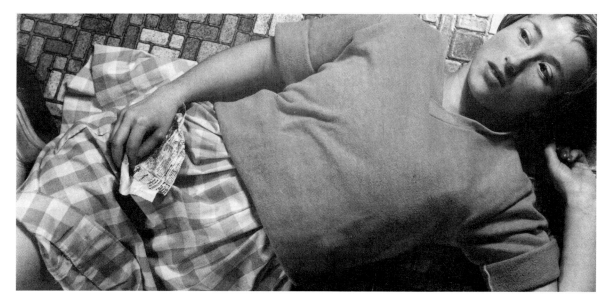

7. **Cindy Sherman.** Untitled. 1981. Color-coupler print, 23⅞ × 48⅛″ (60.6 × 122.2 cm). The Museum of Modern Art, New York. Gift of Carl D. Lobell

most privileged fine-art culture that human history had ever known arrayed in grandeur to perform an *auto-da-fé* upon Judy Jetson and Patty Duke.

In any case, to "deconstruct" (the philosopher's term had sometime early in the eighties lost its original, technical meaning in arguments about the relationship between texts and meanings and become a voguish synonym for "reveal") the manipulative structures of media imagery required no great originality. "Expose the technology" was the new motto of American advertising: take apart your own story before the consumer does it for you. In the age of Joe Isuzu, a hardened knowingness about the value-emptied amorality of media culture, was, far from being the preserve of a small cadre of vanguard thinkers, the sour, commonplace cynicism of the whole commercial culture.

The vision of mass-media culture that occurred in "media art" was therefore selective: it reflected, as much as it opposed, the popular culture around it—which is to say only that it was like all the previous art that we have looked at. But now there was something disingenuous about the difference between the way the art worked and the way it was presented. An element of Beaux-Arts unreality had entered the discussion. The comedy of Pop had depended on the gleeful recognition of a puritanically repressed truth. The low world, good or bad, was one of the worlds we lived in, and to deny it—not to see its punning and parodic and ironic relationships with the world of high art—was to deny facts about the world. The spirit of media art, on the other hand, was itself puritanical, and replaced the comedy of reconciliation with a fiction of disdainful distance.

"Cant," William Hazlitt wrote once, "is the voluntary overcharging or prolongation of a real sentiment; hypocrisy is the setting up of a pretension to a feeling you never had and have no wish for."[6] If the art of the media image was occasionally and perhaps necessarily touched by a kind of cant, an overcharging of a melancholy that these artists could often only affect to feel, the rhetoric that surrounded it was often just hypocritical. Popular culture—the world of the "mass-media representation"—was one that modern art had helped to make. Determining in advance, against the open and anxious example of the modern tradition, that the mass image was deadening and poisonous, the apostles of the new art replaced the inquisitive ardor of the vanguard with the inquisitorial moralizing of academic art. The genuinely "fierce recyclings" of the modern tradition, the alchemy by which the structures of ordinary life were reimagined as art, began to be replaced by a set of in-house revivals—recyclings that began and ended within the museum itself. The art of the media image staked its claim to radical newness on its insistence that it had replaced the delusional purity of high modernism with a disillusioned and unsentimental impurity. But the revolt against "purity" (to the degree that purity had ever actually been held up as an ideal by working artists) had taken place in painting al-

most a quarter century before. As a consequence, the new art could only repeat the strategies and formats of Johns and Rauschenberg and the Pop painters—the assemblage of secondhand images on an epic scale, the deadpan scrutiny of the found thing—and add to them a melodramatic rhetoric of darkened backgrounds and rigid, entropic patterning. In architecture, postmodernism had an undeniable core of things to point at that set it apart from modernism: look at that arch, that Chippendale top, that neoclassical façade. "Postmodern" painting too often was just a familiar kind of modern painting with the brightness knob turned down.

The media image turned out to be as meaningless in the 1980s as the unconscious image had been in the 1930s. In both cases, what promised to be a brave journey into the dark, nether reaches of collective consciousness too often came back with a set of generalized effects and tepid stage properties that had belonged to art all along. In fact, the painting of Salle or Longo, in its weaker moments, looked like nothing so much as the illustrational side of Surrealism: the same black backgrounds and spectral figures, and the same atmosphere of slick, airless pessimism. Secondhand imagery turned out to be no more automatically interesting in art than the dream world had been; the art of the media image too often suggested less the jumpy discontinuities of the electronic box than it did the droning, cheerless didacticism of a salon machine.

If it was no longer credible for a heroic dissenting art to be made from the materials of mass-produced culture, by the early eighties many people felt that a heroically subversive art might still be made from the materials of the street. By then only the very rich among New Yorkers could ignore the ubiquity of a new underground visual culture, which seemed to be rising like a red tide to cover public space: the spray-can art of the graffiti writers.

Graffiti was everywhere. Bleary-eyed commuters waiting for the Number One local at Times Square at eight-thirty in the morning would find the arriving train encrusted from top to bottom with a mad pattern of glittering webs and ballooning letters. Although you knew, in a general way, that what you were seeing was a form of writing—calligraphy—it was hard to read, and left an overwhelming impression, all the more vivid for appearing in such dark and squalid surroundings, of screaming color and ecstatic form.

Inside the cars, of course, the graffiti was a lot less pleasing: a tangle of illegible names scribbled in Magic Marker and spray paint. Although every subway rider knew, in a general way, that this stuff had begun only a few years before and had to be made by particular artists, something about it seemed outside history. It was as though the graffiti had always been there underneath the paint and varnish of the cars and, now that the necessary restraining civic energy had been lost, had just inevitably seeped out into the surfaces of things. To many people, graffiti seemed less an expression of a will to form than the expression of the loss of any will to prevent it.[7]

Subway graffiti, in fact, was modernism made into a folk culture. It was the expression of an independent group of makers who set themselves off from their own society, and began a highly structured competition to one-up the last man through the shock of a new style. The subway writers absorbed what had become by the late seventies the commonplaces of modernism as they had permeated the entire culture—the faith in the glory of individual innovation, the insistence on a fiercely competitive battle of new styles, the sense that the entire history of art, high and low, should be ransacked and recycled and made one's own signature style. The explicit goal of each subway graffiti artist was one that a medieval craftsman, surreptitiously carving obscenities into the back of a choir stall, would have found incomprehensibly daring; it was one that any of Lombroso's criminals, with their desultory scrawls, would have found incomprehensibly constructive. But it was something that Picasso would have understood immediately: it was, simply, to focus your sexual and competitive and form-making energies on the self-sufficient goal of becoming the King of Style.

Although New York walls had, of course, long been covered with graffiti, a new kind of street writing began only in 1970, when a young messenger named Taki decided to put up his "tag"—his own name plus the number of the street on which he lived—on the streets of the Upper West Side neighborhoods he visited: TAKI 183. This was, in some respects, a new kind of graffiti. Its aim was to draw attention to itself as the work of an individual. There is some evidence to suggest that Taki was an unconscious innovator; apparently in his neighborhood, everybody put their names up all the time. But what was commonplace in one neighborhood in Manhattan was daringly original in another, and within months Taki's little gesture had spawned a whole school of imitators.

The sheer density of "tags" on walls and, soon, subway cars made it necessary for each writer to think of a way to make his name stand out from all the others. The answer was style. The name would no longer have to be read; it could just be seen at a glance and its distinctive pattern and color recognized as the signature style of one teenager among all the millions in the city. Then, the writers discovered spray paint. They would "rack" spray cans from art-supply stores. (Eventually, the art-supply stores, overwhelmed by the thefts, just stopped stocking it.) The writers' favorite brands were Rustoleum, Red Devil, Wet Look, and Krylon. With a "fat cap" (a wide nozzle taken from a household spray cleaner) attached to the can, the writers could now think of decorating a sixty-foot-long and twelve-foot-high New York subway car.

The impulse that amplified graffiti from little mark to big balloon, though it obviously involved elements of mischief and minor delinquency, was not simply the expression of an urge to hurt and damage a larger civic culture which the graffiti writer felt had neglected him. Its origins were much more local than that, and more constructive. By the late seventies, the youth-gang culture that had been a permanent feature of New York life since the nineteenth century had become so heavily armed and so feudally entrenched that it left its adherents immobile. A gang member could not be safe outside the few small blocks that his group protected. Against this, the new graffiti writers declared themselves free to move. Their (stolen) spray cans, clipped to their belts, were symbols that they were unaffiliated with any of the warring gangs and that they expected to be considered as neutrals. Because the gang hierarchies were, on the whole, amused and interested in the graffiti writer's work, the writers were usually allowed to pass.

And the city opened up to them. Instead of being pinned in as tightly as serfs to the fiefdoms of the gangs, they could travel anywhere in the five boroughs, making connections between Ocean Park and the South Bronx. The New York subway, which for everyone else had become a symbol of everything decayed and intolerable in the city, became for the graffiti artists a railway to freedom. The express lines that connected one end of the huge city to the other, particularly the Number Five and Four I.R.T. expresses, became for them at once canvas and café and gallery. The blossoming of graffiti was in no sense an expression of the gang culture; it was a rebellion against it.

Graffiti painting went on almost exclusively "in the yards" at night. Its evolution was rapid and focused. Far from being made in a state of existential rage, it was painstakingly considered and sweetly respectable in its ambitions. The graffiti artists would begin with a preparatory sketch drawn in ink in a black notebook. They called this sketch an "original outline" and would spend a very long time getting it right. The elements of these designs were taken over from commercial illustration, from the comics, and, on many occasions, from the high-art sources that by the early seventies had become part of the commonplace language of visual expression (fig. 8). Breaking into the train yards at night, each writer would begin work on his "piece"— short for "masterpiece." First, the original outline would be copied from the notebook in light paint. Then ornamentation would be "faded" in on top of the outline, and finally a second, permanent outline would be laid down over the clouds of fresh paint. It took about eight hours to complete each piece. The ambition was not to scrawl one's name in defiant letters against the cruel and unyielding machinery of an oppressive culture but to somehow manage to finish one's pre-planned design in time for the next day's viewing—a spirit more like varnishing day at the Royal Academy than like anything out of William Burroughs.

Graffiti "art" was structured by two contradictory urges: to "get up" as often as possible—to leave your tag, or pen name, on as many subway cars as you could; and to get up with style—to "make a burner," something that was undeniably a stylistic advance on

8. New York City subway cars with *Soup Cans* by **Lee and Fred**. 1980. Composite photograph by Henry Chalfant

everything that had come before. These advances could take the form of new illusionistic effects—for instance, making simple block letters into "3-D" letters. Or they could take the form of new illustrational ornamentation, for example, adding an icon—the Wizard of Id, the comic-strip character Dondi—to one's own name as part of the tag. An argument about style went on every night in the yards. There were purists, who insisted that the name itself was what mattered. There were minimalists, who favored big silver and gray block letters that stretched from top to bottom of the car and had a blockbuster, impersonal weight. There were colorists, for whom a particular palette of Krylon was as meaningful a signature style as a written name. There were even archaists who kept alive the styles that had been abandoned six months before.

Still one more tension built into graffiti was that between the desire to be "King of the Line" and "King of Style"—between the desire to be the writer who got up most often and to be the writer who got up most beautifully. Speed and style were kept in dialogue, and much of the quality of the work depended on this tension.

Subway graffiti followed the path of individual innovators. The names of the first writers to make an advance were—and still are—recalled and honored by the writers who came after them: Hondo, who made the first top-to-bottom; the Fabulous Five, led by Lee, who made the first "whole train." In the wake of these innovators, the style did follow a general evolutionary path: from simple, scrawled letters, to 3-D letters, to "bubble" letters (in which the accentuated curves and infantile blobs of Disney cartooning were adapted), and, finally, into high "wildstyle," a tense, enfolding web of letters, to which, in certain virtuoso pieces, was sometimes added a complex illusionistic background —crumbling stone walls or exploding buildings. (Each graffiti writer was expected to recapitulate the history of graffiti style in his own evolution as a writer.)

It was on wildstyle that the graffiti writers' claim to real originality as decorative calligraphers—as illuminators—depends. The best of the wildstyle cars were made in a relatively short period in the late seventies and early eighties, and its most original practitioners were A-One, Shy and Kel, Daze, Seen, and Lee (figs. 9, 10). Beginning as a "linking" style, with the letters of the writer's tag overlapping and intertwined, wildstyle quickly developed into a style in which the letters were

collapsed, beyond all understanding, into a hypnotic labyrinth of gaudy and maniacally congested bubbles, a style that recalled and in many ways equaled the maddest excesses of Barcelona *modernista* ornament—the balconies on the Casa Milá imagined in the colors of Walt Disney. The great conundrum of American art since the fifties—how to make a signature emerge from a sign—took on in wildstyle a speeded-up, tasteless imperative which, oddly and touchingly, finally evolved into a form that recalled the most elaborate decorative language of the *fin de siècle*.

The city had always discouraged the subway graffiti writers, but usually in a fairly benign, Our Gang Meets the Truant Officer spirit. But by the early 1980s the Metropolitan Transit Authority, under a new director, had decided to make the elimination of graffiti a priority. The M.T.A.'s reasons were understandable, even indisputable. Whatever the case that might be made for the work of the best of the writers as art, the interiors of the New York subway cars, littered with the tags thrown up by "toys" (young kids and beginners), were just squalid. They suggested a city out of control, in which the most basic premises of civility had been surrendered. The graffiti writers were probably the last people in New York to have romantic notions about the subway, but, however much one admired the writers and their best work, the point was that the subways did belong to the people, and what the people wanted was a tranquil and ordered civic environment. It is hard but necessary to see both that subway graffiti may have been an authentically living art and that the Transit Authority may have been behaving in an authentically democratic spirit in suppressing it.

The graffiti artists saw in their work the same spirit of modern optimism that Léger had found in the billboard: a summons out of the cramped tenement and away from the addiction of indoor overlord culture, into the free world of common public spectacle. Their writings and declarations—indeed, the whole enterprise—were, in every sense, public-spirited. Graffiti art was played out on a public stage that embodied the widest possible contradictions of modern New York life—private initiative and public squalor, individual freedom and communal brutality. The structure that the museum or gallery could provide when graffiti art began to go indoors was by comparison extraordinarily impoverished. When you have had the Number Six line as your daily exhibition space, even a SoHo gallery

9. New York City subway cars with graffiti; top to bottom: *Dusty Shadow*, 1982; *A-One Steph*, 1983; *Nod Tech Daze*, 1980. Composite photograph by Henry Chalfant

10. New York City subway cars with *Style Wars* by **NOC**. Composite photograph by Henry Chalfant

looks like small stuff. In the past, street graffiti had been an unstructured scrawl that offered itself up for individual transformation—a vocabulary in search of a grammar. Subway graffiti, by comparison, offered an extraordinarily rich context from which to derive meaning and a restricted decorative vocabulary from which to make art.

By the early eighties, a few more conventionally ambitious artists had already begun to penetrate the graffiti world. During the high period of wildstyle top-to-bottoms, the art-school-trained Keith Haring also began to draw his signature simple outline figures in the subways (figs. 11, 12). Although these figures had, especially at the beginning, a cryptic fascination, they derived from a conventional vocabulary of "primitive" *faux-naïf* drawing that couldn't have been more distant from the Alhambra-like decorative intensity of the work of A-One and Seen. The career of Jean-Michel Basquiat is more complicated. Basquiat had actually taken part in subway art, where he had used the tag of Samo. Yet Basquiat's paintings (fig. 13) seem more closely aligned to the international style of Neo-Expressionism than they do to the real stylistic innovations of the writers. And for all that it suited people to see the new graffiti as a form of folk expressionism, subway art, with its small vocabulary of secondhand commercial-design elements, endlessly expanded and elaborated and embroidered, could not have been more inhospitable to the free, unmediated gestures and lumpy rhetoric of expressionism. The "modernity" of subway art resided in its faith that pure abstract pattern, allied to a fierce competitive energy and an accelerated search for the new, could itself be a self-sufficient form of expression. The expressive energies of subway graffiti were tightly coiled within a strict language of original outlines; Basquiat's painting, by com-

11. **Keith Haring.** Subway drawing. 1982. Photograph by Tseng Kwong Chi

12. **Keith Haring.** Untitled. 1982. Vinyl ink on vinyl tarp, 10 × 10′ (304.8 × 304.8 cm). Collection Ara Arslanian, New York

parison, looked to a much older and looser and more generalized European tradition of freehand gesture.

The problem with Basquiat wasn't that he could never surpass graffiti style but that he never really ad-

dressed it. Perhaps Basquiat ought to have been a great painter—surely all the ingredients for an intensely personal style, at once enriched by the energies of the street and informed by the modern tradition, seemed available at that moment to an ambitious and fearless artist—and for some people he will always remain one. But no matter how eager one is to embrace the paintings and their tragic maker, there remains a sense that his art belongs less to the particular and extraordinary experience of subway art than to the beiged-out Neo-Expressionist rhetoric of acceptable gestures that had become by the mid-eighties an all-purpose dealer's broadloom, bought and sold by the yard. His paintings finally evoke less the trip on the Number Five line to Pelham than the airless Lufthansa flight, shuttling between SoHo and Documenta.

13. Jean-Michel Basquiat. Untitled. 1984. Oilstick, synthetic polymer paint, and collage on canvas, 66¼ × 60″ (168.3 × 152.4 cm). Collection Dr. David Ramsay, New York

14. New York City subway cars with *What Is Art? Why Is Art?* by **Freedom**. 1983. Composite photograph by Henry Chalfant

By the end of the eighties, graffiti had entirely disappeared from the New York subways. (The M.T.A. held a celebration to mark the passing of the last graffiti-ridden car out of service.) By then, of course, subway art existed only as a style, much prized by European collectors. The complicated story of burners and style wars exists now only in a handful of documentary images, and in the memories of the New Yorkers who experienced them.

In December 1979, a graffiti writer put up one night, as a "window-down whole car," a carefully rendered image of the central icon of Western art—Michelangelo's God the Father reaching out to touch the hand of Adam (fig. 14). Beside it he wrote, WHAT IS ART? WHY IS ART? The questions provide a quiet chorus to any attempt to answer the more peevish and ordinary question that we ask about subway graffiti: Is it (was it) art? For if by art we mean something that extends an accepted tradition of icons and images, and restates the inherited beliefs of our culture, then, no, of course it wasn't art. But if by art we mean, as we have for more than a century, a self-propelled and self-generating competition in style, a serious game that begins as an in-group game that gives meaning to the life of the maker and to his enthralled small audience, and ends by producing a new and widely shared style—well, then, of course it was art. A minor, decorative art, perhaps, no greater than that of an ordinary medieval illuminator or a Bauhaus typographic designer. But no smaller, either.

The problem, of course, is that by now we really want the concept of "art" to mean both things. We want art to remain a private, uncompromised competition in style and at the same time to become the core of an ideal of civic life. We want art to belong both to its makers and to a common culture—to be marginal and central at the same time. We want the King of Style also to be the King of our particular line. The graffiti writers could not achieve this easily, or at all, but then who could?

In the end, subway graffiti mattered less for what it "contributed" to high art than for what it said about it. Graffiti at the beginning of the century had been seen as a series of scrawls that nobody (aside from a handful of archeologists) thought had any meaningful struc-

ture at all. It required the then disruptive new vision of modernist art to make these outsider wall markings seem significant. As the end of the century approached, that once disruptive vision had become so deeply entrenched that it could imprint its own peculiar shape even on the way people drew marks on walls, or on the sides of subway cars. The insistence on the artist's privileged place, on his self-definition through his participation in a restless, competitive struggle for innovation, and on his right to inconvenience a bourgeois audience in his search for authenticity—those beliefs, taken up without irony or cynicism, were what made subway art different from all the other graffiti that had preceded it. When the subway writer A-One once explained why his work was art, not vandalism, he memorialized, perhaps for the last time, an uncritical faith in this uniquely modernist idea of achievement. "A vandal is someone who throws a brick through a window," he said. "An artist is someone who paints a picture on the window. A great artist is someone who paints a picture on the window and then throws a brick through it."[8]

One of the elements in late-period wildstyle subway graffiti had been a new form of cartoon figuration. In the original subway cars, these cartoon heralds functioned a little like saints' attributes in Renaissance painting; rather than taking part in any story, they were present just to identify the writer. The most common of these characters, the big-eyed waif Dondi, was taken from the obscure work of Vaughn Bodé, a largely forgotten cartoonist whose comic strip had flourished in the forties and fifties, and which, for some still unexplained reason, was revived by the graffiti writers. The comic-strip characters one might have expected to appear—the superheroes of the new wave of "dark" comic books for instance—were almost invisible in subway graffiti, while Mickey Mouse and Donald Duck appeared all the time. Nevertheless, the cartoon figures on the subway cars gave license to a new wave of cartoon art that soon became one of the signature styles of the East Village art galleries and artists' co-ops that flourished briefly in New York in the early 1980s. The most famous representative of this brief moment was Kenny Scharf (fig. 15), although it also included

15. Kenny Scharf. *Elroy Mandala II.* 1982. Synthetic polymer paint on canvas, 60 × 60" (152.4 × 152.4 cm). Private collection

the painters Peter Saul (fig. 16), Nicholas Moufaregge, and several others. Theirs was a form of cartoon art that only occasionally looked all the way back to the high period of the comics. Instead, it took for its favorite subject and stylistic influence the imagery of the animated prime-time cartoon programs that the Hanna-Barbera company had produced in the early 1960s: *The Jetsons* and *The Flintstones*. These cartoons rendered the stereotypes of American middle-class life as timeless verities, true to the stone age and space age alike—Smithson's gloomy sense that the

very old and the very new are more or less the same, imagined in sitcom terms. Guston was sometimes claimed as a forefather, but in fact the new cartoon style descended from the Chicago school of cartoon artist who took the collective name of the Hairy Who.

Although they had received fitful attention during the heyday of Pop, the spirit of the Hairy Who wasn't that of Warhol or Lichtenstein by a mile. Instead of bringing into play two different styles, high and low, and then evaluating both by their punning superimposition, the Chicago painters—Jim Nutt and Roger Brown (fig. 17) in particular—were essentially aggressively *faux-naïf* urban cartoonists who liked to work big. They offered a slapdash, high-spirited form of illustration that, like the contemporaneous work of Red Grooms, used a hepped-up style to suggest the "delir-

17. Roger Brown. *Modern, Post-Modern?* 1982. Oil on canvas, 6' × 48" (182.9 × 121.9 cm) Courtesy Phyllis Kind Gallery, New York

ium" of modern urban life—close to Carl Sandburg in their forced, energetic pace, and also in their slightly hyped-up promotion of anti-international American vernacular style.

For many fanciers of cartoon style, the inheritance of the Chicago School was far truer and more authentic than what were perceived as the condescending and cerebral appropriations of Pop. From this point of view, the flourishing East Village cartoon painting of the eighties, with its joining of the Chicago School vision of the cartoon to the permanent rictus of postmodern irony, represented a high point in the dialogue between modern painting and the comics.[9] Yet many other people with no axe to grind against popular imagery in art thought that the problem with this paint-

16. Peter Saul. *Donald Duck Descending a Staircase.* 1979. Synthetic polymer paint on canvas, 6'6" × 52¾" (198.1 × 134 cm). Courtesy Fischer Fine Art, London

ing was that it was made in a vacuum of other visual experience. All previous cartoon art had set up the comic book and vanguard painting as two poles and created an electric field between them. The new painters made their art at one end of the field, and as a result their art had little magnetism. The new cartoon painters chose the cartoon not because it was curiously allied or disturbingly opposed to high aesthetic experience, but because it was just about all the aesthetic experience they had. Their compositional ideas tended to be limited to incongruous juxtapositions or parodies of religious art, as in Scharf's *Elroy Mandala II* (fig. 15).

The work was puerile. On occasions it could become interestingly puerile. For, within this puerility was a new common emotion—a desire to replace the old Romantic/modernist dream of returning to childhood with a new dream of returning to adolescence. Lichtenstein and Oldenburg had retained much of the Baudelairean dandy's attitude toward street style. They had invented a cult of images, which they had scrutinized until their originally inarticulate liking for these things began to reveal new kinds of meaning and symbolic significance. But they had added to the dandy's part the part of the child, the eye too innocent and eager to exclude anything. Warhol, for his part, fulfilled the old modern dream of the absolute, unprejudiced innocent to a greater degree than had any other modern artist, and showed it to be a colder and more sinister dream than anyone had imagined. But the East Village cartoon artists saw cartoons as twelve-year-old boys see them on Saturday mornings—with a certain thin, supercilious irony, knowing perfectly well that this is infantile entertainment but still over-

19. Cover of *Read Yourself Raw,* ed. Art Spiegelman and Françoise Mouly (New York: Pantheon Books, 1987)

whelmed by the panicky desire to sink back into its bright certainties. Their paintings seemed neither defiant nor innocent; they held in solution instead an odd mixture of the tender and the contemptuous, a sense that the best thing in life would be to remain forever twelve. (The paradise from which Americans were expelled was now not the nursery but the den.) Lichtenstein, looking at feeble and undernourished comics, had discovered in them complicated jokes and puns. Scharf and Saul, looking at highly sophisticated cartoons, could not find in them anything except what one already knew to be there: simple drawing, a lot of bright colors, and some jokes about the American desire to see its surfaces as timeless and almost divinely ordained.

If you were going to make cartoons from cartoons, why bother with "art" at all? If the old orders of art were dead, then why not just take up the comics as the living form they were, and deepen and enlarge them? Perhaps the future lay with the comics as comics. This decent and constructive intuition was at the heart of the remarkable New York underground journal *Raw* (fig. 19), edited by the cartoonists Art Spiegelman and Françoise Mouly. Although *Raw* included the work of artists who had at least a foot in the gallery world, among them Sue Coe and Gary Panter, its essential ambition was to revive the cartoon as a serious form—an ambition self-consciously modeled on the turn-of-the-century caricature journals. Spiegelman's own masterful *Maus* (fig. 18) was a profound retelling

18. **Art Spiegelman.** Panels from "Mauschwitz," chapter 7 of *Maus: A Survivor's Tale*, published as an insert to *Raw*, no. 8 (1986), p. 172

of his father's memories of the Holocaust. *Maus* used comic-book style as a way of making horror more immediate by distancing it. Spiegelman tried to find a stylized, ritual language that would suggest the almost sacred nature of the material—the sense that the story of the Holocaust contained within it some fundamental, irreducible kernel of truth about the human soul—without seeming to aestheticize horror. With all Jews drawn as mice, and Germans as cats, *Maus* managed to suggest both the human hopes and fears and endless schemes for escape of the Jews in Europe, and their foreordained doom at the hands of a brute predatory instinct. Painfully truthful both about the great tragedy of the past and its inability to dissipate the small generational impatience of the present, *Maus* was perhaps the single greatest achievement of the comics in the past twenty years.[10] But as the decade wore on it became more and more plain that it was as singular an achievement as Crumb's. Although much of the drawing in *Raw* had considerable graphic power, and was never less than sincere, intense, and original, the magazine could not entirely escape the pervasive sense of the secondhand—of styles recycled less out of a sudden imaginative insight than in a helpless resignation—that burdened the gallery's version of cartoon art, too.

In the early 1980s, a very different imaginative transformation of the comic tradition, made by an older artist out of the intellectual and physical materials of an older idea of painting, also appeared in American art. Elizabeth Murray's first experience of art was her experience of the comics. As a little girl she drew Dagwood and Dick Tracy and the Disney characters. Their forms—the accentuated curve, the exaggerated comic proportions of thinned-out limbs and expanded appendages, Dagwood's shoes and Mickey's glove—all entered her mind by way of her hand. They were for her neither the deadening forms of mass media nor yet the nostalgically recuperated forms of childhood. They were just a way of drawing.

In art school in Chicago in the fifties, Murray discovered American abstraction. De Kooning and Pollock amazed her, and she chose as an almost religious vocation the difficult and austere path of modernist art. When Pop appeared, it had the force of a call from home. From Warhol she took what was perhaps the most far-reaching and easily overlooked part of his inheritance: his American palette, all bright make-up and Day-Glo colors. Yet Pop for her, more than a style to learn from, was a series of permissions, injunctions even, to look at life whole. The importance of Pop for her was to lead her back to James Joyce and Jasper Johns. In *Ulysses* she encountered, instead of the austere difficulty that she been led to expect, an exclaiming joy in the epic intensity of everyday life. "I expected something distant, and it turned out to be about taking kidneys and newspaper ads and making it into *The Odyssey*," she has said. "It was about the epic power of dailiness, and about the tension between what you

experienced right this second and everything that everybody else had experienced all along."[11]

From Johns, with whose art she remains obsessed, she took a similar lesson. For in his art she recognized a laconic, American translation of Joyce's expansive connectiveness. If Pop played a liberating role for her imagination, in many ways the bright, shaped canvases of domestic subjects—coffee cups and shoes and squalling children—that made her reputation in the eighties descend directly from Johns's painting of the fifties: the refined and dense painterly surface, taking intense pleasure in its own mute, primary thingness, always just on the verge of joining the secondary world of signs—things that stand for other things. The banal image—the coffee cup, or flag—releases the artist back into the primary act of painting, and the primary act of painting ends by breathing new life into the banal image.

By the late seventies, Murray felt free, at last, to return to her painting the cartoon draftsmanship that came so readily to her and that she had always before censored from her hand. Pop brought her back to Johns and Joyce, and Johns and Joyce allowed her to repossess Chester Gould. Her work seems so entirely fresh and unpremeditated that it is surprising to realize how often Murray has looked to old comics as a template of poetic drawing (figs. 20–23). Her bright, asymmetrical canvases—for all that they can be enjoyed in terms of purely abstract, high-volume argument between form and ornament, between booming relief and the startled, high, bright apple-and-orange cry of the painted surface—again and again have at their starting point a remembered cartoon image. Her animated kitchen table, alive on spaghetti legs, recalls Winsor McCay, while her most recent repeated format, the upright, foreshortened shoe (fig. 21), derives directly from the shoes that Dagwood wears in *Blondie*. The borrowed and transformed image of Dagwood's shoe released in turn for her a set of associations about her own father's business troubles, which for her as a girl were symbolized by the brave, heavy shoes he wore as he pounded the pavement through the Depression, looking for work.

The way that secondhand form can release primary emotion is the subject at the heart of all Murray's cartoon paintings. The contoured cloud of steam that rises from the coffee cup, the big distended shoe, the dialogue balloon—Murray's work suggests not that these things are the clichés into which the mass media have corralled individual experience, but, rather, that only through a love of these things as a common poetic shorthand can one begin to see the things themselves for what they are. The beautiful ordinariness of familiar things can be captured only in a beautifully familiar style; our husbands and children and the breaking cup at breakfast came to us first as the Sunday funnies, our father's shoes appeared first on Dagwood's feet. The slightly retro look of Murray's style can be associated with Guston, and with Crumb; but her love for the Depression style of her childhood

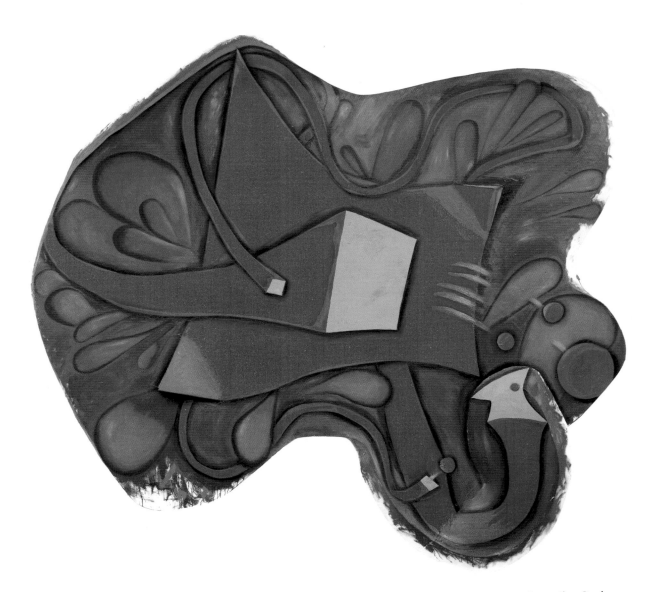

20. **Elizabeth Murray.** *96 Tears.* 1986–87. Oil on canvas, 10′ × 10′9¾″ × 18″ (304.8 × 329.6 × 45.7 cm). The Pacesetter Corporation, Omaha

21. **Elizabeth Murray.** *Tomorrow.* 1988. Oil on canvas; two panels, overall, 9′3″ × 11′3¾″ × 21½″ (218.9 × 337.2 × 54.6 cm). Collection The Fukuoka City Bank, Ltd.

memories is essentially a way to comically cross-reference her life.

Murray is drawn to the cartoon because it registers both the ordinary thing and the ordinary way of seeing it. It is a "seen before" style for things whose claim on our imagination lies precisely in their having been seen so many times before. Hers is the art of a poet struggling to take experience whole, kitchen tables and picture planes together; an art in which remorse for a parent takes the form of a remembered comic image.

> The desert sighs in the cupboard
> The glacier knocks in the bed
> And a crack in the tea-cup opens
> A lane to the land of the dead.[12]

More than any American painter's since Guston, Murray's work takes for its subject the dialogue between low, secondhand form and acute little sensations. Yet for Guston that tension was still imagined in heroic, Old Testament terms: a struggle between

22. **Elizabeth Murray.** *Just in Time.* 1981. Oil on canvas; two panels, overall 8'10½″ × 8'1″ (270.5 × 246.4 cm). Philadelphia Museum of Art. Purchase: The Edward and Althea Budd Fund, Adele Haas Turner and Beatrice Pastorius Turner Fund and funds contributed by Marion Stroud Swingle and Lorine E. Vogt

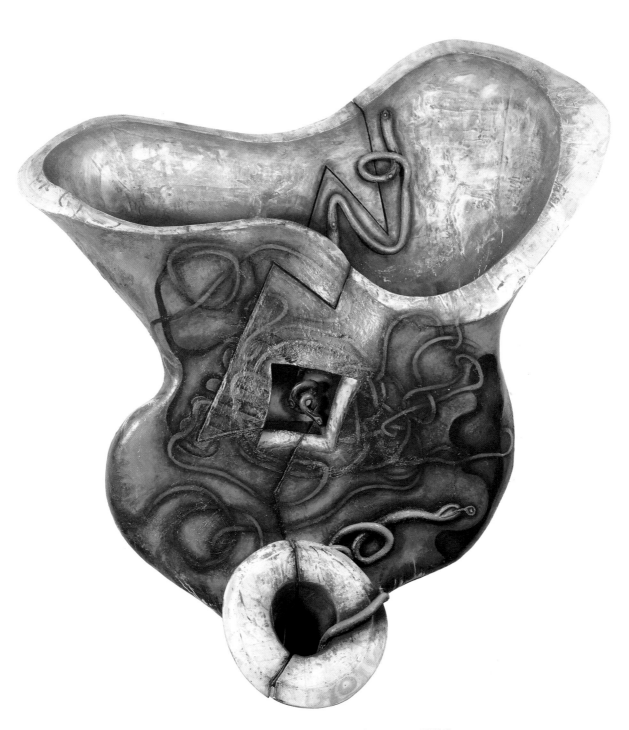

23. **Elizabeth Murray**. *Labyrinth*. 1989. Oil on canvas, 8'10½" × 8'3½" × 27" (270.5 × 252.7 × 68.6 cm). Courtesy Paula Cooper Gallery, New York

damnation and impassioned clay, between images of failure and comic defeat and a dream of painting as still potentially tragic and timeless. Each nail and shoe in Guston's work has the tremulous, almost hysterical edge of an old man's iconoclasm, like the argument of an aging apostate in an old radicals' home. In Murray's work, the dialogue is quieter, and at the same time at least as profound. Less concerned with the rhetorical battles, the arguments between the figural and the flat, in which an older generation had invested an al-

most Talmudic energy, her work rests unselfconsciously on an apprehension of immediate experience seen through unpretentious form. Though it participates completely in the great symposium about secondhand culture and primary experience that is the obsession of our time, Murray's work is completely without hypocrisy or cant, and paints a recognizable picture of bourgeois life—the world seen by the *femme moyenne sensuelle* at the end of the twentieth century. Nor is the change of gender in the phrase unimportant, for there is, in a radical, affirmative sense, something feminine (and feminist) in all of her work. It is the feminism of the women Impressionists, insisting that domestic experience is as heroic a subject as any other. Murray can now present this theme less as mute afternoon emotion than as high morning comedy, Mary Cassatt reinterpreted by Roz Chast. In the tradition of Matisse, she has managed to take comfort as a subject without succumbing to complacency as a theme.

By the middle of the 1980s, the essential conundrum of the media age—how could you make an art that scrutinized pop culture when the artist was at least as enmeshed in the mass media as the imagery he pretended to scrutinize?—had begun to provoke a new response, one that would be ingenious, honest, sometimes comically and charmingly candid, and almost always hair-raisingly cynical. Stripped of any pretenses to heroic individual style, the new art would insist that all that was possible now was a flat recycling of imagery and style from degraded pop culture to degraded modern art. Not even the small melodrama of Salle and Schnabel would be permitted. The pleasure of the new art, if any, for artist and audience alike, would lie, the argument went, in its bitter assertion of bitter truth. Only by refusing to participate in the bourgeois game by which originality was constantly seduced and betrayed could one protest.

This insistence on using mass language against itself in an art that deliberately denied any claims to originality had two wings. One group, who saw themselves as Post-Structuralist Marxists, would try to run the cycles of art and popular culture in reverse, by taking up the forms and techniques of advertising, disorienting them, and then using them against their original class patrons. The second group, who thought of themselves as Marxist Post-Structuralists, thought that the first group's project was much too optimistic. The second group's analysis of the hegemony of logocentric repression showed it to be so powerful, so all-pervasive, so entrenched within language and signs and money, and within the ideas of art and argument themselves, that all one could hope to do was to retreat into deep cover, taking up a position of frozen equanimity within the society which one despised, and participating in its evils so fully and wholeheartedly that in retrospect one's actions could only be understood as a form of irony.

The prophet of the first group was the German-born veteran of Conceptual art, Hans Haacke (fig. 24). Haacke's work tended to be composed of ''documentation,'' photographs and wall labels filled with fine type, revealing the connections between advertising and social evils. One of his *bêtes noires* was the advertising magnate Charles Saatchi, who by the mid-eighties had assembled an extraordinary collection

24. Hans Haacke. *The Saatchi Collection.* **1987. Mixed media installation, 8'5'' × 6'4''
(256.5 × 193 cm). Courtesy John Weber Gallery, New York**

25. **Barbara Kruger.** Untitled (You Invest in the Divinity of the Masterpiece). 1982. Unique photostat, 71¾ × 45⅝" (182.2 × 115.8 cm). The Museum of Modern Art, New York. Acquired through an anonymous fund

to be the assumption that, somewhere, there could be found many people who remained utterly vulnerable to the manipulations of Bartells & Jaymes and the Calvin Girls, and who had to be lectured at in nursery talk to have the scheming of the mass media made plain to them. However sympathetic you might have been to the political position that underlay this work, and however much you might have shared its disgust with a disposable culture of manufactured lies, it was still hard for many people to see how Kruger's strategies and methods differed from those of advertising itself. The flair for the catchy slogan, the preference for the categorical over the complex, for the reductive sales pitch over ambivalent analysis, the faith in the power of a signature mantra—the manipulative language of advertising was simply taken up in this art and re-accented. It wasn't even ironic, since its messages—DON'T FIND YOUR WORLD IN OURS—were, in fact, perfectly sincere: it wasn't a commentary on seductive simplification, just a new and arresting form of it. In the past, the work of artists like Hannah Höch and John Heartfield had, as we have seen, tried to take up the vocabulary of mass persuasion and turn it against itself. They had believed that it was possible to make art that would be structurally immune to anyone's manipulation, a language so intrinsically alogical that it could derange and counteract the language of mass persuasion. This faith had proved unjustified, and perhaps it was partly a dim memory of its failure that led the new

of contemporary art, a lot of it seemingly radical, from the proceeds of his international ad agency. Haacke produced an artwork that consisted of unflattering photographs of Saatchi and sloganeering wall labels that attacked him—unsophisticated people might have called it an "advertising campaign"—and attempted to demonstrate that Saatchi was out to demoralize avant-garde art in the interests of international capitalism. Throughout the eighties, Haacke continued to make an art that consisted of the "deconstruction" of the language of advertising, in the hope that, with its manipulations and lies laid bare, ads would no longer have the hypnotic power that he believed they possessed.

In the work of the word artist Barbara Kruger, the language of anti-advertising art became more sophisticated. Kruger had actually worked as a layout artist, and this led her to begin to make mock ads that used the typographical devices and attention-getting juxtaposition of images that she had learned, in order to expose the machinery of seduction. Kruger's dour slogans—YOU INVEST IN THE DIVINITY OF THE MASTERPIECE; I SHOP THEREFORE I AM; DON'T FIND YOUR WORLD IN OURS; AN IMAGE IS NOT A WORLD—and signature bald, tabloid typeface and red-and-black layouts, in which Constructivist design was skillfully reconciled with the front page of the *New York Post*, became one of the most instantly recognizable of eighties graphic styles (figs. 25, 26). Underlying this striking work, though, seemed

26. **Barbara Kruger.** Untitled (I Shop Therefore I Am). 1987. Photographic silkscreen on vinyl, 9'3" × 9'5" (281.9 × 287 cm). Courtesy Mary Boone Gallery, New York

generation of artists to accept so uncritically that the only language with which to counter mass persuasion was another dialect of the same language—that the answer to advertising was now not art but propaganda. And, as the century-old interchange between propaganda and advertising now seemed to narrow to the duration of a single synapse firing, Kruger's style inevitably became the newest style of mainstream advertising, which by the end of the decade had taken up the deliberately bald, peremptory tone of Kruger's slogans to sell its own things: JUST DO IT; BUY THIS.

DON'T FIND YOUR WORLD IN OURS. But nobody really did; if one small hope seemed justified at the end of the twentieth century, it was that fear of mass manipulation, which had dominated the thinking of so many decent people for much of the century, had turned out to be unfounded. As the experience of Eastern Europe and China made plain, totalitarianism could be kept in power not by the sophisticated manipulation of mass emotion, but only by terror, plain and simple. Once the instruments of terror were removed, the appearance of mass consent passed with it. If this was true of the totalitarian East, where the apparatus of mass persuasion had been maintained as a monopoly by the Party to the exclusion of all other public discourse, how much more true was it likely to be of America and Western Europe, where no one group had a monopoly on mass persuasion, and where the fear of manipulation was at least as vocal and institutionalized an intellectual tradition as its practice? The artists who fearlessly "deconstructed" the language of advertising had first to insist, against all common experience (and against all the rueful testimony of the putative manipulators themselves), that people in an open and skeptical society did not already have a very precise idea about which public speech rang true, and which rang false.

It is the case, of course, that each of us spends great amounts of mental energy fending off the endless importunities, on billboards and television, by mail and by phone, to buy something. But the common resistance is as large a part of the story as the common surrender, and the pleasure of possession as large a part of the experience as the self-reproach at giving in. Denying the lived experience of consumer society, both the hard carapace of skepticism that each of us grew and the ticklish places of pleasure that each of us permitted, the new art could only retreat into a bleak and unreal priggishness—into reaction. "All our culture and aesthetic sense doesn't find anything better to do than to work for the exaltation of well-being and the tickling of the instincts.... Triumphant, exultant, continually sapping our heart and soul by its vibrant futility." The words of Talmeyr, the extreme right-wing Catholic who, as we saw, feared advertising at the end of the nineteenth century because he saw it as an expression of the democratic imagination—an instrument, in every sense, of the Commune—had by the 1990s become the uncritically accepted motto of those who would have liked to think of themselves as the rightful inheritors of the Commune. The alternative and genuinely modern tradition of Seurat, whose intricate embrace and eager assimilation of advertising style rested, finally, on his faith in the power of the modern eye to discriminate—to absorb and select from the new arts of persuasion those elements that might contribute to a poetic art—no longer seemed capable of expansion.

What was perhaps most significant in the work of

Haacke and Kruger was the final break of the Marxist tradition with any affection for popular spectacle. It had after all been Léger, the supreme hero of the Communist avant-garde, who celebrated the billboards in the place de Clichy precisely because they did promise a "society of spectacle" as an overwhelming, open alternative to the mean repressions of bourgeois culture. The world of the billboard, the movie house—the world of which Chaplin was the saint and the place de Clichy the temple—for Léger heralded an emerging civilization in which sheer, vulgar material appetite would triumph over the narrow, repressive pieties and hierarchies of the church and counting-house culture. Against this, it had been Duchamp, with an aesthete's

27. **Sherrie Levine.** Untitled (Lead Checks: 1). 1987. Casein on lead, 20 × 20" (50.8 × 50.8). Collection Carol and Paul Meringoff

fastidiousness, who had insisted that art had no future in a society of spectacle except the tiny infra-mince gesture that prefaced the classic aristocratic Horatian retreat. Now the tiny chess move on the board of art would present itself as the latest extension of radical engagement.

A new generation of radical artists expressed their contempt for modernist art only by taking over its ironic jokes and turning them into memento mori. Sherrie Levine was perhaps the shrewdest of those who redefined the Duchampian joke about the mutability of context as a statement about the death of art. It was Levine's single insight to see that the utopian styles of modern art had become the equivalents of urinals and bicycle wheels and bottléracks. Her readymades were other works of modernist art—generic styles of geometric abstraction or particular modernist drawings and photographs, copied exactly and presented, deadpan, as her own (fig. 27). "Appropriation art," as it came to be called, had at least the virtue of mean truth. The transformation of modern art into popular culture, whose denial had mired so much media art earlier in the decade in an unreal rhetoric, was in this art presented as a hard, sour fact. But this was all the art had to present, and the second, syncopated beat of modern art, in which the appropriated thing became the basis for something newly imagined, was never struck.

By the middle of the eighties, this strange assemblage of emotions—an urge to lay claim to a position of extreme radicalism, coupled with an absolute contempt for popular culture; a desire to declare one's contempt for the forms of mass society coupled with the fixed belief that nothing existed outside them—found an oracle and a dogma in the works of the French philosopher Jean Baudrillard. In one of those comedies of Franco-American life whose point by point transmission someone ought to trace, Baudrillard passed in about five years—from his first sightings in 1982 to his apotheosis in 1987—from a stray figure in the lower reaches of the French establishment to an American art-world oracle, whose books were displayed right next to the cash register at SoHo bookstores, like copies of *T.V. Guide* at a supermarket.

Baudrillard immunized his system in advance against any empirical criticism, or even contact with the real world, by the wonderful "principle of operational negativity." He insisted that all things that seemed to be for his case and all the counter-examples that might be adduced against it were in fact equivalent, since in our culture a fact might easily be "metamorphosed into its inverse in order to be perpetuated in its purged form."[13] There was an element of deliberate, hyperbolic overkill, and even of *blague,* in all of Baudrillard's writings, which his admirers in America did not really understand. It wasn't that Baudrillard wasn't serious; it was just that the last thing he wanted to be was "sincere." As the decade wore on, and his audience in America grew, Baudrillard was inclined continually to inflate his aphorisms until they touched the edge of obvious self-parody. But even when he announced, as he did in 1989, that the key to understanding life on Earth was to see that it was not a real planet at all, but just an advertisement for some other planet, his admirers looked grave, and were disinclined to take it as a joke.

Baudrillard's ideas were meant to be taken less as elements in a coherent argument than as exclamations at a wine tasting: smell, taste, roll it around in your mouth, spit it out, exclaim, and then move on. In America, however, Baudrillard's tasting notes from the society of spectacle were taken as a Prohibitionist tract.[14] What his American admirers wanted was a dogma and a program, and they found one in a Baudrillardian orthodoxy which could, in fact, sometimes actually be glimpsed beneath the churning surface of the prose. Basically, Baudrillard believed that "capital" now enforces its power through the manipulation of representations. We have been purposefully deluged by a sea of representations, he insisted, and now they have drowned reality. We no longer judge our images in terms of how well they resemble our experience; we judge our experience in terms of how much it resembles our images. Baudrillard sees his contemporaries as adrift in the world of the "simulacra"—pure images, floating free, referring to nothing but themselves—and in the world of the spectacle, the endless ribbon of entertainment and news and confession brought by the mass media. Even the most seemingly disruptive and violent images—a hijacking, say—are presented to us not as the reportage of an event but as the playing out of a scenario.

As Baudrillard himself admitted, there was nothing in all of this that couldn't have been found twenty years ago in the writing of Marshall McLuhan. What was new was the tone of unrelieved pessimism. When McLuhan first offered his view of the medium as message, he suggested that by becoming spectators of the great, coming universal spectacle, we all might be brought into a new unity—the global village. But for Baudrillard, the media image, in its free-floating abstraction, had brought nothing but more and more coercive social control and the emptying out of inner life. The global village had become the capitalist Gulag. The function of simulation and spectacle was to eliminate any possibility of rebellion, which depends, ultimately, on individuals being able to control their own use of representations—on their being able to make reliable, concrete maps of their world and its objects.

That Baudrillard became an oracle of New York art institutions was impossibly ironic, for if everything that Baudrillard had the most contempt for in the world could have been summed up in two words they would have been "American art." American art and its rhetoric of the new was the most pathetic diversionary campaign of the spectacular society. Yet Baudrillard was perceived, by an odd bit of American self-delusion, to offer the perfect program for American art. Baudrillard's desperate howl was translated into the terms of American therapeutic culture as an ideology that offered absolute license in the guise of total honesty.

Baudrillard was understood to counsel an art that accepted its own paralyzed place in the world of the spectacle, but that accepted it with a buried detachment. Though the system of manipulation was inescapable, it was possible to make art that showed one's awareness of the processes of manipulation. As Baudrillard had put it, in words that came to serve as a motto for a generation of young artists: "Let us be stoics: if the world is fatal, let us be more fatal than it. If it is indifferent, let us be more indifferent. We must conquer the world and seduce it through an indifference that is at least equal to the world's."[15] Baudrillard's dogma was to many artists like the document that Lucy, in a vintage *Peanuts* strip, made all the other children sign. "Sign this," she said. "It absolves me of all responsibility." As Charlie Brown said wistfully, after signing it himself, "That must be a very convenient document to have."

In the work of the arch-Baudrillardian Peter Halley, for instance, the spectator was offered simple, signature geometric abstractions painted in Day-Glo colors, most often featuring fluorescent rectangles divided by heavy black bars (fig. 28). One could look as deep into

28. **Peter Halley.** *Two Cells with Circulating Conduit.* 1985. Day-Glo synthetic polymer paint and Roll-a-Tex on canvas, 63" × 9' (160 × 274.5 cm). Collection Michael H. Schwartz, New York

these pictures as one chose: they could be read as parodies of hard-edge abstraction, as dumbed-down decoration, or as jeering assertions that abstraction itself was a kind of prison, and that beneath the heroic and pseudo-scientific attitudinizing of geometric abstraction there was never anything more than an urge to aestheticize the airless world of the Third Avenue office building. In the wild rhetoric that accompanied these pictures, Halley insisted that they were demonstrations that life and death were both "pretty outmoded concepts."[16] Only by not supporting ideas, by refusing to participate in the old game in which an image embodied an idea and thus allowed the simulation of communication to perpetuate itself, could art show that it was onto the game. It was a kind of dim parody of the inflated transcendental claims by which geometric abstraction had first been put forward, now offered as a willfully deflated reduction.

If Halley represented the reductive end of the Baudrillardian aesthetic, Ashley Bickerton caught its tone of cool, apocalyptic melodrama. Like Halley, and the rest of the Neo-Geo artists given sustenance by Baudrillard's theory, Bickerton took a device from the American pop tradition and then invested it with despair. Bickerton made slickly finished slabs of anodized aluminum, secured to the gallery walls by rows of heavy steel bolts (fig. 29). The faces of the boxes were covered with commercial type and managed to combine the look of the credits at the end of a P.B.S. documentary with that of the casing of a hydrogen bomb. Though these boxes were obviously inspired by Stuart Davis, they suggested not his vision of entrepreneurial culture calling out to the world like a carnival barker, but a chilling vision of corporate culture whispering to itself in code. A monolithically ceremonial civilization

without private life or public discourse, ominous signs arranged in endlessly reductive patterns—that was the world invoked, and those were the emblems depicted, on Bickerton's shields.

Baudrillardian ideology was a deliberately narrowing program, designed to convince artists that nothing new was possible. To make something from it that had any intensity of feeling, it was necessary to have an imagination so peculiarly laid out that it would see expansive possibilities where everyone else saw narrowing restrictions, goofy and creepy veins of emotion where everyone else saw the death of feeling altogether. This imaginative leap was achieved by Jeff Koons. Koons once worked as a Wall Street trader, and he has taken great pains to insist on his work as a set of impersonal market manipulations, small Duchampian gestures in which objects are traded by the artist as a way of illustrating the processes of commodification, an art in which shopping has replaced making. But if you put aside the rhetoric that Koons has allowed to be decanted into his art and actually look at its structure, the reedy originality of his imagination becomes plain.

Koons first became well known for a small, ironic displacement presented as art: vacuum cleaners placed in plexiglass cases (fig. 31). It was an act, on the face of it, no different from the misplaced urinal or the Campbell's soup can. But Koons's vacuum cleaners were charmless; they didn't have the thrill of the forbidden or the appeal of the overlooked, just the drudge-like presence of the ignored. The *Fountain* depended for its power on its already having a place, if a precarious one, in the array of objects that counted as art; the timid newcomer to the ball, it could be crowned king by Duchamp in order to show up the

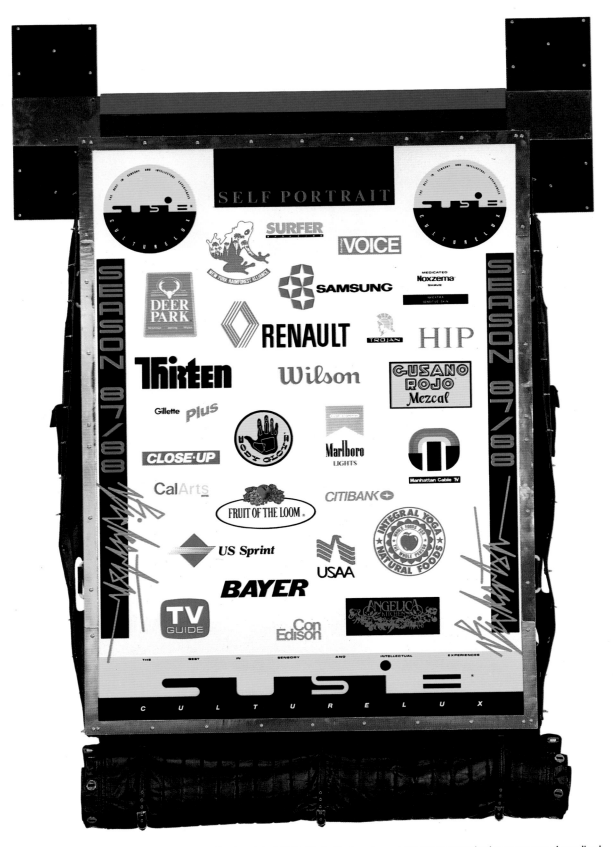

29. Ashley Bickerton. *Tormented Self-Portrait (Susie at Arles).* 1987–88. Synthetic polymer paint, bronze powder, lacquer on wood, anodized aluminum, rubber, plastic, Formica, leather, chrome-plated steel, and canvas, 7'5⅜" × 68¾" × 15¾" (227.1 × 147.5 × 40 cm). The Museum of Modern Art, New York. Purchase

arbitrary pretenses of the entire social masquerade. The soup can derived its power from Warhol's ability to pick out something with which the whole culture had a familiarity so deep that it had already been transformed into a kind of inarticulate love. The vacuum, a necessary thing but in 1987 nobody's idea of either hi-tech glitz or small-is-beautiful honesty, was one of the few household objects for which there was no rhetoric at all. In a culture that was wild about things, crazy about things, Koons had managed to find the one thing for which no one had ever felt any emotion at all. He had a cruel eye for the dead zone of consumerism, for the moment in the evolution of an object when it had neither the energy of innovation nor the charm of nostalgic association.

Next, Koons began to make metal casts of everyday objects: toy trains that were sold as whiskey premiums, portable bars, scuba gear (figs. 30, 32). His most famous work of this kind became the emblem of the eighties: a stainless-steel cast of a cheaply made Taiwanese inflatable toy of a rabbit holding a carrot (fig. 1). The rabbit made Koons into Oldenburg's evil twin. Oldenburg's subject had been the emotional life of inanimate things, and his theme was metamorphosis—the ordinary thing suddenly made animate: soft or big or seductive. Koons's subject was the murder of feeling by selling, and his metaphor was paralysis. Armored in silver, the small, sinister bunny—a toy that was not really quite a crib toy or a beach toy, but was just this . . . thing, that you bought (fig. 33)—became a cool, cybernetic hero, an android, suggesting at once Neil Armstrong on the moon and the arriving alien visitors.

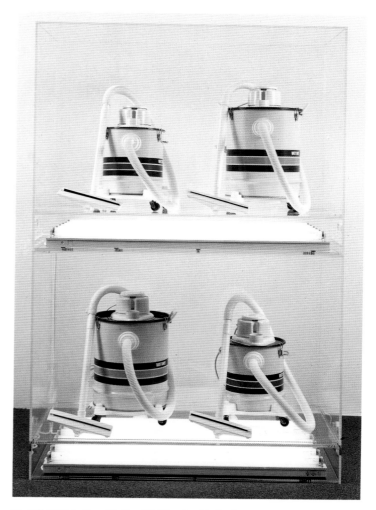

31. Jeff Koons. *New Shelton Wet/Dry Double Decker.* 1981–86. Acrylic case, fluorescent lights, and four Shelton Wet/Dry Vacuums, 6′10″ × 52″ × 28″ (208.3 × 132.1 × 71.1 cm). Collection Emily and Jerry Spiegel Family

30. Jeff Koons. *Baccarat Crystal Set.* 1986. Cast stainless steel, 16 × 16 × 12½″ (40.6 × 40.6 × 31.8 cm). Collection Elaine and Werner Dannheisser, New York

32. Jeff Koons. *Jim Beam J. B. Turner Train.* 1986. Cast stainless-steel Jim Beam bourbon decanters with cast stainless-steel track (edition of three), 9¾″ × 9′8″ × 6¾″ (24.8 × 295 × 171.1 cm). Saatchi Collection, London

In late 1988, Koons managed to do something that most people thought was no longer possible. He shocked them. At the Sonnabend Gallery, he displayed life-size porcelain and polychromed wood sculptures, executed in Italy by craftsmen who usually make the mantelpiece figurines sold in discount shops. The figures included a seven-foot bear in a rainbow-striped

T-shirt looming over a London bobby (fig. 35); a shivering beauty with a Farrah Fawcett hairdo, hugging the Pink Panther to her bare bosom (fig. 34); a pair of midget bears clasping hands and grinning; a five-foot-tall Buster Keaton, astride a donkey and with a chipmunk-cheeked bird perched on his shoulder; and Michael Jackson, recumbent in a cream and gold jack-et, holding his pet chimpanzee, Bubbles.

Koons's work was applauded and attacked as an abstract demonstration of a theory of commodification. If all art in any case aspired to the condition of *chotckes,* then Koons, it was said, had at least got there one-two-three, just like that. But by 1989 no one really could have been shocked or even much affected by those small, ironic platitudes. Koons's figurines were shocking because of the way they looked. They were nightmarish—devil dolls, in which the insipid language of the cartoons' over-accentuated contours and biscuit glazes was suddenly made hard and staring. The contours of each piece were as chubby as a Disney drawing, but glacially hard—like Muppets who had just seen the Medusa. All the soft puerility of the cartoon art of Kenny Scharf, all the hard-glazed stoicism of the dead surfaces of Peter Halley, came together to produce something as cold as it was compellingly absurd. Koons had discovered an *Ur*-kitsch beneath kitsch—a part of pop culture that had never been anathematized because nobody had ever thought about it. Critics in the past had insisted that tap dancing, or comic strips, or hairpiece ads, were taboo, and artists had rushed to violate that decorum. But nobody had ever thought to come up with a rule to cover seven-foot-tall bears in rainbow-colored T-shirts stealing the whistles of London bobbies. For a little while, the

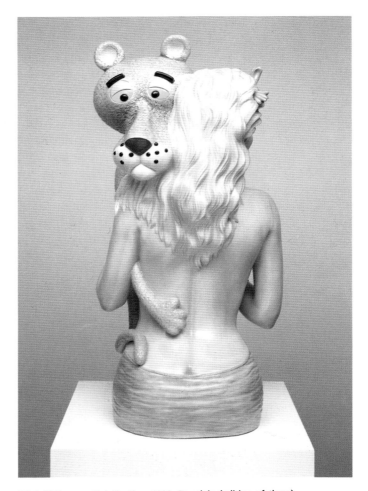

34. Jeff Koons. *Pink Panther.* **1988. Porcelain (edition of three), 41 × 20½ × 19″ (104.1 × 52.1 × 48.3 cm). Collection Elaine and Werner Dannheisser, New York**

33. "Bunny" toy. Inflatable vinyl, approximately 46″ (114.3 cm) high, deflated. Distributed by F. W. Woolworth Co., New York; manufactured in Taiwan

decade's formalized pavane of high and low ground to a halt, as though the art-world audience were so many bemused customs agents, thumbing through their rule books: go find me the regulation for *that.*

Yet the longer one looked at these objects, the more one's amusement passed into a sense of seeing

something personal and strangled. "I wanted them to be irresistible, to get you on every level at once," Koons once said.[17] Beneath the practiced cant of commodification, against the grain of the theory which insisted that thingness was no longer possible at all in a world of desiccated spectacle, there was in these weird objects a desire to make things that could only be taken *as* things. These were relentlessly invented objects, which, far from being haphazardly appropriated from a Fifth Avenue discount shop, derived their imagery and iconography from a narrow, specific band of American popular culture. They came from the narrow, empty interregnum of pop culture in the early seventies (when, as it happened, Koons had been an adolescent)—the world of limited animation, Sid and Marty Krofft Christmas Specials, of *Charlie's Angels*, and *The Pink Panther.*

Koons was the *poète maudit* of American adolescence. His work summoned up the world of a thirteen-year-old's bedroom, the *Mad* magazine reader—the meticulously assembled model planes on the dresser, the rat-fink on the windowsill, the gleaming, polished photo of Miss December on the wall above the bed. As much as Kenny Scharf's painting, it was puerile; but now the puerility was in dialogue with the look of the cold luxury object. Like the little boy in the movie *Big,* Koons's was the adolescent imagination set free in a world of cynical calculation. (Even the ads which he

35. **Jeff Koons.** *Bear and Policeman.* 1988. Polychromed wood (edition of three), 7'5⁄8″ × 43 × 36″ (215 × 109.2 × 91.4 cm). Courtesy Sonnabend Gallery, New York

produced for his exhibitions, and which outraged many people, didn't really look like ads at all. They were amateurish tableaux of the artist with his objects, accompanied by models in bikinis. They had none of the shrewd self-deprecating spirit of contemporary ads; his ads suggested, instead, a thirteen-year-old's ideas of advertising—me, sexy babes, and my stuff.)

Koons's ceramics appeared around the same time as Andrew Wyeth's heavily hyped paintings of his mistress-model, Helga Testorf. Koons's figurines were a kind of Helga phenomenon in reverse: that had been a publicity stunt disguised as a *cri de coeur;* Koons's work was a *cri de coeur* disguised as a publicity stunt. What made his work disturbing was its coupling of an excitable imagination with an affectless and stoical demeanor. A private iconography—as original in its way as Joseph Cornell's—could now enter the world only by presenting itself as part of the enveloping culture of contempt. The desire to make newly imagined things look vitiated and secondhand seemed to express a preference for death over life, and even in a weary time this remained shocking. Writing about Jean Rhys and William Burroughs, John Updike once spoke of them as "Open-eyed tourists in Hell, for reality breaks bare and inconsequent upon their personae. A certain pragmatic dryness, which we feel in their styles, a certain deadness, even, permeates their burnt-out worlds. This deadness, perhaps, proved their mundane salvations, and makes them, as artists, post-modern."[18] It is that same self-protecting morbidity, merged, in this case, with a cheerful entrepreneurial busyness and a strangely ingratiating humor, that radiated from all of Koons's work. For once, the word *postmodern* seemed meaningful—dead on.

At the end of the decade, it would be two installations by the American word artist Jenny Holzer that would seem to many people to have defined the spiritual crisis of the decade and, to a remarkable degree, still managed to bode that crisis forth as art. If Koons's art was made by a perverse imagination feeding on a dead body of theory, Holzer was the first artist of her melancholy order to self-consciously translate a narrowing ideology into a richly ambivalent sensibility. Holzer had done important work throughout the decade, but at the very end of the 1980s she produced two installations that summed up and rearticulated the time's concerns. Both installations took as their medium the "light-emitting diode"—the kind of moving electronic signboard that had once been part of the language of Times Square spectacle but that had become, in the eighties, a commonplace advertising device of the corner deli and take-out restaurant. The first and in some ways the more unforgettable of Holzer's environments was called *Laments,* installed at the Dia Art Foundation. In *Laments,* words passed, at a speed just a little bit too fast to be truly read or absorbed, up and down vertical columns (fig. 36). The observer was left fixed, passive, by the spectacle: if Holzer's medium was the electronic message board, her underlying model of communication was television. Scraps of individual consciousness—fragmentary first-person confessions of pain, fear, greed—flew by in the dark, in glowing reds and greens and yellows.

Occasionally, the spectacle would stop, the room would go black, and then the columns would glow in pure color, before the words began again. (After the experience of the lit columns, spectators could go into an adjoining room and read the texts at leisure; they were there chiseled into sarcophagi [fig. 37]). The words, as one slowly absorbed them, turned out to be flat-footed, arrhythmic confessions—I SUBTRACT PEOPLE KILLED FOR ONE REASON OR ANOTHER, I COUNT INFANTS AND PREDICT THEIR DAYS, I GUESS THE NEW REASONS AND PROJECT THEIR EFFICACY. I DECORATE NUMBERS AND CIRCULATE THEM. Over time, it slowly became apparent that these seemingly disconnected sentences were in fact fragments from monologues spoken by particular contemporary types: many of the messages in the *Laments,* for instance, had to do with the AIDS epidemic. (The lines beginning I SUBTRACT PEOPLE... seemed meant to represent the internal monologue of an epidemiologist.) Yet all these monologues had been processed into one calm, impersonal, electronic spectacle. Holzer's art seemed to insist that at the end of the century the old tension, initiated by Picasso and Braque, between public words and private sensibility has gone slack, and that all private experience could be expressed now only in the homogenized language of public information. In Holzer's work, private feeling has been swallowed up in an affectless strip of public spectacle, pain and sex and remorse vacuumed up by the media machine and then re-presented in an endless ribbon of undifferentiated information.

A few months later, Holzer installed an even grander and more theatrical environment in the great open well of the Guggenheim Museum (fig. 41). Now, the light-emitting-diode displays followed the spiraling path of Frank Lloyd Wright's ramp, and fragments of anonymous confessions snaked majestically up the circumference of the museum. The environment of *Laments* had been intensely private and secretive—a sanctuary of the cult of the misdirected message. The message boards at the Guggenheim managed to suggest something larger. Some of its vocabulary, and its aura of direct, unremitting earnestness descended from the American sculptor Bruce Nauman (fig. 38), whose work, made on the edge between substance and spectacle, seemed more and more prescient as the decade wore on. Yet where Nauman still belonged to the inward-turning orbit of Duchamp and Johns, Holzer on the whole was almost Smithson-like in voicing the kinship of primitive ritual and modern spectacle. The bright electric light, mesmerizing spectators as it dominated the dark museum, suggested both the huddled warmth of the campfire and the cold signs of the Ginza district in Tokyo. Her work depended on a tension between the ancient memorial styles represented by the graven sarcophagi and the new, transient information style represented by the electric sign.

36. **Jenny Holzer.** *Laments.* 1989. Installation at the Dia Art Foundation, New York

37. **Jenny Holzer.** *Laments.* 1989

38. Bruce Nauman. *One Hundred Live and Die.* 1984. Neon and glass tubing, 9'10" × 10'11" × 21" (300 × 335.9 × 53.3 cm). Courtesy Leo Castelli Gallery, New York

Each style communicated some of its power to the other: the lapidary inscriptions made one aware of the elegiac potential residual in the modern sign, and the cool passivity of the contemporary signage made one aware of the chilled impersonality latent in the high memorial style. It was difficult to convey the surprising power of these pieces, for all their apparent simplicity of means and message. At the Dia Foundation, people would come in ones and twos and threes, and remain for hours. The tragedy of the AIDS epidemic, which, more than any other catastrophe of recent times, demonstrated the way in which information did not necessarily produce understanding, much less salvation, was perhaps memorialized there more powerfully and appropriately than anywhere else. At the Guggenheim, crowds gathered on the ground floor of the museum and looked up, raptly, patiently, like a crowd of office workers who have emerged at the end of the day to find the Times Square zipper given over, somehow, to a catalogue of their own private obsessions.

Holzer had always been a word artist, but her path through the decade was a passage from the narrow, hard ironies of Conceptualism to an intense confessional realism. She first became well known for her Truisms, purposefully flat-footed clichés that she had printed in muted, classic type on white posters, and then stuck up around the city, or inscribed on small stones (figs. 39, 40). The Truisms resembled slips plucked from particularly glum fortune cookies at a Chinese restaurant near the New School: PROTECT ME FROM WHAT I WANT; A SENSE OF TIMING IS THE MARK OF GENIUS; MONEY CREATES TASTE; ABUSE OF POWER COMES AS NO SURPRISE. These Truisms were inspired by Holzer's experience at the Whitney Museum's Independent Study Program in early 1977, during which she was expected to read "studies in art and literature, Marx, psychology, social and cultural theory, criticism and feminism."[19] Holzer intended these Truisms as affectionate parodies of the all-purpose art-world reading list. She wanted to draw up an encyclopedia of intellectual clichés that one was somehow not quite aware of as clichés, a textbook of the commonplaces of the avant-garde bibliography.

Many people, however, were inclined to take the purposefully empty Truisms as though they were significant aphorisms. And this was not entirely a mistake, since beneath the deadpan jokes there was in Holzer's art also a completely unironic urge to make a word art that communicated to an audience larger than the usual art-world circuit. Only connect. For most of the eighties, Holzer was seen as one of a generation of artists who had taken up the syntax of the "information" and Conceptual art of the seventies, and put it to use as a public art of a new and touchingly unremitting earnestness.

Yet over the last few years Holzer has translated the common ideology into an intricate personal sensibility, in touch with a deeper melancholy, at once more outward-turning and more self-implicating, than that of her contemporaries. Holzer recognized in the uninflected, flat-footed language that Conceptual art shared with the set forms of media confessions—the 976 party line, the electronic bulletin boards—a visionary ineloquence that was peculiarly American and affecting: a tongue-tied sincerity that could become the means to an anatomy of contemporary melancholy.

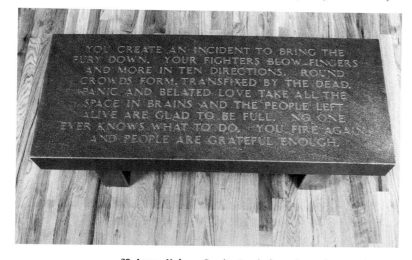

39. Jenny Holzer. *Granite Bench*, from the Under a Rock series. **1986. Misty Black granite bench (edition of three), 17¼ × 48 × 21″ (43.8 × 121.9 × 53.3 cm). Courtesy Barbara Gladstone Gallery, New York**

What makes Holzer's art moving is its connection to the larger river of American confession. If the syntax of Holzer's art derives from the avant-garde traditions of Conceptual and information art, the visual drama of her installations—the dark intimations of violation, loss, and entrapment expressed in an environment of bright public spectacle—is a poetic reduction of the imagery of urban melancholia that has always been part of the inheritance of American art. There has always been in American memorial art a faith in the laconic—a sense, extending from the Gettysburg Address to Maya Lin's Vietnam Veterans Memorial, that real grief is laconic, for fear of seeming insincere. In the long view of history, perhaps Holzer's installations will come to be seen as part of this tradition. Her installations share with the Vietnam Veterans Memorial the uncanny ability to use a seemingly oblique or limited text—a flat list of names, or a series of affectless and almost unreadable confessions—to evoke in a large public a sense of loss and pain that seems no longer available to the more conventional forms of rhetorical pathos. What people wanted at the end of the decade, it seems, was something spectacularly sad.

Standing in the well of the Guggenheim Museum on a winter afternoon, looking up at Jenny Holzer's stately, gloomy words as they spin up toward the roof,

one is put in mind of a different and more recent history of spiraling form. For Frank Lloyd Wright, of course, the shell-like spiral that gave the museum its shape was the ultimate organic metaphor for growth. Robert Smithson summoned a new vision to life by reimagining the spiral as the ultimate entropic form—a symbolic image of culture and nature alike turning in on themselves. Holzer, in turn, adapted Wright's spiral to Smithson's purpose. She found in the forms of the new "information society" a way to rearticulate the old ascending coil as a huge sign, one not to be ascended but just to be observed. Her work suggests that modern art and the popular culture around it no longer seem to be ascending to heaven, or even going down the drain—just running around in circles.

How we all roared when Baudelaire went fey.
"See this cigar" he said "It's Baudelaire's.
What happens to perception? Ah, who cares."
Today, alas, that happy crowded floor
Looks very different: many are in tears:
Some have retired to bed and locked the door;
And some swing madly from the chandeliers;
Some have passed out entirely in the rears;
Some have been sick in corners; the sobering few
Are trying to think of something new.[20]

Auden wrote these lines in 1937, in an attempt to describe what seemed to him a fundamental modern dilemma. Modernist art, it seemed to him, had been shaped by a flight from responsibility—to a common audience, to articulate tradition, to firsthand experience—and had become poisonously infatuated in-

40. Jenny Holzer. Untitled, from the Survival series. 1984. Street installation, New York

stead with the artist's newly discovered ability to make art out of any material that lay at hand. The power to make poetry from one's own cigar ash, and to invest mere banality with the spell of original imagination, though it may have once promised joy and limitless freedom, had ended, Auden thought, in nausea and self-reproach.

Auden's lines may have never seemed more appropriate to the situation of art than they do right now. The retreat from the responsibility of ordering singular firsthand experience, into the dandyish, perverse connoisseurship of the clichés of second-order culture, seems, for many people, to have climaxed in the orgiastic frenzy of Pop, and now has produced something like a permanent hangover. "Some have retired to bed and locked the doors...." On the one hand, we see the attempt to find a space for art completely outside the cycles of seduction and consumption, an attempt that seems, perhaps inevitably, to carry its own burden of puritanical self-righteousness. On the other, the alternative to this accusatory retreat seems to be an increasingly hysterical and mannered insistence that the exhausted party of consumer culture is still all the world there is ("And some swing madly from the chandeliers..."). For many among our own "sobering few," this unhappy scene marks the inevitable outcome of an attempt to make art out of non-art, to substitute secondhand culture for firsthand experience as the subject of art. The only sane future for art, they argue, lies in a complete divorce from the materials of mass culture, and in a return to "perception"—to the specific engagements of realist painting and sculpture. Faces and bodies and landscapes remain as central to experience now as any television image, they argue, and the future of painting relies on art's renewed allegiance to those subjects—in a return to the somatic, the individually observed, the personally felt, the seen.[21]

Yet one of the triumphs of modern art has been to show us that sight is manifold, and that looking hard at secondhand culture can become as meaningful as the scrutiny of first-order nature. Perception itself, after all, cannot operate outside of an inherited vocabulary of schemata. By enlarging and reforming and revising the vocabulary of art to include the new vernaculars of modernity, art has reformed and enlarged the vision of us all. Baudelaire was interested in his own cigar not just because it was his, but because it represented the near-at-hand, the ordinary, the impossible-to-overlook—the real thing. In this sense, Baudelaire's cigar is also Seurat's poster and Picasso's headline and Léger's billboard.

Now, as in 1937, what look like dead ends can still emerge as a new set of individual options for art-making. If the evolution of modern art into a kind of popular culture has seen many artists succumb to the temptation to reduce art to a set of ideological flash-cards, held up to evoke a set of fixed responses—groans from one group and cheers from another—it has also created other sets of possibilities. A broad range of responses to the world around us still seems available to the art of our time; the stubborn experience of art still emerges from what might seem deadening or impossibly narrow rhetorics and announced ambitions. If the emergence of modern art as a central shared experience—a form of popular culture—has reduced the space for the kind of guerrilla raids and abductions that had proved so potent in the past, the new coexistence of art and pop culture leads to no single or simple place. The situation of art today seems to depend less on sustaining a permanent outsider's position than on a constant back-and-forth dialogue between the tiny, individual experience and the giant public platform that is now provided for advanced art.

In Elizabeth Murray's work, for instance, we recognize that popular imagery can be inextricably intermingled with private experience, in a way that intensifies, rather than diminishing, the articulation of feeling; in her painting, pop culture has become, in every sense, the "second nature" of modern life. For Jeff Koons, the seemingly narrowing dogma of the death of originality has led to a kind of challenging irresponsibility, and to an art of mad comedy and excess in which the small, private imagination can treat the museum and gallery as an extension of the den and the playroom. For Jenny Holzer, on the other hand, the new centrality that vanguard art has won has led her (as it has so many other artists of her generation) to a new kind of self-consciously public speech. The extreme literal-mindedness of her art, though it may be rooted in deliberately blank phrases and affectlessness, seems finally less ironic than possessed by an urge to take over the duties and solemnity of ceremonial art through blunt, unmistakable symbols and signs.

What is astonishing is the degree to which the most seemingly resistant and unpromising materials and rhetoric can continue to provide the sense of the double, the troubling, the perpetually unstable, that we recognize as unique to art. If contemporary art teaches a lesson about contemporary mass culture, it is in a sense not a lesson about its brute strength but about its continuing vulnerability to the manipulations of the individual imagination. For all the declarations of the impossibility of the new and original in the world we inhabit, artists continue to allow us to experience sensibility as history, to refract through willfully banal and eccentric objects and orderings of objects—seven-foot-tall polychromed bears and the lights of deli signs and the maxims of fortune cookies—a sense of the way we live now.

What matters most for the future, perhaps, is not the debate of first-order experience versus second-hand schemata—we know now that neither of these things can exist without the other—but the argument between the categorical and abstract idea and the particular and individual emotion. Of all the unsuccessful general theories of art, probably the least bad has been the one that suggests that we use the concept of "art" to call attention to any made thing which seems to unify what we had always thought before were oppo-

41. **Jenny Holzer.** Installation at the Solomon R. Guggenheim Museum, New York, December 1989–February 1990

sites and, in doing so, reminds us of the irreducible complexity of life. Flowing pattern and truthful detail reconciled, as in Raphael; a child's color and Cézanne's drawing, as in Matisse; Chester Gould and Emily Dickinson, as in Elizabeth Murray—what matters is less what the particular opposed terms may be than that the newly made thing recalls to us the "And yet..." and "But also..." and "That, too..." of lived experience rather than the tendentious categories of received ideas.

Since that tension, now shaped by poles of possibility and horror more extreme than those of any previous historical period, continues to shape our lives, there doesn't seem to be any reason that they can't

shape art, too—and pop culture seems still so pervasive and significant that it is difficult to see how it can be left completely out of the articulation of these ambiguities. The motifs and subjects that any culture takes up to express its sense of order—and of disorder—are always unpredictable, and often emerge from the realm of the banal, eccentric, and absurd. For five hundred years, from China to Ireland, one of the most telling and effective motifs in the world's art was the image of a fabulous beast devouring its own tail. What let art go on was that peculiarly gifted people continued to want to make visible the concentrated shock of the struggle between the bite and the beautiful body.

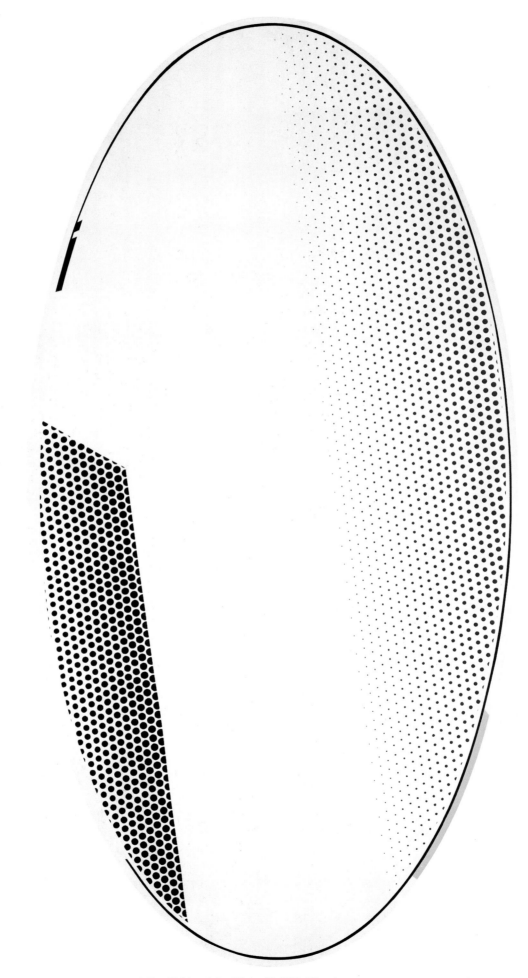

1. **Roy Lichtenstein.** *Mirror #1.* 1971. Oil and magna on canvas
(oval), 72 × 36″ (182.9 × 91.4 cm). Collection the artist

After so many different histories, filled with hundreds of individuals and objects, the time might seem overdue to hold the mirror up to that populous world, and to propose our own organizing principles for the story of modern art and popular culture. In that regard, two very different epigraphs may help point the way. The first is from the zoologist Ernst Mayr, in his introduction to a 1964 edition of Charles Darwin's *The Origin of Species*. Stressing the way evolutionary biology studied nature as a sequence of changing populations, rather than as an array of fixed types, Mayr reflected on the fundamental change Darwin's vision required in the way people thought about the world's variety:

Typological thinking, no doubt, had its roots in the earliest efforts of primitive man to classify the bewildering diversity of nature into categories. The *eidos* of Plato is the formal philosophical codification of this form of thinking. According to it, there are a limited number of fixed, unchangeable "ideas" underlying the observed variability, with the *eidos* (idea) being the only thing that is fixed and real, while the observed variability has no more reality than the shadows of an object on a cave wall, as stated in Plato's allegory. . . .

The assumptions of population thinking are diametrically opposed to those of the typologist. The populationist stresses the uniqueness of everything in the organic world. What is true for the human species—that no two individuals are alike—is equally true for all other species of animals and plants. . . . Averages are merely statistical abstractions; only the individuals of which the populations are composed have reality. The ultimate conclusions of the population thinker and of the typologist are precisely the opposite. For the typologist, the type (*eidos*) is real and the variation an illusion, while for the populationist the type is an abstraction and only the variation is real. And, having abandoned the *eidos* in the context of evolutionary theory, one finds it untenable also in every other way. The philosophical consequences of this aspect of Darwinism have not yet been fully explored.[1]

The second is from Roy Blount, Jr., in his 1974 book, *About Three Bricks Shy of a Load*, which charted a season with the Pittsburgh Steelers in the National Football League. Blount, defending his choice of a title, wrote:

I doubt that Chuck Noll [the coach of the Steelers] . . . would like to think of his team as being three bricks shy of a load, which is comparable to playing with less than a full deck. But what deck that is worth anything can ever be said to be full, and what is so boring as a complete, neatly squared away load of bricks? "We don't have the peaks and valleys," said a

member of the N.F.L. champion Miami Dolphins; neither do expressways through Kansas. The great thing in sports and nature is the way bricks slip and reassemble in unexpected combinations.[2]

Splice Mayr's thoughts on what is true in high science to Blount's on what is arresting in popular entertainment, and you get a pair of truths that are affirmed by everything this book has related about modern art and popular culture: only individual variations are real, and interesting new variations most often appear when familiar things slip and reassemble in unexpected combinations.

Put another way, the emphasis of the previous chapters on the profligate idiosyncrasies of all their different stories has constituted a principle in itself. In the study of modern art and popular culture, it's often been taken for granted that the ultimate goal is to search past the diversity of individual creations for the realities that lie behind the appearances of things—the categories that are supposedly the real stuff of history. In those searches for governing patterns or underlying essences, the particulars of local events, or the complex nature of a given work and a given creator, are typically pushed aside as anecdotal peculiarities, significant only because they may reveal something about the real nature of the "modernist project" or of "mass society." For all the impassioned and even violent political differences that separate rival schools of interpretation, almost all are united by some kind of faith that modernity has what Mayr called an *eidos*, and that this *eidos* is the real and most profound subject of debate.

But such intellectual exercises, undertaken with the announced purpose of restoring art to history, betray the unruly details which make history matter. By emphasizing small stories about people and objects instead of big abstractions about terms and categories, we set out to replace mute, complacent generalities with the eloquence of peculiar facts. And what we have seen in these pages is not an encounter between an immutable ideal of "high" or serious art and an equally unvarying "low" culture. Instead we have seen that high art in our century, far from having a unified "project" or direction, has always included the most disparate attitudes, intentions, gestures, and critiques; and that the forms and intentions of advertising, graffiti, or comics have been diverse, and subject to varying rhythms of change. Between these two general zones there has been, instead of a rigidly fixed line, a constant series of transgressions and redirections, in which the act of an individual imagination has been able to alter in a moment the structure of the high-to-low relationship. Schwitters picks up a tram ticket and sees in it a component of his art; as a result, our ideas about tram tickets, and our ideas about art, change. Picasso reconsiders his grotesques, both as analogues of the tribal and as tools to reform a painted likeness; from there, the genre of caricature is burst, and a form of potently ambiguous physiognomics is released to become an emblem of our century.

These are not uniquely heroic or transcendent instances, bright bubbles that rise only occasionally above a sludge of turbid, anonymous processes. The smaller, less complex but vital responses that rebound back from high to low are made by individual acts as well: Stan Lee, not "the comics," saw something profitable in Lichtenstein, and his attitude changed the look, the content, and the audience of comic illustration; A-One, not "graffiti," brought a version of de Kooning's ambition to the Pelham Local. The real challenge in this still confusing and complex field may be to find out more about such particular stories, and to keep postponing our urge for the safe harbor of the categorical conclusion.

Keeping a steady eye on contingencies does not mean, however, that we renounce all idea of order. Evolutionary thinking of the kind Mayr espouses plots patterns of growth and change, but denies given destinies, permanent foreclosures, and underlying essences. Without forgetting, or lessening our joy at, the sheer variety of creative transformations this hundred-year history has entailed, we can in fact discern in it several recurrent patterns.

Certainly the phenomenon of retrospective vision is such an ongoing order. From Braque and Picasso's preference for quaintly drawn advertisements rather than splashy photomechanical layouts, through Hamilton's homage to the 1957 Cadillac, to Lichtenstein's selection of war comics, modern art has often looked at popular culture through a rear-view mirror—constructing longer-lived secondary worlds from materials of the day-to-day world that are just passing. And by memorializing a disappearing popular culture, modern art has frequently made that memorial take over our imagination of the thing itself. We see the early sixties through the lens of Warhol's nostalgia; and Paris in 1910 looks to us now like Cubist collage. When Cornell wanted to construct his imaginary France, it was with the detritus of forty years before, already sorted by his artist forbears. Popular culture, so often described as a flickering dazzle of restless, momentary novelty, is more frequently presented in modern art as a repertoire of well-worn clichés, threatened familiars, or fallen ideals. It is addressed as a realm of nostalgia and enduring preservation that locks into place the imagery of childhood, the designs of soup cans, the look of comic characters, or the shape of soda bottles, and holds them up unchanged across the century, at the same time that it incessantly churns up and casts off styles in other areas.

A larger, more global pattern has emerged, too, in the way modern art's backward glance has been linked to the reversal of Marx's aphorism about history. The relations of popular culture to modern art have followed the pattern "first time farce, second time tragedy," in at least two ways. In one, what seemed simple jests or straightforward sales pitches in popular culture have often become serious devices of unsettling doubt or ambiguity in art: schoolboy puns reinforce the conundrums of a refined and semiotically complex Cubism, for example, or the comic spaces of the 1930s become the despairing skies and bleak metaphysical interiors of Guston in the 1970s. But in the other, on a longer historical trajectory, the high spirits and iconoclastic irreverence with which artists initially reached out to the material of commerce in the early part of the century seem to congeal into suspicion, cynicism, and disillusioned turgidity in many instances of more recent art. The sense of a potential to be grasped from advertising, as felt by Léger or Davis or Rodchenko, and still by Oldenburg, devolves into wary suspicion and melancholia in the era of Kruger and Holzer; and the elegant puns and disruptive gestures of Duchamp have nurtured a stultifyingly earnest academicism as they have aged.

The most dominant pattern that describes itself in this history, however, moves neither forward nor backward, nor simply up or down, but around in circles. The exchange between high and low has not involved one-way ascents and descents along a ladder, but cycles in the turning of a wheel. Styles, or ways of structuring communication, go round and round from group to group instead of just rising or falling from rung to rung in some rigid vertical hierarchy. From small symbolic motifs, like sans-serif letters or Benday dots, to strategies such as gigantism or jumbo styling, to broad models like the billboard's use of huge, flat planes of color, no style remains fixed in its original place, but passes along the wheel from low to high and back again . . . and back again. Between the recognized and defined positions on this circuit, too, exists an infinite range of interminglings of the different worlds, and they also have a part to play in this process. Few words in modern culture have such an immediate association with mediocrity as "middle"; yet again and again, middle-position figures and institutions—Chéret between the Louvre and the kiosk; Agha between avant-garde and fashion; or the shop window, between artiness and cutthroat come-on, from Duchamp's day to Warhol's—have helped to provoke exchanges that have had radical outcomes.

No less than the growth of consumer culture or the advent of entertainment industries, the development of modern art has been entwined with the messy avidity of modern bourgeois society, which has constantly put a premium on novelty and the assimilation of change. The greatest as well as the most demeaned productions on the wheel of interchange bear the marks of this friction and grinding. Every attempt to quarantine what we like from what we don't seems doomed to betray the often reckless and seamy vitality of the history of art in this era. Our culture is one that seems to operate by a rule of reflex that is at once its chagrin and its hope: nothing so sacred that it may not be made profane—but also nothing so profane that it may not be made sacred.

Modern life is lived in contradictions, without the support of fixed or continuous traditions. Modern art, for all its aspirations to be a firm anchor amid that turbulence, is more like a navigational sighting device that allows a constant renegotiation of positions. Popular culture has been not only the zone where high traditions have met their demise, but also the ground from which they have been revived, often through a parodic affection that has supplanted simple academic fealty. The special end of the parodic tradition in modern art, as Lorenz Eitner writes, is "not to devalue the great traditions, but to give them new life by freeing them from the preciousness of mandarin culture, reanimating them with genuine feeling, and bringing them into the reality of modern experience."[3] To find Tiepolo in Chéret, to identify Duchamp and Gropius and Marinetti all commingled in the tail fin, to recover *japoniste* framing from war comics or see Brancusi in a fire hydrant—this is neither simply to revere nor simply to rebuke the ideals of the past, but to insist that traditions, kept vital by individual reinventions, should direct us to make something of the complexities of life instead of sealing us from them.

In that pursuit, artists have recurrently contradicted what might seem logical fears about the debilitating effects of modern mass culture. Their work has shown, for example, that new technologies of mechanical reproduction do not simply deform our perception of original works of art, or dissipate the "aura" that surrounds such unique objects; these same technologies also generate palettes of easily manipulable imagery and unexpected variations of style. What appears merely parasitic may in fact prove to be productive. In the evolution of caricature, the growth of self-conscious stylization, and of a playful alternative to mimetic illusion, depended to a large degree on the proliferation of peculiar styles through copying, first by hand and then by printing—and on artists' readiness to seize on the puns and parodic resemblances those copies provided, and make them the material of art. In the modern era, that pattern of innovation, which had been a minor sideshow in the history of art, became central to its progress: from Seurat's and van Gogh's appreciation of the robust vulgarity of commercial printing to Lichtenstein's discovery of a formal molecular order within the relentless rows of Benday dots, the proliferation of mechanical reproduction, by its sheer inadvertent production of peculiar stylistic variations, has provided a pool of possibilities that has expanded the language of modern art. In this way, the turning wheel that threatens the special place of art also provides the possibility of its renewal—and often precisely by making the conventions of the past available in altered forms that can become the coin of new treasures.

In a similar contradiction, the realm of popular culture that seems the graveyard of creative originality—the world of the apparently tired cliché, or the hackneyed, mechanical convention—has recurrently been favored by modern artists as a garden from which to garner new forms of sensibility. From Léger's interest in advertising's stereotypes and Schwitters's affection for trivial pleasantries, to Rauschenberg's or Rosenquist's eye for the dead zones of commercial banality, to Holzer's work with the inert grammar of homilies, artists have looked to popular culture to provide, in the form of things over-familiar and too well known, the conditions for a particular kind of freedom of maneuver, and the bases for fresh, unexpected styles of expression. Those common properties that have come down farthest on the wheel have often provided a special point of departure for new ascents into art that is difficult, personal, and unsettling.

Accepting the life of the wheel does not mean encircling ourselves in some hermetic internal dialogue of images. To the contrary, it entails seeing the way the patterns of change in modern art restate those of other patterns of change in modern society, and elsewhere in history. Studies of entirely different aspects of human culture reveal a similar order. We could find the crucial role of the individual affirmed, for example, by sociolinguistic studies of the way dialects or slangs pass from one social class to another, by the mediation of "advanced speakers" who can maneuver in both neighborhoods and speak both tongues.[4] And archeologists know that cycles of passage from high to low and back again may be in unceasing motion even in what appear to be simple and undeveloped societies. In burial sites from ancient Greece to Victorian England, the seemingly logical opposition by which peasants settle for rustic simplicity in their rites, while aristocrats prefer sumptuous elaboration in theirs, has been found to reverse itself within a generation—with the simple graves belonging only to the refined aristocrats, while the peasants take up the aristocratic style (which then becomes, of course, "vulgar overstatement").[5] Here, too, the cycles of fashion intervene between social circumstance and stylistic expression. The incomparably more rapid revolution of the wheel that has made it such a vital engine of change in modern society may thus reveal, as much of modern art does, the expanded potential of systems of convention that existed, ignored or demeaned, before our time.

We don't need, though, to look so far afield for evidence that individual acts and recycled forms are the crucial agents of change in human culture. The history we have examined demonstrates this, and that history is not just some minor strain or secret, alternate current within the modern tradition. These are the patterns of invention that gave us the collages of Picasso and Braque and Schwitters and Hausmann, central images of Miró's Surrealism, the paintings of Twombly and Dubuffet, and so on almost beyond counting. "Painting is impure," Philip Guston once said. "It is the adjustment of impurities that forces its continuity."[6] This history of impurity is not, of course, the only record modern art presents to us. But as Guston's words—written while he was still an abstract painter—suggest, even the dream of purity often proceeds only through the adjustment of impurities, by seizing on and remaking the vernacular at hand. California artists of the 1960s, such as Robert Irwin and John McCracken, seeking a Zen clarity of featureless, seamless surfaces, absorbed the painting techniques of custom car shops to achieve their ends. Matisse found in the 1940s that the ideal vision of *luxe, calme, et volupté* he had begun pursuing as a young man was consonant with the jazz music that blared from the radio in his old age. And Piet Mondrian, this century's most ardent advocate of an art of elevated aspiration and distilled form, showed how even a world of austere platonic form could be a way to take in the variety of a life lived, from glimmering light on the sea to the probity of plain Dutch interiors to the rhythms of boogie-woogie on Broadway.

Yet there are constant pressures to deny this tradition, in part because its open-endedness and indifference to fixed hierarchies evoke such anxiety, and place such burdens of freedom on us. "The plastic life is terribly dangerous," Léger said. "Equivocation is perpetual there. No tribunal exists to settle the dispute over beauty."[7] In order to avoid that danger, rival courts have been established, and laws proclaimed. On the one hand, people have invented an imaginary system of powerful strategies and programmed destinies, usually associated with a notion of uncontaminated aesthetic elevation, and they have called this system "modernism." And in opposition, others have set themselves the task of demythologizing this system of beliefs. This ongoing adjudication sustains whole careers and nourishes vast institutions. But the two sides of the battle need each other more than they need history; and the terms constructed in these wars take on a comfortable life of their own, independent of discrete objects, individual lives, and personal experience.

It is not that the lessons we draw from the history of high and low in twentieth-century art in any way lead to a simple, empiricist skepticism about "theory." Theory is exactly what we need—but we need theory that is emancipated from a pre-scientific and even pre-rational basis in the kind of typological thinking Mayr condemned, which still governs the writing of so much cultural history. We began this book with the discomfiting sense that the "conservative" and "radical" positions on the issue of high and low were peculiarly alike. We may see now that this similarity is rooted in a shared, unconscious allegiance to what some philosophers would call "essentialism." Able to imagine historical understanding only in terms of penetrating the veils of mere appearance to get at an underlying truth, "left" and "right" alike end up arguing over the type rather than charting the variability. And, since no abstract *eidos* can ever sustain itself in the natural world, inevitably the pictures of history they present become

stereotyped fables of beleaguerment and corruption.

More recently, some cultural historians, having grasped that the categories of all theories themselves inevitably rest "ungrounded" in other complex and unjustifiable assumptions, have come to the despairing conclusion that all rational criticism is itself an illusion, or merely the deceptive camouflage by which a system of power perpetuates itself. But this intellectual nihilism requires us to accept in advance the notion that useful knowledge must take the form of authoritative types and essences; the melodramatic and dogmatic skepticism of "deconstruction" is the inevitable offspring of a disappointed essentialism. The critical theory we need is one which recognizes that the abstractions of social thought—the "bourgeoisie," the "mass audience," or high and low themselves—are, at best, provisional constructions, useful conjectures that may sometimes allow us partially to organize or grasp a little piece of history.

One of the comedies (perhaps it is really a tragedy) of contemporary intellectual manners is that, at the very moment when some of the "hard" sciences have begun to look to cultural history for models of storytelling, cultural history is increasingly infected by contempt for its own methods. Natural scientists, formerly thought of as engaged in the search for grand systems of all-shaping law, now more than ever extol the special explanatory power of "just history"—that is, of descriptive chronicles which respect the role of accident and honor the intractable power of the individual case. (A key example of this celebration of historical narrative would be the paleontologist Stephen Jay Gould's recent reconsideration of the branching diversity of early animal forms, *Wonderful Life*.) Yet many contemporary historians of culture, ironically, denigrate such ways of recounting change as unsophisticated—and treat them as delusory distractions from a "real" history, of the hidden working of large, determining forces, supposedly concealed beneath the apparent diversity of observable events and personalities. This denigration of the errant matters of mere contingency is doubly ironic in the case of those who deal with the history of modern art; for the progress of that art, in its bewilderingly different forms, provides us with some of the most telling instances in all of history of the force latent in unpredictable inventions, undetermined responses, and individual idiosyncrasies. Museums of modern art are, among much else, places where we go to replenish our faith in the power and fascination of things that did not have to happen.

To deny categories and types, however, is to risk seeming to deny values: to say that nothing is certain is often understood to be saying that anything goes. If the denial of authority is seen to result only in a surrender to facile subjectivism, then questions of critical judgment easily become just a question of who has the power to impose their views. And this argument, too, is heard from many sides of the debates over modern art and popular culture—the argument that all hierarchies of value in art are delusory artifacts of arbitrary taste, inflicted on a field in which no true discrimination is possible. This view—which is a dim parody of its antithesis, the hunger for authority—informs blissful swoons over the pleasures of kitsch culture solely because they are "pop," as well as tirades against the elitism of attempts to identify better or worse among the achievements of artists.

The forced choice between the authoritarian and the indiscriminate positions isn't adequate either to the best traditions of response to modern art, or to the art itself. The point of the "cult of imagery" that Baudelaire saw as the advancing wave of mass-media society in the nineteenth century was not that this new world of reproduced things stood conventional values on their head, but that it charged the individual's habits of looking with a burden of decision more complex than any ever experienced by a member of the academy; and brought with it for the critic a new task of persuasion. Baudelaire knew, as Robert Storr has written, that it would be necessary for the critic of modern life to "reenter modernity in the fullness of its enduring ambiguity...."[8] Baudelaire said that "a system is a kind of damnation that condemns us to perpetual backsliding; we are always having to invent another and that is a cruel form of punishment. And every time, my system was beautiful, big and spacious, convenient, tidy and polished—or at least so it seemed to me. And every time, some spontaneous unexpected vitality would come and give the lie to my puerile and old-fashioned wisdom...to escape from the horror of these philosophic apostates, I arrogantly resigned myself to be modest; I became content to feel."[9]

From Baudelaire's dissatisfaction with systems to Reyner Banham's frustration with people who talked about cars without looking at them, a higher critical tradition has insisted that we have to see for ourselves. More Baudelaire than Baudrillard, more Banham than Barthes, this tradition rests above all on a relentless and unsettling engagement with particulars, on the detection of high in low and low in high, and on the invention of new kinds of discrimination. We have passed beyond the comforting rules of former academic hierarchies, when judgments about art were made within the confines of a given set of rules that dictated which motifs, which genres, or which materials were inherently more or less noble. Every experience of the art of the past hundred years reinforces the uncomfortable, challenging premise that we cannot delimit the realm of art by any pat, a priori rankings among the categories of the circumstances, the materials, or the subjects in question: matchsticks as well as marble, printers' ink as well as oil paint, found imagery as well as esoteric fantasy may all and equally be the stuff of the most powerful and complex expressions of art in our time. In such a world, the shared cult of modern images must entail a faith in contention and a dedication to constant reassessment, second thoughts, and argument. Modern art, like the open society it inhabits, is a matter of individuals, clubs, communities, factions, and end-

less change. Taste in art, and discriminations between high and low, are in this sense entirely political—if we understand that politics does not begin with ideological categories, but rather when we are emancipated from them into a life of debate.

This vision isn't just truer to the art we know. It also corresponds to the actual experience of life in the urban cultures of the Western world in the twentieth century. We live in a world where BAL and BACH belong to the same experience, in the same day or hour, where Utamaro and *Doonesbury,* Elvis Presley and Jasper Johns, modern art in all its intensity and popular culture in all its pleasures sustain us nearly simultaneously, and each of us has to decide for ourselves what weight or measure to give to each of these things.

No fixed categories, only individual actions and judgments. This isn't a heroic conclusion. The inheritance of the nineteenth century has made us see insistent individualism as inevitably allied to a Romantic faith in heroes. But individualism need not be Romantic; it's simply an inescapable fact about the story at hand, and it is found more often in slow labors than in blinding genius. Clive James, the British critic of television and poetry, once wrote that to be a true pluralist "is a work of patience, of taking pains to attack categories while insisting on values, and there is no valid way of speeding the job up."[10] Better to conclude, then, not with the vision of a vast turning wheel as the image of this progress, but with an inquiry into the smaller human efforts that propel that wheel, step by step. Leave aside the big questions about big cycles, and look at one last little motif, whose image stuck out of this book's frontispiece: the big foot.

When we saw, back at the beginning, Bibendum's huge, studded sole kicking out at us, we recognized a comic motif that was also the announcement of a particular kind of modern energy. *In your face.* But that motif has reappeared often in our story, from Crumb's undaunted "truckers" to Lichtenstein's *Keds* to Guston's pathetic cobbled soles. And when we ask where

2. George Herriman. Panel from *Baron Bean*, 1918. © King Features Syndicate

3. Floyd Gottfredson. Panel from *Mickey Mouse*, April 22, 1948.
© Walt Disney Productions

this funny motif came from, and how it grew, we get a kind of microcosmic recapitulation of the patterns of history we've been recounting, a story of people finding a vehicle for poetic expression in the most improbable low motif, a story of souls and soles.

The big foot, like so much else in modern art, begins in the Renaissance; it's a perspective motif. When we search for its origins we realize that they lie in early experiments in foreshortening, and that the motif has two different emotional effects there. In battle scenes, the foreshortened foot is a motif of energy, in which the inexorable logic of linear perspective and the free description of athletic movement can be joined. But we also see big feet on people who lie down, and most often this means the dead, whether in the defeated warriors of the quattrocento painter Uccello or in such extraordinary images of pathos as Mantegna's radically foreshortened *Dead Christ* of about 1466. The big foot begins both as a bravura demonstration piece of human energy and artistic mastery, and as an image of surrender and defeat.

At the end of the nineteenth century, this motif moves from the margin to the center and becomes, in Chéret's hands, for instance, a motif that suggests the jaunty, dandified syncopation of modern life—a world

of kicks and turns and flying leaps; that is still its meaning in the kick-boxing Bibendum. But by the time it enters the American comic strip, a few years later, the upturned foot has changed its meanings slightly. Now it is more of a clown's big shoe, an exaggerated "adult" feature, that, supporting the tiny head and elongated bodies of Mutt or Baron Bean, makes us laugh at the absurd contrast between the grown-up appearance and the infantile comportment. The constant reiteration of these upturned soles in the early comic strip seems to offer, on a Lilliputian level, a joining of the two traditional meanings of the motif: comic energy and determination on the one hand and an undertone of pathos on the other, a foreknowledge that all the schemes and plots on which the characters are so jauntily launched will be overthrown (fig. 2).

By the early thirties this device of the oversized shoe became part of the standard language of cartooning; it just said "comics." In Gottfredson's Mickey Mouse, for instance, the big, clunky shoe and sudden revelations of nailed-down soles are elements of costume, part of the abstract repertoire of Disney devices, something to place alongside Mickey's accentuated curves and neotenic features (fig. 3). From this perch, the big foot sank down into the lowest reaches of gag-a-day

4. Mort Walker. Panels from *Beetle Bailey*, September 14, 1952. © King Features Syndicate

5. **Robert Crumb.** "Keep on Truckin'...," from *Zap,* 1 (November 1967). © 1983 R. Crumb

comics so that, by the early fifties, the work of hack cartoonists was labeled by their condescending colleagues as simply "big foot" style (fig. 4).[11]

From that low perch, both Crumb and Guston picked up the motif again, and recognized in its degradation a new kind of meaning. In Crumb's hands, the big foot and upturned sole became symbols of the reconciliation of the protest culture with the vernacular of American working-class life; to "keep on truckin'" was essentially an injunction to the counterculture to take on itself some of the buttoned-up stoicism, the uncomplaining, trudging rectitude, of working people (fig. 5). The comic force of the symbol—and it was for a while one of the most pervasive images in America—lay in the utterly unexpected embrace of a degraded comic image of resignation by a subculture seemingly bent on reforming the world.

For Guston, the same image of the upturned sole and the cobbled shoe, which he seems to have recollected from its low point in Gottfredson, became a symbol at once of protest and of exhausted surrender. Choosing the most awkward, unbeautiful of images, Guston insisted that this was a base level of truth—that real souls could only be found in foot soles, and that shoe leather offered an uncompromising, glamorless image of lived experience (count the nails on this sole and then talk to me about "pure aesthetic experience," each Guston shoe whispers). At the same time, Guston restored to the upturned sole its original pathos; for him, too, it is a symbol of death (fig. 6).

The upturned sole and the big foot have also become favorite symbolic motifs of Elizabeth Murray.

6. **Philip Guston.** *Mesa.* 1976. Oil on canvas, 64" × 9'6" (162.5 × 292.1 cm). Courtesy David McKee Gallery, New York

Here, as we've seen, the source lay in low imagery. Her big-shoe reliefs have their origins in the oversize shoes that Dagwood wears in Chic Young's *Blondie*. For Murray, Dagwood's shoe became a found symbolic image of her own father, wearing out his shoe leather, searching for a job—failing. Comic disproportion became for her a symbol of defeat, and this association was reinforced by a famous photograph of Adlai Stevenson (the beaten Democrat in both presidential races of the 1950s), with his foot turned up to reveal a hole in the sole. For Murray, this simple comic vessel—Dagwood's shoes, which are the great liberal loser's shoes, which are her father's shoes—have become a motif of defeat and perplexity generally, freeing her to find in the least inflection of the low image new symbolic meaning. The shoelace, reforming itself into a noose, can, for example, embody an elegiac recollection of the suicide of a friend (fig. 7).[12]

"How beautiful are the feet of them that preach the gospel of peace, and bring glad tidings of good things!" runs the most incongruous exultation in the Bible.[13] "How beautiful are the feet"—what Saint Paul meant, of course, was that feet were beautiful because they could go places, propel works that could only be done by one person trudging over to another, to take a new message from town to town in a way that would eventually change the consciousness of an empire. The big, rolling movements of modern culture, those wheels and whirligigs of exchange, in the end turn out to be just such small, pedestrian movements—not foreordained cycles but the consequence of little, prodding, uncertain motions forward. Look at a funny upturned shoe, and, if you are willing, you can see faith, energy, failure, and your father's life. The modern tradition can continue to bring us glad tidings by taking us on extraordinary journeys to familiar places, but only on its own eccentric terms. The deal is that you have to go without a map, and you can only get there on foot.

7. **Elizabeth Murray.** *Tomorrow.* 1988. Oil on canvas; two panels, overall, 9′3″ × 11′¾″ × 21½″ (218.9 × 337.2 × 54.6 cm). Collection The Fukuoka City Bank, Ltd.

The notes are for the most part limited to sources of quotations and references for individual artists and works. For general references on the main chapter subjects—graffiti, caricature, comics, and advertising—as well as theoretical studies of mass culture, see the relevant headings of the Bibliography.

Translations given in the text are by the present authors, unless a translator is indicated in the note.

Introduction

1. See Max Horkheimer and Theodor W. Adorno, "The Culture Industry: Enlightenment as Mass Deception," in Horkheimer and Adorno, *The Dialectic of Enlightenment,* trans. John Cumming (New York: Continuum Press, 1972); see also Adorno, "Culture Industry Reconsidered," *New German Critique,* 6 (Fall 1975), pp. 12–19.

2. The line is from Clement Greenberg, "Avant-Garde and Kitsch," *Partisan Review,* 6 (Fall 1939), pp. 34–49; reprinted in Greenberg, *Art and Culture: Critical Essays* (Boston: Beacon Press, 1961). For recent considerations of this Greenberg essay, see Robert C. Morgan, "Formalism as a Transgressive Device," *Arts Magazine,* 64 (December 1989), pp. 65–69, and in the same issue, comments by Peter Halley, Lisa Phillips, and Stephen Westfall (pp. 58–64), and Saul Ostrow's interview with Greenberg, "Avant-Garde and Kitsch, Fifty Years Later" (pp. 56–57). See also T. J. Clark's "Clement Greenberg's Theory of Art," Michael Fried's "How Modernism Works: A Response to T. J. Clark," and Clark's "Arguments About Modernism: A Reply to Michael Fried," all in Francis Frascina, ed., *Pollock and After: The Critical Debate* (New York: Harper & Row, 1985); and Robert Storr, "No Joy in Mudville," in Kirk Varnedoe and Adam Gopnik, eds., *Modern Art and Popular Culture: Readings in High and Low* (New York: The Museum of Modern Art and Harry N. Abrams, 1990).

3. Recently, several art historians have taken a far more active interest in creating a body of critical thought specific to the history of the modern visual arts and their relation to mass culture. Following the early lead of Meyer Schapiro's discussions of the social context of early modern art, and particularly of the motifs from the world of Parisian leisure and entertainment favored by the Impressionists and Post-Impressionists, Thomas Crow has attempted to extend some of the analyses of Theodor Adorno into a newly specific consideration of the dialogue between the modern visual arts and modern mass culture, in his essay "Modernism and Mass Culture in the Visual Arts," in Benjamin H. D. Buchloh, Serge Guilbaut, and David Solkin, eds., *Modernism and Modernity: The Vancouver Conference Papers,* The Nova Scotia Series, 14 (Halifax: Press of the Nova Scotia College of Art and Design, 1983); see also the revised version in Frascina, ed., *Pollock and After.* T. J. Clark also concentrates on early modern art's engagement with the new commercial culture of entertainment in late nineteenth-century Paris in *The Painting of Modern Life: Paris in the Art of Manet and His Followers* (New York: Alfred A. Knopf, 1984).

Words

1. *Le Portugais* (fig. 2) was among the canvases Braque brought back with him when he returned to Paris in January 1912; we cannot be certain that it was the first canvas on which the stenciled letters appear, though it is generally thought to be so. See Judith Cousins with the collaboration of Pierre Daix, "Documentary Chronology," in William Rubin, *Picasso and Braque: Pioneering Cubism,* exh. cat. (New York: The Museum of Modern Art, 1989), p. 388.

2. On the collage works by Juan Gris, see Lewis Kachur, "Gris, cubismo, y collage," in *Juan Gris, 1887–1927* (Madrid: Ministerio de Cultura, 1985). My thanks to Lewis Kachur for bringing this article

to my attention, and for providing me with its manuscript.

3. Guillaume Apollinaire, "Zone" (1913), in *Selected Writings of Guillaume Apollinaire,* trans. Roger Shattuck (New York: New Directions, 1971), p. 117.

4. Apollinaire continues, "One wonders why the poet should not have an equal freedom, and should be restricted, in an era of the telephone, the wireless, and aviation, to a greater cautiousness in confronting space." Guillaume Apollinaire, "The New Spirit and the Poets" (1918), in *Selected Writings of Guillaume Apollinaire,* p. 229.

5. See Daniel Pope, "French Advertising Men and the American 'Promised Land,'" *Historical Reflections,* 5 (Summer 1978), pp. 117–38.

6. Girardin played heavily on the *roman feuilleton,* by using citywide ads to build curiosity about developments in the current novels. See H.-R. Woestyn, "Quelques modes bizarres de la publicité," *La Publicité moderne,* 2 (September 1906), p. 7.

7. Pope, "French Advertising Men and the American 'Promised Land,'" p. 123.

8. See Paul Bernelle, *Des restrictions apportées depuis 1881 à la liberté de l'affichage* (Paris: Arthur Rousseau, 1912).

9. Pope, "French Advertising Men and the American 'Promised Land,'" p. 125. In 1917, an American writer commented: "The circulation of these [the Parisian] papers far exceeds those of American dailies—for instance *Le Petit Parisien* has 2,350,000, *Le Matin* has 2,000,000 and *Le Petit Journal* has

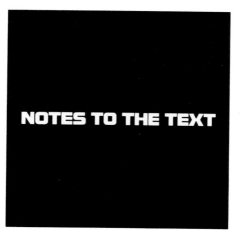

NOTES TO THE TEXT

1,250,000" ("The Lay of the Market in France," *Printers' Ink,* September 20, 1917, p. 85). One might well take these figures with a grain of salt. The notorious inflating of circulation figures and the lack of any objective mechanism to measure circulation were frequent complaints of American advertisers against the French market. In one instance in which the author seems to have been at pains to obtain a hard figure on the actual number of papers printed, D. C. A. Hémet reported a week's figures for the editions of *Le Journal* in October 1910, and they ran consistently in the range of 1,100,000 or more copies per day; see "Le Tirage des journaux," *La Publicité,* 8 (October 1910), p. 419.

10. See Norman L. Kleeblatt, ed., *The Dreyfus Affair: Art, Truth and Justice,* exh. cat. (New York: The Jewish Museum; Berkeley: University of California Press, 1987).

11. On the numerous press scandals of the late nineteenth and early twentieth centuries in Paris, see Claude Bellanger, Jacques Godachot, Pierre Guival, and Fernand Terron, eds., *Histoire générale de la presse française,* vol. 3 (Paris: Presses Universitaires de France, 1973).

12. See Boussalon, "Le Mur," *La Publicité moderne,* 3 (December 1907), p. 7.

13. Pope, "French Advertising Men and the American 'Promised Land,'" p. 125.

14. "On the eve of World War One . . . French newspapers had made notable improvements in their treatment of advertising. Advertisements

spilled over from the rear page onto the inside pages, where they mingled with news and features. A plethora of type faces had entered the major dailies. Illustrated advertisements, some running the entire width of the page, were not uncommon. Nevertheless, major display advertising was rare. *Le Matin,* one of the mass circulation Parisian dailies, ran only two or three full-page ads a month in early 1914" (Pope, "French Advertising Men and the American 'Promised Land,'" p. 126). See also the discussion of newspaper promotions of aviation, with regard to Robert Delaunay's *The Cardiff Team,* in the chapter "Advertising," below.

15. Oswald Spengler, *The Decline of the West,* trans. Charles Francis Atkinson ([1920]; rpt., London: George Allen & Unwin, 1980), vol. 2, pp. 461–62.

16. "Les Kiosques et la publicité," *La Publicité,* 9 (February 1911), p. 81. The Prefect's move was spurred by a protest from the holder of a publicity concession, and kiosk owners were convinced that the intention was only to provoke an incident that would end by extending the rights of the concession holder.

17. On William Morris's Arts and Crafts movement and the flowering of its ideas, see Peter Stansky, *Redesigning the World: William Morris, the 1880s, and the Arts and Crafts* (Princeton, N.J.: Princeton University Press, 1985); Ian Bradley, *William Morris and His World* (New York: Charles Scribner's Sons, 1978); Stephen T. Madsen, *The Sources of Art Nouveau* (New York: George Wittenborn, 1956), and Robert Schmutzler, *Art Nouveau—Jugenstil* (Stuttgart: Gerd Hatje; New York: Harry N. Abrams, 1962).

18. See Rubin, *Picasso and Braque,* p. 20.

19. Robert Rosenblum, "Picasso and the Typography of Cubism," in Roland Penrose and John Golding, eds., *Picasso in Retrospect* (New York and Washington, D.C.: Praeger, 1973); British edition published as *Picasso, 1881–1973* (London: Paul Elek, 1973). For Rosenblum's updated evaluation of the subject, see his "Cubism as Pop Art," in Kirk Varnedoe and Adam Gopnik, eds., *Modern Art and Popular Culture: Readings in High and Low* (New York: The Museum of Modern Art and Harry N. Abrams, 1990).

20. The development of the laws applying to postering in Paris are fully discussed in the chapter "Advertising."

21. Maurice Jardot was the first to deduce the link between Picasso's use of the phrase *ma jolie* with the refrain of the popular song by Fragson. See Maurice Jardot, *Picasso: Peintures, 1900–1955,* exh. cat. (Paris: Musée des Arts Décoratifs, 1955), cat. no. 28. In a letter dated June 12, 1912, Picasso wrote to his dealer, D.-H. Kahnweiler, that Eva "is very sweet. I love her very much and I will write this in my paintings." See Cousins, "Documentary Chronology," pp. 394–95.

22. On the other hand, the association with Kub brand bouillon may have had unintentional nationalist overtones. The accusation that Cubism was somehow the result of pernicious German influences on French art may have received support, around the time of World War I, from the apparent association of the Kub brand name—likely the result of its initial K, which suggested a Germanic origin—with the enemy across the Rhine. See the interesting story of the popular movement to attack and destroy ads for Kub, after war with Germany was declared: "Le Bouillon Kub," *La Publicité,* 18 (April 1920), pp. 160–62.

23. The 1912 pamphlet *Notre Avenir est dans l'air* is a compendium of brief statements by French Army officers asserting the importance of the development of French aeronautics for military power. The rhetoric of this pamphlet gave way to far more bellicose language in the firm's 1919 pamphlet *Notre Sécurité est dans l'air,* which dealt almost exclusively with advances in formation bombing.

24. See Rubin, *Picasso and Braque,* pp. 32–33; and

Cousins, "Documentary Chronology," pp. 401–02.

25. See Rosenblum, "Picasso and the Typography of Cubism," p. 64. See also D.-H. Kahnweiler, *Juan Gris: His Life and Work*, trans. Douglas Cooper ([1946]; rev. ed., New York: Harry N. Abrams, 1969), pp. 49, 261; and E. A. Carmean, Jr., "Juan Gris' *Fantômas*," *Arts*, 51 (January 1977), pp. 116–19.

26. Regarding the hostile reactions to the Armory Show of 1913, Milton Brown comments that "most of the running gags about the Armory Show were not exactly witty. They were usually of the Joe Miller Joke Book variety, like the one about Braque's *Violon*, which included the names Kubelik and Mozart. Two men were looking at the painting and one said, 'Braque is the painter who put cube in Kubelik.' 'No,' said the other, 'he put art in Mozart' " (Milton W. Brown, *The Story of the Armory Show* [New York: Abbeville and The Joseph H. Hirshhorn Foundation, 1988], p. 139).

27. See Meyer Schapiro, "The Nature of Abstract Art" (1937), in Schapiro, *Modern Art: Nineteenth and Twentieth Centuries—Selected Papers* (New York: George Braziller, 1979).

28. On Picasso's frequent clipping of stories related to the Balkan Wars, and the possible relation of these choices to anarchist and pacifist beliefs, see Patricia Leighten, *Re-Ordering the Universe: Picasso and Anarchism, 1897–1914* (Princeton, N.J.: Princeton University Press, 1989).

29. Just such a notice for Mistinguett did appear in the listings that were immediately below the lingerie ad Picasso clipped for the *papier collé* known as *Au Bon Marché* ("Advertising," figs. 33, 34).

30. See Michael Kirby, *Futurist Performance* (New York: E. P. Dutton & Co., 1971), pp. 61, 63.

31. See *The Futurist Imagination: Word + Image in Italian Futurist Painting, Drawing, Collage and Free-Word Poetry*, exh. cat. (New Haven, Conn.: Yale University Art Gallery, 1983); see especially Christine Poggi, "Marinetti's *Parole in libertà* and the Futurist Collage Aesthetic."

32. See *Soviet Commercial Design of the Twenties*, edited and designed by Mikhaïl Anikst, text by Elena Chernevich, translated by Catherine Cooke (New York: Abbeville, 1987).

33. See Selim Omarovich Khan-Magomedov, *Rodchenko: The Complete Work*, ed. Vieri Quilici (Cambridge, Mass.: MIT Press, 1987). See also *Paris/Moscou, 1900–1930*, exh. cat. (Paris: Musée National d'Art Moderne, Centre Georges Pompidou, 1979).

34. On Mayakovsky, see Juliette R. Stapanian, *Mayakovsky's Cubo-Futurist Vision* (Houston, Tex.: Rice University Press, 1986); L. L. Stahlberger, *The Symbolic System of Mayakovsky* (The Hague: Mouton, 1964); and *Mayakovsky: 20 Ans de travail* (Paris: Musée National d'Art Moderne, Centre Georges Pompidou, 1975).

35. John Bowlt, "A Brazen Can-Can in the Temple of Art: The Russian Avant-Garde and Popular Culture," in Varnedoe and Gopnik, eds., *Modern Art and Popular Culture*.

36. Our estimation of the impact of Russian influences on French graphic design after 1925 depends on the recollections of Alexander Liberman, given in a personal interview in November 1989. Mr. Liberman stressed how completely French graphic designers had ignored the avant-garde in Paris until the Russian designers, seen in 1925, opened their eyes.

37. This echo effect may be true of the content, as well as the style, of advertising in the 1930s. One of the most famous posters by the artist Cassandre, for Dubonnet, played on the segmentation of the brand name into parts with independent meanings: DUBO, an aural play on *du beau*, with its echoes of "beautiful" or "handsome"; DUBON, suggesting "good"; and finally DUBONNET. It is precisely the kind of game the Cubists had played, with *Le Journal* for example, but now adapted to sales purposes.

38. See "Mehemed Fehmy Agha," in *The Fifty-first*

Annual of the Advertising Art Director's Club of New York (New York: Art Directors' Club of New York, 1971). See also R. Roger Remington and Barbara J. Hodik, *Nine Pioneers in American Graphic Design* (Cambridge, Mass., and London: MIT Press, 1989), pp. 9–13.

39. See M[ehemed] F[ehmy] Agha, "Sanserif," *Advertising Arts* (supplement to *Advertising and Selling*), March 1931, pp. 41–47.

40. On the history of modern typography, see Herbert Spencer, *Pioneers of Modern Typography* ([1969]; rev. ed., Cambridge, Mass.: MIT Press, 1983); see also Herbert Spencer, ed., *The Liberated Page* (San Francisco: Bedford Press, 1987). For a recent evaluation of typography in America, see *Graphic Design in America: A Visual Language History*, exh. cat. (Minneapolis: Walker Art Center; New York: Harry N. Abrams, 1989).

41. For an argument that modern popular culture inevitably saps the real force of the avant-garde's intransigent resistance to society's dominant powers, and thus makes vanguard art into a mere "research and development" branch of what Theodor Adorno called the "culture industry," see Thomas Crow, "Modernism and Mass Culture in the Visual Arts," in Benjamin H. D. Buchloh, Serge Guilbaut, and David Solkin, eds., *Modernism and Modernity: The Vancouver Conference Papers*, The Nova Scotia Series, 14 (Hailifax: Press of the Nova Scotia College of Art and Design, 1983). See also the later version of this essay in Francis Frascina, ed., *Pollock and After: The Critical Debate* (New York: Harper & Row, 1985).

42. See John Elderfield, *Kurt Schwitters*, exh. cat. (London: Thames & Hudson, for The Museum of Modern Art, New York, 1985), pp. 12–13; and see p. 90, where Elderfield discusses alternate meanings for the term Merz.

43. Ibid, pp. 12–13.

Graffiti

1. *The Merry-Thought: or, the Glass-Window and Bog-House Miscellany*, published by Hurlo Thrumbo, printed for J. Roberts, Part 1 (London, 1731), Parts 2–4 (n.d.). Reprint, Los Angeles: University of California, The Augustan Reprint Society, 1982 (Part 1), 1983 (Parts 2–4).

2. The graffiti of Pompeii were first remarked in the unpublished official reports of the excavation, the *journal des fouilles*, in October 1765, according to Raphael Garrucci, *Graffiti de Pompéi*, 2nd ed., rev. and enl. (Paris: Benjamin Duprat, 1856), p. 8. Garrucci also cites two Nuremberg publications by Christophis Theophilus de Murr, in 1792 and 1793, that briefly discuss the cursive inscriptions.

3. See Jacques-Joseph Champollion, *Monuments de l'Egypte et de la Nubie: Notices descriptives*, vol. 1 (Paris: Firmin-Didot, 1835), plate 53 (bis); F. C. Gau, *Antiquités de la Nubie, ou monuments inédits des bords du Nil situés entre la première et la seconde cataracte, dessinés et mesurés, 1819* (Stuttgart: J. G. Cotta; Paris: Firmin-Didot, 1822). For a comprehensive discussion of the Nubian graffiti, see F[rancis] Ll[ewellyn] Griffith, *Temples immergés de la Nubie: Catalogue of the Demotic Graffiti of the Dodecaschoenus*, 2 vols. (Oxford: University Press, 1935, 1937).

4. Rev. Christopher Wordsworth, *Inscriptiones Pompeianae: Or, Specimens and Facsimiles of Ancient Inscriptions Discovered on the Walls of Buildings at Pompeii* (London: John Murray, 1837).

5. According to Garrucci, *Graffiti de Pompéi*, F. M. Avellino published an article on two inscriptions in an 1831 *Bulletin de l'Institut Archéologique de Rome*. Some images of the graffiti were also reproduced in Guglielmo Bechi, "Relazione degli scavi di Pompei," *Real Museo Barbonico*, 6 (Naples: Stamperia Reale, 1830). The Englishman William Gell noted the inscriptions briefly in his *Pompeiana: The Topography, Edifices and Ornaments of Pompei—The Result of Excavations Since 1819* (London: Jen-

nings & Chaplin, 1832), pp. 30–31. Christopher Wordsworth was the first to devote an entire publication to these records, with *Inscriptiones Pompeianae*.

6. Cav. F[rancesco] M. Avellino, *Osservazioni sopra alcune iscrizioni e disegni graffiti sulle mura di Pompei* (Naples: Stamperia Reale, 1841).

7. Garrucci, *Graffiti de Pompéi*. Note that this 1856 publication, which was widely circulated and remarked upon, is the second edition, greatly enlarged, of an earlier study; see Garrucci's comments, in the Preface, on the limitations of the first edition.

8. On early Christian graffiti, see G[iovanni] B[attista] de Rossi, *La Roma sotterranea cristiana*, 3 vols. (Rome: Cromo Litographia Pontifica, 1864–77); and Abbé Martigny, *Dictionnaire des antiquités chrétiennes*, 3rd ed. (Paris: Librairie Hachette, 1889), p. 335.

9. Rodolphe Töpffer, *Réflexions et menus propos d'un peintre genevois ou essai sur le beau dans les arts* (Paris: J. J. Dubochet, Lechevalier, 1848), vol. 2, pp. 104–11.

10. Champfleury [Jules-François-Félix Husson], *Histoire de la caricature antique* ([1865]; 2nd ed., Paris: Éditions Dentu, 1867), p. 283.

11. Rev. J. W. Horsley, *Jottings from Jail* (London: T. Fisher Unwin, 1887); Dr. Émile Laurent, *Les Habitués des prisons de Paris* (Lyon: A. Storck; Paris: G. Masson, 1890); Cesare Lombroso, *Les Palimpsestes des prisons* (Lyon: A. Storck; Paris: G. Masson, 1894).

12. Havelock Ellis, *The Criminal* ([1890]; 3rd ed., rev. and enl., London: Walter Scott; New York: Charles Scribner's Sons, 1903), p. 211.

13. Of the various articles by Georges Henri Luquet, first see "Sur la survivance des caractères du dessin enfantin dans des graffiti à indications sexuelles," *Anthropophyteia*, 7 (1910), pp. 196–202; see also his other articles: "Dégénérescences alphabétiques du visage humain dans les graffiti contemporains," *Revue d'ethnographie et de sociologie*, 5, no. 3–4 (March–April 1914), pp. 92–96; "Figuration possible de la vulve dans l'écriture pictographique de la Crète minoenne," *Anthropophyteia*, 8 (1911), pp. 215–16; "Représentation de la vulve dans les graffiti contemporains," *Anthropophyteia*, 8 (1911), pp. 210–14; "Sur les caractères des figures humaines dans l'art paléolithique," *L'Anthropologie*, 21 (1910), pp. 409–23; "Sur un cas d'homonymie graphique: Sexe et visage humain," *Anthropophyteia*, 7 (1910), pp. 202–06; and "La Méthode dans l'étude des dessins d'enfants," *Journal de psychologie*, 19 (1922), pp. 193–221. Luquet also wrote a book in which he argued that both children's drawings and graffiti could be used to understand prehistoric art: *L'Art primitif* (Paris: G. Doin, Bibliothèque d'Anthropologie, 1930). For a review of this book, by Georges Bataille, see note 24, below.

14. For pictures and discussion of these works, see Susan Sontag, "The Pleasure of the Image," *Art in America*, 75 (November 1987), pp. 122–32.

15. See Thomas Kren, "*Chi non vuol Baccho*: Roeland van Laer's Burlesque Painting About Dutch Artists in Rome," *Simiolus* 11, no. 2 (1980), pp. 63–80. There is a similarly marked-up wall in the background of Renoir's *Chez la mère Antoine*, a view of artists in a Barbizon inn, of 1867 (National Museum, Stockholm). See also Giulio Briganti, Ludovica Trezzani, and Laura Laureati, *The Bamboccianti: The Painters of Everyday Life in Seventeenth-Century Rome*, trans. Robert Erich Wolf (Rome: Ugo Bozzi, 1983).

16. Restif de La Bretonne, *Mes inscripcions: Journal intime de Restif de La Bretonne, 1780–1787* (Paris: E. Plon, 1889).

17. My thanks to Emily Braun for pointing out the Vittorio Corcos painting. For a discussion of its graffiti, see Emily Braun, "From the Risorgimento to the Resistance: One Hundred Years of Jewish Artists in Italy," in Vivian B. Mann, ed., *Gardens and Ghet-*

tos: *The Art of Jewish Life in Italy*, exh. cat. (Berkeley, Los Angeles, Oxford: University of California Press, 1989), p. 148.

18. For a discussion of graffiti-like inscriptions on works by these artists, and possible other references to graffiti in Russian art of the same period, see John Bowlt, "A Brazen Can-Can in the Temple of Art: The Russian Avant-Garde and Popular Culture," in Kirk Varnedoe and Adam Gopnik, eds., *Modern Art and Popular Culture: Readings in High and Low* (New York: The Museum of Modern Art and Harry N. Abrams, 1990).

19. On Balla and the photographs of lowlife taken by the photographer Primoli, see Gerald Silk, "Fù Balla e Balla Futurista," *Art Journal*, 41 (Winter 1981), pp. 328–36.

20. See Theodore Reff, "Duchamp and Leonardo: L.H.O.O.Q.-Alikes," *Art in America*, 65 (January–February 1977), pp. 82–93.

21. Brassaï, "Du mur des cavernes au mur d'usine," *Minotaure*, 1, nos. 3, 4 (1933), pp. 6–7.

22. Brassaï, "The Art of the Wall," *The Saturday Book*, no. 18 (1958), pp. 237–49. For a different translation, see "Language of the Wall," *U.S. Camera*, 1958, pp. 6–15, 290, 294. See also "Graffiti parisiens," *XXe Siècle*, new series, no. 10 (March 1958), pp. 21–24.

23. Hans Prinzhorn, *Bildnerei der Gefangenen* (Berlin: Axel Juncker, 1926), pp. 11–13.

24. See Marcel Griaule, *Silhouettes et graffiti abyssins*, Introduction by Marcel Mauss (Paris: Larose, 1933). See also Georges Bataille, "L'Art primitif" (review of Luquet's *L'Art primitif*), *Documents*, 2, no. 7 (1930), pp. 389–97; and A. S., "Peintures rupestres de Congo," *Minotaure*, no. 2 (1933), pp. 52–55.

25. The standard source on Dubuffet's writings between 1944 and 1967 remains *Prospectus et tous écrits suivants*, ed. Hubert Damisch, 2 vols. (Paris: Éditions Gallimard, 1967). For a poetic remembrance of common interest in graffiti, see René de Solier, "Au temps des graffiti, et ensuite," in *Dubuffet*, ed. Jacques Berne, *Cahiers de l'herne* series (Paris: Éditions de l'Herne, [1973]), pp. 273–76; on de Solier's earlier statements concerning Luquet, Prinzhorn, Klee, Henri Calet, and Brassaï's interest in graffiti, see "Embarras du beau," *L'Arc*, 35 (1968), pp. 67–73; for the reference to an unpublished letter, dated August 16, 1947, by Dubuffet to Brassaï discussing a publication project concerning graffiti from the *art brut* collection, see *Brassaï*, exh. cat. (Paris: Bibliothèque Nationale, 1963), p. 23. For a view opposing Dubuffet's claim to making subversive art with graffiti, see Clement Greenberg, "Art Chronicle: Jean Dubuffet and 'Art Brut,'" *Partisan Review*, 16 (March 1949), pp. 295–97; for a broader consideration, from a psychoanalytic viewpoint, regarding Dubuffet's use of language, see Michel Thévoz, "Dubuffet: Le casseur de noix," *Critique*, January–February 1988, pp. 77–94. Note that the above-mentioned Henri Calet (1904–1956), a literary figure associated with Dubuffet, recorded the prison graffiti of the French resistance in *Les Murs de Fresnes* (Paris: Les Éditions de Quatre Vents, 1945).

26. For a general introduction to the *nouveau réalisme* movement and for sections on individual artists, see Pierre Restany, *Les Nouveaux réalistes*, preface by Michel Ragon (Paris: Planète, 1968); and *1960: Les Nouveaux réalistes*, exh. cat. (Paris: Musée d'Art Moderne de la Ville de Paris, 1986). On Raymond Hains, see *Hains*, exh. cat. (Paris: Musée National d'Art Moderne, Centre Georges Pompidou, for the Centre National d'Art Contemporain, 1976). On Jacques de la Villeglé, see *Villeglé: Défense d'afficher*, exh. cat. (Paris: Galerie Beaubourg [1974]); *Villeglé: Lacéré anonyme*, exh. cat. (Paris: Musée National d'Art Moderne, Centre Georges Pompidou, 1977); and Christopher Phillips, "When Poetry Devours the Walls," *Art in America*, 78 (February 1990), pp. 138–45. For the artists' writings, see *Urbi & Orbi* (Paris: Éditions W. Macon, 1986).

On Mimmo Rotella, see *Rotella: Décollages, 1954–1964*, Introduction by Sam Hunter (Milan: Electa, 1986); and Tommaso Trini, *Rotella*, Preface by Pierre Restany (Milan: G. Prearo, 1974).

27. Cited in *Villeglé: Lacéré anonyme*, p. 21.

28. Restany, *Les Nouveaux réalistes*, p. 82.

29. On the photographic technique involving the use of special lenses (*verres cannelés*), see Hains's statements of 1952, "Quand la photographie devient l'objet," reprinted in *Hains*, pp. 6–7; on the application of this technique to texts, see pp. 152–66.

30. François Dufrêne was the latecomer. From an interest in the hidden aspects of language and phonetic exploration he came to the discovery of torn posters. He first saw them in December 1957, when accompanying Hains to the Maison Bompaire, a storage for torn posters. See *François Dufrêne*, exh. cat. (Les Sables d'Olonne: Musée de l'Abbaye Sainte-Croix; Nemours: Château-Musée, 1988); and *Hommage à François Dufrêne*, exh. cat. (Paris: Musée National d'Art Moderne, Centre Georges Pompidou, 1983).

31. On Lettrism and its offshoots, including the Situationist International, see Stewart Home, *The Assault on Culture: Utopian Currents from Lettrisme to Class War* (London: Aporia Press & Unpopular Books, 1988); and on the Situationist International movement, see Elizabeth Sussman, ed., *On the Passage of a Few People through a Rather Brief Moment in Time: The Situationist International, 1957–1972*, exh. cat. (Boston: Institute of Contemporary Art; MIT Press, 1989). On Asger Jorn's décollages, see *Asger Jorn: The Final Years, 1965–1973* (London: Lund Humphries, 1980); for his statements on his décollages, see *Asger Jorn au pied du mur et un trilogue de l'artiste avec Noël Arnaud et François Dufrêne*, exh. cat. (Paris: Jeanne Bucher, 1969).

32. On Jorn's interpretation of graffiti, see Asger Jorn, ed., *Signes gravés sur les églises de l'Eure et du Calvados* (Copenhagen: Édition Borger, 1964); and on his views regarding vandalism and Nordic folk art, see Ann-Charlotte Weinmarck, *Nordisk Anarkiism* (Arhus: Kalejdoskop Forlag, 1980), p. 85.

33. On Rauschenberg, see *Robert Rauschenberg*, exh. cat. (Washington, D.C.: National Collection of Fine Arts, Smithsonian Institution, 1976); and Roni Feinstein, "Random Order: The First Fifteen Years of Robert Rauschenberg's Art, 1949–1964" (Ph.D. dissertation, Institute of Fine Arts, New York University, 1990).

34. On the identification of the Twombly drawing in *Rebus*, see Feinstein, "Random Order," p. 210. For an interpretation of *Rebus*, see Charles F. Stuckey, "Reading Rauschenberg," *Art in America*, 65 (March–April 1977), pp. 81–83.

35. For bibliographies on Twombly, see *Cy Twombly: Paintings and Drawings, 1954–1977*, exh. cat. (New York: Whitney Museum of American Art, 1979), pp. 108–11; and *Cy Twombly: Paintings, Works on Paper, Sculpture*, ed. Harald Szeemann, with contributions by Demosthenes Davetas, Roberta Smith, and Harald Szeemann, and a Foreword by Nicholas Serota (Munich: Prestel; New York: distributed in the U.S.A. by Te Neues Pub. Co., 1987), pp. 237–39; for references to graffiti, see Jean-Jacques Levêque, "Twombly: Graffiti-Story," *Nouvelles littéraires*, 54 (July 8, 1976), p. 12. Roland Barthes commented that Twombly is "un écrivain qui accèderait au graffiti" (in *Cy Twombly: Catalogue raisonné des oeuvres sur papier de Cy Twombly*, catalogue by Yvon Lambert, text by Roland Barthes [Milan: Multhipla, 1979], p. 10); and Donald Kuspit discusses "graffiti idealized into memory traces of a time when the prosaic was inherently poetic" (in "Cy Twombly," *Artforum*, 25 [October 1986], p. 129).

Caricature

1. See Irving Lavin, "High and Low Before Their Time: Bernini and the Art of Social Satire," in Kirk Varnedoe and Adam Gopnik, eds., *Modern Art and Popular Culture: Readings in High and Low* (New York: The Museum of Modern of Art and Harry N. Abrams, 1990).

2. See Maurice du Seigneur, "L'Exposition de la caricature et de la peinture de moeurs au xixe siècle," *L'Artiste*, 9 (1888), p. 433.

3. The two seminal essays on the relationship between modern art and popular imagery in the nineteenth century are Meyer Schapiro, "Courbet and Popular Imagery," *Journal of the Warburg and Courtauld Institutes*, 4 (1941), pp. 164–91, reprinted in Schapiro, *Modern Art: Nineteenth and Twentieth Centuries—Selected Papers* (New York: George Braziller, 1978); and E. H. Gombrich, "Imagery and Art in the Romantic Period," *Burlington Magazine*, 191 (June 1949), pp. 153–58, reprinted in *"Meditations on a Hobby Horse" and Other Essays on the Theory of Art* (London: Phaidon, 1963). For a critical review of what has happened since, see Lorenz Eitner, "Subjects from Common Life in the Real Language of Men: Popular Art and Modern Tradition in Nineteenth-Century French Painting," in Varnedoe and Gopnik, eds., *Modern Art and Popular Culture*.

4. See Edmond Pottier, *Les Origines de la caricature dans l'antiquité*, Annales du Musée Guimet, Bibliothèque de Vulgarisation, 41 (Paris: Hachette, 1916), pp. 180–85.

5. See Thomas Wright, *A History of Caricature and Grotesque in Literature and Art* ([1865]; rpt., Hildesheim and New York: Georg Olms Verlag, 1976). See also Werner Hofmann, *Caricature from Leonardo to Picasso* (New York: Crown, 1957); and E. H. Gombrich and E[rnst] Kris, *Caricature* (Harmondsworth, Middlesex, England: Penguin, 1940), p. 6.

6. Vasari tells a story about the origin of Leonardo's grotesques that seems to mark the marriage of satiric form to the Renaissance cult of the individual. Leonardo, Vasari says, was "fascinated when he saw a man of striking appearance, with a strange head of hair or beard; and anyone who attracted him he would follow about all day long and end up seeing so clearly in his mind's eye that when he got home he could draw him as if he were standing there in the flesh." Vasari even goes on to give names to some of these profiles; one of them, he tells us, is a likeness of Amerigo Vespucci, the navigator who gave his name to the new continents. See Giorgio Vasari, *Lives of the Artists*, ed. George Bull (London: Penguin, 1987), vol. 1, p. 261.

7. See E. H. Gombrich, "The Grotesque Heads," in *The Heritage of Apelles: Studies in the Art of the Renaissance* (Ithaca, N.Y.: Cornell University Press, 1976). For an analysis of where and how the grotesque heads came to be cut out, see Carlo Pedretti, ed., *Leonardo da Vinci: Fragments at Windsor Castle from the Codex Atlanticus* ([London]: Phaidon, 1957). See also Kenneth Clark, *The Drawings of Leonardo da Vinci in the Collection of Her Majesty The Queen at Windsor Castle*, 3 vols., 2nd ed., rev. with the assistance of Carlo Pedretti (London: Phaidon, 1968–69).

8. See Gombrich, "The Grotesque Heads."

9. See Pedretti, ed., *Leonardo da Vinci*. See also Adam Gopnik, "From Grotesque to Caricature," M.A. thesis, New York University, 1983. The encyclopedic impulse behind these compilations is something like the rationale Lawrence Gowing has given for the existence of museums: "Museums exist so that future growths may have roots—so that the idiosyncrasies of artists may be allied to the generality of art" (Lawrence Gowing, *Paul Cézanne: The Basel Sketchbooks*, exh. cat. [New York: The Museum of Modern Art, 1988], p. 34).

10. On the invention of caricature, see Gombrich

and Kris, *Caricature*; and Lavin, "High and Low Before Their Time."

11. Lavin, "High and Low Before Their Time."

12. See *The Arcimboldo Effect: Transformations of the Face from the Sixteenth to the Twentieth Century*, exh. cat. (Venice: Palazzo Grassi; Milan: Bompiani, 1987); *Arcimboldo*, text by Roland Barthes, with an essay by Achille Bonito Oliva (Milan: Franco Maria Ricci, 1980); and *Bizzarie: Propos sur Braccelli par Tristan Tzara*, ed. Alain Brieux (Paris: Alain Brieux, 1963). On Braccelli, see in particular Kenneth Clark's still unsurpassed essay, "The 'Bizarie' of Giovanbatista Braccelli," *The Print Collector's Quarterly*, 16 (October 1929), pp. 311–26.

13. It's interesting to note that Arcimboldo, trying to characterize his strange works to a potential patron, called them *macchie* ("spots"), a term that appears previously in art theory only when Leonardo uses it in his treatise on art to refer to the blots and accidents in which one might discover purposeful form. See *The Arcimboldo Effect*, p. 93.

14. Many years ago, Gombrich and Kris suggested that the birth of caricature also marked the death of belief in "image magic." To draw someone else in a grotesque or distorted fashion, or, worse, to give him some of the attributes of an animal, or of a mere object, had never before been completely severed from the magical desire to do harm to the man by doing harm to his image. Only after image-making had been redefined as a form of competitive rhetoric, a game of one-upmanship, could one begin to view mocking portraiture (so to speak) abstractly, as affectionate, provisional teasing—image magic, but held in quotes. Other, less speculative thinkers have considered caricature a form of mannerism, the aftermath of achievement. Only after artists had completely mastered the description of natural appearances could they begin to knowingly depart from them. But then, artists and admirers had at least since the time of Giotto thought that the latest language of appearances was "complete." See Gombrich and Kris, *Caricature*.

See also Gombrich's discussion of Kris's interest in caricature, of his leaving art history for psychiatry, and the tragic historical circumstances that forced them both to abandon the major opus on caricature that they had planned, in *Tributes: Interpreters of Our Cultural Tradition* (Oxford [Oxfordshire]: Phaidon, 1984). We would be proud if the influence of the ideas of Professor Gombrich about the place of caricature in Western art history, as they were expressed in that collaboration and then later in many other writings, could be felt everywhere in this chapter (although the conclusions drawn here might be very different from his own).

15. On Hogarth, see Ronald Paulson, *Hogarth: His Life, Art, and Times*, 2 vols. (New Haven and London: Yale University Press, published for the Paul Mellon Centre for Studies in British Art [London], 1971).

16. On Gillray, see Draper Hill, *Mr. Gillray the Caricaturist: A Biography* ([London]: Phaidon, [1965]). On Gillray and early Romantic painting, see Gombrich, "Imagery and Art in the Romantic Period." See also Jonathan Bate, "Shakespearean Allusion in English Caricature in the Age of Gillray," *Journal of the Warburg and Courtauld Institutes*, 49 (1986), pp. 196–210; and Reva Wolf, "Goya's Satires of Society and the British Tradition of Comic Art," a lecture delivered at The Metropolitan Museum of Art, New York, May 23, 1989.

17. See Gombrich, "Imagery and Art in the Romantic Period."

18. For David and Gillray, see Albert Boime, "Jacques-Louis David, Scatological Discourse in the French Revolution and the Art of Caricature," *Arts Magazine*, 62 (February 1988), pp. 72–81, also printed in *French Caricature and the French Revolution, 1789–1799*, exh. cat. (Los Angeles: Grunwald Center for the Graphic Arts, Wight Art Gallery, University of California, 1988).

19. Daumier may have been familiar with this motif

either through David's *Sabines* or through a caricatural parody of it.

20. There has recently been a renaissance in Daumier studies. For a review of changing evaluations of Daumier in the light of evolving ideas about art and imagery, see Michel Melot, "Daumier and Art History: Aesthetic Judgement/Political Judgement," *Oxford Art Journal*, 11, no. 1 (1988), pp. 3–24. For a thematic index, see Louis Provost, *Honoré Daumier: A Thematic Guide to the Oeuvre*, ed. Elizabeth C. Childs (New York: Garland Publishing, 1989). On Daumier's classical sources, see Jody Maxmin, "A Hellenistic Echo in Daumier's Penelope?," *Art International*, 27 (August 1984), pp. 38–47. On his technique, see Bruce Laughton, "Some Daumier Drawings for Lithographs," *Master Drawings*, 22, no. 1 (1984), pp. 56–63. On Daumier's imaginative reuse of found grotesque material, see Bruce Laughton, "Daumier's Expressive Heads," *RACAR: Revue d'art canadienne*, 14, nos. 1, 2 (1987), pp. 135–42. For a full-scale attempt to integrate Daumier into the aesthetics of his period, see Judith Wechsler, *A Human Comedy: Physiognomy and Caricature in Nineteenth-Century Paris*, Foreword by Richard Sennnett (Chicago: University of Chicago Press, 1982).

21. See Eitner, "Subjects from Common Life in the Real Language of Men." Degas once said, "Daumier had a feeling for the antique"; see Theodore Reff, "Three Great Draftsmen," in *Degas: The Artist's Mind* (New York: The Metropolitan Museum of Art, 1976), p. 71.

22. On Philipon, see James Cuno, "The Business and Politics of Caricature: Charles Philipon and La Maison Aubert," *Gazette des beaux-arts*, ser. 6, 106 (October 1985), pp. 95–112.

23. On Grandville and Philipon, see Clive F. Getty, "Grandville: Opposition Caricature and Political Harassment," *Print Collector's Newsletter*, 14 (January–February 1984), pp. 197–201.

24. On Dantan, see Philippe Sorel, "Les Dantan du Musée Carnavalet: Portraits-charges sculptés de l'époque romantique," *Gazette des beaux-arts*, ser. 6, 107 (January 1986), pp. 1–38, and (February 1986), pp. 87–102.

25. See Thomas Wright, *A History of Caricature and Grotesque in Literature and Art*; and Champfleury, *Histoire de la caricature antique* ([1865]; 2nd ed., Paris: Éditions Dentu, 1867).

26. Charles Baudelaire, "De l'essence du rire et généralement du comique dans les arts plastiques," in *Baudelaire: Oeuvres complètes*, ed. Claude Pichois, vol. 2 (Paris: Gallimard [Bibliothèque de la Pléiade], 1976). For an English edition, see "On the Essence of Laughter," in *The Mirror of Art: Critical Studies by Charles Baudelaire*, trans. and ed. with notes and illustrations by Jonathan Mayne (Garden City, N.Y.: Doubleday & Co., 1956). See also Baudelaire, "1846: Le Salon caricatural," *Le Manuscrit autographe*, 5 (July–August 1930), pp. 1–14; Werner Hofmann, "Baudelaire et la caricature," *Preuves*, 18 (May 1968), pp. 38–43; Beatrice Farwell, *The Cult of Images (Le Culte des images): Baudelaire and the Nineteenth-Century Media Explosion*, exh. cat. (Santa Barbara, Calif.: UCSB Art Museum, University of California, 1977); and Ainslie Armstrong McLees, "Baudelaire and Caricature: *Argot plastique*," *Symposium*, 38 (Fall 1984), pp. 221–33. Although Baudelaire seems to have written the essay on laughter around 1846, it was reorganized sometime in the early 1850s, and not published until 1857. See Claude Pichois, "La Date de l'essai de Baudelaire sur le rire et les caricaturistes," *Les Lettres romanes*, 19 (August 1, 1965), pp. 203–16.

27. Baudelaire, "De l'essence du rire et généralement du comique dans les arts plastiques," pp. 532–34.

28. For a fine discussion of Baudelaire's coinage of this term, see McLees, "Baudelaire and Caricature."

29. Baudelaire, "De l'essence du rire et généralement du comique dans les arts plastiques," p. 536.

30. On Daumier's relationship to organized lan-

guages of gesture and expression, see Wechsler, *A Human Comedy*.

31. On Manet and popular lithography, see particularly Anne Coffin Hanson, "Manet's Subject Matter and a Source of Popular Imagery," *Museum Studies, 3* (Chicago: The Art Institute of Chicago, 1968), pp. 63–80; and her "Popular Imagery and the Work of Édouard Manet," in Ulrich Finke, ed., *French Nineteenth-Century Painting and Literature* (Manchester: Manchester University Press, 1972). See also Farwell, *The Cult of Images*. For a discussion of Manet's popular sources, see Ewa Lajer-Burcharth, "Modernity and the Condition of Disguise: Manet's *Absinthe Drinker*," *Art Journal*, 45 (Spring 1985), pp. 18–26.

32. Paul Gauguin, *The Writings of a Savage*, ed. Daniel Guérin, trans. Eleanor Levieux (New York: The Viking Press, 1978), p. 132. See also the extended discussion of Gauguin's interest in Daumier and caricature as part of a larger arsenal of stylization in Kirk Varnedoe, "Gauguin," in William Rubin, ed., *"Primitivism" in 20th Century Art: Affinity of the Tribal and the Modern*, exh. cat., 2 vols. (New York: The Museum of Modern Art, 1984).

33. See Aimée Brown Price, "Official Artists and Not-So-Official Art: Covert Caricaturists in Nineteenth-Century France," *Art Journal*, 43 (Winter 1983), pp. 365–70.

34. Ibid.

35. On the evolution of the caricature journals and the birth of modernist painting, see Jean Adhémar, "Les Journaux amusants et les peintres cubistes," *L'Oeil*, 4 (April 15, 1955), pp. 40–42.

36. See the discussion of Grosz in Ralph E. Shikes, *The Indignant Eye: The Artist as Social Critic in Prints and Drawings from the Fifteenth Century to Picasso* (Boston: Beacon Press, 1969), pp. 286–94.

37. Klee's interest in caricature included a peculiarly prescient comment about Rodin. At an exhibition in Rome in 1902, he wrote that "The only good displays are the drawings, etchings and lithographs by the French. Above all, Rodin's caricatures of nudes!—caricatures!"; this is an early application of the term to high figurative art in a way that is meant to be entirely complimentary. See *The Diaries of Paul Klee, 1898–1918*, ed. Felix Klee (Berkeley and Los Angeles: University of California Press, 1964), p. 105.

38. See Adam Gopnik, "High and Low: Caricature, Primitivism, and the Cubist Portrait," *Art Journal*, 43 (Winter 1983), pp. 371–76. What follows is adapted in part from that essay.

39. There have been relatively few discussions of Picasso's early caricatures in the context of his later art. For a brief discussion with illustrations, see Anthony Blunt and Phoebe Pool, *Picasso: The Formative Years—A Study of His Sources* ([Greenwich, Conn.]: New York Graphic Society, 1962).

40. See William Rubin, "Picasso," in Rubin, ed., *"Primitivism" in 20th Century Art*, pp. 285–86, especially n. 118.

41. Ibid., p. 285.

42. For Picasso's punning awareness of the relationship between primitive form and his own graphic shorthand, see the chapter "Primitivism" in Kirk Varnedoe, *A Fine Disregard: What Makes Modern Art Modern* (New York: Harry N. Abrams, 1990).

43. See Roland Penrose, *Picasso: His Life and Work* (London: Victor Gollancz, 1958), p. 126. Picasso added, when he told this story to Penrose, that this remark of Fénéon's was not as dumb as it sounded, since all good portraits contained an element of caricature.

44. See Rubin, "Picasso," p. 282.

45. Ibid., p. 284.

46. Ibid.

47. On the practitioners of this strategy, see Jurgis Baltrusaitis, "Têtes composées," *Médecine de France*, no. 19 (1951), pp. 29–34; Bernard Champigneulle, "A Forerunner of Surrealism in the Seventeenth Century," *Graphis*, 16, no. 33 (1950), pp. 458–61; and John Grand-Carteret, *Les Moeurs et la* *caricature en France* (Paris: La Librairie Illustrée, [1888]).

48. See Rudolf Arnheim, "The Rationale of Deformation," *Art Journal*, 43 (Winter 1983), pp. 319–24.

49. See Ernst Kris, "The Psychology of Caricature," *International Journal of Psycho-Analysis*, 17 (July 1936), pp. 285–303.

50. For cognitive studies of caricature, see David N. Perkins, "Caricature and Recognition," *Studies in the Anthropology of Visual Communication*, 2 (Spring 1975), pp. 10–23; and David N. Perkins and Margaret A. Hagen, "Convention, Context and Caricature," in *The Perception of Pictures*, ed. Hagen (New York and London: Academic Press, 1980), vol. 1. See also the writings of the psychologist Julian Hochberg, particularly "The Representation of Things and People," in E. H. Gombrich, Julian Hochberg, and Max Black, *Art, Perception, and Reality*, ed. Maurice Mandelbaum (Baltimore and London: Johns Hopkins University Press, 1972).

Of course, debate still continues about the psychology of caricature, and many recent studies recognize that the early notion that "the mind's eye sees caricatures" is oversimplified. A fascinating recent line of investigation, which may shed some light on the underlying structure of the historical invention of caricature, has involved trying to understand how people draw caricatures by figuring out ways of getting machines to draw them. It turns out that a successful computer program for caricature-making can't work just by taking coordinates of a face and distorting them. Instead, the program has to invent a complicated abstract set of comparative operations in what the programmers call "face space": the computer has first to make a line drawing of a given face, then compare that drawing with a drawing of a so-called "norm" face—a homogenized, neutral face—and then emphasize and exaggerate those areas of the first face that most differ from the norm.

The computer scientists, naturally and understandably, treat the line-drawing styles in which they instruct the computer to work as though they were simply "given," styles without any history. But from the historical point of view, we can recognize in this program some of the elements of the history we have been examining. The "norm" faces for the early caricaturists seem to have been earlier "grotesque" faces, and what made caricature interesting, and what made it grow, was the constant "feeding in" of new and more surprising norms into the "face space" of early caricature. The "norm" of the computer program is a straightforward, purposefully banal, neutral face. Perhaps what Bernini and Arcimboldo did was, intuitively, to choose more and more challenging norms—bowls of fruit, insect bodies—as templates for caricature. Certainly, the thought that caricature takes place not through a simple routine of distortion, but through a dialogue between a generic norm and a particular face, is one that seems to fit the history of caricatural invention remarkably well.

For more on this subject, see A. K. Dewdney, "Computer Recreations: The Compleat Computer Caricaturist and a Whimsical Tour of Face Space," *Scientific American*, 255 (October 1986), pp. 20–24, 27–28.

51. The argument between "economical" and "expansive" theories of humor reflects larger twentieth-century arguments between economical and expansive theories of art. See the discussion of Mach and his opponents among the Russian Formalists in Varnedoe, *A Fine Disregard*, pp. 265–66.

52. Quoted in Gombrich and Kris, *Caricature*, p. 11.

53. Henri Bergson, *Le Rire: Essai sur la signification du comique* (Paris: F. Alcan, 1900); English trans. in Wylie Sypher, ed., *Comedy* ([1956]; rpt. Baltimore and London: John Hopkins University Press, 1980), p. 64.

54. For the key discussion of this strategy, see E. H. Gombrich, "The Mask and the Face: The Perception of Physiognomic Likeness in Life and in Art," in *Art, Perception, and Reality*.

55. See Adhémar, "Les Journaux amusants et les peintres cubistes."

56. For Covarrubias, see *Masters of Caricature: From Hogarth and Gillray to Scarfe and Levine*, Introduction and commentary by William Feaver, ed. Ann Gould (New York: Alfred A. Knopf, 1981), p. 159. See also *Miguel Covarrubias: Caricatures*, Beverly J. Cox and Denna Jones Anderson with essays by Al Hirschfeld and Bernard F. Reilly, Jr., Foreword by Alan Fern (Washington, D.C.: Smithsonian Institution Press, for the National Portrait Gallery, 1985); and *Miguel Covarrubias: Homenaje*, ed. Lucía García-Noriega y Nieto (Mexico City: Centro Cultural Arte Contemporaneo, 1987).

57. See Eduard Fuchs, *Geschichte der erotischen Kunst*, vol. 1 (Munich: Albert Langen, [1912]).

58. See James Cuno, Introduction to *French Caricature and the French Revolution*; and Alexander Meyrick Broadley, *Napoleon in Caricature, 1795–1821* (London and New York: John Lane, 1911).

59. Paul Éluard, "Les Plus Belles Cartes postales," *Minotaure*, 1, nos. 2, 3, nos. 3, 4 (1933), pp. 85–100. The Surrealists' interest in body/face transformations is traced in *The Arcimboldo Effect*. See also Tristan Tzara, "Le Fantastique comme déformation du temps," *Cahiers d'art*, 12, nos. 6, 7 (1937), pp. 195–206.

60. Éluard, "Les Plus Belles Cartes postales . . . ," p. 86.

61. Maurice Raynal, "Dieu, table, cuvette," *Minotaure*, nos. 3, 4 (1933), p. 40.

62. On Léautaud, see Kenneth Tynan, *Curtains: Selections from the Drama Criticism and Related Writings* (New York: Atheneum, 1961), pp. 397–98.

63. Kris, "The Psychology of Caricature," p. 293.

64. Tynan was, of course, paraphrasing the ideas of the Polish theater historian and critic Jan Kott, as they had been set down in Kott's book, *Shakespeare, Our Contemporary* (trans. Boleslaw Taborski [Garden City, N.Y.: Doubleday & Co., 1964]), and exemplified in Peter Brook's great production of *King Lear*, in the mid-sixties. See Kathleen Tynan, *The Life of Kenneth Tynan* (New York: William Morrow, 1987), pp. 241–42.

65. See Gert Schiff, *Picasso: The Last Years, 1963–1973* (New York: George Braziller in association with the Grey Art Gallery and Study Center, New York University, [1983]).

Comics

1. See David Kunzle, "Goethe and Caricature: From Hogarth to Töpffer," *Journal of the Warburg and Courtauld Institutes*, 48 (1985), pp. 164–88. Professor Kunzle's work, in this article and many others, has set a new standard of scholarship in this field.

2. Ibid, p. 188.

3. Comics historian Maurice Horn was generous enough to allow the authors to see an unpublished paper of his on this subject. For an argument of a much earlier date, see David Kunzle, *The Early Comic Strip: Narrative Strips and Picture Stories in the European Broadsheet from c.1450 to 1825* (Berkeley and Los Angeles: University of California Press, 1973). See also Richard Marschall, *America's Great Comic-Strip Artists* (New York: Abbeville, 1989).

4. David Kunzle, *The History of the Comic Strip: The Nineteenth Century* (Berkeley and Los Angeles: University of California Press, 1990).

5. See Clive F. Getty, "Grandville: Opposition Caricature and Political Harassment," *The Print Collectors' Newsletter*, 14 (January–February 1984), pp. 197–201.

6. Grandville's transition from caricature to comedy is essentially the same transformation that gave Dickens's *Pickwick Papers*, for instance, its special shape. It was only after Dickens emancipated himself from his original illustrator and employer, the caricaturist Robert Seymour (one of the remaining pillars of the Gillray/Rowlandson tradition) that he was able to transcend the simple, sour mockeries of the first chapters of *Pickwick* and create a much deeper and more potent comedy built around the invention of heightened mythopoeic worlds—Dingley Dell and the Fleet.

For a discussion of Dickens's relations with Seymour, see Edgar Johnson, *Charles Dickens: His Tragedy and Triumph* (rev. ed., New York: Penguin, 1986).

7. For a discussion of Grandville's key role in remaking certain perspective devices for modern art, see the chapter "Overview: The Flight of the Mind," in Kirk Varnedoe, *A Fine Disregard: What Makes Modern Art Modern* (New York: Harry N. Abrams, 1990).

8. See Michael Hancher, *The Tenniel Illustrations to the "Alice" Books* (Columbus, Ohio: Ohio State University Press, 1985), pp. 77–79.

9. See John Canemaker's excellent *Winsor McCay: His Life And Art* (New York: Abbeville, 1987).

10. For a superb account of Hearst's role in the invention of the comic strip and his relationship with Swinnerton, see Bill Blackbeard, "Max, Maurice, and Willie: The Saga of a Little Yellow Book," *Nemo*, 2 (August 1983), pp. 48–53.

11. See Canemaker, *Winsor McCay*, p. 25.

12. Ibid., pp. 161–203.

13. Ibid., p. 211.

14. For a history of Dart's "The Explorigator" and a more general discussion of the development of fantasy comics, see Richard Marschall, "The Explorigator: Dreamship of the Universe," *Nemo*, 5 (February 1984), pp. 7–21.

15. One may find this error in, for example, Adam Gopnik, "The Genius of George Herriman," *The New York Review of Books*, 33 (December 17, 1986), p. 20.

16. These artists have all been the subject of fine biographical and analytic essays in Richard Marschall's invaluable magazine of comics history, *Nemo*. On Jimmy Swinnerton, see Donald Phelps, "Jimmy and Company," *Nemo*, 22 (October 1986), pp. 36–37. For Cliff Sterrett, see Gary Groth, "The Comic Genius of Cliff Sterrett," *Nemo*, 1 (June 1983), pp. 21–26. On Tad, see "The Incomparable Dorgan: Giving the Once-Over to One-of-a-Kind," *Nemo*, 13 (July 1985), pp. 37–56. A compendium of statements by Bud Fisher and Tad is presented in John Wheeler, "The Reminiscences of John Wheeler, Newspaperman," in *Nemo*, 25 (April 1987), pp. 47–60. An entire issue was devoted to Rube Goldberg: *Nemo*, 24 (February 1987).

17. See Wheeler, "The Reminiscences of John Wheeler, Newspaperman," p. 49.

18. For details of the relations between Bud Fisher and Pancho Villa, see Wheeler, "The Reminiscences of John Wheeler, Newspaperman," pp. 53–58.

19. Lyonel Feininger, to his friend Alfred Vance Churchill, March 1913; cited by Ernst Scheyer in *Lyonel Feininger: Caricature and Fantasy* (Detroit: Wayne State University Press, 1964), p. 133.

20. Gilbert Seldes, *The Seven Lively Arts* (New York: Sagamore Press, 1924). See especially the pioneering chapter on Herriman, "The Krazy Kat That Walks by Himself."

21. The Herriman literature is large and growing. See Patrick McDonnell, Kevin O'Connell, and Georgia Riley de Havenon, *Krazy Kat: The Comic Art of George Herriman* (New York: Harry N. Abrams, 1986). See also E. E. Cummings, Introduction to George Herriman, *Krazy Kat* (New York: Holt, 1946), pp. 10–16; Umberto Eco, "On Krazy Kat and Peanuts," trans. William Weaver, *The New York Review of Books*, 32 (June 13, 1985), pp. 16–17; Franklin Rosemont, "Surrealism in the Comics I: Krazy Kat," in Paul Buhle, ed., *Popular Culture in America* (Minneapolis: University of Minnesota Press, 1987); and Gopnik, "The Genius of George Herriman."

22. For Herriman's early years, see Bill Blackbeard, "The Forgotten Years of George Herriman," *Nemo*, 1 (June 1983), pp. 50–60.

23. See W. H. Auden, "Dingley Dell and The Fleet," in Auden, *The Dyer's Hand* (London: Faber & Faber, 1963).

24. See Mikhaïl Mikhaïlovich Bakhtin, *Rabelais and His World*, trans. Helene Iswolsky (Cambridge, Mass.: MIT Press, 1968).

25. See Marschall, *America's Great Comic-Strip Artists*, p. 118.

26. Joan Miró, "Sur le carnaval d'Arlequin," *Verve*, 4 (1939), p. 85.

27. Joan Miró, quoted in Robert Hughes, *The Shock of the New* (New York: Alfred A. Knopf, 1981), p. 235.

28. See *Joan Miró: Carnets catalans, dessins et textes inédits*, ed. Gaëten Picon (Geneva: Éditions Albert Skira, 1976), p. 72. The authors are grateful to Robert Rosenblum for bringing this drawing to their attention. See Rosenblum's discussion of it in *The Dog in Art* (New York: Harry N. Abrams, 1988), pp. 83–86.

29. See Johan Huizinga, *Homo Ludens: A Study of the Play Element in Culture* ([1938]; rpt., New York: Harper & Row, 1970).

30. Ibid., pp. 190, 191.

31. See Phyllis Tuchman, "Guernica and *Guernica*," *Artforum*, 21 (April 1983), pp. 44–51.

32. See E. H. Gombrich, "Imagery and Art in the Romantic Period," *Burlington Magazine*, 191 (June 1949), pp. 153–58; reprinted in Gombrich, "*Meditations on a Hobby Horse*" and Other Essays on the Theory of Art (London: Phaidon, 1963).

33. See Antonio Martín, *Historia del comic español, 1875–1939* (Barcelona: Editorial Gustavo Gili, 1978).

34. For a good overview of the history of the comic book, see Michael Barrier and Martin Williams, eds., *A Smithsonian Book of Comic-Book Comics* (Washington, D.C.: Smithsonian Institution Press; New York: Harry N. Abrams, 1977).

35. On the work of Jerry Siegel and Joe Shuster, see Richard Marschall, "Of Superman and Kids with Dreams," *Nemo*, 2 (August 1983), pp. 6–12, 14–28.

36. On Chester Gould, see Bill Crouch, ed., *Dick Tracy, America's Most Famous Detective* (Secaucus, N.J.: Citadel Press, 1987). See also *Nemo*, 17 (February 1985), a special issue devoted to Gould, including Max Allan Collin's interview, "Bringing in the Reward," pp. 7–22.

37. See the conversation recorded between Floyd Gottfredson and Carl Barks (who drew the Donald Duck comic books), reprinted as "A Century's Worth of Disney Memories," *Nemo*, 17 (June 1984), pp. 12–15.

38. See Clement Greenberg, "Avant-Garde and Kitsch," *Partisan Review*, 6 (Fall 1939), pp. 34–49; reprinted in Greenberg, *Art and Culture: Critical Essays* (Boston: Beacon Press, 1961). See also Robert Storr's essay on Greenberg, titled "No Joy in Mudville," in Kirk Varnedoe and Adam Gopnik, eds., *Modern Art and Popular Culture: Readings in High and Low* (New York: The Museum of Modern Art and Harry N. Abrams, 1990).

39. For a history of William Gaines and E.C. Comics, see James Van Hise, *The E.C. Comics Story* (Canoga Park, Calif.: Psi Ei Movie Press, 1987). See also Barrier and Williams, eds., *A Smithsonian Book of Comic-Book Comics*, pp. 295–98.

40. See Fredric Wertham, *The Seduction of the Innocent* (New York: Rinehart, 1954). See also United States Senate, Judiciary Committee, *Juvenile Delinquency (Comic Books): Hearings Before the Subcommittee to Investigate Juvenile Delinquency of the Committee on the Judiciary—United States Senate, 83rd Congress, Second Session, April 21, 22, and June 4, 1954* (Washington, D.C.: U.S. Government Printing Office, 1954). For a contemporaneous assessment of the weaknesses and prejudices of Wertham's argument, see Frederick M. Thrasher, "The Comics and Delinquency: Cause or Scapegoat?," *Journal of Educational Sociology*, 23 (1949), pp. 195–205; see also Robert Warshow's

1954 essay "Paul, the Horror Comics and Dr. Wertham," reprinted in *The Immediate Experience* (New York: Doubleday, 1962). Both authors conclude that no correlation between aggressive behavior and the reading of comic books could ever be seriously adduced, and that Wertham's methods and conclusions were unsound.

The recent past has witnessed a similar campaign, undertaken by The Parents' Music Resource Center, which, under the direction of the wives of prominent politicians, claimed that listening to certain rock songs led to rape, suicide, preoccupation with the occult, and various forms of sexual misconduct.

41. Cited in *The Fredric Wertham Collection: Gift of His Wife Hesketh*, exh. cat. (Cambridge, Mass.: Busch-Reisinger Museum, Harvard University, 1990), p. 18.

42. Ibid.

43. Ibid., p. 12.

44. On Hamlin's *Alley Oop*, see Rick Norwood, "King of the Jungle Jive," *Nemo*, 6 (April 1984), pp. 39–49.

45. See Pontus Hulten and Björn Springfeldt, *Öyvind Fahlström*, exh. cat. (Paris: Musée National d'Art Moderne, Centre Georges Pompidou, 1980). See also, *Öyvind Fahlström*, exh. cat. (New York: Solomon R. Guggenheim Museum, 1982).

46. See Harold Rosenberg, *Saul Steinberg* (New York: Alfred A. Knopf, 1975). See also Adam Gopnik, *Saul Steinberg's Gift*, exh. cat. (New York: The Pace Gallery, 1987).

47. On Jess, see Madeleine Burnside, *Jess*, exh. cat. (New York: Odyssia Gallery, 1989). See also Michael Auping, *Jess: Paste Ups (and Assemblies), 1951–1983*, exh. cat. (Sarasota, Fla.: John and Mable Ringling Museum of Art, 1983).

48. Irv Novick, conversation with the authors, June 1989.

49. See *Real Love: The Best of the Simon and Kirby Romance Comics, 1940s–1950s*, ed. Richard Howell (Forestville, Calif.: Eclipse Books, 1988); and Bruce Bailey, "An Inquiry into Love Comic Books: The Token Evolution of a Popular Genre," *Journal of Popular Culture*, 10 (Summer 1976), pp. 245–48.

50. John Romita, conversation with the authors, June 1989.

51. Ibid.

52. See John Coplans, "Interview: Roy Lichtenstein" (1970), in Coplans, ed., *Roy Lichtenstein* (New York: Praeger, 1972).

53. Conversation with John Romita. See also Stan Lee, *The Origins of Marvel Comics* (New York: Simon & Schuster, 1974).

54. On Oldenburg and Mickey, see Coosje van Bruggen, *Claes Oldenburg: Mouse Museum/Ray-Gun Wing*, exh. cat. (Cologne: Museum Ludwig, 1979); and Barbara Rose, *Claes Oldenburg*, exh. cat. (New York: The Museum of Modern Art, 1970).

55. For varying accounts of the origin and development of Mickey Mouse, see Robert D. Field, *The Art of Walt Disney* (New York: Macmillan, 1942), pp. 31–39; Christopher Finch, *The Art of Walt Disney: From Mickey Mouse to Magic Kingdom* (New York: Harry N. Abrams, 1973), pp. 49–65; and Bob Thomas, *Walt Disney, an American Original* (New York: Simon & Schuster, 1976), pp. 88–89. For an intelligent and purely schematic treatment of the stylistic evolution of Mickey Mouse, see Stephen Jay Gould, "This View of Life: Mickey Mouse Meets Konrad Lorenz," *Natural History*, 88 (May 1979), pp. 30, 32, 34, 36.

56. See Richard Schickel, *The Disney Version: The Life, Times, Art and Commerce of Walt Disney* (New York: Simon & Schuster, 1968), pp. 113–14.

57. The spare, uncluttered look perfected by Gottfredson may be due in great part to the intervention of Disney himself, who was known to have written to the artist, enclosing copies of his work and a note saying, "There's too damn much junk in this strip." See Thomas, *Walt Disney*, p. 107.

58. See Germano Celant, *Il corso del coltello/The*

Course of the Knife: Claes Oldenburg, Coosje van Bruggen, Frank O. Gehry, ed. David Frankel (New York: Rizzoli, 1986).

59. On Harvey Kurtzman, William Gaines, and *Mad* magazine, see Frank Jacobs, *The Mad World of William F. Gaines* (Secaucus, N.J.: Lyle Stuart, 1972); and Glen Bray, *The Illustrated Harvey Kurtzman Index* (Sylmar, Calif.: Glen Bray, 1976).

60. See Paul Goodman, *Growing Up Absurd: Problems of Youth in the Organized System* (New York: Random House, 1960).

61. The literature on Crumb is surprisingly large. See *The Complete Crumb Comics*, 4 vols., ed. Gary Groth and Robert Fiore, with introductory essays by Marty Pahls (vols. 1–3, Westlake Village, Calif: Fantagraphics Press, 1987–89), and by Robert Crumb (vol. 4, Seattle, Wash.: Fantagraphics Press, 1989). (Owing to Pahls's death, Crumb wrote the introduction to the most recent volume himself.) See also Harvey Pekar, "Rapping About Cartoonists, Particularly Robert Crumb," *The Journal of Popular Culture*, 3 (Spring 1970), pp. 677–88. For the most incisive account, see Gary Groth's marathon interview, "The Straight Dope from R. Crumb," *Comics Journal*, 121 (April 1988), pp. 48–120.

On the general background of the development of the underground comic, see Clinton R. Sanders, "Icons of Alternate Culture: The Themes and Functions of Underground Comics," *The Journal of Popular Culture*, 8 (Spring 1975), pp. 836–52; and M. J. Estren, *A History of Underground Comics* (2nd ed., Berkeley: Ronin Publishing, 1986).

62. Robert Crumb, *Sketchbook: November 1983 to April 1987* (Frankfurt: Zweitausendeins, 1988), pp. 336–38.

63. "The Straight Dope from R. Crumb," p. 50.

64. Ibid., p. 67.

65. Crumb, *Sketchbook*, p. 215. The entire entry reads: "Message to Myself: DON'T LET WHAT HAPPENED TO HARVEY KURTZMAN HAPPEN TO YOU!! ESCAPE! Run away! Break out! Go Crazy! Do something desperate! Think about it... Invent a strategy for yourself ... Don't throw your life away... Hold on... Fight back! Survive!!... I can't... It's too hard... Sob whimper...."

66. Robert Crumb, Introduction to *The Complete Crumb Comics*, vol. 4, p. viii.

67. Ibid.

68. Fredric Wertham, *The World of Fanzines: A Special Form of Communication* (Carbondale and Edwardsville, Ill.: Southern Illinois University Press, 1973), p. 130.

69. Crumb, *Sketchbook*.

70. Quoted in Musa Mayer, *Night Studio: A Memoir of Philip Guston* (New York: Alfred A. Knopf, 1988), p. 170.

71. For the best discussion of late Guston, see Robert Storr, *Philip Guston*, Modern Masters series (New York: Abbeville, 1986). See also Dore Ashton, *Yes, But... A Critical Study of Philip Guston* (New York: Viking, 1976).

72. Storr, *Philip Guston*, p. 64.

73. Storr, "No Joy in Mudville."

74. Storr, *Philip Guston*, p. 99.

75. David McKee, Guston's dealer at that time, in conversation with the authors, October 1989.

76. Robert Crumb, conversation with the authors, May 1989.

Advertising

1. Robert Hughes, "Memories Scaled and Scrambled," *Time*, August 11, 1986, p. 69.

2. Théophraste Renaudot is credited with the first newspaper, and newspaper ad, in 1631; see Daniel Pope, "French Advertising Men and the American 'Promised Land,'" *Historical Reflections*, 5 (Summer 1978), pp. 121–22. In 1715 the first poster with an illustration appeared in Paris, and six years later a law was passed (the law of October 29, 1721) to limit the number of licensed poster-mounters in the city to forty; see *La Grande Encyclopédie* (Paris:

H. Lamitault & Cie, 1890), p. 687.

3. In 1791 a law was passed requiring all those involved in printing and posting a notice to affix their signatures to it; the same law reserved for the government the exclusive use of black print on white paper (all other notices had to be printed on colored paper, a requirement that continued through the nineteenth century); see Claude Bellanger, Jacques Godacat, Pierre Guival, and Fernand Terron, eds., *Histoire générale de la presse française* (Paris: Presses Universitaires de France, 1973), vol. 3, pp. 13–14.

In 1817, after the return of private industry, a law was passed allowing the government to receive revenue benefits, via stamp tax, on posters; see Alain Weill, *L'Affiche française* (Paris: Presses Universitaires de France, 1982), p. 24.

4. The law of April 28, 1816 (annulled in 1818), first made it obligatory for posters to be printed only on paper having a stamp from the authority which governed posters. Taxation by stamp on posters remained high until the law of July 18, 1866. See "Le Régime fiscal de l'affichage, son evolution ainsi que les taxes actuelles," *La Publicité*, 24 (February 1927), p. 61.

5. The story of the LU cookie is an instructive capsule history of business in the Second Empire. In 1846, Jean Romain Lefèvre arrived in the port city of Nantes and began a pastry shop specializing in the kind of sweet cookies known as *biscuits de Reims*. The business grew, and in 1860, after one of the sons, Louis Lefèvre, had bought the business from his family, he incorporated under the name Lefèvre-Utile. When Louis took over, the French were heavy importers of English biscuits, and he determined to cut into the market of this foreign industry (which, he noticed, was drawing a great deal of its raw material, in butter and refined sugar, from his own region). The new factory he opened in 1855 used the latest English machinery and produced a whole new range of cookie types. The one that soon dominated the line was the *petit beurre*, for which Louis had himself designed a special crenulated cookie mold, with the firm's initials, L.U., pressed into the product. The recipe and form of this product have remained unchanged since then. The ornate typeface Louis used on the cookie itself was not the bold, simple, sans-serif face used in the company's ads; the simple LU mark, redesigned several times (as, for example, by Raymond Loewy in 1957) still maintains that original style. See Daniel Cauzard, Jean Perret, and Yves Ronin, *Images de marques, marques d'images* (Paris: Ramsay, 1989), pp. 90–94.

6. "Le Régime fiscal de l'affichage", p. 61

7. See Michael Barry Miller, *The Bon Marché: Bourgeois Culture and the Department Store, 1869–1920* (Princeton, N.J.: Princeton University Press, 1981). See also Rosalind H. Williams, *Dream Worlds: Mass Consumption in Late Nineteenth Century France* (Berkeley: University of California Press, 1982), especially pp. 67–68, on the Bon Marché as the inspiration for Zola's *Au bonheur des dames*. The founding editor of the French advertising journal *La Publicité*, D. C. A. Hémet, wrote in 1910 that "Among the most incontrovertible causes of the progress of advertising, we have to cite the department stores, which form one of the characteristic traits of modern societies, and where the amount and the rapidity of transactions are an indispensable element of success. They gave birth to ads of a new kind, for example the announcement of weeks specially consecrated to a type of object, or of exceptional days, reduced-price sales, exhibitions of merchandise offered at determined prices.... The public has gotten used to advertising, it waits on it and counts on it to become informed about what it calls 'opportunities' [*occasions*]" ("La Réclame appréciée par les économistes," *La Publicité*, 8 [October 1910], pp. 417–18).

Purchase by credit, a crucial adjunct to this new structure of shopping, is also evident in the Dufayel ads in the later photos. Georges Dufayel's scheme

to facilitate purchase on an installment plan, begun in the 1870s in a chain of household-goods stores across France, was centered at the turn of the century in an immense emporium in Paris, complete with a movie theater and other sideshow attractions; see Williams, *Dream Worlds*, pp. 93–94.

8. *Dictionnaire de l'industrie et des arts industriels* (Paris: Librarie des Dictionnaires, 1881), vol. 1, p. 69.

9. Paul Bernelle, *Des restrictions apportées depuis 1881 à la liberté de l'affichage* (Paris: Arthur Rousseau, 1912), pp. 25–27.

10. For the history of the development of trademarks for Uneeda biscuits, Ivory Soap, and Quaker Oats, and the general shift to pre-packaged goods, see Susan Strasser, *Satisfaction Guaranteed: The Making of the American Mass Market* (New York: Pantheon Books, 1989), especially pp. 47–48, 78, 118–19. See also Daniel Pope, *The Making of American Advertising* (New York: Basic Books, 1983), pp. 48–49.

11. For articles touting or criticizing the poster as the dominant ad form in France, see "The Lay of the Market in France," *Printers' Ink*, September 20, 1917, pp. 85–87; Pope, "French Advertising Men and the American 'Promised Land'"; and "Une Technique scientifique de l'affiche," *La Publicité*, 25 (January 1928), pp. 967–70.

12. See Phillip Dennis Cate, *The Color Revolution: Color Lithography in France, 1890–1900* (Santa Barbara, Calif., and Salt Lake City, Utah: Peregine Smith, 1978), pp. 3–5.

13. Ibid., pp. 1–6.

14. See Ambroise Vollard, *Recollections of a Picture Dealer*, trans. Biolet M. MacDonald ([1936]; rpt., New York: Dover Publications, 1978); Una E. Johnson, *Ambroise Vollard, Éditeur: Prints, Books, Bronzes*, exh. cat. ([1944]; rev. ed., New York: The Museum of Modern Art, 1977). On the development of posters and their increasing appeal to collectors, see Philip Dennis Cate, ed., *The Graphic Arts and French Society, 1871–1914* (New Brunswick, N.J.: Rutgers University Press, 1988).

15. Maurice Talmeyr, "L'Age de l'affiche," *Revue des deux mondes*, 137 (September 1896), pp. 201–06.

16. Ibid., pp. 208–09.

17. Ibid., p. 212.

18. Ibid., p. 202.

19. "Georges Seurat," *La Société nouvelle*, 7 (1891), p. 434, quoted in Robert L. Herbert, "Seurat and Jules Chéret," *The Art Bulletin*, 40 (June 1958), p. 157.

20. Herbert (ibid., n. 6, p. 157) cites this information from unpublished correspondence between Madeleine Knobloch, Seurat's common-law wife, and the painter Paul Signac.

21. Ibid., p. 158.

22. See Robert L. and Eugenie W. Herbert, "Artists and Anarchism: Unpublished Letters of Pissarro, Signac, and Others," *Burlington Magazine*, 102 (November 1960), pp. 473–82.

23. See Camille Mauclair, *Jules Chéret* (Paris: Maurice Le Garrec, 1930), especially chapters 2 ("L'Affiche et l'historien de Paris") and 7 ("Le Dessin et la couleur"). See also Felix H. Man, "Lithography in Colour," in Man, *Artists' Lithographs* (New York: G. P. Putnam's Sons, 1970); and Jane Abdy, *The French Poster: Chéret to Cappiello* (London: Studio Vista, 1969), pp. 28–32.

24. See Robert L. Herbert, "*Parade de cirque* de Seurat et l'esthétique scientifique de Charles Henry," *Revue de l'art*, 50 (1980), pp. 9–23.

25. See William Innes Homer, *Seurat and the Science of Painting* (Cambridge, Mass.: MIT Press, 1964), pp. 188–217. See also Henri Dorra, "Charles Henry's 'Scientific' Aesthetic," *Gazette des beaux-arts*, 73 (1969), pp. 81–94.

26. There are, of course, other possible sources for the rhythmic repetition in the chorus line of *Le Chahut*. Staggered lines of legs in parallel, as a proto-cinematic formula for motion, can be found at least

as far back as the Parthenon frieze, which we know Seurat admired, and even earlier in Assyrian relief sculpture. Moreover, in Seurat's day, the physiologist Étienne-Jules Marey was pursuing chronophotographic documentation of figures in motion, which resulted in multiple-image photographs with distinct repetitive structures. Degas, too, had begun to work with images of dancers in which several figures seemed to move in parallel, one to another. For a consideration of such structures of repetition in the 1880s and 1890s, see the chapter on "Fragmentation and Repetition" in Kirk Varnedoe, *A Fine Disregard: What Makes Modern Art Modern* (New York: Harry N. Abrams, 1990). The possible connection of *Le Chahut* to repetitive posting is one of many instances in which advertising practices may have made immediately available to an artist, in simplified or degraded form, a visual device that had been a part of art for ages.

27. Seurat's enthusiasm for laws of the kind Henry proposed finds echoes in books like Henry Foster Adams's *Advertising and Its Mental Laws* of 1916. As Ann Uhry Adams explains in "From Simplicity to Sensation: Art in American Advertising, 1904–1929" (*The Journal of Popular Culture*, 10 [Winter 1976], p. 624), Adams broke down all aspects of composition into analyzable parts, and maintained that ad artists could, through science, learn to arouse any human sensation. See also Jules Lallemand, "Une Expérience cruciale de la 'suggestion' publicitaire," *La Publicité*, 18 (February 1921), pp. 23–25; and M. Igert, "Une Technique scientifique de l'affiche," *La Publicité*, 25 (January 1928), pp. 967–70.

28. Norma Broude, "New Light on Seurat's Dot: Its Relation to Photo-Mechanical Printing in France in the 1880s," *Art Bulletin*, 56 (December 1974), pp. 581–89.

29. Vincent van Gogh, letter to Theo van Gogh, January 28, 1889, in *The Complete Letters of Vincent van Gogh* (Boston: New York Graphic Society, 1978), vol. 3, p. 129.

30. See Pope, "French Advertising Men and the American 'Promised Land,'" p. 130.

31. "Until a few years ago the advertising-agency situation was in bad shape. Such agencies as existed were space brokers pure and simple, with never a thought of such things as writing copy, carrying on merchandising investigations, or laying out campaigns" ("The Lay of the Market in France," *Printers' Ink*, September 20, 1917, p. 86).

Daniel Pope explains that the innovation of the Compagnie Générale des Annonces was regarded as a "mixed blessing" by advertising men of the early twentieth century. Newspapers that had leased their space to such brokers were more costly than others that sold space without a middleman, and had less incentive to make their ad pages more lively as a way of pleasing customers. Even as late as the period between the two world wars, the specter of monopolization lingered, as the five major daily newspapers in Paris persisted in the attempt to "cartelize" the market for their space—a phenomenon Pope sees as typical of French "economic Malthusianism, a propensity to seek stability and avoid risks at the expense of potential profit and growth" (Pope, "French Advertising Men and the American 'Promised Land,'" pp. 122–23).

32. On the French response to these developments, see D. C. A. Hémet, "La Réclame appréciée par les économistes," *La Publicité*, 8 (October 1910), p. 418.

33. The founder of the French trade journal *La Publicité*, D. C. A. Hémet, said in 1907 that "advertising these days is almost exclusively pharmaceutical or medical" (*La Publicité moderne*, 3 [September 1907], p. 1, cited in Pope, "French Advertising Men and the American 'Promised Land,'" p. 131). The American counterpart magazine, *Printers' Ink*, still reported in 1917 that "the patent-medicine business is by far the heaviest class of advertising in the French press" ("The Lay of the Market in France," p.

86). As late as 1938, thirty percent of the ads in France still promoted pharmaceuticals, according to Pope (pp. 130–31).

34. Pope, "French Advertising Men and the American 'Promised Land,'" pp. 130–31.

35. For a French lament over the poor reputation of advertising in France, and the greater success of the Americans in gaining public acceptance, see Édouard Dupont, "Les Deux Méthodes, New-York et Paris," *La Publicité moderne*, 2 (September 1906), pp. 1–3.

36. See Merle Curti, "The Changing Concept of 'Human Nature' in the Literature of American Advertising," *Business History Review*, 61 (Winter 1967), pp. 335–57, especially the section titled "The Dominant Rationalistic Image of Man Challenged, 1890–1910," pp. 337–45.

37. For a symptomatic discussion of "modernization" in poster art, see "Les Murs de France," *La Publicité*, 17 (December 1919), pp. 445–46: "We can conclude that posters with modern tendencies — simple, fresh, and colored—are also the most economical and the most profitable for him who makes the announcement." See also the late example, still devoted to Cappiello, by M. Igert, of the Psychology Laboratory of Braqueville, titled "Une Technique scientifique de l'affiche" (note 27).

38. For the dog Nipper and the White Rock Girl, see "How Trade Marks Originate," *Printers' Ink*, September 5, 1935, pp. 61–69. The genealogy of Mr. Peanut can be found in *Modern Packaging*, 23 (August 1950), pp. 78–80.

39. For the speech in which the phrase was initially used, see M. A. Michelin, *De la vélocipédie et des progrès que le bandage pneumatique lui a permis de réaliser* (Paris: Mémoires de la Société des Ingénieurs Civils de France, 1893), p. 19.

40. "Phrases et personnages types," *La Publicité moderne*, 2 (October–November 1906), pp. 9–16. I am also greatly indebted to M. d'Arpiany of the Michelin corporation for his invaluable assistance in reassembling the intricate history of the formation of the firm and its early advertising campaigns.

41. On Michelin's interest in the formation of an air army, and hence the company's sponsorship of the aerial-bombing contests, see the chapter titled "Words."

42. See Alain Jemain, *Michelin: Un Siècle de secrets* (Paris: Calmann-Lévy, 1982).

43. The use of Latin here suggests a moment when it seemed that the classical culture men like Delaunay had acquired in the traditional French educational system might be compatible with, not threatened by, the advent of commerce's mass appeals. As with the name Bibendum, the phenomenon on view here seems to be that of the unexpected new public life given to a "dead" language, or an ossified elite culture, by the appropriations of advertising.

The phrase SOCIÉTÉ CONSTRUCTION AEROPLANE, beneath ASTRA, is treated in Cubist fashion, with the elimination of parts of each word. As for the relation between Delaunay's painting and the contemporaneous experiments of Picasso and Braque with *papiers collés*, it seems entirely likely that the segmented AL at the left edge of the painting may echo the frequent recurrence of the last letters of the masthead of *Le Journal*—NAL, AL, and so on—in the Cubist works.

44. The international emphasis may also include the plane above. In another painting, titled *Homage to Blériot*, Delaunay featured the monoplane the Frenchman used in his Channel flight. In the present work, however, he clearly shows a biplane, closer in type to that used by the Wright brothers, who were singular heroes in the French imagination.

45. The image of the rugby team is taken from a photograph in a news clipping, which was preserved among Delaunay's belongings. See Gustav Vriesen and Max Imdahl, *Robert Delaunay: Light and Color* (New York: Harry N. Abrams, 1967), p. 55.

46. On the background of nationalist and vitalist ideals leading toward the institution of the first modern Olympics in 1896, see Richard D. Mandell, *The First Modern Olympics* (Berkeley and Los Angeles: University of California Press, 1976). See also *Delaunay und Deutschland*, exh. cat. (Munich: Staatsgalerie Moderner Kunst, 1986), pp. 373, 381.

47. For an account of the competition to cross the Channel, and the role of the *Daily Mail* and *Le Matin*, see Henry Serrano Villard, *Contact! The Story of the Early Birds* (Washington, D.C.: Smithsonian Institution Press, 1987), pp. 62–73. Aviators, like professional athletes today, were also sought after to endorse products in ads; that vogue for using airplanes and aviators to sell was already widespread, and open to much criticism, by 1909; see G. Espinadel, "L'Art et ses inconvénients," *La Publicité moderne*, 2 (December 1906), p. 492.

48. This version is in the Stedelijk van Abbemuseum, Eindhoven. In a drawing for the painting, in the Musée National d'Art Moderne, Centre Georges Pompidou, the same wall bears the ubiquitous DUFAYEL (see note 7, above)..

49. V. L. Bocjanovkij, "Cto takoe futuristy," *Novoe Slovo*, 12 (1913), p. 57. Many thanks to Professor Radu Stern for this reference.

50. "Industry and commerce, pulled into a wild race of competition, were the first to lay a heavy hand on anything that could make an attraction. They admirably sensed that a shop window, a department store, must be a spectacle. They had the idea of creating an enveloping, pressing atmosphere, using only the objects at their disposition.... Crushed by the enormous *mise-en-scène* of life, what is there to do for the artist who wants to conquer his public? A single opportunity remains for him to pursue: to raise himself up to the level of beauty in considering everything that surrounds him as raw material, to choose in the turbulence that rolls under his eyes, the possible plastic and scenic values, to interpret them in the sense of a spectacle, to arrive at a scenic unity and to dominate at any cost.... *He has to invent*, cost what it will.... Life today never adapts, it creates; every morning, nonstop, good or bad, but it invents. If adaptation is admissable from the point of view of theater, it is not from the point of view of spectacle." Fernand Léger, "Le Spectacle: Lumière, couleurs, images mobiles, objet-spectacle" (1924); reprinted in Léger, *Fonctions de la peinture* (Paris: Éditions Gonthier, 1965), pp. 132–33.

51. See Guy Debord, *La Société du spectacle* (Paris: Buchet & Chastel, 1967). See also T. J. Clark, *The Painting of Modern Life: Paris in the Art of Manet and His Followers* (New York: Alfred A. Knopf, 1984).

52. France passed national laws regarding posting in 1887, 1902, 1906, and again in 1910, each allowing the prefect of the Seine to delimit excessive posting in Paris. Prefectural edicts in 1902 and 1908 explicitly prohibited posting on a designated list of protected sites and monuments. See "Les Abus de l'affichage," *La Publicité*, 21 (December 1923), p. 799. See also Bernelle, *Des restrictions apportées depuis 1881*, pp. 158–60. For a thorough history of French law concerning posting in the suburbs and countryside, see Roland Engerand, "La Lèpre des routes," *L'Illustration*, September 6, 1930, pp. 6–8.

53. The 1906 law protecting natural sites from billboards is discussed in Bernelle, *Des restrictions apportées depuis 1881*, p. 158. For a reaction to the 1910 law, and a call to have it extended within Paris, see the article by the anti-poster activist Charles Beauquier (president of the Society for the Protection of the Landscape), "L'Affiche, voilà l'ennemie," *La Publicité*, 9 (May 1911), pp. 149, 151.

54. P. Raveau, "La Guerre à l'affiche," *La Publicité*, 9 (December 1911), pp. 149–50.

55. Bernelle, *Des restrictions apportées depuis 1881*, pp. 155–77.

56. Ibid., p. 175.

57. "Les Abus de l'affichage," p. 799.

58. "Notes et échos," *La Publicité*, 12 (January–February 1914), pp. 57–58.

59. England's advertising regulation act of 1907 had given local authorities the right to forbid posters that spoiled the landscape; laws of 1902 and 1907 in Prussia, and 1909 in Saxony, put posting on certain sites under the control of police or other local administrators. See Hémet, "La Réclame appréciée par les économistes," p. 418.

60. "The Forward Movement in Poster Advertising," *Advertising and Selling*, 23 (July 1913), p. 36.

61. For a French reaction to this law of September 1, 1911, see "La Guerre aux affiches," *La Publicité*, 9 (November–December 1911), p. 427.

62. See *Code of Ordinances of the City of New York*, ed. Arthur F. Cosby (New York: Banks Law Publishing, 1913), pp. 257–58.

63. See the commission's report of August 1, 1913, titled *The Mayor's Billboard Advertising Commission* (New York, 1913). See also *The Billboard Nuisance in New York City*, pamphlet no. 1 (Washington, D.C.: Division of Municipal Art, Council of National Advisors, National Highway Association, 1916).

64. "Naturally, to find in this rupture of everything that habit has entrenched, a motive for a new pictorial harmony and a plastic means of life and movement, required an artistic sensibility that stays always ahead of the normal visual [sensibility] of the crowd.

"In the same way, modern means of locomotion have completely upset relationships that had been known for an eternity. Before them, a landscape was a value in itself, that a white, dead road crossed without changing anything in the surroundings.

"Now, trains and cars, with their mixture of smoke and dust, take all the dynamism for themselves, and the landscape becomes secondary and decorative.

"Posters on the walls, [and] illuminated signs are of the same order of ideas" (Fernand Léger, "Les Réalisations picturales actuelles," a talk given at the Académie Wassilieff in 1914, originally published in *Soirées de Paris* in 1914, reprinted in Léger, *Fonctions de la peinture*, pp. 21–22).

65. Robert Rosenblum explored the possibility of a sexual reference in the words TROU ICI ("hole here"), inserted in the cutout opening in the lower center of the work and perhaps referring to the genitalia of the woman who is shown above them. See Rosenblum, "Picasso and the Typography of Cubism," in Roland Penrose and John Golding, eds., *Picasso in Retrospect* (New York and Washington: Praeger, 1973), p. 53.

66. See the catalogue *Manufacture Française d'Armes et Cycles de Saint-Étienne* (1913), p. 448. This resemblance was first pointed out by Michel Sanouillet in "Marcel Duchamp and the French Intellectual Tradition," in Anne d'Harnoncourt and Kynaston McShine, eds., *Marcel Duchamp*, exh. cat. (New York: The Museum of Modern Art; Philadelphia: Philadelphia Museum of Art, 1973), p. 53.

67. Katherine Kuh, "Marcel Duchamp," in Kuh, *The Artist's Voice: Talks with Seventeen Artists* (New York: Harper & Row, 1962), p. 83.

68. See the facsimiles of Duchamp's 1914 notes for the *Large Glass* printed in *Marcel Duchamp: Notes*, ed. and trans. Paul Matisse (Boston: G. K. Hall & Co., 1983), nos. 47–166. For a thorough analysis of the "program" of sexual encounters Duchamp conceived as the subject of the *Glass*, see George Heard Hamilton, "The Large Glass," in d'Harnoncourt and McShine, *Marcel Duchamp*.

69. E[dward] V[erral] L[ucas] and G[eorge] M[orris], *What a Life!* ([1911]; rpt., with an Introduction by John Ashberry, New York: Dover Publications, 1975).

70. Ashberry (Introduction to *What a Life!*, pp. v–xii), discusses this aspect of the cliché and gives a persuasive reading of the larger import of the satire for Lucas.

71. Pages from the book were shown in the exhibition "Fantastic Art, Dada, and Surrealism" at The

Museum of Modern Art, New York, in 1936. See Alfred H. Barr, Jr., *Fantastic Art, Dada, and Surrealism*, exh. cat. ([1936]; rpt., New York: The Museum of Modern Art, 1946), p. 109. See also Ashberry, ibid., pp. v–vi.

72. See David Steel, "Surrealism, Literature of Advertising and the Advertising of Literature in France, 1910–1930," *French Studies*, 41 (July 1987), p. 287.

73. See Dawn Ades, *Photomontage* (London: Thames & Hudson, 1976). See also Robert A. Sobieszek, "Composite Imagery and the Origins of Photomontage," *Artforum*, 17 (September 1978), pp. 58–65, (October 1978), pp. 40–45. For contemporaneous advice to admen on montage technique, see "Making Practical Use of the Cutout," *Advertising and Selling*, 24 (January 1915), pp. 9–10. Hannah Höch told an interviewer that she and her friends got the idea for photomontage from a trick used by the Prussian armed forces, of setting photo portraits into holes made in prepared prints of cavalry troops; see Hannah Höch, interviewed by Édouard Roditi, in Lucy R. Lippard, ed., *Dadas on Art* (Englewood Cliffs, N.J.: Prentice-Hall, 1971), p. 73.

74. "Yes, our whole purpose was to integrate objects from the world of machines and industry in the world of art. Our typographical collages or montages set out to achieve this by imposing, on something which could only be produced by hand, the appearances of something that had been entirely composed by a machine; in an imaginative composition, we used to bring together elements borrowed from books, newspapers, posters, or leaflets, in an arrangement that no machine could yet compose" (Höch, in Lippard, ed., *Dadas on Art*, p. 73).

75. Max Ernst, "Au-delà de la peinture," *Cahiers d'art*, nos. 6, 7 (1936), pp. 169–70.

76. See Werner Spies, *Max Ernst: Collagen*, exh. cat. (Cologne: Dumont, 1988), p. 29.

77. Ibid., pp. 58–59.

78. For a consideration of Picabia in the larger context of the sexualization of the automobile in the modern imagination, see *Automobile and Culture*, exh. cat. (Los Angeles: Los Angeles Museum of Contemporary Art, 1984).

79. On the Dadaists' fascination for drafting-style execution, see Molly Nesbit, "Ready-Made Originals: The Duchamp Model," *October*, 37 (Summer 1986), pp. 53–64.

80. The advertisements could have been culled from any number of American magazines. *The Saturday Evening Post*, however, is the most likely source.

81. See Willard Bohn, "Apollinaire and de Chirico: The Making of the Mannekins," *Comparative Literature*, 27 (1975), pp. 153–65.

82. See Arturo Schwarz, *The Complete Works of Marcel Duchamp* (New York: Harry N. Abrams, 1969), p. 521.

83. As an adjective applying to mass-produced wares, especially clothing, "ready-made" dates to the eighteenth century. As a noun, the word was in use long before 1900. See *The Oxford English Dictionary*, prepared by J. A. Simpson and E. S. C. Weiner (Oxford: Clarendon Press, 1989), vol. 13, p. 270.

84. William A. Camfield, *Marcel Duchamp: Fountain* (Houston: The Menil Collection, 1989).

85. See the interview with Duchamp in Otto Hahn, "Passport No. G255300," *Art and Artists*, 1 (July 1966), p. 10.

86. Duchamp's remarks on Dada aesthetics, made in response to Pierre Cabanne's question on the choosing of Readymades, have achieved the status of legend. "In general," he said, "I had to beware of its 'look.' It's very difficult to choose an object, because, at the end of fifteen days, you begin to like it or hate it. You have to approach something with an indifference, as if you had no aesthetic emotion. The choice of readymade is always based on visual indifference and, at the same time, on the total ab-sence of good or bad taste." Pierre Cabanne, *Dialogues with Marcel Duchamp*, trans. Ron Padgett (New York: Viking Press, 1971), p. 48.

87. Camfield, *Marcel Duchamp: Fountain*, pp. 34–42.

88. Ibid., pp. 44, 65.

89. See, for example, Amy Conger, "Edward Weston's Toilet," in Peter Walch and Thomas F. Barrow, eds., *Perspectives in Photographs: Essays in Honor of Beaumont Newhall* (Albuquerque, N.M.: University of New Mexico Press, 1986).

90. "The Richard Mutt Case," *The Blind Man*, no. 2 (May 1917), p. 5.

91. *Sanitary Pottery*, 7 (May 1915), p. 3.

92. *The Plumbers' Trade Journal*, February 15, 1915, p. 1.

93. *Modern Plumbing, No. 6* (Trenton, N.J.: J. L. Mott Ironworks, 1911), p. 7.

94. *Sanitary Pottery*, 7 (July 1915), p. 8.

95. *The Plumbers' Trade Journal*, August 15, 1915, p. 240.

96. "The Richard Mutt Case," p. 5.

97. H. Glévéo, "L'Étalage moderne, puissance de suggestion par l'objet," *La Publicité*, 21 (November 1923), pp. 731–33.

98. H. Glévéo, *Vitrines et étalages modernes* (Paris: G. & M. Ravisse, 1922), p. 3. The author recommends that the smart urban shop-owner will place his objects "dans un cadre recherché qui leur communique un cachet de chic, d'exclusivité." He also recommends that the merchant look to the art of the past for inspiration, studying Watteau or the Greeks, for example, for hints on draping.

99. Glévéo, "L'Étalage moderne," p. 731.

100. J-R. d'H., "Les Étalages," *La Publicité moderne*, 3 (July 1907), pp. 6–7.

101. See Leonard S. Marcus, *The American Store Window* (New York: Whitney Library of Design, 1978), pp. 62–63.

102. Preceding quotations from "Sur la peinture" (1937); reprinted in *Europe*, 49 (August–September 1971), p. 70. The text also asserts: "A new order tries to come out of [the chaos and speed of modern life]. In a certain way, the street gets organized: I mean the street, the shop windows, the displays, become spectacular. There a will to order establishes itself. Instead of a thousand objects stacked up one against the other, one shows ten well presented, given value.... [This shows that] the merchant understood that the object he was selling had an artistic value in itself, if he knew how to bring it out."

In an earlier homage to the various styles of shop-window display in Paris, Léger recognized that the "aesthetic of the isolated object" was basically a style of the chic shops around the Champs-Élysées, and that the old style of crowding in as many objects as possible still obtained in the popular quarters. (In this regard, Duchamp's isolation of the urinal could be seen as giving an 8th-*arrondisement* treatment to a 17th-*arrondisement* object.) See "La Rue: Objets, spectacles" (1928), in *Fonctions de la peinture*, pp. 68–69.

103. "...the *present* element, the central element of the street is the object more than the poster, which passes to a secondary plane and disappears. *The direct advent of the object as a decorative value*...belongs to the domain of pure plasticity, to the world of sculpture and construction.

"In Paris, if the modern street has a style, it is certainly thanks to this new taste for the object itself, for the form.

"...Economic pressure has put the seller on his knees before his merchandise; he has discovered it; he has recognized that these objects have a beauty. One fine day, stepping back, he exhibited a shoe or a rack [of meat] in his window. His imagination, his taste do the rest. A style is born, very up-to-date—a revolution has happened without drums or trumpets. The street can now be considered one of the fine arts, because it is magisterially dressed by the thousand hands that every day make and unmake the pretty *mise-en-scènes* that are called modern stores. The poster isn't up to this level. Only the Bébé Cadum, that enormous object, persists" (Léger, "La Rue: Objets, spectacles," p. 68).

"There are displays, absolutely perfect modern arrangements of shop windows, impossible [for an artist] to use; they are no longer raw material, it [the artistic work] is already done. That becomes a question of numbers, because if this production satisfied the human demand, there would be nothing more to do.... I repeat, the situation of the artist before these objects is often worrisome" (Léger, "Note sur l'élément mécanique" [1923], in *Fonctions de la peinture*, p. 51).

104. Léger, "Note sur l'élément mécanique," pp. 51–52. This text should also be read for Léger's long, appreciative description of one window-designer's arrangement of vests, and for the artist's delighted tour of several quarters of Paris, with their differing styles of window display.

105. See Léger, "Le Spectacle: Lumière, couleur, image mobile, objet-spectacle," p. 133.

106. With a partially digested notion of evolutionary natural selection as their guide, they felt that the human organism had been refined to a kind of functional perfection over the ages, and that in the same way, many of the things humans frequently use had acquired a well-adapted "design" of classic simplicity. These ideas are summarized by Christopher Green, *Léger and the Avant-Garde* (New Haven and London: Yale University Press, 1976), p. 207. Green is careful to distinguish Léger's ideas from those of the more theoretical Purist thinkers, but he underlines how Léger's taste for industrial objects does reflect the Purist approach; see Green, p. 273.

107. In "Revue de la publicité" (*La Publicité*, 11 [January 1914], p. 35), a closely similar ad (fig. 103) was reviewed, with the comment: "Here again is an excellent ad.... The drawing isn't complicated and makes itself understood easily."

108. "I am inspired by diagrams or mechanical elements," he said, "[and] sometimes even the stereotypes of advertising, like in this drawing of a syphon, which I found in *Le Matin*" (cited in Green, *Léger and the Avant-Garde*, p. 273).

109. Quoted in Jacques Gaucheron, "Fernand Léger et Blaise Cendrars," *Europe*, 49 (August–September, 1971), p. 98.

110. Léger, "Le Spectacle: Lumière, couleur, image mobile, objet-spectacle," p. 135.

111. See Léger's remarks on the mask in ancient theater, and its relation to the present sense of spectacle, in "Le Spectacle: Lumière, couleur, image mobile, objet-spectacle," pp. 134–35.

112. "More than ever, contemporary history...is the rule of the masses, therefore of propaganda. Because propaganda is to the mass of humanity what a bar of soft iron is to a magnetic field: just as the iron condenses the lines of force into a narrower flux, so propaganda permits the unification of thought and the simultaneity of actions.... The war was only possible because of propaganda... [which] alone was capable of creating a 'collective spirit' among the armies and the reservists.... [Now] propaganda plays a role in the moral world like that ultraviolet rays play in the material world, attempting to realize, in its own way, organic syntheses" (Jules Lallemand, "L'Art de la propagande," *La Publicité*, 19 [October 1921], pp. 537–38).

113. Jules Lallemand, "Propagande et publicité," *La Publicité*, 19 (November 1921), pp. 610–13.

114. E. Gautier, "La Propagande nationale et la publicité," *La Publicité*, 21 (April 1923), pp. 161–63; and Louis Angé, "L'Organisation de la propagande," *La Publicité*, 21 (January 1924), pp. 913–16.

115. Lallemand, "Une Expérience cruciale sur la 'suggestion' publicitaire," pp. 23–25.

116. Curti, "The Changing Concept of 'Human Nature' in the Literature of American Advertising," p. 347.

117. Ray Calt, "Advertising's Debt to Dr. Freud," *Advertising Agency/Advertising and Selling*, 45 (June 1952), p. 67.

118. Lallemand contributed an article on "Psychologie de la subconscience" to *La Publicité*, 19 (May 1921), pp. 219–21. He also foresaw the day when a properly rationalized science of persuasion would be a licensed profession on the model of medicine.

In his Foreword to a 1922 edition of D. C. A. Hémet's *Traité pratique de publicité* of 1912, Louis Angé (who began teaching a course on the psychology of advertising in 1908) traced the science of his trade as descending from a properly French, Cartesian tradition that had been revived in the experimental method of Claude Bernard and the positivist thought of Auguste Comte; Louis Angé, Foreword to D. C. A. Hémet, *Traité pratique de publicité commerciale et industrielle* ([1912]; rev. ed., Paris: 1922). M. Igert, of the psychology laboratory of Braqueville, in examining "the scientific technique of the poster" with controlled tests, referred to a similar heritage in analyzing how ads "modify the soul of the crowd"; Igert, "Une Technique scientifique de l'affiche," pp. 967–70.

119. Jules Lallemand, in "Psychologie et publicité," declared: "We know today that the collaboration of technicians is, in every industry, absolutely indispensable for the complete and rational realization of labor and of the primary matter, that is to assure for capital as high a remuneration as possible. On this subject, the experience of the war and the contact with the labor procedures—as much intellectual as physical—employed by our American friends, the comparison with our own, all this is decisive: production, in the full sense of the word, imperiously requires the collaboration of non-manual technicians, of scholars tested in research and in the methods of the laboratory" (p. 151). On the question of a Taylor-like concern with the factor of fatigue in repetition, see Jean Waldusberger and Charles Gonset, "Vente et psychologie," *La Publicité*, 21 (June 1923), pp. 357–58.

120. See Le Corbusier's comments in "L'Esprit moderne 1918," reprinted in *Léger and the Modern Spirit, 1918–1931*, exh. cat. (Paris: Musée d'Art Moderne de la Ville de Paris, 1982), p. 9.

121. "...an educational war where all values were laid bare. Total revision of moral and material values"; Léger, "Le Spectacle: Lumière, couleur, image mobile, objet-spectacle," p. 133.

122. "A nail, a bit of a candle, a shoelace, can cost the life of a man or a regiment. If, in today's life, we look at such things twice—and that's what's admirable—*there are no longer any negligible values*, everything counts, everything competes and the order of usual, conventional values is overturned" (Léger, "L'Ésthétique de la machine, l'ordre géometrique et le vrai," [1925]; reprinted in *Fonctions de la peinture*, p. 66).

123. Ibid.

124. Léger, "Sur la peinture," p. 69.

125. Christopher Green (in *Léger and the Avant-Garde*, p. 182) cited the importance of the following exchange between Cendrars and Léger. The conversation in its entirety was published as *Entretiens de Fernand Léger avec Blaise Cendrars et Louis Carré sur le paysage dans l'oeuvre de Léger* (Paris: Louis Carré, 1956) and includes the following remarks:

B.C.: *"The City" is very important. We used to stroll a lot around Paris; we often agreed to meet in very different locales, often the place Clichy. That's why I, myself, situate "The City" in place Clichy.*

F.L.: *That's it, yes; it dates from that period.*

B.C.: *As a composition, even as a distribution of masses, don't you see, and also for the extraordinary colors, which were those of place Clichy. You remember that, there, were the largest posters in Paris?*

F.L.: *Yes, it's the birth of advertising, isn't it.*

B.C.: *...of high advertising...*

F.L.: *Which would expand till it became nauseating.*

B.C.: *You had the largest Bébé Cadum in Paris, at place Clichy. Then one day, they brought out an astonishing black man, at place Clichy. I don't know, anymore, for what advertising that could have been...Black Lion shoe polish, or something like that...Ménélik, which you used one fine day like you use things, that's to say without knowing why.*

126. In 1946, Léger would remember billboards as indebted to, rather than inspirational for, this picture: "After the war, in 1919, I composed the picture *The City* uniquely with pure colors, laid down flat. The picture is technically a revolution in plasticity. It was possible, without chiaroscuro, without modulation, to obtain a depth and a dynamism. It was advertising that was first to utilize the consequences. The pure tone, the blues, reds, yellows escaped from the picture and went to inscribe themselves on walls, in windows, on the roadsides, in signalization. Color had become free" ("L'Architecture moderne et la couleur ou la création d'un nouveau espace vital" [1946]; reprinted in *Fonctions de la peinture*, p. 99).

127. Christopher Green discusses at length the cinematic aspects of this painting and compares its structure with the poetry of Blaise Cendrars, in *Léger and the Avant-Garde*, pp. 182–84.

128. At the time he was painting this and other pictures of modern commercial packaging, Davis made some relevant notations in his journal. The entry for March 11, 1921, includes his statement that he wished to make paintings, not from geometric shapes, but from "an alphabet of letters, numbers, canned-goods labels, tobacco labels, in a word let these well-known, purely objective things be used to indicate location and size." And in an entry made the following month he declared, "I do not belong to the human race but am a product made by the American Can Co., and the New York *Evening Journal*." See John R. Lane, *Stuart Davis: Art and Art Theory*, exh. cat. (Brooklyn: The Brooklyn Museum, 1978), p. 94.

129. On the stylistic development of American cigarette packs and the strategies of their marketing, see Chris Mullen, *Cigarette Pack Art: A Unique Blend of Cigarette Pack Design* (New York: St. Martin's Press, 1979), pp. 94–95. For an in-house history of the style changes in the packaging of Lucky Strikes, see *"Sold American!": The First Fifty Years* (n.p.: American Tobacco Company, 1954), pp. 53–54, 74–76.

130. A sample: Rene Clarke, reviewing the history of advertising in the United States in 1934, declared that "the fifteen [sic] years between 1921 and 1930 were the golden age of advertising" ("Cavalcade," *Advertising Arts*, September 1934, p. 12).

131. In an unpublished paper to which we have had access, Victoria de Grazia of Rutgers University discusses these and other aspects of the situation between the wars: "The 'Publicity Machine' in the Garden: American Advertising in the Remaking of European Commercial Culture, 1920–1945." By the same author, see "Americanism for Export," *Wedge*, nos. 7, 8 (Winter–Spring 1985), pp. 74–85.

132. "Futuristic Monstrosities Are All the Rage: (By a Commercial Art Manager)," *Printers' Ink*, November 12, 1925, pp. 57–60. "Things that people can't quite understand seem to interest and hold them. It keeps them guessing," the author surmised, as he counseled tolerance on the pragmatic premise that modern inflections worked for certain markets.

133. L. B. Siegfried, "Modernism Emerges Full-Fledged," *Advertising and Selling*, new series, 10 (February 8, 1928), pp. 24–25, 40, 67.

134. Pierce Johnson, "The Sane Use of Modern Art in Advertising," *Advertising and Selling*, new series, 14 (October 30, 1929), pp. 17–19.

135. On the new typography, see Douglas C. McMurtrie, "The Fundamentals of Modernism in Typography," *Printers' Ink*, January 1930 pp. 33–35, 70, 81; and McMurtrie, "The Future of Advertising Composition," *Printers' Ink*, April 1930,

pp. 39–40, 90, 93–94.

136. An analysis of this phenomenon can be found in *The Machine Age in America*, exh. cat. (New York: The Brooklyn Museum in association with Harry N. Abrams, 1986).

137. E. E. Calkins, "Beauty in the Machine Age," *Printers' Ink*, September 25, 1930, pp. 72–73, 77–78, 83.

138. Louis Chéronnet, "La Publicité, art du XXe siècle," *L'Art vivant*, 3 (March 1927), p. 192.

139. "Have you thought about the sadness that would represent the streets, the squares, train stations, the subway, palaces, dance halls, movie theaters, dining cars, trips, automobile roads, nature, without the countless posters, without the shop windows...without the illuminated signs, without the *boniments* of loudspeakers" (Blaise Cendrars, *Aujourd'hui*, in Cendrars, *Oeuvres complètes* [Paris: Denoël, 1960]; cited in Steel, "Surrealism, Literature of Advertising and the Advertising of Literature in France, 1910–1930," pp. 283–84).

140. Cendrars, *Oeuvres complètes*, pp. 229–30; cited in Steel, "Surrealism, Literature of Advertising and the Advertising of Literature in France, 1910–1930," p. 285.

For a further literary appreciation of advertising from the same date, see Aldous Huxley, *Essays Old and New* (Freeport, N.Y.: Books for Libraries Press, 1927) pp. 126–31. Huxley maintained that "The story of the development of advertising...is an essential chapter in the history of democracy."

141. Louis Chéronnet, "La Publicité moderne: La Gloire du panneau," *L'Art vivant*, 2 (August 1926), p. 618.

142. Steel, "Surrealism, Literature of Advertising and the Advertising of Literature in France, 1910–1930," note 3, p. 295.

143. Max Jacob, letter to Marcel Jouhandeau, July 1923, *Lettres à Marcel Jouhandeau* (Geneva: Droz, 1979), p. 59; cited in Steel, "Surrealism, Literature of Advertising and the Advertising of Literature in France, 1910–1930," p. 283.

144. Léger, "La Rue: Objects, Spectacles," p. 68.

145. See Robert Desnos, *La Liberté ou l'amour!* (Paris: Aux Éditions du Sagittaire, 1927); cited in Steel, "Surrealism, Literature of Advertising and the Advertising of Literature in France, 1910–1930," p. 295. Desnos's title puns on the patriot's cry, "Liberty or death!" (*La liberté ou la mort!*).

146. For a thorough discussion of Magritte's career in advertising, and of the subsequent influence of his imagery on advertising, see G. Roque, *Ceci n'est pas un Magritte: Essai sur Magritte et la publicité* (Paris: Musée de la Publicité, 1983). For specific consideration of display, see Silvano Levy, "René Magritte and Window Display," *Artscribe*, no. 28 (March 1981), pp. 24–28.

147. See Michel Foucault, "Ceci n'est pas une pipe," *Cahiers du chemin*, no. 2 (1968), pp. 79–105; cited in André Blavier, *Ceci n'est pas une pipe* (Brussels: Fondation René Magritte, 1973), p. 27.

148. "The public wants more facts and less fancy, for there is a great deal it will no longer take for granted," said Gurden Edwards, advertising director of the American Bankers Association in his "Training Course for Salesman," in 1935; cited by Curti, "The Changing Concept of Human Nature," p. 353.

149. M. F. Agha wrote: "This year of grace 1932 begins under auspices highly unfavorable to European art in American advertising. Some observers think that even the local brands of art, including the modest commercial art, are under a cloud. Even the advertising agencies rise to the occasion, and, at the risk of undermining the prestige of the profession, write: 'This is a hard year for the nuances in advertising. The Graphic Arts have gone graphic, gentlemanly copy has been given the bum's rush. It is a hard-boiled year, a year of plug-ugly type-sets, of copy full of more-for-the-money'" ("Leave European Art in Europe," *Advertising Arts* [January 1932],

p. 15). For a full discussion of the change in the look of ads during the Depression years, see "Depression Advertising as a Shift in Style," in Roland Marchand, *Advertising the American Dream* (Berkeley and Los Angeles: University of California Press, 1985), pp. 300–06. See also E. E. Calkins, "1934," *Advertising Arts* (January 1934), pp. 9–12.

150. E. E. Calkins, "Design and Economic Recovery," *Advertising Arts* (July 1933), pp. 9–13.

151. Calkins, "1934," pp. 11–12. From the same article: "Instead of pointing the camera from a surprising angle, or photographing patterns made by the shadows of commonplace objects, we now have the natural conventional group.... A further instance of the endeavor to get nearer the popular mind and interest is the employment of the comic strip formula, the cartoon serial, and the tabloid make-up....The screaming Gothic headlines, scrambled layout and general air of excitement of the tabloid press have been adopted by several advertisers.... All these trends and changes have one characteristic in common. They are away from the cherished ideal which prevailed during the high water era, away from the precious, the distinguished, the fine, toward something coarser, more direct, even, if necessary, uncouth, in the effort to get down to brass tacks."

152. Heyworth Campbell, "Going Buckeye Vengefully...But Intelligently," *Printers' Ink Monthly*, 24 (February 1932), pp. 22–23, 58. From the same article: "Especially these days, when advertising must do a strenuous job, the hard-boiled fans are wondering if getting their advertisement into the Art Director's Show isn't, after all, an art achievement, but a selling liability.... The cult of the 'buckeye' is again coming into its own. The devotees of the plug-ugly are now having a Roman holiday."

153. W. K. Nield, "The Disloyal Art Director," *Advertising and Selling*, new series, 19 (August 18, 1932), p. 21.

154. See Michael Schudson, *Advertising: The Uneasy Persuasion—Its Dubious Impact on American Society* (New York: Basic Books, 1984), pp. 209–33.

155. Miró created another fanciful painting from a similar point of departure in a machine ad: his 1929 *Queen Luisa of Prussia*. See Jacques Dupin, *Joan Miró: Life and Work* (New York: Harry N. Abrams, 1962), pp. 182–85, 195–96, and figs. 27–42.

156. For several fine essays and an extensive bibliography on Cornell, see Kynaston McShine, ed., *Joseph Cornell*, exh. cat. (New York: The Museum of Modern Art, 1980). Also see Diane Waldman, *Joseph Cornell* (New York: George Braziller, 1977); and Dore Ashton, ed., *A Joseph Cornell Album* (New York: Viking Press, 1974).

157. On Cornell's fascination with tattered carnival ephemera, see Harold Rosenberg, "Object Poems," *The New Yorker*, June 3, 1967, pp. 112, 114–18.

158. Clement Greenberg, "The Situation at the Moment," *Partisan Review*, 15 (January 1948), p. 82; cited by Francis Frascina, Introduction to Frascina, ed., *Pollock and After: The Critical Debate* (New York: Harper & Row, 1985), p. 97.

159. Douglas D. Paige, "Should Copy Writers Be Cultured?," *Printers' Ink*, October 1, 1954, p. 25.

160. For a summary of Golden's career, see Cipe Pineles Golden, Kurt Weihs, Robert Strunsky, eds., *The Visual Craft of William Golden* (New York: George Braziller, 1962).

161. See "Mehemed Fehmy Agha," in *Fifty-first Annual of the Advertising Art Directors' Club of New York* (New York: Art Directors' Club of New York, 1971), n.pag.

162. "Agha introduced a radically new principle in the conception of American publications—that of the participatory role of the Art Director at every level. The visual articulation of a magazine was not an act after the editorial fact; it was, as Agha saw it, an integral function of the editorial process" (ibid).

163. Thomas B. Stanley, "Has Modern Layout Come to Stay?," *Printers' Ink*, August 28, 1953, pp. 38–40, 87.

164. See Stanley, "Has Modern Layout Come to Stay?" pp. 38–40, 87. "Modern display...is no longer primarily a matter of layout. In it, the traditional distinction between layout as arrangement, and visualization as pictorial expression of the advertising appeal has largely disappeared.... Modern advertising comes honestly by its three most important characteristics: *unconventional approach*, *striking design*, and *imaginative, personal treatment*." Stanley singles out the Ohrbach ad as his prime example of merging layout with visualization. See also Sanford H. Margolis and Morton Silverstein, "This Week Is Really Going to Be Something!," *Printers' Ink*, January 2, 1953, pp. 28–32, for a complimentary look at Bernbach. The authors divide advertising into three camps: old patricians from the Harvard-Princeton axis, play-it-safe people who work from market research and proven techniques, and on "the far left we have Bill Bernbach and his imitators. Strongly influenced by modern art and convinced that copy and art should be integrated so fully that one cannot stand without the other."

165. Margolis and Silverstein, "This Week Is Really Going to Be Something!," p. 28.

166. The "amount of money a person makes is no index of his buying motivations," Dichter wrote in 1956. "It is much more important to establish what is the source of a person's income, what is the background against which he lives, what social and personal forces direct his life goals and ambitions" (Dr. Ernst Dichter, "The Case for Motivational Research," *Advertising Agency*, 49 [March 2, 1956], p. 43). In a note of hope for a utopian program of advertising, Dichter allowed that "our deepest wish is to see a unified field of market research established, where conventional statistical research and motivational research work hand in hand in complete scientific harmony."

167. See "You Can't Escape MR," *Advertising Agency*, 51 (January 3, 1958), pp. 20–23, 26–33; there, John J. Reilly of Esso Standard Oil complains, "It is very difficult to get a client to consider motivation research if he thinks it deals only with sex concepts, as reported by the press."

For another consideration of Dichter's effect on advertising, see Philip Gold, *Advertising, Politics, and American Culture: From Salesmanship to Therapy* (New York: Paragon House, 1987), pp. 45–56.

168. "William Bernbach: Portrait of an Artist as a Young Agency President," *Printers' Ink*, July 31, 1959, p. 51.

169. "Is a masculine product acquiring connotations of daintiness or weakness? Does an expensive item have the necessary social status? Is the tone of a promotional campaign in tune with the changing cultural conventions of the day?" (Dichter, "The Case for Motivational Research," p. 43). One of Dichter's followers echoed: "In our motivation studies, it becomes obvious how important is the personality of the product or institution. This is the composite of attitudes people have formed toward it. Regardless of its truth, this is what people think it is, and this is the way they patronize it.... Keen-minded retailers are aware that their customers do the largest part of their shopping in terms of these attitudes toward the store rather than through specific advertised items" (Pierre Martineau, "New Look at Old Symbols," *Printers' Ink*, June 4, 1954, pp. 85, 88). Compare this to Bernbach's comments on the Ohrbach campaign: "No individual garment is ever described. No price is quoted. We sell the idea that the Ohrbach label is one that can be worn proudly" (quoted in Margolis and Silverstein, "This Week Is Really Going to Be Something!," p. 29). See also Donald David, "Image Building Is an Unexplored Advertising Horizon," *Advertising Agency*, 51 (January 3, 1958), pp. 12–16.

170. The eye patch did not begin as calculated strategy. The model had already been photographed eighteen times at the session, when Ogilvy decided to try the patch to add a note of distinction.

See David Ogilvy, *Confessions of an Advertising Man* (New York: Atheneum, 1963), p. 116.

171. Bill Tyler, in his regular "Copy Clinic" column for *Advertising Agency* of June 8, 1956, cites a Hathaway ad of the previous month as the first ad he had seen with no copy of any kind; but he also discusses the "de-emphasis on copy in recent years" and the new importance of color photography (p. 44). In 1957, in "Visual Impact Provides the Big Picture," Marilyn Hoffner refers to "a strong and continuing trend toward more visual material and less copy," illustrating several examples, including a Bernbach ad for Levy's Jewish rye bread (*Printers' Ink*, May 17, 1957, p. 28).

172. Mort Weiner, "What's Happened to Creativity?," *Printers' Ink*, July 19, 1957, pp. 19–20: "Today the means has become the end; instead of drawing a picture that makes a point, we're satisfied to just draw a picture."

173. The key term "personality," used again and again in advertising planning of the day, seems to derive ultimately from the revisionist, neo-Freudian idea that the "total personality" of the individual be the subject of analysis. This revisionist school, which played down the importance of childhood and biological factors while focusing on the individual's adjustment to social institutions, was emergent in the 1930s and came to prominence precisely in the early 1950s. See Clara Thompson, *Psychoanalysis: Evolution and Development* (New York: Heritage House, 1951). See also Herbert Marcuse, "Critique of Neo-Freudian Revisionism," in Marcuse, *Eros and Civilization* (New York: Vintage, 1962), pp. 217–51. For an early plea to rethink advertising in terms of the findings of the social sciences, see Edward L. Bernays, "Advertising Is Behind the Times—Culturally," *Printers' Ink*, March 30, 1951, pp. 25–27.

174. See Dr. Howard D. Hadley, "What Psychology Offers to Advertising," *Advertising Agency / Advertising and Selling*, April 1953, pp. 70–71, 142.

175. Vance Packard, *The Hidden Persuaders* (New York: David McKay, 1957).

176. Roland Barthes, "The World of Wrestling," in Barthes, *Mythologies*, trans. Annette Lavers ([1957]; English ed., New York: Hill & Wang, 1972).

177. Roland Barthes, "Publicité de la profondeur"; cited in Philip Thody, *Roland Barthes: A Conservative Estimate* (Chicago: University of Chicago Press, 1973), pp. 52–53.

178. See Marshall McLuhan, *Understanding Media: The Extensions of Man* (New York: McGraw-Hill, 1964).

179. Barthes said that popular culture fascinated him *"jusqu'à la nausée"* ("to the point of nausea"); Barthes to Raymond Bellour, in *Les Lettres française*, May 20, 1970; cited in Thody, *Roland Barthes*, p. 52.

180. Christopher Ricks, *Times Higher Education Supplement*, April 21, 1972 (when the English edition of Barthes's *Mythologies* appeared); cited in Thody, *Roland Barthes*, p. 49.

181. John Kenneth Galbraith, *The Affluent Society* (Boston: Houghton Mifflin, 1958).

182. William Whyte, *The Organization Man* (Garden City, N.Y.: Doubleday, 1956). On horror movies of the fifties and social meanings imbedded in them, see Susan Sontag, "The Imagination of Disaster," in *"Against Interpretation" and Other Essays* (New York: Octagon Books, 1966). See also Sloan Wilson, *The Man in the Grey Flannel Suit* (New York: Simon & Schuster, 1955).

183. Alison and Peter Smithson, "Personal Statement, 1: But Today We Collect Ads," *Ark*, no. 18 (Fall 1956), pp. 49–50.

184. See Thomas Lawson, "Bunk: Eduardo Paolozzi and the Legacy of the Independent Group," in *Modern Dreams: The Rise and Fall and Rise of Pop*, exh. cat. (New York: The Institute for Contemporary Art, The Clocktower Gallery; Cambridge, Mass., and London: MIT Press, 1988), p. 22.

185. For articles on the Independent Group and its exhibitions, see *Modern Dreams*.

186. "This was the most hotly debated aspect of American car styling at the time—'fins,' someone has said, 'were the Vietnam of product design.' Everything that boiled over in American politics about Cambodia and Vietnam was, in a way, trailered or run through in rough form already in the argument about tail-fins. Tail-fins divided Left and Right, divided hawk from dove, divided everything from everything. Tail-fins were a really good convenient symbol that everyone could get hold of. In the end tail-fins were held to be responsible for the fact that America lagged behind in the space-race: while the Russians had been developing 'Sputnik' and pushing on into the great blue 'out there,' the Americans had been debauching themselves with tail-fins. More than chrome, more than the implications of sex, etc., the tail-fin in the end, which means 1955/56, focussed the whole issue" (Reyner Banham, "Detroit Tin Re-Visited," in *Design 1900–1960: Studies in Design and Popular Culture of the 20th Century* [Newcastle-on-Tyne: Petras, 1976], p. 134.)

187. Quoted, from *Design Review*, in Banham, "Detroit Tin Re-Visited," p. 121.

188. Reyner Banham, *Theory and Design in the First Machine Age* (London: The Architectural Press, 1960). For the annotated translation of the 1909 manifesto, see "Futurist Manifesto," *Architectural Review*, 126 (August–September 1959), pp. 77–80.

189. For Banham's critique of Corbusier's ideas about automobiles, see Reyner Banham, "Machine Aesthetic," *Architectural Review*, 117 (April 1955), pp. 225–28.

190. See Reyner Banham, "Vehicles of Desire," *Art*, 1 (September 1, 1955); reprinted in *Modern Dreams*. Banham cites Barthes's praise for the 1955 DS, but ultimately prefers the observant, hard-headed writing of Deborah Allan in *Industrial Design* (see the discussion of Hamilton's *Hers Is a Lush Situation*). The same kind of preference was later expressed by other British critics when *Mythologies* appeared in English. Graham Hough complained that "in some of the pieces, the depth of actual social observation is not much beyond that of the sophisticated woman's page: sharper than Jilly Cooper, but not sharper than Katherine Whitehorn" (cited in Thody, *Roland Barthes*, p. 46).

191. Lawson, "Bunk," p. 25: "It is a cozy little future-world pictured here, very British in its claustrophobia."

192. See the articles on product design in Richard Hamilton, *Collected Words* (London: Thames & Hudson, 1982).

193. See Richard Hamilton's review of the role of design in 1950s manufacturing, "Persuading Image," *Design*, February 1960: reprinted in *Modern Dreams*.

194. See Banham, "Vehicles of Desire," pp. 65–69.

195. Hamilton, *Collected Words*, pp. 28–32. Banham quotes the crucial part of Allan's text in "Detroit Tin Re-Visited," pp. 130–31.

196. Banham, "Detroit Tin Re-Visited," pp. 135, 138. "Suddenly, the whole game was transformed—it became a sporting relationship between the two great companies [Chrysler and General Motors] and the buying public...who were not now asking what next year's model would look like but what the 1973 model would look like when it became available in 1968! The general level of expectation was to hurtle on into wilder and more abstract kinds of design, and more uninhibited design, as fast as possible."

197. Robin Boyd, in *Architect's Journal*, late 1956; cited in Banham, "Detroit Tin Re-Visited," p. 134.

198. Bill Tyler, "Copy Clinic," *Advertising Agency*, December 20, 1957, p. 20.

199. See "Ford Will Offer a Shorter, Sleeker, More Streamlined Model for 1960," *Advertising Week*, May 1, 1959, p. 9.

200. Ernst Dichter and Albert Shephard, "Psychological Engineering: Detroit's Future Approach to Automobile Design?," *Printers' Ink*, November 21, 1958, p. 66.

201. "Visual Ads Introduce France's Peugeot to the U.S. Import-Car Market," *Printers' Ink*, December 5, 1958, p. 40.

202. Robert Rauschenberg, "Note on Painting Oct. 31–Nov. 2, 1963" (1963); reprinted in John Russell and Suzi Gablik, *Pop Art Redefined* (New York: Praeger, 1969), pp. 101–02.

203. It may count for something that Atlanta-based Coca-Cola, sometimes referred to affectionately as "the wine of the South," had a program of buying back its bottles, each of which carried the glass stamp of a local bottler on the bottom. These empties—collected for their different imprints of faraway, exotic places like Tallahassee and Roanoke, and traded in for candy money—were the coin of childhood in the South of the 1950s. They were items of variety within standardization, and of personal, nickel-and-dime entrepreneurship within big-time manufacturing.

204. Michael Crichton, *Jasper Johns*, exh. cat. (New York: Harry N. Abrams in association with the Whitney Museum of American Art, 1977), pp. 42–43.

205. Robert Rosenblum, "Pop Art and Non-Pop Art," *Art and Literature*, 5 (Summer 1965); reprinted in Russell and Gablik, eds., *Pop Art Redefined*, pp. 53–56.

206. Max Kozloff, "Pop Culture, Metaphysical Disgust, and the 'New Vulgarians,'" *Art International*, 6 (March 1962), p. 38.

207. Marvin Davis, quoted in Marilyn Hoffer, "Idea Art Does Sales Job for I. Miller," *Printers' Ink*, November 18, 1955, p. 30.

208. Peter Palazzo, quoted in Hoffer, "Idea Art Does Sales Job for I. Miller," p. 30.

209. See "The Great Debate," in Gold, *Advertising, Politics, and American Culture*, pp. 57–61. In 1961, an analyst for *Advertising Age* noted that an intensely competitive market was bringing these two approaches into fierce contention: "One is the 'let's-blow-their-house-down' school. This one uses money as a sledgehammer. It says that the only important thing is to have a strong selling idea. Then you jam this down people's throats by repetition.... The other school says that since it's so hard to get attention today, your advertising should devote most of its effort to getting attention.... This is an entirely new advertising cult—the off-beat.... It has as its crusading objective the goal of a dramatically compelling ad every time out.... One says that advertising is nothing more than the science of mass selling...the other says that success in advertising depends on the art of dramatic presentation" (William D. Tyler, "Two Ad Factions Struggle for Attention as the Problem of Getting Heard Gets Harder," *Advertising Age*, October 9, 1961, pp. 95–96).

Also, contrast Warhol's repetition with earlier advertising's frequent use of repetition as a decorative device; see W. Livingston Larned, "Showing the Product in Pictorial Patterns," *Printers' Ink*, May 8, 1930, pp. 100, 105–06, 108.

210. William D. Tyler, "Here Are the '60 All-Star Ads," *Advertising Age*, March 13, 1961, p. 78.

211. Charles W. Hurd, "The Package as a Strong Medium," *Printers' Ink*, April 11, 1912, p. 28.

212. W. Livingston Larned, "Designing the Label with the Sales 'Punch,'" *Printers' Ink*, June 10, 1915, pp. 25–35.

213. See Claes Oldenburg and Emmett Williams, *Store Days: Documents from "The Store" (1961) and "The Ray Gun Theatre" (1962)* (New York: Something Else Press, 1967).

214. See Peter Plagens's remarks on the importance, for Los Angeles artists of the 1960s, of rejecting the bohemian model of the artist, and becoming businessmen; Plagens, "Golden Days," in Kirk Varnedoe and Adam Gopnik, eds., *Modern Art and Popular Culture: Readings in High and Low* (New York: The Museum of Modern Art and Harry N. Abrams, 1990).

215. Oldenburg, *Store Days*; cited in Russell and Gablik, *Pop Art Redefined*, pp. 97–99. See also the earlier, 1961 version of this statement, excerpted in Barbara Rose, ed., *Readings in American Art Since 1900* (New York: Praeger, 1967), pp. 166–67.

216. See J. Lemagny, *Visionary Architects: Boullée, Ledoux, Lequeu* (Houston, Tex.: University of Saint Thomas, 1968).

217. W. H. Heath, "'Jumbo' Display That Dominates," *Printers' Ink*, July 7, 1921, pp. 41–48.

218. "Curiously, this [rebel] school had, as its immediate progenitor, the studied simplicity of fashion advertising plus the product-oriented directness of retail advertising. Mostly photographic, the illustrations employed are far from what used to be called candid photography. It is their presentation, rather, that is candid—they announce unashamedly that they are carefully and ingeniously contrived advertising illustration" (Walter Weir, "'Look of the Sixties' Replaces 'Readership School' of Ads, with Accent on Personal Element," *Advertising Age*, October 8, 1962, pp. 75–76).

219. Conversation with the artist, January 1990. The "Injun" was a favored persona of Oldenburg's early performance pieces, representing, among other things, a part of American history (i.e., the violent suppression of Native American tribes) that had often been either concealed or slighted.

220. For a discussion of the rage for "creativity" in later 1960s advertising, and the effect of a large hiring of younger, more eccentric people by ad agencies, see Gold, *Advertising, Politics, and American Culture*, pp. 71–84.

221. In a taped discussion with Stuart Wrede, in June 1968, Marcuse said of the possible construction of one of Oldenburg's proposed giant object-monuments: "Strangely enough, I think that would indeed be subversive. If you could ever imagine a situation in which this could be done, you would have the revolution. If you could really envisage a situation where at the end of Park Avenue there would be a huge Good Humor ice cream bar and in the middle of Times Square a huge banana, I would say—and I think safely say—this society has come to an end. Because then people cannot take anything seriously: neither their President, nor the cabinet, nor the corporation executives...." (*Perspecta 12: The Yale Architectural Review*, [1969], p. 74).

222. "When they say the Rosenquist style is very precise, maybe they just know that painting style as they know it is going out of style. Ways of accomplishing things are extended to different generations in oblique places. Billboard painting techniques are much like Mexican muralist techniques. Few people extend themselves in it at the time because it is not very much considered" (James Rosenquist, "What Is the F-111?" [interview with G. R. Swenson], *Partisan Review*, 32 [Fall 1965]; reprinted in Russell and Gablik, *Pop Art Redefined*, p. 105).

223. "I would bring home colors that I liked, associations that I liked using in my abstract painting, and I would remember specifics by saying this was a dirty bacon can, this was a yellow T-shirt yellow, this was a Man-Tan suntan orange. I remember these like I was remembering an alphabet, a specific color. So then I started painting Man-Tan orange and—I always remember Franco-American spaghetti orange" (James Rosenquist, in G. R. Swenson, "What Is Pop Art? Interviews with Eight Painters—Part 2," *Art News*, 62 [February 1964]; reprinted in Russell and Gablik, *Pop Art Redefined*, p. 111).

224. Contrary to, say, the fascination of the British for the latest in Detroit design in the mid-fifties, Rosenquist wanted to avoid the taint of timely styling. "In 1960 and 1961 I painted the front of a 1950 Ford. I felt it was an anonymous image.... I use images from old magazines—when I say old, I mean 1945 to 1955—a time we haven't started to ferret out as history yet. If it was the front end of a new car there would be people who were passionate about it, and the front end of an old car might make some people nostalgic. The images are like no-images. There is a freedom there" (ibid., p. 110).

225. Ibid.

226. Hughes, "Memories Scaled and Scrambled," p. 69.

227. "The tire is a crown, a celebration of the town and country winter tire. The design, magnified, appears regal. I'd never thought of what rubber tires or wheels meant to me, and I looked at the tire tread and it seemed very strong and cruel or at least very, very visual. It also looked like it was rising up, like a crown, and so I used the image on top of the cake that way. And of course the two images have similar shapes" (Rosenquist, "What Is the F-111?" p. 107).

228. Rosenquist specified that the three bulbs were in pink, yellow, and blue to touch the "three basic colors of the spectrum," and said: "In that area of the picture they allowed me to try experiments in color and scale that I could not have tried in another painting in smaller size. That huge area allowed me to paint with regular artist's oil paint, the pink-grey and yellow-grey and blue-grey, on top of a fluorescent background. The dark red fluorescent paint appears to be lighter than the three light bulbs but the paint in the three light bulbs lets you get the idea that the bulbs are glowing, but not that they are turned on. It seemed to be like force against force" (ibid., p. 107).

229. In his words, "The picture is my personal reaction as an individual to the heavy ideas of mass media and communication and to other ideas that affect artists. I gather myself up to do something in a specific time, to produce something that could be exposed as a human idea of the extreme acceleration of feelings" (ibid., p. 104).

230. Robert Scull's decision to buy all the units, and thus keep the work intact, was a last-minute surprise. Rosenquist liked the idea that symbolic pieces of the plane's image would be bought by the same taxpayers who had, perhaps unknowingly, funded the plane itself; and he intended that the different elements of the painting remain separate and in some sense incoherent. G. R. Swenson suggested to Rosenquist in 1965 that "it might have been better, closer to your intention, if it had been sold piece by piece." Rosenquist replied, "Yes," and elaborated that "it would be to give the idea to people of collecting fragments of vision. One piece of this painting would have been a fragment of a machine the collector was already mixed up with, involved in whether he knew it or not. The person has already bought these airplanes by paying income taxes or being part of the community and the economy. Men participate in the world whether it's good or not and they may have physically bought parts of what this image represents many times" (ibid., p. 106).

231. Léger, "Les Réalisations picturales actuelles," p. 21.

Contemporary Reflections

1. The aphorism itself has a curious history. Marx's *The Eighteenth Brumaire of Louis Bonaparte* begins "Hegel observes somewhere that all great incidents and individuals of world history occur, as it were, twice. He forgot to add: the first time as tragedy, the second as farce." The historian Eugene Kameka notes that "Generations of scholars have been unable to find this remark in Hegel, though in his *Lectures on the Philosophy of History* (published 1837) Hegel refers to seemingly accidental events—such as a *coup d'état*, the defeat of Napoleon or the driving out of the Bourbons—gaining respectability and acceptance through their being repeated. Marx was probably echoing, inaccurately, a remark made by Engels in a letter to Marx of 3 December 1851, where Engels writes: 'It really seems as if old Hegel in his grave were acting as world writ and directly history, ordaining most conscientiously that it should all be unrolled twice over, once as a great tragedy and once as a wretched farce.'" See *The Portable Karl Marx*, ed. Eugene Kameka (New York and London: Penguin, 1983), p. 287.

2. Robert Venturi, Denise Scott Brown, and Charles Izenour, *Learning from Las Vegas: The Forgotten Symbolism of Architectural Form* ([1972]; rev. ed., Cambridge, Mass., and London: MIT Press, 1977).

3. On Smithson, see Adam Gopnik, "Basic Stuff: Robert Smithson and Primitivism," *Arts Magazine*, 57 (March 1983), pp. 74–80. See also Kirk Varnedoe, "Contemporary Explorations," in William Rubin, ed., *"Primitivism" in 20th Century Art: Affinity of the Tribal and the Modern*, exh. cat. (New York: The Museum of Modern Art, 1984).

4. This sensibility was often expressed in what was called, grimly, "post-apocalyptic" art—if there was going to be art about the apocalypse, you had better make it now—that summoned up the forms of Stonehenge to express the approaching doom of the space age. See Varnedoe, "Contemporary Explorations."

5. See Lisa Phillips, "His Equivocal Touch in the Vicinity of History," in Janet Kardon, ed., *David Salle*, exh. cat. (Philadelphia: Institute of Contemporary Art, University of Pennsylvania, 1985).

6. William Hazlitt, *Selected Writings* (London: Penguin, 1970), p. 447.

7. Probably more nonsense has been written about subway graffiti in New York than about any other urban phenomenon of recent years. Shortly after the first recognition of graffiti in the early eighties, for instance, Norman Mailer leapt into print with a "study" based on zero hours of actual scrutiny, which cast the graffiti writers as existential heroes, Kierkegaardian man armed with a spray can.

Fortunately, at least three witnesses took the trouble to document the events as they took place. Two photographers, Henry Chalfant, a scholar of classical Greek, and Martha Cooper, a news photographer, spent years "on the lines" recording the subway writers' work and their world. (Chalfant and Cooper were for a very long time unaware of each other's work; the graffiti writers themselves brought them together.) The present discussion of subway graffiti is based on their definitive study: see Martha Cooper and Henry Chalfant, *Subway Art* (New York: Holt, Rinehart & Winston, 1984). Craig Castelman, a gifted urban anthropologist, spent years living with graffiti artists at about the same time, and wrote a doctoral thesis about them which later became his remarkable book, *Getting Up: Subway Graffiti in New York* (Cambridge, Mass.: MIT Press, 1982).

8. See Adam Gopnik, "Buffed Out," *The New Yorker*, February 20, 1990.

9. See, for example, John Carlin and Sheena Wagstaff, *The Comic Art Show: Cartoons in Painting and Popular Culture*, exh. cat. (New York: Fantagraphics Books, for the Whitney Museum of American Art, Downtown Branch, 1983). See also Sheena Wagstaff, *Comic Iconoclasm*, exh. cat. (London: Institute of Contemporary Art).

10. See Adam Gopnik, "Comics and Catastrophe," *The New Republic*, June 22, 1987, pp. 29–34.

11. Elizabeth Murray, conversation with the authors, January 1990.

12. W. H. Auden, "As I Walked Out One Evening," in Auden, *Collected Shorter Poems, 1927–57* (London: Faber & Faber, 1966).

13. Jean Baudrillard, *Simulations*, trans. Paul Foss, Paul Patton, and Philip Beitchman (New York: Semiotext[e], 1983), p. 37.

14. For a brilliant dissection of Baudrillard's reasoning, see the review of his *America* in Robert Hughes, "America's Pop Guru," *The New York Review of Books*, June 1, 1989, pp. 29 ff.

15. Jean Baudrillard, *The Ecstasy of Communication*, trans. Bernard and Caroline Schutze, ed. Slyvere Lotringer (Brooklyn: Semiotext[e], 1988), p. 101.

16. Peter Halley, interview with Dan Cameron, in *New York Art Now: The Saatchi Collection* (London: Saatchi, 1987), p. 45.

17. Jeff Koons, interview with the authors, February 1989.

18. John Updike, *Hugging the Shore* (New York: Alfred A. Knopf, 1984), p. 556.

19. Diane Waldman, *Jenny Holzer*, exh. cat. (New York: Solomon R. Guggenheim Museum, 1989), p. 10.

20. W. H. Auden, "Letter to Lord Byron," in Auden, *Collected Longer Poems* (London: Faber & Faber, 1983).

21. For a passionate and brilliant presentation of this view, see Robert Hughes, Introduction to *Lucian Freud: Paintings*, exh. cat. (London: The British Council in association with Thames & Hudson, 1987).

Coda

1. Ernst Mayr, Introduction to Charles Darwin, *On the Origin of Species* (facsimile of 1st ed.; Cambridge, Mass: Harvard University Press, 1964), pp. xix–xx.

2. Roy Blount, Jr., *About Three Bricks Shy of a Load: A Highly Irregular Low-Down on the Year the Pittsburgh Steelers Were Super but Lost the Bowl* (Boston: Little, Brown & Co., 1974), p. 5.

3. Lorenz Eitner, "Subjects from Common Life in the Real Language of Men: Popular Art and Modern Tradition in Nineteenth-Century French Painting," in Kirk Varnedoe and Adam Gopnik, eds., *Modern Art and Popular Culture: Readings in High and Low* (New York: The Museum of Modern Art and Harry N. Abrams, 1990).

4. See, for instance, William Labov, ed., *Locating Language in Time and Space* (New York: Academic Press, 1980).

5. See Aubrey Canon, "The Historical Dimension in Mortuary Expressions of Status and Sentiment," *Current Anthropology*, August–October 1989, pp. 437–57.

6. Cited in Robert Storr, "No Joy in Mudville," in Varnedoe and Gopnik, eds., *Modern Art and Popular Culture*.

7. Fernand Léger, "Note sur l'élément mécanique" [1923], in Léger, *Fonctions de la peinture* (Paris, Éditions Gonthier, 1965), p. 52

8. Storr, "No Joy in Mudville."

9. Charles Baudelaire, "The Universal Salon of 1855: Fine Arts, 1. Critical Method," in *Baudelaire: Selected Writings on Art and Artists*, trans. P.E. Charvet (Cambridge: Cambridge University Press, 1972), pp. 117–18; cited in Storr, "No Joy in Mudville," and in Roger Shattuck, *The Innocent Eye: On Modern Literature and the Arts* (New York: Farrar Straus Giroux, 1984), p. 354.

10. Clive James, *The Metropolitan Critic* (London: Faber & Faber, 1974), p. 148.

11. Dik Browne, interview with Richard Marschall, "Browne the Magnificent: On Comics, Commentary and Contentment," *Nemo*, 1 (June 1983), pp. 35–36.

12. Elizabeth Murray, conversation with the authors, January 1990.

13. Romans 10:15.

The bibliography is devoted to the general topics treated in the body of this book—graffiti, caricature, comics, and advertising—as well as to theoretical writings on mass culture. For references on individual artists, see the Notes to the Text.

Mass Culture

This section includes major theoretical writings on twentieth-century mass culture as well as a number of articles representing lesser-known critical viewpoints. It does not include those critiques of mass culture offered in studies focusing primarily on other issues. Critical anthologies are listed separately, after works having a single author.

Theories of Mass Culture

Adorno, Theodor W. "Culture Industry Reconsidered." *New German Critique,* 6 (Fall 1975), pp. 12–19.

————. "Veblen's Attack on Culture." In Adorno, *Prisms.* Translated by Samuel and Shierry Weber. Cambridge, Mass.: MIT Press, 1981.

Aronowitz, Stanley. *The Crisis in Historical Materialism: Class, Politics, and Culture in Marxist Theory.* New York: Praeger, 1981.

Bagdikian, Ben H. *The Media Monopoly.* Boston: Beacon Press, 1987.

Banham, Reyner. *Design by Choice.* Edited by Penny Sparke. New York: Rizzoli, 1981. See especially "The Atavism of the Long-Distance Mini-Cyclist," in which Banham defends modern mass culture against Richard Hoggart and Raymond Williams, who, he asserts, misrepresent British working-class life before World War II.

Barthes, Roland. *Système de la mode.* Paris: Éditions Seuil, 1967. Examines the intricacies inherent in the transformation of objects into language which purports to describe them, providing a platform to discuss structuralism, semiology, sociology, the politics and structures of linguistics, and artifacts of modern bourgeois life.

————. *Mythologies.* Translated by Annette Lavers. English ed., New York: Hill & Wang, 1972. Collection of essays on the ideological critique of the language of mass culture, amalgamating Marxism with Ferdinand de Saussure's systemization of events.

Baudrillard, Jean. *America.* Translated by Chris Turner. London: Verso, 1989.

————. *Selected Writings.* Edited by Mark Poster. Stanford, Calif.: Stanford University Press, 1988.

Benjamin, Walter. "The Work of Art in the Age of Mechanical Reproduction." In Benjamin, *Illuminations: Essays and Reflections.* Edited by Hannah Arendt, translated by Harry Zohn. New York: Schocken Books, 1968. The art object, stripped of its "aura," or ritual cult status, is considered as a tool of political control.

Berger, John. "The Cultural Snob: There Is No 'Highbrow' Art." *The Nation,* November 5, 1955, pp. 380–82. Distinctions between "high" and "low" art as nonexistent, while seeming differences nonetheless fulfill the functions of distracting and flattering the viewer, rather than eradicating social inequities.

Boorstin, Daniel J. *The Image: A Guide to Pseudo-events in American Life.* New York: Atheneum, 1962. Surveys the downward-tending spiral of American culture and "how we have used our wealth, literacy, technology and our progress to create the thicket of unreality which stands between us and the facts of life." Depersonalized mass-produced art vulgarizes high art, eviscerates its original intentions, and leads to widespread cultural deterioration.

Bourdieu, Pierre. *Distinction: A Social Critique of the Judgment of Taste.* Translated by Richard Nice. Cambridge, Mass.: Harvard University Press, 1984. Portrays modern France according to the taste of socio-economic groups determined by educational, social, and cultural capital.

Brantlinger, Patrick. *Bread and Circuses: Theories of Mass Culture as Social Decay.* Ithaca and London: Cornell University Press, 1983. Analyzes the development of the idea of mass culture as a symptom or cause of social decay, concentrating on writers working before 1940.

Brecht, Bertolt. *Brecht on Theatre.* Translated by John Willet. New York: Hill & Wang, 1957. Plots an integration of mass media and radical Marxist aesthetics, to fan the flames of social discontent and arouse the audience to a critical participation in reorganizing society.

Brogan, D. W. "The Problem of High Culture and Mass Culture." *Diogenes,* 5 (Winter 1954), pp. 1–13. Mass culture seen as being without value, yet in no way threatening high art.

Collins, Jim. *Uncommon Cultures: Popular Culture and Post-Modernism.* New York: Routledge & Kegan Paul, 1989.

Crow, Thomas. "Modernism and Mass Culture in the Visual Arts." In Benjamin H. D. Buchloh, Serge Guilbaut, and David Solkin, eds., *Modernism and Modernity: The Vancouver Conference Papers.* The Nova Scotia Series, 14. Halifax: Press of the Nova

BIBLIOGRAPHY

Compiled by Matthew Armstrong and Fereshteh Daftari

Scotia College of Art and Design, 1983. Revised text printed in Francis Fascina, ed., *Pollock and After: The Critical Debate.* New York: Harper & Row, 1985.

Edwards, Thomas R. "High Minds, Low Thoughts: Popular Culture." *Raritan,* 1 (Summer 1981), pp. 88–105.

Eliot, T. S. *Notes Towards the Definition of Culture.* London: Faber, 1948. Maintains that true culture cannot be shared outside its own class, is threatened from below, and can be salvaged only through a return to a society governed by an aristocracy and the church.

Enzensberger, Hans Magnus. *The Consciousness Industry: On Literature, Politics and the Media.* New York: Seabury Press, 1974.

Fishwick, Marshall. "Confessions of an Ex-Elitist." In Ray B. Browne, ed., *Popular Culture and the Expanding Consciousness.* New York and London: John Wiley & Sons, 1973. Popular culture as the barometer of democracy; to disregard it is to disregard the real interests of the people.

Fiske, John. *Understanding Popular Culture.* Winchester, Mass.: Unwin Hyman, 1989. Sees both apologists and critics of popular culture as not understanding how mass culture's ideological intentions can be ignored or altogether subverted by society's subcommunities.

Gans, Herbert J. *Popular Culture and High Culture:*

An Analysis and Evaluation of Taste. New York: Basic Books, 1974. An argument for cultural pluralism; insists that hierarchies of cultures are ultimately meaningless and indefensible, and that all strata of expression are valid, vital, and meaningful.

Gowans, Alan. *The Unchanging Arts: New Forms for the Traditional Functions of Art in Society.* Philadelphia and New York: J. B. Lippincott, 1971. Newer, less traditional forms of image-making, such as film, cartoons, advertising, said to replace the old-fashioned mediums of painting and sculpture.

Gramsci, Antonio. *Selections from Cultural Writings.* Edited by David Forgacs and Geoffrey Nowell-Smith, translated by William Boelhower. Cambridge, Mass.: Harvard University Press, 1985.

Greenberg, Clement. "Avant-Garde and Kitsch." *Partisan Review,* 6 (Fall 1939), pp. 34–49. Reprinted in Greenberg, *Art and Culture: Critical Essays,* Boston: Beacon Press, 1961. For recent considerations of this essay, see Robert C. Morgan, "Formalism as a Transgressive Device," *Arts Magazine,* 64 (December 1989), pp. 65–69, and in the same issue, comments by Peter Halley, Lisa Phillips, and Stephen Westfall (pp. 58–64), and Saul Ostrow's interview with Greenberg, "Avant-Garde and Kitsch, Fifty Years Later" (pp. 56–57). See also T. J. Clark's "Clement Greenberg's Theory of Art," Michael Fried's "How Modernism Works: A Response to T. J. Clark," and Clark's "Arguments about Modernism: A Reply to Michael Fried," all in Francis Frascina, ed., *Pollock and After: The Critical Debate,* New York: Harper & Row, 1985; and Robert Storr, "No Joy in Mudville," in Kirk Varnedoe and Adam Gopnik, eds., *Modern Art and Popular Culture: Readings in High and Low,* New York: The Museum of Modern Art and Harry N. Abrams, 1990.

Halloran, James D. "Mass Media and Mass Culture." In *Control or Consent?* London: Sheed & Ward, 1963. An integrated overview of the arguments against mass culture in Britain and in the United States.

Hoggart, Richard. *The Uses of Literacy: Aspects of Working Class Life with Special References to Publications and Entertainments.* London: Chatto & Windus, 1957. Critique of working-class culture before and after World War II; like George Orwell, seeks to preserve the texture of "authentic" working-class life from Americanization and prefabricated "disposable culture."

————. "Mass Communications in Britain." In Boris Ford, ed., *The Modern Age.* Harmondsworth, Middlesex, England: Penguin, 1973. Both high culture and folk culture are eroded by the standardization and stereotyping of mass culture.

Horkheimer, Max, and Theodor W. Adorno. "The Culture Industry: Enlightenment as Mass Deception." In Horkheimer and Adorno, *The Dialectic of Enlightenment.* Translated by John Cumming. New York: Continuum Press, 1972. Without its "true" role as a critique, culture has become a commodity and an instrument of oppression.

Kaplan, Abraham. "The Aesthetics of Popular Culture." In James B. Hall and Barry Ulanov, eds., *Modern Culture and the Arts.* New York: McGraw-Hill, 1967. The problem with popular culture is not that it is base but that it has yet to realize its great potential.

Kaplan, E. Ann. *Postmodernism and Its Discontents.* London: Verso, 1988.

Kellner, Douglas. "Critical Theory and Culture Industries." *Telos,* 62 (Winter 1984–85), pp. 196–206.

Kristol, Irving. "High, Low, and Modern." *Encounter,* 83 (August 1960), pp. 33–41. Modernism seen as having defied and replaced high culture, undermining standards of quality and decency in cultural production and, by pandering to public ignorance, threatening democracy. Proposes that democracy be governed by the "natural aristocracy" of the virtuous and wise.

Lazere, Donald, ed. *American Media and Mass Culture: Left Perspectives.* Berkeley: University of California Press, 1987. See especially Lazere, "Conservative Media Criticism: Heads I Win, Tails You Lose."

Leavis, F. R. *Mass Civilization and Minority Culture.* Cambridge, Mass.: Minority Press, 1930. Defends the values of an elitist culture against the vulgarities of the popular arts, proposing an educational system that would create audiences skeptical of mass culture.

Levine, Lawrence W. *Highbrow/Lowbrow: The Emergence of Cultural Hierarchy in America.* Cambridge, Mass.: Harvard University Press, 1988. Argues that in nineteenth-century America, "highbrow" culture intermixed freely with "lowbrow." This "kaleidoscopic, democratic" pluralism was later narrowed by an elite anxious to protect what it saw as high art, and "tame" the public into a passive, respectful mass.

Lipsitz, George. *Time Passages: Collective Memory and American Popular Culture.* Minneapolis: University of Minnesota, 1990.

MacDonald, Dwight. "A Theory of Mass Culture." *Diogenes,* 3 (Summer 1953), pp. 1–17. Argues that "Mass culture is imposed from above. It is fabricated by technicians hired by businessmen; its audiences are passive consumers, their participation limited to the choice between buying and not buying. The lords of kitsch, in short, exploit the cultural needs of the masses in order to make a profit and/or maintain their class rule."

———. "Masscult and Midcult." In MacDonald, *Against the American Grain: Essays on the Effects of Mass Culture.* New York: Vintage, 1962. Argues that mass culture lacks standards and fosters a society which is inchoate and uncreative. Proposes a separation of high art for the *cognoscenti* and a low art for the masses.

McLuhan, Marshall. *The Mechanical Bride: Folk Lore of Industrial Man.* (1951). 2nd ed., New York: Vanguard Press, 1967.

———. *The Gutenberg Galaxy: The Making of Typographic Man.* Toronto: Toronto University Press, 1962. Investigating the shift in communications from content to manner of presentation, argues that information flows to modern man not in a rational, linear fashion but as a "mosaic" of random patterns which are codified and organized only by the individual. Sees mass media as helping to create an egalitarian, utopian society.

Malraux, André. "Art, Popular Art and the Illusion of the Folk." *Partisan Review,* 18 (September–October 1951), pp. 487–95.

Marcuse, Herbert. *One Dimensional Man.* Boston: Beacon Press, 1964. Fuses the ideas of Marx and Freud in a complex critique of modern society, arguing that artistic creativity is the catalyst for developing a sociopolitical alternative to the dominant capitalist state.

———. *An Essay on Liberation.* Boston: Beacon Press, 1968.

———. *Eros and Civilization.* Boston: Beacon Press, 1974. Sees the power of art arising from its primal impulse to express forbidden images of freedom.

Mills, C. Wright. *The Power Elite.* New York: Oxford University Press, 1956. Condemns the mass media for fostering "psychological illiteracy" among a populace whose interests and beliefs are now manufactured for them.

———. "The Cultural Apparatus." In Wright, *Power, Politics and People: The Collected Essays of C. Wright Mills.* Edited by Irving Horowitz. New York: Oxford University Press, 1963.

Mintz, Lawrence E. "Recent Trends in the Study of Popular Culture Since 1971." *American Studies International,* 1983, pp. 88–105.

Nye, Russell B. "Notes for an Introduction of Popular Culture." *The Journal of Popular Culture,* 5 (Spring 1971), pp. 1031–38. Catalogues the reasons why popular culture is studied and accepted; insists that once artificial boundaries based on snobbery and cultism are erased, greater understanding of our culture will result.

Ortega y Gasset, José. *The Revolt of the Masses.* London: Allen & Unwin,1932. Argues that genuine culture cannot exist on a mass basis and must be protected by, and for, an aristocracy of intellectuals.

Reisman, David, Nathan Glazer, and Reuel Denney. *The Lonely Crowd: A Study of the Changing American Culture.* New Haven, Conn.: Yale University Press, 1950. Modern man's desire to "fit in" to a society whose values are increasingly superficial and materialistic.

Rollin, Roger B. "Against Evaluation: The Role of the Critic of Popular Culture." *The Journal of Popular Culture,* 9 (Fall 1975), pp. 355–65.

Rosenberg, Harold. "Pop Culture and Kitsch Criticism." *Dissent,* 5 (Winter 1958), pp. 14–19. Studying mass culture is itself seen as a form of kitsch.

Ross, Andrew. *No Respect: Intellectuals and Popular Culture.* New York and London: Routledge, 1989. American intellectuals overlook the political tensions fueling popular culture's production, failing to see its origins in "the desires and fantasies that do not always 'obey' politically conscious ideas about correctness."

Rosten, Leo. "The Intellectual and the Mass Media." In Norman Jacobs, ed., *Culture for the Millions?* Princeton, N.J.: D. van Nostrand, 1959. Argues that most of modern mass culture's intellectual adversaries know very little about what they criticize, and that the technological transformation and dissemination of cultural information bring as much good as harm.

Schiller, Herbert I. *Culture, Inc.: The Corporate Takeover of Public Expression.* New York and Oxford: Oxford University Press, 1989. Analysis of the media, information agencies, multinational corporations, covert political and governmental agencies, and the resultant strain such bodies impose on civil liberties and creative expression.

Singleton, Gregory H. "Popular Culture or the Culture of the Populace." *The Journal of Popular Culture,* 11 (Summer 1977), pp. 254–66. An introduction to the problems inherent in the study of popular culture.

Sobel, Robert. *The Manipulators: America in the Media Age.* New York: Doubleday, 1976. Argues that the mass media have smashed the party system and replaced it with a "plebiscitary democracy, run more by polls than by election."

Sontag, Susan. "One Culture and the New Sensibility." In Sontag, *"Against Interpretation" and Other Essays.* New York: Farrar Straus Giroux, 1966. Argues that the gulf between "high" and "low" art is illusory. The new cross-cultural media evidence "not a conflict of cultures [but] the creation of a new kind of sensibility [which is] defiantly pluralistic" and dedicated both to "excruciating seriousness and to fun, wit and nostalgia."

Swingewood, Alan. *The Myth of Mass Culture.* Atlantic Heights, N.J.: Humanities Press, 1977. Considers the very idea of mass culture—whether from the right or from the left—a myth which "demands a passive adaptation to existing society and a rejection of all forms of activity to achieve social change."

Toffler, Alvin. "Excellence for What?" In Toffler, *The Culture Consumers.* New York: St. Martin's Press, 1964. While the rise of mass culture has ushered in a good deal of trash, the availability of classical music, high art, Shakespearean drama, and world literature has also grown.

Warshow, Robert. *The Immediate Experience: Movies, Comics, Theatre & Other Aspects of Popular Culture.* New York: Doubleday, 1962. A collection of Warshow's liberal postwar essays, on diverse aspects of American popular culture, that originally appeared in *Commentary* and *Partisan Review.*

Williams, Raymond. "Conclusion." In Williams, *Culture and Society, 1750–1950.* New York: Columbia University Press, 1958. Assesses mass culture as that which "depends, essentially, on a minority in some way exploiting a majority" and argues for the creation of a modern common culture to be shared by all.

———. *Communications.* New York: Barnes & Noble, 1967. Mass culture as a threat to both high culture and folk culture since its power is to "reduce us to an endlessly mixed, undiscriminating, fundamentally bored reaction."

Williamson, Judith. *Consuming Passions: The Dynamics of Popular Culture.* London: Boyars, 1986. Mass culture serves to perpetuate capitalism's consumption ethic.

Critical Anthologies

Arato, Andrew W., and Eike Gebhardt, eds. *The Essential Frankfurt School Reader.* New York: Continuum Press, 1982.

Bennett, Tony, Colin Mercer, and Janet Woollacott, eds. *Popular Culture and Social Relations.* Philadelphia: Open University Press, 1986. Essays on popular culture and its political ideology, social relations, and the historiography of its critical literature.

Bigsby, C. W. E., ed. *Superculture: American Popular Culture and Europe.* Bowling Green, Ohio: Bowling Green University Popular Press, 1975. See especially Bigsby, "Europe, America and the Cultural Debate."

———, ed. *Approaches to Popular Culture.* London: Edward Arnold, 1976. Traces the history of the criticism of mass culture.

Browne, Ray B. "Popular Culture: Notes Towards a Definition." In Browne, ed., *Popular Culture and the Expanding Consciousness.* New York and London: John Wiley & Sons, 1973. A survey of postwar and contemporary attitudes toward popular culture, attempting to clarify distinctions between elite, popular, mass, and folk cultures. See especially Russell Kirk, "Anti-Culture at Public Expense," where the idea of studying popular culture is viewed as a step toward the vulgarization of society. Includes reprint of Sontag, "One Culture and the New Sensibility."

Buhle, Paul, ed. *Popular Culture in America.* Minneapolis: University of Minnesota, 1987. Collection of American writings from a leftist or a cultural pluralist point of view. Includes Franklin Rosemont, "Surrealism in the Comics," and Robert Crumb and Bill Griffith, "As the Artist Sees It: Interviews with Comic Artists."

Curran, James, Michael Gurevitch, and Janet Woollacott, eds. *Mass Communications and Society.* London: Edward Arnold, Ltd., 1977. See especially Stuart Hall, "Culture, Media, and the 'Ideological Effect,'" a useful survey of the history of Marxist literature on culture and mass culture since the nineteenth century.

Dorfles, Gillo, ed. *Kitsch: The World of Bad Taste.* 2nd ed. New York: Universe Books, 1970. Essays evaluating vulgar and pseudo-artistic elements found "in politics, religion, advertising, film, architecture and design, 'porno-kitsch,' and the modern trappings that surround birth, family life and death." Contributors include John McHale, Clement Greenberg, Hermann Broch.

Ferguson, Russell, William Olander, Marcia Tucker, and Karen Fiss, eds. *Discourses: Conversations in Postmodern Art and Culture.* Images by John Baldessari. New York: The New Museum of Contemporary Art; Cambridge, Mass.: MIT Press, 1990.

Foster, Hal, ed. *The Anti-Aesthetic: Essays on Post-*

modern Culture. Port Townsend, Wash.: Bay Press, 1983. Includes contributions by Jean Baudrillard, Frederic Jameson, Rosiland Krauss, Edward Said, and Craig Owens, among others.

Fox, Richard Wightman, and T. J. Jackson Lears, eds. The Culture of Consumption: Critical Essays in American History 1880–1980. New York: Pantheon Books, 1983.

Gardner, Carl, ed. Media, Politics and Culture: A Socialist View. London: Macmillan, 1979.

Geist, Christopher D., Ray B. Browne, Michael T. Marsden, and Carole Palmer. Directory of Popular Culture Collections. Phoenix: Oryx Press, 1989. A directory of American and Canadian libraries, picture collections, museums, archives, colleges, associations, book centers and societies that specialize in popular culture. Indexed and annotated.

Gurevitch, Michael, Tony Bennett, James Curran, and Janet Woollacott, eds. Culture, Society, and the Media. New York: Methuen, 1982.

Hall, Stuart, and Paddy Whannel, eds. The Popular Arts. New York: Random House, 1964. See especially Hall, "Mass Society: Critics and Defenders," a compendium of arguments.

Inge, M. Thomas, ed. Handbook of American Popular Culture. 3 vols. Westport, Conn: Greenwood Press, 1981. Historical summaries and bibliographies of popular-culture topics ranging from boating to stamp collecting to magic tricks.

Jacobs, Norman, ed. Culture for the Millions? Princeton, N.J.: D. van Nostrand & Co, 1959. See especially Hannah Arendt, "Society and Culture," on mass culture as inculcating conformity and acceptance: "... as soon as the immortal works of the past become the object of 'refinement' ... they lose their most important and elemental quality," rendering the very word "culture" suspect; mass society wants not culture but entertainment, and transforms cultural objects into objects for mass consumption. See also Edward Shils, " Mass Society and Its Culture," which interprets burgeoning mass culture as promoting greater individuality and freedom than did elitist high art;"A General Theory of Mass Culture," with comments by Arthur Schlesinger, Jr., Patrick Hazard, Sidney Hook, and Bernard Rosenberg; and Ernest van den Haag, "A Dissent from Consensual Society," on mass culture as the degradation of high art to its lowest common denominator.

Kroes, Rob, ed. High Brow Meets Low Brow: American Culture as an Intellectual Concern. Amsterdam: Free University Press, 1988. Contributors include David E. Nye, Gordon Hutner, Marian Janssen, Marc Chénetier, and others.

Lazere, Donald, ed. American Media and Mass Culture: Left Perspectives. Berkeley and Los Angeles: University of California Press, 1987. A vast collection of essays on the history of mass culture, encompassing the development of media, literacy, political ideology, economics, marketing, manipulation, and systems of government. Contributors include Donald Lazere, Ariel Dorfman, Douglas Kellner, Todd Gitlin, Kate Ellis, Stanley Aronowitz. Each section contains a lengthy bibliography.

Modleski, Tania, ed. Studies in Entertainment: Critical Approaches to Mass Culture. Bloomington: Indiana University Press, 1986.

Nelson, Cary, and Lawrence Goldberg, eds. Marxism and the Interpretation of Culture. Urbana and Chicago: University of Illinois Press, 1988.

Oliver, Michael, ed. Social Purpose for Canada. Toronto: University of Toronto Press, 1961. See especially Neil Compton, "The Mass Media," which views the media as the "characteristic expressions of modern industrialism and ... the capitalistic system [which subordinates] all motives for expression to the pursuit of profit"; mass culture held to destroy both high and folk culture, and increase the difficulties of making art.

Partisan Review, 19, nos. 2–5 (May–June 1952). See "Our Country and Our Culture," a symposium on American culture; participants include Irving Howe, Norman Mailer, Arthur Schlesinger, Jr., Louis Kronenberger, David Reisman, Philip Rahv, Delmore Schwartz, and others.

Rosenberg, Bernard, and David White, eds. Mass Culture: The Popular Arts in America. Glencoe, Ill.: Free Press, 1957. An early anthology of important writings on the subject of mass culture. See especially Leslie Fiedler, "The Middle Against Both Ends," an early defense of popular culture and aesthetic pluralism. Other contributors include Robert Warshow, José Ortega y Gasset, and Dwight MacDonald.

Taylor, Ronald, ed. and trans. Aesthetics and Politics. London: New Left Books, 1977. Collection of writings by European Marxists of the 1930s, including Theodor W. Adorno, Walter Benjamin, Ernst Bloch, Bertolt Brecht, Georg Lukacs, and others.

Waites, Bernard, Tony Bennett, and Graham Martin, eds. Popular Culture: Past and Present. London: Croom Helm & Open University, 1982. See especially Dick Hebridge, "Towards a Cartography of Taste, 1936–1962," which assesses the various arguments over the "Americanization" of British cultural life following World War II.

Graffiti

This section focuses on the historical development and scientific study of graffiti. For references on modern graffiti as a form of art, see the Notes to the Text.

Pre-Modern and Non-Western Graffiti

Avellino, F[rancesco] M., Cav. Osservazioni sopra alcune iscrizioni e disegni graffiti sulle mura di Pompei. Naples: Stamperia Reale, 1841. Among the first Italian sources recognizing importance of Pompeian graffiti. At various times, the author was director of the Real Museo Borbonico, general superintendent of the excavations, professor at the Royal University, and editor of the Bullettino archeologico Napoletano (1843–48), where inscriptions and graffiti were occasionally reported.

Bechi, Guglielmo. "Relazione degli scavi di Pompei." Real Museo Borbonico, 1 (1824), 2 (1825), 6 (1830). Reports of archeological excavations, noting some graffiti.

Le Blant, Edmond. L'Epigraphie chrétienne en Gaule et dans l'Afrique romaine. Paris: Ernest Leroux, 1890. Contains a section on religious graffiti and includes an extensive bibliography of Christian epigraphy.

Blindheim, Martin. Graffiti in Norwegian Stave Churches c.1150–c.1350. Oslo, Bergen, and Stavanger: Universitetsforlaget, 1985.

Bresciani, Edda. Graffiti démotiques du dodecaschoene, Qertassi, Kalacha, Dendour, Dakka, Maharaqqa. Cairo: Centre de Documentations et d'Études sur l'Ancienne Egypte, 1969.

Briganti, Giuliano, Ludovica Trezzani, and Laura Laureati. The Bamboccianti: The Painters of Everyday Life in Seventeenth-Century Rome. Translated by Robert Erich Wolf. Rome: Ugo Bozzi Editore, 1983. Includes some works by artists who incorporated graffiti.

Bruzza, L. "Sopra alcuni graffiti di vasi arcaici ritrovati in Roma." Bulletino della Commissione Archeologica Comunale di Roma, 6 (1878), pp. 177–98. The relation of signs found on archaic vases to figures from the old Latin alphabet.

Bucherie, Luoc. "Mise en scène des pouvoirs dans les graffiti anciens (XVe–XVIIIe siècles)." Gazette des beaux-arts, 6th series, 103 (January 1984), pp. 1–10.

The Cambridge Ancient History, vol. 3, part 3: The Expansion of the Greek World, Eighth to Sixth Centuries B.C. Edited by John Boardman and N.G.L. Hammond. 2nd ed., Cambridge, London, and New York: Cambridge University Press, 1982. The section "The Greeks in Egypt," by T. F. R. G. Braun, includes an illustration and translation of a graffito from 591 B.C. scratched by a Greek mercenary on the leg of a colossal statue at Abu Simbel, p. 50.

Cerny, Jaroslav. Graffiti hiéroglyphiques et hiératiques de la nécropole thébaine. Cairo: Imprimerie de l'Institut Français d'Archéologie Orientale, 1956.

Cerny, Jaroslav, Charles Desroches Noblecourt, and M. Kurz. Graffiti de la montagne thébaine. 2 vols. Cairo: Centre de Documentations et d'Études sur l'Ancienne Egypte, 1969, 1970. Graffiti used to ascertain sociological information.

Champfleury [Jules-François-Félix Husson]. Histoire de la caricature antique. [1865]. 2nd ed., Paris: Éditions Dentu, 1867. Pompeian graffiti recognized as comparable to an artist's première pensée.

Champollion, Jacques-Joseph. Monuments de l'Egypte et de la Nubie: Notices descriptives. 4 vols. Paris: Firmin-Didot, 1835–45.

———. Monuments de l'Egypte et de la Nubie: Notices descriptives. 2 vols. Paris: Firmin-Didot, 1844–89.

Correra, Luigi. "Graffiti di Roma." Bullettino della Commissione Archeologica Comunale di Roma, 4th series, 21 (1893), 22 (1894), 23 (1895). Graffiti's value to studies in archeology, paleography, and philology.

Della Corte, Matteo. Iwentus: Un nuovo aspetto della vita pubblica di Pompei finora inesplorato, studiato e ricostruito con la scorta dei relativi documenti epigrafici, topografici, demografici, artistici e religiosi.... Arpino: Giovanni Fraioli, 1924.

———. Amori e amanti di Pompei antica: Antologia erotica Pompeiana. Cava dei Tirreni: E. di Mauro, 1960. Hampered by the author's refusal to discuss Pompeii's "obscene" graffiti.

Dacos, Nicole. "Visitatori di Villa Adriana." Palatino, 9 (January–March 1965), pp. 9–11.

———. "Graffiti de la Domus Aurea." Bulletin de l'Institut Historique Belge de Rome, 1967, pp. 145–76.

Dayot, Armand Pierre Marie. Histoire contemporaine par l'image d'après les documents du temps, 1789–1872. Paris: Ernest Flammarion, n.d. Dayot's illustrated books include some graffiti.

———. L'Invasion, le siège 1870, la Commune 1871. Paris: Ernest Flammarion, n.d.

———. Journées révolutionnaires, 1830–1848. D'Après des peintures, sculptures, dessins, lithographies, médailles, autographes, objets du temps. Paris: Ernest Flammarion, n.d.

———. Les peintres militaires Charlet et Raffet. Paris: Librairies-imprimeries réunies, n.d.

Field, Henry. "Camel Brands and Graffiti from Iraq, Syria, Jordan, Iran and Arabia." Supplement to the Journal of the American Oriental Society, no. 15 (October–December 1952).

Garrucci, Raphael. Graffiti de Pompéi. 2nd ed., revised and enlarged, Paris: Benjamin Duprat, 1856. A key paleographic study which stresses graffiti's usefulness as an archeological and philological tool, noting the variety of languages and alphabets used in Pompeii. Extensively illustrated.

Gau, F. C. Antiquités de la Nubie, ou monuments inédits des bords du Nil situés entre la première et la seconde cataracte, dessinés et mesurés, 1819. Stuttgart: J. G. Cotta; Paris: Firmin Didot, 1822. Classification of graffiti according to location, use, and the ability to elucidate aspects of history, religion, and language.

Gell, William. Pompeiana: The Topography, Edifices and Ornaments of Pompei—The Result of Excavations Since 1819. 2 vols. London: Jennings & Chaplin, 1832. Summary study referring to Pompeian graffiti and inscriptions, citing several examples of Latin graffiti.

Griaule, Marcel. Silhouettes et graffiti abyssins. Introduction by Marcel Mauss. Paris: Larose, 1933.

Griffith, F[rancis] Ll[ewellyn]. Temples immergés de la Nubie: Catalogue of the Demotic Graffiti of the Dodecaschoenus. 2 vols. Oxford: University Press, 1935, 1937. A crucial study of proscynemata (formulas of prayer), official graffiti which were the work of temple employees whose inscriptions were paid for by pious visitors.

Helck, Wolfgang. "Die Bedeutung der ägyptischen Besucher-schriften." Zeitschrift der deutschen Morgenländischen Gesellschaft, 102 (1952), pp. 39–46. Explores the shifts of the visitors' attitudes toward monuments where graffiti have been found.

"Jeux et divertissements anciens." Magasin pittoresque, 3 (1835), pp. 329–36.

Jorn, Asger, ed. Signes gravés sur les églises de l'Eure et du Calvados. Copenhagen: Édition Borger, 1964.

Kampen, Michael. "The Graffiti of Tikal, Guatemala." Estudios de cultura maya, 11 (1978), pp. 155–80.

Kren, Thomas. "Chi non vuol Baccho: Roeland van Laer's Burlesque Painting About Dutch Artists in Rome." Simiolus, 11, no. 2 (1980), pp. 63–80. Includes substantial discussion of graffiti.

Krenkel, Werner. Pompejanische Inschriften. Leipzig: Koehler & Amelang, 1961.

Lacour-Gayet, Georges. "Graffiti figurés du temple d'Antonin et Faustine, au Forum romain." École française de Rome: Mélanges d'archéologie et d'histoire, 1 (1881), pp. 226–48.

Lanciani, Rodolfo. "Miscellanea epigrafica." Bullettino della Commissione Archeologica Comunale di Roma, 5 (1877), pp. 161–83.

Lang, Mabel L. Graffiti in the Athenian Agora. Princeton, N.J.: American School of Classical Studies at Athens, 1974.

———. Graffiti and Dipinti. Princeton, N.J.: American School of Classical Studies at Athens, 1976.

Lindsay, Jack. The Writing on the Wall: An Account of Pompeii in Its Last Days. London: Frederick Muller, 1960. Life in Pompeii re-created through information obtained from graffiti, notices, and inscriptions on walls.

Martigny, Joseph Alexandre (L'Abbé). Dictionnaire des antiquités chrétiennes. 3rd ed., enlarged, Paris: Hachette, 1889. On Early Christian graffiti.

Massmann, Joannes Ferdinandus. Libellus aurarius sive tabulae ceratae et antiquissimae et unicae romanae in Fodina Auraria. Leipzig: T. O. Weigel, 1840. A catalogue of inscriptions including Pompeian graffiti.

de Murr, Christophorus Theophilus. Specimina antiquissima scripturae Graecae tenuioris sev cursivae ante Imperatoris Titi Vespasiani tempora ex inscriptionibus extemporalibus classiariorum pompeianorum. Nuremberg: Bibliopolio Bavero-Manniano, 1792. One of the earliest publications on Pompeian inscriptions.

Nougier, Louis-René, and Romain Robert. The Cave of Rouffignac. Translated by David Scott. London: George Newnes, 1958. Eighteenth- and nineteenth-century graffiti found in the cave of Rouffignac.

Paranavitana, S. Sigiri Graffiti: Being Sinhalese Verses of the Eighth, Ninth and Tenth Centuries. London, New York, Bombay, and Madras: Oxford University Press, 1956. Ancient Sinhalese graffiti as a key to the study of Sinhalese philology and paleography.

Pritchard, Violet. English Mediaeval Graffiti. Cambridge: Cambridge University Press, 1967. A tightly focused study of inscriptions and drawings in churches near Cambridge, from the twelfth to the sixteenth century.

Restif de La Bretonne, Nicolas-Edme. Mes inscriptions: Journal intime de Restif de La Bretonne, 1780–1787. Paris: Éditions Plon, 1889. When the author, "the founding father of the Naturalist School," learned that his graffiti at the Île Saint-Louis were being erased, he began recording them in a manuscript which lends insight into the "confessional and therapeutic" motivations of a graffitist.

Rosa, P. "Scavi del Palatino." Annali dell'Istituto di Corrispondenza Archeologica, 1865, pp. 346–67.

de Rossi, G[iovanni] B[attista]. Roma sotterranea cristiana. 3 vols. Rome: Cromo Litografia Cristiana, 1864–77. Graffiti as an echo of ancient history. Includes a thorough discussion of the various types of graffiti (names, statements, invocations, epitaphs) and exceptional images.

———. "Sui graffiti del Palatino." Bullettino di archeologia cristiana, 5 (1867), p. 75.

Sheon, Aaron. "The Discovery of Graffiti." Art Journal, 36 (Fall 1976), pp. 16–22. History of mid-nineteenth-century assessment of the artistic value of graffiti, children's art, caricature, primitive and folk art, and popular prints.

Sontag, Susan. "The Pleasure of the Image." Art in America, 75 (November 1987), pp. 122–31. Includes a discussion of graffiti in seventeenth-century Dutch paintings.

Tanzer, Helen H. The Common People of Pompeii: A Study of the Graffiti. Baltimore: Johns Hopkins University Press, 1939.

Töpffer, Rodolphe. Réflexions et menus propos d'un peintre Genevois, ou essai sur le beau dans les arts. 2 vols. Paris: J. J. Dubochet, Lechevalier, 1848. An early recognition of the artistic value of graffiti.

Trik, Helen, and Michael E. Kampen. The Graffiti of Tikal. William R. Coe, volume ed. Philadelphia: The University Museum, University of Pennsylvania, 1983.

Väänänen, Veikko, ed. Graffiti del Palatino. Helsinki: Akateeminen Kirjakauppa, 1966. Graffiti of the Palatine seen as a way of understanding antiquity. Includes extensive bibliography and illustrations.

Walker, Lester, "Maya Graffiti as Art." Southwestern Louisiana Journal, 3 (Fall 1959), pp. 193–200.

Walker, Raymond J. " 'Kilroy Was Here': A History of Scribbling in Ancient and Modern Times." Hobbies, 73 (July 1968), pp. 98/N–98/O.

Weege, Fritz. "Das goldene Haus des Nero." Jahrbuch des Kaiserlich deutschen archaologischen Instituts, 28 (1913), pp. 127–244.

Wordsworth, Christopher, Rev. Inscriptiones Pompeianae: or, Specimens and Facsimiles of Ancient Inscriptions Discovered on the Walls of Buildings at Pompeii. London: John Murray, 1837. One of the first extensive treatments of graffiti. Wordsworth, who visited Pompeii in 1832, writes about examples which elucidate the orthography and language. About salacious examples he comments only that they "show us with what moral depravity these graceful embellishments were allied."

Zangmeister, Karl, ed. Corpus inscriptionum latinarum, vol. 4: Inscriptiones parietariae Pompeianae, Herculanenses Stabianae. Berolini: G. Reimerum, 1871. A well-illustrated catalogue including Latin inscriptions and graffiti found in Pompeii.

Graffiti and the Social Sciences

Abel, Ernest, and Barbara E. Buckley. The Handwriting on the Wall: Toward a Sociology and Psychology of Graffiti. Westport, Conn., and London: Greenwood Press, 1977. Graffiti seen as expressing the character of a society. Employs a Freudian approach.

Adler, Alfred. "Über Kritzeleien." Internationale Zeitschrift für Individual Psychologie, 12 (October–December 1934), pp. 201–03. Adler, in examining his own scribblings, is led to study man's inclination toward symmetry.

Ahmed, S. M. S. "Graffiti of Canadian High School Students." Psychological Reports, 49 (October 1981), pp. 559–62. Classifies sex and cultural differences as reflected by inscriptions in washrooms with results strikingly different from earlier studies.

Albrecht, Gunter. "Zur Stellung historischer Forschungsmethoden und nicht-reaktiver Methoden im System der empirischen Sozialforschung." Kölner Zeitschrift fur Soziologie und Sozialpsychologie, 16, pp. 242–93. Mainly on methodology; argues for graffiti as a useful tool.

Alexander, Bob. "Male and Female Restroom Graffiti." Maledicta: The International Journal of Verbal Aggression, 2 (Summer–Winter 1978), pp. 42–59. Tests traditional hypotheses of sex differences.

Anderson, Stephen J., and William S. Verplanck. "When Walls Speak, What Do They Say." The Psychological Record, 33 (Summer 1983), pp. 341–59. Graffiti as a social barometer.

Arluke, Arnold, Lanny Kutakoff, and Jack Levin. "Are the Times Changing? An Analysis of Gender Differences in Sexual Graffiti." Sex Roles, 16 (January 1987), pp. 1–7. Examines the assumption that the gender gap has narrowed over time in the writing of graffiti.

Barick, Mac E. "The Growth of Graffiti." Folklore Forum, 7 (October 1974), pp. 273–75.

Bates, John A., and Michael Martin. "The Thematic Content of Graffiti as a Nonreactive Indicator of Male and Female Attitudes." The Journal of Sex Research, 16 (November 1980), pp. 300–15. Contradicts earlier studies, such as Kinsey's, in showing that women write more graffiti than do men and express more hostile, sexual, or issue-related content.

Baudrillard, Jean. "I graffiti di New York, ovvero l'insurrezione attraverso i segni." La Critica Sociologica, 29 (Spring 1974), pp. 148–50 (Part I); 31 (Autumn 1974), pp. 6–10 (Part II). Graffiti as modern urban alternatives to the languages and signs of an oppressive and racist society.

Bilodau, Denyse. "Du cru sur le mur." Études Littéraires, 19 (Fall 1986), pp. 67–79. The subversive thrust of graffiti found in Quebec.

Blake, C. Fred. "Graffiti and Racial Insults: The Archaeology of Ethnic Relations in Hawaii." In Richard A. Gould and Michael B. Schiffer, eds., Modern Material Culture: The Archaeology of Us. New York: Academic Press, 1981. Ethnological study of racial remarks.

Bourke, John G. Scatological Rites of All Nations. Washington, D.C.: W. H. Lowdermilk & Co., 1891.

Bratley, Carol. "Boston's Graffiti Board." The American City, 86 (April 1971), pp. 138, 140. Reports on a "graffiti board," set up by the city's Municipal Public Relations Department, on which people were allowed to write.

Brown, Waln K. "Graffiti, Identity and the Delinquent Gang." International Journal of Offender Therapy, 22 (1978), pp. 46–48. Graffiti as a means of transmitting messages, securing individual recognition, displaying personal associations, and delineating territorial boundaries.

Bruner, Edward M., and Jane Paige Kelso. "Gender Differences in Graffiti: A Semiotic Perspective." Women's Studies International Quarterly, 3 (1980), pp. 239–52. Restroom graffiti understood as communication for the same sex, with the distinctions between the writings of each gender reflecting its social position.

Buser, Mary M., and Fernanda Ferreira. "Models, Frequency, and Content of Graffiti." *Perceptual and Motor Skills,* 51 (October 1980), p. 582. Frequency and content of graffiti largely determined by the content and number of preexisting graffiti.

Calet, Henri. *Les murs de Fresnes.* Paris: Les Éditions des Quatre Vents, 1945. Records prison graffiti left by inmates involved in the anti-fascist resistance.

Castleman, Craig. *Getting Up: Subway Graffiti in New York.* Cambridge, Mass.: MIT Press, 1982. An in-depth study of the graffiti-writing phenomenon, by an anthropologist.

Collins, Thomas B., and Paul Batzle. "Method of Increasing Graffito Responses." *Perceptual and Motor Skills,* 31 (December 1970), pp. 733–34.

D'Angelo, Frank J. "Fools' Names and Fools' Faces Are Always Seen in Public Places: A Study of Graffiti." *The Journal of Popular Culture,* 10 (Summer 1976), pp. 102–09.

Davitt, Michael. *Leaves from a Prison Diary: or, Lectures to a Solitary Audience.* London: Chapman & Hall, 1885. Contains a section on prison graffiti.

Deiulio, Anthony M. "Desk Top Graffiti: Scratching Beneath the Surface." *Journal of Research and Development in Education,* 7 (Fall 1973), pp. 100–04. Graffiti on students' desks provide insights which can be useful in reforming curricula.

Doyle, Charles Clay. "Folk Epigraphy by Subtraction." *Midwestern Journal of Language and Folklore,* 7 (Spring 1981), pp. 49–50. On defacing written instructions or official messages.

Dundes, Alan. "Here I Sit: A Study of American Latrinalia." *Kroeber Anthropological Society Papers,* 34 (Spring 1966), pp. 91–105. Coins the term *latrinalia;* advances the ideas that graffiti writing derives from the impulse to smear feces or dirt on walls and that there are more male than female graffiti because men, envious of pregnancy, concentrate on anal creativity.

Ellis, Havelock. *The Criminal.* (1890). 3rd ed., revised and enlarged, London: Walter Scott; New York: Charles Scribner's Sons, 1903. A study of prison inscriptions viewed from the standpoint of "criminal anthropology."

Farr, Jo-Ann, and Carol Gordon. "A Partial Replication of Kinsey's Graffiti Study." *The Journal of Sex Research,* 11 (May 1975), pp. 158–62. Kinsey hypothesized that sexual graffiti reflected the extent and nature of the suppressed sexual desires of men and women. The present study shows an increase in the percentage of erotic homosexual graffiti made by both sexes.

Feiner, Joel S., and Stephan Marc Klein. "Graffiti Talks." *Social Policy,* 12 (Winter 1982), pp. 47–53. Graffiti interpreted as the display of mainstream adolescent development, its style deriving from comic books, signs, and from the need to write quickly, with large muscle movements.

Fenn, E. A. Humphrey. "The Writing on the Wall." *History Today,* 19 (June 1969), pp. 419–23. Investigates prison graffiti from the sixteenth century.

Ferenczi, Sandor. *Sex in Psychoanalysis.* New York: Basic Books, 1950. Discusses a case study whereby toilet inscriptions of an obscene nature resulted in neurotic repression in one of Ferenczi's patients.

Fraser, Bruce. "Meta-Graffiti." *Maledicta: The International Journal of Verbal Aggression,* 4 (Winter 1980), pp. 258–60. Study of creators of graffiti.

Gadpaille, W. J. "Graffiti: Its Psychodynamic Significance." *Sexual Behavior,* 2 (November 1971), pp. 45–51. A key study, discussing motivations.

Glazer, Nathan. "On Subway Graffiti in New York." *Public Interest,* Winter 1979, pp. 3–11. Graffiti writing viewed as criminal behavior.

Gonos, George, Virginia Mulkern, and Nicholas Poushinsky. "Anonymous Expression: A Structural View of Graffiti." *Journal of American Folklore,* 89 (January–March 1976), pp. 40–48. Contradicts the idea that graffiti directly reflect the collective conscience; maintains that graffiti express taboos, rather than socially accepted values.

"Graffiti Helps Mental Patients." *Science Digest,* 75 (April 1974), pp. 47–48. On Chicago psychiatrists who encourage patients' graffiti as a way of promoting communication.

Grider, Sylvia Ann. "*Con safos*: Mexican-Americans, Names and Graffiti." *Journal of American Folklore,* 88 (April–June 1975), pp. 132–42. Study of the untranslatable Chicano expression *con safos,* which, inscribed with one's name, acts as a safeguard. The author concludes that the conception of graffiti varies from culture to culture and that Mexican-Americans do not regard graffiti as defacement of public property.

Grotjahn, Martin. *Beyond Laughter.* New York, Toronto, London: McGraw-Hill Book Co., 1957. A psychoanalytic interpretation of the Kilroy phenomenon.

Horsley, Rev. J. W. *Jottings from Jail.* London: T. Fisher Unwin, 1887. Frequently referred to by social scientists; maintains that only inscriptions made by prisoners are worth considering.

Hougan, Jim. "Kilroy's New Message." *Harper's Magazine,* 245 (November 1972), pp. 20, 22, 24, 26. The politicization of graffiti in men's restrooms.

Jefferson, Roland S. "Black Graffiti: Image and Implications." *The Black Scholar,* 7 (January–February 1976), pp. 11–19. Graffiti understood as an alternative form of expression for problems of the black community, traditional avenues often being blocked by white America.

Jiménez, A. *Picardía mexicana.* (1960). 15th ed., Mexico City: Libro Mex, 1963.

Jorgenson, Dale O., and Charles Lange. "Graffiti Content as an Index of Political Interest." *Perceptual and Motor Skills,* 40 (April 1975), pp. 616–18.

Jorgenson, Dale O., Phillip Guadabascio, Claudia Higginson, David Sutton, and Janet Watkins. "Contents of Graffiti and Bumper Stickers as Measures of Political Behavior." *Perceptual and Motor Skills,* 45 (October 1977), p. 630.

Kinsey, Alfred Charles, Wendell Baxter Pomeroy, and Clyde E. Martin. *Sexual Behavior in the Human Female.* Philadelphia and London: W. B. Saunders Co., 1953. Includes comparative study of men's and women's toilet inscriptions.

Kohl, Herbert, and James Hinton. "Names, Graffiti and Culture." In Thomas Kochman, ed., *Rappin' and Stylin' Out.* Urbana, Chicago, and London: University of Illinois Press, 1972. Early recognition of importance of street graffiti to the sociological investigation of urban youth.

Klofas, John M., and Charles R. Cutshall. "The Social Archeology of a Juvenile Facility: Unobtrusive Methods in the Study of Institutional Cultures." *Qualitative Sociology,* 8 (Winter 1985), pp. 368–87. Proposes the study of graffiti as an unobtrusive method for understanding the process of socialization.

Korytnyk, Natalie, and David V. Perkins. "Effects of Alcohol Versus Expectancy for Alcohol on the Incidence of Graffiti Following an Experimental Task." *Journal of Abnormal Psychology,* 92 (August 1983), pp. 382–84.

Kris, Ernst. *Psychoanalytic Explorations in Art.* New York: International University Press, 1952. A reprint of articles first published in the 1930s and 1940s; includes brief comments on a blasphemous Roman graffito.

Landy, Eugene, and John M. Steele. "Graffiti as a Function of Building Utilization." *Perceptual and Motor Skills,* 25 (December 1967), pp. 711–12. Study of whether specific graffiti are unique to a particular type of building and the population using that building.

Laurent, Émile. *Les Habitués des prisons de Paris.* Preface by A. Lacassagne. Lyon: A. Storck; Paris: G. Masson, 1890. Includes a chapter on the "beaux-arts" in prisons and another on tattoos.

Legman, Gerston. *The Hornbook: Studies in Erotic Folklore and Bibliography.* New York: University Books, 1964. Graffiti interpreted by an authority on erotic folklore.

Ley, David, and Roman Cybriwsky. "Urban Graffiti as Territorial Markers." *Annals of the Association of American Geographers,* 64 (December 1974), pp. 491–505. Graffiti used by teenage gangs to mark off their turf or area of control.

Loewenstine, Harold V., George D. Ponticos, and Michele A. Paludi. "Sex Differences in Graffiti as Communication Style." *The Journal of Social Psychology,* 117 (August 1982), pp. 307–08.

Lomas, Harvey D. "Graffiti: Some Observations and Speculations." *The Psychoanalytic Review,* 60 (Spring 1973), pp. 71–89.

———. "Graffiti: Some Clinical Observations." *The Psychoanalytic Review,* 63 (Fall 1976), pp. 451–57. Writing on walls is a destructive act.

Lombroso, Cesare. *Le piu recenti scoperte ed applicazioni della psichiatria ed antropologia criminale.* Turin: Fratelli Bocca, 1893.

———. *Les Palimpsestes des prisons.* Lyon: A. Storck; Paris: G. Masson, 1894. This important sourcebook uses prison graffiti to investigate the moral and psychological state of prisoners.

Longenecker, Gregory J. "Sequential Parody Graffiti." *Western Folklore,* 36 (October 1977), pp. 354–64.

Lucca, Nydia, and Angel M. Pacheco. "Children's Graffiti: Visual Communication from a Developmental Perspective." *The Journal of Genetic Psychology,* 147 (December 1986), pp. 465–79. Graffiti revealing children's self-identity and affective-romantic interpersonal relationships.

Luquet, Georges Henri. "Sur la survivance des caractères du dessin enfantin dans des graffiti à indications sexuelles." *Anthropophyteia,* 7 (1910), pp. 196–202. Identifies spontaneous characteristics that survive in adult contemporary graffiti; distinguishes between "visual" (optical) and "logical" (conceptual) realism.

———. "Sur un cas d'homonymie graphique: sexe et visage humain." *Anthropophyteia,* 7 (1910), pp. 202–06.

———. "Représentation de la vulve dans les graffiti contemporains." *Anthropophyteia,* 8 (1911), pp. 210–14. Concentrates on the inherent characteristics of graffiti.

———. "Figuration possible de la vulve dans l'écriture pictographique de la Crète minoenne." *Anthropophyteia,* 8 (1911), pp. 215–16. Contemporary graffiti used to decode a pictographic sign.

———. "Sur les caractères des figures humaines dans l'art paléolithique." *L'Anthropologie,* 21 (1910), pp. 409–23. Modern graffiti used to explain prehistoric art.

———. "Dégénérescences alphabétiques du visage humain dans les graffiti contemporains." *Revue d'ethnographie et de sociologie,* 5 (March–April 1914), pp. 92–96. Asserts that studying graffiti can shed light on primitive and prehistoric art.

McGlynn, Paul. "Graffiti and Slogans: Flushing the Id." *The Journal of Popular Culture,* 6 (Fall 1972), pp. 351–56.

McLean, William. "Graffiti." In *Encyclopedia Universalis,* vol. 7. Paris: Encyclopaedia Universalis France, 1968. A good introduction to the subject.

————. *Contribution à l'étude de l'iconographie populaire de l'érotisme.* Paris: G. P. Maisonneuve et Larose, 1970.

Macioti, I., and M. d'Aurato. "I graffiti dell'università." *Critica Sociologica*, 41 (Spring 1977), pp. 122–51. On the opposition expressed by Italian students who viewed the whitewashing of university walls as an act signifying the elimination of the "creative inheritance of the movement."

Mailer, Norman. *The Faith of Graffiti.* Photographs by Mervyn Kurlansky and Jon Naar. New York: Praeger, 1974. Graffiti as modern collective cave painting.

The Merry-Thought: or, the Glass-Window and Bog-House Miscellany. Published by Hurlo Thumbo, printed for J. Roberts. Part 1 (London, 1731), Parts 2–4 (n.d.). Reprint, Los Angeles: University of California, The Augustan Reprint Society, 1982 (Part 1), 1983 (Parts 2–4). Includes what is believed to be one of the earliest collections of graffiti.

Mockridge, Norton. *The Scrawl of the Wild: What People Write on Walls and Why.* Cleveland and New York: World Publishing Co., 1968. Popularized notions borrowed from the social sciences.

Olowu, A. A. "Graffiti Here and There." *Psychological Reports,* 52 (June 1983), p. 986. Graffiti from lavatories of British universities compared to those of Nigeria.

Pennebaker, James W., and Deborah Yates Sanders. "American Graffiti: Effects of Authority and Reactance Arousal." *Personality and Social Psychology Bulletin,* 2 (Summer 1976), pp. 264–67.

Peretti, Peter O., Richard Carter, and Betty McClinton. "Graffiti and Adolescent Personality." *Adolescence,* 12 (Spring 1977), pp. 31–42. Graffiti as outward manifestations of the early stages of adolescent personality: sexual maturity, self-identity, idealism, gender, iconoclasm, and rebelliousness.

Praetorius, Numa [Magnus Hirschfeld]. "Homosexuelle Pissoirinschriften aus Paris." *Anthropophyteia,* 8 (1911), pp. 410–22.

Prinzhorn, Hans. *Bildnerei der Gefangenen.* Berlin: Axel Juncker, 1926. A critique of earlier studies (by Laurent, Ellis, Gross, and Lombroso) of the visual productions of prisoners, arguing that a great number of drawings are found in museums of criminology and that some of them belong to a kind of which Kubin and Goya are the legitimate masters. Believes that prison graffiti do not provide a glimpse into the individual psyche, but if viewed collectively can be revealing.

Read, Allen Walker. *Lexical Evidence from Folk Epigraphy in Western North America: A Glossorial Study of the Low Element in the English Vocabulary.* Paris: [privately printed], 1935. Graffiti as a universal form of folklore invaluable to historians, folklorists, psychologists, sociologists, and linguists.

Reich, Wendy, Rosalie Buss, Ellen Fein, and Terry Kurz. "Notes on Women's Graffiti." *Journal of American Folklore,* 90 (October–December 1977), pp. 188–91. Discussion of differences between women's and men's graffiti and the social factors contributing to these differences, with emphasis on lesbian and feminist graffiti.

Reiskel, K. "Skatologische Inschriften." *Anthropophyteia,* 3 (1906), pp. 244–46.

Reisner, Robert. *Graffiti: Two Thousand Years of Wall Writing.* New York: Cowles Book Co., 1971.

"Revolution on the Walls." *The Nation,* August 5, 1968, pp. 84–85. On the graffiti associated with the 1968 student uprising in Paris.

Rhyne, Linda D., and Leonard P. Ullmann. "Graffiti: A Nonreactive Measure." *The Psychological Record,* 22 (Spring 1972), pp. 255–58.

Romotsky, Jerry, and Sally R. Romotsky. "L.A. Human Scale: Street Art of Los Angeles." *The Journal of Popular Culture,* 10 (Winter 1976), pp. 653–66.

Rudin, Lawrence A., and Marion D. Harless. "Graffiti and Building Use: The 1968 Election." *Psychological Reports,* 27 (October 1970), pp. 517–18. Suggests that far more research is needed before graffiti can be considered unobtrusive measures of social and political predilections.

Schwartz, Marc J., and John F. Dovidio. "Reading Between the Lines: Personality Correlates of Graffiti Writing." *Perceptual and Motor Skills,* 59 (October 1984), pp. 395–98. Graffiti writing not as a destructive act but as one that allows individuals to express themselves.

Sechrest, Lee, and Janet Belew. "Nonreactive Measures of Social Attitudes." *Applied Social Psychology Annual,* 4 (1983), pp. 23–63. Assesses methodology for using graffiti in studying attitudes between the sexes and between different cultures and socioeconomic levels.

Sechrest, Lee, and Luis Flores. "Homosexuality in the Philippines and the United States: The Handwriting on the Wall." *The Journal of Social Psychology,* 79 (October 1969), pp. 3–12. Comparative study of graffiti from men's restrooms in Chicago and Manila with respect to homosexuality.

Sechrest, Lee, and A. Kenneth Olson. "Graffiti in Four Types of Institutions of Higher Education." *The Journal of Sex Research,* 7 (February 1971), pp. 62–71. Study of socio-economic effects on the content of graffiti in male latrines.

Solomon, Henry, and Howard Yager. "Authoritarianism and Graffiti." *Journal of Social Psychology,* 97 (October 1975), pp. 149–50. Examines the relationship of authoritarianism to graffiti, positing graffiti as a safety valve for repressed impulses.

Stewart, Susan. "*Ceci tuera cela*: Graffiti as Crime and Art." In John Fekete, ed., *Life After Postmodernism: Essays on Value and Culture.* New York: St. Martin's Press, 1987. Graffiti and the paradoxes of consumer culture.

Stocker, Terrance L., Linda W. Dutcher, Stephen M. Hargrove, and Edwin A. Cook. "Social Analysis of Graffiti." *Journal of American Folklore,* 85 (1972), pp. 356–66. Graffiti as an accurate barometer of social attitudes.

Wales, Elizabeth, and Barbara Brewer. "Graffiti in the 1970s." *The Journal of Social Psychology,* 99 (June 1976), pp. 115–23. Females write more graffiti than males, and while females predominantly write romantic inscriptions, this depends on socioeconomic level, upper levels writing less romantic and more erotic material.

Webb, Nick. "Borderline Creativity." *Interchange,* 16 (1985), pp. 94–102. Examines the creative value of graffiti, an example of borderline art; concludes that art educators should be open to such "creative" endeavors.

"Women's Wallflowerings." *Psychology Today,* 13 (August 1979), p. 12. Graffiti in women's restrooms seen as collective conversation.

Caricature

Publications relating to metamorphic imagery are given in a separate section following the general listings on caricature.

Adhémar, Jean. "Les Journaux amusants et les peintres cubistes." *L'Oeil,* 4 (April 15, 1955), pp. 40–42. On contributions of artists such as Villon and Gris to journals like *L'Assiette au beurre* and *Le Rire.*

————. *Imagerie populaire française.* Milan: Electa, 1968.

Alexandre, Arsène. *L'Art du rire et de la caricature.* Paris: Quantin, Librairies-Imprimeries Réunies, [1892]. A comprehensive history of caricature from Egypt to France.

Arnheim, Rudolf. "The Rationale of Deformation." *Art Journal,* 43 (Winter 1983), pp. 319–24.

Baecque, Antoine de. *La Caricature révolutionnaire.* Preface by Michel Vovelle. [France]: Presses du CNRS, Librairie du Bicentenaire de la Révolution Française, 1988.

Bate, Jonathan. "Shakespearean Allusion in English Caricature in the Age of Gillray." *Journal of the Warburg and Courtauld Institutes,* 49 (1986), pp. 196–210.

Baudelaire, Charles. "1846: Le Salon caricatural, critique en vers et contre tous, illustrée de soixante caricatures dessinées sur bois." Paris: Charpentier, 1846. Published in *Le Manuscrit autographe,* 5 (July–August 1930), pp. 1–14. Illustrated poems.

————. "De l'essence du rire et généralement du comique dans les arts plastiques"; "Quelques Caricaturistes français"; "Quelques Caricaturistes étrangers." In *Baudelaire: Oeuvres complètes,* vol. 2. Edited by Claude Pichois. Paris: Gallimard [Bibliothèque de la Pléiade], 1976.

————. "On the Essence of Laughter." In *The Mirror of Art: Critical Studies by Charles Baudelaire.* Translated and edited by Jonathan Mayne. Garden City, N.Y.: Doubleday, Anchor Books, 1956.

Bayard, Émile. *La Caricature et les caricaturistes.* Paris: Librairie Ch. Delagrave, [1901]. Primarily on nineteenth-century French caricaturists.

Bergson, Henri. *Le Rire: Essai sur la signification du comique.* Paris: F. Alcan, 1900. English translation in Wylie Sypher, ed., *Comedy.* (1956). Reprint, Baltimore and London: Johns Hopkins University Press, 1980.

Blum, André. "L'Estampe satirique et la caricature en France au XVIIIe siècle." *Gazette des beaux-arts,* 1910. A series of seven articles.

————. *La Caricature révolutionnaire: 1789–1795.* Paris: Jouve & Cie, 1916.

————. *L'Estampe satirique en France pendant les guerres de religion.* Paris: M. Giard & E. Brière, 1916. Sixteenth-century caricatures within their political and religious contexts.

————. "La caricature politique sous la monarchie de juillet." *Gazette des beaux-arts,* 62 (March–April 1920), pp. 257–77.

Boime, Albert. "Jacques-Louis David, Scatological Discourse in the French Revolution, and the Art of Caricature." *Arts Magazine,* 62 (February 1988), pp. 72–81.

Brinton, Selwyn. *The Eighteenth Century in English Caricature.* London: A. Siegle, 1904.

Caricature and Its Role in Graphic Satire (exh. cat.). Providence: Brown University; Museum of Art, Rhode Island School of Design, 1971.

"La Caricature": Bildsatire in Frankreich 1830–1835 aus der Sammlung von Kritter (exh. cat.). Westfälisches Landesmuseum für Kunst und Kulturgeschichte; Göttingen: Kunstgeschichtliches Seminar der Universität Göttingen, 1980.

"Caricatures françaises et étrangères d'autrefois et d'aujourd'hui." *Arts et métiers graphiques,* 31 (September 15, 1932). A special issue devoted to European caricatures.

Champfleury [Jules-François-Félix Husson]. *Histoire de la caricature antique.* Paris: Éditions Dentu, [1865].

————. *Histoire de la caricature moderne.* Paris: Éditions Dentu, [1865].

————. *Histoire de la caricature sous la République, l'Empire et la Restauration.* Paris: Éditions Dentu, [1874].

————. *Histoire de la caricature au moyen âge et sous la renaissance.* 2nd ed., enlarged, Paris: Éditions Dentu, [1875].

————. *Histoire de la caricature sous la réforme et la ligue: Louis XIII à Louis XVI*. Paris: Éditions Dentu, [1880].

————. *Le Musée secret de la caricature*. Paris: Éditions Dentu, 1888.

Clark, Kenneth. *The Drawings of Leonardo da Vinci in the Collection of Her Majesty The Queen at Windsor Castle*. 3 vols. 2nd ed., revised with the assistance of Carlo Pedretti, London: Phaidon, 1968–69.

Miguel Covarrubias: Caricatures (exh. cat.). Beverly J. Cox and Denna Jones Anderson, with essays by Al Hirschfeld and Bernard F. Reilly, Jr., Foreword by Alan Fern. Washington, D.C.: Smithsonian Institution Press, for the National Portrait Gallery, 1985.

Miguel Covarrubias: Homenaje. Edited by Lucía García-Noriega y Nieto. Mexico City: Centro Cultural/Arte Contemporáneo, 1987.

Cuno, James. "Charles Philipon and La Maison Aubert: The Business, Politics, and Public of Caricature in Paris, 1820–1840." Ph.D. dissertation, Harvard University, 1985.

————. "The Business and Politics of Caricature: Charles Philipon and La Maison Aubert." *Gazette des beaux-arts*, 106 (October 1985), pp. 95–112.

Dayot, Armand Pierre Marie. *Les Maîtres de la caricature française au dix-neuvième siècle*. Paris: Maison Quantin, 1888.

Deberdt, Raoul. *La Caricature et l'humour français au dix-neuvième siècle*. Paris: Librairie Larousse, [1898]. Recognition of the sociopolitical importance of caricatures.

Le dessin d'humour, du XVe siècle à nos jours (exh. cat.). Paris: Bibliothèque Nationale, 1971.

Dewdney, A. K. "Computer Recreations: The Compleat Computer Caricaturist and a Whimsical Tour of Face Space." *Scientific American*, 255 (October 1986), pp. 20–24, 27–28. Relation of computer-generated caricatures to cognitive processes.

Dolan, Therese. "Upsetting the Hierarchy: Gavarni's *Les Enfants terribles* and Family Life During the 'Monarchie de Juillet.'" *Gazette des beaux-arts*, 109 (April 1987), pp. 152–57. Analysis of how Gavarni's series of satirical prints sheds light on the sociopolitical realities of the 1840s.

Duché, Jean. *Deux siècles d'histoire de France par la caricature, 1760–1960*. Paris: Éditions du Pont Royal, 1961.

English Caricature, 1620 to the Present: Caricaturists, Their Art, Their Purpose and Influence (exh. cat.). London: Victoria and Albert Museum, 1984.

"English Caricature, 1620 to the Present." *Art and Artists*, August 1985, p. 34.

Everitt, Graham. *English Caricaturists and Graphic Humourists of the Nineteenth Century: How They Illustrated and Interpreted Their Times*. London: S. Sonnenschein, Le Bas & Lowrey, 1886.

Farwell, Beatrice. *The Cult of Images (Le Culte des images): Baudelaire and the Nineteenth-Century Media Explosion* (exh. cat.). Santa Barbara, Calif.: UCSB Art Museum, University of California, 1977. Shows that Baudelaire's interest in popular imagery was shared by the practitioners of "high art."

————. *French Popular Lithographic Imagery, 1815–1870*, vol. 8: *Contemporary Events and Caricatures*. Chicago and London: University of Chicago Press, 1988. Lithographic imagery from the restoration to the Commune which comments on contemporary events.

Ferment, Claude. "Le Caricaturiste Traviès, la vie et l'oeuvre d'un 'prince du guignon' (1804–1859)." *Gazette des beaux-arts*, 99 (February 1982), pp. 63–78.

Fingesten, Peter. "Delimitating the Concept of the Grotesque." *Journal of Aesthetics and Art Criticism*, 42 (Summer 1984), pp. 419–26.

The Franco-Prussian War and the Commune in Caricature, 1870–71. London: Victoria and Albert Museum, 1971. On a collection of caricatures in the Department of Prints and Drawings of the Victoria and Albert Museum since 1887.

French Caricature and the French Revolution, 1789–1799 (exh. cat.). Los Angeles: Grunwald Center for the Graphic Arts, Wight Art Gallery, University of California, 1988.

Freud, Sigmund. *The Standard Edition of the Complete Psychological Works of Sigmund Freud*, vol. 8: *Jokes and Their Relation to the Unconscious*. Translated by James Strachey. (1960). Reprint, London: Hogarth Press, 1986.

Fuchs, Eduard. *Die Karikaturen der europäischen Völker vom Altertum bis zur Neuzeit*. Berlin: A. Hofmann, 1901.

————. *Die Karikaturen der europäischen Völker vom Jahre 1848 bis zur Gegenwart*. 2nd ed., Berlin: A. Hofmann, 1906.

————. *Die Frau in der Karikatur*. Munich: Albert Langen, 1906.

Gaertner, Susanna. "Europe's Biggest and Best Cartoons Museum." *Connoisseur*, 218 (March 1988), pp. 162, 164. Addresses the collection of caricatures and cartoons in Basel.

Garcin, Laure. *J. J. Grandville: Révolutionnaire et précurseur de l'art du mouvement*. Paris: Eric Losfeld, 1970.

Gaultier, Paul. *Le Rire et la caricature*. Paris: Hachette, 1906.

George, Mary Dorothy. *English Political Caricature 1793–1832: A Study of Opinion and Propaganda*. Oxford: Clarendon Press, 1959.

————. *Hogarth to Cruikshank: Social Change in Graphic Satire*. London: Allen Lane, Penguin, 1967. Concentrates on graphic social satire, including caricatures, before the advent of illustrated journalism.

Getty, Clive F. "Grandville: Opposition Caricature and Political Harassment." *The Print Collector's Newsletter*, 14 (January–February 1984), pp. 197–201. Investigates why Grandville's career as a political caricaturist came to an end.

Gianeri, Enrico. *Storia della caricatura europea*. Florence: Vallecchi, 1967.

Goldstein, Robert Justin. "Approval First, Caricature Second: French Caricaturists, 1852–81." *The Print Collector's Newsletter*, 19 (May–June 1988), pp. 48–50. On the effects of the "authorization rule" on caricatures.

Gombrich, E[rnst] H[aas]. "Imagery and Art in the Romantic Period." *Burlington Magazine*, 191 (June 1949), pp. 153–58. Reprinted in *"Meditations on a Hobby Horse" and Other Essays on the Theory of Art*. London: Phaidon, 1963. Maintains that the Romantic movement sanctioned a marriage between art and popular imagery.

————. "The Experiment of Caricature." In *Art and Illusion: A Study in the Psychology of Pictorial Representation*. The A. W. Mellon Lectures in the Fine Arts, 1956. Bollingen series XXXV, 5. New York: Pantheon Books, 1960. Supports his views with arguments advanced by Rodolphe Töpffer, thereby taking issue with earlier definitions of caricature. Posits his own definition based on independence of caricature from the study of nature.

————. "The Mask and the Face: The Perception of Physiognomic Likeness in Life and in Art." In Gombrich, Julian Hochberg, and Max Black, *Art, Perception and Reality*. Edited by Maurice Mandelbaum. Baltimore and London: Johns Hopkins University Press, 1972. Elaboration of ideas first propounded in "The Experiment of Caricature."

————. "The Grotesque Heads." In *The Heritage of Apelles: Studies in the Art of the Renaissance*. Ithaca, N.Y.: Cornell University Press, 1976. An interpre-

tation of Leonardo's drawings of grotesque heads.

Gombrich, E[rnst] H[aas], and E[rnst] Kris. *Caricature*. Harmondsworth, Middlesex, England: Penguin, 1940. A key study examining the functions of the comic in history (e.g., moralizing, propagandistic, black magic), the reasons for the late appearance of caricature proper, and its history.

Gopnik, Adam. "High and Low: Caricature, Primitivism, and the Cubist Portrait." *Art Journal*, 43 (Winter 1983), pp. 371–76.

Gould, Ann. "La Gravure politique de Hogarth à Cruikshank." *Revue de l'art*, 30 (1975), pp. 39–50.

Grose, Francis. "Rules for Drawing Caricaturas with an Essay on Comic Painting." In *The Analysis of Beauty by William Hogarth and Rules for Drawing Caricaturas with an Essay on Comic Painting by Francis Grose*. London: Printed for Samuel Bagster, 1791. Brief instructions, with illustrations, on how to draw caricatures and make a comic picture.

Olaf Gulbransson: Werke und Dokumente (exh. cat.). Nuremburg: Archiv für Bildende Kunst am Germanischen Nationalmuseum Nürnberg; Munich: Prestel Verlag, 1980.

Hanson, Anne Coffin. "Manet's Subject Matter and a Source of Popular Imagery." *Museum Studies, 3*. Chicago: The Art Institute of Chicago: 1968.

————. "Popular Imagery and the Work of Édouard Manet." In Ulrich Finke, ed., *French Nineteenth-Century Painting and Literature*. Manchester: Manchester University Press, 1972.

Henderson, Ernest Flagg. *Symbol and Satire in the French Revolution*. New York and London: G. P. Putnam's Sons, 1912.

Herding, Klaus, and Otto Gunter, eds. "*Nervöse Auffangsorgane des inneren und äusseren Lebens*" *Karikaturen* (exh. cat.). Giessen: Anabas Verlag, 1980. A series of essays with an excellent bibliography.

Hill, Draper. *Mr. Gillray the Caricaturist: A Biography*. [London]: Phaidon, [1965].

————. *Fashionable Contrasts: Caricatures by James Gillray*. London: Phaidon, 1966.

Hofmann, Werner. *Caricature from Leonardo to Picasso*. Translated by M.H.L. New York: Crown, 1957. A short history of Western caricature; includes a discussion of caricature's relation to high art.

————. "Baudelaire et la caricature." *Preuves*, 18 (May 1968), pp. 38–43.

Holme, Charles. *Daumier and Gavarni*. London, Paris, and New York: Offices of "The Studio," 1904.

Huart, Louis. *Museum parisien: Histoire physiologique, pittoresque, philosophique et grotesque de toutes les bêtes curieuses de Paris et de la banlieue—350 vignettes par MM. Grandville, Gavarni, Daumier, Traviès, Lecurieur et Henri Monnier*. Paris: Beauger & Cie, 1841.

Kahn, Gustave. *Das Weib in der Karikatur Frankreichs*. Stuttgart: H. Schmidt, [pref. 1907]. Profusely illustrated.

Klingender, Francis Donald, ed. *Hogarth and English Caricature*. London and New York: Transatlantic Art, 1944.

Kozloff, Max. "The Caricatures of Giambattista Tiepolo." *Marsyas*, 10 (1961), pp. 13–33.

Kris, Ernst. "The Psychology of Caricature." *International Journal of Psycho-Analysis*, 17 (July 1936), pp. 285–303. Originally published in *Imago*, 20 (1934), pp. 451–66.

————. *Psychoanalytic Explorations in Art*. New York: International University Press, 1952. Reprints Kris's articles published in the thirties and forties, including the two on caricature cited here.

Kris, Ernst, and Ernst [Haas] Gombrich. "The Principles of Caricature." *The British Journal of Medical Psychology*, 17 (1938), pp. 319—42. Brief survey of caricature, followed by inquiry into underlying psychological mechanism and why this form of pictorial play developed later than verbal play.

Kunzle, David. " 'Les Misérables de Victor Hugo, lus, médités, commentés et illustrés par Cham' (1862—63)." *Gazette des beaux-arts*, 106 (July—August 1985), pp. 22—34. On the series of caricatures by Cham published in the *Journal amusant*.

————. "Goethe and Caricature: From Hogarth to Töpffer." *Journal of the Warburg and Courtauld Institutes*, 48 (1985), pp. 164—88.

Lajer-Burcharth, Ewa. "Modernity and the Condition of Disguise: Manet's *Absinthe Drinker*." *Art Journal*, 45 (Spring 1985), pp. 18—26. Rag-picker in popular publications considered as a source for Manet.

Lambourne, Lionel. *An Introduction to Caricature*. London: Her Majesty's Stationery Office, 1983.

Langlois, Claude. *La Caricature contre-révolutionnaire*. [France]: Presses du CNRS, Librairie du Bicentenaire de la Révolution Française, 1988.

Laughton, Bruce. "Some Daumier Drawings for Lithographs." *Master Drawings*, 22, no. 1 (1984), pp. 56—63.

————. "Daumier's Expressive Heads." *RACAR: Revue d'art canadienne*, 14, nos. 1, 2 (1987), pp. 135—42.

Lavin, Irving. "Bernini and the Art of Social Satire." In *Drawings by Gianlorenzo Bernini from the Museum der Bildende Künste, Leipzig, German Democratic Republic* (exh. cat.). Princeton, N.J.: The Art Museum, Princeton University; Princeton University Press, 1981.

Léger, Charles. *Courbet selon les caricatures et les images, avec 190 reproductions en couleurs et en noir et blanc d'après Baudelaire, Daumier, André Gill. . . .* Preface by Théodore Duret. Paris: Paul Rosenberg, 1920.

Lethève, Jacques. *La Caricature et la presse sous la IIIe République*. Paris: Armand Colin, 1961.

Lortel, J. "David, caricaturiste." *L'Art et les artistes*, 18 (March 1914), pp. 273—75.

Lucie-Smith, Edward. *The Art of Caricature*. Ithaca, N.Y.: Cornell University Press, 1981.

Lynch, John Gilbert Bohun. *A History of Caricature*. Boston: Little, Brown, 1927.

McIntosh, Malcolm. "Baudelaire's Caricature Essays." *Modern Language Notes*, 71 (1956), pp. 503—07.

McLees, Ainslie Armstrong. "Baudelaire and Caricature: *Argot plastique*." *Symposium*, 38 (Fall 1984), pp. 221—33.

————. *Baudelaire's "argot plastique": Poetic Caricature and Modernism*. Athens, Ga.: University of Georgia Press, 1989.

Maeterlinck, L. "La Satire animale dans les manuscrits flamands." *Gazette des beaux-arts*, 29 (February 1903), pp. 149—66.

Malcolm, James Peller. *An Historical Sketch of the Art of Caricaturing with Graphic Illustrations*. London: Longman, Hurst, Rees, Orme & Browne, 1813. Inclusive approach.

Masters of Caricature: From Hogarth and Gillray to Scarfe and Levine. Introduction and commentary by William Feaver, edited by Ann Gould. New York: Alfred A. Knopf, 1981. An invaluable reference work.

Maurice, Arthur B., and Frederic Taber Cooper. *The History of the Nineteenth Century in Caricature*. New York: Dodd Mead & Co., 1904. Covers Europe and America.

Maxmin, Jody. "A Hellenistic Echo in Daumier's Penelope?" *Art International*, 27 (August 1984), pp. 38—47.

Melot, Michel. *L'Oeil qui rit; le pouvoir comique des images*. Fribourg: Office du Livre, 1975.

————. "Daumier and Art History: Aesthetic Judgement / Political Judgement." *Oxford Art Journal*, 11, no. 1 (1988), pp. 3—24. Maintains that aesthetic discourse is motivated by ideology.

Murrell, William. *A History of American Graphic Humor*. Vol. 1 (1747—1865), New York: Whitney Museum of American Art, 1933; vol. 2 (1865—1935), New York: Macmillan, 1938. Reprint, New York: Cooper Square, 1967.

Le Musée pour rire: Dessins par tous les caricaturistes de Paris. Text by Maurice Alhon, Louis Huart, and Ch[arles] Philipon. 3 vols. Paris: Aubert, 1839—40. Humorous text precedes each illustration.

Parton, James. *Caricature and Other Comic Art in All Times and Many Lands*. New York: Harper & Bros., 1877. From Pompeian wall drawings to American caricature, this profusely illustrated book provides a panoramic view.

Paston, George. *Social Caricature in the Eighteenth Century*. (1905). Reprint, New York: Benjamin Blom, 1968.

Paulson, Ronald. *Hogarth: His Life, Art, and Times*. 2 vols. New Haven, Conn.: Yale University Press, for the Paul Mellon Centre for Studies in British Art (London), 1971.

Perkins, D[avid] N. "Caricature and Recognition." *Studies in the Anthropology of Visual Communication*, 2 (Spring 1975), pp. 10—23.

Perkins, D[avid] N., and Margaret A. Hagen. "Convention, Context and Caricature." In Hagen, ed., *The Perception of Pictures*. New York and London: Academic Press, 1980.

Pichois, Claude. "La Date de l'essai de Baudelaire sur le rire et les caricaturistes." *Les Lettres romanes*, 19 (August 1, 1965), pp. 203—16.

Pichois, Claude, and François Ruchon. *Iconographie de Charles Baudelaire*. Geneva: Pierre Cailler, 1960. Includes illustrations of Baudelaire's caricatures.

Piddington, Ralph. *The Psychology of Laughter: A Study in Social Adaptation*. 1933; New York: Gamut Press, 1963. Incorporates summaries of various theories of laughter.

Pottier, Edmond. *Les Origines de la caricature dans l'antiquité*. Annales du Musée Guimet, Bibliothèque de Vulgarisation, 41. Paris: Hachette, 1916.

Price, Aimée Brown. "Official Artists and Not-So-Official Art: Covert Caricaturists in Nineteenth-Century France." *Art Journal*, 43 (Winter 1983), pp. 365—70.

Provost, Louis. *Honoré Daumier: A Thematic Guide to the Oeuvre*. Compiled by Provost, edited by Elizabeth C. Childs. New York: Garland Publishing, 1989. Includes extensive bibliography, 1837 to 1980.

Ragon, Michel. *Le Dessin d'humour; Histoire de la caricature et du dessin humoristique en France*. Paris: Librairie Arthème Fayard, 1960. Charts a history of caricatures from the Middle Ages to today, arguing that humor and the rejection of conventional notions of beauty are elements which mark the beginning of modern art and its link to caricature.

Refort, Lucien. *La Caricature littéraire*. Paris: Librairie Armand Colin, 1932. Chronicles French caricature and its relation to French history and literature.

Revel, Jean-François. "L'Invention de la caricature." *L'Oeil*, 109 (January 1964), pp. 12—21. Discerns origins of French caricature in sixteenth-century Italy.

Rifkin, Adrian. "Well-Formed Phrases: Some Limits of Meaning in Political Prints at the End of the Second Empire." *The Oxford Art Journal*, 8, no. 1 (1985), pp. 20—28.

Roberts-Jones, Philippe. "L'Antiquité selon Grandville et Daumier." *Gazette des beaux-arts*, 111 (January—February 1988), pp. 71—75. Interprets Daumier's series of caricatures, "Histoire ancienne," as a critique of false classicism, and Grandville's references to antiquity as an earlier example of mythology used as pretext for social satire.

————. *De Daumier à Lautrec: Essai sur l'histoire de la caricature française entre 1860 et 1890*. Paris: Les Beaux-Arts, 1960.

Die Rückkehr der Barbaren: Europäer und "Wilde" in der Karikatur Honoré Daumiers (exh. cat.). Edited by André Stoll. Hamburg: Hans Christians Verlag, 1985.

The Satirical Etchings of James Gillray. Edited by Draper Hill. New York: Dover Publications, 1976.

Schapiro, Meyer. "Courbet and Popular Imagery." *Journal of the Warburg and Courtauld Institutes*, 4 (1941), pp. 164—91. Reprinted in Schapiro, *Modern Art: Nineteenth and Twentieth Centuries—Selected Papers*. New York: George Braziller, 1978.

Schmied, Wieland. "Die Karikatur als Wegbereiterin der modernen Kunst." *Neue deutsche Hefte*, 4, no. 40 (November 1957), pp. 728—35. Caricature as paving the way for an understanding of modern art.

Schneider, Mechthild. "Pygmalion: Mythos des schöpferischen Künstlers. Zur Aktualität eines Themas in der französischen Kunst von Falconet bis Rodin." *Pantheon*, 45 (1987), pp. 111—23.

du Seigneur, Maurice. "L'Exposition de la caricature et de la peinture de moeurs au dix-neuvième siècle." *L'Artiste*, 9 (1888), pp. 433—39.

Sheon, Aaron. "Caricature and the Physiognomy of the Insane." *Gazette de beaux-arts*, 88 (October 1976), pp. 145—50. Contemporary scientific illustrations, concerning the physiognomy of the insane and phrenology, as sources for political caricatures.

————. "Courbet, French Realism, and the Discovery of the Unconscious." *Arts Magazine*, 55 (February 1981), pp. 114—28. Caricatures as bearers of the knowledge French artists and writers had about the unconscious.

Shikes, Ralph E. *The Indignant Eye: The Artist as Social Critic in Prints and Drawings from the Fifteenth Century to Picasso*. Boston: Beacon Press, 1969.

Shikes, Ralph, and Steven Heller. *The Art of Satire: Painters as Caricaturists and Cartoonists from Delacroix to Picasso*. New York: Pratt Graphics Center and Horizon Press, 1984.

Signorini, Telemaco. *Caricaturisti e caricaturati al Caffè Michelangelo, con 48 caricature del tempo*. Florence: F. le Monnier, 1952.

Simplicissimus: Eine satirische Zeitschrift, München 1896—1944 (exh. cat.). Munich: Haus der Kunst, [1977].

Sorel, Philippe. "Les Dantan du Musée Carnavalet. Portraits-charges sculptés de l'époque romantique." *Gazette des beaux-arts*, 107 (January 1986), pp. 1—38; (February 1986), pp. 87—102. The life and work of the nineteenth-century caricatural sculptor Jean-Pierre Dantan.

Sutherland Harris, Ann. "Angelo de' Rossi, Bernini, and the Art of Caricature." *Master Drawings*, 13, no. 2 (1975), pp. 158—60.

Töpffer, Rodolphe. *Essai de physiognomie*. (1845). Reprint, Siegen: Massenmedium und Kommunikation an der Universität-Gesamthochschule, 1980.

Veth, Cornelius. *Comic Art in England*. Introduction by James Greig. London: Edward Goldston, 1930. Includes an especially cogent chapter on George Cruikshank. .

Veyrat, Georges. *La Caricature à travers les siècles*. Paris: C. Mendel, 1895.

Wechsler, Judith. *A Human Comedy: Physiognomy and Caricature in 19th Century Paris*. Foreword by Richard Sennett. Chicago: University of Chicago

Press, 1982. Examines the language of caricature in relation to the tradition of classification and codification of human types.

————. "Editor's Statement: The Issue of Caricature." *Art Journal,* 43 (Winter 1983), pp. 317–18. An invaluable summary of caricature historiography; the editor's preface to eleven articles in a special issue devoted to caricature.

Wright, Thomas. *A History of Caricature and Grotesque in Literature and Art.* [1865]. Reprint, Hildesheim and New York: Georg Olms Verlag, 1976.

Metamorphic Imagery

Arcimboldo. Text by Roland Barthes, with an essay by Achille Bonito Oliva. Milan: Franco Maria Ricci, 1980.

The Arcimboldo Effect: Transformations of the Face from the Sixteenth to the Twentieth Century (exh. cat.). Venice: Palazzo Grassi; Milan: Bompiani, 1987.

Baltrusaitis, Jurgis. "Têtes composées." *Médecine de France,* no. 19 (1951), pp. 29–34. Sources and diffusion of the Arcimboldesque device.

————. *Le Moyen âge fantastique: Antiquités et exotismes dans l'art gothique.* Paris: Armand Colin, 1955.

————. *Réveils et prodiges. Le gothique fantastique.* Paris: Armand Colin, 1960.

Berliner, Rudolf, and Gerhart Eggert. *Ornamentale Vorlageblätter des 15 bis 19 Jahrhunderts.* 3 vols. Munich: Klinkhardt & Biermann, 1981. Illustrations of prints from Germany, the Netherlands, France, and Italy.

Bizzarie: Propos sur Braccelli par Tristan Tzara. Edited by Alain Brieux. Paris: Alain Brieux, 1963. Includes a facsimile of the 1624 series of etchings by Braccelli.

Bossi, Benigno. *Raccolta di disegni originali di Franco Mazzola detto il Parmigianino tolti dal gabinetto di sua eccellenza il sigre. conte Alessandro Sanvitale. Incisi da Benigno Bossi Milanese stuccatore regio, e Professore della Reale Accademia delle Belle Arti.* Milan: Giochimo Betalli e C., 1794.

Broadley, Alexander Meyrick. *Napoleon in Caricature, 1795–1821.* 2 vols. London and New York: John Lane, 1911.

Caillois, Roger. *Au coeur du fantastique.* Paris: Gallimard, 1965. Proposes ornaments as the most plausible source for the Arcimboldesque invention.

Champigneulle, Bernard. "A Forerunner of Surrealism in the Seventeenth Century." *Graphis,* 6, no. 33 (1950), pp. 458–61. Imagery wherein objects associated with various professions are combined to represent figures, a genre popularized in France by Nicolas de Larmessin, Gillot, and Petitot.

Clark, Kenneth. "The 'Bizarie' of Giovanbatista Braccelli." *The Print Collector's Quarterly,* 16 (October 1929), pp. 311–26. Interprets Braccelli's etchings in relation to three seicento discoveries: mannerism, mechanism, and conceits.

Cruikshank, George. Illustrations by George Cruikshank; Comprising a Collection of About 800 Pages of Illustrations, Including About 40 Colored Plates, Many Proof Impressions, Clippings from Books Illustrated by Cruikshank. Album in 6 vols. London, [1820–60]. The New York Public Library. Print Collection, Miriam and Ira D. Wallach Division of Art, Prints and Photographs.

————. *George Cruikshank's Omnibus.* London: Tilt & Bogue, 1842.

Dacos, Nicole. *La Découverte de la Domus Aurea et la formation des grotesques à la Renaissance.* London: Warburg Institute; Leiden: E. J. Brill, 1969. Important discussion of the development of grotesques.

Éluard, Paul. "Les Plus Belles Cartes postales." *Minotaure,* 1, nos. 3, 4 (1933), pp. 85–100. Poetic text by Éluard and illustrations of postcards, among them a series of composite heads.

Fantasy in Prints: An Exhibition (exh. cat.). New York: The New York Public Library, Division of Prints, 1951. Includes composite figures by Nicolas de Larmessin and Petitot.

Fierens, Paul. *Le Fantastique dans l'art flamand.* Brussels: Editions du Cercle d'Art, 1947.

Fuchs, Eduard. *L'Elément érotique dans la caricature.* Vienna: C. W. Stern, 1906. A concise version of material the author later published under the title of *Geschichte der erotischen Kunst.*

————. *Geschichte der erotischen Kunst.* 3 vols. Munich: Albert Langen, [1912–28]. Includes discussion of metamorphic and scatological caricatures.

Grand-Carteret, John. *Les Moeurs et la caricature en Allemagne, en Autriche, en Suisse.* Preface by Champfleury. Paris: Louis Westhausser, 1885. Religious figures and architectural schema caricatured in an Arcimboldesque manner.

————. *Les Moeurs et la caricature en France.* Paris: La Librairie Illustrée, [1888]. The tradition of prints wherein the entire body and not merely the face is composed of occupational objects.

————. *Vieux papiers, vieilles images: Cartons d'un collectionneur.* Paris: A. Le Vasseur, 1896. Chapter seven includes eccentric caricatical images.

————. *L'Histoire, la vie, les moeurs et la curiosité par l'image, le pamphlet et le document (1450–1900).* 5 vols. Paris: Librairie de la curiosité et des beaux-arts, 1927–28. A limited number of metamorphic caricatures of religious leaders and illustrations of figures physically defined by the attributes of their professions.

Harpham, Geoffrey Galt. *On the Grotesque: Strategies of Contradiction in Art and Literature.* Princeton, N.J.: Princeton University Press, 1982. Treats the development of the grotesque from Nero's Domus Aurea to the spread of *grottesche,* coinciding with and largely indebted to the rise of printing and the medium of engraving.

Hocke, Gustav René. *Die Welt als Labyrinth: Manier und Manie in der europäischen Kunst.* Hamburg: Rowohlt, 1957.

Hofmann, Werner. *Luther und die Folgen für die Kunst* (exh. cat.). Hamburg: Prestel Verlag, 1983. Includes discussion of satirical imagery using multiple heads and Arcimboldesque devices.

L'Humour dans l'imagerie populaire allemande: Collection de Günter Böhmer (exh. cat.). Paris: Goethe-Institut, 1974. See the section on metamorphosis.

Koch, Carl. *Eine folge phantastischer Radierungen von Wendel Dietterlin D.J.* Berlin: Albert Frisch, 1928.

Legrand, Francine-Claire, and Félix Sluys. " 'Têtes composées' du XVIe siècle à nos jours: Arcimboldo et Arcimboldeschi." *Les Beaux-Arts,* June 19, 1953, pp. 1, 8–9.

————. "Giuseppe Arcimboldo, joyau des cabinets de curiosités." *Les Arts plastiques,* 6 (July–September 1953), pp. 243–58.

————. "Some Little-Known 'Arcimboldeschi.' " *The Burlington Magazine,* 96 (July 1954), pp. 210–14. Prints illustrating the occupations of everyday life and trades with a style combining those of Braccelli and Arcimboldo, particularly the work of Bernard Caillot [sic].

————. *Arcimboldo et les arcimboldesques.* Paris: La Nef de Paris, 1955. Hypotheses on the sources of Arcimboldo, from Indian miniatures and antique Dionysian representations to sixteenth-century caricatures of religious leaders, and on the diffusion of metamorphic imagery.

Marguery, Henry. "Les Figures bizarres de G. B. Braccelli." *L'Amateur d'Estampes,* 7 (October 1928), pp. 141–44; (December 1928), pp. 173–79.

della Porta, Giovanni Battista. *De humana physiognomonia.* Vici Aequensis: I. Cacchium, 1586. Physiognomic comparisons between men and animals.

Porzio, Francesco. *L'universo illusorio di Arcimboldi.* Milan: Fabbri Editori, 1979. Traces influences on Arcimboldo (Indian miniatures, Pompeian paintings) as well as his influence on Gaillot, Hogarth, and others.

Quatre Siècles de surréalisme: L'Art fantastique dans la gravure. Preface by Marcel Brion. Paris: Pierre Belfond, 1973.

Grandville: Das gesamte Werk. Introduction by Gottfried Sello. 2 vols. Munich: Rogner and Bernhard, 1969.

Soupault, Philippe. *Histoire de l'insolite.* Paris: Robert Laffont, 1964.

Tzara, Tristan. "Le Fantastique comme déformation du temps." *Cahiers d'art,* 12, nos. 6, 7 (1937), pp. 195–206.

Veth, Cornelis. *Geschiedenis van de nederlandsche caricatuur.* Leiden: A. W. Sijthoff, 1921.

Warncke, Carsten-Peter. *Die ornamentale Groteske in Deutschland 1500–1650.* 2 vols. Berlin: Volker Spiess, 1979. An important source, abundantly illustrated from Cornelis Floris, René Boyvin, Aloisio Giovannoli, Bodeneher the Elder, Tobias Stimmer, Heinrich Göding, Christoph Jamnitzer, Paul Flindt, Wendel Dietterlin the Younger, and the series of prints entitled *Songes drôlatiques.*

Wescher, Paul. "The 'Idea' in Giuseppe Arcimboldo's Art." *Magazine of Art,* 43 (January 1950), pp. 3–8. Claims that the origin of Arcimboldo's idea lies in the Italian ornamental grotesques of the early sixteenth century. Follows development of this idea through Surrealism.

Comics

Commentary and Criticism

American Civil Liberties Union. *Censorship of Comic Books: A Statement in Opposition on Civil Liberties Grounds.* New York: American Civil Liberties Union, 1955.

Bagdikian, Ben H. "Stop Laughing: It's the Funnies." *The New Republic,* January 8, 1962, pp. 13–15.

Bakwin, Ruth M. "The Comics." *Journal of Pediatrics,* 42 (May 1953), pp. 633–38.

Bataille, Georges. "Les Pieds nickelés." *Documents,* 4 (1930), pp. 214–16. Surrealist appraisal of French comics.

Bender, Lauretta, and R. S. Lourie. "The Effects of Comic Books on the Ideology of Children." *The American Journal of Orthopsychiatry,* 11 (1941), pp. 540–50. "The comic strip is the folklore of the times" and enables children to "solve the individual and sociological problems appropriate to their own lives."

Berger, Arthur Asa. "Comics and Culture." *The Journal of Popular Culture,* 5 (Summer 1971), pp. 164–77. American cultural attitudes evinced in comics.

————. *The Comic-Stripped American.* New York: Walker & Co., 1973. A history of the criticism of comics; draws parallels between American social life and comic strips, highlighting *The Yellow Kid, Buck Rogers, Batman, Pogo, Zap Comics,* and others.

Berkman, Aaron. "Sociology of the Comic Strip." *American Spectator,* 4 (June 1936), pp. 51–54.

Bogart, Leo. "Comic Strips and Their Adult Readers." In Bernard Rosenberg and David M. White, eds., *Mass Culture: The Popular Arts in America.* Glencoe, Ill.: Free Press, 1957.

Boime, Albert. "The Comics Stripped and the Ash Canned: A Review Essay." *Art Journal,* 32 (Fall 1972), pp. 21 ff. The significance of comics within the formation of modern art.

Borgardus, Emory Stephen. "Sociology of the Cartoon." *Sociology and Social Research,* 30 (November–December 1945), pp. 139–47.

Dorfman, Ariel, and Armand Mattelart. *How to Read Donald Duck: Imperialist Ideology in the Disney Comic.* Translated by David Kunzle. New York: International General, 1975. Disney comics as covert forms of capitalist propaganda in the Third World.

Faust, Wolfgang Max, and R. Baird Shuman. "Comics and How to Read Them." *The Journal of Popular Culture,* 5 (Summer 1971), pp. 195–202. A "linguistic-visual" analysis of a single *Superman* image, proposing a method by which comics can be best understood.

Fiedler, Leslie A. "The Comics: Middle Against Both Ends." *Encounter,* 5 (1955), pp. 16–23. Defense of comic books and attack on both their "elitist" and "middlebrow" critics.

Fresnault-Dervelle, Pierre. *La Chambre à balles: Essai sur l'image du quotidien dans la bande dessinée.* Paris: Union Generale d'Éditions, 1977.

Gilbert, James. *Mass Culture and the Fear of Delinquency: The 1950s.* College Park, Md.: University of Maryland Press, 1985. The origins and impact of the notion that mass culture, particularly comic books, were responsible for increase of juvenile crime.

Goldwater, John L. *Americana in Four Colors: A Decade of Self-Regulation by the Comics Magazine Industry,* 1964. Discusses the history, origins, and result of the institution of the Comics Code Authority and includes the text of the 1954 code, which was to keep the industry "morally acceptable to reasonable people."

Harrison, R. P. *The Cartoon: Communication to the Quick.* Beverly Hills, Calif.: Sage Publications, 1981. The cartoon considered as a means of communication within the context of its society and history; the creation of cartoons, from inception to reproduction.

Masson, Pierre. *Lire la bande dessinée.* Lyon: Presses Universitaires de Lyon, 1985. Semiologist's evaluation of French comic books.

McLuhan, Marshall. "The Comics." In Edward M. White, ed., *The Pop Culture Tradition.* New York: W. W. Norton & Co., 1972.

Muhlen, Norbert. "Comic Books and Other Horrors." *Commentary,* 7 (1949), pp. 80–88. Like Fredric Wertham, Muhlen asserts that the anarchy of comics contributes to the decay of modern society, "helping to create a whole generation for an authoritarian rather than a democratic society."

Ryan, John K. "Are the Comics Moral?" *Forum,* 95 (May 1936), pp. 301–04. Early article campaigning against comic books as instruments in the vulgarization and perversion of young minds.

Schwartz, Delmore. "Masterpieces as Cartoons." *Partisan Review,* 19 (July–August 1952), pp. 461–71. Discusses the bowdlerization of literary masterpieces when interpreted by "classic comic books."

Tan, Alexis S., and Kermit Joseph Scruggs. "Does Exposure to Comic Book Violence Lead to Aggression in Children." *Journalism Quarterly,* 57 (Winter 1980), pp. 579–83. Concludes that no significant correlation can be established between comic-book reading and subsequent physical or verbal aggression.

Thorndike, Robert L. "Words and the Comics." *Journal of Experimental Education,* 1941, pp. 110–

13. Appraisal of the value of comics in teaching children to read.

Thrasher, Frederick M. "The Comics and Delinquency: Cause or Scapegoat." *Journal of Educational Sociology,* 23 (1949), pp. 195–205. Disputes Fredric Wertham's supposition that comics foment criminal behavior in adolescents. Wertham's "extreme position . . . is not substantiated by any valid research. . . . Juvenile delinquency is the result of pent-up frustration and bottled-up fear. The comics are a handy, obvious, uncomplicated scapegoat."

Tucker, Nicholas. *Suitable for Children? Controversies in Children's Literature.* Berkeley: University of California Press, 1977.

United States Senate, Judiciary Committee. *Juvenile Delinquency (Comic Books): Hearings Before the Subcommittee to Investigate Juvenile Delinquency, of the Committee on the Judiciary—United States Senate, 83rd Congress, Second Session, April 21, 22 and June 4, 1954.* Washington, D.C.: U.S. Government Printing Office, 1954.

Wagstaff, Sheena. *Comic Iconoclasm* (exh. cat.). London: Institute of Contemporary Art, 1987. Catalogue essay views comics as a hunting ground for modern artists, surveys the development of comics and those painters influenced by them.

Warshow, Robert. "Paul, the Horror Comics and Dr. Wertham." (1954). In Warshow, *The Immediate Experience,* Garden City, N.Y.: Doubleday, 1962.

Wertham, Fredric. *The Seduction of the Innocent.* New York: Rinehart, 1954. Claims that the "moral and ethical confusion" of comic books is a primary cause of moral degeneracy and juvenile crime: "There is a significant correlation between crime-comics reading and the more serious forms of juvenile delinquency."

West, Mark I. *Children, Culture, and Controversy.* Hamden, Conn.: Archon Books, 1988. Assesses the attacks from both the left and right on dime novels, children's radio, rock music, television, and comic books, arguing that all such attacks are based on a faulty and uninformed presumption of the "innocence" of childhood.

General Histories and Encyclopedias

Abbott, Lawrence L. "Comic Art: Characteristics and Potentialities of a Narrative Medium." *The Journal of Popular Culture,* 19 (Spring 1986), pp. 155–76. Examines the relation between text and image and the "inherent structures and artistic potentials of comics as art."

Alessandrini, Marjorie. *Encyclopédie des bandes dessinées.* Paris: Éditions Albin Michel, 1979. Worldwide in scope, containing synopses of histories of comics and lengthy biographies of artists.

Bailey, Bruce. "An Inquiry into Love Comic Books: The Token Evolution of a Popular Genre." *The Journal of Popular Culture,* 10 (Summer 1976), pp. 245–48. "Love Comics" as culturally conservative and unaffected by social developments.

Becattini, Alberto, and Luca Boschie. *The Disney Index.* Florence: Al Fumetto, 1984. Catalogues the newspaper comics of Walt Disney Productions.

Becciu, Leonardo. *Il fumetto in Italia.* Florence: G. C. Sansoni, 1971. Charts the historical development of illustration as it relates to its political and cultural use in Italy. Contains a vast bibliography of Italian commentary on the subject.

Becker, S. D. *Comic Art in America.* New York: Simon & Schuster, 1959.

Bera, Michel, Michel Denni, and Philippe Mellot. *Trésors de la bande dessinée.* Paris: Éditions de l'Amateur, 1984. An encyclopedia and catalogue for collectors.

Carlin, John, and Sheena Wagstaff. *The Comic Art Show: Cartoons in Painting and Popular Culture* (exh. cat.). New York: Fantagraphics Books, for the

Whitney Museum of American Art, Downtown Branch, 1983.

Les Chefs-d'oeuvre de la bande dessinée. Edited by Jacques Sternberg and Michel Caen. Paris: Éditions Planète, 1967.

Colloque international education et bandes dessinées. Aix-en-Provence: Edisud, 1977.

Comics and Visual Culture: Research Studies from Ten Countries. Alphons Silbermann and H. D. Dyroff, eds. Munich and New York: K. G. Saur, 1986.

Comics Journal (published monthly, 1977–). Edited by Gary Groth. Agoura, Calif.: Fantagraphics. Originally issued as *The Nostalgia Journal.*

Couperie, Pierre. *A History of the Comic Strip.* Translated by Eileen B. Hennessy. New York: Crown, 1968. Collection of essays on the history of American comics and the French *bandes dessinées,* their audiences, the development of their graphic and narrative techniques, and their defense.

Craven, Thomas. *Cartoon Cavalcade.* New York: Simon & Schuster, 1943.

Crawford, Herbert H. *Crawford's Encyclopedia of Comic Books.* Middle Valley, N.Y.: Jonathan David, 1978. Publishing history of D.C. Comics, King Features, Dell, E.C. Comics, and others.

Daniels, L. *Comics: A History of Comic Books in America.* New York: Outerbridge & Dienstfrey, 1971.

Donahue, Don, and Susan Goodrick, eds. *The Apex Treasury of Underground Comics.* New York: Quick Fox, 1974.

Estren, M. J. *A History of Underground Comics.* 2nd ed., Berkeley: Ronin Publishing, 1986. Mostly illustrations.

Feiffer, Jules. *Great Comic-Book Heroes.* New York: Dial Press, 1965.

Filippini, Henri, and Michel Bourgeois. *La Bande dessinée en 10 leçons de Zig et Puce à Tintin et Astérix.* Paris: Éditions Hachette, 1976.

Fisher, Edwin, Mort Gerberg, and Ron Wolin. *The Art in Cartooning: Seventy-five Years of American Magazine Cartoons.* New York: Charles Scribner's Sons, 1975.

Foster, David William. *From Mafalda to Los Supermachos: Latin-American Graphic Humor as Popular Culture.* Boulder, Colo.: L. Rienner, 1989.

Gifford, Denis. *The British Comics Catalogue, 1874–1974.* London: Mansell Information Publishing, 1975. Annotated survey of British cartoons.

———. *Victorian Comics.* London: George Allen & Unwin, 1976. A picture book of late nineteenth-century English comics.

———. *Encyclopedia of Comic Characters: Over 1200 Characters.* Harlow, Essex: Longman, 1987.

Goulart, Ron. *Great Comic Book Artists.* New York: St. Martin's Press, 1986. Concentrates on well-known mid-century American artists and provides one-page biographies facing samples of their work. Ignores underground comics.

Hess, Stephen, and Milton Kaplan. *The Ungentlemanly Art: A History of American Political Cartoons.* New York: Macmillan, 1975. Outstanding reproductions, histories, and bibliographies.

Horn, Maurice. *The World Encyclopedia of Comics.* New York: Chelsea House, 1976. Vast and comprehensive indexed guide to characters, illustrators, publishers, and writers of comic books from all over the world, supplemented with an essay which traces the development of this largely American-based art form.

———. "Comix International." *Heavy Metal,* November 1980, p. 7. Essay on postwar Japanese comics.

———. *The World Encyclopedia of Cartoons.* Detroit: Gale Research Co., 1980. Vast international catalogue of comic strips, caricatures, political cartoons completes Horn's earlier *Encyclopedia of Comics.*

————. *Sex in the Comics.* New York: Chelsea House, 1985. Illustrated history of the depiction of the female in various comic-book genres.

Inge, M. Thomas. "Comic Art." In Inge, ed., *Handbook of American Culture.* Westport, Conn.: Greenwood Press, 1978. Bibliographic essay on the history, development, and criticism of comics.

————. *Comics as Culture.* Jackson, Miss.: University of Mississippi, 1990.

Jacobs, Will, and Gerard Jones. *The Comic Book Heroes: From the Silver Age to the Present.* New York: Crown, 1985. Superheroes produced by D.C. and Marvel, 1956–85.

Kempkes, Wolfgang. *International Bibliography of Comics Literature.* Detroit: Gale Research Co., 1971.

Kunzle, David. *The Early Comic Strip: Narrative Strips and Picture Stories in the European Broadsheet from c. 1450 to 1825.* Berkeley: University of California Press, 1973. Traces the history of narrative imagery from pre-Reformation Germany to the aftermath of Goya's *Disasters of War.*

————. *The History of the Comic Strip: The Nineteenth Century.* Berkeley and Los Angeles. University of California Press, 1990.

Lecigne, Bruno. *Avanies et mascarade: l'evolution de la bande dessinée en France dans les années 70.* Paris: Éditions Futuropolis, 1981.

Loveday, L., and Satomi Chiba. "Aspects of the Development Toward a Visual Culture in Respect of Comics: Japan." In *Comics and Visual Culture,* Munich and New York: K. G. Saur, 1986. The comics style as it proliferates within all aspects of modern Japanese culture.

Marschall, Richard. *America's Great Comic-Strip Artists.* New York: Abbeville, 1989. Documents the growth of the art form from its beginnings through the mid-twentieth century.

Martin, Antonío. *Historia del comic español, 1875–1939.* Barcelona: Editorial Gustavo Gili, 1978. A history of Spanish comic art and its criticism.

Murrell, William. *A History of American Graphic Humor.* Vol. 1 (1747–1865), New York: Whitney Museum of American Art, 1933; vol. 2 (1865–1935), New York: Macmillan, 1938. Reprint, New York: Cooper Square, 1967.

Nemo: The Classic Comics Library (published 1983–). Edited by Richard Marschall. Stamford, Conn.: Fantagraphics Books. Indispensable source for the history of American newspaper comics and illustration. Predominantly reprints of old stories, *Nemo* also contains interviews, features on artists, favorite strips, and short histories.

O'Brien, Richard. *The Golden Age of Comic Books, 1937–1945.* New York: Ballantine Books, 1977.

O'Neil, Dennis, ed. *Origins of the D.C. Super Heroes.* New York: Crown-Harmony Books, 1976.

O'Sullivan, Judith. *The Art of the Comic Strip.* College Park, Md.: University of Maryland Press, 1971. Introductory essay treats the history of newspaper comics, relating them to the history of continuous pictorial narrative. The book is primarily reprintings of comics, accompanied by biographies of the artists.

Overstreet, Robert M. *The Official Overstreet Comic Book Price Guide.* 18th ed., New York: House of Collectibles, 1990.

The People's Comic Book: Red Women's Detachment, Hot on the Trail, and Other Chinese Comics. Translated from the Chinese by Endymion Williamson. Introduction by Gino Nebidlo, translated from Italian by Frances Frenaye. Garden City, N.Y.: An-

chor, 1973. History of the ideological battles waged in Chinese comics since the 1949 revolution.

Perry, George, and Alan Aldridge. *The Penguin Book of Comics.* Revised ed., London: Penguin, 1971. Short, engaging pictorial history of American and British comics.

Reitberger, Reinhold C., and Wolfgang Fuchs. *Comics: Anatomie eines Massenmediums.* Munich: Heinz Moos Verlag, 1971. Examines the sociopolitical ramifications of European and American comic books.

Rey, Alain. *Les Spectres de la bande: Essai sur la B.D.* Paris: Éditions de Minuit, 1978.

Robbins, Trina, and Catherine Yronwode. *Women and the Comics.* Guerneville, Calif.: Eclipse Books, 1985. International summary of the history of women artists, editors, and writers in the comics industry from 1880 to the present.

Robinson, Jerry. *The Comics: An Illustrated History of the Comic Strip.* New York: Putnam, 1974. An epigrammatic history of the comic strip in the context of film, radio, and television.

Sanders, Clinton R. "Icons of Alternate Culture: The Themes and Functions of Underground Comics." *The Journal of Popular Culture,* 8 (Spring 1975), pp. 836–52. Well-researched history of the underground comics of the late 1960s, their themes, functions, and style; contains a good bibliography.

Schodt, Frederik L. *Manga! Manga!* New York: Harper & Row, 1983. English-language sourcebook for the history of modern Japanese comics.

Scott, Randall William. *Comic Books and Strips: An Information Sourcebook.* Phoenix: Oryx Press, 1988. Invaluable bibliographic index of all aspects of twentieth-century cartooning, comic books, their creators, artists, critics, and compilers.

Sheridan, Martin. *Comics and Their Creators.* Boston: Hale, Cushman & Flint, 1942. Reprint, Arcadia, Calif.: Post-Era Books, 1973. Illustrated synopses of popular American comics and their histories.

Skinner, Kenneth A. "Salaryman Comics in Japan: Images of Self-Perception." *The Journal of Popular Culture,* 8 (Summer 1979), pp. 141–51. The world of the Japanese white-collar worker as reflected in the immensely popular *sarariman manga.*

A Smithsonian Book of Comic-Book Comics. Edited by Michael Barrier and Martin Williams. Washington, D.C.: Smithsonian Institution Press; New York: Harry N. Abrams, 1977. Focuses on twelve major artists, including Walt Kelly, Will Eisner, and the early work put out by Marvel, accompanied by several color plates for each artist.

Smithsonian Collection of Newspaper Comics. Edited by Bill Blackbeard and Martin Williams, Foreword by John Canaday. Washington, D.C.: Smithsonian Institution Press; New York: Harry N. Abrams, 1977. Reprints of mainstream American comics from 1896 to 1970; little commentary.

Tucker, K. "Cats, Mice, and History: The Avant-Garde of the Comic Strip." *The New York Times Book Review,* May 26, 1985, p. 3.

Van Hise, James. *The E.C. Comics Story.* Canoga Park, Calif.: Psi Ei Movie Press, 1987.

Von Bernewitz, Fred, and Joe Vucenic. *The Full Edition of the Complete E.C. Checklist (Revised).* Los Alamos, N.M.: Wade M. Brothers, 1974.

Waugh, Coulton. *The Comics.* New York: Macmillan, 1947. Pioneering history of American comics includes economic, publishing, and biographical histories from *The Yellow Kid* to *Terry and the Pirates.* Comics are seen as "democratic," but not as modern "folk" art.

The Who's Who of American Comic Books. Edited by Jerry Bails and Hames Ware. 4 vols. Detroit: Jerry Bails, 1973–76.

Young, William H. "The Serious Funnies: Adventure

Comics During the Depression, 1929–1938." *The Journal of Popular Culture,* 3 (Winter 1969), pp. 404–26.

Artists and Creators

Adams, John Paul. *Milton Caniff, Rembrandt of the Comic Strip.* Philadelphia: David McKay Co., 1946.

Barks, Carl, and Floyd Gottfredson. "Two Disney Legends Share Their Memories." *Nemo,* 7 (June 1984), pp. 12–15. Barks and Gottfredson were Disney's "pre-eminent Duck and Mouse artists" of the forties, fifties, and sixties.

Berger, Arthur Asa. *Li'l Abner: A Study in American Satire.* New York: Twayne Publishers, 1970. *Li'l Abner* proposed as an example of the exemplary richness of modern popular culture, which "like 'High Culture,' can contribute much towards understanding our society."

Blackbeard, Bill. "The Forgotten Years of George Herriman." *Nemo,* 1 (June 1983), pp. 50–60. Documents and analyzes the proto-Surrealist work Herriman undertook before beginning *Krazy Kat.*

Bray, Glenn. *The Illustrated Harvey Kurtzman Index.* Sylmar, Calif.: Glenn Bray, 1976.

Bridwell, E. Nelson. *Batman: From the 1930s to the 1970s.* New York: Bonanza Books, 1971. A pictorial history of Batman.

Brown, Slater. "The Coming of Superman." *New Republic,* 103 (September 1940), p. 301.

Canemaker, John. *Winsor McCay: His Life and Art.* New York: Abbeville, 1987. A thorough and intelligent biography of the creator of *Little Nemo in Slumberland.*

Caniff, Milton. *Terry and the Pirates.* Edited by Bill Blackbeard. 12 vols. New York: Nantier-Beall-Minoustchine, 1984–87. Reprints entire run of this hugely influential strip for 1934–46.

Capp, Al. *The Best of "Li'l Abner."* New York: Holt, Rinehart & Winston, 1978. Capp's selection of the best of his well-known strip, 1952–72.

The Complete E.C. Segar Popeye. 3 vols. Westlake Village, Calif.: Fantagraphics, 1986. Includes essays by Jules Feiffer, Richard Marschall, Bill Blackbeard, Mort Walker, Dik Browne, and others.

Coudouy, Josiane. *Le Phénomè Astérix.* Toulouse: Institute de Recherches sur la Bande Dessinée, 1972. Sociological reflections on France's immensely popular comic character.

Crouch, Bill, ed. *Dick Tracy, America's Most Famous Detective.* Secaucus, N.J.: Citadel Press, 1987. A general history with essays by creator Chester Gould and later illustrator Max Allan Collins.

Crumb, Robert. *The Complete Crumb Comics.* Edited by Gary Groth and Robert Fiore, introductory essays by Marty Pahls. Vols. 1–3, Westlake Village, Calif.: Fantagraphics, 1987, 1988, 1989; vol. 4, Seattle, Wash.: Fantagraphics, 1989. Elaborately detailed biography accompanies an unusually thorough survey of Crumb's influential comics.

Crumb, Robert, and Bill Griffith. "As the Artist Sees It: Interviews with Comic Artists." In Paul Buhle, ed., *Popular Culture in America.* Minneapolis: University of Minnesota Press, 1987.

cummings, e. e. Introduction to George Herriman, *Krazy Kat.* New York: Holt, 1946. Herriman, Krazy Kat, and democratic principles.

Desnos, Robert. "Imagerie moderne." *Documents,* 7 (December 1929), pp. 377–79. A Surrealist's appreciation of *Fantômas.*

Dick Tracy and the Art of Chester Gould (exh. cat). Port Chester, N.Y.: The Museum of Cartoon Art, 1978.

Eco, Umberto. "On Krazy Kat and Peanuts." Translated by William Weaver. *The New York Review of Books,* 32 (June 13, 1985), pp. 16–17.

————. "A Reading of *Steve Canyon*." Translated by Bruce Merry. In Sheena Wagstaff, *Comic Iconoclasm* (exh. cat.). London: Institute of Contemporary Arts, 1987.

Fifty Who Made D.C. Great. New York: D.C. Comics, 1985.

Fisher, Harry Conway. *The Mutt and Jeff Cartoons by Bud Fisher*. Boston: Bell Publishing, 1910.

Foster, Hal. *Prince Valiant in the Days of King Arthur*. Franklin Square, N.Y.: Nostalgia Press, 1974.

Gallick, Rosemary. "The Comic Art of Lyonel Feininger, 1906." *The Journal of Popular Culture*, 10 (Summer 1976), pp. 667–75.

Gopnik, Adam. "The Genius of George Herriman." *The New York Review of Books*, 33 (December 18, 1986), pp. 19 ff.

Gould, Stephen Jay. "This View of Life: Mickey Mouse Meets Konrad Lorenz." *Natural History*, 88 (May 1979), pp. 30, 32, 34, 36. The stylistic development of Mickey Mouse and its increasing dependence on physiognomic traits that suggest juvenility.

Gray, Harold. *Arf! The Life and Times of Little Orphan Annie, 1935–1945*. Introduction by Al Capp. New Rochelle, N.Y.: Arlington House, 1970.

Groth, Gary. "The Straight Dope from R. Crumb." *The Comics Journal*, 121 (April 1988), pp. 48–120. Encyclopedic interview encompassing Crumb's life and art, postwar American society, copyright law, and the development of underground comics.

Gruenwald, Mark, and Peter Sanderson. *The Official Handbook of the Marvel Universe*. 7 vols. New York: Marvel Comics Group, 1986. Encyclopedia of Marvel characters and stories.

Hollis, Richard, and Brian Sibley. *Walt Disney's Mickey Mouse: His Life and Times*. New York: Harper & Row, 1986.

Jacobs, Frank. *The Mad World of William F. Gaines*. Secaucus, N.J.: Lyle Stuart, 1972. Biography of the publisher of E.C. Comics and *Mad* magazine.

Kelly, Walt. *Ten Ever-Lovin' Blue-Eyed Years with Pogo, 1949–1959*. New York: Simon & Schuster, 1959. Commentary by Kelly.

Lee, Stan. *The Origins of Marvel Comics*. New York: Simon & Schuster, 1974. Reprints those stories in which the Fantastic Four, The Incredible Hulk, Spiderman, and others made their initial appearances.

Lerman, Alain. *Histoire du journal "Tintin."* Grenoble: J. Glenat, 1979.

McCay, Winsor. *The Complete "Little Nemo in Slumberland,"* vol. 1: *1905–1907*. Edited by Rick Marschall. Westlake Village, Calif.: Fantagraphics, 1988. Exceptionally high quality color reprints with a good introductory text.

McDonnell, Patrick, Karen O'Connell, and Georgia Riley de Havenon. *The Comic Art of George Herriman*. New York: Harry N. Abrams, 1986.

Marzio, Peter C. *Rube Goldberg: His Life and Work*. New York: Harper & Row, 1973.

Mendelson, Lee. *Charlie Brown and Charlie Schulz*. New York: New York World, 1970.

Pekar, Harvey. "Rapping About Cartoonists, Particularly Robert Crumb." *The Journal of Popular Culture*, 3 (Spring 1970), pp. 677–88. The development of underground comics and the art of Robert Crumb.

————. *American Splendour: The Life and Times of Harvey Pekar*. Introduction by Robert Crumb. Garden City, N.Y.: Doubleday, 1986.

Raymond, Alex. *Flash Gordon*. Franklin Square, N.Y.: Nostalgia Press, 1967.

Read Yourself Raw: Pages from the Rare First Three Issues of the Comics Magazine for Damned Intellectuals. Edited by Art Spiegelman and Françoise Mou-

ly. New York: Pantheon Books, 1987. Reprints from *Raw*, the most innovative graphics magazine of the alternate press since *Zap* comics of the late 1960s. Includes work by Art Spiegelman, Mark Beyer, Gary Panter, Charles Burns, José Muñoz, Jacques Tardi, Bill Griffith, and others from 1980–86.

Real Love: The Best of the Simon and Kirby Romance Comics, 1940s–1950s. Edited by Richard Howell. Forestville, Calif.: Eclipse Books, 1988.

Rivière, G. H. "Couvertures illustrées de *Fantômas*." *Documents*, 1 (1930), pp. 50, 53.

Rosemont, Franklin. "Surrealism in the Comics, Part I: *Krazy Kat* (George Herriman); Part II: *Dick Tracy* (Chester Gould)." In Paul Buhle, ed., *Popular Culture in America*. Minneapolis: University of Minnesota Press, 1987.

Schulz, Charles. *Peanuts Jubilee: My Life and Art with Charlie Brown and Others*. New York: Holt, Rinehart & Winston, 1975.

Seldes, Gilbert. "The Krazy Kat That Walks by Himself." In Seldes, *The Seven Lively Arts*. New York: Sagamore Press, 1924. Seldes writes that "*Krazy Kat*, the daily comic strip of George Herriman, is, to me, the most amusing and fantastic and satisfactory work of art produced in America today."

Shannon, Lyle W. "The Opinions of Little Orphan Annie and Her Friends." *Public Opinion Quarterly*, 18 (Summer 1954), pp. 169–79. Attempts to rebalance the public attitude toward comics, asserting that American middle-class sociopolitical ideals can be detected in the funny papers.

Superman from the 30s to the 80s. Introduction by E. Nelson Bridwell. New York: Crown, 1983. Reprinted stories.

Warshow, Robert. "Krazy Kat." *Partisan Review*, 13 (November–December 1946), pp. 587–90. *Krazy Kat*, though one of the best items to be produced by *lumpen*-culture, exists wholly outside of the domain of the respectable.

Witek, Joseph. *Comic Books as History: The Narrative Art of Jack Jackson, Art Spiegelman, and Harvey Pekar*. Jackson, Miss.: University of Mississippi Press, 1990.

Young, Dean, and Richard Marschall. *Blondie and Dagwood's America*. Introduction by Bob Hope. New York: Harper & Row, 1981. Reprints from 1930 to 1980 and a short biography of creator Chic Young.

Yronwode, Catherine. *The Art of Will Eisner*. Princeton, Wis.: Kitchen Sink Press, 1982. Reprints of Eisner's work, 1933–81.

Advertising

A complete bibliography on all aspects of Western advertising would be larger than the entire present volume. What follows, therefore, focuses primarily on the history and criticism of modern print advertising since the late nineteenth century and related typography, design, display techniques, signage, and marketing strategies.

Attacks and Defenses

Advertising and the Public Interest. Washington, D.C.: American Enterprise Institute for Public Policy Research, 1976.

Babson, Roger W., and C. N. Stone. *Consumer Protection: How It Can Be Secured*. New York: Harper & Bros., 1938. Consumers urged to fight fraud and deceitfulness in advertising.

Barmash, Isadore. *The World Is Full of It: How We Are Oversold, Overinfluenced, and Overwhelmed by the Communications Manipulators*. New York: Delacorte Press, 1974. Human values and basic human dignity undermined by "the great deceivers in our society."

Batten, Henry A. "An Advertising Man Looks at Advertising." *Atlantic Monthly*, 150 (July 1932), pp. 53–57. The "blatancy, vulgarity, charlatanism" of advertising blamed less on the advertising industry than on the consumer, who alone can bring reform, through boycott and protest.

Beeman, William O. "Freedom to Choose: Symbols and Values in American Advertising." In Hervé Varenne, ed., *Symbolizing America*. Lincoln, Nebr., and London: University of Nebraska Press, 1986. Analyzes the pervasive advertising appeals to conformity; summarizes modern marketing techniques.

Berman, Ronald. "Advertising and the Rational State" and "Advertising and Mass Society." In Ronald Berman, ed., *Advertising and Social Change*. Beverley Hills, Calif., and London: Sage Publications, 1981. Gripes against advertising are really complaints against larger social issues involving capitalism.

Boorstin, Daniel J. "Advertising and the American Civilization." In Yale Brozen, ed., *Advertising and Society*. New York: New York University Press, 1974. Advertising as a destructive replacement of the folk culture of preceding centuries.

Borden, Neil H. *The Economic Effects of Advertising*. Chicago: Richard D. Irwin, 1942. Highly influential and often-quoted "classic" demonstrates the beneficent economic effects of advertising.

Borsodi, Ralph. *National Advertising vs. Prosperity*. New York: Arcadia Press, 1923. The advertising industry as economically wasteful and morally leprous.

Buzzi, Giancarlo. *Advertising: Its Cultural and Political Effects*. Translated by B. David Garmize. Minneapolis: University of Minnesota Press, 1968. Advertising "acts as a corrosive greatly contributing to the obsolescence of today's values, opening the way for a maturer conscience" (i.e., socialism).

Calkins, Earnest E. *Business the Civilizer*. Boston: Little, Brown & Co., 1928. Highly regarded, defensive presentation of advertising; much information on the relation of image and text, on the development of ideas and styles, and the opening of foreign markets.

Carpenter, Charles E. *Dollars and Sense*. Garden City, N.Y.: Doubleday, Doran & Co., 1928. A response to Chase and Schlink's *Your Money's Worth*; proposes that advertising plays a responsible role in the economic system.

Chase, Stuart, and F. J. Schlink. *Your Money's Worth: A Study in the Waste of the Consumer's Dollar*. New York: Macmillan, 1927. Primarily a catalogue of quackery and fraud, but also a telling document in the history of American consumer protection.

Clark, Eric. *The Want Makers: Lifting the Lid Off the World Advertising Industry*. New York: Viking, 1988. Investigates the paucity of hard information in modern ad campaigns, and the strategies by which advertisers appeal to consumers' fantasies. Advertising seen as a powerful influence over virtually all current cultural enterprises.

Cone, Fairfax M. "The Good Life Didn't Just Happen." In *Printers' Ink: Yesterday, Today and Tomorrow*. New York: McGraw-Hill, 1963. Cogent and vigorous defense of advertising on economic grounds, against the attacks of Arthur Schlesinger, Jr., John Kenneth Galbraith, and Arnold Toynbee.

Demsetz, Harold. "Advertising in the Affluent Society." In Yale Brozen, ed., *Advertising and Society*. New York: New York University Press, 1974. Advertising itself as productive, saving shopping costs and preventing overly specialized production.

Douglas, Mary Tew, and Baron Isherwood. *The World of Goods*. New York: Basic Books, 1979. Anthropologically oriented argument states that consumption cannot realistically be understood in John Kenneth Galbraith's categories of essential versus frivolous needs, since all goods have meaning and help to define a social group.

Duesenberry, James S. *Income, Saving, and the Theory of Consumer Behaviour*. Cambridge, Mass.: Harvard University Press, 1949. Influential theory of consumer behavior which posits that tastes and preferences within a culture are not dictated by advertising but in fact by growth and changes from within.

Ewen, Stuart. *Captains of Consciousness: Advertising and the Social Roots of the Consumer Culture*. New York: McGraw-Hill Book Co., 1975. A critique of the American ad industry's "imperialization of the psyche" in the 1920s, when the industry "promoted itself as a new patriarch" and lulled consumers with goods.

————. *All Consuming Images: The Politics of Style in Contemporary Culture*. New York: Basic Books, 1988. Argues that the images constructed by advertising manipulate American consumers into defining their own lives largely in terms of "style" and consumption.

Firestone, O. J. "An Economist Looks at Advertising." In Hugh W. Sargent, ed., *Frontiers of Advertising Theory and Research*. Palo Alto, Calif.: Pacific Books, 1972. Attempts to establish a middle ground in the debate over advertising's usefulness.

Galbraith, John Kenneth. *The Affluent Society*. Boston: Houghton Mifflin, 1958. Key anti-advertising book of the mid-century asserts that modern advertising creates synthetic needs that would otherwise never have existed.

Greyser, Stephen A. "Advertising: Attacks and Counters." *Harvard Business Review*, 50 (March–April 1972), pp. 22–24, 26, 28, 140–46. Allegations against advertising held to be unfair and based on intuitive assumptions, not fact.

Griff, M. "Advertising: The Central Institution of Mass Society." *Diogenes*, 68 (Winter 1969), pp. 120–37. "The real and deep purpose of advertising is to reduce men to a condition in which they lose all capacity for individual reaction," and to more easily make them candidates for "all types of indignities and enslavement."

Harris, Ralph, and Arthur Seldon. *Advertising and the Public*. London: Institute for Economic Affairs, 1959. Survey of economic issues, advertising's critics, the efficacy of advertising, and evaluations of consumers. A standard defense of the ad business.

Henry, Jules. "Advertising as a Philosophical System." In Henry, *Culture Against Man*. New York: Random House, 1963, pp. 45–99. A condemnation of advertising's "pecuniary psychology," focusing on adman Rosser Reeves and the president of Motivation Research, Ernst Dichter.

Hoyt, Elizabeth. "Aggressive Methods of Sales Making." In Hoyt, *The Consumption of Wealth*. New York: Macmillan, 1928. Maintains that "The huge wastes of competitive advertising would not take place if the consumer used his head."

————. "Advertising and Aggressive Salesmanship." In Hoyt, *Consumption in Our Society*. New York and London: McGraw-Hill, 1938. This later work by Hoyt no longer criticizes the consumer but instead the industry itself, for being rapacious, misleading, crass, and wasteful.

Inglis, Fred. *The Imagery of Power: A Critique of Advertising*. London: Heinemann Educational Books, Ltd., 1972.

Jhally, Sut. *The Codes of Advertising: Fetishism and Political Economy of Meaning in the Consumer Society*. New York: St. Martin's Press, 1987. The author calls advertising "fetishistic," i.e., as filling goods with a meaningfulness for consumers largely unrelated to use.

Key, Wilson Bryan. *Subliminal Seduction*. New York: Prentice-Hall, 1973. How advertising aims at the subconscious by using disguised eroticism in unexpected contexts. The book was highly popular with the American public but seen as little more than an irritant by advertisers.

Knight, Frank H. *Risk, Uncertainty, and Profit*. Boston and New York: Houghton Mifflin, 1921. Discounts the importance of whether information in ads is true, asserting that the existence of the ad itself creates part of the commodity's value.

Larrabee, C. B. "Thunder on the Right!" *Printers' Ink*, March 7, 1952, pp. 39 ff. Assesses public and governmental attacks on advertising abuses.

Larsen, Roy. "Advertising and the Affluent Society." In C. H. Sandage, ed., *The Promise of Advertising*. Homewood, Ill.: Richard D. Irwin, 1961. Advertising and America's responsibility to spread its affluence around the world.

Lears, T. J. Jackson. "From Salvation to Self-Realization: Advertising and the Therapeutic Roots of the Consumer Culture, 1880–1930." In Richard Wightman Fox and T. J. Jackson Lears, eds., *The Culture of Consumption*. New York: Pantheon Books, 1983. Explores the relationship between advertising and the health movement of the early twentieth century, a period when American culture was transformed from one based on production, morality, and sensibility to one based on consumption, permissiveness, and passivity.

Leduc, Robert. *La Publicité*. Paris: Éditions Dunod, 1970. Akin to the work of Roland Barthes, to whom this and other of Leduc's Structuralist studies of European advertising are dedicated; elucidates advertising's elaborate linguistic techniques.

Lewis, Sinclair. "Sinclair Lewis Looks at Advertising." *Advertising and Selling*, new series, 13 (May 15, 1929), pp. 17 ff. Resentment against the fatuous claims of an arrogant advertising industry.

Lipovetsky, Gilles. *L'Empire de l'ephemere: La Mode et son destin dans les sociétés modernes*. Paris: Gallimard, 1988. By promoting an economic system based on ephemeral "style," advertising does not give cause for despair, since such insubstantial fantasy is itself a desired and marketable commodity.

Mayer, Martin. *Madison Avenue, U.S.A.* New York: Harper & Row, 1958. Discussion of Madison Avenue strategies, asserting that the public manipulates the mass media, not the other way around. A useful encapsulation of the industry's response to Vance Packard's *Hidden Persuaders*.

————. "The American Myth and the Myths of Advertising." In C. H. Sandage, ed., *The Promise of Advertising*. Homewood, Ill.: Richard D. Irwin, 1961. Response to John Kenneth Galbraith, Arthur Schlesinger, Jr., and Arnold Toynbee. Although advertising operates through the myth of progress, it is a healthy myth which arises from public wish as much as from advertising craft.

Mayers, Henry. "How Well Are We Selling the World's Best Account." *Advertising Age*, March 29, 1961, pp. 83–84, 86, 88, 90. The "world's best account" is democracy; its "selling" is said to be encumbered by liberals in government.

Meyers, William. *The Image Makers: Power and Persuasion on Madison Avenue*. New York: Time Book Co., 1984. Attempts to understand advertising from the agencies' point of view, discussing the development of consumer assessment and the internal politics of the firms; condemns the industry as contributing "little of tangible value to our society . . . its only purpose is to keep us spending, spending, spending."

Murray, Barbara B., ed. *Consumerism: The Eternal Triangle*. Pacific Palisades, Calif.: Goodyear Publishing Co., 1973. Collection of essays by economists and marketing specialists Jules Backman, Yale Brozen, Gaylord Jentz, Theodore Levitt, and others.

Nadel, Mark V. *The Politics of Consumer Protection*. New York: Bobbs-Merrill, 1971. Thorough history of the consumer movement in the twentieth century.

Ohmann, Richard. "Doublespeak and Ideology in Ads: A Kit for Teachers." In Donald Lazere, ed., *American Media and Mass Culture*. Berkeley: University of California Press, 1987. Examination of the ways in which large corporations use advertisements to gain the sympathy, support, and money of the public.

Orman, Felix. *A Vital Need of the Times*. New York: F. Orman, 1918. Defense of advertising in the face of wartime criticism that it was wasteful and dishonest. Savagely anti-Bolshevik; promotes advertising as a primary and edifying force in a modern democracy.

O'Toole, John. *The Trouble with Advertising*. New York and London: Chelsea House, 1981. Largely an inventory of historical suppositions, statistics, and gossip. States that most academicians, journalists, and consumer advocates criticize and dislike advertising because it isn't something else.

Packard, Vance. *The Hidden Persuaders*. New York: Washington Square Press, 1957. Bestselling exposé of the devices of consumer manipulation, asserting that these devices are not only flourishing but inescapable, effective, and inevitable.

Potter, David H. "The Institutions of Abundance: Advertising." In Potter, *People of Plenty: Economic Abundance and the American Character*. Chicago: University of Chicago Press, 1954. Advertising's most powerful effects are "not upon the economics of our distributive system but upon the values of our society. Its influence is as great as religion or education, yet unlike these, it does not seek—nor is it able—to make better individuals."

Preston, Ivan L. *The Great American Blow-up: Puffery in Advertising*. Madison, Wis.: University of Wisconsin Press, 1975. On the ethics and legality of fraudulent advertising, the uses of misleading information and permissible exaggeration, and Federal Trade Commission regulations. Informative and extensive.

Sandage, C. H., and Vernon Fryburger, eds. *The Role of Advertising: A Book of Readings*. Homewood, Ill.: Richard D. Irwin, 1960. Essays on consumer protection, mass communication, persuasion, ethics.

Schudson, Michael. "Criticizing the Critics of Advertising: Towards a Sociological View of Marketing." *Media, Culture, and Society*, 3 (1981), pp. 3–12. Examination and rebuttal of the major criticisms of advertising, exemplified by Vance Packard's (that it is manipulative) and John Kenneth Galbraith's (that it is wasteful). Concludes that studies of advertising need more sociological fact and less theorizing.

————. *Advertising: The Uneasy Persuasion*. New York: Basic Books, 1984. Argues that advertising affects sales only very slightly and instead primarily works to reinforce existing patterns of consumption; suggests that the effectiveness of modern advertising remains almost impossible to determine.

Sheldon, Roy, and Egmont Arens. *Consumer Engineering: A New Technique for Prosperity*. New York: Harper & Bros., 1932. Advertising as a stimulus to consumption, manipulating taste and creating obsolescence.

Smith, Ralph Lee. *The Bargain Hucksters*. New York: Thomas Y. Crowell, 1962. Advertising documented and condemned as unlawful and deceitful; proposes new guidelines for government watchfulness and public awareness, with the expressed intent of creating a marketplace "where the American family can go without fear of being cheated, gouged, and gypped."

Strasser, Susan. *Satisfaction Guaranteed: The Making of the American Mass Market*. New York: Pantheon, 1989. The concept of name brands in creating desire for products.

Tinkham, Julian R. *Advertising is Non-Essential—Tax It!* Upper Montclair, N.J.: [Privately printed], 1918. A crusade against competitive advertising, which is seen as synonymous with hucksterism and superfluous for a country at war.

Toynbee, Arnold. "Arnold Toynbee Speaks About Advertising." In Vernon Fryburger, ed., *The New World of Advertising*. Chicago: Crain Books, 1975. Advertising as an instrument of moral and intellectual miseducation and an arm of competitive business practices which implore modern man to consume incessantly. Asserts that such practices reflect a mentality that is not only dangerous, but antithetical to the teachings of Christ.

Tuerck, David G., ed. *Issues in Advertising*. Washington, D.C.: American Enterprise Institute for Public Policy Research, 1978. A collection of intelligent legal debates over the proper role of government in regulating advertising.

Warne, Colston E. "Advertising: A Critic's View." *Journal of Marketing*, 26 (October 1962), pp. 10–14. Advertising as wasteful and deceptive promotion of rival brands.

Wight, Robin. *The Day the Pigs Refused to Be Driven to Market: Advertising and the Consumer*. New York: Random House, 1974. How Ralph Nader and other advocates have made consumers more critical and aware.

Williamson, Judith. *Decoding Advertisements: Ideology and Meaning in Advertising*. London: Marion Boyars, 1978. Examines the underlying capitalist implications in Western print advertisements using Structuralist and Marxist methods.

Advertising History and Practice

Adams, H. F. *Advertising and Its Mental Laws*. New York: Macmillan Co., 1916. Early attempt to apply "scientific" laws to advertising; chapters on attention, memory, use of color, and informing the consumer.

Adams, James D. "What IS This Modern Advertising?" *Advertising and Selling*, new series, 6 (March 10, 1926), pp. 27, 68.

Advertising and Consumer Psychology. Edited by Jerry Olson and Keith Sentir. New York: Praeger, 1986. Papers presented at the 1984 Consumer Psychology Conference, on subliminal cues, measuring consumer attitudes, semiotics, stimuli, brand personality.

"Advertising Increasing in 'Non-Commercial' Uses." *Advertising Age*, April 30, 1980, pp. 104, 108, 112, 114.

"American Advertisers Forge Ahead in France." *Printers' Ink*, November 27, 1919, pp. 43–44.

"Anticipating the 90s." *Advertising Age*, November 6, 1989, pp. 28–29. Predicts a greater emphasis on direct marketing, typography, and "realism," and "less frivolity."

Arren, J. *Sa Majesté, la Publicité*. Tours: Alfred Mame & Fils, 1908. Prewar French advertising considered from social and political points of view. Includes essays on advertising and political leverage, protectionism, appeals to human weakness, and tactics for enlarging a campaign. Like all of Arren's writings, seeks to legitimize the new industry in the eyes of a presumably suspicious populace.

———. *La Publicité lucrative et raisonnée*. Paris: Bibliothèque des Ouvrages Pratique, 1909. Crucial text examines the use of reason and suggestion, modern visual methods, American advertising devices, and testimonials by French manufacturers.

———. *Comment il faut faire de la publicité*. Paris: Pierre Lafitte, 1912. More a textbook than Arren's earlier, more polemical, texts.

Barton, Bruce. *The Man Nobody Knows*. Indianapolis: Bobbs-Merrill, 1924. A biography of Christ, presented as "the greatest businessman ever" whose parables contain a special message for those in business. Well known, highly influential, and the epit-

ome of what Sinclair Lewis attacked.

Beaver, Allan. "Advertising's Demise Greatly Exaggerated." *Advertising Age*, August 7, 1989, pp. 20, 32.

Bensman, Joseph. "The Advertising Man." In *Dollars and Sense: Ideology, Ethics and the Meaning of Work in Profit and Non-Profit Organizations*. New York: Macmillan, 1967. Internal workings of ad agencies, their ethics, management, and responsibilities. Concludes that advertising is a cutthroat enterprise ideally suited for hard-hearted, non-creative types.

Bernbach, William. "The Danger Is Mistaking Technical Skill for Creative Ability." *Advertising Age*, February 1, 1960, pp. 57–58, 60.

———. "It's One Thing to Have Selling Proposition, Another to Sell It . . ." *Advertising Age*, May 29, 1961, pp. 59, 60, 62.

———. "Facts Are Not Enough." *Advertising Age Yearbook, 1983*. New York: Crain Books, 1983. Retrospective summary of Bernbach's ideas.

Bogart, Leo. *Strategy in Advertising: A Worldwide Study*. New York: Harcourt, Brace & World, 1967. Exhaustive account of "new advertising," strategies in spending and marketing, using media, "reach vs. frequency," concepts of audience, measuring effects. Informative advertising contrasted with the harmful effects of appeals to emotion and the unconscious.

Bunting, Henry S. *The Elementary Laws of Advertising—And How to Use Them*. Chicago: Novelty News Press, 1913. Manual exemplifying the early "rational" approach to advertising; warns against advertisers who think their job is merely to attract attention, proposing instead "attraction and instruction."

Calkins, Earnest E. *The Business of Advertising*. New York: D. Appleton & Co., 1915. Pioneering work describing how an agency works; includes summations of how to place ads, find markets. Exemplifies "rational" approach to product selling by one of the century's most influential copywriters.

———. "Some Advertising Methuselahs." *Printers' Ink*, January 13, 1948, pp. 32–33.

Carrier, Émile. "La Suggestive Publicitaire." *La Publicité*, 27 (April 1929), p. 169.

Casson, Herbert N. *Advertisements and Sales: A Study of Advertising and Selling from the Standpoint of the New Principles of Scientific Management*. Chicago: A. C. McClurg and Co., 1911. Believes in a "reasonable predictability of the public"; much anecdotal history of wily "scientific" business schemes.

Chambonnaud, L., Émile Gautier, and F. Thibaudeau. *Les Affaires et l'annonce*. Paris: Dunod, 1921. Fuses economic theory with new fashion of "scientific" selling. Scott's laws of attention, space, intensity, and suggestion are applied to notions of customer satisfaction, illustration, typography, and poster construction.

Coleman, Loyd Ring. "Out of Witchcraft by Psychoanalysis." *Advertising Age*, June 30, 1958, pp. 67–68. "Subliminal advertising is a 'scientific absurdity,' like table rapping or Ouija boards."

Colford, Steven W. "Hail to the Image; The Reagan Legacy: Marketing Tactics Change Politics." *Advertising Age*, June 27, 1988, pp. 3, 32. Celebrates advertising's triumph of the image and crafted reality, focusing on the ways in which Ronald Reagan, "the greatest salesman ever," used marketing's manipulative devices.

Coolsen, Frank G. "Pioneers in the Development of Advertising." *Journal of Marketing*, 12 (July 1947), pp. 80–86. A review of books on American marketing practices prior to 1910.

"Creatives Bemoan Current State of Advertising." *Advertising Age*, May 26, 1980, p. 10.

Cumings, Tax. "Profusion of Ads is Ushering in the Era of the One-Two Punch." *Advertising Age*, January 6, 1964, pp. 53–54.

Cummings, Bart. *The Benevolent Dictators: Interviews with Advertising Greats*. Chicago: Crain Books, 1984. Collection of interviews with former agency directors charts growth and change of the ad industry since 1930.

Curti, Merle. "The Changing Context of Human Nature in the Literature of American Advertising." *Business History Review*, 41 (Winter 1967), pp. 335–57. Surveys American advertising's shifting notions of "human nature" and consequent changes in strategy from the 1880s to the 1950s.

Della Famina, Jerry, and Charles Sopkin. *From Those Wonderful People Who Brought You Pearl Harbor: Front-Line Dispatches from the Advertising Wars*. New York: Simon & Schuster, 1970. Exposé of Madison Avenue practices.

Dermée, Paul, and Eugène Courmont. *Les Affaires et L'affiche*. Paris: Dunod, 1922. Adapts scientific principles of attention, repetition, visibility, color, and suggestion from psychologist Wilhelm Wundt and Chicago adman W. D. Scott and their application to poster advertising.

DeWeese, Truman A. *The Principles of Practical Publicity*. Philadelphia: George W. Jacobs, 1906. Addresses the popular but conservative "reason why" approach to marketing, outdoor advertising, and rules for the successful creation of advertising imagery.

[Dichter, Ernest, and Albert Shepard]. "Psychological Engineering: Detroit's Future Approach to Automobile Design?" *Printers' Ink*, November 21, 1958, pp. 65–66.

Dichter, Ernst. *The Strategy of Desire*. Garden City, N.Y.: Doubleday, 1960. Asserts that advertisers should strive to make people "consciously discontent" by providing them with product "information" while exploiting every conceivable dissatisfaction with their present. Humanity progresses only by the extent to which it is dissatisfied so "hedonism . . . must be brought to the surface once again."

———. "Dichter Lists Nine Things to Keep in Mind." *Advertising Age*, September 5, 1966, pp. 63, 64, 66.

Dickinson, Roy. "How U.S. Could Use Paid Advertising." *Printers' Ink*, July 11, 1941, pp. 9–12, 77, 79.

Dietz, W. Stephens. "Are Ad Trends Changing? Yes, with Public Moods." *Advertising Age*, May 12, 1969, pp. 51–52.

"Directe et Indirecte." *La Publicité*, 25 (March 1927), pp. 160–62.

Donaton, Scott, and Pat Sloan. "Ad 'Printaculars' Under Scrutiny." *Advertising Age*, February 12, 1990, p. 32. Growing criticism of gimmicky insertions in print advertising.

Dornbush, Sanford, and L. Hickman. "Other-directedness in Consumer Goods Advertising: A Test of Riesman's Historical Theory." *Social Forces*, 38 (December 1959), pp. 99–104.

"Le Droit Publicité." *La Publicité*, 18 (April 1920), p. 159.

Dupont, Édouard. "Les Deux Methodes: New York et Paris." *La Publicité Moderne*, 2 (September 1906), pp. 1–3.

"The Eighties: What a Decade!" *Advertising Age*, January 1, 1990, pp. 13–15, 21–29, 32–35. Nostalgic picture-history surveys consumer values and interests as seen by the advertising community.

Eisner, David M. "Leo Burnett: The Solid Sell." *The Wall Street Journal*, January 12, 1977, p. 39.

Elinder, Eric. "Needed: Advertising That Passes All Boundaries." *Advertising Age*, November 27, 1961, pp. 91, 92, 94, 96.

Fisher, Karen. "Say Goodbye to Soft Sell." *Advertis-*

ing Age, March 17, 1980, p. S1.

Fonteix, J. B., and Alexandre Guérin. *La Publicité Méthodique.* Paris: Société Française de Publications Périodiques et de Publicité, 1922. A *manuel pratique* which urges the use of various means; printing techniques, uses of typography, methods and means of newspaper advertising are all treated.

Fox, Frank W. *Madison Avenue Goes to War: The Strange Military Career of American Advertising, 1941–1945.* Provo, Utah: Brigham Young University Press, 1975. Content analysis of American advertisements during World War II and their complex relations to the financial interests of American industry, the advertising community, and the U.S. Government.

Fox, Stephen. *The Mirror Makers.* New York: Vintage Books, 1984. Intelligent "group biography" of American advertisers; charts the rise and fall of advertising's powers, arguing that since the Depression, the industry has had to contend with an increasingly skeptical public and, therefore, has chosen to employ increasingly elaborate and scurrilous practices.

Fremont, Louis. *La Publicité, son historique, sa technique.* Verdun: H. Fremont & Fils, 1924. The early twentieth century's "scientific advertising," its laws and applications; a short history of the subject and its use in the modern city.

French, George. *Advertising: The Social and Economic Problem.* New York: Ronald Press, 1915. Emphasis on advertising reform, application of science to art of selling, ethics, social effects.

Garrett, Paul. "Advertising and the Economics of U.S. Defense." *Advertising and Selling,* June 1941, unpaginated supplement.

Gautier, Émile. "La Propagande Nationale et la publicité." *La Publicité,* 21 (April 1923), pp. 161–63.

————. "L'Evolution de la publicité." *La Publicité,* 21 (January 1924), pp. 865–67.

Gérin, Octave-Jacques, and C. Espinadel. *Publicité suggestive: Theorie et technique.* Paris: H. Dunod & E. Pinat, 1911. W. D. Scott's "psychological" approach to advertising as adopted by the French advertisers Gérin, Hémet, and Arren, France's most important advertising theorists and promoters in the early century.

Ginsburgh, A. Robert (Lt. Col.). "An Army Spokesman Outlines Advertising's Job in War." *Advertising and Selling,* 35 (January 1942), pp. 25, 26, 42.

Gossage, Howard. *Is There Any Hope for Advertising?.* Urbana and Chicago: University of Illinois Press, 1986. Brilliant essays on billboards, advertising psychology, creativity, copywriting, gimmicks, and designing campaigns.

Gould, Philip. *Advertising, Politics, and Popular Culture: From Salesmanship to Therapy.* New York: Paragon House, 1987. Attempts to cover internal debates within the industry and thereby draw parallels between ad campaigns and America's public sensibility and political ideology since World War II.

Gunther, John. *Taken at the Flood: The Story of Albert D. Lasker.* New York: Harper & Bros., 1960. Lasker, Madison Avenue's first tycoon, was to the first half of the century what Ogilvy and Bernbach were to the second. Lasker built his empire by surrounding himself with innovative copywriters who redirected the nineteenth-century notion that advertising was simply to display goods, arguing instead that the industry's role was to convince and persuade, to provide reasons, and to assert.

Harper, Paul C., Jr. "Consumers See Ads Through Filters." *Advertising Age,* June 7, 1965, pp. 121, 122.

Harris, Ralph, and Arthur Seldon. *Advertising and the Public.* London: Institute for Economic Affairs, 1959. Survey of advertising's economics, critics, efficacy, and customers.

Hart, Gifford R. "Comes Now the Claimless Era." *Printers' Ink,* August 12, 1955, pp. 26–28. After the ads of David Ogilvy, the trend away from competitive claims toward a simple, positive presentation.

Hémet, D. C. A. "La Réclame appréciée par les économistes." *La Publicité,* 8 (October 1910), pp. 417–19.

————. *Traité pratique de publicité.* Paris: Éditions du Bureau Technique de "La Publicité," 1922. Introduction to the advertising profession; chapters on consumer relations, the uses of typography, the construction of newspaper ads, modern selling psychology, and the effective use of illustration.

"Here Come the Super Agencies." *Fortune,* August 27, 1979, p. 46.

Hervier. "L'Évolution de la publicité." *Nouvelle Revue,* 160 (1906), pp. 377–91. A history of the newspaper, advertising, and the public since the French Revolution.

Higham, Sir Charles F. *Scientific Distribution.* New York: A. A. Knopf, 1918. Advertising's early attempts to legitimize itself by using "scientific" methods. Advertising seen as a beneficent educator, a denouncer of fraud, and, being the modern world's greatest tool for the distribution of information, part of the advance toward a higher civilization.

Hollingworth, Harry Levi. *Advertising and Selling: Principles of Appeal Response.* New York and London: D. Appleton & Co., 1913. Pop psychology advertising textbook. Bowdlerized versions of W. D. Scott's ideas, reworked in an attempt to address matters of visual formation, its relation to memory and persuasion.

Hopkins, Claude. *My Life in Advertising.* New York: Harper & Bros., 1927. Explication of the "hard-sell" technique of the early century. One of the most influential books in the history of advertising; read avidly in the U.S., Britain, and France.

Hotchkiss, George Burton. *An Outline of Advertising.* New York: Macmillan, 1933.

"How Advertising Can Help the U.S. Win Both War and Peace." *Printers' Ink,* July 3, 1942, p. 29.

"How the War Affected Marketing." *Printers' Ink,* September 21, 1945, pp. 22, 143–48.

Howard, Ainsworth. "More Than Just a Passing Fancy." *Advertising Age,* July 30, 1979, p. 50.

Hower, Ralph M. *History of an Advertising Agency: N. W. Ayer and Son at Work, 1869–1939.* Cambridge, Mass.: Harvard University Press, 1939. A vast, scholarly, and highly regarded work long valued for its intelligence and its abundance of material.

Jacoby, Jacob, Wayne D. Hoyer, and Mary R. Zimmer. "To Read, View or Listen?" In James H. Leigh and Claude R. Martin, eds., *Current Issues and Research in Advertising.* Ann Arbor, Mich.: University of Michigan Press, 1983. Cross-media analysis of information receptivity; finds print media most effective.

Jaffe, Robin. *The Advertising Index.* Los Angeles: Los Angeles Advertising Club, 1918. Guide for students and professionals.

Jereski, Laura Konrad. "Do You Know Your Consumers?" *Marketing and Media Decisions,* 18 (February 1984), pp. 76–78, 142, 144.

Jurist, Stewart S. (Sgt.). "Leaflets Over Europe: Allied Propaganda Used Some Advertising Principles." *Printers' Ink,* October 26, 1945, pp. 23–24.

Koepp, S. "The British Admen Are Coming." *Time,* April 28, 1986, p. 53.

Kurnit, Shep. "Creativity: Nothing New in '82." *Advertising Age Yearbook 1983.* New York: Crain Books, 1983. Surveys advertising's deepening "creative depression" of the 1980s.

Lallemand, Jules. "Psychologie et publicité." *La Pub-*

licité, 17 (May 1919), pp. 151–53. Postwar application of new theories of repetition, suggestion, and "les lois de la psychologie" to French advertising community.

————. "Psychologie de la subconscience." *La Publicité,* 19 (May 1921), pp. 219–21.

————. "L'Art de la propagande." *La Publicité,* 19 (October 1921), pp. 537–38.

————. "Propaganda et publicité." *La Publicité,* 19 (November 1921), pp. 610–13.

Larrabee, C. B. "Importance as Well as Truth in Advertising." *Printers' Ink,* August 25, 1944, pp. 21–22.

Lasker, Albert D. "The Personal Reminiscences of Albert Lasker." *American Heritage,* 6 (December 1954), pp. 74–84. Encapsulates the accomplishments of one of America's most influential advertising men.

Lears, T. J. Jackson. "Some Versions of Fantasy: Toward a Cultural History of American Advertising, 1880–1930." *Prospects,* 9 (1984), pp. 349 ff.

"Let Creative Men, Not Researchers, Control Agency Research." *Advertising Age,* November 16, 1964, pp. 1, 147.

Ludgin, Earle. "Advertising Must Be Unexpected and Believable." *Advertising Age,* January 19, 1959, pp. 81–82, 84.

Lyons, R. S. "War Creates New Advertising Themes." *Printers' Ink,* October 10, 1941, pp. 13–16.

McCreary, E. "The Uncommon Market: Advertising." Chapter in McCreary, *The Americanization of Europe.* Garden City, N.Y.: Doubleday, 1964. Review of the practices undertaken by American advertisers selling American goods in Europe.

McFee, William E. "Emotionalism Takes 'Why' from Reason-Why Copy." *Printers' Ink,* November 24, 1932, pp. 44–45. Depression-era article asserting that a rational approach to selling is always less effective than appeals to emotion.

McMahon, Michael. "An American Courtship: Psychologists and Advertising Theory in the Progressive Era." *American Studies,* 13 (Fall 1972), pp. 5–18.

Marchand, Roland. *Advertising the American Dream: Making Way for Modernity, 1920–1940.* Berkeley: University of California Press, 1985. A study of American advertising techniques from 1920 to 1940; arguably the best history to appear to date.

Martineau, Pierre. *Motivation in Advertising: Motives That Make People Buy.* New York: McGraw-Hill, 1957. Amalgamates pop-Freudianism with elaborate rhetoric to convince advertisers that ads are most effective when they dispense with logic and use subliminal visual devices.

Mataja, Victor. "La Réclame au point de vue economique et social." *Revue d'économie politique,* 25 (Paris, 1911), pp. 587–600.

Miller, A., and D. Tsiantar. "Psyching out Consumers." *Newsweek,* February 27, 1989, pp. 46–47.

Miller, Rod. "No Escaping Ads: The Response to Clutter—More Clutter." *Advertising Age,* December 11, 1989, p. 34.

Millman, Nancy. *Emperors of Adland: Inside the Advertising Revolution.* New York: Warner Books, 1988. Chronicles advertising's powermongering of the seventies and eighties.

Norins, Hanley. "Join the Revolution: Get Ad Readers into the Act." *Advertising Age,* December 1, 1969, pp. 85–86, 88.

O'Connor, Richard D. "The Future of Advertising." *Vital Speeches of Our Day,* 55 (July 15, 1989), pp. 583–87.

O'Dea, Mark. "The Power of Fear." *Printers' Ink,* April 23, 1936, p. 29. Fear is not only one of the most effective selling techniques, but a prime means of motivating people in any collective undertaking: "It is our national salvation."

Ogilvy, David. *Confessions of An Advertising Man*. New York: Ballantine Books, 1963. Rule book for successful advertising from one of the industry's leaders. Proposes that superior advertising requires a superior product, a wealth of factual data rather than a single pitch, and a "suggestive" approach that will charm and impress, not harangue, the prospective buyer.

Opdycke, John Baker. *Advertising as a Selling Practice*. Chicago and New York: A. W. Shaw Co., 1918. Rails against the use of decoration and promotes the use of large formats, heraldry, repetition, direct and terse language, and uplifting sentiments.

"L'Organisation de la propaganda." *La Publicité*, 22 (January 1924), pp. 913–16.

Pease, Otis. *The Responsibilities of American Advertising*. New Haven, Conn.: Yale University Press, 1958. Scholarly history of American advertising, 1920–40, dealing primarily with challenges to advertising, weapons of persuasion, socio-economic pressures, and cultural contexts.

Percy, Larry. "A Review of the Effect of Specific Advertising Elements upon Overall Communication Response." In James H. Leigh and Charles P. Martin, Jr., eds., *Current Issues and Research in Advertising 1983*. Ann Arbor, Mich.: University of Michigan Press, 1983. Modern psycholinguistics, visual imagery, and their effect upon consumer response to implicit and explicit strategies.

Percy, Larry, and John R. Rossiter. *Advertising Strategy*. New York: Praeger, 1980. Advertising as affected by recent findings in cognitive psychology, linguistics, information processing, and communication theory; discusses repetition, memory, and visual emphasis.

Piteraerens, Jules. "Publicité et suggestion." *La Publicité*, 17 (December 1919), p. 433.

Politz, Alfred. "The Dilemma of Creative Advertising." *Journal of Marketing*, 25 (October 1960), pp. 1–6. The merits of creativity and its relationship to effective marketing.

Pollay, Richard W. *Information Sources in Advertising History*. Westport, Conn.: Greenwood Books, 1979. Richly annotated bibliography indispensable for any study of advertising history.

———. "The Subsiding Sizzle: A Descriptive History of Print Advertising, 1900–1980." *Journal of Marketing*, 49 (Summer 1985), pp. 24–37.

Pope, Daniel. "French Advertising Men and the American 'Promised Land.'" *Historical Reflections*, 5 (Summer 1978), pp. 117–38. Socio-economic evaluation of the distinctions between French and American attitudes toward advertising from 1900 to 1918.

———. *The Making of Modern Advertising*. New York: Basic Books, 1983. A superb analysis of American advertising from the 1880s to the 1920s. Charts the history of shifts within the industry and discusses advertising journals, criticism, marketing strategies, and social effects.

Powell, Richard P. (Lieut.). "How U.S. Army Cooperates with Advertisers in Wartime." *Printers' Ink*, July 10, 1942, pp. 48–52.

———. "The War Department's Advertising Policy." *Advertising and Selling*, new series, 35 (August 1942), pp. 44, 74, 76.

Presbrey, Frank Spencer. *The History and Development of Advertising*. New York: Greenwood Press, 1929. Long considered a standard, this study of advertising concentrates on the late nineteenth century, though it includes a discussion of the early twentieth century and catalogues the tactics and rhetoric of advertising as it attempted to legitimize itself.

Printers' Ink: Fifty Years, 1888–1938. New York: Printers' Ink Publishing, 1938. An invaluable account of the shifting attitudes, approaches, and ideologies within the industry.

"Propagande Ingenieuse." *La Publicité*, 30 (January 1933), p. 20.

"La Publicité dans la construction mécanique." *La Publicité*, 21 (March 1923), pp. 95–97.

"La Publicité en France." *La Publicité Moderne*, 1 (November 1905), pp. 14–17.

"La Publicité sous la dictature nazie." *La Publicité*, 31 (January 1934), p. 32.

Ray, Michael L. *Advertising and Communication Management*. Englewood Cliffs, N.J.: Prentice-Hall, 1982. Intelligent textbook of high repute; provides good summaries of strategies prevalent in the 1970s and early 1980s.

Reeves, Rosser. *Reality in Advertising*. New York: Alfred A. Knopf, 1961. Adman's job is to "prove" the superior qualities of one product over another through a Unique Selling Proposition, or "hard sell," hinging on a single, forceful claim driven home with a vengeance, and coupled with the implication that all competitors' statements were no more than hot air.

Reid, Leonard N., and Sandra Ernst Moriarty. "Ideation: A Review of Research." In James H. Leigh and Claude R. Martin, Jr., eds., *Current Issues and Research in Advertising 1983*. Ann Arbor, Mich.: University of Michigan Press. Explores "ideation"—the conceiving of original ideas through imagination—and its application to marketing.

"La Reglementation de la publicité." *La Publicité*, 21 (January 1924), pp. 893 ff.

Rothenberg, Randall. "Brits Buying Up the Ad Business." *The New York Times Magazine*, July 2, 1989.

———. "Shifts in Marketing Strategy Jolting Advertising Industry." *New York Times*, October 3, 1989.

Rowsome, Frank. *They Laughed When I Sat Down*. New York: McGraw-Hill, 1959. A picture book of successful American advertising campaigns; also includes a great deal of campaign history and marketing strategy.

Russell, Thomas, and Glenn Verrill. *Otto Kleppner's Advertising Procedure*. 9th ed., Englewood Cliffs, N.J.: Prentice-Hall, 1986. Modernized revision of Otto Kleppner's 1925 original, with updated information on advertising history, theory, and practice in the media-saturated 1980s.

Ryckman, Peter. "Write the Ad Before You Design a Product." *Advertising Age*, December 17, 1979, p. 41.

Saatchi, Maurice. "The Future According to Saatchi." *Advertising Age*, March 21, 1988. Proposes and predicts a "global philosophy" to guide advertising on an increasingly international scale.

Sampson, Henry. *A History of Advertising from the Earliest Times*. London: Chatto & Windus, 1874. The best of the early histories of advertising and selling.

Sawyer, Howard G. "The Consumer Is a Jerk!" *Printers' Ink*, March 1, 1946, pp. 23–25.

Schultze, Quentin J. "Advertising and Progressivism." *Journal of Advertising History*, no. 3 (March 1980), pp. 90–110. Charts history of American advertising's self-legitimization, 1900–30; argues that its prosperous growth and social standing were due to scientific advancements and the "elevation of the businessman" from his earlier status as a mere purveyor of goods.

Scott, Walter Dill. *The Psychology of Advertising*. Boston: Small, Maynard & Co., 1908. The most influential of the "psychological" advertising textbooks of the early century. Scott promoted the use of "suggestion" and implied value rather than the popular "reason-why" method of selling or the ear-

lier, more understated, simple presentation of goods. He viewed the populace as impulsive, unthinking, and easily manipulated, insisting that any appeal to reason was based on a flawed assessment of human character.

Seldin, Joseph. *Golden Fleece: Selling the Good Life to Americans*. New York: Macmillan, 1963. Excellent source for postwar marketing history and various aspects of advertising, including promotion, packaging, public relations, and the media.

Serstevens, A. "La philosophie de la publicité." *La Publicité*, 19 (June 1921), p. 285.

Shepard, T. Mills. "Defense as an Advertising Theme." *Advertising and Selling*, new series, 34 (November 1941), pp. 16–17.

———. "What the War Theme Is Doing to Advertising Readership." *Advertising and Selling*, new series, 35 (October 1942), pp. 13–15.

"Sicken 'em; Sell 'em." *Printers' Ink*, July 14, 1939, pp. 21–22. Examines increasing use over the preceding decade of the ploy of inventing a "disease" ("razor-blade skin," "halitosis") and then presenting its cure: the product.

Skelley, Florence R. "The Impact of Advertising on the Social Sciences." *Advertising Age*, April 30, 1980, pp. 68, 70.

Smith, Roland B. "Can Advertising Prevent World War III?" *Printers' Ink*, December 5, 1942, pp. 32–33, 60.

Smith, Willard K. "A Primer of Propaganda." *Advertising and Selling*, new series, 23 (June 21, 1934), pp. 32, 34, 36. An admiring appraisal of the persuasive techniques American advertisers could learn from Adolph Hitler, who had come to power the year before.

Snyder, A. H. "Puissance de suggestion de la publicité." *La Publicité*, 7 (December 1909), p. 495.

Snyder, Kenneth C. T. "Use Humor in Ads When You Have a Lot to Say." *Advertising Age*, September 28, 1964, pp. 89–90.

Starch, Daniel. *Principles of Advertising*. Chicago and New York: A. W. Shaw Co., 1923. Vast investigation of advertising business, analysis of techniques, notions of "human nature," discussions of color, layout, media, trademarks, economics, and changes in the industry. This, Frank Presbrey's, and W. D. Scott's were the three key "in-house" texts of the early century.

———. "What Consumers Really Think About Advertising." *Printers' Ink*, July 24, 1942, pp. 26–27.

"Subliminal Advertising." *Advertising Agency*, May 23, 1958, pp. 14–19, 22. The best contemporaneous account on the questionable effectiveness of attempts to sell through indirect unconscious appeals.

Thibaudeau, F. "L'Annonce française." *Annuaire graphique*, 39 (1910–11), n. pag.

"Trade-marks Don't Detract from Messages Donated to Government." *Printers' Ink*, November 27, 1942, p. 58. Ploy by which advertisers cloaked themselves in nationalist rhetoric.

Trout, Jack, and Al Reis. "Positioning Era Cometh." In Vernon Fryburger, ed., *The New World of Advertising*. Chicago: Crain Books, 1975. "Positioning" presented not as a change in advertising technique but as a concept with which advertisers could better define their markets, and thus sell to them. The appeal of a product based on the position of its particular "slot" in relation to others.

———. "The Decline and Fall of Advertising: 'Positioning' 20 Years Later." *Advertising Age*, June 26, 1989, p. 20. Asserts that the emphasis on "creativity" is crippling advertising; proposes an increase in the use of candor and fact, and a sharpening of the ad's perception in the consumer's mind.

True, Herbert G. "How to be Creative." *Printers' Ink*, January 4, 1957, pp. 19–23.

Turner, Ernest S. *The Shocking History of Advertising.* London: M. Joseph, 1952. Compilation of the amusing and seamy aspects of British advertising, hucksterism, and blatant fraud, entirely symptomatic of the postwar skepticism held by the public, akin to American bestsellers by Wakeman and Vance Packard.

"Two Different Animals: Brand Awareness and Corporate Image." *Forbes,* March 6, 1989, p. 20.

Tyler, William D. "Corporate Ads Must Influence a Hostile Public." *Advertising Age,* October 18, 1971.

Unwin, Stephen. "How Culture Affects Advertising Expression and Communication Style." *Journal of Advertising,* 2 (January–February 1974), pp. 24–27.

Wadsworth, Gerald B. *Principles and Practices of Advertising.* New York: G. B. Wadsworth, 1913. Primarily economic advice for advertisers. More concerned with the application of "scientific laws" than the construction of advertisements themselves. Chapters on psychology, belief in appealing to consumers' ambitions, fears, and "sense of purity."

Waldsberger, Jean, and Charles Gonset. "Vente et psychologie." *La Publicité,* 21 (June 1923), pp. 357–58.

Walley, Wayne. "Advertisers 'Up in Arms.'" *Advertising Age,* March 27, 1989, pp. 1, 68. Deals with the industry's reaction to what it sees to be a "new Puritanism" among consumers.

"A War Message in Every Ad." *Advertising and Selling,* new series, 36 (July 1943), p. 26.

"We Are the Ad World." *Creativity* (supplement to *Advertising Age*), November 6, 1989, pp. 20–22, 26–27. Profile of "adland's new kids on the block."

Weir, Walter J. "Fighting Mad!" *Printers' Ink,* April 3, 1942, p. 65. The advertising community and the promoting of a wartime mentality.

———. "Opportunity!" in *Printers' Ink,* April 10, 1942, pp. 13–14.

———. "'Look of the Sixties' Replaces 'Readership School' of Ads." *Advertising Age,* October 8, 1962, pp. 75–76.

Weiss, E. B. "Propaganda Idea." *Printers' Ink,* January 17, 1941, pp. 37, 40.

———. "How to Get More Draftee Business." *Advertising and Selling,* new series, 34 (May 1941), pp. 34–35, 86–89.

———. "Advertising's Crisis of Confidence." *Advertising Age,* June 26, 1967, pp. 138, 140, 142, 144.

———. "Fifty-One New Advertising-Marketing Regulations Offer Lively Future." *Advertising Age,* October 25, 1971, pp. 67, 68, 70.

Weld, L. D. H. "French Advertising, Judged by American Standards, Seems Backward." *Printers' Ink,* January 27, 1933, pp. 96, 98, 100, 102, 106.

———. "Why Wartime Advertising Is Most Important of All." *Printers' Ink,* September 25, 1942, pp. 29–30.

West, Paul B. "Advertising Can Provide the Leadership That Will Save Our Democracy." *Printers' Ink,* July 5, 1946, pp. 64–73.

Wiener, Mort. "What's Happened to Creativity?" *Printers' Ink,* July 19, 1957, pp. 19–20. Advertising man rails against the trend of presenting an appealing image, rather than remaining within the time-honored tradition of persuasively presenting information.

Winski, Joseph M. "The Decade of the Deal." *Advertising Age,* January 1, 1990, pp. 3–4. Celebrates "the excessive 80s, the me-first years, the ultra consumers," and the marvels of government deregulation.

Woestyn, H. R. "Quelques modes bizarres de publicité." *La Publicité moderne,* 2 (September 1906), pp. 7–8.

Wood, James Playsted. *The Story of Advertising.* New York: Ronald Press, 1958. Biographically oriented history of advertising from the colonial period to the 1950s, examining changes in the industry during international conflicts, the development of media, the use of language, and the emergence of the modern advertising agency.

"You Can't Escape M.R." *Printers' Ink,* January 3, 1958, pp. 20–23, 26–33. Appraisal of the work of Ernst Dichter and the craze for the controversial Motivation Research.

Advertising Art

Agha, M[ehemed] F[ehmy]. "Leave European Art in Europe." *Advertising Arts* (supplement to *Advertising and Selling*), January 1932, pp. 15–18.

———. "Art and Art Directors." *Advertising Arts* (supplement to *Advertising and Selling*), May 1935, p. 13. Rise of the status of the art director and tension between art and business.

Aldersay-Williams, Hugh. "Double Vision." *Advertising Age,* April 4, 1988, pp. 20–22, 43. Asserts that although print advertising and "the lofty realm of art have never been further apart," attempts are being made in advertising to merge the two, "to make something beautiful."

"Les Annonces de langue anglais: Les chez eux et chez nous." *La Publicité,* 18 (January 1921), pp. 593–96.

"Les Annonces de langue anglaise." *La Publicité,* 18 (April 1920), pp. 155–57.

"Les Annonces de langue anglaise: La Publicité française en Amerique." *La Publicité,* 18 (October 1920), pp. 411, 413.

Art Directors Annual. New York: Art Directors' Club, 1921–. Annual report on art directors' best designs.

"Art for Art's Sake." *Printers' Ink,* November 19, 1925, pp. 145–46, 148, 151.

Aymar, Gordon. *An Introduction to Advertising Illustration.* New York and London: Harper & Bros., 1929.

Baker, Stephen. *Advertising Layout and Art Directions.* New York: McGraw-Hill, 1959. Written at outset of the "creative revolution" in advertising of the late 1950s. Contains invaluable information on the relation between word and image, the uses of photography, brand image. The book itself is a fine example of the "new" layout and design of the period.

———. *Visual Persuasion.* New York: McGraw-Hill, 1961. Catalogue of current graphic design in all media.

Bedell, Clyde. "Money's No Object with Us." *Advertising Age,* February 16, 1959, p. 67. A recent spate of shoe illustrations seen as "innovative" but not as good advertisements, even though they were prize-winning designs by Andy Warhol.

Berdanier, Paul F. "Art for Ad's Sake." *Printers' Ink,* May 28, 1943, pp. 15–16.

"Blended Pictures." *Printers' Ink,* August 24, 1933, pp. 25–26. Conservative endorsement of composite photography: "The very nature of photomontage is likely to lead to confusion."

Brennan, John E. "Power Through Simplicity." *Printers' Ink,* January 17, 1958, p. 70.

Buchanan, C. M. "Post-war Advertising Will Need More Realism." *Printers' Ink,* September 8, 1944, pp. 34, 36.

Burkhardt, Ron. "A Creative Mind: Will It Return in the 1980s." *Advertising Age,* March 31, 1980, pp. 45–52.

Calkins, Earnest Elmo. "What Has Art to Do with Advertising." *Advertising and Selling,* new series, 8 (January 12, 1927), pp. 28, 84–85.

———. "Modern Art and the Stock Market." *Advertising and Selling,* new series, 11 (September 19, 1928), p. 21. The skillful use of modern art in advertising as a key to higher profit.

———. "Beauty in the Machine Age." *Printers' Ink,* September 25, 1930, pp. 72 ff. Beauty in modern design can never rival fine art, but does "awaken some sense of taste in millions of minds." Business is encouraged to help stimulate and create a taste for mass-made beauty.

———. "Design and Economic Recovery." *Advertising and Selling,* new series, 21 (July 1933), pp. 9–13. Champions the combined forces of modernism and industry to help the economy since "in the middle ages, religion was an ideal—and men made it pay. . . . Today beauty is an ideal—and we can make it pay."

———. "1934." *Advertising Arts,* January 1934, pp. 9–12. Senses a turn away from "modernism to realism," because "advertising is beginning to make its appeal to a lower intellectual stratum."

Calkins, H. "Is Advertising Art Only the Stepchild of Fine Art?" *Advertising and Selling,* new series, 5 (May 20, 1925), p. 30.

Campbell, Heyworth. "Going Buckeye Vengefully . . . But Intelligently." *Printers' Ink Monthly,* 24 (February 1932), pp. 22–23, 58. Rails against "art" in advertising, proposing a shift toward a more direct, more emotional, tabloid approach.

Campbell, James M. "They Don't Think Much of Business Men in Europe." *Advertising and Selling,* new series, 16 (November 13, 1929).

Clarke, Rene. "Cavalcade." *Advertising Art,* September 1934, pp. 9–13. Review of advertising design and uses of photography, 1900–34.

Coiner, Charles T. "Annual Thirteenth Art Directors' Show." *Printers' Ink Monthly,* 28 (May 1934), pp. 18–19.

———. "What Are the Limits of Fine Art in Advertising?" *Advertising and Selling,* new series, 34 (October 1941), pp. 14–15.

"Comment employer l'art en publicité." *La Publicité,* 18 (January 1921), pp. 589–90.

Comstock, J. B. "Considerations for the Use of Color." *Printers' Ink,* March 12, 1914, pp. 44–47.

"Les Conditions techniques." *La Publicité,* 18 (June 1920), pp. 223–25.

Cone, Fairfax. "Picking Ten out of Eleven." *Advertising Age,* September 28, 1959, pp. 121–22.

Craven, Thomas. "Men of Advertising Art." *Printers' Ink Monthly,* 28 (May 1934), pp. 18–19. While spurning excesses in the artwork of both avant-garde modernists and advertising artists, the author urges a compromise between the two as a way to improve both.

Day, William L. "Fundamentals and Decadence." *Printers' Ink,* March 5, 1936, pp. 17–18, 22, 24. Short assessment of what was good and bad in thirty years of advertising design.

Dean, Arthur W. *Modern Publicity: A Plea for Art in Advertising.* London: Sir Isaac Pitman & Sons, Ltd., 1921. Praises the "unified" imagery of American advertisements wherein a "singleness of effect" is created, but shuns the aggressive and manipulative "psychological" rhetoric which is its invariable counterpart.

Deiss, Jay. "How Modern Art Is Influencing Advertising." *Advertising and Selling,* new series, 42 (November 25, 1949), pp. 33–37.

Delano, Frank. "Image Power: How It Is Acquired." *Advertising Age,* March 24, 1980, pp. S1, S4.

Deutsch, David. "Three Telling Tales in the Life of an Agency Art Director." *Advertising Age,* October 8, 1979, p. 61.

Divry, P. "Chef de fabrication et imprimerie." *La*

Publicité, 31 (March 1933), pp. 218–20.

Dobrow, Larry. *When Advertising Tried Harder: The 60s—The Golden Age of Advertising.* New York: Friendly Press, 1984. Collection of successful campaigns of the 1960s: Avis, Clairol, Volkswagen, Benson & Hedges, Eastern Airlines.

"Exhibit of Decorative Advertising Art." *Printers' Ink,* May 21, 1914, pp. 90–94.

"Exhibit of Prize Posters in New York." *Printers' Ink,* November 18, 1915, p. 84.

Feasley, Florence G., and Elnora W. Stuart. "Magazine Advertisement Layout and Design." *Journal of Advertising,* 16 (1987), pp. 20–25. Survey of the history of style in American advertising layout.

Feulner, Cliff. "Skip Subheads: Your Ad Is Stronger Without Them." *Advertising Age,* July 8, 1968, pp. 77–78.

Fitzgerald, Henry. "There Is Too Much Art in American Advertising." *Printers' Ink,* October 15, 1931, pp. 49–50.

"Forward Movement in Poster Advertising." *Advertising and Selling,* 23 (July 1913), p. 36.

Frankfurt, Stephen O. "Advertising and the Arts." *Advertising Age,* April 30, 1980, pp. 74–77.

Frederic, Joseph E. "Does the Design of an Ad Help Sell the Product?" *Printers' Ink,* April 10, 1953, pp. 38–39.

French, George. *How to Advertise: A Guide...* New York: Doubleday, Page & Co., 1919. Advertising art should attract the eye "not for art's sake but as trade promoters.... The simpler [the design] the better." The best sourcebook of the era on visual presentation and sales.

"Futuristic Monstrosities Are All the Rage." *Printers' Ink,* November 12, 1925, pp. 57–58, 60. Dismisses the artistic value of Futurism but argues that since it appears to be popular with the public, it can be effective in advertising.

Gallagher, James E. "White Space Is Part of Every Layout." *Printers' Ink,* July 25, 1952, pp. 29–30.

Gaw, Walter A. "Visualisation and Layout." In Gaw, *Advertising: Methods and Media.* San Francisco: Wadsworth Publishing, 1961, pp. 100–23.

Gérin, O. J. "Vue plongeante ou vue remontante." *La Publicité,* 16 (February 1919), pp. 11–13.

Gerrish, Sarah Lee. "Why This Ad Sells A State of Mind." *Printers' Ink,* September 6, 1957, pp. 25–27.

Gerry, Roberta. "How Agencies Are Solving Today's Creative Problems." *Printers' Ink,* October 1956, pp. 23–25, 49–50.

Gidley, Don. "Is Modern Advertising Art Modern Enough." *Printers' Ink,* April 2, 1925, pp. 81–82.

Giellerup, S. H. "What the Depression Years Have Done to the Ads." *Advertising and Selling,* new series, 23 (August 30, 1934), pp. 25–26.

Giles, Ray. "Must 'New Copy' Step Forward to Join the 'New Art'?" *Advertising and Selling,* new series, 11 (August 22, 1928), pp. 31 ff.

Glatzer, Robert. *The New Advertising: The Great Campaigns from Avis to Volkswagen.* New York: Citadel Press, 1970. Informative picture book of successful ads of 1950s and 1960s; includes sketches of creative processes undertaken by Doyle Dane Bernbach, David Ogilvy, Shirley Polykoff, and Leo Burnett.

Glim, Aesop. "European Advertising Art: In Europe and in America." *Printers' Ink,* March 19, 1931, pp. 41–42, 44. Appraisal of European advertising illustration and its differences from that in America.

Goode, Kenneth M. "The Art Editor in an Iron Mask." *Advertising and Selling,* new series, 13 (July 10, 1929), pp. 19–20. Most modern stylizing im-

pedes sales and confounds viewer as to what the product is.

Gossage, Howard. "Feel About Your Audience as an Actor Must." *Advertising Age,* March 9, 1959, p. 59.

Gossop, Robert Percy. *Advertisement Design.* London: Chapman & Hall, Ltd., 1927. Conservative but useful handbook of layout and design. Chapters include "Vitality in Design," "The Public Taste," and "The Treatment of Natural Form."

Gottscholl, Edward, and Arthur Hawkins, eds. *Trends in Visual Advertising, 1959–1964.* New York: Art Direction Books, 1965.

———. *Trends in Visual Advertising, 1965–1974.* New York: Art Direction Books, 1974.

Green, Ernest S. "Double Duty Illustrations." *Printers' Ink,* February 9, 1933, pp. 48–49.

Gropman, Paul. "Why Artists Shouldn't Be Art Directors." *Advertising Agency,* 45 (September 1952), pp. 87, 164, 166.

Gundlach, E. T. "Art Versus Advertising." *Advertising and Selling,* new series, 8 (December 29, 1926), pp. 27, 63–64. "Good artwork" detracts from the selling potential of any advertisement and should be replaced by a simple and clear presentation of facts.

Hadley, Howard D. "Is the Direct Appeal the Most Effective?" *Advertising Agency,* 45 (October 1952), pp. 85, 126.

Harper, Marion. "What Poster Illustrations Are Most Effective?" *Advertising and Selling,* new series, 42 (December 1949), pp. 68, 122, 126.

Heath, W. H. " 'Jumbo' Display That Dominates." *Printers' Ink,* July 7, 1921, pp. 41–48. An appraisal of the technique in which vast scale changes and colossal enlargements of products were used in print advertisements.

"Here's What the Art Directors Like." *Printers' Ink,* June 11, 1954, pp. 30–31.

Hermann, Edgar Paul. "Easy on the Eyes, Boys." *Printers' Ink Monthly,* 22 (March 1930), pp. 49, 78.

Hoffner, Marilyn. "Idea Art Does Sales Job for I. Miller." *Printers' Ink,* November 18, 1955, pp. 30–31. Andy Warhol's ads for I. Miller.

———. "Visual Impact Provides the Big Ad Picture." *Printers' Ink,* May 17, 1957, pp. 28–29.

Hollister, Paul. "Yes It Does Sell Goods!" *Advertising and Selling,* new series, 11 (June 13, 1928), pp. 1, 20, 44–51. Defense of modern art in advertising.

Hopkins, Claude. "Acrobatic Advertising." *Advertising and Selling,* new series, 12 (February 6, 1929), pp. 22, 61. Warns against the use of "eccentric" modernist trends: "Nothing unusual should distract attention from the subject."

Johnson, Pierce. "The Sane Use of Modern Art in Advertising." *Advertising and Selling,* new series, 14 (October 30, 1929), pp. 17–19.

Judy, Clayton. "What Is Advertising Creativity?" *Printers' Ink,* October 19, 1956, pp. 30, 32.

Karl, Sandra. "Creative Man Helmut Krone." *Advertising Age,* October 14, 1968, pp. 107–08. Interview with advertising man responsible for many of the innovations at the Doyle Dane Bernbach agency.

Kaye, Joyce Rutter. "Design and Conquer." *Creativity* (supplement to *Advertising Age*), August 7, 1989, pp. 10–12. Predicts a millennial domination of design by four or five conglomerates.

Kemble, Arthur. "A Lesson from the Campbell Kids." *Printers' Ink,* January 26, 1933, pp. 49–51.

King, A. Rowden. "Art Versus Commercial Art." *Advertising and Selling,* 26 (October 1911), pp. 49–53. Raises distinctions between art which "provides rapture and beauty" and that designed to sell. Insists that the best advertising art is that which *sells*

by concentrating on the product, and that stylistic considerations are irrelevant at best and distracting at worst.

Kleppner, Otto. *Advertising Procedure.* New York: Prentice-Hall, 1928. A fine, if rather old-fashioned, textbook on advertising design.

Lallemand, Jules. "Une Experience cruciale." *La Publicité,* 19 (February 1921), pp. 23–25.

Larned, William Livingston. "The Convincing Advertisement Illustration." *Printers' Ink,* January 21, 1915, p. 41.

———. "Choosing a Trademark That Will Last for Generations." *Printers' Ink,* March 11, 1915, pp. 37–40.

———. "Pictorial Themes That Confuse the Eye." *Advertising and Selling,* 24 (March 1915), p. 15.

———. "Designing the Label with Sales 'Punch.'" *Printers' Ink,* June 10, 1915, pp. 25–35.

———. "How Much Illustration Should an Advertisement Carry?" *Printers' Ink,* July 29, 1915, pp. 45–46, 47, 50, 53.

———. "New Tendencies in Poster Art." *Printers' Ink,* June 19, 1919, pp. 28–32, 137–42.

———. "The Artistic Juggling of White Space." *Printers' Ink,* July 10, 1919, pp. 57–60.

———. "Illustration Novelties That Catch the Eye." *Printers' Ink,* March 31, 1921, pp. 95–99.

———. *Advertising Illustration.* Scranton, Penn.: International Textbook Co., 1929.

———. "When Text Must Be Split Up Into Parts." *Printers' Ink,* October 2, 1930, pp. 89–95.

———. "When Headlines Are Unnecessary." *Printers' Ink,* October 16, 1930, pp. 76–77, 80–81.

———. "Should Every Advertisement Have One Primary Focal Point?" *Printers' Ink,* April 24, 1930, pp. 105–06, 113.

Larrabee, C. B. "Is Advertising Art Art?" *Printers' Ink,* January 11, 1946, p. 7.

Latham, LeRoy. "The Making of a Poster." *Printers' Ink,* June 29, 1916, pp. 146–50.

Lathrop, Donald E. "Rule of Simplicity Improves Industrial Advertising Layouts." *Printers' Ink,* October 12, 1945, pp. 24–25.

———. "Layout of Heading Is an Important Part of the Ad." *Printers' Ink,* June 6, 1947, pp. 38–39.

———. "Modern vs. Fashionable Layout in Advertising." *Printers' Ink,* October 24, 1947, pp. 40–42.

Laville, C. *L'Imprime de publicité.* Paris: Éditions Topo, 1928. Collection of international advertisements with French commentary, assessing what makes for good advertisements, with emphasis on visual rather than verbal presentation, color, and the influence of modern art.

"Let the Picture Do the Job." *Printers' Ink,* October 13, 1944, p. 120.

Levinson, Bob. *Bill Bernbach's Book.* New York: Vintage Books, 1987. Selection of Bernbach's highly successful magazine and television campaigns; contains a succinct history of his highly influential work and includes several of his aphorisms.

"Les Limitations de l'illustration." *La Publicité,* 19 (September 1921), pp. 482–83.

Lois, George, and Bill Pitts. *The Art of Advertising: George Lois on Mass Communications.* New York: Harry N. Abrams, 1977. Punchy, up-beat picture book of visually innovative work by graphic designers from the late 1960s and 1970s.

Lyons, John. *Guts: Advertising from the Inside Out.* New York: Amacom, 1987. Textbook which includes many plates and discussions of successful ads, 1960–87.

McFee, William E. "What a Copywriter Thinks

ADVERTISING

About Art and the Artist." *Advertising and Selling,* new series, 23 (September 13, 1934), pp. 32, 48.

"Making Pictorial Contrast Sharp." *Printers' Ink,* May 20, 1920, pp. 113–16.

Margolin, Victor. *The Promise and the Product: Two Hundred Years of American Advertising Posters.* New York: Macmillan Co., 1979.

Martineau, Pierre. "New Look at Old Symbols." *Printers' Ink,* June 4, 1954, pp. 32 ff.

Matasek, Ray J. *Commercial Art and Design.* New York: Bruce Publishing, 1931. Though simplistic and conservative, this textbook for the graphic artist is an informative period piece and includes sections on the use of lettering and halftone imagery and their application to advertising composition.

Miller, C. E. "Paris Couturiers Shy at Advertising." *Advertising and Selling,* new series, 6 (January 27, 1926), pp. 34, 58.

Morris, C. K. "A Defense of American Advertising Art." *Printers' Ink,* November 5, 1931, pp. 101 ff. A defense of the beauty in American advertising art.

Nield, W. K. "The Disloyal Art Director." *Advertising and Selling,* new series, 19 (August 18, 1932), p. 21. Art directors should concern themselves with selling, not art: "There should be as much difference between fine art copy and advertising as there is between literature and copy."

Norton, Cy. "Exhibit of Wartime Advertising." *Printers' Ink,* November 27, 1942, pp. 17–20, 50.

Parsons, Frank Alvah. *The Principles of Advertising Arrangement.* New York: Prang Co., 1912. Early account and demonstration of visual effectiveness from an art director's point of view.

———. *The Art Appeal in Display Advertising.* New York and London: Harper & Bros., 1921. Analyzes period and typography styles and vigorously disdains talk about business and "new psychology."

Peake, Leonard. "Giving the Photograph an 'Art Quality.'" *Printers' Ink,* August 4, 1921, pp. 123–27.

Phillips, Edgar N. "Punch Versus Aesthetics." *Printers' Ink,* March 9, 1916, pp. 25–32.

"Phrases et personnages types." *La Publicité Moderne,* 2 (October–November 1906), pp. 9–16. Charts Michelin company's use of the Bibendum figure in its advertising.

"Please Keep Your Pictures Simple." *Printers' Ink,* April 15, 1920, pp. 81–89.

Poppe, Fred C. *The 100 Greatest Corporate and Industrial Ads.* New York: Van Nostrand Reinhold Co., 1983. Picture book of advertisements, 1970–82.

Pousette-Dart, Nathaniel. "Modern Art: Its Genesis and Destination." *Printers' Ink,* October 23, 1930, pp. 150, 152.

Powel, Harford. "Pictures Versus Art." *Advertising and Selling,* new series, 10 (January 26, 1928), p. 26.

Preston, John F. *Advertising, Printing and Art in Commerce.* London: Chapman and Hall, Ltd., 1927. Information on halftone printing, the mechanics of type, names and trademarks, psychology, layout, and poster design.

Price, George Logan. "Over-Smartness in Advertising." *Printers' Ink,* December 11, 1930, pp. 17–19. Epitomizes the shift away from advertising that was castigated for having used "too much imagination, too much originality, too much atmosphere, too many fancy pictures that no one could understand," and toward blunt, anti-intellectual ads preying on consumer fears and insecurities.

"La Publicité en France." *La Publicité,* 17 (February–March 1920), pp. 7–10.

"Putting Speed into Your Pictures." *Printers' Ink,*

September 28, 1916, pp. 58–68.

Read, Hall. "The Bolshevik Billboard." *Advertising Arts,* January 8, 1930, pp. 57–58. Soviet posters, though at the service of political propaganda, use techniques that advertising men would do well to emulate.

Reed, Louis C. M. "The American Salesman Abroad." *Printers' Ink,* June 8, 1916, pp. 53–56.

Rock, Johanna T. "Best Technique Depends on Product." *Advertising Age,* February 6, 1961, pp. 75–76, 78.

"Le Rôle des symboles en publicité." *La Publicité,* 18 (June 1920), pp. 221–23.

Rondell, Lester. "Advanced Art Is Good Business When Used in the Right Ads." *Printers' Ink,* April 15, 1949, pp. 35–37.

Rosenberg, Manuel. *The Art of Advertising.* New York: Harper & Brothers, 1930.

Russell, Thomas. "Pictures That Tell a Story." *Printers' Ink,* May 4, 1916, pp. 33–35.

Sandage, C. H., and Vernon Fryburger. "Preparing and Reproducing the Advertisement." In *Advertising Theory and Practice.* 5th ed., Homewood, Ill.: Richard D. Irwin, 1958. Originally published in 1936, this highly respected and reliable textbook contains a comprehensive section on visual strategy.

Schlemmer, Richard M. *Handbook of Advertising Art Production.* Englewood Cliffs, N.J.: Prentice-Hall, 1966.

Siegfried, L. B. "Modernism Emerges Full Fledged." *Advertising and Selling,* new series, 10 (February 8, 1928), pp. 24–25, 40, 67.

Sohn, Monte W. "Misbehaviorism in Advertising Art." *Printers' Ink Monthly,* 34 (January 1932), pp. 21–22.

Sparrow, Walter S. *Advertising and British Art.* London: J. Lane, 1924. Aesthetics of advertising art: imagery, public taste, French commercial artists and their influence in Britain.

Stanley, Thomas B. "What Makes a Picture Interesting?" *Printers' Ink Monthly,* 33 (October 1936), pp. 24–25, 60.

———. "Has Modern Layout Come to Stay?" *Printers' Ink,* August 28, 1953, pp. 38–41.

Starch, Daniel. "How Do Size and Color of Advertisements Affect Readership?" *Advertising Agency,* 48 (June 1955), pp. 72–74.

———. "How Does Form of Presentation Affect Readership?" *Advertising Agency,* 48 (August 1955), pp. 79–81.

Sumner, G. Lynn. "But Does It Sell Goods?" *Advertising and Selling,* new series, 11 (May 30, 1928), pp. 19–20, 68–69.

———. "Isn't It All a Question of Understandability?" *Advertising and Selling,* new series, 11 (June 27, 1928), pp. 21–22. Response to Paul Hollister on the use of modern imagery.

———. "Return of the Artist." *Advertising and Selling,* new series, 34 (January 1941), pp. 28–29.

Tarcher, J. D. "Will There Be 'Commercial' Artists in 1950?" *Advertising and Selling,* new series, 12 (October 3, 1928), pp. 30, 32.

Tasker, G. W. "Drawing vs. Photograph." *Printers' Ink,* January 22, 1943, pp. 18–19.

Teague, W. D. "This Modern Style—If Any." *Advertising and Selling,* new series, 10 (April 4, 1928), pp. 23–24, 70–71.

Thibaudeau, F. "La Publicité moderne: L'Annonce française." *Annuaire Graphique,* 39 (1910–11), pp. 97–117. Reviews popular trends in typography and layout of newspaper and magazine advertisements.

Townsend, A. L. "The Part that Pictures Play in Mod-

ern Advertising." *Printers' Ink,* May 29, 1929, pp. 17–20.

Varga, Arnold. "Big Picture, Brief Copy Ads." *Printers' Ink,* January 1, 1960, p. 28. The growing trend of huge, laconic images as due to the growing importance of television, "where the success of a TV commercial is hinged on the visual."

"Visite au salon de la publicité." *La Publicité,* 18 (June 1920), pp. 195 ff.

Walsh, Thomas F. "Realism or Modern Impressionism in Food Illustration." *Printers' Ink Monthly,* 21 (July 1930), pp. 44–45.

Whittier, Charles L. *Creative Advertising.* New York: Henry Holt & Co., 1955. Chapters on "The Illustrative Idea" and "Layouts and Illustrations" clearly enumerate the visual strategies of mid-century American advertising.

Wiener, Mort. "What's Happened to Creativity?" *Printers' Ink,* July 19, 1957, pp. 19–20.

Wiseman, Mark. "What Is an Effective Layout?" *Advertising and Selling,* new series, 34 (October 1941), pp. 19 ff.

Woolf, James D. "Salesense in Advertising, Concerning the Eye Patch." *Advertising Age,* January 16, 1959, p. 82. Against the dangerous overabundance of "brand-image" advertising.

Young, Frank H. *Modern Advertising Art.* New York: Covici & Friede, 1930. Modern art for the businessman and advertiser; addresses questions such as how modern art can help layout, lettering, illustration, and presentation.

Outdoor Advertising

"Les Abus de l'affichage." *La Publicité,* 21 (December 1923), p. 799.

"Affichage." In Henri Gaisser, ed., *Annuaire Général de la publicité.* Paris: Maison Alfred Mame & Fils, 1922.

"Affichage." *La Publicité,* 9 (February 1912), p. 66.

"L'Affichage en ville et à la campagne." *La Publicité,* 8 (January 1911), pp. 37, 39.

"L'Art et la publicité: À propos d'affiches." *La Publicité,* 18 (June 1920), pp. 189–90.

Babcock, Richard F. *Billboards, Glass Houses, and the Law.* Colorado Springs, Colo.: Shephard's Ink, 1977. Surveys the intricate and complex issues of state and federal law, aesthetics, private and public property, government protection, and artistic freedom.

Bernelle, Paul. *Des restrictions apportées depuis 1881 à la liberté de l'affichage.* Paris: Arthur Rousseau, 1912.

The Billboard Nuisance in New York City. Washington, D.C.: Council of National Advisors, National Highways Association, 1916.

"Billboards: Unique, Controversial." *Advertising Age,* March 10, 1986, p. S7.

Campbell, W. C. "An Ordinance to Regulate Outdoor Advertising." *American City,* 31 (December 1924), pp. 585–86.

Dunn, S. Watson, and Arnold M. Barban. "Visual Communication." In Watson and Barban, *Advertising: Its Role in Marketing.* 6th ed., New York: Dryden Press, 1986.

Engerand, Roland. "La Lèpre des routes." *L'Illustration,* September 6, 1930, pp. 6–8.

———. "Il faut déliver nos paysages de la plaie des panneaux-réclame." *Comoedia,* October 6, 1930, p. 4.

Ewald, William R., and Daniel R. Mandelker. *Street Graphics.* Washington, D.C.: American Society of Landscape Architects Foundation, 1971. Various aspects of outdoor advertising (design, visual psychology, ordinances, regulation, and aesthetics). Refutes ideas that outdoor advertising is a dangerous, inconsiderate, or visually distasteful medium.

Flachat, C. "La Visibilité des affiches, panneaux et enseignes." *La Publicité,* 10 (January 1913), pp. 62–64.

Gage, Theodore J. "Will 80s Belong to Outdoor Industry?" *Advertising Age,* March 10, 1986, pp. S1, S4.

Hémet, D. C. A. "L'Affiche: Prolongement de l'enseigne." *La Publicité,* 9 (August 1911), pp. 283–84.

Henderson, Sally, and Robert Landau. *Billboard Art.* San Francisco: Chronicle Books, 1980.

"How the Experts See Outdoor Ad Art Today." *Advertising Agency,* May 10, 1957, pp. 40–41.

Howe, Andrew M. "Writing in Lights." *Printers' Ink Monthly,* 30 (June 1935), pp. 69–80.

"In '58, Outdoor Field Shifted Execs, Fought Hostile Law." *Advertising Age,* June 15, 1959, pp. 3, 68, 70, 72.

"Jurisprudence—Affichage." *La Publicité,* 20 (February 1923), pp. 21–22.

"Des Lamentations devant le mur." *La Publicité,* 28 (December 1930), pp. 786–87.

Le Musée de la Publicité. *Le Livre de l'affiche.* Paris: Éditions Alternatives, 1985.

"Les Murs de France." *La Publicité,* 12 (May 1914), p. 132.

"Les Murs de France." *La Publicité,* 17 (December 1919), pp. 445–46.

Nelson, R., and A. E. Sykes. *Outdoor Advertising.* London: George Allen & Unwin, 1953.

"Outdoor Advertising: Basically Urban, Not Rural, Business." *Advertising Age,* January 15, 1963, pp. 117–31.

"Outdoor Wins." *Printers' Ink,* September 13, 1957, p. 12.

Paver, John M. "Population Explosion into Suburbs Stimulates Outdoor Advertising." *Advertising Agency,* May 1954, pp. 60–61, 86.

"Le Question de l'affichage." *La Publicité,* 18 (July–August 1920), pp. 257–61.

Raveau, P. "La Guerre à l'affiche." *La Publicité,* 9 (December 1911), pp. 149–50.

"Special Report: Outdoor Advertising." *Advertising Age,* October 9, 1989, pp. S1–20. Recent survey of laws, styles, prices, and international outlook of outdoor advertising.

Stelle, B. Drake. "New Methods Spruce Up Billboards." *Advertising Age,* March 10, 1980, p. S30.

Stuart, Robert D. "Outdoor Advertising Should Prove Its Case." *Printers' Ink,* May 10, 1957, p. 12.

"Les Taxes sur l'affichage dans Paris." *La Publicité,* 12 (March 1914), pp. 69, 71, 73.

Ulmer, Bruno, Thomas Plaichinger, with Daniel Boulogne. *Les Murs réclames: 150 Ans de murs peints publicitaires.* Paris: Éditions Alternatives, 1986. Well-documented, illustrated legal and visual history of French urban painted-wall advertising.

Ulmer, Bruno, and Thomas Plaichinger. *Les Écritures de la nuit.* Paris: Éditions Alternatives, 1987.

"Whatever Happened to Billboard Removal? States Drag Their Feet." *U.S. News and World Report,* February 14, 1977, p. 68.

Advertising Typography

Agha, M[ehemed] F[ehmy]. "Sanserif." *Advertising Arts* (supplement to *Advertising and Selling*), March 1931, pp. 41–47. A history of the development of sans-serif typefaces, their application in advertising, and use by modern painters.

Allen, C. N. "Hand Lettering . . . Tells a Story For Advertisers." *Printers' Ink,* February 7, 1942, pp. 16–17.

Brodie, Charles. "Tricky Typography Isn't Modernism." *Printers' Ink,* July 3, 1930, pp. 98–99.

Divry, P. "La Typographie d'hier et d'aujourd'hui." *La Publicité,* 24 (February 1927), pp. 81–84.

Elam, Kimberly. *Expressive Typography: The Word as Image.* New York: Van Nostrand Reinhold, 1990.

Farrar, Gilbert P. "Something New, Old, Strong and Bold." *Printers' Ink Monthly,* 20 (May 1930), pp. 36–37.

———. "Modern Typography Is Good Advertising." *Printers' Ink Monthly,* 21 (September 1930), pp. 34–35, 106, 109.

———. "Modern Types Do Not Guarantee Modern Advertisements." *Printers' Ink Monthly,* 22 (January 1931), pp. 43, 103

Heller, Steven, and Seymour Chast. *Graphic Style: From Victorian to Post-Modern.* New York: Harry N. Abrams, 1988.

Hornung, Clarence. "Modernising the Trademark." *Advertising Arts* (supplement to *Advertising and Selling*), January 8, 1930, pp. 42–45.

———. "The German Trademark." *Advertising Arts* (supplement to *Advertising and Selling*), January 8, 1930, pp. 36–40.

Hornung, Clarence, and Fridolf Johnson. *Two Hundred Years of American Graphic Art: A Retrospective Survey of the Printing Arts and Advertising Since the Colonial Period.* New York: George Braziller, 1976. Illustrated history of the development of American printing and resultant alterations in typefaces used by advertisers.

Larned, William Livingston. "Doing the Unusual in Advertising with Typography." *Printers' Ink,* April 17, 1930, pp. 76, 80, 84, 88.

Lewis, John. *Printed Ephemera: The Changing Uses of Type and Letterforms in English and American Printing.* New York: Dover Publications, 1962. A picture book of typefaces and labels.

McMurtrie, Douglas C. "The Fundamentals of Modernism in Typography." *Printers' Ink Monthly,* 20 (January 1930), pp. 33–35, 70, 81. "Form follows function" as the major concern of modernist typography, which should be dynamic, "expressive of motion rather than rest," and used with an abundance of white space.

———. "The Future of Advertising Composition." *Printers' Ink Monthly,* 20 (April 1930), pp. 39–40, 90, 93, 94.

Miller, Paul M. "Modern Advertising Can Be Beautiful and Readable." *Printers' Ink,* July 17, 1930, pp. 120, 125. Asserts that modern typefaces are no less readable than the old-fashioned sorts.

Moriarty, Sandra Ernst. "Novelty vs. Practicality in Advertising Typography." *Journalism Quarterly,* Spring 1984, p. 188. Summary of longstanding issue.

O'Dea, Mark. "The Curse of Bad Typography." *Printers' Ink,* July 22, 1937, p. 48.

Paschal, P. "Quelques notions de typographie . . ." *La Publicité,* 17 (May 1919), pp. 132–34.

Pavey, Van R. "Futura, Erbar and Kobel." *Advertising and Selling,* new series, 13 (May 29, 1929), pp. 26–27. Positive assessment of the highly popular typefaces from Germany.

Phillips, Fred N. "Beautiful and Not So Dumb—That's Modern Typography." *Printers' Ink,* June 26, 1930, pp. 33–34.

Remington, R. Roger, and Barbara J. Hodik. *Nine Pioneers in American Graphic Design.* Cambridge, Mass., and London: MIT Press, 1989.

Roberts, William L. "Harmonizing Type with Your Product." *Advertising and Selling,* 24 (April 1915), pp. 33–35.

Rowe, Brian. "Beautiful But Dumb Advertising." *Printers' Ink,* June 12, 1930, pp. 3 ff. Argues that popular typefaces are counterproductive: interesting to look at but virtually unreadable.

Smith, Sherman. "Serif or Sans Serif, Type's Job Is to Convey Ideas Clearly." *Printers' Ink,* June 4, 1948, pp. 36–37.

Spencer, Herbert. *Pioneers of Modern Typography.* 2nd ed., Cambridge, Mass.: MIT Press, 1983. Short, well-illustrated history of avant-garde designers working in typography in the 1920s.

Stanley, Thomas B. "Trends in Popularity of Type Faces." *Printers' Ink, Advertisers' Annual 1954,* pp. 392–95. Documents the shifts in taste in the use of typography in American advertisements.

"Sur la 'lettre' typographique." *La Publicité,* 25 (July 1927), pp. 455, 457, 459; August 1927, pp. 557, 559–60.

Zamboni, Hal. "Influence of Modern Art on Design and Typography." *Advertising and Selling,* 41 (February 1948), pp. 39, 88, 90–91.

Window Display

Artley, Alexandra. *The Golden Age of Shop Design: European Shop Interiors 1880–1939.* London: Architectural Press, 1939. Brief and primarily pictorial history of shop display.

Bernard, Frank J. *Dynamic Display.* Cincinnati: Display Publishing, 1952. A "how-to" book for window designers.

Bos. "Quelques Indications pour constituer des étalages attractifs." *La Publicité,* 27 (April 1929), pp. 165–67.

Bremond, C. "L'Art de l'étalage." *La Publicité,* 11 (October 1913), p. 375.

"Un Concours de devantures des magasins." *La Publicité,* 21 (March 1923), p. 93.

"La Decoration d'une vitrine berlinoise." *La Publicité,* 18 (February 1921), p. 37.

Donmery. "Pour ameliorer les mannequins d'étalage." *La Publicité,* 25 (November 1927), p. 825.

"Les Étalages." *La Publicité moderne,* 3 (July 1907), pp. 6–8.

"Étalages et catalogues." *La Publicité,* 27 (May 1929), p. 297.

"Les Étalages qui favorisent les affaires." *La Publicité,* 19 (April 1921), pp. 151–53.

"Études d'étalages." *La Publicité,* 25 (May 1927), pp. 353–54.

Façades de magasins Parisiens. Edited by C. Massin. Paris, n.d.

"Faites des étalages attrayants." *La Publicité,* 17 (November 1919), pp. 373–74.

Gaba, Lester. *The Art of Window Display.* New York and London: Thomas Y. Crowell, 1952. A "how-to" book by one of the most respected window-dressers of the first half of the century.

Gallotti, Jean. "Boutiques nouvelles." *L'Art vivant,* 3 (October 1927), pp. 886–87.

———. "Étalages." *L'Art vivant,* 4 (June 1928), pp. 482–83.

Gardo, Jose. "L'Evolution de l'étalage." *La Publicité,* 21 (January 1924), pp. 881–82.

Goldman, Judith. *The Art of Gene Moore.* New York: Harry N. Abrams, 1980. Monograph on the most creative window designer of the era; includes a fine summary of the history of window dressing in New York.

Gonda, Francis D. "Window Display in Europe." *Printers' Ink,* April 5, 1934, pp. 41–44.

Leydengrost, Robert J. *Window Display*. New York: Architectural Book Publishing, 1950.

"Un Mannequin au Salon d'automne." *La Publicité*, 26 (February 1929), p. 45.

Marcus, Leonard S. *The American Store Window*. London: Architectural Press, 1978. A history of window dressing that includes much good information on exchanges between the Surrealists and the designers of shop windows.

Montfleury, M. "La Vitrine moderne." *La Publicité*, 25 (October 1927), pp. 741–42.

Plowman, A., and V. Pearson. *Display Techniques*. London: Blanford, 1966.

Présentation deuxieme série: Le Décor de la rue, les magasins, les étalages, les stands d'exposition, les éclairages. Paris: Les Éditions de "Parade," 1929.

Taft, William Nelson. *The Handbook of Window Display*. New York: McGraw-Hill, 1926.

Townsend, A. L. "Stage Craftsmanship in the Modern Window Display." *Printers' Ink*, September 15, 1921, pp. 127–33.

The following list, keyed to page numbers, applies to photographs for which a separate acknowledgement is due.

© A.D.A.G.P., Paris: 38, 48 top, 176 bottom, 177, 178

Franziska Adriani, Stuttgart: 185, 320

© American Brands, Inc.: 297

Matthew Armstrong, New York: 72 bottom right, 199, 201, 235 center right and left, 270 lower right, 274 center left, 275 bottom left, 276 bottom right, 277 center and bottom, 278 top, 281 bottom, 282 top, 331, 345 center

© 1990 The Art Institute of Chicago; all rights reserved: 240 bottom

Artothek, Munich: 290

Courtesy Vrej Baghoomian, New York: 387 bottom

Courtesy Heiner Bastian, Berlin: 95, 96, 97

Lars Bay: 91 left

Bibliothèque Nationale, Paris: 137, 138 top left

Courtesy Blum Helman Gallery, New York: 344

Courtesy Mary Boone Gallery, New York: 340 top right (photo: Zindman Fremont, New York), 372, 373, 390 bottom, 391, 393, 404 (photo: Zindman Fremont)

Scott Bowran, New York: 45

© G. Brassaï: 80; 81 (by permission of Chr. Belser Verlag)

Will Brown: 274 top

Rudolph Burckhardt: 333 bottom, 350 top

Bryan Burkey, New York: 16, 60 bottom, 114 bottom, 149 bottom, 158 bottom, 169 top, 181, 186, 191, 228, 256 top, 275 bottom right, 278 bottom, 289 right, 297, 299, 343 bottom, 384, 409, 410 bottom

Courtesy Christie, Manson & Woods, Int'l, New York: 53, 147 top, 258

© Cliché Musées de la Ville de Paris: 88 top, 247

Lee Clockman: 29

Ken Cohen Photography: 293 bottom

Courtesy Paula Cooper Gallery, New York: 386 top (photo: Geoffrey Clements), 386 bottom, 387, 388 (photo: Clements), 413

© 1990 CBS, Inc.: 316 left

© 1990 Cosmopress, Geneva: 37, 62, 63, 64 (photo: courtesy Marlborough Fine Arts, Ltd., London), 65, 66, 123 top left, 296, 321

Courtesy Andrew Crispo: 229

Culver Pictures, Inc., New York: 19, 42 top right

Nicole Dacos, *La Découverte de la Domus Aurea et la formation des grotesques à la Renaissance*

(London: Warburg Institute; Leiden: E. J. Brill, 1969): 109 top right and top left

Ivan Della Tana, New York: 383 top

Courtesy Rick Dingus: 70

© Eastman Kodak Company: 269

© Allan Finkelman: 24 center left, 353, 355 bottom

Brian Forrest: 355 top

Jerry D. Friedman, Miami: 356

Courtesy Frumkin/Adams Gallery, New York: 383 bottom

Courtesy Gagosian Gallery, New York: 341 bottom

© 1990 General Motors Corporation; all rights reserved; reproduced with permission: 323 (photo: Jim Strong, Hempstead, New York)

E. H. Gombrich, *"Meditations on a Hobby Horse" and Other Essays on the Theory of Art* (Chicago: University of Chicago Press, 1985): 107 top right

Carmelo Guadagno, Venice: 60

Tom Haartsen: 239

Courtesy Richard Hamilton: 319 bottom

David Heald: 403

Peter Heman: 46

Paul Hester, Houston: 33 top, 359

Hickey-Robertson, Houston: 294

Colorphoto Hans Hinz, Allschwill-Basel: 24 top left, 200

Inkiri-Manninen: 358

Bill Jacobson Studio: 399

Hermann Kiessling, Berlin: 87 bottom

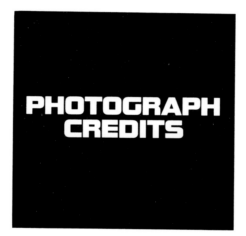

Ken Kirkwood: 2, 245 bottom

Walter Klein, Düsseldorf: 65 top, 296 bottom

Bert Koch, Cologne: 262 bottom

Courtesy Kunsthaus Zurich: 98

Courtesy Galerie Louise Leiris, Paris: 40 right, 279 top

© Luce Marinetti: 51 top

Masters of Caricature, from Hogarth and Gillray to Scarfe and Levine (New York: Alfred A. Knopf, 1981): 138 top right

Robert R. McElroy: 349 top left and bottom

Courtesy David McKee Gallery, New York: 220–22, 224, 225 (photos: Steve Sloman, New York)

Courtesy The Metropolitan Museum of Art, New York: 314

Allen Mewbourn: 103 top

André Morain, Paris: 91 right

The Museum of Modern Art, New York: 18, 24 center right, 26 top, 31 bottom, 34 top right, 36, 43 bottom, 44 top, 50 top, 55, 59 bottom, 86, 87 top right, 90 top, 99, 102 top and bottom left, 140, 143 bottom, 145 top, 146, 152, 166, 167, 179, 198, 203, 237, 238, 244, 245 left center, 263, 271 bottom, 273, 279 bottom, 281 top, 282 bottom, 283 top, 285, 291, 304 center, 306, 307, 312 top, 313, 325, 345 bottom, 348 top, 374 bottom, 390 top, 394, 350, 351

O. E. Nelson: 184 bottom

New York Public Library, Astor, Lenox and Tilden Foundations; General Research Division: 74, 115, 135 top left, top right; Print Collection, Miriam

and Ira D. Wallach Division of Art, Prints and Photographs: 75 top right, 108 bottom, 109 bottom, 110 center, 111 bottom right, 114 top, 116 bottom, 120 top

© Claes Oldenburg, New York: 210 center left, 211 top and bottom (photos: © Dorothy Zeidman, New York)

Courtesy Claes Oldenburg and Coosje van Bruggen, New York: 363 (photo: Shunk-Kender, New York)

Bill Orcutt, New York: 76, 295

Courtesy Pace Gallery, New York: 312 bottom

Courtesy Philadelphia Museum of Art: 119, 334

Tom Powell: 338 top

Courtesy Aimée Brown Price: 120 bottom

James Prince: 311

Nathan Rabin: 361

© Reunion des Musées Nationaux, Paris: 240 top

Rheinisches Bildarchiv, Cologne: 68, 90 bottom, 267 bottom

© Roger-Viollet, Paris: 14, 29 top, 34 bottom, 46 top and bottom left, 232 top right, 241, 243, 283 bottom, 300 top, 345 top

Courtesy Tony Shafrazi Gallery, New York: 383 top left

© S.I.A.E., Rome: 51 bottom (photo: courtesy Christie, Manson & Woods, Int'l, New York)

Courtesy Aaron Siskind: 83 top

Steve Sloman, New York: 223, 411

Courtesy Sonnabend Gallery, New York: 332 top, 368, 395 top, bottom left, 396 top, 397

Courtesy Sotheby's, New York: 93, 326, 341 bottom, 367

© S.P.A.D.E.M., Paris: 22, 24 bottom right, 26 bottom, 38, 47 top, 48 top, 60 top, 88 top, 89 center, 111, 117 top right and left, 126 top and center, 131, 132, 144, 145 bottom, 150, 180 top, 247

Squidd & Nunns, Los Angeles: 327, 329 lower left

Staatsbibliothek Bamberg: 110 top right and left

Courtesy Städtisches Kunstmuseum Bonn: 261 bottom, 262 top, 264 top, 265 top, 266 left (photos: Wolfgang Morell, Bonn)

Lee Stalsworth: 192, 296 top

Jim Strong, Hempstead, New York: 20, 26 top, 28, 29 bottom left and bottom right, 32, 33 bottom, 37 bottom right, 42 right center, 71, 72 top and left, 73, 117 bottom, 155–57, 158 top, 159–65, 169–74, 180 center left and center right, 182, 183, 184 top, 188, 189, 194, 195, 197, 202, 205 bottom, 206, 207, 208 bottom, 210 top, center right, 212–17, 219 bottom, 230, 248, 252 bottom, 255 bottom, 256 bottom, 257, 268 bottom right, 269 bottom, 276 bottom left, 289 left, 301 top, 303, 304 top, 316, 323, 396 bottom, 410 top, 411 top

Studio Chevrojon Frères, Paris: 17

© Succession Picasso: 22, 24 bottom right, 26 bottom, 37 center right, 47 top, 48 top, 60 top, 126 top and center, 131, 132, 144, 145 bottom, 150

Joseph Szaszfai: 364

Aug. Taevernier, *James Ensor: Catalogue illustrée de ses gravures* ([Brussels?]: 1973): 75 bottom right

Michael Tropea, Chicago: 339

© V.A.G.A., New York: 268 bottom left

Paolo Vandrasch, Milan: 89 top

Malcolm Varon, New York: 43 top

© VG Bild-Kunst, Bonn: 39

© Volkswagon of America, Inc.; reproduced with permission: 324

Courtesy Walker Art Center, Minneapolis: 330

Courtesy Walker, Ursitti & McGinnis, New York: 56 top left, bottom righ and bottom left, 57 top, 58, 59 top, 271 top

Dan Walworth: 343 top right

Windsor Castle, Royal Library, © 1990 Her Majesty Queen Elizabeth II: 104, 105 bottom left

Courtesy Yale Center for British Art, New Haven: 322 (photo: Richard Caspole)

© Dorothy Zeidman, New York: 41, 302, 341 top, 342, 343 top left, 360, 361 top, 362, 365 bottom

451

LENDERS TO THE EXHIBITION

Stedelijk Museum, Amsterdam
Fundació Joan Miró, Barcelona
Museu Picasso, Barcelona
Kunstmuseum Basel
Städtisches Kunstmuseum Bonn
Albright-Knox Art Gallery, Buffalo
The Cleveland Museum of Art
Musée d'Unterlinden, Colmar
Museum Ludwig, Cologne
Dallas Museum of Art
Des Moines Art Center
Kunstsammlung Nordrhein-Westfalen, Düsseldorf
Hood Museum of Art, Dartmouth College, Hanover, New Hampshire
Sprengel Museum, Hannover
The Menil Collection, Houston
Saatchi Collection, London
The Tate Gallery, London
Los Angeles County Museum of Art
Museum of Contemporary Art, Los Angeles
Museo Teatrale alla Scala, Milan
Yale University Art Gallery, New Haven, Connecticut
Dia Art Foundation, New York
Grey Art Gallery and Study Center, New York University Art Collection
The Metropolitan Museum of Art, New York
The Museum of Modern Art, New York
The National Gallery of Art, Osaka
Musée d'Art Moderne de la Ville de Paris
Musée National d'Art Moderne, Centre Georges Pompidou, Paris
Musée Picasso, Paris
Philadelphia Museum of Art
Marion Koogler McNay Art Museum, San Antonio, Texas
Staatsgalerie Stuttgart
Kunsthalle Tübingen
Musée d'Art Moderne, Villeneuve-d'Ascq
Hirshhorn Museum and Sculpture Garden, Smithsonian Institution, Washington, D.C.
National Gallery of Art, Washington, D.C.
Kunsthaus Zurich

Mr. and Mrs. William Acquavella
Mrs. James W. Alsdorf
Merrill C. Berman
Ernst Beyeler
Irving Blum
Mr. and Mrs. Marcel Boulois
Adele Bishop Callaway
Jean-Christophe Castelli
The Joseph and Robert Cornell Memorial Foundation
Andrew Crispo
Robert Crumb
Elaine and Werner Dannheisser

Dorthea Elkon
Natasha Elkon
Ernst and Inge Fischer
Dr. and Mrs. Phillip T. George
Arnold and Milly Glimcher
Kathy Goodell
Stephen Hahn Collection
Dieter Hauert
Marcia Riklis Hirschfeld
Anne and William Hokin
Richard E. Jacobs
Carroll Janis
Mrs. Edwin Janss
Jasper Johns
Jean-Jacques Lebel
Roy and Dorothy Lichtenstein
Sally Lilienthal
Ludwig Collection
Harry and Linda Macklowe
Mr. and Mrs. Martin Z. Margulies
Mr. and Mrs. Donald B. Marron
Richard Marschall
Mrs. Robert B. Mayer
Robert and Meryl Meltzer
Mr. and Mrs. S. I. Newhouse, Jr.
Muriel Kallis Newman
Claes Oldenburg and Coosje van Bruggen
S. and G. Poppe
Robert Rauschenberg
James Rosenquist
Judith Rothschild
Dr. Werner Schmalenbach
Ileana and Michael Sonnabend Collection
Emily and Jerry Spiegel
The Swid Collection
Hans Thulin
Thyssen-Bornemisza Collection
Michael Tiefenbacher
Harry Torczyner
Garry Trudeau
Cy Twombly
The Estate of Andy Warhol
David Whitney
Anonymous lenders

Michelin, S.A., Clermont-Ferrand
Galerie Reckermann, Cologne
The Fukuoka City Bank, Ltd.
Marlborough Fine Art, Ltd., London
Studio Marconi, Milan
Gotham Book Mart, New York
David McKee Gallery, New York
Sidney Janis Gallery, New York
Pacesetter Corporation, Omaha
Fuji Television Gallery, Tokyo

In the index, works are cited by artist. In addition, a general listing is given for each of the four principal topics—graffiti, caricature, comics, and advertising—treated in the body of the book; anonymous works are included within those general listings. An artist's name given in parentheses after a title indicates that there is a separate entry for the artist. In a few cases, mediums are noted to distinguish between works having identical titles. Numbers refer to pages.

INDEX OF ILLUSTRATIONS

459